A

critical
action
research
READER

Studies in the
Postmodern Theory of Education

Shirley R. Steinberg
General Editor

Vol. 433

The Counterpoints series is part of the Peter Lang Education list.
Every volume is peer reviewed and meets
the highest quality standards for content and production.

PETER LANG
New York • Bern • Frankfurt • Berlin
Brussels • Vienna • Oxford • Warsaw

A
critical
action
research
READER

PATRICIA H. HINCHEY,
EDITOR

PETER LANG
New York • Bern • Frankfurt • Berlin
Brussels • Vienna • Oxford • Warsaw

Library of Congress Cataloging-in-Publication Data

A critical action research reader / edited by Patricia H. Hinchey.
pages cm. — (Counterpoints: studies in the postmodern theory of education; v. 433)
Includes bibliographical references.
1. Action research in education. I. Hinchey, Patricia H.
LB1028.24.C74   370.72—dc23   2015014328
ISBN 978-1-4331-1759-6 (hardcover)
ISBN 978-1-4331-1760-2 (paperback)
ISBN 978-1-4539-1621-6 (e-book)
ISSN 1058-1634

Bibliographic information published by **Die Deutsche Nationalbibliothek**.
Die Deutsche Nationalbibliothek lists this publication in the "Deutsche
Nationalbibliografie"; detailed bibliographic data are available
on the Internet at http://dnb.d-nb.de/.

The paper in this book meets the guidelines for permanence and durability
of the Committee on Production Guidelines for Book Longevity
of the Council of Library Resources.

To the classroom teachers who generously contributed their work to this book and so patiently waited for its publication—Jessica Blanchard, Rachel Klimke, Lisa Sibbett, Nien N. Tran, Inga Wilder, and Jennifer Zapata—and to all teachers working toward a better world.

Preface

All words are pegs to hang ideas on.——Henry Ward Beecher

While the title of this book may suggest that it's about critical action research ... it's not. Instead, this book is about *ideas about* critical action research. And it offers examples of what some ideas about critical action research have looked like when someone, or a pair or group of someones, translated them into practice.

Any reader with the most rudimentary familiarity with the term *action research* already understands that those particular words have been used so many ways to mean so many things that the phrase has become no more than a holograph, a shadow that seems real but that fades at a firm grasp toward its meaning. A tool to leverage change, action research has been used to name such disparate efforts as doggedly driving eight-year-olds toward higher standardized test scores and helping urban youth name and devise ways to resist stereotyping in their neighborhoods. Individual classroom teachers have used it to explore how their classrooms and schools might be made more democratic and relevant; teacher educators have used it to explore how to awaken their students to the effects of institutionalized racism, sexism, and homophobia; university researchers have partnered with communities to identify important community concerns and to work toward new and better policies.

Over time, as a way to signal important differences among such varied versions of action research, theorists have added adjectives to breathe new life into what has become an empty descriptor, so that we now talk of *educational action research, participatory action research (PAR), youth participatory action research (YPAR)*, and *socially critical action research (SCAR)*. Or they've relied on other phrases entirely to detail meaning: *teacher inquiry* or *practitioner* inquiry or *teacher research*. Meanings refuse to stay pinned down, however: one person's *research* is another person's *inquiry*, and attempts at better definitions merely beget more theoretical wrangling and more words that mean different things to different people.

Such wrangling is a good thing. As theorists and practitioners work toward greater clarity about what exactly it is they want to do and how they think it should be done, practice expands and improves. That is, as we get better at thinking about and explaining what we do, we get better at doing it. This description of the fairly chaotic field is not an indictment. Rather, it is an alert to readers that, although I have worked hard to herd a comprehensive sampling of readings into thematic sections that help make sense of the chaos, the organization I've imposed is inevitably fairly arbitrary. Like all experience, each reading has more than one meaning: a piece written by an individual classroom teacher about working with Latino students to confront racism might have appeared in a thematic group centered on teacher research or as an example of the intersection of critical action research and borderlands scholarship or as an example of youth participatory action research. Or I might have used entirely different themes, resulting in very different groupings. I urge readers to bear this point about arbitrariness in mind and to look for resonance among examples across thematic groupings.

What is consistent in these selections is their commitment to critical action research: research in the interest of creating a more just world, peopled by citizens with the skills to name oppression and to take practical action to resist it. Perhaps even more important, what is consistent in these selections is the authors' faith that educators can help effect significant change in people, institutions, and policies. Readers currently discouraged by a dehumanized educational and political environment where high stakes testing has become an effective whip to drive teachers and students into numbing, meaningless routines are likely to take from this body of work a precious gift: hope.

My own hope is that each reader will take heart in realizing that those of us engaged in this struggle for freedom and dignity are not alone—and we can indeed make a difference, as our colleagues teach us in the following pages.

Acknowledgments

Part 1. Toward an Understanding of Critical Action Research

Chapter 1: Reprinted from Boog, B. W. M. (2003). The emancipatory character of action research, its history and the present state of the art. *Journal of Community & Applied Social Psychology, 13*(6), 426–438.

Chapter 2: Reprinted from Cannella, G. S. & Lincoln, Y. S. (2012). Deploying qualitative methods for critical social purposes. In S. R. Steinberg & G. S. Cannella (Eds.), *Critical qualitative research reader* (pp. 104–113). New York: Peter Lang.

Chapter 3: Reprinted from Kinsler, K. (2010). The utility of educational action research for emancipatory change. *Action Research, 8*(2), 171–189. doi: 10.1177/1476750309351357

Chapter 4: Reprinted from Brennan, M. & Noffke, S. (2001). Uses of data in action research. In T. R. Carson & D. J. Sumara (Eds.), *Action research as a living practice* (23–43). New York: Peter Lang.

Chapter 5: Reprinted from Shields, C. M. (2012). Critical advocacy research: An approach whose time has come. In S. R. Steinberg & G. S. Cannella (Eds.), *Critical qualitative research reader* (pp. 2–13). New York: Peter Lang.

Part 2. Critical Teacher Research in Urban Contexts

Chapter 7: Reprinted from Esposito, E., & Evans-Winters, V. (2007). Contextualizing critical action research: Lessons from urban educators. *Educational Action Research, 15*(2), 221–237.

Part 3. Participatory Action Research (PAR)

Chapter 13: Reprinted from Cahill, Caitlin. (2007). Doing Research with Young People: Participatory Research and the Rituals of Collective Work. *Children's Geographies, 5*(3), 297–312. doi: 10.1080/14733280701445895

Chapter 14: Reprinted from Fox, M. & Fine, M. (2012). Circulating critical research: Reflections on performance and moving inquiry into action. In S. R. Steinberg & G. S. Cannella (Eds.), *Critical qualitative research reader* (pp. 153–165). New York: Peter Lang.

Chapter 15: Reprinted from Muñoz Proto, C. (2012). In search of critical knowledge: Tracing inheritance in the landscape of incarceration. In S. R. Steinberg & G. S. Cannella (Eds.), *Critical qualitative research reader* (pp. 479–490). New York: Peter Lang.

Chapter 16: reprinted from Ayala, J. (2009). Split scenes, converging visions: The ethical terrains where PAR and borderlands scholarship meet. *Urban Review, 41,* 66–84.

Part 4. New Bottles for New Wine—Report Formats

Chapter 17: Reprinted from Canagarajah, A. S. (1996). From critical research practice to critical research reporting. *TESOL Quarterly, 30*(2), 321–331.

Chapter 18: Reprinted from Fisher, K., & Phelps, R. (2006). Recipe or performing art?: Challenging conventions for writing action research theses. *Action Research, 4*(2), 143–164. doi: 10.1177/1476750306063989

Chapter 21: Reprinted from Luce-Kapler, R. Reverberating the action research text. In T. R. Carson & D. J. Sumara (Eds.), *Action research as a living practice* (pp. 187–197). New York: Peter Lang.

Chapter 22: Reprinted from Olberg, A., Collins, C., Ferguson, C., Freeman, D., Levitz, R., McCaskell, M. L. & Walters, B. Sojourning: Locating ourselves in the landscape. In T. R. Carson & D. J. Sumara (Eds.), *Action research as a living practice* (pp. 231–245). New York: Peter Lang.

Part 5. Complexities

Chapter 24: Reprinted from Miller, J. L. Disruptions in the field: An academic's lived practice with classroom teachers. In T. R. Carson & D. J. Sumara (Eds.), *Action research as a living practice* (pp. 199–213). New York: Peter Lang.

Chapter 27: Reprinted from Couch, S. R. (2004). A tale of three discourses: Doing action research in a research methods class. *Social Problems, 51*(1), 146–153.

Table of Contents

PART 3

PARTICIPATORY ACTION RESEARCH (PAR)

PART 4

NEW BOTTLES FOR NEW WINE—REPORT FORMATS

PART 5
COMPLEXITIES

PART ONE

Toward an Understanding of Critical Action Research

Introduction
The Contested Terrain of
Critical Action Research

Theorists have been working for decades to be clear about what type of research might be termed "critical" as well as to be clear about what versions of action research merit that description. While there is some agreement about some things—for example, that any research termed "critical" must have as its ultimate objective greater social equity and justice—there are also many disagreements about other elements. Part 1 is intended to allow readers to build a basic definition of critical action research, to become familiar with some of its many manifestations, and to explore a sampling of related theoretical and practical issues.

In Chapter 1, Ben Boog presents his work as a close look at the characteristics of what he terms "action research." However, many theorists and researchers are likely to understand his description a bit differently, as the editor does—as a basic history and description of "critical action research." This is true because Boog asserts that the central defining characteristic of what he terms "action research" is the explicit objective of advancing empowerment and social equity. As many other researchers and theorists have noted, however, the term "action research" has in fact often been used to describe other forms of action research lacking any empowering, democratic goal.[1] Much of Boog's discussion, then— especially of contemporary strands of action research—can serve as a general introduction to critical action research terrain. The discussion includes the history of the seminal terms "emancipation" and "empowerment," the roots of contemporary practice, and recent trends.

In describing recent approaches, Boog identifies four distinct strands—one of which he names "critical action research" and defines as "a family of models." The other three strands include pragmatic action research, co-operative inquiry, and action research within the tradition of systems thinking. However, he identifies "convergences" among the four strands—and those convergences are widely accepted by many others as characteristic of critical action research. In addition to the common goal of empowerment, each approach includes a cyclical process in which action is an integral component and which requires mutual understanding among research partners. This bare-bones sketch of what makes critical action research "critical" helps explain why efforts as varied as one classroom teacher working to improve high school health curriculum and several research partners working to understand how incarceration of parents affects youth can be considered critical action research. This piece also details the many skills a critical action research practitioner needs, including mastery of theories and methodologies, an explicit ethical stance, strategies for nurturing self-awareness, and the ability to assess effects as the project unfolds. In general, Boog's piece provides a useful survey of the history and geography of critical action research.

Given that the hallmark of critical work is to advance empowerment and social equity, Gaile Cannella and Yvonne Lincoln pose a provocative question in Chapter 2: "Since critical perspectives are powerfully engaged with powerful issues of our time, why is it that so little critical research becomes a part of civic debate?" Certainly any critical researcher, and especially a critical action researcher, intends to nudge the world toward change. Why does so little happen so routinely? The authors posit three influences, each of which merits consideration by those who would help change the world. The first is the issue of complex language, which has been debated within the field for some time. Critical researchers routinely write employing the lexicon of critical theory, and lay readers cannot—or perhaps reasonably will not—struggle through such abstractions as "conscientization" and "double-hermeneutic process" to access what writers intend to convey. While detailing and agreeing with arguments in favor of avoiding dominant discourse in presenting oppositional ideas, Canella and Lincoln insist that critical researchers nevertheless must find a way to make critical work readily accessible to a much larger public than the relatively few specialists who read highly specialized academic journals. The second issue the authors identify is that of well-funded government and politically conservative organizations reifying a particular kind of "evidence-based research" as the only type of research considered credible. The authors explain the many ways that such groups have helped silence critical voices in the interest of maintaining existing, inequitable power arrangements. Finally, the authors explain how corporatization of universities has altered the nature and goals of administrators and faculty in ways that undermine interest in anything other than institutional and personal financial profit—hardly a hospitable climate for researchers pursuing more equitable social relations. Any critical researcher would do well to digest—and adopt—the authors' four suggestions for increasing efficacy of critical work in the face of such strong oppositional forces. After all, there is little point to mastering the theory and process of critical action research if, in the end, it has little or no effect on the world we seek to change.

In Chapter 3, Kimberley Kinsler also takes up the question of why critical action research has ultimately produced little real change—in particular for marginalized students who so often fare badly in schools. After reviewing various methodological models, as well as frequent criticisms of them, she takes issue with those theorists who insist that any action research seeking to improve student achievement is not truly critical. Like Cannella and Lincoln, she points to the ways in which much educational action research has been tightly interwoven with interests within the academy rather than with the interests of marginalized students and their families. After noting that critics frequently consider action research seeking improved academic achievement as technical rather than critical, Kinsler insists that it is—and should be recognized as—inherently critical and emancipatory:

> In industrialized nations there is still a great deal of race and class discrimination and masked institutional oppression, and for those who have been historically marginalized, undereducated and denied access to the cultural capital needed for a viable existence in these societies, technical and practical educational AR that results in significant advances in these students' academic achievement and passing rates on critical 'gate keeping' tests is emancipatory research.

That is, she argues that much classroom research qualifies as critical because empowerment includes helping marginalized students acquire the education—and cultural capital—that they are routinely denied and that equips them to effectively participate in efforts to realize a more just society.

Marie Brennan and Susan Noffke, in Chapter 4, shed considerable light on the difficulty of living critical action research in the teacher education classroom, where action research is often assigned to students and where structural power is bestowed on faculty experts. As the student teachers they supervised conducted individual action research projects, the authors conducted action research on their own teaching. This chapter details how ongoing analysis of data from faculty and student projects helped a seminar group cohere as co-researchers who continually came together for "constant questioning … [of] both positions and propositions." In exploring the meaning and function of what the authors term "data-in-use," the authors candidly discuss not only their successes but also their challenges, acknowledging "many points in [their] own practice which seem to contradict [their] most deeply held and articulated positions." Their discussion is a thoughtful consideration of the nature and function of data, and it uncovers some of the many factors that make critical action research one of those things "easier said than done."

Although Carolyn Shields does not address action research specifically in Chapter 5, she confronts head-on the criticism so often thought to damn critical action research: that in its explicit ideological commitments, critical research is advocacy and not truly research at all.[2] In contrast, Shields argues that the privilege and power most researchers hold in fact confers the responsibility—perhaps even the moral obligation—to become public intellectuals who work toward greater social equity. Within the article she defines what she terms "critical advocacy research" and discusses how the quality of such work might be assessed without defaulting to standards, such as "trustworthiness," derived from the positivist paradigm. She argues further that action strategically designed to realize change must become an integral part of such work. To illustrate, she details her earlier studies in Navajo schools, where she found and reported dominant discourses constructing Navajo youth as inferior—a deficit perspective on the students with damaging effects. Looking back at the lack of progress subsequent to her work, Shields believes that she erred in not taking more action to widely change stakeholders' understanding of the situation and to promote strategic action to remedy it—that is, to be a more active advocate for the youth. While she acknowledges the practical risks to those who are outspoken in critique and in lobbying for greater equity, she nevertheless urges researchers to develop the courage necessary to answer this question affirmatively: "Has our research done anything to level the playing field, to overcome disparity, to promote a more mutually beneficial democratic society?"

Closing out this segment of the text is Phil Carspecken's exploration of the sense that "critical" has had in the development of critical theory. Tracing some of the philosophical paths from Kant to Hegel that explore human identity, existential need, and freedom, Carspecken argues that both mainstream social research and much of what has been presented as challenges to the mainstream assume the subject-object paradigm of knowing without recognition of the associated knowledge limits. Carspecken's arguments lead the reader toward the subject–subject paradigm of knowing, a paradigm most directly employed with critical action forms of research. According to this article, in critical action research humans produce knowledge together through collective action—a process that simultaneously advances human freedom.

Together, these chapters sketch the contested terrain of critical action research and offer some sense of the variety of perspectives on and issues within it, providing context for the highly diverse work appearing in subsequent parts of this text.

Notes

1. For perhaps the best-known (if not uncontested) exploration of noncritical action research, see Kemmis, S. (2006). Participatory action research and the public sphere. *Educational Action Research, 14*(4), 459–476.
2. For a more detailed discussion and refutation of such criticism, see Carr, W. (2000). Partisanship in educational research. *Oxford Review of Education, 26*(3/4), 437–449.

CHAPTER 1

The Emancipatory Character of Action Research, Its History and the Present State of the Art

Ben W. M. Boog

Introduction

The historical development of action research reveals that it had emancipatory intentions from the very beginning and that this basis has become increasingly sophisticated with the refinement of action research into different approaches. Action research is designed to improve the researched subjects' capacities to solve problems, develop skills (including professional skills), increase their chances of self-determination, and have more influence on the functioning and decision-making processes of organizations and institutions from the context in which they act. Emancipation implies that the generated results of action research are two sided. On the one hand are the specific improved action competencies of the researched subjects in the local situation in the specific research project. On the other hand are the general enhanced action competencies in other comparable problematic situations in the future, sometimes even in broader contexts. In addition, every action research project also aims to enhance the theory and methodology of action research as a distinct social science approach, as well as the professional skills of action researchers.

In the last few decades, emancipation has come to be equated with empowerment. Although they initially represented different perspectives, both emancipation and empowerment are closely connected to what is called a participatory worldview. This implies that all people must be equal participants in society, which means that they must have equal opportunities for schooling and jobs, have the opportunity to share in all goods and services in society and participate in decision making, both public and private. However, success in the sense of realizing emancipation and empowerment cannot be guaranteed by the wide range of action research theories available for designing a practice-oriented research project. Since the main characteristic is the communicative interaction between researchers and the researched subjects, action researchers have to be experienced in handling this relationship as a minimum success factor, over and above their skills as adequate social researchers.

In order to outline the state of the art of action research as an explicitly emancipatory research approach the following steps will be taken. First, the content of the concepts of emancipation and empowerment and the notion of participatory democracy, which is closely connected to these concepts, will be outlined. Second, the history of action research, keeping close to the concepts of emancipation, empowerment and participatory democracy and modalities and submodalities such as self-actualization and self-determination will be briefly sketched. Third, the different fully grown approaches of action research that we know today will be described. In the last paragraph, in which the focus is on the relationship between the researcher and researched subjects, some recommendations to improve the practice of action research will be made.

Emancipation, Empowerment and Participatory Democracy

To emancipate means to free oneself from restraint, control or the power of someone else, especially to free oneself from any kind of slavery. Emancipation was the main goal of large social, political and religious groups during the eighteenth, nineteenth and twentieth centuries. They struggled for equal rights and social justice and made efforts to create more power, including political power, for the poor, cultural and ethnic minorities, religious groups, women, and homosexuals. Emancipation was the main political preoccupation of critical theory and critical action research.[1] Although one could be emancipated as an individual, the concept applied to the collective. Critical theory, and the majority of Marxist approaches in the social sciences, criticized the all-embracing structural power of the dominant classes in the economical, political and cultural (or so-called ideological) systems and subsystems in society. Their purpose was to get the dispossessed into power; the dominated labour classes were to become the historical subject of a new fully democratized classless society. Thus critical reflection on the power structures of the dominating classes, for example family and community life, work, and urban politics, was the core activity of critical action research. This was done through adult educational work such as community education, community development and communal action, literacy projects and also through socialist feminist group work. Thus, emancipation was not only freeing oneself from domination but also transforming society and achieving a more equal distribution of power and control within society. Its purpose was to achieve freedom from the power exercised by the dominant groups and classes and to obtain the power to be free to exert influence and give direction to one's own life. It is easy to see that emancipation is a worldview concept, closely connected to the aforementioned participatory worldview. Nowadays, however, the more recent concept of empowerment is often used.

The concept of empowerment has a somewhat different history. At first it was used by radical feminist groups. These groups of women used a form of group work that combined methods developed by Lewin and Moreno (two of the founding fathers of action research; see next page) and within humanistic psychology and radical psychoanalysis (Vermeulen & Boog, 1994). As in Lewin's group work method, the emphasis of these groups was on direct or participative democracy. Group members worked on personal growth and personal empowerment, within the safe boundaries of the group. Thus, at first, empowerment was a more 'individual' concept. Empowerment was connected to raising self-consciousness, learning to stand up for yourself (self-advocacy) and self-actualization. However, in the last few decades empowerment has also been used in the sense of collective and group empowerment. Jacobs (2002, p. 248) writes: 'The basic assumption in an empowerment approach is that people cannot fully realise their potential in life if they have no control over the (internal and external) factors that determine their lives.'

Empowerment enriched the concept of emancipation with notions about personal being and competencies and motivational elements. Paradigmatic for this enrichment are the themes which the faction of radical feminists added to those of the socialist feminists. Although at first there was tension between both factions, soon most women in the feminist movement saw the necessity of combining the socialists' goal of the structural transformation of society with the radical feminists' notions of personal growth and personal strength. In practice this meant the combination of reflection in political consciousness-raising groups with getting to know yourself.

The concepts of emancipation and empowerment are closely connected with the concept of participatory democracy. The values of equal rights, social justice, and solidarity with the socially deprived can only be realized within a community that is organized along the principles of participatory democracy. Participatory here means communication and participation in decision making. Participatory democracy is not only seen as a goal inherent to emancipation or empowerment but must also be experienced in the practice of action research: in the relationship between researcher and researched subjects. Thus learning by reflection and self-research in small 'direct democratic' groups where the participants are regarded as equals, though nevertheless recognized as different—unique—human beings became one of the core activities in action research.

A Brief History of Action Research

Action research in the West started with Aristotelian thinking (Toulmin, 2000), but the distinct social research approach started in the US prior to World War II. This American current of action research had two sources: the tradition of philosophical pragmatism and, somewhat later, the work of the European gestalt psychologist Lewin and the radical psychoanalyst Moreno.

The first research practice that can be labelled as action research was based on the philosophical pragmatism of Dewey. It was Collier, of the Bureau of Indian Affairs, who initiated community education projects in the Indian reserves in the US (Noffke, 1997). Philosophical pragmatism, especially the works of the philosopher of education Dewey and his close friend the philosopher and social psychologist Mead, was the first grand theory to provide a firm foundation for action research. It aimed to improve people's social and democratic participation in society and to establish social equality and social justice. Mead and Dewey's theories were what I will call genuine action theories, as opposed to behavioural theories. Central to these theories were the notions of human development through 'transaction' (Dewey) and interaction-communication (Mead). In behavioural theories human beings are seen only as reacting units, black boxes, or similar to the doves and dogs of Skinner's 'operant conditioning'. Philosophical pragmatism generated a base for the development of professional practices such as social casework, community education and community organization, directed at facilitating people to learn to stand up for themselves, to participate in civil society, and in this way to decrease structural social injustice. Later, just after World War II, it also generated strategies of 'social action' as developed by Alinsky for the civil rights movement (Dubost, 2001). These became popular in the community action committees and the self-organizations in neighbourhoods in Europe and Great Britain at the end of the 1960s.

About a decade later, the 'gestalt psychologist' Lewin started an action research practice. Lewin had fled from Nazi Germany and from 1934 he worked in the US. In Germany, Lewin was a member of the Socialist Party, and his scientific work was directed at the emancipation of minorities. 'His particular concerns appear to have been the combating of anti-Semitism, the democratisation of society, and the need to improve the position of women. Along with other students he organised and taught an adult education program for working-class women and men' (Smith, 2001, p. 1). In the US, he had contact with Dewey and worked for some time together with Moreno, a psychiatrist from Vienna. Lewin coined the term 'action research,' which he understood to be 'a comparative research on the conditions and effects or various forms of social action, and research leading to social action' (Lewin, 1948, pp. 202–203, as quoted in Smith, 2001, p. 9). In Lewin's work, all the important elements of action research can be found. He developed a dynamic field theory and started experiments in the field. Furthermore, he developed an approach called dynamic group work. This group work (with the so-called T-group model) was meant to facilitate learning by group members (Smith, 2001). In these groups, participants worked on democratic leadership. To this end, Lewin changed the role of the researcher from distanced outsider to involved participant (Greenwood & Levin, 1998) and used a multi-method approach based on social psychological 'concepts that were more sociological than psychological' (Fachbereich Sozialpädagogiek an der Pädagogischen Hochschule Berlin, 1972). Greenwood and Levin (1998) mention two other elements in Lewin's approach. First, Lewin's (and Moreno's) work started from an open system view, and second, Lewin was the inventor of the cyclical model of social change as a three-stage process: 'dismantling former structures (unfreezing), changing the structures (changing), and finally locking them back into a permanent structure (freezing)' (Greenwood & Levin, 1998, p. 17). Ever since, group work to facilitate social change and adult learning following this cyclical development has been central to the methodology of all kinds of action research.

Before he started the neo-positivistic movement of sociometrics, Moreno worked with a combination of the living sociogram, psychodrama and sociodrama (Boog, 1989; Moreno, 1951). He combined group work with an interpretation of Freudian psychoanalysis which was less verbal and more non-verbal. Instead of the interaction between psychoanalyst and analysand, he used group work in which the role of the analyst was non-authoritative. Creativity and spontaneity were considered to be more important concepts than Freud's unconscious impulses. As in Lewin's group work, the researcher participated in the group, but Moreno went further and explicitly invited the researched subjects to become coresearchers.

The British Tavistock Institute picked up on Lewin's work where it was used, for instance, for group psychotherapies and team building as well as for professional work in industrial relations (sociotechnics). Its goals were personal empowerment and team building in social situations or (democratic) participation so that an organization could grow into what later would be called a 'learning organization.'

With the democratic movements of 1968, action research received a new impulse. Critical theories delivered new starting points for action research approaches with explicit emancipatory intentions. Approaches such as participatory action research, emancipatory action research and critical action research were developed. The most important impulse came from the theory of Habermas (Habermas & Luhmann, 1971, pp. 101–141; Moser, 1975). Habermas was the key scientist of the second generation of the Frankfurter Schule. Like all theorists of this school, his work reflected explicit emancipatory preoccupations. Later on, in the 1980s, his action theory in particular (Habermas, 1981)[2] was taken as a basis for action research approaches. In addition, critical psychology (Holzkamp, 1983) and especially critical pedagogy and adult education (Freire, 1970, 1998) played important roles as basic impulses for action research approaches. Action research at this time was also influenced by the critical approach as advocated by radical feminism.

During the second half of the 1970s and in the 1980s, action research disappeared in Germany and became scarce in many other Western countries. This was partly due to the fact that action research was seen as the research of Marxist militants (Coenen, 1987; Moser, 1975). However, it revived in England and other English-speaking countries, especially Australia and New Zealand, around 1985.

In this period, Touraine developed his action theory, called actionalism, which he and his team in Paris combined with an action research model known as sociological intervention (Touraine, 1978). This was a group work method in the tradition of Lewin and Moreno. This sociological intervention methodology was extensively used in research on new social movements (Boog, 1989; Dubost, 2001). In these interventions, militants of social movements were stimulated to reflect on their collective identity as part of the 'historicity' (the dynamic social world) they lived in. This reflection was to result in a clear collective narrative, a project for the social world as they wanted it to be. Touraine called this project a cultural orientation, which referred to this particular movement's ideal and holistic view on the economic, cultural and political institutional framework of society. The underlying idea was that once they were able to formulate such a project they would also be able to formulate action strategies. Empowerment in this approach meant being able to formulate this project, to appropriate it as your own collective identity and to know how to translate it into action strategies.

A special place is taken by action research as developmental work in so-called developing countries. In particular, the experiences and perceptions from Africa, Asia and Latin America played an inspiring role in the theory and practice of action research in Western European countries. As early as the 1950s, a great deal of interest arose in the views of Mahatma Ghandi in India. This concerned not only his views on non-violent action but also his ideas about community development. Community development became an important part of the strategies of the UN for developmental processes. Other influences on action research included the ideas of Mao Zedong in China (Huizer, 1993). The experiments with Ujamaa in Tanzania, Africa, and with *kibbutzim* in Israel also caught the attention. Initiatives in Latin America were influential, for instance the many initiatives in the areas of *desarrollo communal, acción comunal, educación fundamental,* and *participación popular.* Orlando Fals Borda's study *Acción comunal en una vereda Colombiana* (1961) became well known, just as the *Centro Regional de Educación Fundamental* (CREFAL) of the Union Panamericana and UNESCO were established in the Mexican city of Patzcuaro. However, the greatest influence has to be attributed to the experiences and perceptions of Paulo Freire. Freire developed an (adult) literacy approach that focussed on learning to read and write about the concrete everyday life and social contexts of the learners. This activated them to reflect on their social situation (conscientization) and thus enabled them to become empowered. His ideas influenced participatory and educational action research all over the world (Keune & Boog, 2000).

Four Recent Action Research Approaches

In the last two decades, action research has revived, especially in the Anglo-Saxon countries. Elsewhere, social scientists have generally followed this interest in action research slowly. Action research has profited from the enormous upheaval in qualitative research. According to Todhunter (2001), this has been caused by the growing popularity of the so-called interactive research methodologies. Just as in action research, this is a kind of research in which the interaction between researchers and researched subjects is explicitly used for the processes of data gathering and data analysis. Researchers and researched subjects interact. In this interaction there is a subject–subject relationship between researchers and researched subjects. However, the researcher usually owns the 'data' and controls the interpretation of it as well as the way it is used to answer the research question. The intended effects of the research are owned and controlled by the commissioners and researchers and are not an issue in the interaction between researchers and researched subjects. The research is, for instance, meant to improve an organization or to reach an agreement on issues of public policy.

Nowadays, action research is a fully fledged, respected social research practice. All elements and preoccupations of the aforementioned approaches can be synthesized into four broad approaches: pragmatic action research, co-operative inquiry, 'critical' action research, and action research within the tradition of systems thinking. Though these approaches differ, they share many theoretical and methodological assumptions and even take each other's theoretical and methodological elements into account as co-grounding. Action research practices are increasingly converging, caused by the developments and positive experiences with communicative methodologies such as, for example, group work and the cycle of experiential learning. Therefore, I will briefly characterize the approaches and pay some attention to their convergence.

Pragmatic action research is based on the philosophical-pragmatic works of Dewey and Mead (Greenwood & Levin, 1998). It has two central parameters: 'knowledge generation through action and experimentation, and the role of participatory democracy,' according to Levin and Greenwood (2001, p. 104). They 'argue for knowledge construction processes that involve both researchers and local stakeholders in the same learning-action process, thereby fulfilling both a participative democratic ideal and achieving knowledge generation through learning from action.'

The English scientists Reason, Rowan and Heron (Heron, 1996; Reason & Rowan, 1981) developed an action research approach which has become known as co-operative inquiry. It places strong emphasis on personal growth, self-actualization, and inquiry into personal strengths. It owes much to the works of Lewin and Moreno and the work of the Tavistock Institute but also to the diversity of methods and techniques that were used in the radical feminist therapy groups, such as encounter, art therapy, gestalt therapy, and transactional analysis. Their underlying worldview is participatory and integrates elements from holistic-spiritualistic alternative cultures (Heron, 1996; Reason, 2002). The philosophical pragmatism of Dewey has also influenced co-operative inquiry.

Critical action research is a family of models, grounded by critical hermeneutics and often by neo-Marxist theories in sociology (Habermas, Negt), psychology (Holzkamp) and education (Freire). It has different adjectives applied to it: participatory, emancipatory and exemplary. Strong practices of critical and participatory action research can be found, for instance, in Australia and New Zealand (Hoogwerf, 2002; Kemmis & McTaggert, 1988; Zuber-Skerritt, 1996), and Austria (Boog, 2002). Exemplary action research is a specific mode developed by Coenen (1987) and his group in the Netherlands. Besides the critical sociological, psychological and pedagogical inspirations, this approach is strongly influenced by philosophical pragmatism (Mead's interactionalism) and Giddens's structuration theory.

Finally, there is action research that is grounded in systems thinking. Systems thinking views action as embedded in unpredictable complex systems which are in a continual process of self-creation and re-creation. In action research, it challenges people to reflect on the place and function of what you do or do not do as part of a dynamic whole. This reflection can provide more insight into the potentialities and possibilities to act otherwise and in this way can enhance human emancipation (Flood, 2001).

Despite their differences, these action research approaches share six important characteristics:

(1) The cycles of research, experiential learning and action.
(2) A common goal-orientedness and 'ethics': emancipation, individual and social empowerment and participatory democracy.
(3) A general action theoretical approach. Following Nijk (1978, 1984), the theoretical and methodological stance in action theory is inherently critical and grounded in an emancipatory worldview. Active experiential learning is fundamental to the notion of the human being as the active creator of his or her world.

In the last decades of the twentieth century, Giddens (1976, 1984), Habermas (1981), and Touraine (1965, 1978) developed general action theories which transcended the existing disciplinary division, as did Dewey and Lewin in their time. In particular, the dualism of psychology and sociology was transcended into a dynamic synthesis. Both disciplines gained knowledge about two sides of one and the same coin: social action. Thus they criticized and went beyond the existing conventional approaches in the social sciences, which were still based on the methodologies of seventeenth-century natural sciences (Giddens, 1976; Smith, 1998; Toulmin, 2001). Moreover, these action theories went beyond the dualisms that were usually applied in the explanation and understanding (epistemology) of action. Rationalism and historicism, individualism and collectivism, structure and action, inside and outside, and subject and object were not opposed but taken into account side by side. Different founding theories were also synthesized. For instance, despite their differences, Habermas's communication theory and Giddens's structuration theory synthesized elements of hermeneutics, philosophical pragmatism, language philosophy, open systems theory, communication theory and structuralism. Such action theories are essential for the foundation of action research projects, as well as for the enhancement of action research as a special kind of fundamental scientific social research. It provides rationality for researchers for the (ex-post) reconstruction of concrete research projects. For researchers and their scientific community it is important to work on the sophistication of this role of action theory. Action is 'intentional action' (Weber) and transaction (Dewey), which means that it is embedded in a social context, an intersubjective social cultural space. Action is learned in the transactional processes of socialization. Human beings' lives consist of socio-cultural performances that are controlled by the possibilities permitted by the social system they are part of. However, what they do or do not feel and think is basically unpredictable. Human beings have the capacity to learn and to develop new action strategies based on new insights. Right from the start of their lives, they are pressed to learn and to socialize, which also develops their capacity to learn, which in turn empowers them to do 'otherwise' or 'make a difference.' They can reflect, but only in interaction and depending on the social system they live in. In action research processes, researchers and researched subjects try to get a grip on the action processes of the researched subjects and develop new action scripts through co-operative reflection. These new action scripts are tried out in practice on a small scale, evaluated, and then adjusted or rejected. Furthermore, action and reflection are seen to reinforce each other, which results in a cyclical or narrative development of individual lives or life projects. Action is reflexively monitored continuously (Giddens, 1984). Reflection must not be disconnected from action; otherwise one runs the risk of estrangement, utopianism, dogmatism, scientism or fundamentalism.

(4) Another important point in which all four action research approaches converge is that the underlying action theories imply that (new) knowledge in social research is basically gained through a process of mutual understanding, a so-called double hermeneutic process. Researchers interpret an already interpreted world; researched subjects comment on that interpretation, and so on. In the process of mutual understanding, the research partners try to get to know and trust each other as equals in self-knowledge about their other-ness (Ricoeur, 1992). This dialogically acquired self-knowledge is a necessary condition for, primarily, the researched subjects to learn their possibilities for self-determination. The researchers also learn to improve their capacities as action researchers to facilitate the personal or other growth of the researched subjects.

(5) This subject–subject relationship has implications for the criterion of the validity of the new action scripts gained, based on (new) self-knowledge (empowerment, emancipation). Validation is achieved by the procedures of 'communicative or dialogical validity' (Smaling, 2000). It also implies that the research process must be able to function as a catalyst for structural change. This is validated by 'catalytic validity.' 'Catalytic validity represents the degree in which the research process reorients, focuses and energises the participants toward knowing reality in order to transform it, a process Freire (1972) called conscientisation' (Bernard, 2000, p. 183).

(6) All research approaches share a co-generative research assessment procedure. Researcher, researched subjects and other involved actors reconstruct the research process and weigh the possible effects (including both intended and unintended outcomes). This assessment has to occur at the individual and at the collective level. At the individual level, this assessment consists of learner reports about the growth of the capacity for self-determination in the domain on which the research focuses, but also in other domains of one's life. At the collective level the assessment focuses on the question of whether the researched subjects and other actors involved obtain more transforming power and influence on the processes of decision making in organizations and institutions (political empowerment and emancipation).

Some Recommendations to Improve the Practice of Action Research

A theoretical basis is no guarantee of a positive end result for any particular action research. Which criteria does a model of action research have to fulfil if it is to realize its emancipatory content and effects?

To start with, researchers have to implement the heuristics of an action research approach with a sincere emancipatory intention. If there is no explicit emancipatory or empowering vision guiding the project from the outset, it will prove difficult to realize any emancipatory effects, or even worse, the research might turn out to be non-emancipatory or result in the de-emancipation of the researched subjects.

A further requirement is that the research project has to be a mutually supported learning process for both the researcher and the researched. The last few decades have shown a remarkable comeback and revival of all kinds of qualitative research approaches, especially action-oriented or 'interactive' qualitative research. According to Todhunter (2001), action research holds a special place. It is interactive research where emancipation, empowerment and democratization form the criteria for the demarcation between action research and other research designs.

However, whether a project will succeed or not is highly dependent on the core process of action research: the interaction between researchers and the researched subjects that forms the basis for the quality of the produced knowledge. At the same time, this interaction represents an experimental microcosm of the problematic social situation of the researched subjects, which was the initial reason for setting up an action research project. Since the professional skills of the researcher to handle this situation form the basis for a good action research project, it is important to formulate some recommendations for researchers. These recommendations stem from the specific foundation of action research in action theory and meet the test of its criteria: empowerment, emancipation and democratization.

First of all, researchers should be able to formulate and set up the action research in accordance with its basic assumptions. They must know the ins and outs of sophisticated action theories and how to use a broad range of communicative methods and techniques, learning methods and techniques, and research methods and techniques.

Moreover, the researcher should have an overview of the chances that the research will be successful. An analysis of the specific situation of the researched subjects is necessary, including the history, power structure, and network of actors, public policies and laws. This may be done in a pilot study, which could also be a way of getting to know the researched subjects better. At this stage it is important that the researchers start to interest the researched group, or at least some of its individual members, in the first global design of the research: they have to create a basis of support. They might start a so-called group of critical friends, a small group selected from the researched subjects, which will stay close to the researcher, especially at the beginning.

Initially, an action research design cannot be anything but rather sketchy. As soon as possible the researched subjects must be engaged in their role as co-researchers. In that role, they must be able to co-control the research process and participate in the decisions about the following steps. This has to be communicated clearly to possible commissioners of the project. It is also important to organize good communication lines with the other actors who play a role in the research situation. The empowerment of the primary researched subjects depends to a large degree on whether the stakeholders allow them to be empowered. In his experiences in Latin America and the Netherlands, Keune (1993) found that people in power reacted very repressively, even before the researched subjects started to develop the slightest idea of self-determination. He describes the situation where the stakeholders surrounding the primary researched subjects have a disempowering influence as the 'boomerang effect.'

Basically, the relationship between researcher and researched subjects is a dialogue, but frequently the research entails a multilogue in which others besides the primary subject are involved. Therefore, in some cases it might be wise for researchers to first try to empower other stakeholders, because in this way they can pave the path for the empowerment of the primary researched subject. For instance, a research project might start with the development of a participatory professional practice as a first step (a necessary though not *per se* sufficient condition) towards empowering their clients.

Although the research partners are equals, they are different because their expertise lies in different domains and aspects. The researched subject is an expert in the matters of his or her everyday life. The researcher is an expert and the one responsible for proposing the application of certain methods and techniques. The researcher must be an expert in (adult) education processes. The researcher must be explicit and open about his or her social ethics. Many researchers use the concept of 'facilitator' to capture all the practical, methodological, theoretical, analytical, pedagogical, and teaching skills of the researcher. Greenwood and Levin (1998) are more modest and describe the role of the researcher as a 'friendly outsider.' But it is clear that action researchers need a larger range of skills than just those of a social researcher.

Researchers need enough self-knowledge to be able to know how to delegate research tasks to others (researched subjects, critical friends, other researchers). This delegation might also have the function of enhancing the process of trustworthy communication, the learning processes of the researched subjects and/or the empowering effects of the research process. Therefore, it is important that researchers have the patience and the insights of a good teacher.

To Conclude

Researchers and researched subjects have access to a growing number of methods and techniques. Action research nowadays is sophisticated on the level of practices and applications in concrete projects as well as on the level of their theoretical and methodological foundations. The sophistication of action research is a result of the growth and diversification of approaches. This has been caused by a growth in projects, both as regards numbers of projects and the scope of the projects in different domains, and the increasing reflection and communication that goes along with this, resulting in numerous publications.

In this article it has been argued that in the history of action research, the concepts of emancipation, empowerment and participatory democracy have always played a significant role, at least theoretically. However, these concepts are difficult to assess within the limited time-spatial happenings of a concrete action research project. In the history of action research, social scientists have worked on the sophistication of the content of these concepts. They were skilled in fundamental theoretical and methodological matters and, at the same time, were skilled practitioners and researchers. A considerable part of this refinement developed out of their experiences as learners in research projects. Epistemologically this sophistication occurred through action theoretical perspectives, which see the transactions between researcher and researched subjects as a microcosm of macrosocial processes. Concepts like individual empowerment, self-actualization, raising self-consciousness, learning to stand up for yourself and self-advocacy can be used as goals for a broad range of learning, communication and research techniques on the transactional level of researcher and researched subjects. In this way flesh is put onto the bones of emancipation and social participation.

Action research is social research connected to an educational intervention. From the start, the scientists who developed it shared a utopia. They wanted a social science that enhanced the capacities of the researched subjects to become self-determining people who define themselves as being free, as individuals who have self-knowledge, who know how to manage difficult situations and how to get access to resources to support their efforts (Mithaug, 1996). They wanted a social science that helped create active citizenship. But action research projects can only be assessed discursively in their emancipatory effects during and after the research. Action research establishes participatory ethics in the hearts and minds of all participants, which is a starting point for democratized societies. To be an adequate action researcher the social scientist must:

- juggle action theories and methodology;
- be explicit in his ethical stance;
- know numerous methods and techniques to facilitate experiential learning, in order to raise the self-consciousness and self-knowledge of the subjects involved in the research project;
- have gained experience in the application of methods to assess different empowering effects during and after the research process.

Notes

1. The approaches within the stream of critical action research are based on critical social theory, which I see as broader than the Frankfurter Schule of Adorno and Horkheimer and others. Many scientists in even more disciplines were inspired by Marx and Engels's critique of capitalism. Habermas is a social philosopher/sociologist and the most important theoretician of the so-called second-generation Frankfurter Schule. Critical action research was developed within critical sociology (e.g. Habermas, Offe, and Negt), critical psychology (e.g. Holzkamp) and critical pedagogy (Freire). Apart from emancipation, critical action research approaches share the following three theoretical and methodological preoccupations. First, these approaches are characterized by a subject–subject relationship between researchers and the researched subjects. Second, they contain a critique of the state and state apparatus and other cultural institutions representing the dominating ideology of the ruling classes, based on the critique of capitalist economy. Third, they were influenced by Freud's psychoanalytic interpretation approach. Moreover, they thematized an important distinction between 'the situation that we have now' (Sein) which is repressive, etc., and the transformation thereof into a new (utopian) future which is characterized by social justice and where all men are equals, etc. (Sollen). This theme is emancipation and is connected to the search for a 'subject' which came into being with Enlightenment. This implies a critical hermeneutic action theory which has as its central theme the possibility of the 'free' human meaningful action of a subject against the determining forces of nature and society in which this action is necessarily situated.
2. Though this was first outlined in an essay in 1971 (Habermas & Luhmann, 1971).

References

Bernard, W. T. (2000). Participatory research as emancipatory method. Challenges and opportunities. In D. Burton (Ed.), *Research training for social scientists* (pp. 167–185). London and Thousand Oaks, CA: Sage.

Boog, B. (1989). *Het aktionalistisch paradigma van Alain Touraine cs*. Hoogezand: Stubeg.

Boog, B. (2002). Handelingsonderzoek: Een update. *Sociale Interventie, 11*(4), 27–40.

Coenen, H. (1987). *Handelingsonderzoek als exemplarisch leren. Een bijdrage aan de fundering van de methodologie van handelingsonderzoek*. Groningen and Utrecht.

Dewey, J. (1999). *Ervaring en opvoeding*. Houten: Bohn Stafleu Van Loghem.

Dubost, J. (2001). Réflections sur les passés de la recherche-action et son actualité. *Revue Internationale de Psychosociologie, VII*(16–17), 9–19.

Fachbereich Sozialpädagogiek an der Pädagogischen Hochschule Berlin. (1972). Überlegungen zur Handlungsforschung in der Sozialpädagogiek. In F. Haag, H. Krüger, W. Schwärzel, & J. Wildt (Eds.), *Aktionsforschung. Forschungsstrategieen, Forschungsfelder und Forschungspläne* (pp. 56–75). München: Juventa Verlag.

Flood, R. L. (2001). The relationship of 'systems thinking' to action research. In P. Reason & H. Bradbury (Eds.), *Handbook of action research participative inquiry and practice* (pp. 133–144). Thousand Oaks, London, New Delhi: Sage Publications.

Freire, P. (1970). The adult literacy process as cultural action for freedom. *Harvard Educational Review, 40*(2), May.

Freire, P. (1998). *Pedagogy of freedom*. Lanham and Oxford: Rowman & Littlefield Publishers.

Giddens, A. (1976). *New rules of sociological method*. Cambridge: Polity Press.

Giddens, A. (1984). *The constitution of society–an outline of the theory of structuration*. Cambridge: Polity Press.

Greenwood, D. J. (2002). Action research: Unfulfilled promises and unmet challenges. *Concepts & Transformation, 7*(2), 117–139.

Greenwood, D. J., & Levin, M. (1998). *Introduction to action research. Social research for social change*. London and Thousand Oaks, CA: Sage.

Habermas, J. (1981). *Theorie des Kommunikativen Handelns 2Bd* (Erste Auflage). Frankfurt am Main: Suhrkamp Verlag.

Habermas, J., & Luhmann, N. (1971). *Theorie der gesellschaft oder Sozialtechnologie*. Frankfurt: Suhrkamp Verlag.

Heron, J. (1996). *Co-operative inquiry. Research into the human condition*. London and Thousand Oaks, CA: Sage.

Holzkamp, K. (1983). *Grundlegung der Psychologie*. Frankfurt am Main and New York: Campus Verlag.

Holzkamp, K. (1993). *Lernen. Subjektwissenschaftliche Grundlegung*. Frankfurt am Main and New York: Campus Verlag.

Hoogwerf, L. (2002). *Innovation and change in a rehabilitation unit for the elderly through action research*. Utrecht: Proefschrift.

Huizer, G. (1993). Participatory action research in rural development. In B. Boog, H. Coenen, J. Foolen, & L. Keune (Eds.), *De actualiteit van handelingsonderzoek* (pp. 57–75). Tilburg: Tilburg University Press.

Jacobs, G. (2002). Humanistics. Reflection and action in the transitional space of the political and the existential. In A. Halsema & D. van Houten (Eds.). *Empowering humanity. State of the art in humanistics*. (pp. 243–255). Utrecht: De Tijdstroom Uitgeverij.

Kemmis, S., & McTaggartt, R. (Eds.). (1988). *The action research planner* (3rd ed.). Victoria, Australia: Deakin University.

Keune, L. (1993). Participatie en boemerangs—Ervaringen uit Colombia, Nederland en Mexico. In B. Boog, H. Coenen, J. Foolen, & L. Keune (Eds.), *De actualiteit van handelingsonderzoek* (pp. 77–95). Tilburg: Tilburg University Press.

Keune, L., & Boog, B. (2000). *Investigación Acción Ejemplar: Conceptos y applicaciones*. San José, Costa Rico: DEI.

Levin, M., & Greenwood, D. (2001). Pragmatic action research and the struggle to transform universities into learning communities. In P. Reason & H. Bradbury (Eds.), *Handbook of action research*. London: Sage.

Lewin, K. (1948). *Resolving social conflicts: Selected papers on group dynamics*. In G. G. Lewin (Ed.). New York: Harper & Row.

Mithaug, D. H. (1996). Fairness, liberty and empowerment evaluation. In D. M. Fetterman, S. J. Kaftarian, & A. Wandersman (Eds.), *Empowerment evaluation, knowledge and tools for self-assessment and accountability* (pp. 234–255). Thousand Oaks, London, New Delhi: Sage Publications.

Moreno, J. L. (1951). *Sociometry, experimental method and the science of society.* New York: Beacon House.

Moreno, J. L. (1952). *Who shall survive?* New York: Beacon House.

Moser, H. (1975). *Aktionsforschung als kritische Theorie der Sozialwissenschaften.* München: Kösel.

Nijk, A. J. (1978). *The mythe van de zelfontplooiing en andere wijsgerig-andragologische opstellen.* Meppel: Boom.

Nijk, A. J. (1984). *Handelen en verbeteren. Wijsgerig andragologische voorstudiën.* Meppel: Boom.

Noffke, S. (1997). Themes and tensions in US action research. Towards historical analysis. In S. Hollingworth (Ed.), *International action research. A casebook for educational reform* (pp. 2–16). London: The Falmer Press.

Reason, P. (2002). Justice, sustainability, and participation: Inaugural professorial lecture. *Concepts and Transformation, 7*(1), 7–29.

Reason, P., & Rowan, J. (Eds.). (1981). *Human inquiry: A sourcebook of new paradigm research.* Chichester: John Wiley.

Ricoeur, P. (1992). *Oneself as another.* Chicago, IL, and London: The University of Chicago Press.

Smaling, A. (2000). Inductieve, analoge en communicatieve generalisatie. In F. Wester, A. Smaling, & L. Mulder (Eds.), *Praktijkgericht kwalitatief onderzoek* (pp. 155–171). Bussum: Coutinho.

Smith, M. J. (1998). *Social science in question.* London: Sage (The Open University Press).

Smith, M. K. (2001). Kurt Lewin, groups. Experiential learning and action research. *The encyclopedia of informal education.* Retrieved August 4, 2003 from http://www:infed:org/thinkers/et-lewin:htm

Todhunter, C. (2001). Undertaking action research: Negotiating the road ahead. Retrieved September, 2002, from Social Research Update, 34, University of Surrey. website: http://www:soc:surrey:ac:uk/sru/SRU34:html.

Toulmin, S. (2000). Be reasonable, not certain. *Concepts and Transformation, IV*(2).

Toulmin, S. (2001). *Terug naar de rede.* Kampen: Agora/Pelckmans.

Touraine, A. (1965). *Sociologie de l'action.* Paris: Seuil.

Touraine, A. (1978). *La voix et le regard.* Paris: Editions du Seuil.

Touraine, A. (1992). *Critique de la Modernité.* Paris: Fayard.

Touraine, A. (1994). *Qu'est-ce que la Démocratie?* Paris: Fayard.

Vermeulen, D., & Boog, B. (1994). *Een nieuw perspectief voor emancipatie. Verslag onderzoek FORT-Friesland.* Groningen: Andragogiek RuG.

Zuber-Skerritt, O. (Ed.). (1996). *New directions in action research.* London: Falmer Press.

CHAPTER 2

Deploying Qualitative Methods for Critical Social Purposes

Gaile S. Cannella and Yvonna S. Lincoln

Twenty years ago, in her *Harvard Educational Review* article, Elizabeth Ellsworth (1989) questioned the assumption that critical perspectives or critical research were either empowering or transformative. She argued that critical theory was embedded within patriarchal forms of reason, Enlightenment logic, and male domination, such that the attempted adoption of a critical lens can easily create the illusion of justice while actually reinscribing old forms of power.

Beyond Ellsworth's criticisms, it is also clear now that critical inquiry cannot be described utilizing traditional research language like models, predetermined linear methods, or any forms of unquestioned methodologies (Richardson, 2000). Indeed, even several of the foundational terms of critical theory—divided consciousness, false consciousness—imply a singular truth to which adherents must pledge allegiance, lest they be charged with failing to see or own this singular truth. Further, some critical perspectives would challenge the notion of a singular truth while remaining concerned about power and oppression. Although many contemporary researchers claim to use critical qualitative research methods (and we are among those), these inquiry practices often do not transform or even appear to challenge the dominant or mainstream constructions.

Our intent here is to explore why much of the critical/critical theorist work that has been done has not always resulted in any form of increased social justice. We echo Ellsworth's question: Why does this not feel empowering? Our own questions, however, go further, and we explore the issues of how we filter research through a critical lens. How do we deploy qualitative methods (which are by and large far less linear than conventional experimental and quantitative methods) for critical historical, social justice and policy purposes? How can we be more explicit about critical methodologies and make both our methodologies and our analyses clearer and more accessible to a larger set of publics? How do we construct an environment that values a critical perspective? Is it possible to construct critical research that does not simultaneously create new forms of oppressive power for itself or for its practitioners? What does a critical perspective mean for research issues and questions, for frames that construct data collection and analyses, and forms of interpretation and re-presentation? How do we effect a wider dissemination of critical studies such that we prompt a broader civic debate around our analyses?

The Criticism Inherent in Critical Perspectives

One of the major, but unexplored, issues surrounding critical perspectives is what, precisely, is meant by them. Thus, we are offering a preliminary definition of how we are using the term "critical perspectives." By critical perspectives, we mean any research that recognizes power—that seeks in its analyses to plumb the archaeology of taken-for-granted perspectives to understand how unjust and oppressive social conditions came to be reified as historical "givens." These taken-for-granted perspectives might include, for example, unequal educational opportunity, racism, the acceptance of an inevitability of poverty, the relegation of women to second-class political and economic status, the systematic devaluation of homemaking and childrearing as productive economic activity, romanticized views of children and childhood that actually create forms of oppression for those who are younger (Cannella, 1997), and the like. The foundational questions to critical work are: Who/what is helped/privileged/legitimated? Who/what is harmed/oppressed/disqualified? In addition to poststructural analyses and postmodern challenges to the domination of grand narratives, the range of feminist perspectives, queer theory and its critique of forms of normalization, as well as anti-colonialist assessments of empire, are included in our broad definition. Such research, in addition to searching out the historical origins of socially and politically reified social arrangements, also seeks to understand how victims of such social arrangements come to accept and even collaborate in maintaining oppressive aspects of the system.

Further, critical perspectives seek to illuminate the hidden structures of power deployed in the construction and maintenance of its own power and the disempowerment of others (e.g., groups, knowledges, ways of being, perspectives). Frequently, these power structures (whether hidden or obvious) are/can be tied to late capitalism and more currently, neoliberalism and its counterpart, invasive hyper-capitalism. Neoliberalism, with its political roots in globalization and the discourse of "free" markets (however inequitably these markets actually function), serves as an economic backdrop to the redistribution of wealth in the guise of liberal political theory. The real power of neoliberalism has been to create corporate states and individuals who are more powerful and more wealthy than many nations, but further, to facilitate corporate power (Said, 1979) that is not restricted by national boundaries, and, finally, to concentrate wealth in an ever-smaller set of hands. As capital has been created, so has more extensive and dire impoverishment, both at home and abroad.

Critical perspectives also inquire deeply into the usages of language and the circulation of discourses which are used to shape all of social life, from advertising to decisions regarding the candidate for whom we should vote. Primarily, however, critical researchers are interested in the "language games" which maintain power relations, which appear to prevent transformative action, and which insistently shape a dulled, misled, and/or false public consciousness. Language gives form to ideologies and prompts action and consequently is deeply complicit in power relations and class struggles.

Next, critical perspectives are profoundly engaged with issues of race, gender and socioeconomic level, as major shapers as well as components of historically reified structures of oppression. Often, a given scholar's focus will be on one of the three, but increasingly, consciousness of how various forms of oppression and privilege intersect (Collins, 2000) results in a focus on the interactive nature and institutionalization, of power, oppression, and injustice. An example would be the hybrid condition of injustice suffered by individuals based on race, economic status, or class and the particular political destitution of women. More recently, scholars have also been deconstructing whiteness, the invisible advantage assumed because of it, and the oppressions suffered by the intersecting of societal power structures based on gender, sexual orientation, and economic status.

Finally, along with race, class, and gender, indigenous scholars virtually always approach relations between themselves and imperialist forms of power from the perspective of colonialism, neocolonialism, and postcolonialism. Relations shaped by conquest and occupation inevitably demand critical interrogation, for the lasting vestiges of cultural, linguistic, and spiritual destruction alter forever the cultural landscape of an indigenous people (Spivak, 1999).

So Why Are Critical Perspectives Not Empowering?

One might well ask, since critical perspectives are profoundly engaged with powerful issues of our time, why is it that so little critical research becomes a part of civic debate? Why does so little important work make it to the editorial pages of newspapers or into venues routinely perused by intellectuals and engaged citizens, such as the *Atlantic Monthly* or *Harper's*, but is instead aimed at the even smaller audiences captured by such publications as *Daedalus* or *Tikkun?* Certainly, the lack of wider public discussion surrounding such research is one reason most of such work has not yet resulted in any measurable increase in social justice, nor has it had any real visible transformative effect on social policy or education.

Critical perspectives have already acknowledged the role of the research "construct" in the generation and perpetuation of power for particular groups, especially knowledge and cultural workers such as academics (Greenwood & Levin, 2000; Knorr-Cetina & Mulkay, 1983). Indeed, knowledge production, traditionally the province of the scholarly profession, has finally seen its flowering in the information age and the information society. However, even when we recognize this research/power complicity, we must still, as academic knowledge generators and producers, conduct research, both because of the influence that it holds within dominant discourses and, more selfishly, because that is what we are hired to do in certain kinds of institutions. Critically inclined academics, however, continue to struggle with how to rethink our fields in ways that generate critically oriented questions and methods, even while addressing issues such as voice, representation, and the avoidance of new forms of oppressive power. Although qualitative methods and alternative paradigm inquiry offer possibilities for the generation of epistemologies and methodologies that insist upon the examination of themselves, even qualitative inquiry creates power for, and all too frequently, a focus on the researcher herself. Thus, we are caught in the paradox of attempting to investigate and deconstruct power relations, even while we are ourselves engaged in a project which creates and re-creates power accruing primarily to us.

We believe that three issues can be identified that contribute to the continued marginalization of critical theorizing and critical pedagogy. One issue is endogenous to critical theories themselves, while two others are exogenous, but each of the issues can be addressed by the community of critical knowledge workers. First, we discuss things that academics do to keep their work from being read by broader audiences. These practices are tied both to training and to the insulated environment that is the academy. Second, we believe that there are political forces, particularly on the political right, that have a large stake in quelling serious critiques of schooling practices, critical research, and critical researchers (Horowitz, 2006). Conservative forces within and external to the academy mount rigorous efforts at systemic and systematic disqualification of critical qualitative research and those who produce it, the most serious effort thus far having been to "capture" federal resources sufficiently to deny funding to qualitative and critical researchers, while mandating that "what works" is primarily or solely randomized experiments (Mosteller & Boruch, 2002; National Research Council, 2002). Third, we believe the effects of neoliberal and hyper-capitalism have created additional social problems (e.g., increasing poverty of some segments of Western society, demands for goods and services which outstrip the global ability to produce or deliver them, unquestioned nationalisms) which in turn have led to a de-emphasis on certain forms of academic knowledge production. We would like to deal with each of those in turn.

"Repressive Myths," Difficult Language, and Writing Complexities

When Ellsworth (1989) speaks of "repressive myths" associated with critical theorizing and critical pedagogy, she refers to forms of language which "operate at a high level of abstraction" (p. 300), the overall effect of which is to reinscribe certain forms of oppression within the classroom. In part, this occurs because

> … when educational researchers advocating critical pedagogy fail to provide a clear statement of their political agendas, the effect is to hide the fact that as critical pedagogues, they are in fact seeking to

appropriate public resources (classrooms, school supplies, teacher/professor salaries, academic requirements and degree) to further various "progressive political agendas that they believe to be for the
public good—and therefore deserving of public resources …" As a result, the critical education "movement" has failed to develop a clear articulation for its existence, its goals, priorities, risks, or potentials.
(p. 301)

Some of the foregoing criticism has since been answered by the critical community, but some
critical theorizing remains connected to patriarchy and rationalist abstraction. Ellsworth found, in
her media course, that concepts borrowed from the critical pedagogy literature were singularly un-
helpful in uncovering the experiences of racism and other "isms" brought to her classroom and recognized that she and her students needed to move away from the regulating aspects of rationalism,
which "operate[s] in ways that set up as its opposite an irrational Other,"[1] as it "has become a vehicle
for regulating conflict and the power to speak" (p. 301), silencing some voices and marginalizing
others.

Rationalistic argumentation, however, is not the only issue the critical educationists face. The
issues of abstraction, of difficult languages and "complicated writing styles" make the work of many
critical researchers appear less transparent than it might be and appears to create a smaller audience than the ideas warrant. At times, we have been guilty of the same charge, so we abstain from
adopting some sort of literary high ground here. Indeed, at times, the material we undertake to
deconstruct and de-mystify demands a complex political and philosophical treatment, circling as
it does around abstruse social and democratic theory. Nevertheless, as Lather (1996) makes clear,
language itself possesses a "politics" wherein "Clear speech is part of a discursive system, a network
of power that has material *effects*" and thus, "Sometimes we need a density that fits the thought
being expressed" (p. 3). Additionally, St. Pierre (2000) reminds us that the "burden of intelligibility" lies with the reader/receiver as well as with the writer/constructor. She asks the question:
"How does one learn to hear and 'understand' a statement made within a different structure of
intelligibility?" (p. 25). We would argue, however, that Lather's analysis regarding the deskilling
effects of "clear and concise plain prose" and its relationship to a pervasive anti-intellectualism in
American society, while true, does not mitigate the necessity of making our theories and arguments
more accessible to a broader set of audiences in order to further public scrutiny and debate about
these ideas.

Consequently, while we strongly hold to the premise that sound theorizing is both academically
necessary and epistemologically moral and that there indeed might be some "violence of clarity," a
kind of "non-innocence" in plain prose, it is also clear that many who would like to understand the
foundational elements of what is being argued either cannot or will not struggle with our terminologies
and languages. The requirement that thinking differently necessitates speaking differently becomes a
barrier. Rather than being the rational argument makers, we are unfortunately cast in the mold of being
Ellsworth's "irrational Other." Thus, in part, the problem of critical pedagogues and theorists is partially
one of our own making and partially one of difficult circumstance. When dominant understandings are
so thoroughly embedded within truth orientations, critical language and abstract terminologies sometimes ensure that ideas will not be received by a patient audience that has learned to expect answers to
generalizable solutions.

There are, however, greater reasons so little critical qualitative research makes it into the public
realm of debate. One of these reasons is linked to the backlashes against feminisms and other traditionally marginalized knowledges. As Patricia Hill Collins (2000) explains in her discussion of Black feminist thought, as critical work and resistance become evident related to intersecting oppressions, new
forms of power are generated to silence/ignore the traditionally oppressed and to reinscribe/reinstate
power for those who have been traditionally privileged.

Reinscribing Oppressive Forms of Knowledge:
Attacking Diversity and Discrediting Critique

As we and others have written, the civil rights successes of the 1960s resulted in new possibilities for academia and the acceptance of the voices and knowledges of those who have been traditionally marginalized. In academia, women and gender studies, ethnic studies, and diverse research philosophies and methodologies emerged and gained credibility. Yet there were those who were not happy with these gains across society in general and in academia specifically. For example, as women made gains in the workplace and elsewhere, actions were taken to resubjugate them/us (Faludi, 1991). As women made gains in traditional domains of academia, there was/is a backlash against their leadership styles, their research topics, their publication outlets, and so on.

In society in general, a movement was specifically designed and funded to (re)inscribe a monocultural conservative agenda in the media, the judiciary, and in academia. Foundations and think tanks were created that funded a range of broad-based societal activities including particular forms of literature used to discredit feminisms, qualitative research methods, and constructs like affirmative action and multiculturalism. Most are familiar with these activities by now because of the past seven years of a U.S. government administration that has been entirely supported by this monocultural agenda. However, most (even academics) do not notice the ways that this activity has entirely transformed the expectations for intellectual engagement; for example, when an academic discussion is conducted via the media, most listeners are not aware that three out of four panel members are employed by "right of center" foundations or think tanks.

An Example of Narrowed Scholarship: Privileging Evidence-Based Research

Specific academic activities have ranged from publications designed to discredit feminist, critical, postmodern, and postcolonial voices to funding for students whose purposes would be to build careers using the narrowed academic agenda to the redeployment of public grant funding privileging monocultural practices (Lincoln & Cannella, 2004). Contemporarily, a major example is the discourse of evidence-based research infused throughout government agencies and invading academic fields like medicine, education, and business within nation states and globally. Constructs like controlled experiments, replicability, efficiency, validity, and generalizability are again imposed as superior, more sophisticated, and representing quality (Cannella & Miller, 2008). All the language is present, from designs that use 'randomized experiments' to quantitative orientations like 'correlational,' 'disciplined,' and 'rigorous'—reference terms used as legitimation like 'medicine' and 'technology' as academic fields of power, the degrading of the field of education, calls for what our 'children deserve'—to actions that would redeploy 'funding.' This discourse is not simply found in academic journals, but it is used in testimony of academics before Congress as illustrated in the words of Jeffrey Pfeffer in March 2007: "Organizations … ought to base policies NOT on casual benchmarking, on ideology or belief … but instead should implement evidence-based management." He goes on to promote notions like high-performance culture, gold standard, and "what we know" (Evidence-Based Management, 2007).

Critiques have come from a range of perspectives. Two articles in different fields demonstrate this further. In the *Journal of Management Studies*, Morrell (2007) uses Russian Formalism to illustrate the ways that the evidence-based systematic review technique is used to defamiliarize the conventional notion of systematic and the ways that the term 'transparency' is reinvented to reinforce assumptions and values within the evidence-based discourse. Further, credibility is generated by invoking a powerful discipline like medicine, as well as calls for thoroughness and rigor, while referring to practices like narrative as older or obsolete. The discourse methods privilege a perspective in which critique of the evidence-based construct is not permitted. In *Social Theory & Health* (2008), Wall uses feminist post-structural analyses to demonstrate how the discourse of evidence-based research positions and labels nurses as subjects of humanist individualism who are blamed for rejecting research and interpreted as 'laggards' yet are excluded from the very game that would control them. Further, feminine and nursing ways of knowing, like esthetics, personal, and ethical knowledges are excluded. As Wall states, "What passes for objective research is a search for what elites want knowledge about" (p. 49). And, in contemporary times, those elites want knowledge to be about efficiency, measurement, objectives/outcomes/benchmarks, profiteering, and corporate capitalism. Other critiques of evidence-based research call attention to a lip service that is paid to qualitative methods while practices are put forward that would exclude its possibilities (Freshwater & Rolfe, 2004), the ways that postmodern (or other such) critiques reveal the choices, subjectivities, and genres through which particular authors/researchers choose to function (Eaglestone, 2001), and the limits of evidence-based perspectives even in the legitimating 'power' field of medicine (e.g., the interplay between observation and theory even in critical realist work, the subjectivity even within 'randomized trials,' the denial of individual patient circumstances and variations, the limitation of patient rights within the assumptions of evidence-based research; Cohen, Stavri, & Hersh, 2004).

Critiques and deconstructions have occurred, yet evidence-based research discourses are alive, expanding, and most likely invading locations that would surprise us all. Recently a Google search resulted in 35,500,000 sites, with over 14,000,000 of those devoted to the U.S. government and evidence-based research/practice. Examples of the actual funded entities related to the sites abound, like the U.S. Department of Health & Human Services, Agency for Healthcare Research and Quality, *Evidence-based Practice Centers*. In October 2007, a third wave of 14 centers in the U.S. and Canada were funded to "review all relevant scientific literature on clinical, behavioral, and organization and financing topics to produce evidence reports and technology assessments." Funded centers include the ECRI Institute, RTI International, Minnesota and Oregon Evidence-Based Practice Centers, and the Blue Cross and Blue Shield Association, as well as U.S. and Canadian universities like Duke, Johns Hopkins, and Vanderbilt (Canadian examples include the Universities of Alberta and Ottawa).

In the U.S., the Council for Excellence in Government (2008) has created alliances like the *Coalition for Evidence-Based Policy* with corporate partners like the Annenberg, Bill and Melinda Gates, Ford, and William T. Grant Foundations as well as Geico, Goldman Sachs, Google, Johnson & Johnson, and Microsoft, just to name a few. The coalitions' mission is to "promote government policymaking based on rigorous evidence." Conducting activities like the April 2008 workshop "How to Read Findings to Distinguish Evidence-Based Programs from Everything Else" and deploy funds like $10,000,000 to an HHS evidence-based home visitation program, the coalition claims (through an independent evaluation conducted by the William T. Grant Foundation) to have been "instrumental in transforming a theoretical advocacy of evidence-based policy among certain (federal) agencies into an operational reality." One could go on and on with examples, but here we would rather note that the discourse is invasive, often hidden from the public eye (and even the gaze of many politicians) through legislation embedded within hundreds of pages of text. The discourse (and its agents) literally restructures public agencies and redeploys research funds to support itself. Further, it creates ties with and gives a greater voice to the financial elite of society. The obvious next step, in addition to the controlling and discrediting of a range of people, perspectives, and ways of being, is to further produce and support the discourse through neoliberal, hyper-capitalist, free-market profiteering that commodifies and industrializes everything; this 'next step' is much less of a 'next step' than corresponding insidious function. Examples of this also abound, like the corporation *Evidence Based Research, Inc. (EBR)* with headquarters located in Vienna, VA. Organized in two divisions, Military Studies and Decision Systems, the company sells its ability to address problems all around the globe, ranging "from creating systems to measuring political and economic reform ... to designing improved systems for decision making ... (to) improving the ability of coalition forces to provide disaster relief and peacekeeping services" (2008). Does anyone hear (read) further construction of the 'military industrial complex' using evidence-based discourses here? But there are also many other examples that we can find familiar in our own fields—like the selling of school 'turnaround specialist' programs for 'evidence-based failing' schools (read evidence and failing as industry-created test scores, by the way). And, again, we could go on and on.

Challenges to postpositivist science (or critical realism) are certainly *prohibited* (excluded), while the *ritual* of experimental science is certainly reinscribed. Critical perspectives (and critical research) are certainly silenced. Further, the discourse on evidence-based research creates an elite group who become so because of their willingness to accept and use the discourse—those who would invoke validity, generalizability, replicability, and intervention are given the *right to speak and act*. The notion of evidence is used to reinforce the reinscribed *appeal to reason*, the will to truth that creates the claim to reason versus folly, labeling those who would be discredited as half truths, without intellect, as relativist or nonsensical. Evidence-based research further constructs, and is constructed by, a range of *disciplinary technologies* that are broad based from appeals to surviving illness (for everyone, as in medicine) to publishing in 'upper-tier' journals (as representing quality and intellectual sophistication), to specific area technologies like evidence-based research that would raise achievement test scores. This discourse can literally erase critical and qualitative research methods, as well as critical voices of those who have been traditionally placed in the margins (whether as people of color, women, children/students, nurses, patients, or anyone who would challenge positivist 'evidence-based' science).

Perhaps the main, and interconnected, reason for the almost invisibility of critical qualitative research in attempts to transform inequitable societal conditions is the corporatization of knowledge. As illustrated in our discussion of the ways that the discourse of evidence-based knowledge is used to redeploy resources and control fields of understanding, a neoliberal hyper-capitalism has invaded all aspects of scholarship, values that influence decision making, and administration. While this invasion is certainly monocultural and masculinist, it certainly goes beyond the imposition of these particular ideologies because of the importance played by resources and finances in societies dominated by capitalism. A major example in the corporatization of knowledge is the construction of the contemporary corporate university.

Corporatization of Knowledge

While colleges and universities have always been more closely connected to capitalism and the business community than many of us would like, recent discourse practices that have supported decreases in percentages of public taxes designated for higher education have resulted in an increased openness to neoliberal capitalism as a means of survival. As a fundamentalist hyper-capitalism has invaded (and, we would add, has been strategically infused into) all of society (in the U.S. and probably globally), so too has higher education been transformed. Even historically cultural knowledge is now being commodified, patented, labeled as 'wonderfully entrepreneurial,' and sold for a profit. Further, a hypercapitalist perspective has been/is being used to interpret all of life, whether to explain human action as self-benefiting, knowledge as valuable because of market possibilities, or 'saving' the environment as a profitable venture (Cannella & Miller, 2008), and again, we could go on and on.

This corporate fundamentalism is probably the most profound influence on higher education today. University presidents are hired to function like CEOs; deans are employed as fund raisers; faculty 'stars' are recruited with large salaries that increase pay inequities in their fields; yet the general faculty workforce is becoming increasingly female, temporary, and low paid. This larger group of faculty has little voice in the governance of the institution.

In 1969, over 96 percent of academic faculty were in tenure-track appointments. Currently, less than 40 percent of faculty members are in tenure-track appointments (Washburn, 2005). Even if the newly constituted workforce is talented and informed, it is not protected by freedoms of scholarship that would counter CEO administrators or customers that are not satisfied. The reconstituted workforce is expected to go easy on customers and teach whatever content is predetermined (by those with power—whether financial, legislative, or administrative). Research 'superstars' are employed with tenure for exorbitant amounts of money and often named to 'chaired' positions funded by wealthy donors; less than 50 percent of the remaining faculty are employed in tenured or tenure-track positions. The workforce has become one in which faculty votes concerning academic issues can potentially be carried by low-paid academic workers who have no choice but to be controlled by the administrators who hire them. Salaries are increasingly inequitable across the range of individuals employed to teach, with the larger group of temporary, low-paid workers being women. Inequity and corporatized power abound.

If this corporatization of the workforce continues as retirements occur of those who are tenured, the voices of faculty who have actually been the determiners of both research and curricular content will be silenced. Examples of this academic erasure can be easily found generally, but especially in colleges/schools that do not have alumni donors who can be used to 'leverage' (in business terminology) power. Overall, attempts by administrators to require program faculty to determine curricular benchmarks (another business term) and to prove the quality of research, while on the surface appearing justifiable, actually fosters a perspective that assumes faculty incompetence and need for regulation. Some administrators have even imposed curricular content on entire universities without faculty governance by creating required courses for all students (like freshman courses literally constructed and imposed on all programs by university presidents). Faculty of public institutions of higher education have been forced by administrators to accept partnerships with private charter school corporations, to offer graduate programs strictly designed to generate revenue, and to offer online courses and programs using social content that is not appropriate for learning at a distance, just to name a few.

Those who are rewarded as faculty appear to be those who 'buy into' the corporate entrepreneurial function. Short- or long-term profit is privileged over education gains. Professors are commodities to be traded, as the institution gives up those who are less likely to generate money for those who are proven grant writers or 'inventors' whose work can be patented and sold for great profits (Andrews, 2006; Mohanty, 2004). Professors are expected to be entrepreneurs by constructing courses, workshops, conferences, and academic programs that generate profits, as well as obtaining grants. Further, as with capitalism in general, this entrepreneurial perspective demonstrates a remasculinizing of academia (Baez, 2008) in that the privileging of competition and the call for training a particular type of worker is also focused on the fields that have not accepted notions of hyper-capitalism, entreprenurialism, and competition. For example, teacher education (a traditionally female-gendered field) is blamed for all the problems in education (although those problems are constructed from a neoliberal, market perspective); yet business schools are not held responsible for the fate of the U.S. economy (Saltman, 2007).

This context privileges knowledge that can be converted into profit—either as a direct commodity for financial gain, as the knowledge that is preferred by an outside donor, or as the knowledge that would attain grants redeployed for positivist and masculinist purposes like evidence-based research knowledge. Fields that do not result in a profit or that would actually challenge the free-market perspective are certainly placed in the margin, if not entirely erased. Critical forms of research and knowledges certainly fall into this category.

Can We Create Critical Transformations?

We believe that qualitative methods can be used for critical social purposes. However, academics will most likely need to be strategic and persistent in this endeavor.

(1) First, knowledge of what's happening in society is necessary to understand the discourses that dominate; many of us have not been aware of the agendas and actions that surround us, and further, have not engaged in informed critique. In "Meetings Across the Paradigmatic Divide," Moss (2007) uses the work of Mouffe (2000) that focuses on agonistic pluralism to suggest that we construct an

agonistic politics that searches for common ground, continually fosters engagement with diverse paradigms, and values pluralism in democracy.

(2) Second, researchers will need to determine if there are, in unexpected locations, specific investigations/circumstances in which qualitative methods have been successful in addressing critical social purposes. Since research would no longer accept the objectivity of positivist science, research would no longer be appropriately located in the 'objective,' protected ivory tower. Research conceptualizations, practices, and researchers themselves would be inextricably interconnected to human communities (e.g., locally, academically, nationally, racially). Therefore, in addition to research purposes, researchers would serve as informed reflexive community members, as well as scholars who conduct research as informed by human community relations. Rather than statistical technicians, scholars could be expected to spend time exploring the range of interconnected societal structures that impact individuals and communities.

(3) Third, a *revolutionary* critical social sciences (e.g., feminisms, postcolonial perspectives) will need to be strategically placed at the center of academic research discussions, conceptualizations, and practices. Successful strategies will necessitate networking, collaborative planning, and persistent support for each other (Mohanty, 2004). Research conceptualizations, purposes, and practices would be grounded in critical ethical challenges to social (therefore science) systems, supports for egalitarian struggle, and revolutionary ethical awareness and activism from within the context of community. Directly stated, research would be relational (often as related to community) and grounded within a critique of systems, egalitarian struggle, and revolutionary ethics.

Revolutionary critical inquiry could ask questions (and take actions) similar to the following that challenge social (and therefore science) systems:

How are particular groups represented in discourse practices and social systems?
What knowledges are silenced, made invisible, or literally erased?
What are examples of oppressions (and/or new exclusions) that are being made to sound equitable through various discourses?
How do elite groups define values, constructs, and rhetoric in ways that maintain matrices of power?

Research that supported egalitarian struggles for social justice would ask questions like:

How are particular discourses infused into the public imaginary (e.g., media, parenting, medicine)?
How are power relations constructed and managed through?

Perhaps the most important for us as researchers is the development of a nonviolent revolutionary ethical consciousness. As researchers who are concerned about equity and regulation, we would ask how we construct research practices that facilitate our becoming aware of societal issues, rhetoric, and practices that would continue forms of marginalization or that would construct new forms of inequity and oppression.

(4) Finally, critical work is likely not possible without the construction of alliances within/between academia and the public that would place at the forefront concern for equity and justice. Scholarship in higher education must actively work to counter corporatization of knowledge from within by challenging controlling, narrow discourses of accountability, quality, and excellence. Further, to inquire into the regulatory and equity issues that are most important to a range of communities, both inside and outside of academia, and to construct new ways to share those inquiries, we must be involved with them. Networks, collaborations, and strategic forms of dissemination are necessary that address foundational issues like enlarging the public's understanding of the research imaginary; generating unthought discursive spaces; and public critique of the ways that groups are privileged and silenced by various forms of research, science, and academic practice.

Note

1.   For an interesting note on this same topic, see the brief discussion of rationalism and a-rationalism in Lincoln (1985).

References

Andrews, J. G. (2006, May/June). How we can resist corporatization. Academe, Retrieved May 27, 2006, http://www.aaup.org/publications/Academe/2006/06mjandrtabl.htm

Baez, B. (2008, March). *Men in crisis? Race, gender, and the remasculinization of higher education.* Paper presented at the American Educational Research Association Meeting. New York, NY.

Cannella, G. S. (1997). *Deconstructing early childhood education: Social justice and revolution.* New York: Peter Lang.

Cannella, G. S., & Miller, L. (2008). Constructing corporatist science: Reconstituting the soul of American higher education *Cultural Studies-Critical Methodologies, 8*(1), 24–38.

Cohen, A. M., Stavri, P. Z., & Hersh, W. R. (2004). Criticisms of evidence-based medicine. *Evidence-based Cardiovascular Medicine, 8,* 197–198.

Collins, P. H. (2000). *Black feminist thought: Knowledge, consciousness, and the politics of empowerment.* New York, NY: Routledge.

Council for Excellence in Government. (2008). *Coalition for Evidence-Based Policy.* Retrieved May 8, 2008, http://www.excelgov.org/index.php?keyword=a432fbc34d71c7

Eaglestone, R. (2001). *Postmodernism and Holocaust denial.* Duxford: Icon Books.

Ellsworth, E. (1989). Why doesn't this feel empowering? Working through the repressive myths of critical pedagogy. *Harvard Educational Review, 59*(3), 297–324.

Evidence-Based Management. (2007). Jeffry Pheffer testifies to congress about evidence-based practices. Retrieved April 28, 2007, http://www.evidence-basedmanagement.com/research_practice/commentary/pfeffer_congressional_testimony

Evidence Based Research, Inc. (2008). Retrieved May 5, 2008, http://www.ebrinc.com/html/about_organization.html

Faludi, S. (1991). *Backlash: The undeclared war against American women.* New York, NY: Anchor Books, Doubleday.

Freshwater, D., & Rolfe, G. (2004). *Deconstructing evidence-based practice.* Abbingdon: Routledge.

Greenwood, D. J., & Levin, M. (2000). Reconstructing the relationships between universities and society through action research. In N. K. Denzin & Y. S. Lincoln (Eds.), *Handbook of qualitative research* (2nd ed., pp. 85–106). Thousand Oaks, CA: Sage.

Horowitz, D. (2006). *The professors: The 101 most dangerous academics in America.* Washington, DC: Regnery Publishing.

Knorr-Cetina, K., & Mulkay, M. (Eds.). (1983). *Science observed: Perspectives on the social study of science.* London: Sage.

Lather, P. (1 996). Troubling clarity: The politics of accessible language. *Harvard Educational Review, 66*(3), Retrieved 5/6/08, from http://www.edreview.org/harvard/1996/fa96/f96lath.htm

Lincoln, Y. S. (1985). Epilogue: Dictionaries for languages not yet spoken. In Y. S. Lincoln (Ed.), *Organizational theory and inquiry: The paradigm revolution.* (pp. 221–228). Thousand Oaks, CA: Sage.

Lincoln, Y. S., & Cannella, G. S. (2004). Qualitative research, power, and the radical right. *Qualitative Inquiry, 10*(2), 175–201.

Mohanty, C. T. (2004). *Feminism without borders: Decolonizing theory, practicing solidarity.* Durham, NC: Duke University Press.

Morrell, K. (2007). The narrative of "evidenced based" management: A polemic. *Journal of Management Studies, 45*(3), 614–635.

Moss, P. (2007). Meetings across the paradigmatic divide. *Educational Philosophy and Theory, 39*(3), 239–245.

Mosteller, F., & Boruch, R. (2002). *Evidence matters: Randomized trials in education research.* Washington, DC: Brookings Institution Press.

Mouffe, C. (2000). *The democratic paradox.* London: Verso.

National Research Council. (2002). *Scientific research in education* (Committee on Scientific Principles for Education Research, R. Shavelson & L. Town (Eds.), Center for Education, Division of Behavioral and social Sciences and Education). Washington, DC: National Academies Press.

Richardson, L. (2000). Writing: A method of inquiry. In N. K. Denzin & Y. S. Lincoln (Eds.), *Handbook of qualitative research* (2nd ed, pp. 923–948). Thousand Oaks, CA: Sage.

Said, E. (1979). *Orientalism.* New York, NY: Vintage Books.

Saltman, K. J. (2007). *Capitalizing on disaster: Breaking and taking public schools.* Boulder, CO: Paradigm Publishers.

Spivak, G. C. (1999). *A critique of postcolonial reason: Toward a history of the vanishing present.* Cambridge, MA: Harvard University Press.

St. Pierre, E. A. (2000). The call for intelligibility in postmodern educational research. *Educational Researcher, 29*(5), 25–28.

U.S. Department of Health and Human Services. (2008), Evidence-based practice centers. Agency for Healthcare Research and Quality. Retrieved May 8, 2008 http://www.ahcpr.gov/clinic/epc/

Wall, S. (2008). A critique of evidence-based practice in nursing: Challenging the assumptions. *Social Theory & Health, 6,* 37–53.

Washburn, J. (2005). *University Inc: The corporate corruption of higher education.* New York, NY: Basic Books.

CHAPTER 3

The Utility of Educational Action Research for Emancipatory Change

Kimberly Kinsler

S ince its original promulgation, action research in general, and educational action research in particular, appear to have fallen short of significantly advancing social justice and emancipatory change, particularly in industrialized nations. More often, educational action research has been used as a technical tool to facilitate the use of particular teaching techniques; increase practical professional efficacy; and implement government policies. This may, in part, be due to the primacy advocates give to its meeting key theoretical and practical university-based considerations. While there has been significant debate and advocacy for particular forms of action research as best suited to produce emancipatory consciousness and work, it is here asserted that each form has its own unique emancipatory potential and challenges. It is also asserted that too little attention has been paid to the practical outcomes of much educational action research, suggesting the need to rethink the esoteric nature and narrow range of criteria used to determine what counts as emancipatory research.

The Emancipatory Challenge of Action Research

The roots and emancipatory nature of AR have variously been attributed to John Collier (Neilsen, 2006) and to Kurt Lewin. Carr and Kemmis (1986) state that Lewin (1952) 'saw action research as based on principles which could lead "gradually to independence, equality and cooperation" and effectively alter policies of 'permanent exploitation' which he saw as 'likely to endanger every aspect of democracy' (p. 163). He is said to have presaged three characteristics of modern AR: its participatory character, democratic impulse, and a simultaneous contribution to social science and social change. Consistent with this tradition, Carr and Kemmis (1986) in their seminal work, *Becoming Critical*, asserted both the practical problem-solving role of AR, specifically for the field of education, and its critical use by classroom teachers.

Even at the time of this publication and increasingly thereafter, advocates of educational AR began to criticize its bureaucratic appropriation and its failure to maintain an emancipatory focus. In *Becoming Critical*, Carr and Kemmis lamented that after a decade of growth, educational AR had already gone into decline, attributing the problem to a growing separation of research from action and theory from practice. Two decades later, while acknowledging that in the years following the 1986 publication, AR had become a full grown international movement sustained by a large number of teachers, teacher educators, and educational researchers, Carr and Kemmis (2005) complained that accompanying this surge in popularity was its increasing appropriation as an institutionalized model of in-service teacher education, detached from any emancipatory aspirations, transformed into little more than a research method that could be readily assimilated to and accommodated within the broader requirements of the orthodox research paradigms it was intended to replace.

Multiple causes for this failure have been posited, including the realities of teaching in an increasingly globalized market economy. In support, Groundwater-Smith (2005) asserted that 'action research has been popularized and appropriated as an implementation tool instead of as a social change method' (p. 335). Commenting on conditions in Australia and in the United Kingdom, she stated that educational institutions have been forced into 'highly specified outcome-driven curriculum frameworks', simultaneous with the development of standards-driven reforms. These government-mandated reform efforts were seen as a re-imposition of an outcome-oriented, market-driven economic ideology to educational institutions and to a narrowing in the decision-making space for practitioners. Relative to the United States, Noffke (2005) similarly remarked on the increasing shift in capital and culture to a more centralized and global scale 'where action research is more often connected to issues of professional development, only loosely and infrequently articulated with social justice agendas let alone challenges to dominant research paradigms' (p. 323). Kemmis (2006) labeled these trends as the domestication of educational AR, that is, more technical approaches to AR being adopted by many educational action researchers rather than the critical form. Observing that as much of the AR that proliferated in many parts of the world in the preceding two decades had not been the vehicle for educational critique, he proclaimed that 'some—perhaps most—action research no longer aspires to having this critical edge, especially in the bigger sense of social or educational critique aimed at transformation of the way things are' (p. 459).

This article assumes a position consistent with Carr and Kemmis's (2009) subsequent rethinking of this issue, critiquing the privileging of any one form of AR over another. Its purpose is to assert that all forms of educational AR have emancipatory potential and that without an emancipatory intent, such research is not true AR, but rather an oxymoron and a cynical cooptation. This work also suggests the need to expand the criteria for emancipatory AR to one not primarily defined in terms of consciousness and theory to include actual praxis, or the outcomes of the research. In explanation, one needs first to unpack the various taxonomies and criteria associated with educational AR and to consider the current and potential use of each to meet the standard for emancipatory research/practice.

Forms and Functions of Action Research

Educational AR has multiple forms and levels that permit a range of possible design capabilities (e.g. see Chandler & Torbert, 2003). Below, I briefly review three taxonomic classifications relative to the goal of emancipatory change, that is, the distinction among first-, second- and third-person research/practice (Chandler & Torbert, 2003; Reason & Torbert, 2001); work distinguishing technical, practical, and emancipatory AR (Grundy & Kemmis, 1981); and Kemmis's (2006) five forms of non-emancipatory AR. Commentary on these design types is reserved for the following section.

First-, Second- and Third-Person Research/Practice

The most well-known taxonomy of AR is the distinction among first-, second-, and third-person research/practice. First-person AR 'addresses the ability of the researcher to foster an inquiring approach to his or her own life, to act awarely and choicefully, and to assess the effects in the outside world while acting' (Reason & Torbert, 2001, p. 17). This design is synonymous with an individual experimenter model.

With second-person research/practice, a researcher engages with others in a face-to-face group. The most clearly articulated form of second-person research is co-operative inquiry in which all those involved function both as co-researchers and co-subjects, jointly generating ideas, designing the project, and drawing conclusions (Reason & Torbert, 2001).

Third-person research/practice aims to create a wider community of inquiry involving persons who cannot be known to each other face to face. 'In addition, third-person research/practice may aim to speak out to a yet wider audience to influence and transform popular opinion, organization strategy, and government policy' (pp. 23–24).

Technical, Practical and Emancipatory Action Research

AR theorists also distinguish among technical, practical, and emancipatory AR (Grundy, 1987; Grundy & Kemmis, 1981; Kemmis, 2001). Technical AR is oriented toward functional improvement measured in terms of success in changing particular outcomes of practice (Kemmis, 2001). To Grundy (1987), this kind of AR is a form of problem solving, where a project is viewed as 'successful' when outcomes match some predetermined aspirations. Such research is characteristically instigated by a person or group, who by reason of their greater expertise or qualifications would be viewed as 'expert' or an authority. Other study participants function in the realization of the expert's ideas. The aim is usually more effective practice.

Practical AR seeks to improve practice through the development of personal wisdom derived from 'true and reasoned' deliberation. It aspires for technical change, but also aims to 'do good', that is, to inform and aid the practitioner in 'wise and prudent' practical decision making. This form of AR involves a process of self-education for the practitioner, that is, acquiring a disposition toward 'good' rather than 'correct' action (phronesis; Grundy, 1987).

Emancipatory AR seeks not only to improve outcomes and the self-understanding of practitioners, but is also a critique of their work and social milieu. Its purpose is the emancipation of participants engaged in strategic action from the dictates of compulsion, tradition, precedent, habit, coercion and self-deception (Grundy, 1987). It seeks to reconstruct not only the practice and the practitioner but the practical setting as well. Its goal is to connect the personal and the political and to transform situations so as to overcome felt alienation, dissatisfactions, ideological distortion, and the injustices of oppression and domination (Kemmis, 2001). Based on Habermas's three developmental phases in action-oriented critique, that is, theory, enlightenment, and action, emancipatory strategic action is believed to arise from a disposition of critical intent, or social consciousness, toward critically assessing the extent to which the social milieu impedes the fostering of the 'good' (Grundy, 1987, p. 28).

Kemmis's Five Non-Emancipatory Forms of Action Research

Critiquing much of the existing educational AR, Kemmis (2006, p. 460) delineated five criteria for non-emancipatory AR, forms of research that he states fail to bring about 'parrahesiastes', that is, unwelcome and uncomfortable news necessary for advancing social justice. They are:

1) AR that aims only at improving techniques of teaching, for example, classroom questioning or assessment, without seeing these as connected to broader questions about the education of students for a better society.

2) AR aimed at improving the efficiency of practices rather than their efficacy and effectiveness evaluated in terms of the social, cultural, discursive and material, for example, the economic and/or historical consequences of practices.

3) AR conducted solely to implement government policies or programs, without subjecting their intentions, presuppositions, and frameworks of justification to critical examination.

4) AR that understands the improvement of practice only from the perspectives of professional practitioners (e.g. teachers), without genuinely engaging the voices and perspectives of others involved in the practice (e.g. students or family members).

5) AR conducted by people acting alone rather than in open communication with other participants (like students, their families, or others in the wider community) whose lives and work are involved in or affected by the practices being investigated.

Reflections on the Forms and Functions of Action Research

Before discussing these forms of AR, it is important to position myself in this arena. I am a black female trained as an educational psychologist and school improvement agent. My personal commitment has long been to empower public school stakeholders and advance the achievement of historically marginalized students. Consequently, I have worked as a school reform facilitator for over 25 years. In the early 1990s, I participated in the second wave of school reform and sought to empower teams of teachers and parents through collaborative site-based inquiry and problem solving. I and a colleague subsequently developed our own school improvement model, the Inquiry Based School Improvement Project (IBSIP; Kinsler, 2008), to aid these teams in the circular 'reflection-plan-action' problem solving loop, to both better understand and resolve site-based problems and raise students' academic performance. When second wave reforms fell out of favor with the NYC DOE, to keep site-based inquiry and collaborative problem solving alive in and relevant to these schools, IBSIP adopted an AR umbrella. Now functioning to advance teacher/participants' knowledge and use of AR as a problem-solving tool, we asked them to self-select a form of AR, that is, individual, small group, or representative school-wide projects, as well as the focal topics in which they would engage. IBSIP continued with its AR facilitation in eight historically under-performing public schools for approximately three years, until these efforts were stopped by my college's IRB.[1] Below, I discuss the forms and functions of AR from the combined perspectives of the literature, my professional experience with school improvement and IBSIP, as well as my own personal emancipatory goals for historically marginalized groups of individuals. This discussion is organized in terms of the first, better-known, classification system, embedding discussion of the other two taxonomies, as appropriate.

First-Person Research/Practice

For both theoretical and practical reasons, first-person research/practice has been the most prominent design in the educational AR literature. Theoretically, two contrasting views support a focus on the reflective, individual teacher/inquirer, that is, Habermasian critical theory and Stenhouse's professional development theory. According to the former, emancipatory action is believed to emanate from a disposition of critical intent. Consequently, for teacher/researchers to engage in emancipatory work, they must first acquire an emancipatory consciousness, that is, a disposition toward the critical assessment of the extent to which the social milieu impedes the fostering of the 'good' (Grundy, 1987, p. 28). This vision of the teacher/researcher is inherently political in nature. Conversely, advocates of the alternate view are said to depoliticize the teacher research process. While similarly focused on the development of an inquiring mindset in the individual teacher, AR here is viewed as a tool for in-service teacher education, that is, as a means to develop the teachers themselves 'without group effort guided by a social vision' (Noffke, 1992, p. 19). Its goal is to advance teacher productiveness, effectiveness and autonomous decision making. Thus, from both perspectives first-person research/practice is the model best suited to these two theory-based aims.

What is more, first-person research/practice is also practically expedient based on the knowledge dissemination structure characteristic of university systems. In this context, the most common dissemination pattern relative to potential teacher/researchers is for teachers, either pre- or in-service, to be requested to engage in AR as part of coursework for a credential or degree (Feldman & Atkin, 1995).

As in-service teachers tend to come from varied sites and pre-service teachers' field placements also tend to be dispersed over a range of schools, classes and grades, it is difficult for them to engage in authentic second-person, or team-based, research with either their classmates or other site-based teachers. Also characteristic of this structure is the positioning of the college-based research professional (e.g. the course instructor) as an 'expert', instructing program candidates in the research process while guiding them in the conduct of their individual AR projects.

A number of issues have been raised concerning the relative contribution of first-person inquiry toward the advancement of an emancipatory intent or practice. In terms of theory, Elliott (2005) has asserted that Habermas's position falls short, as an enlightened and critical self-understanding cannot in itself justify strategic action. He states that '(O)ne cannot derive future action merely on the basis of a transformed consciousness' and that 'critical self reflection(s) do not necessarily translate into empowering people to take action for the sake of an ideal. This requires further conditions to apply, such as having the "power motivation" and capabilities necessary for exercising agency in a situation' (p. 362). Referencing Bernstein (1976, pp. 216–217), Elliott points out that 'the liberation of the mind is not yet concrete freedom, and can arise in a world where nothing has substantially changed'.

Elliott's challenge is borne out in practice. On the one hand, the literature finds that an emancipatory mindset may be difficult for pre- and in-service teachers to acquire through university-initiated first-person research/practice and that pre- and in-service teachers may, in fact, actually resist acquiring this mindset through this instructional format. For example, McKinney (2005), citing Rosenberg (1997), states that in raising issues of race and racism in teaching and learning with pre-service teachers in a predominantly white teacher education program, the topic elicited 'general discomfort' and little support from both students and the system. Similarly, Hutchinson (1996), reviewing the articles in Noffke and Stevenson's (1995) book, found that in the first section, where four of the five educational AR articles sought to advance an emancipatory consciousness, all four studies fell short of their goal. Moreover, even when pre-service teachers were found to have acquired a sense of social justice, translating this knowledge into action proved quite difficult. Thus, Peters (2004), reflecting on her work with teacher candidates, states that 'most teachers found that it was not a simple process to translate changes in their thinking into changes in practice because of the complex range of student needs and contextual factors that impacted on their decisions' (pp. 550–551).

What is more, the 'academic commodity production mode' of pedagogic training characteristic of the university system—with 'individual projects, methodological individualism' (Stringer, personal communication, 2008), and radical self-reflection—predisposes local teacher/researchers trained in this manner to be less connected to colleagues and the 'other' oriented needs of their school communities, and renders them unskilled in and unprepared to collaborate in the shared problem-solving tasks most valued in high-need schools today. Equally problematic is the potential transformation of the research objective from the development of an emancipatory awareness to participants' instrumental achievement of predetermined objectives set by faculty, as research 'experts', as well as the failure to democratize the research process. Reflecting on Habermas, Grundy (1987) states that when the facilitator directs the outcome of the deliberative process by attempting to thrust enlightenment upon research participants, rather than being emancipatory, such research/practice becomes technical (1987). This may be particularly true for pre- or in-service teachers, who operate within an intellectual framework established not by the site-based teacher but by a professor and the academy (Feldman & Atkin, 1995). Additionally, this design model also fails to teach by example the democratization of the knowledge creation process as it tends to perpetuate the self-referential belief in and the practice of looking to the university as both the primary source of expertise and the site of the knowledge-creation process. However, if as Carr and Kemmis (2009, p. 80) now assert, 'all action research is personal, and one of its fruits is the *self-transformation* of participants through their developing understandings achieved through enquiry', then the emancipatory potential and challenge of first-person inquiry is its ability to truly achieve and act upon self-transformation.

My own work with IBSIP participants who chose first-person research/practice echoes many of the challenges raised above. While all developed projects focused on very real and immediate site-level problems, by definition, all were technical or practical in nature, for example, intended either to improve students' attainment of externally imposed learning standards or to acquire personal wisdom to inform and aid their own practice. All, without exception, also exhibited one or more of Kemmis's criteria for non-emancipatory research, most often failing to connect the personal and the political. Even when environmental events supported institutional critique, participants always avoided the political. For example, in several schools, IBSIP inquiry teams had engaged in site-based problem solving and had variously planned to initiate new instructional or ancillary support programs to raise student achievement. At the end of that academic year, unexpectedly, the newly elected NYC mayor and his appointed school chancellor mandated the system-wide institution of their own mathematics and literacy programs, nullifying the year-long work of these teams. Despite my urging teachers to critique this dynamic in their AR projects for the next cycle, these teachers sought to avoid any such discourse. That next year, a number of IBSIP participants chose first-person AR to 'protect themselves', they said, from future devastation by confining their work within the walls of their own classrooms—a space over which they had more control. Ironically, such isolationist practices were major targets of second-wave school reforms in the 1980s, which sought figuratively to break down these walls as a means to empower teachers. Moreover, even when such projects obtained positive results and individual researchers changed their personal classroom practices, there was little or no extension of their results beyond their own immediate classroom settings, as the institutional expansion of these results was always dependent on the teacher/researcher's inclination and ability to convince other local stakeholders, for example, school administrators and other teachers, of their benefit. It, thus, seems that this form of AR, as currently practiced, has potential but faces critical challenges if its intent is to instill an emancipatory consciousness in teacher/researchers or to advance social justice on a larger scale.

Second-Person Research/Practice

In the last several years, increasing attention has been focused on second-person research/practice, based in part on Kemmis's later reconceptualization of AR as ideally a social, collaborative process (Kemmis, 2008; Kemmis & McTaggart, 2005). Labeling this reconceptualization critical participatory AR and situating it at the nexus of (developmental) participatory research and critical theory, Kemmis now privileged the social/communicative and transformative/action aspects of grounded research. Kemmis and McTaggart (2005) state:

> The most morally, practically, and politically compelling view of participatory action research is one that sees participatory action research as a practice through which people can create networks of communication, i.e., sites for the practice of communicative action … (which) aim to engender practical critiques of existing states of affairs … and the shared formation of emancipatory commitments. (p. 580)

Still, much of second-person educational AR reported in the literature continues to be accused of falling short of its emancipatory goals, both in developing countries (Cooke & Kothari, 2001) but particularly in industrialized nations. In 2003, Gustavsen challenged the emancipatory ability of both first- and second-person AR/practice. Focusing on the aspect of social change, Gustavsen stated that most researchers interested in society-level issues pose their questions and concerns in general terms, while the questions and answers provided by action research are generally 'local cases'. This was not adequate for Gustavsen, who then asked, '(A)re there ways in which action research can transcend the single case without losing the action element along the road?' At the time, his answer was scale, or critical mass, the 'idea of which is not to replace the single case with a number of cases but to create or support social movements' (pp. 95–96). This form of AR is the essence of what Reason (2003) refers to as third-person inquiry/practice.

Ironically, Reason (2003) took issue with Gustavsen's (2003) comments on the failure of first- and second-person AR toward these ends. In particular, Reason challenged Gustavsen's focus on the 'distributive' nature of social change (p. 282). Reasserting the primacy of an emancipatory, or enlightened, disposition, Reason countered that

> we need not only to build large scale networks of inquiry but also to engage in transformations of consciousness and behavior at personal and interpersonal levels. While it is true that we cannot make large scale change on the basis of small cases, neither can we build truly effective and liberating political networks of inquiry without developing significant capacities for critical inquiry in the individuals and small communities which constitute them. (p. 282)

Reason did, however, concede the need to explore how to expand the emancipatory communicative space created by second-person inquiry groups through the creation of 'first-order democracies', that is, inquiry sites where participants can examine their practice closely and carefully, and change what they do as a result. Only cursorily developing this concept, Reason commented that '(O)pening such inquiry spaces can be highly challenging, even subversive, to the established order' (p. 284). In contrast, Kemmis explored in depth the dynamics of such collaborative communicative spaces, which he interpreted as potentially a direct application of Habermas's concepts of communicative action and in the public sphere to the AR process (Kemmis, 2008; Kemmis & McTaggart, 2005). By 2008, Gustavsen had also evolved beyond the belief that only a good diffusion strategy was needed to now assert that the challenge 'lies first and foremost in linking different spheres to each other so that they can reinforce each other and contribute to a "mass effect on society"' (p. 435).

In this light, the emancipatory challenges facing second-person educational research/practice are the development of an emancipatory consciousness, scale or the extension of this research into the larger social system and creating democratic communicative spaces. In regard to the first, one of the greatest dangers to local researchers' development of a critical disposition remains the facilitation by the externally based research 'expert'. When such 'experts' macro-manage a school's or educators' research process, regardless of any efforts to democratize the communicative space, the risk remains that the 'ideas' of this one individual will come to dominate the group's consciousness through her superior ability to 'sell' her ideas. When this occurs, irrespective of the expert's intent, the research/practice that results becomes technical in nature, a point noted by Kemmis and McTaggart (2005, p. 569) as one of their earlier 'myths, misinterpretations and mistakes.'

Relative to the issue of scale, my own personal experience with both school improvement and second-person AR has bearing on Gustavsen's challenge. I have found that when IBSIP participants engaged in second-person research/practice, their topics of study were also invariably of a technical or practical nature. For example, chosen topics included why a school's fifth-grade students performed so poorly on the newly instituted standardized test in social studies, and why were students from a school's lower grades so poorly prepared to address the cognitive demands of third grade, including standardized testing in several subject areas. While such topics are specific to a school, the widespread effects of federal and state legislation, like NCLB, as well as the increasing trend toward educational standardization in the current global economy, render the outcomes of such AR of interest to a considerable number of chronically under-performing schools and school systems servicing high populations of historically marginalized student groups, both nationally and internationally. Moreover, as the participant numbers increase to include whole grades and schools, the sample size begins to approximate those of small-scale positivist research. What is more, even with general educational principles derived from grand theories or positivist research, they too must be adapted to the conditions of their application. Thus in my mind, knowledge acquired from some second-person research/practice, while not framed in general societal terms, can be of such significance and relevance so as to 'transcend the single case without losing the action element along the road' (e.g. see Elliott, 2009, pp. 31–32).

On the issue of communicative space, both the school improvement literature and my own experience suggest a very complex dynamic often out of the control of site-level participants but more in line with Kemmis's Habermasian perspective than with Reason's (2003) under-developed description of 'first-order democracies'. This complexity is apparent in two seemingly contradictory statements made by Kemmis. In his 2006 publication, Kemmis was quite clear that he regards AR that is the result of government mandates as non-emancipatory, while in 2005, he (and McTaggart) stated, in contrast, that 'many PAR projects came into existence because established structures and authorities wanted to explore possibilities for change in existing ways of doing things, even though the new ways would be in a contradictory relationship with the usual way of operating' (p. 582). Indeed, both the literature on second-wave school reform and current initiatives related to data-driven school improvement strongly suggest that then, as now, the motivation for the creation of site-based inquiry teams is often external (e.g. in response to NCLB). Moreover, irrespective of the voluntary or involuntary origins of these spaces, achieving a truly democratic and participatory problem-solving process, while possible, is fraught with obstacles. One well-known risk is that site-based research teams tend to privilege teacher knowledge in comparison to or the exclusion of the views of other stakeholder groups, for example, the voices of parents and students. Even when teachers try to involve parents in the process (e.g. several IBSIP inquiry teams focused on increasing parent participation in their schools' decision-making process), language barriers, a general distrust of and reluctance to believe that their voices would be honored, as well as time constraints in attending regularly scheduled meetings all worked to decrease their presence on these teams. Where IBSIP schools were able to achieve decent levels of parent attendance, many parents never spoke at meetings due to a felt lack of knowledge on the topics of discussion. Finally, I have found there to be no inevitable relationship between the nature of the communicative space and the larger school's adoption of their products. Even with a democratic problem-solving process, there is no guarantee that the outcomes will be respected and implemented in the larger school community. Much depends on the willingness of other school stakeholders to honor the work of these inquiry teams. When they don't, team members can experience feelings of extreme disempowerment. However, as a larger proportion of the school community is involved, there is a greater likelihood that the results of such local research will reach beyond the study participants to effect changes in the larger community and advance the democratization of the school's decision-making process. Still, there is no guarantee that this work will involve consideration of the larger socio-political milieu or issues of social justice.

Third-Person Research/Practice

Third-person research/practice seeks to create non face-to-face communities of inquiry which awaken and support the inquiring qualities of first- and second-person AR. Consistent with this criterion are transformative communicative activities undertaken by large group organizations and large participatory professional and community networks (e.g. conferences and reflexive journals). According to Torbert (2004), such inquiry/practice should speak to a yet wider audience to influence and transform popular opinion, organization strategy, government policy, etc. They are one significant way that first- and second-person educational research/practice may address Gustavsen's (2003) emancipatory criterion of scale.

While growing in number, third-person AR communities are still few, and rare are those that embrace the interests and professional priorities of those other than at the forefront of various AR movements. Thus, existing third-person AR networks, most notably scholarly journals, continue almost exclusively to be targeted to and to prioritize the values and dialogues of the university community, in sharp contrast to the more instrumental and practical interests of elementary and secondary school educators and parents of marginalized and underachieving students. For example, the exemplary work of Cochran-Smith and Lytle (1993, 2009), while doing much to advance the existence of first-, second-, and third-person teacher/practitioner inquiry communities, largely involves AR conducted by doctoral students, student teachers, cooperating teachers associated with university-based professional preparation programs and networks, and college faculty. This research also disproportionately privileges self-studies; first-person research voice; and knowledge construction consistent with Stenhouse's emphasis on teacher professional development. AR emanating from such organizational structures still risks ventriloquism and co-optation by AR professionals and can perpetuate the social and knowledge stratifications AR is intended to redress. Despite Cochran-Smith and Lytle's (2009) tracing of the origins of teacher inquiry back to critical theory, initiatives to deepen educators' sense of social responsibility and movements for social justice, the focus of much of such work remains on enhancing the sensibilities and professional knowledge of university-associated educators, in fact, changing little in the daily or future lives of historically marginalized and underachieving students whom they may serve at the elementary and secondary school levels. Ironically, teacher/researchers at these levels focused on such instrumental change may not only find dissemination of their work within their own systems threatening to existing power structures but may also find such work devalued within larger third-person AR networks (see section below). While third-person educational AR networks are growing in number, have great potential and achieved some success in creating social movements, in industrialized nations, their greatest acceptance and involvement are still among teacher/researchers associated with academe. Still, too little affected is the knowledge-creation hierarchy and even less affected are the lives of those most needy of social justice in the field, that is, historically marginalized and undereducated students.

A Re-conceptualization of Emancipatory Educational Action Research

In an article, Groundwater-Smith (2005) asks if the idea of an emancipatory critical social science is an impossible goal, based in part on a rigid adherence to Habermasian theoretical principles that, in actual practice, have been very difficult to attain. In seeming response, Gustavsen (2004) declared that he and others have 'progressively abandoned' the idea of a theoretical foundation of the type proposed by Habermas in favor of a pragmatic one, based on 'what works'. Concurring with Shotter (1993), Gustavsen challenges the use of theory primarily to establish the one and only true or right way—which theory can seldom do—seeing its value rather to test ideas, generate new associations, and generally enrich our thoughts and actions. Building upon Shotter and Gustavsen's re-conceptualization, that is, to privilege 'what works', an even greater shift is suggested here, away from the exclusive primacy of theory and pure, or even actionable, knowledge generation to allow the equality of real-world praxis, that is, to attend to the actual and/or potential outcomes of educational AR to change discriminatory systems and/or their impact on the lives of others for the better.

Now, almost exclusively focused on theory-based concerns, for example, researcher dispositions or theoretical stance, design features, and the experimental process, characteristically subordinated to near incidental status are the real-world effects of the research, particularly on the lives of students and the larger social system. Even Kemmis's view of the aim of critical participatory AR is primarily in intellectual terms. Kemmis and McTaggart state (2005, p. 590):

> Public spheres do not affect social systems … directly; their impact on systems is indirect. In public spheres, participants aim to change the climate of debate, the ways in which things are thought about and how situations are understood … It is only by the force of better argument, transmitted to authorities who must decide for themselves what to do, that they influence existing structures and procedures.

Cochran-Smith and Lytle echo this view, categorizing the work of professional learning communities oriented toward school reform and student achievement as wrongly focused on 'test outcomes rather than on learning more expansively defined' (2009, p. 57). These statements seem to miss or dismiss the fact that such criteria, standards and tests are among the instruments currently used by industrialized nations and their school systems to continue to deny historically marginalized groups access to the cultural capital needed to reap the rewards of these societies. Granting that these school systems are not the sole vehicle for group disenfranchisement, still, should educators eschew targeting and equipping such students with the tools to surmount these barriers until they are removed through critique and debate? Also cognizant that teaching is not best done through top-down mandates, as it involves a complex, contextualized and inter/personal dynamic, how much more time should academics devote primarily to a focus on self-reflection, consciousness raising, and on process, as generations of marginalized students continue to fail and are prepared more for these systems' jails than for institutions of higher education? I too deny the assumed greater inherent efficacy in the use of 'scientifically based research', but where are the voices of parents of underachieving students and educators' sense of urgency in setting the AR goals and agenda in these children's learning and instruction? Hendriks (2009, p. 32) alludes to these quandaries and a possible need to broaden her reflexive boundaries when noting the disparities between her and her students, who were in-service teachers, regarding the perceived value and consequences of scripted instruction. She states that

(W)hen I brought up the issue of teacher autonomy, I was the only person in the conversation passionate about it. Everyone else agreed autonomy is important, but felt student achievement is more important … I have to admit my values get messy in light of the realities educators face. There are issues here of social justice, which I hadn't considered before—the right of students to learn to read and the right of teachers to be treated as professionals.

Not only do most academicians, including action researchers, tend to devalue these exigencies in the instrumental objectives of local educators' AR, but more importantly they negate the emancipatory potential of directly aiding historically marginalized students in surmounting these very real institutional obstacles impeding their access to societal rewards. Thus, Cochran-Smith and Lytle (2009, pp. 58–59), in comparing teacher inquiry to the more instrumental school reform work of teacher professional communities, laud the former as 'enhancing educators' sense of responsibility and social action in the service of a democratic society', linking this work with 'larger movements for social justice and social change', warning that the latter 'may reify rather than challenge dominant epistemologies and values about the purposes of schooling'. Kemmis (2006) takes a similar perspective, asserting and simultaneously warning that technical and practical AR 'may even become the vehicle for domesticating students and teachers to conventional forms of school' (p. 459), going as far as to term it schooling at the expense of education.

It is my view, however, that in industrialized nations there is still a great deal of race and class discrimination and masked institutional oppression, and for those who have been historically marginalized, undereducated and denied access to the cultural capital needed for a viable existence in these societies, technical and practical educational AR that results in significant advances in these students' academic achievement and passing rates on critical 'gate-keeping' tests is emancipatory research. It is an error to view emancipatory AR as primarily confined to PAR in developing countries while limiting its role in industrialized nations to enhancing educators' sense of social responsibility, consciousness raising, and professional development. Such efforts should continue; however, in prioritizing our understanding of ourselves as the oppressor, we cannot lose sight of freeing the oppressed. Thus, equally as important as the existing criteria for emancipatory educational AR is the need also to focus on changing the actual 'lifeworlds' and achievement rates of historically undereducated student populations. Consequently, while many local teacher/researchers may lack an appropriate theoretical consciousness and their inquiry process may at times be less than fully rigorous, if their goal is the actual elimination of class- and race-based achievement gaps and the equitable passage of historically oppressed student groups through gated access routes, should not this work also be regarded as emancipatory AR?

It is critical to state that it is not my vision for schools to become test prep mills, but rather to become sites for dedicated instruction in and the learning of substantive content, the arts, critical thinking, problem solving and citizenship. My goal is to see actual change in the cultural capital, life trajectories, and aspirations of historically marginalized and chronically underachieving groups of students in industrialized nations. However, to achieve these other-oriented lifeworld ends, such outcomes need to be the stated foci of educational AR.

Finally, the proposed shift or, more accurately, the broadening of the criteria for emancipatory educational AR/practice to include consideration of immediate or potential outcomes has significant implications. First and foremost, it means that site-level teachers have the ability to create a significant and valuable knowledge base on successful instructional practices found to advance the learning and achievement of historically marginalized and heretofore chronically underachieving students. This alone is profound, as currently college-based academics have limited access to this population, most recently constrained by the IRBs. What is more, it appears to address one of Reason and Bradbury's (2006) criteria for emancipatory status, that is, to produce practical knowledge that is useful to people in the everyday conduct of their lives and through this knowledge to contribute to the increased well-being of human persons and communities to a more equitable and sustainable relationship with the wider ecology, leading not just to new knowledge, but to new abilities to create knowledge. Third, it would lead to a new respect for the instrumental work of primary and secondary school teachers, opening the doors of existing or leading to the creation of new third-person communicative networks that would help this work achieve the level of a 'societal movement', or scale consistent with Gustavsen's notion. And last, teacher/researchers, now practically motivated to reflect on the institutional and societal obstacles to their work and to their students' achievement, may spontaneously begin to develop their own grounded self- or group understanding of the elements of a critical emancipatory consciousness.

Conclusions

There are thousands of elementary and secondary school teachers in the US alone, many if not most of whom have exited the university system without a theory-based emancipatory intent. This number is exponentially magnified across the industrialized world. Over the next several years, a majority may well be mandated or voluntarily elect to engage in first- or second-person research/practice often aimed at increasing the successful instruction and passing rates of historically marginalized and chronically underachieving students. To continue to privilege theory, self-reflection, process, and knowledge production for the sake of researcher self-enlightenment while ignoring if not denigrating the actual outcomes of this research on students and school systems, or the lack thereof, is to be myopic and elitist. It takes a stance superior to these others and assumes the privilege and greater wisdom to decide when, where and how historically marginalized and undereducated groups should be emancipated rather than directly and immediately working to obtain their societal access and letting them decide for themselves.

While action research comes in many forms and 'flavors', each with differential potential and risks for advancing social justice and emancipatory change, its fulfillment is not in constricting the criteria for its achievement; and pooh-poohing the role and emancipatory significance of aiding historically marginalized people in surmounting institutional barriers to their societal advancement. Ethnic and class oppression and stratification are still very much a part of industrialized nations, reproduced in their educational systems. We must fight these injustices, not only in our theories, research processes, and attitudinal intent but also in the focus and outcomes of our AR. Our work must also seek to produce change in the real lives of oppressed people everywhere, not just in educators' attitudes, knowledge and theories.

Note

1. Institutional Review Boards (IRBs) are regulatory and screening committees established for the purpose of reviewing all proposed research emanating from an institution to preclude or stop any research that is deemed potentially abusive to human subjects.

References

Bernstein, R. J. (1976). *The restructuring of social and political theory. Part IV.* Oxford: Blackwell.

Carr, W., & Kemmis, S. (1986). *Becoming critical: Education, knowledge and action research.* Abingdon: Routledge Falmer, Taylor and Francis Group.

Carr, W., & Kemmis, S. (2005). Staying critical. *Educational Action Research, 13*(3), 347–357.

Carr, W., & Kemmis, S. (2009). Educational action research: A critical approach. In S. Noffke & B. Somekh (Eds.), *Handbook of educational action research* (pp. 74–84). London: Sage.

Chandler, D., & Torbert, B. (2003). Transforming inquiry and action: Interweaving 27 flavors of action research. *Action Research, 1*(2), 133–152.

Cochran-Smith, M., & Lytle, S. (1993). *Inside/outside: Teacher research and knowledge.* New York: Teachers College Press.

Cochran-Smith, M., & Lytle, S. (2009). *Inquiry as stance: Practitioner research for the next generation.* New York: Teachers College Press.

Cooke, B., & Kothari, U. (2001). *Participation: The new tyranny?* London: Zed Books.

Elliott, J. (2005). Becoming critical: The failure to connect. *Educational Action Research, 13*(3), 359–373.

Elliott, J. (2009). Building educational theory through action research. In S. Noffke & B. Somekh (Eds.), *Handbook of educational action research* (pp. 28–39). Sage: Thousand Oaks, CA.

Feldman, A., & Atkin, J. M. (1995). Embedding action research in professional practice. In S. E. Noffke & R. B. Stevenson (Eds.), *Educational action research: Becoming practically critical* (pp. 127–140). New York: Teachers College Press.

Groundwater-Smith, S. (2005). Painting the educational landscape with tea: Rereading *Becoming critical. Educational Action Research, 13*(3), 329–345.

Grundy, S. (1987). Three modes of action research. *Curriculum Perspectives, 2*(3), 23–34.

Grundy, S., & Kemmis, S. (1981). *Social theory, group dynamics and action research.* Paper presented at the Annual Meeting of the Pacific Association of Teacher Educators, Adelaide.

Gustavsen, B. (2003). Action research and the problem of the single case. *Concepts and Transformations, 8*(1), 93–99.

Gustavsen, B. (2004). Theory and practice: The mediating discourse. In P. Reason & H. Bradbury (Eds.), *Handbook of action research* (pp. 18–26). London: Sage.

Gustavsen, B. (2008). Action research, practical challenges and the formation of theory. *Action Research, 6*(4), 421–437.

Hendriks, C. (2009). *Improving schools through action research: A comprehensive guide for educators.* Upper Saddle River, NJ: Pearson.

Hutchinson, N. (1996). Action research: Being teachers or freeing teachers? *Teaching & Teacher Education, 12*(1), 109–114.

Kemmis, S. (2001). Exploring the relevance of critical theory for action research: Emancipatory action research in the footsteps of Jurgen Habermas. In P. Reason & H. Bradbury (Eds.), *Handbook of action research* (pp. 94–105). London: Sage.

Kemmis, S. (2006). Participatory action research and the public sphere. *Educational Action Research, 14*(4), 459–476.

Kemmis, S. (2008). Critical theory and participatory action research. In P. Reason & H. Bradbury (Eds.), *Handbook of action research: Participative inquiry and practice* (2nd ed., pp. 121–138). London: SAGE.

Kemmis, S., & McTaggart, R. (2005). Participatory action research: Communicative action and the public sphere. In N. K. Denzin & Y. S. Lincoln (Eds.), *Handbook of qualitative research* (3rd ed., pp. 559–604). London: Sage.

Kinsler, K. (2008). Teaming for success in underperforming schools. *Kappa Delta Pi, 44*(3), 128–131.

Lewin, K. (1952). Group decision and social change. In G. E. Swanson, T. M. Newcomb, & F. E. Hartley (Eds.), *Readings in social psychology.* New York: Holt.

McKinney, C. (2005). A balancing act: Ethical dilemmas of democratic teaching within critical pedagogy. *Educational Action Research, 13*(3), 375–391.

Neilsen, E. (2006). But let us not forget John Collier: Commentary on David Bargal's 'Personal and intellectual influences leading to Lewin's paradigm on action research'. *Action Research, 4*(4), 389–399.

Noffke, S. E. (1992). The work and workplace of teachers in action research. *Teaching and Teacher Education, 8*(1), 15–29.

Noffke, S. E. (2005). Are we critical yet? Some thoughts on reading, rereading and *Becoming critical. Educational Action Research, 13*(3), 321–327.

Noffke, S. E., & Stevenson, R. B. (1995). Action research and democratic schooling. In S. E. Noffke & R. B. Stevenson (Eds.), *Educational action research: Becoming practically critical* (pp. 1–12). New York: Teachers College Press.

Peters, J. (2004). Teachers engaging in action research: Challenging some assumptions. *Educational Action Research, 12*(4), 545–555.

Reason, P. (2003). Action research and the single case: A response to Bjorn Gustavsen and Davydd Greenwood. *Concepts and Transformations, 8*(3), 283–294.

Reason, P., & Bradbury, H. (2006). *Handbook of action research* (2nd ed.). Thousand Oaks, CA: Sage.

Reason, P., & Torbert, W. R. (2001). The action turn: Toward a transformational social science. *Concepts and Transformations, 6*(1), 1–37.

Shotter, J. (1993). *Conversational realities.* London: SAGE.

Torbert, W. R. (2004). The practice of action research. In P. Reason & H. Bradbury (Eds.), *Handbook of action research* (pp. 207–217). London: Sage.

CHAPTER 4

Uses of Data in Action Research

Marie Brennan and Susan E. Noffke

Data in Our Action Research

Action research is a highly personal as well as political activity. It is not merely a technique—an instrument or method for educational research. Rather, we see it as a way to problematize many of the assumptions and practices of social research, including educational research. Our version of action research in education, and there are many versions circulating,[1] is particularly concerned with exploring reflexively how research can contribute to the empowerment of teachers and student teachers and thereby alter what occurs in schools and in teacher-education programs. Because of this, we see ourselves contributing to the tradition of recent critical curriculum and feminist efforts "to create empowering and self-reflexive research designs"[2] and share Lather's assumption that: "an emancipatory social science must be premised upon the development of research approaches which both empower the researched and contribute to the generation of change enhancing social theory."[3] We do not, however, suggest that action research is automatically "liberatory": like any other social practice it can be used for co-option and for avoiding action on significant issues. However, in our view, the push to become explicit about our practices and make them problematic in an action research group is more likely than with other forms of research and reform to contribute to greater equality within the group as well as to better our understanding of the issues involved and the improvement of practice.

This particular action-research project arose as part of existing work on action research on teacher education already being done. Noffke and Zeichner at the University of Wisconsin-Madison had already raised a number of issues requiring more attention, among them the importance of ensuring that as supervisors, our action research is on action research and our own practice rather than on the students'[4] and that our work is with and for teachers rather than on teachers.[5] Our basic assumption is that we cannot study things using a research methodology that is based on a fundamentally different epistemology to which we are committed, and then use the epistemology of "normal science" in order to study the process. Action research is a way for our students and for ourselves to problematize the nature of teaching. This task has both epistemological and methodological implications and therefore includes issues of ethics and politics. For us, the relationship between issues of knowledge and issues of ethics was the "general idea" of this "cycle" of an ongoing action-research project. In this chapter, we specifically consider the role of data in action research. This will be shown to be not merely an issue of choosing a "research technique" for the accumulation of information. Instead, data are crucial to redefining the relationship among "knowers" and between those "knowers" and what is to be learned.

Our action research with our student teachers took place in the context of a weekly group seminar and separate supervisory visits to the school to observe and discuss progress in teaching with each student and his or her cooperating teacher. Our work as supervisors of student teachers in the Elementary Education program at the University of Wisconsin-Madison provided the opportunity for us to undertake action research ourselves and to ask our students to do it as a university project requirement, forming part of their final placement in schools for student teaching experience.[6] We undertook our own action-research project alongside theirs so that the two kinds of projects could work together in dialogue about action research and student teaching. In this chapter, we are focusing on the way data were used in and about action research and, because of our own action-research project, how this was interwoven with our teaching. There was no neat dividing line between our teaching and our research. Rather, we tried to improve our teaching as we reflected on our project, often with input from the students as to how our approach to action research was contributing to their development as student teachers. Evidence that could be said to be based in our research efforts became part of our teaching, in the following week or in the following semester.

In this chapter, we address only a small number of issues about the uses of data as they relate to action research. Our major question is how data can be used as part of both the teaching and research processes in ways that explore how redefining research and teaching occurs in practice. Such action research on action research would, of necessity, be reflexive—contributing to both the process of learning to teach and the process of learning to teach teachers. We summarize our learning to date about the role of data in group action research under what we define as emerging propositions about the use of data in action research. Examples from the student teacher seminar and the supervisory process are used to illustrate this learning. The first section considers the contribution of data to the development of a group and explores the place of interpreting data together in building different and more equal kinds of relationships among the seminar group of student teachers, and among the triad of the student teacher, the cooperating teacher, and the supervisor in various moments of the relationship. The second section emphasizes the importance of group articulation of issues to define what counts as evidence on an issue and illustrates the proposition that work on data ought to be able to support group members in articulating their own theoretical issues.

Using Data in Becoming a Group

Methodologically, we consider the interpretations of actions and statements by the actor-speaker her- or himself within the context of the group as a mutual, interpretive process, going well beyond "support" to conceptualizing interpretation as an interactive process. Data—its collection, presentation and discussion within a group—can thus be a catalyst for mutuality and reciprocity. In turn, this has implications for the very way in which we use data for evidence in and about action research as a research commitment within teacher education.

To understand the role of evidence in and about action research, it is not enough to look merely at separate pieces of data. Techniques for gathering data, which become used as "evidence" in an investigation, may well be common across several approaches to educational research yet function entirely differently when embedded in their particular project. Sandra Harding's formulation of the relationship and distinctions between method, methodology, and epistemology have been useful to us in helping to flesh out how and why we think evidence takes on a different role in action research than it does in other forms of research:

A research method is a technique for (or way of proceeding in) gathering evidence ... A methodology is a theory and analysis of how research does or should proceed ... An epistemology is a theory of knowledge. It answers questions about who can be a 'knower' ... what tests beliefs must pass in order to be legitimated as knowledge ... what kinds of things can be known.[7]

In focusing on evidence in action research, we are trying to throw light on the interconnections of method, methodology and epistemology around which our major questions lie. We are under no illusions that we can address these issues thoroughly in this short chapter, but it is necessary to situate this investigation about the particular place and role of evidence in action research within a larger context of the definitions of and approaches to research in the social sciences in general. "Evidence," as we see it, is a shorthand concept which describes the use of data in ways that are congruent with the epistemological assumptions and methodological commitments embodied in our version of action research. For data to be used as "evidence" presupposes shared assumptions of validity. We see this paper as a contribution to understanding more about the context in which validity claims can be developed and used. Within our context, evidence becomes a relational concept grounded in two or more people as they proceed around issues of joint practice and conversations over separate, but related, activities.

There are three particular kinds of data used for evidence in the task of building dialogue in our work on action research. First, we had data in the form of information gathered on a topic under discussion or investigation. Each student, as well as the supervisor, had data on her or his own project which could be shared with the group. Dealing with this data became the focus of a second phase of data gathering: data about how the group processes were working in meeting our goals, whether jointly set as coresearchers or individually in relation to our own specific situation. Finally, there was the data about what we were learning about action research—the focus of our project as supervisors. All three foci for data gathering could be seen as fitting within Harding's "method" category. At the same time, though, each fits within a particular view of how data are to be used and within a commitment to all members of the group as the producers of knowledge. The point of collecting the data is to further the communicative action of members of the group: their understanding of themselves and others, the setting, and their capacity to act. In so doing, we hoped to promote greater articulation and understanding of the specific interests and tasks of student teaching within contemporary schooling in the United States.

Students brought various forms of data to the weekly university seminar as a way of contributing to the seminar topic under discussion. Sometimes the particular item was a result of conversations during classroom supervision in which the cooperating teacher took part. Discussing their data allowed students to take a leadership role in the class, particularly as there were usually many forms of data available on the same topic intersecting in the discussion and allowing for a wide variety of interests and emphases. Some of this data was collected expressly for a class topic, some arose from the student teachers' existing journal and observation materials in relation to their action-research project, and some was suggested or offered by the cooperating teacher. Calling on Brown's[8] delineation, we understood and explained different kinds of data to our students as: primary—an artifact already existing within the situation, secondary—organized and collected specifically to follow up a question or issue, and tertiary—reflecting on the first two groups of data. Students could choose what data to present and thus determine their own level of personal engagement in the class project as a whole.

For discussion of the topic of classroom management, for example, a seminar group brought copies of school policies about the discipline system for the school, individual shadow studies of "problem" children, notes from interviewing a principal and a teacher, observation notes about two different teachers with the same class, copies of student reports and student class work, and a wealth of journal entries and anecdotes from the student teachers' own experiences and, particularly, their problems. As well, the supervisor brought to class, as her data, a list of relevant issues discussed in student journals, her notes from observing the students and discussing these issues with them at their schools, and photocopies of some of the students' material already existing in the form of written observations. There were also a number of class readings on the topic, covering different points of view and different levels of abstraction.

For most students, the topic of classroom management was closely related to their current concerns in the classroom. In fact, the topic had been moved forward on the seminar calendar because of this interest. During the meeting the supervisor took notes on the discussion, forming data on the processes in which the group was engaged, for use in later discussion with the other supervisor and with students. Discussion of observational data and reflections from the seminar on the classroom data formed occasions for promoting conversation.

At times, our data on the students' progress in meeting agreed goals or outlined expectations contributed directly and immediately to the topic at hand. One example of this is a collage the students created on the topic of the curriculum in their classrooms. Three students had nothing about content anywhere in their presentations, which were mainly concerned with representing loving and caring relationships among pupils and between teacher and class. Reflections about this on the part of the supervisor were brought up in class, using the immediate data as a way of raising the question of what the role of curriculum content was in a teacher–student relationship.

This strategy could be seen merely as an attempt at good teaching rather than as an exercise in research. However, the emphasis on the reflexive use of data over time is what distinguishes this approach to research from other teaching efforts. In endeavoring to make the students' learning the focus of the seminar, this strategy of gathering data about the overtly discussed agenda of the supervisor forms a necessary cornerstone. The presence of constant feedback from the supervisor also encourages open discussion of the role of the seminar, which the students sometimes felt understandably as a tension, a conflict with their placement in the schools.

Instead of the university as the site of theory and the school as a place of practice, we were able to examine in the seminar the practice and the theory of both school and university and the tensions between them. Discussion of students' data also rehearsed or modeled the way that the data for their action-research projects could be dealt with, both for its contributions to their practice in the classroom and for the potential for understanding that practice. It could make problematic the embedded theories in daily practice in schools and show quite well how much is already shared among teachers who think of themselves as having very different styles, commitments, and interests in teaching.

For the group analysis of data to work, there has to be a level of trust, knowledge, and respect within the group—the seminar group, the university supervisor, and the cooperating teacher in the school. Otherwise, the process runs the danger of reinforcing the idea of the university as the site of abstracted expertise and the school as the site of practice. Data in our experience formed a bridge between two sites of theorizing and practice. This was particularly important in bringing the cooperating teacher into ongoing discussions of issues.

For the supervisor to become part of the ongoing relationship between student teacher and cooperating teacher is difficult but necessary if the university program is to offer any assistance and challenge to classroom teachers on whom the program as a whole depends. It helps immensely if the supervisor and cooperating teachers already know each other and if the cooperating teachers are interested in using the opportunity of having a student teacher in the room for thinking about their own practice. Without the capacity for the supervisor to make established classroom practice problematic as a participant in an ongoing conversation, the stereotypic gap between university and school is maintained.

Cooperating teachers have noted in their feedback that they enjoyed the action-research project because it allowed them to have an equal part in the ongoing conversations: they could contribute much to the data gathering, the reflection, and the planning of future steps, if the student teacher felt able to let them in. Some continued the project beyond the student teacher's experience.[9] Copies of data from the supervisor's observations and conferences with student teacher and cooperating teacher were given to the student and cooperating teacher after each session, so that they had the same records for their own purposes. Some of these conferences were audiotaped, mainly for the supervisor's data interests. As a result of the collection and reuse of data, we have found that the level of preparation for such conferences on the part of the student increased over time and that there was a tendency to become more reflexive in the choice of topics discussed at the later conferences.

For example, one student, Kathleen,[10] came to the midterm conference totally unprepared to discuss her own views on her progress although this had been suggested earlier. While this conference was productive, especially in beginning the processes of articulated self-reflection on growth, the final conference showed a much clearer partnership in the determination of the agenda. That discussion also included topics of supervisory and, to an extent, cooperating teacher practices, as well as the student teacher's own articulation of progress. The relationship itself, as a factor in the student teacher's development, had come to be seen as equally problematic and in need of exploration. Specific relationships among individuals, such as in the triad of student teacher, cooperating teacher, and supervisor, also contributed to the growth of trust and mutuality in the seminar group as a whole.

Using our evidence as part of the teaching process is an important means of achieving some measure of symmetry in the seminar group. This is the only time in the week that the student teachers are a group. The rest of the time they are in separate classrooms with their cooperating teacher, with whom an intense and very personal relationship usually develops. To develop the commitment towards group reflection in twelve seminar meetings, against most of their previous university experiences, was perhaps the most difficult challenge for us as teacher educators. Mostly, we did not succeed as well as we would have liked. However, there were some encouraging signs from seminar discussions and from comments from cooperating teachers about the projects that this was an aspect of our work that was valued and worth working on further. Since we saw each of the student teachers in their classrooms, we were in a position to draw out links with other students' experiences and strengths, to suggest foci for conversations, and to demonstrate the links between readings and their own experience. Given this pivotal role for the supervisor in the group, it was difficult to ensure that we did not remain the focus of attention and that real conversations developed among the student teachers as a group. Such an effort should not be seen as just a contribution to improved teaching or teacher education, or as a way to create better "group dynamics." Rather, it also contributes to the redefinition of the "knower" in research. If there is no reflexivity in the use of data and no recognition of the necessary interdependence of "knowers," then the data are not being properly used.

Over the semester we, as supervisors, learned to be more patient, and in listening and reacting in conversational dialogue with students, we were gradually able to raise critical points with students more directly than we have been able to do in other situations. We were able to see that the conversational-dialogue mode did grow over time and fostered more profound attention to issues than ever before experienced in our teaching. In this, we were able to explore earlier frameworks suggesting that the technical, practical, and critical dimensions of reflection are not hierarchically arranged and should not be treated as such in our seminars or supervisory conferences. All three dimensions are important and connected.[11] Living with that advice is not always easy, just as it is not easy to be patient enough to allow students to follow their own judgment and surface those judgments through identifying embedded theories.

It might need to be pointed out that being patient and allowing for all three dimensions of issues to be explored does not imply a passive stance on the part of the teacher, in this case the supervisor. We did not wait for them to "rediscover the wheel," nor did we refrain from entering into conversations that grew progressively more "symmetrical"[12] as time passed. The equality of conversation partners is an important focus in our research quest for a "reciprocally educative process."[13] Unless and until there can be some symmetry in the conversation, there cannot be mutual reflection, let alone a group investigation. Schweickart's notion of the "coherence" of a conversation is an image for the way difference and disagreement can work to build a group effort without removing the separate interests and locations for different participants' activities.[14] Without such difference among participants, the group is diminished in its potential to affect each individual as well as the group as a whole.

An example of this process could be seen in one of the final seminar sessions and in Kathleen's final conference the next day. At the beginning of the seminar, the supervisor described again her own action-research project, its purpose, and some of her tentative thoughts on the data accumulated so far. These, then, became the topic for a group discussion, the central focus of which was the idea of the students' "context-specific knowledge" versus the supervisor's use of abstract concepts and general principles. Through an open discussion, wherein both the seminar agenda and the supervisor's practice were made problematic, several issues emerged. First, the students felt a real need to begin with their own direct experience in the classroom and in supervision and then look for patterns before discussion of abstract concepts. This was felt not just as a way to better understand the abstract but as a valuing of their needs, tensions, and joys.

The second area had to do with the supervisor's form of feedback, especially at the beginning of the semester, of probing for the student's beliefs embodied in their feelings of satisfaction and dissatisfaction with particular practices. The students felt this to be a conscious attempt at suspending judgment, which they felt was necessary. But it also led at times to a certain "fuzziness" as to alternative practices. Kathleen expressed her feelings:

> I was just thinking about it, when was it? Last week. I need input … It's like I'm trying to find all these answers and I have nowhere else to look and I … was this, am I doing this the right way? Or am I, should I be doing something different? Is there something else I should try? And I didn't feel I had enough of that.

She commented further:

> It was always kind of like "we don't want to step on eggshells and tell her she's doing anything wrong. We don't want to think for her." So it's been going over and over in my mind and I keep thinking 'I wish someone would just help me.'

That "help" came from other students as well as the supervisor. They shared their own reactions, how they saw the tension between developing their own thoughts and the need for concrete suggestions, leading to the generation of an alternative "practical" suggestion to the supervisor as to how she might deal with future groups. That group's discussion, it seemed, made it possible for the topic to reemerge in the context of Kathleen's final conference. For the first time that semester, not only her progress in teaching but the progress of the relationship itself became the substance of real conversation.

Our first proposition arising from our action-research project is that data should be able to contribute to the dialogue of a group, with an emphasis on building towards more symmetrical relationships. As Carr and Kemmis put it, drawing on Habermas, "the conditions for truth telling are also the conditions for democratic discussion."[15] If action research in teacher education is to challenge the existing power relations, especially in the way theory and practice are seen to relate, then the research design must pay particular attention to how knowledge production works in student teaching practice and to the interaction of supervisor and student teacher. We do not want to see one version of imposition—by university-based research or by the press of the status quo in practice—replaced by another kind of imposition, also university based but clothed in the rhetoric of emancipation. There is thus a need for the development of action research as part of an explicit group process where different agendas are laid out for negotiation.

Within this conceptualization of the projects, both ours and the student teachers', the relationships among students in the seminar group and between student and supervisor are critical elements of the research. Data are important because they can provide the focus for developing the relationship of "coresearchers" among group participants. The presence of data emphasizes and embraces different perspectives and biographies within the group while also building a commonality of procedures for reaching understanding; data act as a catalyst to promote "communicative action." They contribute to the possibility of "an understanding among participants in communication about something that takes place in the world."[16] Because data, in our situation, are about actions of the participants in the group, the individual interests and normative judgments are brought into the conversation and then are able to be interrogated.

Building Theories and Professional Ethical Judgment: Living Action Research

This section considers the interconnections between action research and the development of better teaching by student teachers in their own classrooms. In showing how this worked, most of our examples are drawn from the students' concern with classroom management and discipline. When so many of our students chose action research foci concerning discipline and classroom management, we were initially somewhat apprehensive, reflecting our skepticism about the fruitfulness of this topic. We had a series of concerns: Would this focus eliminate the more curriculum-oriented aspects of teaching, which we felt were crucial to changing teacher practice? Was the choice of topic merely an effect of the timing of the project early in the semester? Would the students themselves find it restricting later on in the semester? Would this really be an opportunity for us to help students to see and live the interconnection of issues? Would students focus mainly on the technical elements of discipline, particularly given the prevalence of setting up school-wide policies to promote systems of "assertive discipline" then proliferating in the local school district? Given the time constraints on student teachers and the pressure to build skills appropriate within their classroom and school setting, would this focus allow for open and honest three-way conversations among the student teacher, cooperating teacher, and supervisor, with the potential to problematize existing practice?

After examining a number of the students' action-research final reports and other data from seminar and cross-seminar groups, we came to realize that for students, "classroom management" and "discipline" were often shorthand terms to cover a whole area of teacher–student relationships. While there is a literature around issues of ethics and nurturance[17] separate from that dealing with race, class, gender and teaching technique, for these students and for us, building professional, ethical judgment was an integral part of the practical challenges facing them. Close examination of the data on the topic of classroom management and discipline became a way to explore how these issues were interconnected.

The connections between curriculum and issues of technique and ethical judgment can be seen more clearly by looking at the students' projects. Laurie's action-research project looked, on the surface, especially in its written form, as though all she was concerned about was how to make her first- and second-grade students pass the time in transitions more easily and how to help them to relax, become "centered" and aware of their own reactions and tiredness. Certainly these foci were a strong part of her interest, especially in the early stages of the semester. She used music and relaxation techniques with her class to help them to settle down and act as a group as well as individuals. This was important since the class was "squirrelly" and not skilled in group activities. However, both Laurie and her cooperating teacher were interested in building a nonauthoritarian, "open" classroom. They used Laurie's project as a way to focus on how this goal was being achieved with a group who posed difficulties for them both. Laurie's questions guiding different stages of her investigation were seemingly simple and technical:

> Is the rug too crowded? Dirty? Do some children prefer to sit up and relax? Is there too much stimulus in the room for some children who can't leave it alone? Why was there resistance by K? The day was quite hectic; perhaps I needed to take more time to help them relax? Is spontaneity better than planned activities?

The data she gathered in her journal looked in particular at students who were experiencing trouble in relaxing and in staying on task. This focus formed the basis of Laurie's discussions with her cooperating teacher, as well as of her requests for the supervisor to gather data when observing.

According to Laurie, the impetus for the project lay in its links with her own experiences: "I knew the benefits of positive self-image and overall well-being that I had received from doing yoga and listening to music." When this was linked to problems in the classroom in the early part of the semester and the readings and discussions in seminar, Laurie's project became an important aspect of her teaching. Other student teachers' experiences had also influenced her understanding, even though their classrooms were not, on the whole, oriented towards some form of democracy in their practice of "management." Hearing about the assertive discipline approaches of other rooms and schools added to Laurie's interest in her own investigation as a viable option for contributing to better learning. By the end of the semester, Laurie was excited to discover the interactions between what was happening in the class curriculum and students' behavior. She wrote:

> The best part of the research and the practice was the realization that I was seeing teaching as bits and pieces that seemed unrelated when in reality they all work together to make teaching effective (or not effective!). Classroom management is not an isolated issue, but rather it ties in with the curriculum, my attitude/composure for the day, how prepared I am, whether it is going to rain or snow, or if there has been a long vacation, or a vacation coming up ... Vital to the success of a classroom is the mutual trust and respect that is developed among all the participants in the class. When the group feels like a "community," everyone takes part in the responsibility of maintaining a classroom that is conducive to learning. (Laurie, December 1987)

Six weeks into the semester, Laurie said she was concerned about whether she was making progress and how she could tell in an open classroom. Her supervisor suggested that there were some data she could look back on to chart her progress, e.g., her own journal. She commented that she could now see how the things she was noticing became more complex, overlapping, building patterns. She also noted that she "hadn't been sure till recently what all the data collection was on about. Last week, it clicked" (Supervisor journal, October 13, 1987). Where before she was using the journal to record isolated bits of plans, information, observation data, and ideas for the future, now she began to make explicit interpretations.

This conversation was "replayed" to the seminar as a whole and used as the springboard for three related discussions: about how people felt about their journals and the supervisor's responses, about action research and how it related to their teaching, and about the principles behind discipline approaches in different situations. In this way, the connections and tensions between school and seminar requirements could become part of the overt questioning of the seminar group. The curriculum of the seminar and the curriculum of the student teaching experience were fruitfully played against each other in the context of a discussion about the relationship of discipline and curriculum issues for the classroom, a discussion which would not have been so detailed and precisely contributing to the articulation of the student's theory without the availability of data and its regular analysis.

To treat the so-called practical separately and/or as prior to ethical issues is to misrepresent quite seriously the experience and the concerns of student "neophyte" teachers. Building theory requires attention to the practical as well as the abstract. Two examples illustrate this point.

For one student, Jane, issues of "control" in her kindergarten classroom, especially during large group meetings for "sharing," formed the beginning point of her action research. In one sense, her growth over the semester mirrors stage theories of teacher development. She did alter her perspective from a focus on discipline techniques to a growing concern for the children's feelings and a concern with curricular and structural factors (e.g., room arrangement, time of day, etc.). Yet to note this as a "given" pattern is to obscure the way that ethical thought was continually intertwined with technical skill development. For instance, an early supervisory visit raised questions of purpose—Why did she see "sharing time" as valuable to children? What do both the listeners and the sharers gain?—that were then tied to particular possible courses of action such as sticking with the sharing time rather than choosing another activity, trying to involve the children more in discussion, focusing attention better.

As Jane explored these themes, she did develop skills, e.g., attention focusing techniques and clear consequences for inappropriate behavior. Yet she also raised new questions: How should one "be" with children? How can one focus more attention on appropriate rather than inappropriate behavior? Gradually the center of her attention became less the individual "misbehaving" child and more her own actions. This new set of skills (clearer directions, positive comments, question asking) developed with and through moral deliberation, not after a set of "secure" competencies had been established.

The last phase of Jane's project built on the first. Realizing that her purpose in using "sharing time" had a lot to do with personal knowledge and that issues such as student interest and self-control were valuable to her, Jane changed her focus to concentrate more on curriculum. She spent more time on her planning, chose activities that allowed for greater participation, gave the children a simple questionnaire on their activity preferences, and encouraged children to resolve some of their own conflicts. Rather than a process of proceeding through a series of "natural stages," changes in her actions were a reflexive process of deliberate thought, bringing into consciousness previously unarticulated and unquestioned moral issues, along with technical skill development.

For another student, Kathleen, the shifts in foci for learning and the intertwining of curricular, ethical, and technical deliberation and actions occurred in a quite different manner and included many autobiographical justifications. At her midterm conference (November 3, 1987), she noted:

> I'm thinking … I learned the most listening to myself, listening to the things I said to the students and then thinking about the implications … I shouldn't have said that, I should have said something else, or let it go.

When asked if she knew why she focused more on listening to herself during this field experience, she responded:

> My main concern before was the material. That's what I thought teaching was about. But being with kids as often, just seeing their emotions, how much they're a part of it. It doesn't matter what you're teaching, it's how you're saying things.

Two central aspects to this new concern seem salient. First, she saw it as tied to a need to know more about each child, especially how they learned. Second, her whole definition of "classroom management" and her desire to "work on" this area more, hinged on her definitions of "fairness" and "caring." In relation to the last example, she outlined a definition of "fairness" that strongly indicated a belief in the need to treat each child equally, to make sure that the same rules and procedures applied to all children. By the end of the semester (final conference, December 10, 1987), both aspects were merged:

> I was thinking about what I said [at the midterm conference] about being equal. I don't think it's possible to be equal as far as how you treat people. Fair is a much better word for it. Because kids are so different. How can you be equal? Because, equal—I mean, they're not equal. There are so many differences and there's no way they're going to be treated equally because they have so many different needs.

Kathleen's attention throughout the semester, in her journal, in supervisory conferences, and in her action research, was expressed as a concern with her "discipline and classroom management style." Yet clearly the focus was not on developing a set of techniques for "control" but rather on an ongoing process of examining the relationship one has with others in terms both of ethical principles of caring and justice and of instructional strategies. Some of the impetus for this reflexive process seemed closely connected, too, to her own biography. Often, her discussions of the need for sensitivity to the social and emotional needs of children were punctuated with descriptions of episodes from her own contrasting experiences in a Catholic grade school. These were used to describe changes in beliefs about teaching:

> … before, when I started, it was—I'm back in a Catholic grade school where I take your hands and slap you with a ruler. You know, turn your picture [on the bulletin board] over if you didn't have a handkerchief or clean fingernails … That was humiliating in third grade.

Curriculum questions, too, were considered in light of personal experience. Part of her rationale for her action-research project on class discussion (outlined in seminar, December 9, 1987) was given in terms of helping children to learn to see knowledge as "problematic":

> I found in my own schooling that passive learners are more likely to accept things without question. I came from a school where there was one right answer, it seemed, for everything. This is one of the reasons why I chose to pursue this. It wasn't until I got to college that I realized—I have a say. I can argue this. What the textbooks say doesn't mean that it's the truth.

There was in Kathleen's learning, then, no clear, linear progression in focus from management to children to curriculum. Rather, each was intertwined with the other and used as the topic for her own individual reflections and those of the supervisory and seminar groups. Teaching practice and theorizing teaching are learned through a complex process in which judgment and practical techniques are intertwined. The surfacing of the developing theories of these student teachers can be seen as making connections and articulating these connections. The multiple representations of the actions taken in the classroom found in the data of each student teacher and shared in the different settings of the group provided an important impetus to this articulation.

This, then, leads to our second main proposition about data in action research: Data ought to have the potential to assist group members to build and articulate their own theories. In our situation, student teachers and supervisors used the opportunity of the group to build up their understanding of what it is to be a student teacher and what it means to teach, of what schooling can be in the United States, and of the relationship of schools and the university. Often, students are unaware that their own "commonsense" language is full of embedded theories, each with a history in their own biography and their culture's priorities. To address these embedded theories will often involve them in understanding how issues in education are interconnected—that they have institutional as well as personal aspects, and that they operate within particular historical and contemporary time frames, with ideological and experiential/sensory dimensions.[18] The data and the methodological framework in which they are used should throw light on the constructed institutional and structural framework of their world in relation to themselves constructed as individual and group actors. Since we are interested in the action-research group for its potential to change practice and theory, it is important for method and methodology to be part of the living dynamic of understanding and action as they are in the process of transformation.

Rethinking Research and the Place of Data

If we start from the epistemological position that knowledge is social, then we have to give attention to the interpersonal and institutional circumstances of the situations in which our student teachers find themselves. As teacher educators, we have put much of our pedagogical effort into working out ways to develop groups and group communication at the university and some equality of communication among students and between students and supervisor. Because of this, our work has tended to focus on discourse, and we have found the arguments of Habermas in his *Theory of Communicative Action*[19] useful in our conceptualization of these processes:

Communicative action relies on a cooperative process of interpretation in which participants relate simultaneously to something in the objective, the social, and the subjective worlds, even when they thematically stress only one of the components in their utterances.[20]

Traditionally, data have been seen as a way to objectify an aspect of the relationship of subject and world, in order for the detached observer to subject it to critical scrutiny. However, if our epistemological stance is such that we do not accept either the detached, unitary subject or this particular representation of the separation of subject and world, then this function of data in the research process is no longer viable.

Data do not exist, except under the social conditions of their making. Data must be part of the relationship among a group. If data are seen as a way of furthering relationships among knowers, then they can no longer be seen to have an existence separate from that relationship. Rather, they provide the opportunity for normative debate within the group, subject to the same practical and ethical demands that the rest of the relationship requires. Since our epistemological concerns have a moral and political dimension, this dimension must also be part of both method (data collection) and methodology. Given our commitment to setting up group processes as a way for students to produce their own knowledge, the following characteristics are a tentative delineation of the potential for using data reflexively to contribute to the life of a group in formation and in action.

While the truth tests of more conventionally understood research emphasize an "objectivity" which is seen to exist outside of the researcher and the researched, validity measures in action research have to be developed within the group itself. Habermas argues that "validity claims of propositional truth, normative rightness, and sincerity or authenticity" can only be developed and tested within the framework of the group and its communicative action.[21] If, as our program goals imply, we are trying to work towards students who see themselves as producers of knowledge as well as consciously reproducing knowledge, then data must enable them to articulate, argue, and critique not only their own ethical stance but also the criteria that lie behind those positions.

In the context of communicative action, only those persons count as responsible who, as members of a communication community, can orient their actions to intersubjectively recognized validity claims.[22]

The use of data is not an attempt to distance the self and the world but to allow interpretation of the relationship/s existing between self and world and thereby to allow to be called into question the way in which those relationships are reconstructed and the criteria of truth and justice embedded in the actions under consideration. In this context, data provide a representation of and catalyst for questioning the principles, intentions, relationships and actions of participants; they give a common focus for the participants to put themselves and each other under scrutiny and challenge. They provide an opportunity for developing intersubjective validity claims and procedures. The ethical issues requiring judgment arise from the consideration of validity. As Habermas argues, truth claims are not a separate issue from "freedom" and 'justice."[23]

A further qualification to this outline of group-based validity is needed at this point. We do not suggest that the group is a closed and self-sufficient circle. That would be to fall into the trap of much of phenomenological research, where the only form of validity is bounded by the participants' own subjective interpretations and tends to ignore the structural and institutional boundaries that help form that consciousness. If the group is conceived of as an expanding conversation, which draws in others, either in their actions or in their written record of theorizing and practice, then wider understandings can be made relevant by the individual. This also implies that individual consciousness does not provide the measuring stick for validity, enabling group work to push beyond both the philosophy of consciousness[24] and the philosophy of the subject.[25] The objectivity-subjectivity split, inherent in most forms of research, we try to transcend here through attention to the links between the personal, the theoretical, and the practical, which come together in the student's classroom practice and in the seminar through the action-research project based in that classroom.

As a catalyst for surfacing debate about validity and the criteria for normative judgment within the group, data have an important role in ensuring that the action-research processes are self-reflexive for the participants. Consideration of new data or revisiting old data with new questions and issues by a group of coresearchers rather than by an individual researcher allows for constant questioning in a shared forum of the basis for both positions and propositions.

These explorations of data-in-use in action research have been built out of our experience in trying to use evidence with our students in promoting better student teaching experiences. As we worked, we kept tripping over unexamined assumptions about research and, although reasonably clear about our goals, we found that they, too, need constant reexamination. It was only after looking at how we use data in our teaching that we saw the connections with others' work such as Lather or Habermas.[26] Pursuing the theoretical through and with the practical act of teaching through action research, we found each other's company on the journey not only personally sustaining but also, as with our students, necessary to promote challenges to existing positions.

Such challenges underscore the relationship of the substantive work in teacher education to the metatheoretical work. For instance, since the history of group work in the United States is often more closely tied to co-option and social control than it is to collaborative work, [27] we have had many debates about how to avoid such pitfalls by addressing them explicitly. Other issues we continue to debate are more a matter of detail, within our framework. Triangulation, for example, is often seen to be the means to gain validity through cross-checking of one data source with another. In the process, a richer and more complex picture is to be built. However, our hunch is that action research alters the emphasis: triangulation is undertaken not so much to get internal validity from other sources, although coherence among sources is still important, but rather to expose for argumentation the various possible validity claims that might be in operation. There is not one reading of a text or item of datum, but many are possible. Keeping the conversation going within the group, even over a single semester, appears at this stage to offer the possibility of uncovering many more different options within the one set of data and within the mind-constructions of members of the group. Revisiting may perhaps be a more important approach to validity than cross-checking with other data sources.

In learning about the uses of data and some characteristics of how data can be used within our epistemological framework, we also learned about some aspects of action research. In the process, we certainly taught better and thought more deeply about our teaching. If knowledge is socially constituted and historically embedded, then we recognized that students have to see and analyze their positions on this, as well as experience it. That is, the articulation of their analysis is an important and necessary part of the group process. The work on classroom management and discipline has definitely contributed to a different understanding of the relationship of the ethical and the practical through personal and group action—with practical teaching implications for us as well as our students. The literature on caring, often seen in feminist works, takes on another dimension, adding to our understanding of the way that women students in particular learn to analyze and articulate their beliefs in practice. It also adds to our understanding of the way the practical has been separated from moral/ethical issues in the very language in which we conceptualize issues of discipline and classroom management.

However, merely understanding these things in our teaching and supervisory practice is not enough. We see this work as part of a much broader effort to redefine educational research, building on the work of feminist and other critical social scientists. There are many points in our own practice which seem to contradict our most deeply held and articulated positions. Through examining them together, we uncover more of the contradictions as the next place to start our questioning. For instance, while we are trying to practice this form of action research, we remain part of an unjust and unequal society. This affects not only how much we can make our relationships symmetrical and dialogic but also acts back on the institution and our teaching within it. Injustices and problems become more apparent, and seemingly intractable, especially in the limited sphere of action of undergraduate student teachers and even their supervisors. The pessimism which may result has to be overcome, not merely rejected or ignored. Uncovering contradictions helps us all to see those spaces in which strategic rather than naive or idealistic action is possible.

Notes

1. Other versions of action research include: action research as the investigation of the application of university-based research findings to the school practice: Gary Griffin, "Interactive research and development on schooling: Antecedents, purposes, and significance for school improvement" (paper presented at the annual meeting of the American Educational Research Association, Montreal, Quebec, 1983); action research as a means of gaining understanding, interest and adoption of particular ideas or practices: John Elliott, *Action research for educational change* (Philadelphia: Open University, 1991); action research as the action-oriented phase of a larger research project: Sharon N. Oja and Lisa Smulyan, *Collaborative action research: A developmental approach* (London: Falmer Press, 1989). We prefer not to engage in purist-oriented arguments about definitional issues concerning action research, since our own understanding is changing as we undertake more action research and see both its potentials and disadvantages with our student teachers. However, we do emphasize that action research is research on one's own practice, undertaken systematically, over time. This may, and usually does, involve interaction with others' ideas in the form of theoretical and practical issues, but this interaction is as a result of one's own investigation and the questions posed there. We also emphasize the importance of sharing at least the reflection and planning elements of the research process with others, even if action cannot be undertaken jointly.
2. Patti Lather, *Getting smart: Feminist research and pedagogy with/in the postmodern* (New York: Routledge, 1991), 70.
3. Patti Lather, "Feminist perspectives on empowering research methodologies" (paper presented at the annual meeting of the American Educational Research Association, Washington, D.C., April 1987), 4.
4. Susan E. Noffke and Kenneth M. Zeichner, "Action research and teacher thinking" (paper presented at the annual meeting of the American Educational Research Association, Washington, D.C., April 1987).
5. Stephen Kemmis, "Action research and the politics of reflection," in *Reflection: Turning experience into learning*, ed. David Boud, Rosemary Keogh, and David Walker (London: Kogan Page, 1985), 139–163.
6. In the Elementary Education program at the University of Wisconsin-Madison, students take an introductory course, three times a week, before proceeding to twenty-seven credits of methods-related courses in a variety of subject areas. Two two-credit practicums, with three half-days per week in schools for eight weeks are associated with the major areas of language arts/reading, and science/social studies/math. In their final semester, students are placed in schools for four and one-half days per week, and in addition have a weekly seminar with their supervisor who observes them approximately six times during the semester.
7. Sandra Harding, "Is there a feminist method?" in *Feminism and methodology*, ed. Sandra Harding (Bloomington: Indiana University Press, 1987), 1–14.
8. L. Brown, "Notes on evaluation" (unpublished paper, Curriculum Services Unit, Victoria, Australia, 1982).
9. P. Wood, "Action research: A field perspective," *Journal of Education for Teaching* 14, no. 2 (1988): 135–150.
10. All names used in this chapter are pseudonyms.
11. We have pursued this line of thought in four works: Susan E. Noffke, "The dimensions of reflection" (unpublished paper, University of Wisconsin-Madison, 1986); Marie Brennan, "Reflection as socialization? The colonization and liberation of minds and action" (unpublished paper, University of Wisconsin-Madison, 1987); Susan E. Noffke and Marie Brennan, "The dimensions for reflection: A conceptual and contextual analysis" (paper presented at the annual meeting of the American Association for Educational Research, New Orleans, LA, April, 1988): and Susan E. Noffke and Marie Brennan, "Action research and reflective student teaching at the U. W.-Madison: Issues and examples," in *Issues and practices in inquiry-oriented teacher education*, ed. B. Robert Tabachnick and Kenneth M. Zeichner (London: Falmer Press, 1990), 186–201.
12. Jurgen Habermas, *The theory of communicative action, vol. 1: Reason and the rationalization of society*, trans. Thomas McCarthy (Boston: Beacon Press, 1984).
13. Lather, "Feminist perspectives on empowering research ...," 8.
14. Patrocinio P. Schweickart, "What are we doing, really? Feminist criticism and the problem of theory," *Canadian Journal of Political and Social Theory* 9, no. 1–2 (1985): 148–164.
15. Wilfred Carr and Stephen Kemmis, *Becoming critical: Education, knowledge and action research* (London and Philadelphia: Falmer Press, 1986).
16. Habermas, *The theory of communicative action, vol. I*, 11.
17. Daniel P. Liston and Kenneth M. Zeichner, "Reflective teacher education and moral deliberation," *Journal of Teacher Education* 38, no. 6 (1987): 2–8; Nel Noddings, *Caring: A feminine approach to ethics and moral education* (Berkeley: University of California Press, 1984).
18. Noffke and Brennan, "Action research and reflective student teaching ..."

19. Habermas, *The theory of communicative action, vol. 1* and Jurgen Habermas, *The theory of communicative action, vol. 2: Lifeworld and system: A critique of functionalist reason,* trans. Thomas McCarthy (Boston: Beacon Press, 1987).
20. Habermas, *The theory of communicative action, vol. 2,* 120. 21.
21. Ibid., 137.
22. Habermas, *The theory of communicative action, vol. 1,* 14.
23. Jurgen Habermas, *Legitimation crisis,* trans. Thomas McCarthy (Boston: Beacon Press, 1975).
24. Habermas, *The Theory of Communicative Action, vols. 1 and 2.*
25. Seyla Benhabib, *Critique, norm, and utopia: A study of the foundations of critical theory* (New York: Columbia University Press, 1986).
26. Patti Lather, "Issues of validity in openly ideological research: Between a rock and soft place," *Interchange* 17, no. 4 (1986): 63–84; Habermas, *The theory of communicative action, vols. 1 and 2.*
27. Susan E. Noffke, "The social context of action research: A comparative and historical analysis" (paper presented at the annual meeting of the American Educational Research Association, San Francisco, CA, 1989).

CHAPTER 5

Critical Advocacy Research

An Approach Whose Time Has Come

Carolyn M. Shields

I n the current educational research climate dominated by quasi-experimental scientific studies and sophisticated statistical analyses, randomized controlled trials and replicable analyses have become the new "gold standard" (Hargreaves, 2003). Nevertheless, not everyone is enamored with the currency; Lather (2004) wrote that "the movement towards 'evidence-based policy and practice' oversimplifies complex problems and is being used to warrant governmental incursion into legislating scientific method." She continued, "It calls for critical readings of current policy and direct engagement in policy forums—putting critical theory to work" (p. 759). Despite considerable confusion about "what constitutes credible research and how to interpret it for practical purposes" (Manzo, 2004, p. 16), there often seems to be little room for qualitative research studies, let alone those called for by Lather, studies firmly grounded in critical ontologies, epistemologies, and methodologies.

In 1998, Maxine Greene asserted that we live in a "society of unfulfilled promises"—one in which a gap in school performance between majority and minoritized youth is indicative and reflective of disparities in opportunities for our country's citizens. Further, and even more distressing to many, is the fact that, despite America's claims to be the best and most powerful democracy in the world, there are still huge disparities in health care, income, insurance coverage, high school and university graduation rates, incarceration rates and so forth. Education has not fulfilled its mandate to be the "great equalizer." Moreover, the situation is not solely confined to the United States but is repeated in most developed countries worldwide.

As we consider the appropriate role of educational leaders and researchers in these contexts of wealth and disparity, we note considerable frustration with repeated attempts to implement educational reform and considerable discouragement on the part of many with apparent minimally successful results. Research that fails to take account of this reality holds little promise for redressing wrongs and making a difference in social, cultural, political, or economic outcomes of individuals or societies. Hence, the need for critical research—research that is both rigorous and activist, that has the potential to inform both policy and practice and, at the same time, to empower both researcher and participants alike—to be taken seriously is long overdue. In fact, the potential of critical research has barely been tapped, in that many scholars from critical perspectives tend to produce eloquent conceptual writing and de-emphasize needed empirical studies.

Purpose

This chapter has two purposes: first, to clarify the term "critical advocacy research," including reflection on some appropriate standards of rigor and quality; and, second, to consider the ability of such research both to empower its participants and to influence the social fabric of the nation. From the outset, therefore, it is apparent that critical research is openly ideological and hence (as all doctoral students are taught) must have a clear thread of argumentation running through the research problem, the purpose, theoretical lens, methodology, analysis, interpretations, and conclusions. The ideological position must no longer be "the clandestinely ideological research conducted by quantitative and more traditional qualitative researchers that helped legitimate societal inequality" identified by Lather (1986). Given today's polarized and politicized climate of accountability and conservatism, it is not surprising to note that taking such an openly ideological position is still not, however, generally accepted by all members of the research community.

For that reason, conceptual and methodological clarity and explicitness of research perspective must enable research designs to withstand the inevitable charges of bias and lack of rigor. In critical advocacy-oriented research, the researcher must both carefully reflect on the role of critical epistemologies in grounding research that is intended to highlight inequities in our current systems and also be willing to advocate meaningful change. At the same time, given the unabashed intent to use the outcomes of critical research for advocacy, the researcher must take special care to construct and conduct research that is rigorous, trustworthy, and authentic. Clearly, the researcher must distinguish between identifying one's ideology up front as a basis for identifying the parameters of the investigation and shaping the findings to conform with one's predetermined ontological biases. For that reason, careful attention must also be paid to the development of some well-designed standards of conduct and excellence.

Critical Advocacy Research

In this chapter, then, I argue, with Bourdieu (1977), Said (1994), and others, that most researchers enjoy a social location of power and privilege, one that requires that we take a stance as public intellectuals. I assert that critical research which begins with questions of inequity and disparity holds the most promise for promoting policies and practices that can lead to economic, ecological, and human justice and a sustainable global future. Hence, in this chapter, I will elucidate theoretically and demonstrate through examples from practice how it is possible to conduct critical research that is rigorous and ethical, and that, at the same time, has as its goal both empowerment and significant change. The time has come for critical advocacy research to come into its own.

Clarifying the Term

Critical research begins with the premise that research's role is not to describe the world as it is, but also to demonstrate what needs to be changed. Although initially influenced by Marxist thinkers and arguments and assumptions arising from a group of scholars known as the Frankfurt School, critical research has expanded to embrace various theoretical perspectives focused on elucidating inequity (queer theory, critical race theory, critical poverty theory, critical feminism, post-colonialism, and so forth). As Foster (1986) clarified a quarter of a century ago, critical researchers "do not presume to give a positivist and unilateral definition of history and society" but instead probe "foundational assumptions that are normally taken for granted" (p. 71). Primarily, critical researchers "examine sources of social domination and repression, but with the caveat that since we ultimately make our worlds, we can ultimately change them" (p. 71). Or as Lather (1992) describes it, critical inquiry "takes into account how our lives are mediated by systems of inequity such as classism, racism, and sexism" (p. 87).

Critical researchers, steeped in evidence of social and structural inequities that include and privilege some groups and members of society to the exclusion and marginalization of others, are often so passionate about redressing these inequities that they begin with the assumption that their views are widely understood and generally shared. Yet they must begin by recognizing that due to the very multiple perspectives they claim to value, not everyone sees the world in the same way. Some people, for example, have myopically lived their lives oblivious to the inequities around them. Indeed, the myth of the American dream, with its stories of people who have overcome adversity, worked hard, and pulled themselves up by their own bootstraps, have seemed so convincing that many people have failed to recognize the inherent error of that storyline. Thus, we commonly encounter school principals and superintendents who have never considered that a "no tolerance" policy may adversely target some elements of the population; that differential minority immigrant status (Ogbu, 1992) may be associated with disparate and conflicting attitudes and assumptions about education. Some educators have never reflected on the hegemonic roots of the educational norms, policies, curriculum, or accountability procedures they implement, support and perpetuate, or on the ways in which they often continue to perpetuate inequitable student outcomes.

For that reason, critical educators must not take awareness of the "unfulfilled promises" and social inequity for granted. Several years ago, for example, a young colleague and I were making a presentation at a prominent national conference. Early in the presentation, when my colleague made reference to Maxine Greene's notion of "a society of unfulfilled promises," she was amazed to be interrupted by a senior faculty member (coming from a different tradition), who asked, "What do you mean by unfulfilled promises?" Obviously our starting assumption was neither universally understood nor shared. More recently I experienced more dramatic evidence of the need to be explicit about our starting point and our goals. I had asked my doctoral students to read several articles that drew on Foucault's (1980) use of the panopticon to develop such concepts as surveillance, discipline, a regime of truth, and performativity.[1] Much to my surprise, when I read what had been intended as a critical reflection on these articles, one student, reading with an unquestioning positivist lens, had assumed their discussions to be normative descriptions rather than critical analyses.

Thus, to avoid obvious misunderstanding, the critical researcher must carefully delineate the problem to be researched, clarify his or her epistemological assumptions, and ensure both data and analyses are presented explicitly. Anderson, for example, in his critique of the ISLLC standards, had stated, "I will in this article explore the standards as a disciplinary practice and as ideology, using a critical approach to discourse analysis developed by Fairclough (1992)" (2001, p. 202). He went on to state, "My analysis is also informed by an approach to discourse analysis developed by Foucault (1984), who emphasizes that dominant discourses are determined by power struggles." My point is not to criticize Anderson's strong and compelling analysis of the standards as "disciplinary practice" but to demonstrate how easily the very basis of the argument being made by critical researchers can be misconstrued. Hence, the student (who arguably missed many textual cues) believed that the dominant discourse, arising from the power struggle, was now an irrefutable norm and that disciplinary practice was to be taken at face value as the way "discipline" should be enacted in a school.

Once a critical researcher has developed a clear line of argument from the problem prompting a particular investigation, his or her epistemological location, and the selected critical, theoretical framework, it may be useful to take an abductive reasoning (see Evers & Wu, 2006) approach to the analysis, investigating alternative explanations for one's findings, before concluding systemic inequity. Evers and Wu pose the question: "How is it possible to approach data in a theoretically sensitive way so that patterns are able to emerge unforced without the antecedent theory functioning either as a preconception that imposes an interpretation on the data or as a set of hypotheses that the data may confirm or disconfirm?" (p. 517). How do critical researchers avoid "confirmation bias"—seeing "in the case only whatever is brought to it in the prior theory" (Evers & Wu, 2006, p. 522) or "the tendency to emphasize evidence that supports a hypothesis and ignore evidence to the contrary" (Littell, 2008, p. 1300). Could

Anderson usefully have offered alternative possible explanations of the standards before concluding that the accompanying teacher test exemplified a continued negative and hegemonic influence of a power elite on education?

Because critical researchers still struggle to swim upstream in a positivistic current of quasi-experimental design and interpretation, it is important to work to ensure that research data are carefully embedded in a reasonable "inferential network" about socially just education, the presence of an uneven playing field, and the need for a more equitable and more inclusive approach to education. The key here is "reasonable" because critical researchers must avoid the trap of treating the data and inferential network in a positivistic way, as though it represents the only possible interpretation or valid perspective. Hence, despite our conviction that our lens, focused on "unfulfilled promises," provides the necessary perspective on the inequities inherent in a given phenomenon, we must avoid falling into the trap of denying that other legitimate perspectives also exist. Evers and Wu (2006) argue that in abductive reasoning, "the justification of a generalisation relies on the fact that it explains the observed empirical data and no other alternative hypothesis offers a better explanation of what has been observed" (p. 513); in other words, it uses "inference to the best explanation" (p. 528). The critical researcher may accept this challenge, recognizing that it must be taken up in a way that holds true to their critical perspective—in other words, avoiding the positivist and unitary explanation earlier rejected by Foster but also rejecting a relativism that assumes the equal validity of each alternative interpretation.

Thus, Tooms (2007) can justifiably argue that "*the Right Kind of Queer* is an educational leader who lives and works within a double bind of 'don't-ask-don't tell' politics that reproduces heteronormative power through their efforts to fit as a leader" (p. 36); she can further argue that "this particular kind of leader is an overachiever and workaholic who lives with a different, lesser, set of Civil Rights" (p. 36). At the same time, she will not (and does not) negate the possibility that others will disagree with this conclusion, arguing instead that their sexual orientation is not necessarily a "civil right."

My point here is that critical researchers will gain credibility as they do not fall into the same error made by those they critique—that of ridiculing or rejecting out of hand differing interpretations, whether based on differing ideologies or on erroneous factual grounds. As Foster urged in 1986, "critical theory has three tasks: understanding, critique, and education" (p. 72); hence the need to raise consciousness, to develop understanding, to urge reflection, and to advocate redress—but at the same time to avoid (insofar as possible) further polarizing an already emotionally and ideologically charged research landscape.

Justifying Interpretations

It is interesting that, although in the early days of qualitative research, scholars such as Guba, Lincoln, and Marshall were urging a break from trustworthiness standards that were derivative of quantitative research, the early standards for qualitative research, all of which were derivative of qualitative standards, still dominate the fields of qualitative and critical research. In 1985, Marshall asked researchers to consider whether the quest for trustworthiness (emphasizing credibility, transferability, dependability, and neutrality) "sacrifices something valuable" (p. 356). She argued that, among other reasons, "researchers choose qualitative methodology … for research that cannot be done experimentally for practical or ethical reasons" (p. 356). A similar argument can be made today: researchers choose critical advocacy research for studies that cannot be done experimentally and that require an ethical advocacy stance to address injustice and/or inequity. Hence, similar questions must be asked: what are we sacrificing by continuing to focus on outdated derivative standards? Marshall (1985) wrote that the radical critique requires us to examine how the "education system functions in the interests of more powerful social classes" and hence that it maintains the "myths of meritocracy and democracy" (p. 361) while it continues to marginalize and disadvantage some students and to advantage and privilege others. She argued that we need "research designed to capture the words of the underclass, the hidden structured connections among organizations, the informal policies or the unanticipated outcomes of policies on particular populations" (p. 367). This research, she argued 25 years ago, must "explore its unique goodness—its ability to explore multiple and competing perspectives and ideologies, to identify under-represented voices, to challenge commonly accepted 'truths.'" It must therefore be judged by different standards, those she called "goodness standards"—standards that can be undermined by an excessive emphasis on the typical "trustworthiness criteria."

A year later, Lincoln and Guba (1986) also emphasized the derivative nature of commonly ac-cepted trustworthiness criteria, the criteria that, as Huberman and Miles (1983) argued, test research "in context." To move beyond this paradigm, Lincoln and Guba developed and urged the adoption of "unique criteria of authenticity"—fairness, ontological authentication (raising consciousness), edu-cative authentication (increasing understanding of constructions rooted in different value systems), catalytic authentication (getting theory into action), and finally, tactical authentication (ensuring em-powering action).

Only a few years later, Lather (1992) wrote about how the proliferation and legitimacy of para-digms with such competing goals as prediction, understanding, emancipation, or deconstruction had contributed to a "transdisciplinary disarray regarding standards and canons" (p. 89). She, too, focused on the emergence of critical inquiry as a means of emphasizing meaning making in the human sciences. More recently, Schwandt (2007) argued that although "the very act of generating evidence or identify-ing something as evidence is itself an interpretation" and that "every interpretation is made in some context or background of beliefs, practices, or traditions," it does not mean that every interpretation is the subjective, personal view of the interpreter (p. 11). In fact, he argues, "interpretation is not simply an individual cognitive act but a social and political practice" (p. 12). Moreover, he acknowledges that this view stands in "sharp contrast to what is, more or less, a standard epistemological account of estab-lishing the objectivity and truthfulness of claims that we make about the world" (p. 12).

It is clear that although the "orthodox consensus about what it means to do science has been dis-placed" (Lather, 1992, p. 89)—and, indeed, has been displaced for more than a quarter of a century—normative views related to the need for objectivity and trustworthiness die hard. Nevertheless, there are other, clearly articulated and equally valid standards of interpretation that one can use for critical advocacy research. The necessity, it seems to me, is to ensure that one selects standards appropriate to the intent and design of the research and then makes those standards explicit.

Moral Courage: Taking an Advocacy Approach

Before I continue, I need to clarify my use of the terms advocacy and activist—for I use them here relatively interchangeably. Both imply taking a stance on behalf of a person or a position in which one believes. Both imply moral action and, hence, the need for the researcher to take a courageous stance. Neither implies that the educational researcher must take up a banner and march in a protest rally, demonstrating for the urgency of a particular position (although one may do so on occasion). Despite the fact that *activist* has connotations that may suggest a more public stance, I am persuaded that both activism and advocacy are marks of the public intellectual who takes a reasoned, moral, and public stance based on the information and understanding one has.

Thus, in 2006, when Oakes and Rogers argued that Dewey was on the right track when he decried the "absence of a robust public sphere" and called for "'public intelligence' to confront the cultural norms and politics of privilege that sustain structures of inequity both in and out of school" (p. 16), they were supporting a position of both advocacy and activism. Given our levels of higher education and our positions of public trust with respect to society's children and youth, educational leaders and educational researchers occupy a position of relative power and privilege in today's society. Hence, we are in a strong position to exercise roles as activists and public intellectuals and to advocate for the kind of dialogue that might constitute a more robust public sphere. Said (1994) argued that those who oc-cupy a position as public intellectuals must play a role that "has an edge to it"—a role that

> cannot be played without a sense of being someone whose place it is publically to raise embarrassing questions, to confront orthodoxy and dogma (rather than to produce them), to be someone who can-not easily be co-opted by governments or corporations, and whose raison d'être is to represent all those people and issues that are routinely forgotten or swept under the rug. The intellectual does so on the basis of universal principles: that all human beings are entitled to expect decent standards of behavior concerning freedom and justice from worldly powers or nations, and that deliberate or inadvertent violations of these standards need to be testified and fought against courageously. (p. 9)

Similarly, Bourdieu (1977) stated that "the primary contribution of social scientists to society is to illuminate the mechanisms of domination and to show how these mechanisms reproduce social inequi-ties, thus making the social sciences inherently critical" (p. 29). And yet in the current context of public scrutiny and high levels of public accountability, many educational leaders feel deskilled and silenced, reluctant to take on a role they perceive to be increasingly bureaucratized. Many researchers fear that if they do not conform to the current "gold standard," they will be successful neither in grant applica-tions nor in tenure bids. There seems to be a fear of speaking out, of engaging constituents in broader debate about how to overcome the persistent inequities in school and society, or of advocating action or policy that might polarize rather than unite powerful stakeholders. Instead of confronting orthodoxy and dogmas, as urged by Said, we are more likely to be co-opted by them.

Nevertheless, as Baker (in Oakes & Rogers, 2006) stated: "We are going to have to learn to think in radical terms" if we want to make a difference. To promote "enlightened understanding" (Bode, 2001) and participation of the general public in dialogue and debate about conflicting ideologies; to pres-ent alternative and relevant interpretations, strategies, and solutions, educational researchers will need to take a more active role in informing, empowering, and legitimizing public participation. Critical research provides the basis for such advocacy.

Moreover, critical researchers must be clear that taking a stand as an advocate does not imply biased, distorted, or sloppy research but can (and must) be associated with rigor and relevance. It does imply that those with power and privilege should work on the side of those without. In other words, for the critical researcher, taking an advocacy position is, in many ways, a moral imperative.

Illustrating a Critical Advocacy Approach

Let me give an example from my own research. Some years ago, I conducted a number of studies in schools on a portion of the Navajo reservation in the United States. My quest was to determine why, despite being extraordinarily well equipped and having a rich array of material resources, Navajo stu-dents in these schools continued to be less successful than their non-Navajo peers and to experience even less success if they enrolled in post-secondary programs at local or regional colleges or universities. I surveyed both students and parents and found no statistically significant differences in the family lives (parental education, books in the home, income levels) of students who were successful and those who were not. I interviewed students and parents and found that the Navajo parents were as interested in, and supportive of, their children's education as non-Navajo parents. I interviewed teachers and school administrators and found little difference in their teaching philosophies, in their postgraduate training, or in their linguistic ability. In short, from a relatively objective (modernist, or positivistic perspective), the continued lesser school achievement of Navajo children seemed to be mysterious and unexplain-able. It must, one might have argued, simply be due to different levels of motivation and interest on the part of the children themselves.

However, my research did not stop with these preliminary investigations. I subsequently conduct-ed a series of critical investigations in which I took as my starting point a post-colonial, domination perspective (Ashcroft, Griffiths, & Tiffin, 2002; Gandhi, 1998; Prasad, 2003). In these critical studies, I was careful not to speak *for* the Navajo, but to talk *with* them and to share ways in which I and my colleagues as White educators were not only complicit in the current minoritized and dominated state of American Indian students but to consider ways in which we could begin to address implicit racism and hegemonic power (see, for example, Shields, 1993, 2002; Shields & Lopez, 1993; Shields & Seltzer, 1997). Through this critical lens, I recognized that the Navajo students, although in the numerical majority, were still minoritized in that they were studying a dominantly White, middle-class curriculum, primarily taught by educators steeped in the dominant culture. Moreover, for the most part, their education followed the domination perspective of Cummins (1986) instead of an empowerment perspective, in that the instruction was mostly transmissive, the community played no viable role in the education of its children, the Navajo language and culture were largely ignored in the schools, and evaluation and assessment were for the purpose of legitimation and not advocacy. Using a critical lens that began with Foster's (1986) recognition of the need to challenge taken-for-granted assumptions that perpetuate "sources of social domination and repression" (p. 71), I began a new series of interviews with parents, teachers, and school principals. And, as a result, in an early publication (Shields & Lopez, 1993), I examined the planning effort of a small Navajo school attempting to effect changes to improve student learning. I concluded that planners would have to pay more attention to the creation of a shared vision and asked a number of questions about how to overcome a "dysfunctional culture."

When I asked teachers what would help the students achieve more academic success, the blunt response of one teacher, "better parents!", was reiterated in various ways. Another stated:

> The Navajo students who are doing the very best in school are going to come from those families who have probably not taught them the language, but have insisted that they get a good education and prepare to go to college.

Teachers told me that parents were duplicitous in that they said they supported education but kept their adolescents home to help with transportation or look after younger children—especially if a family member needed to be taken to the doctor. My critical lens immediately required I challenge the assumption undergirding the statement, recognizing that here, two valid, valuable, and competing values were coming into conflict. Parents did value education, but in the remote and isolated expanse of the Navajo reservation, families living in traditional hogans out in the semi-desert valley had no public means of transportation and no nearby neighbors or child-care facilities to expedite the medical appointment. Hence, having older children help with the medical appointment was not a rejection of the value of schooling but a strong validation of the importance of family.

When parents were asked about incorporating Navajo language and culture into the curriculum, numerous hegemonic statements were made. Some made such illogical comments about the Navajo as "We live in a society of English. They chose to come here and so they need to learn to speak English" or "We are an English country," "English is the language of the United States and English is an international language!" or "Indian peoples in this area live in America and should be required to learn English." Others said that culture "should be taught at home, if the parents want it." Others believed that schools should focus on helping students "who struggle with English" to become better able to use the language in which they must function and not "force them to learn a language of limited use."

Subsequent analysis of these and other data showed a very different picture of some possible reasons for the apparent lack of academic success. Educators clearly were operating from deficit perspectives, pathologizing the Navajo students, and seeking as much to "fix" or to "cure" them as to educate them (Shields, Bishop, & Mazawi, 2005). Some parents also believed that the Navajo should have long ago been better assimilated into the White, English-speaking, dominant culture and that if they had chosen to resist, their failure should be attributed to this resistance.

From this critical perspective, it is absolutely inappropriate to simply report the perspectives of stakeholders; instead they must be understood and explicated through a critical lens, using as starting points notions of colonization (Prasad, 2003; Said, 1994), hegemony, or domination. The findings demonstrate that pathologizing—a mode of colonization used to govern, regulate, manage, marginalize, or minoritize students primarily through hegemonic discourses—is operating in these schools. Thus, regardless of how hard working the students, how supportive the parents, how dedicated some teachers, the dominant discourses position the students as inferior. Educators in general do not expect them to succeed and certainly do not hold them to the same high expectations as their non-Navajo peers.

Such discourses serve to disempower; they give the clear message that school is not for the likes of—in this case—the Navajo, who are not represented in the curriculum or in the assignments and activities of the textbooks. Clearly a science project in which students are asked to record and analyze the family's use of electricity by reading the meter is an impossibility for students living in a traditional hogan, far from any source of electricity except the battery of their car or truck. Similarly, being asked to create a piñata to celebrate the Mexican festival of Cinco de Mayo would not only have little meaning, but be almost impossible when there is only one general store within 50 miles and it does not carry papier-mâché. Moreover, asking the students to make models of hogans, shade houses, and to bake fry bread for one week of the year (as I have seen on several occasions) in order to celebrate Native American week seems more than slightly incongruous in a community in which 98% of the students are Navajo, and hence, in which Navajo culture should figure prominently all year round.

Using a less critical research lens is likely to lead to the essentializing of the Navajo students, the exoticizing of their lifestyle, and perhaps to the conclusion that to be successful in school, they must abandon their traditional lifestyle. Nevertheless, during my series of critical ethnographic studies (as reported elsewhere; see for example, Shields, 1999; Shields & Seltzer, 1997), I have found students have been able to boot up the school computers, connect to the Internet to seek information for an assignment, travel in a rented limousine formally dressed in long gowns or tuxedos for the prom one day, and dress in ornate costumes covered with tinkling brass decorations or feathers to energetically perform an intricate jingle dance or hoop dance the next day. They do not need to give up their traditional language, culture, or traditions in order to be successful in school; indeed, as Cummins (1986) argues, education must be additive rather than subtractive, for it is immoral and unconscionable to ask students to renounce what is important at home to succeed at school.

Let me be clear: for critical advocacy-oriented research, the analysis is only the beginning. Given that very few (some would argue 10–20) people read any given peer-reviewed scholarly article, publishing an analysis that argues for the elimination of deficit thinking and the adoption of a more empowering and additive curriculum is unlikely to have any positive effect or to bring about any significant change. Moreover, even having a brief follow-up discussion with the school principal or making a formal presentation to the school board (as I did) will effect little if any change.

What I now firmly believe, advocate, and argue as an essential component of critical advocacy-oriented research is for the researcher to engage the stakeholders on an ongoing basis with the findings and implications of a critical research study, to emphasize the authenticity criteria described earlier, to ensure that people's understandings are indeed changed, and that such new comprehension leads to action that is tactical and strategic (in this case, towards a more empowering approach to educating the Navajo). Ten years after my critical studies of Navajo schooling, I wonder what might have occurred had I specifically advocated for educational discourses that depathologized the students, not just holding one meeting in which I stated that the change was necessary but modeling it, demonstrating instances of deficit thinking, and providing alternatives. What if I had then (as I try to now) taken Lincoln and Guba's (1986) authenticity criteria more seriously? Could I have facilitated new discourses focused not on deficits but on agency, community, social justice, deep democracy, and academic excellence? I wonder how I might have worked with the board and the school administrators to help them reposition members from both the dominant and the minoritized groups—providing an impetus for the full inclusion of all community members, and perhaps offering training for elders who (because of their own experiences with residential schools) were unfamiliar with ways in which parents could be productively involved in their children's schooling (and by this I do not mean finding ways to encourage more parents to come into the school on hegemonic White, middle-class terms).

I did try to exemplify *fairness*, trying to provide evidence of differing educator and stakeholder perspectives. It could also be said that *ontological authenticity*—"improvement in the individual's (and group's) conscious experiencing of the world" (Lincoln & Guba, 1986, p. 22)—was achieved—at least for members of the school board who considered my findings. Nevertheless, how could I have helped parents and teachers with differing perspectives to hear and understand each other; what dialogic fora could I have initiated and facilitated? Doing so might also have helped me fulfill the *educative authenticity* criteria, helping participants not only to hear each other's perspectives but to increase their understanding of the "whys of various expressed constructions" (p. 23), at the same time enhancing their understanding of "the groups they represent" (p. 23). Hence, school board members might have better understood, and then decided to address, some of the underlying racism and deficit assumptions of the teachers they had hired. *Catalytic authenticity* is sometimes known as "feedback-action validity" (p. 23). Hence helping participants to not only hear and understand the data but to decide on and implement action strategies to redress wrongs is the next step. Finally, *tactical authenticity* would ensure that the selected action was an appropriate response to the findings. Helping school board members and the superintendent to respond in educative ways to the parents who believed that the Navajo had chosen to go to America, and hence should learn English, might be a positive tactical example. Ignoring the inappropriateness and incorrectness of parental perceptions and instead canceling all Navajo instruction would not be an appropriate tactical response.

I recall, almost 20 years ago now, asking my university department advisor how much time I should spend in the field doing research. His unequivocal answer was "As little as possible, because your job is to get tenure." My answer today would be quite different; to an inquiring young researcher who might ask that question, I would respond, "As long as it takes to make a difference." In other words, conducting critical, advocacy-oriented research requires a commitment of the researcher to support and advocate for those whose voices are not always clearly heard. It implies a commitment to work to influence policies and practices that perpetuate marginalization and exclusion rather than integration and membership in school communities. It is a commitment never addressed when I was a graduate student and one that was (and still is) often rejected out of hand by other researchers and scholars whose path to tenure and respectability is more traditional.

Yet, despite my strong conviction that educational research that is worth doing has an activist edge, it is appropriate to issue a caution. Because it is more difficult to fund research that does not meet the current "gold standard," and because taking an advocacy stance often brings the researcher into conflict with people who hold the power—legislators, school district administrators, university tenure committees—it is not without risks. Thus, it is incumbent on each researcher selecting the critical, advocacy path to reflect on the advice I received two decades ago, to calculate the risks, and to make an informed decision.

Summary

A critical, advocacy-oriented approach to research requires both a clearly articulated epistemological stance up front and a courageous and-long term engagement and follow-through. Critical research, as with all other kinds of research, *is* in some way promotional (Schwandt, 2007). It promotes a particular question, gives prominence to certain values, ideologies, and methodologies—but that recognition does not inherently distort or negate it. Indeed, the challenge is to conduct research with as much independence, credibility, rigor, and discipline as possible, but then, once one has drawn some conclusions, to take on the role of activist and ensure that the findings are not only understood but, where appropriate, acted upon.

This is quite different from taking an activist or advocacy position up front and selecting respondents, cases, or variables *in order to prove a point*. Hence, I am not advocating what Bob Stake (2008) has described as "sneaky undeclared advocacy of programs or practices" but a reasoned advocacy based on solid findings and interpretations. Thus the foundation for any advocacy is not the desire of a sponsor or the impassioned beliefs of a researcher but research that has been both designed and conducted with as much detail, care, and accuracy as possible.

Identifying the theoretical framework at the outset assists the reader to develop both an understanding of the research but also of its parameters But this is not "sneaky undeclared advocacy"—indeed it is not advocacy at all. If, for example, in a given study, a researcher discovers that, in a particular school, refugee students are impeded from engagement in learning because the teacher repeatedly makes derogatory comments about their lack of previous schooling experiences and communicates an expectation they will fail, action is called for—action I call activism, not based on a predetermined position but on the outcome of the research study itself and my moral imperative as a public intellectual. To do otherwise would be unethical and immoral. If a critical investigation results in contradictory or inconclusive findings, it may not be possible or ethical to advocate action; instead, ensuring that all perspectives are clearly explicated and examined is warranted. But if we have conducted careful and accurate investigation that permits us to identify potential problems that must be addressed, challenges to overcome, behaviors that impede the success of some children, or inappropriate outcomes of certain policies, then it is incumbent on us to act.

Indeed, it seems to me that taking a stand, engaging with the school district and its educational leaders about the detrimental impact of deficit thinking and hegemonic programming on Navajo students is the most credible way to conduct authentic inquiry and ethical research. This is particularly true when one is conducting studies focused on people who have been typically underrepresented, silenced, or marginalized by the mainstream culture, but who are striving for agency, authentic voice, and empowerment.

Eisenhart (2006), in a discussion of the gold standard of quasi-experimental design, commented that "experimental research on causal effects isolates variables … and investigates their relationship to other variables …" She went on to say:

> This procedure will work if the variables being measured do not change over time, are not variably influenced by circumstances and are not affected by human intention or desire … The problem is that in education and other social practices all else is not equal, and little if anything remains constant. (pp. 699–700)

As I have attempted to illustrate here, one cannot control for attitudes, assumptions, hegemonic use of power, or deficit assumptions. One cannot easily control for competing and conflicting cultural variables such as those I described earlier.

The important issues for educational researchers revolve around ways to create educational opportunities and learning environments that offer equitable access and outcomes to all students. We must name power and privilege where we find it and challenge its inappropriate uses when we identify them. These deep-seated, politicized ideologies are clearly affected by, and affect, human intention and desire. They must be identified, surfaced, and challenged if more researchers, educators, and members of the general public are to work, with Maxine Greene, to ensure that ours becomes a society of fulfilled promises.

Educators and educational researchers must turn the mantra that "all are created equal" into practice so that all members of our global society can experience equitable access, opportunities, and outcomes.

We are not simply literary critics, scholars of the classics looking for a new angle for a dissertation, or historians looking for a new story. I am persuaded that for *educational* researchers to be responsible is to use our power, privilege, and position in the field to promote justice and enlightenment and not just advance my career or add to the archives. We must be able, when all is said and done, to ask of ourselves, "Has our research done anything to level the playing field, to overcome disparity, to promote a more mutually beneficial democratic society?" It is my hope that we will find the necessary courage to be able to answer in the affirmative.

Note

1. They included Anderson's (2001) critical analysis of the ISLLC standards, Perryman's (2009) analysis of an OfSTED inspection in England, and Tooms's (2007) examination of the challenges facing closeted LGBTQ administrators.

References

Anderson, G. L. (2001). Disciplining leaders: A critical discourse analysis of the ISLLC national examination and performance standards in educational administration. *International Journal of Leadership in Education, 4*(3), 199–216.

Ashcroft, B., Griffiths, G., & Tiffin, H. (Eds.). (2002). *The empire writes back: Theory and practice in post-colonial literatures* (2nd ed.). London, England: Routledge.

Bode, B. H. (2001). Reorientation in education. In S. J. Goodlad (Ed.), *The last best hope: A democracy reader* (pp. 92–100). San Francisco, CA: Jossey-Bass.

Bourdieu, P. (with Passeron, J. C.). (1977). *Reproduction in education, society and culture*. London, England: Sage.

Cummins, J. (1986). Empowering minority students: A framework for intervention. In N. M. Hidalgo, C. L. McDowell, & E. V. Siddle (Eds.), *Facing racism in education* (Reprint Series No. 21). Cambridge, MA: Harvard Educational Review. (First published in *Harvard Educational Review, 56*(1), 1986, 18–36)

Eisenhart, M. (2006). Qualitative science in experimental time. *International Journal of Qualitative Studies in Education, 19*(6), 697–707.

Evers, C. W., & Wu, E. H. (2006). On generalising from single case studies: Epistemological reflections. *Journal of Philosophy of Education, 40*(4), 511–526.

Foster, W. (1986). *Paradigms and promises: New approaches to educational administration.* Buffalo, NY: Prometheus.

Foucault, M. (1980). *Power/knowledge: Selected interviews and other writings 1972–77.* New York, NY: Pantheon Books.

Foucault, M. (1984). The order of discourse. In M. Shapiro (Ed.). *Language and politics.* Oxford, England: Blackwell.

Gandhi, L. (1998). *Postcolonial theory: A critical introduction.* New York, NY: Columbia University Press.

Greene, M. (1998). Introduction: Teaching for social justice. In W. Ayers, J. A. Hunt, & T. Quinn (Eds.), *Teaching for social justice* (pp. xxvii–xlvi). New York, NY: Teachers College Press.

Hargreaves, D. (2003). *Education epidemic: Transforming secondary schools through innovation networks.* London, England: Demos.

Huberman, A. M., & Miles, M. (1983). Drawing valid meaning from qualitative data: Some techniques of data reduction and display. *Quality and Quantity, 17,* 281–339.

Lather, P. (1986). Research as praxis. *Harvard Educational Review, 56*(3), 257–277.

Lather, P. (1992). Critical frames in educational research: Feminist and post-structural perspectives. *Theory into Practice, 31*(2), 87–99.

Lather, P. (2004). Scientific research in education: A critical perspective. *British Educational Research Journal, 30*(6), 759–772.

Lincoln, Y. S., & Guba, E. G. (1986). But is it rigorous? Trustworthiness and authenticity in naturalistic evaluation. In D. D. Williams (Ed.), *Naturalistic evaluation.* San Francisco, CA: Jossey-Bass.

Littell, J. H. (2008). Evidence-based or biased? The quality of published reviews of evidence-based practices. *Children and Youth Services Review, 30,* 1299–1317.

Manzo, K. K. (2004). Leading commercial series don't satisfy "Gold Standard." *Education Week, 24*(3), 16–17.

Marshall, C. (1985). Appropriate criteria of trustworthiness and goodness for qualitative research on educational organizations. *Quality and Quantity, 19,* 353–373.

Oakes, J., & Rogers, J. (2006). *Learning power: Organizing for education and justice.* New York, NY: Teachers College Press.

Ogbu, J. U. (1992). Understanding cultural diversity and learning. *Educational Researcher, 21*(8), 5–14; 24.

Perryman, J. (2009). Inspection and the fabrication of professional and performative processes. *Journal of Education Policy, 245*(5), 611–631.

Prasad, A. (2003). *Postcolonial theory and organizational analysis: A critical engagement.* New York, NY: Palgrave Macmillan.

Said, E. W. (1994). Representations of the intellectual. In E. W. Said (Ed.), *Representations of the intellectual: The 1993 Reith lectures* (pp. 3–17). London, England: Random House.

Schwandt, T. A. (2007). Judging interpretations. In S. Mathison (Ed.), Enduring issues in evaluation [Special issue]. *New Directions for Evaluation, 114,* 11–25.

Shields, C. M. (1993). A planning paradox: One school's effort to restructure to meet the needs of a Native American student body. *Educational Planning, 6*(3), 48–61.

Shields, C. M. (1999). Learning from students about representation, identity, and community. *Educational Administration Quarterly, 35*(1), 106–129.

Shields, C. M. (2002). *Understanding the challenges, exploring the opportunities, and developing new understandings: Examining the effects of the past four years* (Unpublished report completed for San Juan School District).

Shields, C. M., Bishop, R., & Mazawi, A. E. (2005). *Pathologizing practices: The impact of deficit thinking on education.* New York, NY: Peter Lang.

Shields, C. M., & Lopez, C. G. (1993). What I want for my children is what I want for all children: Planning to serve the needs of minority students. *Planning and Changing, 24*(1/2), 69–85.

Shields, C. M., & Seltzer, P. (1997). Complexities and paradoxes of community: Toward a more useful conceptualization of community. *Educational Administration Quarterly, 33*(4), 413–439.

Stake, R. (2008, March). The price of playing a superhero: Why researchers should eschew advocacy and concentrate on inquiry. In *Inquiry and advocacy: Reconsidering the distinction for a postmodern era still committed to scientific research.* Symposium conducted at the annual meeting of the American Educational Research Association, Chicago, IL.

Tooms, A. (2007, April). *"Is that a wedding ring?" A look at the panopticons of identity politics lived by gay school administrators serving homophobic communities.* Paper presented at the annual meeting of the American Educational Research Association, Chicago, IL.

CHAPTER 6

Limits to Knowledge and Being Human
What Is "Critical" in Critical Social Research and Theory?

Phil Francis Carspecken

Introduction

This chapter discusses limits to knowledge and their relevance to critical action research. Limits to knowledge are not just constraints on what we can know: they are also core structures of what we are. They are in the place where ontology and epistemology are one—where knowing is united with being rather than a representation separated from what it represents. The ontological significance of limits to knowledge cannot be understood from within an empiricist framework, nor can they be understood from the perspective of many currently popular anti-empiricist understandings of knowledge. This is because it is difficult to escape what Hegel called "picture-thinking." Many, probably most, versions of post-empiricism, post-structuralism, social constructivism, classical pragmatism, and other theories of knowledge opposing empiricism reproduce a fundamental version of subject-object thinking that also supports empiricism. This is a version of the subject-object relation in which the "subject" side is hidden. It is easy to hide since it is fundamentally not an object, not objective, not picturable, and impossible to model. Yet it is at the heart of being human, being persons. The subject, which is not the same as subjectivity, is ontologically prior to the differentiation of knowing and being.

In what follows I seek to clarify these opening claims of this chapter through an examination of limits to knowledge that moves us from thinking within a subject-object framework toward that framework's conditions of possibility: the subject-subject relation. An examination of the sense "critical" has had in the ongoing project of critical theory will be my main method. In critical theory "critique" has everything to do with the existential significance of limits to knowledge. It doesn't simply mean that a researcher or theorist finds serious moral and ethical problems with existing social-political-cultural orders and wants his or her work to directly challenge them.

Although there are many ways to do critical action research, the general idea includes putting together things that are usually held apart. Critical action researchers work with communities of people to make changes in social systems and cultures. Research practices are integrated with activism. Research results are not entirely in the form of providing means to achieve ends but are themselves ends in the form of raised collective consciousness, the expansion of identities, the enrichment of culture and social relationships. These are not easy tasks because within contemporary social systems researchers and those they research are two different groups having different and sometimes conflicting needs and interests. Moreover, the knowledge produced by social researchers studying other people will for the most part be used by still other groups of people: policymakers, marketing experts, public relation firms, and many others working within government and corporate institutions. And that is the case, of course, only when such knowledge is put to any socially relevant use at all. Many social research projects result in academic publications where they receive some attention from academics but otherwise remain unknown.

Critical action research is pitted against these separations among knowledge, those who produce knowledge, those about whom the knowledge is produced, those who use knowledge, and those affected by the use. It is a practice with an at least implicit theory of knowing that transcends mainstream understandings of knowledge and research. The word "mainstream" is used here to refer to an understanding that is most widespread in terms of numbers of people within a diversity of occupations, but in addition it refers to ideology: beliefs, in this case about knowledge, that are deeply ensnared with social institutions and function to maintain those institutions as well as support, not counter, certain directions in which they are changing. This mainstream understanding of knowledge-in-general has the form of representation at its heart. Knowledge is like a picture of what is, taken from a position any possible sapient being can in principle occupy. Paradigmatically for the sciences, knowledge is a *model*. Knowledge and being are, then, ontologically distinct. Taking a picture cannot catch the act of taking the picture. What, then, is the understanding of knowledge implicit to the practice of critical action research?

This chapter is a work in philosophy and social theory. It does not share the experiences and results of a critical action field project nor does it attempt to specify practical guidelines for engaging in critical action field projects. But critical action research is all about the unification of practice and theory and that applies in both directions: activities in the field are a way of producing theory, and writing explorations like this one is practice. It's a contribution to conversational practices taking place within communities of action and critical researchers.

Critique

Of course, words have meanings through their uses within discourses. And discourses mutate and proliferate. It is silly to look for original meanings or uses of words if the idea is to find out what the "right" meaning is. I make this point to clarify what I am not doing in this chapter. I'm not arguing for a correct meaning of "critical"; I am rather trying to retrieve, refresh, and push forth. Many people doing social research and theorizing in our qualitative research communities who call their practices "critical" mainly mean that their work is meant to significantly change social-political-cultural orders. There is an understanding that knowledge has intimate relations to power and social organization and that this cannot be understood within the confines of empiricist epistemologies. Well, the history of uses of "critical" in social theory certainly accords with those meanings but also, and because, there is profound grasp of limits to knowledge in that history. The basic epistemological framework enabling empiricist research has limits that are transcended in critical theory. Today most qualitative social researchers object to empiricist epistemology, and yet popular challenges to empiricism actually fail to escape the same basic framework within which empiricism resides.

The expression "critical theory" was first used in 1937 by founders of what we now call the Frankfurt School to hide what they were doing from the Nazis. They were producing theory incompatible with fascism, drawing upon authors banned by National Socialists, such as Marx and Freud. "Critical" was chosen for this purpose with deliberate reference to Kant's famous use of the word "critique" in his development of critical philosophy. And "critical" in Frankfurt School usage alludes as well to the work of philosophers after Kant, especially Hegel and Marx, who understood the significance of Kant's discoveries.

Kant published three critiques—*The Critique of Pure Reason*, *The Critique of Practical Reason*, and *The Critique of Judgment*[1]—plus a number of related books during the last two decades of the eighteenth century. Kant's critique of "pure reason" supplies a core sense to critique as this term has been understood by critical theorists. This is a work about limits to knowledge when knowledge is thought of as empiricists and physical scientists do: that is, knowledge that has its ground in sense experience. In what follows I will sometimes use *CPR* for *Critique of Pure Reason*.

Kant famously wrote that reading the works of the radical empiricist David Hume woke him from "dogmatic slumbers." Applying empiricist principles as rigorously as he could, Hume became a philosophical skeptic. There are many basic things people believe in that cannot be grounded empirically and thus, for a true empiricist, cannot be known to be true or false. We cannot be sure of concepts like "self," "causation," "induction," and "laws of nature" because we cannot ground their meaning on sense experiences or on strict logical inference. Thus, argued Hume, we should be philosophically skeptical of them.

Using Kantian terminology we can say that Hume regarded concepts like "cause" and "self" to be concepts of transcendent realities, features of transcendent metaphysics that, he believed, science and modern philosophical thinking have grown beyond. Concepts of transcendent realities refer to beings, objects, forces, and/or processes that we cannot access through our senses. They can resemble the postulated entities used in scientific models today, such as neutron, electromagnetic field, gravitational force, and so forth. But unlike the supersensible postulates of modern science, the transcendent realities claimed in metaphysical systems are not defined operationally; that is, they are not tied in their meanings to observations and measurements and thus are not falsifiable.

Transcendent metaphysical systems have been and still are used in many cultures and modern subcultures to provide ways of making sense of events and life experiences.[2] One of the central aims of empiricism from the start has been to remove beliefs in transcendent realities. In the strictest forms of empiricism, like logical positivism, even the operationalized but still transcendent postulates of contemporary physical science are regarded as "useful fictions" only. They are useful because they are operationally defined and because they are components of models that are successful in making predictions.

The Difference between Transcendent and Transcendental

The stimulation Kant received from Hume's radical and convincing version of empiricism resulted in Kant's critical philosophy, beginning with *CPR*. Kant noted that some of the concepts we use in our interpretations of the world can indeed never be grounded in sense experiences, just as Hume claimed. But that only results in skepticism if we think these concepts to be of objective entities, forces, substances, and the like—that is, as being about transcendent, supersensible realities. For example, we can never have "cause" as an object of our experience, just as Hume said. We see patterns of contiguous events, or one event regularly followed by another, but we don't see or in any way experience a "cause" connecting one of the events to the other. Kant agreed with Hume's reasoning, adding "space" and "time" to the list of such non-empirically grounded concepts as well. He also developed a theory of 12 "categories of the understanding," each category pertaining to things and relations between things that cannot ever be objects of sense experience. Space, time, and the 12 categories of the understanding—one of which is cause—are not empirically grounded in the sense of being objects of experience. For Hume, these concepts and categories should be set aside because their use cannot be legitimized through empiricist principles.

However, Kant noticed the concepts of space and time as well as his 12 categories of the understanding appear to *accompany* experiences rather than to refer to existing objects. Whatever the object of an experience may be, it will be accompanied by some of these categories that cannot themselves be directly experienced. Experience cannot seem to do without them. They are not concepts of transcend*ent* realities; rather they are transcend*ental*[3] conditions necessary for the possibility of experience. As transcendental categories they make experience possible while not being sensually experienceable themselves.

The key idea we wish to take away from this is that of "transcendental conditions of possibility" in general. Regarding both physical and social research, are there conditions having a transcendental or transcendental-like status? If so, then we have limits to knowledge. They would be conditions necessary to produce knowledge through conducting research that cannot themselves be known or studied within the framework they make possible. To be clear on the basic idea, take Kant's claims about space and time as a paradigmatic example. Space and time are transcendental in Kant's philosophy because it is not possible to conceive of any experience that does not involve temporal distinctions (for example, an experience of an emotion as well as of a rock are framed in relation to a before and an after); and in the case of experiences involving "external sense"[4] (of a rock but not of an emotion, for example), it is not possible to conceive of any experience that does not involve both spatial and temporal distinctions. Hence, space and time cannot themselves be studied empirically because everything that is empirical is already framed by either time alone or both space and time together.[5]

Here is what we want to generalize from. According to Kant there is no empirical investigation that can be done to prove or disprove the existence of any transcendental conditions necessary for all possible empirical phenomena. And this is because everything and anything empirical is, so to speak, already shaped by these conditions. These conditions cannot be doubted within the framework of knowledge they make possible.

In addition to transcendental categories and concepts, Kant's theory develops an insight he called "the transcendental unity of apperception," which is related to what he called "the transcendental 'I'" and "transcendental self-consciousness." This insight has specific importance to critical theory and will receive extended discussion later. But I am not concerned with whether or not Kant's claims of transcendental status for space, time, and the 12 categories are correct. Aside from the transcendental "I," I will concentrate on the generalized idea of transcendental conditions of possibility.

Are there transcendental or transcendental-like conditions of possibility associated with empirical forms of knowing that cannot themselves be known empirically? If so, then we will have found limits to knowledge associated with empirical inquiry. Such conditions would enable empirical inquiry and simultaneously limit it.

The next section will list transcendental-like conditions necessary for the empirical sciences of objects and objective events, processes, energies, and substances as well as just sense experiences if one wishes to be a strict positivist. Before beginning that section I will end this one by specifying three topics rooted in Kant's philosophy that are important for critical theory.

1. *The general idea of transcendental conditions of possibility.* Kant's theory of transcendental conditions of possibility has had an impact on a number of philosophical and social-theoretical schools that emerged after his time. The idea of transcendental-like conditions of possibility for knowledge is important in critical theory and theories of culture and ideology more generally. The next section will illustrate two uses of this idea for a critical theory of knowledge and society.

2. *Reflection.* Kant reasoned about reasoning to generate his critiques. The process of knowing was applied to the process of knowing. This sort of thing is called "reflection." Reflection is enormously important in critical theory and intimately related to limits of knowledge. Thus, there is a section ahead on the topic of reflection.

3. *Transcendental unity of apperception.* Kant's philosophical explorations of what he called the "transcendental unity of apperception" are profound. In a later section the basic idea will be

reviewed as well as the associated concepts of the transcendental "I" and transcendental self-consciousness. This insight, I believe, is one of the most important insights under development, in diverse ways, by critical theorists and one of the least understood insights outside critical theory and philosophy.

1. The General Idea of Transcendental Conditions of Possibility

Conditions of possibility for observational-empirical inquiry

To return to a question posed above: Are there something like transcendental conditions of possibility for the empirical sciences? Before proceeding I need to make a few distinctions. If you look up a definition of "empirical," you will find something like this: "originating in or based on observation or experience."[6] The word "experience" is usually used to mean *sense* experience. But everyday experiences are holistic experiences of meaning *from within which* a deliberate effort can be made to isolate sensual and perceptual components. *Meaning* is what is basic to experience and meaning cannot be observed. Physical scientists depend upon a limited form of experience, observational experience only, and observations require training to be done properly because they are not really a natural way of experiencing the world. That means that the competency for holistic, communicatively pre-structured (in the case of humans) experiences of meaning is a precondition for observational experience in the strict sense. When we "observe" people interacting with each other in qualitative social research we actually experience meanings, and we usually do this through barely conscious virtual participation. If we observe other people interacting from a different mode, from within a project of describing what is going on in the terms of a community that is other than the one being studied, then virtual participation takes place between ourselves and anonymous and generalized members of this other community. Of course, that is something a qualitative social researcher usually wishes to avoid because it can fail to result in actually understanding those we observe.

So by "empirical inquiry" I shall mean any inquiry focused on experience-in-general, of ongoing natural or social processes. Empirical inquiry then divides into two types: (1) holistic/non-restricted experiences of nature and other people, and (2) experience deliberately restricted to sense-based perceptions. Qualitative social researchers do empirical research of the first type and they primarily seek understandings of other people and of themselves through their relationships with other people. This kind of inquiry I will call "hermeneutic"; it is a subcategory of the first general type. Physical scientists and social-psychological researchers who use highly quantified methods are of the second general type. I will call the kind of inquiry they practice "observational-empirical."

Now back to conditions of possibility associated with formal inquiry. The best work I am familiar with on the topic of conditions of possibility for the various sciences was written by Jürgen Habermas early in his career: *Knowledge and Human Interests* (*KHI*) (1968), a work in critical theory. Habermas discusses what he calls the "empirical-analytic sciences," (equivalent to what I am calling "observational-empirical" inquiry) brings out their conditions of possibility, shows how these sciences themselves cannot be used in an investigation of what makes those sciences possible, and shows that those very conditions can be and are topics of study in the "historical-hermeneutic sciences" (what I am calling "hermeneutic inquiry"). This is an analysis resembling Kant's in that conditions of possibility are revealed for a form of inquiry that cannot itself be used for knowledge of those conditions. Hence, they are like transcendental conditions (Habermas calls them "quasi-transcendental"). But a number of aspects of this analysis differ from Kant. The conditions of possibility for observational-empirical inquiry are accessible to us through the structures of a more general form of knowledge: the hermeneutic form of knowing. These are social-communicative conditions upon which observational-empirical inquiry depends. This exceeds Kant's framework.

Below I list conditions that enable observational-empirical inquiry and characteristics of this form of inquiry. All items on this list (and a few more) can be extracted from the rich and detailed explorations provided in *Knowledge and Human Interests*, but I word them in my own way and I have different emphases and interpretations (especially when it comes to ontology, something explicitly avoided, with reasons provided, in *KHI*). So readers should understand that the items on this list come from my reading of Habermas and my own uses and interpretations of his analysis but that what I write ought not to be taken as representing Habermas. To find out what Habermas's analysis and conclusions are, you must read *Knowledge and Human Interests*.

1. Truncated experience: Human experience is limited to that of observing through the senses, with seeing as the paradigm sense.

2. Interest in disinterest: Knowledge is acquired from a disinterested position (more precisely, it is an interested-disinterested position; the interest in disinterest shapes it). Disinterest is assured through instrumentalizing and rigorously controlling observation procedures so that any possible person (sapient being) could in principle perform them identically.

3. Formal language: It is necessary to produce a strict factual language with operational definitions at its heart. Explicit rules give strict unambiguous and singular relations between symbols and measurements. The theory language is then another formalized language, distinct from the factual language, allowing for the specification of external relations, causal or correlational, between measurements. The distinction between a factual language and a theory language enables hypothesis testing (the same facts, measurements, can be hypothesized in different relations).

4. Validity as prediction: Valid knowledge is knowledge that provides successful predictions. The instrumental manipulation of initial conditions and interventions is paradigmatic: hypotheses take the form of conditionals, "*If* measurements are x in conditions y; *then* measurements z will subsequently result."

5. Reality is transcendent: Physical reality is conceptualized in an abstract manner, composed of basic elements and forces we never experience. Models explain what we do experience as phenomena caused by a reality that can never be directly accessed. Relations between phenomena alone are not sufficient for successful explanatory models, so metaphors based on phenomena are employed in the positing of supersensible entities and forces.

6. Knowledge is separated from being: Knowledge of reality cannot itself have a form of being unless it is described as a physical state (in the brain) related to another physical state (whatever is known) that, if attempted, will result in contradictions.[1] The separation of knowledge and being is isomorphic with the impossibility of a physical model, in quantum physics, to include the observer.[2]

7. The subject is effaced: Knowledge is disclosed through observations and measurements to an "I" that cannot itself be observed or measured. The position of universal observer/universal instrumental actor (who can conduct a measurement) is attained by bracketing away all that individuates one subject from another. This transcendental "I" is a cognitive "I" (privileging third-person position) rather than a moral "I" (privileging, in ways I don't have space to explain, the second-person position and first-person plural) or an expressive "I" (privileging the first-person singular position).

1. Can knowledge of physical states be itself a physical state, like a brain state? This is a contentious issue. My claim that a contradiction results if we think of knowledge as a physical state is supported by my discussion of the subject-object frame later in this essay and what happens when the frame itself is conceptualized as a meta-object within a new level of subject-object relation. The recently advocated philosophical orientation called "transcendental materialism" grapples explicitly with this issue of knowledge and ontology and may be of interest to some who read this essay (Johnston, 2014a). Meanwhile, many, perhaps most, contemporary analytic philosophers endorse physicalism, making it distinct from materialism, and recognize that we cannot reduce our "mentalistic" vocabulary to our physical one though the former, they argue, can be explained in terms of such things as secondary functionalist properties supervening over primary, physical properties (several books by Jaegwon Kim provide good summaries and discussions; for example Kim, 1993, 2000).
2. The choice of a measurement and its subsequent implementation in quantum experiments cannot be included in the physical model that gives the rationale for the measurement, even if choices are believed to be determined by the same laws that govern physical nature. In addition, the von Neumann chain argument tells us that any effort to trace a chain of caused events (stimulation of sense organ, transmissions along nerves to the brain, stimulation of parts of the brain) end with something nonphysical and thus not included in the model (for a good presentation of this argument see Rosenblum & Kuttner 2011, p. 238). Many other arguments can be made from what is involved in quantum physics research to demonstrate this same point.

Table 6.1. Observational-Empirical Inquiry: Conditions of Possibility and Characteristics

"Scientism" is the ideological belief that all knowledge in the end must be testable and acquirable within the framework of these conditions and characteristics (there could be more conditions; I don't claim to have caught them all). Those of us in the social sciences have had ample exposure to scientism. The above list of conditions should be familiar to all of us because they are applied in quantitative social science and psychology. Somewhere in our personal histories most of us have been taught ways of understanding validity, reliability, objectivity, measurement, observation, instrumentation (as when surveys, attitude scales and such are called "instruments") and so on. We are taught these things in conformity with the conditions and characteristics listed above. If you practice and teach qualitative research methods please don't say that "the researcher is the instrument." That is a very misleading expression. And a similar irritant is the expression "colored lenses," used often as a metaphor to try to capture the fact that people from different backgrounds, genders, races, and so on, living within different regions of social systems, interpret and experience social events differently. This and similar ocular-centric metaphors reproduce the fundamentals of scientism by suggesting the primacy of observation and the third-person position generally for all forms of knowledge.

The enabling conditions I've listed for observational-empirical inquiry are *deliberate constructions* that people have to learn and receive training in. This is why calling them "enabling," as well as necessary and transcendental-like is especially appropriate. Deliberately constructing these conditions enables the form of knowledge that so far has been very successful in producing useful models of our physical world. This kind of inquiry is also helpful for a number of domains in the social sciences: economics, demography, opinion polling, and so on. But this is a restricted form of inquiry dependent upon a more general framework for knowing. The ideology of scientism is responsible for the belief that *only* this way of knowing counts. This ideology runs deep in most of the disciplines involved in research of one kind or another. Yet simply talking and writing about the enabling or limiting conditions of observational-empirical inquiry demonstrates a form of knowing that is not confined by them. They are dependent upon the enabling/limiting conditions of subject-subject knowing, a topic that follows directly from the arguments in this chapter and one that I have written about elsewhere (Carspecken 2009).

The truncation of experience to that of third-person position observation can only be accomplished from within fully lived holistic experience. Maintaining a third-person observer position requires an understanding of its differentiation from the first-, second-, and third-person performative positions—that is, it requires intersubjectivity and communicative competence.

- The formalization of language into explicit rules for taking measurements and acting in replicable instrumental ways has everyday informal linguistic competence as a prerequisite. Everyday languages involve large domains of implicit understandings. There is no way to formalize everyday languages; they must have the ever-receding riverbed of implicit knowing. Efforts to seek an explicated semantic ground for all meanings in a language fail because the rules needed to fix meanings to procedures have to be communicable already.
- Observational-empirical inquiry models reality in relation to a featureless "I" position—something like the transcendental "I" considered below. It is the "I" that has no qualities to individuate it. Anything that differentiates me from you must be stripped away to attain observation-based objectivity. But, again, this requires deliberate effort and training. It is not possible without full human identity already in place. A bit later we shall see that full human identity is complex, requiring distinctions between "I," "me," "we," "thou," and self-narrative.

In summary, the general idea of transcendental conditions of possibility helps us to understand the limits to knowledge that the very enabling conditions of observation-empirical inquiry entail. Simply becoming aware of these conditions transcends them, and puts us back to where human beings have always been and from where and within the specialized conditions of inquiry for observational-empirical science were historically developed. Coming back in this way is a form of reflection. It is a reflection that reveals what was always the case but perhaps originally difficult to notice and thematize. The development of the scientific method during the sixteenth and seventeenth centuries in Europe gave us something to reflect *from*. And what results from this reflection is the thematization of what has been with us, as part of our being, all along: knowing within the subject-subject relation.

The transcendental-like conditions that both enable and limit observational-empirical inquiry are within the scope of hermeneutic-inquiry, the domain within which qualitative social research takes place. Now we can ask whether there is a new set of limits to knowledge, those of hermeneutic-inquiry, that enable this form of inquiry but escape hermeneutic understanding. Are there such conditions? The answer is yes but I am not yet at the place for writing about them.

Culture as conditions of possibility

Consider the concept of culture used by sociologists, anthropologists, ourselves. Now, within what circumstances would the culture of a people enable its members to come up with the concept of culture? We would expect the concept of culture to have risen only recently within the tens of thousands of years humans have lived on this planet. It is the product of reflection upon transcendental-like structures[7] people use for acting, interacting, experiencing, and thinking within a form of life. These structures (that is, concept structures, identity-enabling structures, normative structures) are drawn upon, instantiated, and reproduced in and through human activities that could not take place without them. Cultural structures are transcendental-like conditions of possibility. But unlike Kant's transcendental conditions of possibility, portions of culture can be changed, one important way being through thematization (making them explicit) and enabling critique. In addition, culture supplies the conditions required for reflection upon itself. It enables forms of knowing, including knowing as reflection.

Many philosophers, social theorists, and anthropologists have developed theories about culture that capture some of its transcendental-like features. Hegel and Marx were early contributors to this idea and the work of both is important to the sense "critical" has in critical theory. But in different ways structuralism, post-structuralism, and the many versions we have of cultural relativism also recognize the transcendental-like role played by culture. The key difference between understandings of culture coming from, on the one hand, Hegel, Marx, and the ongoing project of critical theory, and on the other hand, structuralism, post-structuralism, and some of the ways text is used to conceptualize society and culture, is that the former recognize the capability of persons and groups to reflect from within their cultures and societies to generate change through critique; whereas the latter, to put it mildly, have trouble with this. Reflection from within cannot be understood without understanding the concept of "subject" as something transcending cultural and social conditions rather than as something determined by those conditions. To understand the issue let's take a closer look at culture and reflection.

2. "Reflection" as a Form of Knowing and Being

I put quotation marks around "reflection" because it is easy to misunderstand the process it refers to. "Reflection" is a metaphor suggesting a process of looking into a mirror in order to see what had been previously invisible. That way of understanding reflection isn't quite right because the intersubjective constitution of self-understanding has more to do with shapes of body feeling than visual perception, and it is not about seeing what already is so much as it creates claims about what is. Yet I will still use "reflection" here because I can't think of a better word to use in this section of a sequence of arguments leading from and out of subject-object knowing to intersubjectivity.

When we humans become reflectively aware of cultural themes, beliefs, norms, identity categories, and ideologies we can, at least in some cases, change what we are at the same time. For example, people changed when feminism began to expand awareness in popular culture as well as within the cultures of feminist-activist communities. The changes of significance are a growth of freedom within one's being.

Reflection and critique result in knowledge that is also a change in being, not because the knowledge is first produced and next used to change something, but because knowing in this case is internal to what we are. The feminist movement is an example of a process of knowing through consciousness raising, resulting in changed women and men.

The distinctions between cognition, affect, and morality we are accustomed to are not evident within knowing as reflection. Reflection is felt, entails moral consciousness, and has cognitive content. Cultural structures and ideologies work like "transcendental conditions of possible experience/understanding."[8] They work in this way until we become aware of them, explicate them, and critique them.[9] But why does this activity of making something we had not previously noticed explicitly noticeable (often) change who we are? And why does that feel like freedom?

The process seems to go something like this: we live within and through intersubjective structures that are historically, culturally, and ideologically contingent. Our very being as persons requires such structures. The cultural, intersubjectively structured conditions that make it possible to be a person will not be noticed without undergoing some sort of reflective process. Many of these conditions making it possible to be a person also constrain being a person because they are sexist, homophobic, racist, classist, ageist, separate us from nature, give us misleading ideas about happiness, and so on. Critical theory excels at making sense of the process by which the being of a person, the form of person-ness, involves conditions of possibility that are inherently transcendable, or "capable of being transcended."

What we refer to with the word "self" and similar words (human identity, ego, and so on) is something that necessarily, ontologically, transcends its enabling conditions. To transcend is to pass beyond limits. "Transcend" comes from the old French word "transcender" which came from the Latin word "transcendere" which both meant "to climb over, step over, surpass." We are onto what Kant was referring to with his use of "transcendental" except that we are making ontological claims rather than merely epistemological ones, saying that transcendental-like conditions of possibility are different in different cultures, subcultures, and historical periods.

How is self-transcending a characteristic of human being? For many thousands of years we have had people living within racist, sexist, elitist, homophobic cultures of different colors, stripes, and shapes without any person in them articulating critique. I suspect that limits on the being of persons are felt in most cases, but thematizing the ideological conditions that constitute those limits is difficult and has likely been rare during the many thousands of years of human presence on this planet. So how can the being of person-being be said to be precisely the process of transcending, through forms of self-knowing, the conditions of possibility for its being? Well, being more than any description of ourselves, any judgment of ourselves, is built into all human actions that have anything to do with norms. This then includes language, because the distinction between correct and incorrect ways of speaking is normative. When someone is told they have behaved well, admirably, poorly, or despicably, the assumption is that this someone can maintain or change the ways they act and that they understand and agree with why they ought to. So when someone who is female acts in a way that isn't "suitable" or "proper" for a girl or woman within the horizons of a particular culture, she will usually get feedback to this effect. She will be chastised, scolded, scorned, and so on, with the assumption that she not only can change what she says and does but also understand and agree with why she should. The key to the idea here resides within that word "agree."

For norms to be norms, there has to be at least an implicit assumption that person-ness entails continuous self-transcending. Person-ness is a kind of being that is aware of itself such that it can judge itself, regard itself from the perspective of a community, a culture, and is therefore capable of being responsible for what it does and does not do and say. When monitoring ourselves or judging ourselves, to put it too simply, we exist as the repeated instantiations of a relationship—a relationship between identifications with the generalized position of a group and with an individuated "me" belonging to that group. The group is a generalized other that originates in a culture or subculture but that can expand beyond its empirical origin, which it does when there is critique. In general people exist as inter-subjectively structured activity, involving self-monitoring movements between individuated and group subject positions. Norms require self-application, and thus humans transcend who they are reflectively all the time. Ideologies work because we apply them to ourselves; they can be thematized and criticized because the self-transcending practice of applying cultural themes to ourselves is also our potentiality for changing who we are as part of changing the cultures we live within.

3. "I": The Transcendental Unity of Apperception

Human identity involves applying self-judgments, being accountable to others, taking responsibility, and doing things with (and sometimes for) reasons rather than being caused to do things. Kant's *Critique of Pure Reason* includes a subtle insight that can help us to understand the complexities of human identity.[10] It is not sufficient on its own in this respect, but it is crucial to an understanding of the limits of subject-object thinking. Later, it will also help with a grasp of the conditions of possibility for subject-subject forms of knowing.

All of us have probably wondered at times how it is that we perceive objects like rocks and pens and cars as single things. Any object we perceive as singular can be examined to reveal parts. But the oneness of an object is not the collection of parts, nor their arrangement, nor is oneness itself a kind of part that we can separate from the object. This is a version of the long-discussed "problem of the one and the many" in Western philosophy (an excellent recent book on this topic is *One*, by Graham Priest, 2014). The problem comes up in domains other than experience: in theories of concepts, of meaning, mathematical concepts of infinity, and other topics and fields as well. Kant, like many philosophers, had a number of things to say on this topic but one of them is especially of relevance to the themes of this essay. How is it that experience is unified?

In Kant's theory, the oneness of a perceived object, like a rock, involves those 12 transcendental categories of the understanding. Three categories, grouped together as "quantity," are "unity," "plurality," and "totality." Totality is the unity of a plurality. The reason we experience an object like a rock as a "one" is that, according to Kant, a preconscious judgment took place involving the transcendental category of "unity." This sort of unity Kant calls "categorical unity."

But our interest is in what Kant called "non-categorical unity." Kant provides a number of arguments to lead to a grasp of this non-categorical unity, but the one I like best concerns the fact that, for each of us, experience is always inescapably "mine," or "my" experience. There is a singularity to experience that has to do with "mine-ness." Kant expressed this by writing that all experiences can in principle be accompanied by "I think." "There is a cup on the table over there" can be expressed "*I think* there is a cup on the table over there." Strawson, in his meticulous examination of *The Critique of Pure Reason* published as *The Bounds of Sense* (1966), words the insight in terms of self-ascription: all experiences can in principle always be self-ascribed but in an odd sort of way. It is not correct to think of the self to which experience can always be ascribed as "Phil," or "Heyoung," or any person individuated from other persons. We do not have any empirical experiences of the "I" to which experience is self-ascribed. An example given by Strawson is helpful for awakening to the main idea here: "When I am in pain, for example, I do not have to look and see that it is *I* who is in pain." And this is unlike our knowledge of objects and even our knowledge of other people. This "I" is not an object of experience. It has no determinations; no qualities.

Kant got the idea of "apperception" from Leibniz, who wrote of the difference between perception and apperception in both *The Monadology* (1890, pp. 218–232) and *The Principles of Nature and Grace* (1890, pp. 209–217). In *The Monadology* Leibniz writes that perception is a state representing multitude in unity (p. 219). In *The Principles of Nature and Grace* he writes:

Therefore it is well to make a distinction between the perception, which is the internal condition of the monad representing external things, and apperception, which is consciousness or the reflective knowledge of this internal state; the latter not being given to all souls, nor at all times to the same soul. (pp. 210–211)

Apperception is a kind of reflective awareness of the unity-of-a-multitude that is perception. It is the consciousness of the unity, not the object or any of the contents, of perception.

Kant adapted and expanded Leibniz's idea to produce his theory of the transcendental unity of apperception. The "one" of experience is not attributable to any region or moment that analysis can separate but rather to the mine-ness of experience. Kant thus believed that there is "a pure original unchangeable consciousness" (*CPR* A, p. 107) that can be named "the transcendental 'I'." The transcendental "I" is an identity without content that enables all (categorical) forms of unity. Kant writes, "The original and necessary consciousness of the identity of the self is thus at the same time a consciousness of an equally necessary unity of the synthesis of appearances according to concepts" (*CPR* A, p. 108; 1965, p. 136[11]). Because it is a consciousness of the identity of the self, it is "self-consciousness." But this is "the unity of *transcendental* self-consciousness" (*CPR* B, p. 132). It is not empirical self-consciousness. It is not the consciousness of being a shy person or a fast runner or a person with an open mind. It is not consciousness of being a person or anything else at all. It is necessary for those forms of self-awareness but it has no content, no qualities, is not an entity, is not distinguishable from other things in terms of qualities, and has no parts. It cannot be an object of experience ever, in any way. It cannot really be thought of as an "it" or an object ontologically. All we can say of it, writes Kant, is "I am": "In the synthetic original unity of apperception I am conscious of myself not as I appear to myself, nor as I am in myself, but only that I am" (*CPR* B, p. 157; 1965, p. 168).

In *CPR* Kant writes of the transcendental "I" or transcendental apperception: "that self-consciousness which, while generating the representation '*I think*' (a representation which must be capable of accompanying all other representations, and which in all consciousness is one and the same) cannot itself be accompanied by any further representation" (*CPR* B, p. 132; 1965, p. 153). All experiences can be relativized to "mine," but transcendental apperception itself cannot be relativized in this manner. There is no "transcendental 'I'" for me.

This is a subtle but important insight. Because it is subtle, it is difficult to include in theories. One has to move beyond what Hegel, in *Phenomenology of Spirit*, called "picture-thinking" (1977, p. 34) to bring it into a philosophy or theory. If you have a picture of the transcendental "I," then that picture should simultaneously act as a mnemonic, sparking the memory that what is represented in your picture is unrepresentable. The insight Kant articulated as the transcendental "I" concerns the common confusion, notes Strawson, between "the experience of unity" (categorical unity, or the oneness of an object perceived) and the "unity of experience" (non-categorical, transcendental unity). As Strawson points out, this insight helps us catch the fact that *self*-knowledge is unique in relation to *all* other forms of knowledge (1966, p. 38). As we have seen, self-consciousness is a condition of possibility for all knowledge of the observational-empirical type. Self-knowledge is also a condition of possibility for knowing within the subject-subject framework as we discover when we move from Kant to a more general understanding of knowledge.

Observational-empirical knowledge is a subset within the subject-object framework; the "empirical" specification it makes prohibits full reflection and dialectics, both of which are features of the subject-object framework in its general form. The general subject-object frame is used in such things as Hegelian dialectics, paraconsistent logic, and the ontology of dialetheism (see Priest, 2002, 2005, 2014 on paraconsistent logic and dialetheism). But dialectics and paraconsistent logic do not lead us from subject-object thinking to intersubjectivity. And it is toward intersubjectivity that we are moving.

Limits of the Subject-Object Framework: If You Can Picture It, It Is Not Subject;
If You Ignore It, You Contradict Yourself

The reason it is so very difficult to escape what I have been calling the "subject-object" framework of knowing is that the subject side of this relation is transcendental or "negative" in the Hegelian sense I will summarize below. It cannot be pictured. A model will not capture it. Thinking of it already transcends it. Even a very basic understanding of Kant's "transcendental turn" reveals the necessity but also the difficulty of the concept of the subject (which is not the same as subjectivity; everything that is subjective is also not the subject, a point I cannot explain here).

There are a number of possible responses to the insight Kant called the transcendental "I." The most prevalent one taken is to ignore Kant. Most scientists and secular subcultures basically take on a materialist worldview, and other populations in modern societies (to which plenty of scientists also belong outside their professional work) live within transcendent metaphysical worldviews (non-reflective beliefs in souls, in a mental domain made of a special kind of non-material substance, in spirits, and so on).

Another response to Kant is to understand the significance of his work and develop philosophy so as to better clarify transcendence and limits to reason. Habermas's work integrates and advances the work of many diverse schools of philosophy and social theory, including (but not at all limited to) Frege's revolutionary writings on the internal connections between truth and meaning, Weber's closely argued thesis of the rationalization of Western societies and cultures, Kant, and the particular post-Kantian direction taken by Fichte, Hegel, and Marx. Kant's major contributions to philosophy are reinterpreted in more compelling ways within Habermas's critical theory of communicative reason (1984, 1987). Kant's critiques of reason were themselves limited by understanding reason monologically rather than intersubjectively. It is this response to Kant's philosophical insights that informs my own work in critical theory. The arguments in this chapter present the discovery and significance of limitations to subject-object forms of knowing so as to arrive at the subject-subject framework for understanding knowledge. It is not possible in a chapter of this length to discuss subject-subject epistemology, but readers should know that it is the most compelling response to the insights Kant brought to light.

One more way of interpreting the significance of Kant's work is worth mentioning since it is one pursued by Foucault, who subsequently influenced many others, including people working within cultural anthropology, cultural studies, and some communities of qualitative researchers. The transcendental subject, argues Foucault (1970), is a feature of the "modern episteme." But so is the empirical human subject. The self, during the period of the modern episteme, is thought of as a necessary transcendental condition for all possible experience and knowledge (hence it cannot be in any sense empirical) and yet human selves can be regarded as objects of study and pursued empirically (as they are in psychology, criminology, psychotherapy, pedagogic theories, "scientific management" theories of work organization, and so on). Western philosophy from Kant to Heidegger recognized this contradictory concept of the subject and tried unsuccessfully to develop philosophies that could make sense of it. Meanwhile the psychological and social sciences emerged and grew within this same episteme, basically blind to the transcendental side of the contradiction and thus to something like Nietzsche's "will to power," which operated through the discourse-practices of such things as criminology, psychiatry, pedagogic theories, and theories of personnel management to construct and then subjugate the empirical human subject.

There is no "will," however, in Foucault's objectivistic concept of power. The modern episteme's notion of the subject and associated ideas like that of will is contradictory and hence should be rejected. "The subject" in the postmodern period is therefore "dead." Subjectivities, as opposed to the subject, are real but ontologically secondary to objective forces, the "power," that determine them. Power manifests as "power-knowledge," and "discourse-practices" in relation to which subjectivities and ways of knowing are internal and subordinate. However, if we have a theory of knowledge that relativizes all knowledge to something objective—power in the case of Foucault, matter in the case of a materialist—we have a number of contradictions that are not visible within the theory (for an extended discussion see

Carspecken, 2003). Thus, if we try to deny the subject by basically taking the object side of an unac-knowledged subject-object framework, we simply hide it. I've never quite understood the popularity of this version of post-structuralism, and its widespread take-up in the social sciences has deeply frustrated me. Relatively recently, however, the work of Žižek and other contemporaries, calling their perspective "transcendental materialism" (Johnston, 2014a), has been growing in popularity, producing work that counters the post-structuralist denial of the subject in enormously welcome ways. A famous sentence of Hegel's from his preface to *The Phenomenology of Spirit* (1977) is central to the project of transcendental materialism: "In my view, which can be justified only by the exposition of the system itself, everything turns on grasping and expressing the True, not only as *Substance*, but equally as *Subject*" (pp. 9–10). Hegel's philosophy is very important to critical theory. In fact, Hegel is so important to the project of critical theory and practice we need a special section devoted to him.

Hegel, Self-certainty, and Pure Negativity

Hegel's philosophy is impossible to summarize. He writes many times in many places that all of the key concepts central to his philosophy cannot be understood without understanding his philosophy as a whole. His philosophical writings all fall within an integrated system having three main dialectical progressions, with the ending of one major dialectical course leading directly to the beginning of the next and the end of that next dialectic leading directly back to the beginning of the first. The three divisions are Logic (very different from what is normally meant by "logic"), Philosophy of Nature, and Philosophy of Spirit.

The Phenomenology of Spirit

Hegel's *Phenomenology of Spirit* (1977) is distinct from the three divisions of his actual philosophical system in that it is devoted to the dialectical progression of forms of knowing. The contents of this work are considered to be something like the prerequisite to his system. *Phenomenology* takes readers through forms of knowing we are supposed to recognize internally (and in fact many of them are indeed recognizable) because our present way of knowing has within it all the forms that it took during a process of self-development. Our present way of knowing is internalized from and recapitulates the structures of our existing culture and society, which Hegel believed to be the result of an historical dialectical progression.

The idea is similar to the ways in which Piaget's cognitive stages are recognizable to us; for example we take object-permanence for granted, but when reading Piaget the stage of object-impermanence makes internal sense to us. We can sort of "put ourselves" back within it. And we realize that object-permanence is not just a stage of cognition but a stage of experience itself. Hegel regarded experience itself to be the ground of what we call knowing. Experiencing is knowing. Hegel would have had to agree that the later stages of knowing described in *Phenomenology* have not yet been attained by most of us, but his idea was that those stages reside within our capabilities because they have been established within the culture of our historical period, the culture and society into which we were born and socialized.

Of course it is his own historical period and culture that Hegel meant. If Hegel were right, the culture of today might differ on the surface from the culture of his day but the historical stage reached by his day would simply have been in a state of self-maintenance and self-reproduction ever since. Two untenable aspects of Hegel's philosophy are here evident: the idea that cultures progress in a sort of linear way, and the idea that this progression can reach an end. But still alive is his idea that culture and social activities are necessary conditions for human thinking. And the idea of a possible but not necessary direction in cultural change also makes good sense today and can be understood through the subject-subject paradigm.

At the end of *Phenomenology* is a section called "Absolute knowledge." Absolute knowledge is knowledge that is totally certain. Hegel doesn't mean the huge number of knowledge claims made every day from claims like "there are the carrots" to "we need to use a nickel-based alloy like C-276 for the rocket engine." Those sorts of knowledge claims can be understood as necessarily fallible without threatening Hegel's main idea. Hegel's main idea pertains to fundamental beliefs about knowledge that differ within different cognitive modes. Hence the idea that all knowledge claims are fallible would be an example of one of these fundamental beliefs about what knowledge is in general. How can we know that all knowing is fallible? It is a contradiction. In Hegel's view it would be at bottom between certainty and conceptually articulated knowledge claims meant to explicate the ground of certainty.

Today we would want to assess Hegel's connections between certainty and fundamental notions of knowledge in general to all types of validity claims—normative and subjectivity-referenced claims included. What is "certainty"? Hegel describes a progression of implicit, structure-forming beliefs residing in our typical states of "being certain." These are the commonsense certainties of a form of life (a culture and society; today we would break it down to subcultures and ideologies) that philosophers of an era attempt to make explicit for examination.

Hegel's stages of cognition dialectically move forward when efforts are made to make conceptually explicit knowledge claims of the most taken-for-granted ways that "being certain" have within a mode of knowing. Those efforts result in contradictions. If you reach out to touch a cup of coffee cautiously, without much thought about what you are doing, and I ask you why you did this you would articulate what was a certainty constituting that activity: the coffee cup might be really hot. If I ask you why you think it could but might not be hot your answer might include mention of the substance the cup is made of—perhaps it is a metal cup. And if I keep asking you questions to explain the basic concepts, what is a metal, what are atoms, and so forth, that you used in previous answers, you will reach horizon boundaries eventually. Your most basic beliefs in the fundamental components of nature, human senses, and so on would be found. Trying to articulate those most fundamental beliefs explicitly results in contradictions between your everyday certainties and the best you can do to make them conceptually explicit. And then, according to Hegel, you might be able to move into a higher cognitive mode that dialectically reconciles that contradiction.

In addition, modes of knowing, as mentioned above, are at bottom modes of experience. Modes of experience are associated with forms of life. And the ways of being certain through the action routines common to a form of life are the milieu within which self-certainty is embodied. Self-certainty and human-being are to be thought of as two sides of the same coin. What we humans are is our self-knowledge, and our self-knowledge is fundamentally uncertain. To put this into more contemporary terms, what we humans are is a matter of action and interaction routines that contain self-claiming. The experience of the results of self-claiming are socially mediated, based on how others respond to our identity claims and how we internally respond to them through taking other possible subject positions in relation to them. Cultures and subcultures (this is also adapting Hegel to more contemporary theoretical frames) enable and constrain the actualization of our human-being. We are actualized in degrees of self-certainty had within action routines that are socio-culturally specific.

Those are very basic features of *Phenomenology*. Most important are the connections Hegel discerned among certainty, self-certainty, the actualization of human-being as self-certainty and its embodiment within a socio-cultural milieu that both enables and constrains actualization. The limit case of fully attained self-certainty would be a state requiring no more action because all the basic desires and motivations humans experience are understood to be forms of seeking self-certainty that fail to fully deliver it. They fail because: (1) what comes back from identity claims will not last in time (hence identity claims are repeated in routines of life); and (2) what comes back from identity claims is usually at best confirmation through intersubjective recognition of a finite self, which contradicts the ever-transcending feature of the "I" of the identity claim. We claim finite "me" selves to find the self-certainty of the "I." But the "I" transcends all finite forms in ways partly clarified by Kant as discussed above and explained more below.

Hegel believed that at a certain stage of the dialectics of knowing the "I" at the heart of self-certainty, the certainty of "I am" is no longer identified with an individual like Phil Carspecken or Hilda Feuerbach or any other person as an individual. Instead it is identified with something trans-individual: "spirit" in forms such as the intersubjective milieu of a culture (and eventually the "spirit" that is the substance and subject of all potential and actual being: *Geist*). But existentialists and many Eastern schools of religion and philosophy teach the impossibility of transcending individuality in a conceptual and communicative manner. It can only happen in non-communicable states like Samadhi and Nirvana, or it must be surrendered with faith in a monotheistic God.[12] These teachings about the limit case of self-certainty can be understood fairly well when we shift from subject-object dialectics (Hegel) to subject-subject thinking. But meanwhile we have much to learn from Hegel.

The above sketch of core themes in *Phenomenology* cannot be understood very well in such a brief overview so I want to connect them in more refined terms to my earlier discussion of Kant's transcendental "I." The next few sections bring out and clarify more themes from *Phenomenology* important to critical theory and practice.

The transcendental unity of apperception and contradiction

In *Phenomenology* all modes of knowing, called "modes of certainty" by Hegel, can only be initially understood from within themselves because more developed modes have not yet developed. Reflection is required for a holistic subject-object form of knowing to be cognitively understood as holistic within the manner of knowing it enables. This should remind us of Kant and the transcendental. Kant's writings about the transcendental unity of apperception and its relation to the transcendental "I" and transcendental self-consciousness involve a contradiction whose general form is examined by Graham Priest in his book *One* (2014). When a subject-object frame is used reflectively, so as to include itself in the knowledge it makes possible, we get inclusion-paradoxes. These come up in set-theory, theories of the unity of meaning, mathematical concepts of infinity, and a number of fields of academic work reviewed by Priest.

In the case of Kant's writings on the transcendental "I," we can ask whether or not we should regard his expression to name a "concept." If it is a concept, then what sort of concept is it, given that all possible concepts for Kant entail the transcendental "I"? I have not fully explained transcendental unity of apperception in terms of concepts for want of space, but the idea can be put across with a few sentences. All experience is transcendentally unified in a way that can be understood by understanding that all experience can be found to be "my" experience for each of us. But all experience is also unified through concepts. We see a pen on a desk in a way that can be described as *recognizing* a pen on a desk. We don't experience "raw sense data" and next integrate it with the concept "pen." The concept and the experience are one and the same but can be differentiated in next thoughts or in talk. A concept like "pen" is learned but all learned concepts like this are nested within more general concepts leading back, for Kant, to the transcendental categories of space and time and the 12 categories of the understanding. A pen is a kind of object-in-general involving the transcendental category of "totality" (unification of parts into a one).

Hence the transcendental unity of apperception is the apperception of—now let's use an important Hegelian term—experience as "mediated" by concepts. All concepts pertaining to sense experiences are indistinguishable from experience in terms of origin: differentiations that reveal concepts as concepts occur after the fact of experience. And all concepts entail, and are distinguished from, the transcendental "I" through the unity of apperception. A concept of the transcendental "I" would similarly entail the transcendental "I." So can *it* be a concept? What is the status of a concept that tries to include itself in all it applies to? It is a problem because the transcendental "I" is necessary to all concepts of the type considered in *CPR* in a manner that distinguishes it from each and every one of them. How can the concept of transcendental "I" distinguish itself from itself? Hegelian philosophy makes sense of this.

Therefore, Kant had difficulties, it seems, in articulating what he meant by the transcendental "I." In some places he calls it a "purely empty" idea, a mere logical correlate to transcendental apperception (*CPR* A, pp. 396, 398). Those would be ways to conceptualize it. But he also writes of it like this: "We cannot even say that this is a concept, but only that it is a bare consciousness which accompanies all concepts" (*CPR* A, p. 436, B, p. 404). Isn't that also a way of conceptualizing it though? The transcendental "I" is a concept as soon as we start to talk, think, and write about it; but it can't be a concept really. It is self-consciousness but it can't be anything at all. It is a limit to knowing that enables subject-object thinking; thus when we try to understand it within the form of knowing it enables, we get contradictions.

This exemplifies one basic form, among several, of the contradictions we find analyzed by Priest (2002, 2005, 2014). Hegel takes contradictions as real (so does Priest, but in a different way, leading to Buddhism). Kant gives us one subject-object framework that, it can be argued, cannot be used to understand itself without contradictions. Hegel gives us a self-developing series of subject-object relations that also entail this contradiction produced by reflection: but when the contradictions of a mode of certainty are articulated, a new and higher-level mode of certainty results. This is the famous Hegelian dialectic expressed in the form of knowing. It can also be expressed in the form of being—particularly human-being. Hegel's presentation of dialectical stages of knowing moves the Kantian insight into a much more subtle form. Unity of apperception and conceptual mediation are keys to this.

Self-certainty and the transcendental "I"

Kant's discernment of transcendental apperception is something we can all awaken to. Let's look again, briefly, at Kant's ways of awakening his readers to the concept of transcendental apperception through his arguments involving the "I think." We are to notice[13] that all experience is inescapably "my" experience. This is one of several ways of awakening the understanding Kant called "transcendental unity." Kant used several different arguments and I believe the same insight is central to a great many diverse teachings and philosophies we can find across cultures and centuries. When learning yoga and yogic meditation I was taught various methods of awakening to the transcendental "I": at least, this is how I understand both Kant and my experiences with meditation. One method is to "seek the 'I-feeling'" meditatively. This project often leads to our first-person awareness of our body in a state of slowed thinking so that attention on body awareness can be maintained and, so to speak, "examined" carefully. In the case of this exercise, inner-body awareness is the "experience" whose unity can be considered. Its mine-ness is more obvious than is the mine-ness of visual perception. It is possible, meditatively, to experience our body in a singular, holistic manner so that we are not attending to different feelings in different places of the body but are aware of the body as a whole. It is even possible, but not necessary for the purpose of making sense of apperceptive unity, to integrate the unity of body feeling with all the sounds that happen to be within our environment at the time.

When body feeling comes into awareness because of the project of seeking an "I feeling," one can experience a strong but momentary flicker of the sense of "I am." But this is against that body feeling, as not that body feeling. And it is very important that the flicker of that strong sense of "I am" is in a just-was temporal mode. We cannot have any experience of existing, of being, that is simultaneous with knowing that we are having it. The reason there is the structure of the momentary flicker of "I am" in exercises like this is that noticing it takes us away from it. In a deep meditation one can, so to speak, "remain within" the sense of "I am" for long periods of time, but in those cases one only remembers moving into it and moving back out. To be aware of any sort of sense experience is to have something distinguished from it: this something distinguished from experience is related to a potentiality for memory and for next actions of thinking about it, talking about it, acting in relation to it. If we experience our finger burning, we usually act in relation to the experience by moving our finger away from heat, but we can also hold our finger still for a while. These are actions in relation to an experience. If we are watching a beautiful sunset, we usually will have the separation of the potential for thinking about, writing about, telling another person about that beautiful sunset. The unity of apperception is the unity of a next act.

The transcendental "I" pertains to the moment of bare differentiation between experience and first-person movement having that experience as its object. And this is how experience is unified. We almost "feel" the "I" when experience becomes something we can act in relation to: our "I" is on the side of next possible actions (keep remembering that thought and even bare shifts of awareness are actions). It is not an object we are aware of because if we were aware of it, then "it" would be what is distinguished from next possible self-movements, and it is the next possible self-movements that "it" is supposed to be. However, one can experience brief moments of "I feeling" as "just was." And this suggests a sort of process of having our being, our existence, always embedded within something else, like body sensation in our example, such that when that something else is objectivated we sense our being, our "I am" in immediate difference from the objectivation. The "stream of experience" is not like continuous movement of various things before an audience but more like a continuous self-movement out of embodiments; and this movement is also the movement of objectivation: becoming aware of what we were previously fully embodied within.

But what moves out of embodiments (and yet always is embodied, since the movements are more like changing embodiments)? Well, we could call it the transcendental "I," or we could call it just the "I" distinguished from such things as the "me." These expressions are often useful but also risk a false picture: that of something that moves. It seems more accurate, less misleading, to just use the word "movement." But even calling it "movement" can be misleading because the concept of movement, the idea of movement, the thought of movement is distinct from what we are trying to catch in explicit linguistic and conceptual form. "First-person movement" is a bit better than "movement" because we don't wish to bring our observational experiences of moving things like cars and the water in rivers to mind; we rather wish to bring to mind something closer to what it feels like when we are running, picking something up, talking, thinking, and even just shifting our attention from one direction to another. We could write "first-person experience of action" except that, remember, when we use the word "experience" we encounter the unity of experience inescapably and that means we encounter a relationship between something and a movement out of that something. So the concept of "experience" is now more complex for us—there is no experience without the "moving out" accompanying it and giving it its unity.

So the "I" is not an experience, but requires experience. It is something we can awaken to in a moment of absolute certainty, which is also self-certainty. And it is very difficult to express what it is in a way that catches the certainty of it conceptually. It is not an experience and above it was argued that it cannot be a concept either. Let's look at that a little more closely.

Not an experience, not a concept

The "I" is also not a concept, as the short discussion above about finding a name for it like, for example, self-movement, shows. In our quest for a good expression to capture the elusive transcendental "I" we are simultaneously seeking a concept adequate to it. If we call it "first-person movement" we find that doesn't work because the sense of the concept is still distinct from what we are trying to catch in exactly the same way that "experience" is distinct from the unifying "I." If we call it "the first-person experience of acting" we have exactly the same problem.

This transcendental "I" insight pertains to both experience and concepts but is neither. Experience is unified but is not itself its unity. And an articulated concept (articulated even in bare form, as an image or a sense) is other than the process of articulation separating it from experience. We can say all concepts when explicated are other than the thinker or the "I" but by now we understand that it is not really correct to think in terms of an "I" or "thinker."

Pure negativity

We should be ready for Hegel's understanding of "I" now. Instead of "transcendental 'I'" we can do this: consider everything that can be called an experience or an object of experience or a thought or a concept or idea "positive." All of these things only are what they are through a unity that comes about from something like a "movement-out" of them. Call that movement "the negative" or "negation." This is getting close to Hegel but we must add the following instruction. Remember that using a name or concept such as negative or negation is making something positive. There is no simple name or concept for what we are trying to name and conceptually capture. "Negative," however, is helpful in many ways: better than "transcendental 'I,'" because it helps us to remember that as soon as something is thought or experienced it is in positive form and "the negative" is not it.

This is all sort of tricky so here are some sentences meant to summarize, expand, and extend. In the exercise of seeking the "I-feeling" we get to sensations without thought (or at least without much thought, slowed thought) and find the flicker of self-certainty as something just gone, as if we just were embedded within the sensations (usually body feeling) but have moved out. This moving out is the process of objectivation that gives us a unified experience. The sensation is objectivated when it is noticed to be a sensation. It is unified by the movement away. But this is metaphor: what actually moved? Well, nothing moved. There is no transcendental "I" if we think of it as something that just is or as something that moves. There is simply movement that we also call time. But as soon as it is thought of as movement there is another objectivation and movement again.

Hence, my summary continues, why use the expression "transcendental 'I'" for the unity of experience? Hegel doesn't. Hegel writes of the negative and negativity instead. The pure "I" that Kant called transcendental is pure negativity in Hegel's philosophy. The movement that is the negative also differentiates, from within a moment of experience, concepts from their objects. The first differentiation from within a moment of experience via reflection to a next moment results in concepts distinguished from what they are of. We recognize a pen on the desk with certainty, acting to pick it up. But what is the basis of that certainty? Is it that there is a pen existing on the desk, or is it that we subjectively interpret an object on the desk to be a pen, or is it something else? The movement we can call "I" is the movement differentiating the conceptual mediations of experience. Much more should be written on that to make it clear but just a basic sense of the idea is good enough for our place in this essay. Hegel writes in *Phenomenology*:

> For mediation is nothing beyond self-moving selfsameness, or is reflection into self, the moment of the 'I' which is for itself pure negativity or, when reduced to pure abstraction, *simple becoming*. (1977, p. 11)

The unity of experience is the unity of movement, "simple becoming." It is the "I." Both the unity of self-movement and the self-certainty that is in some senses identical with it are "caught" only as what has happened but is over. This is because we can only try to catch self-certainty cognitively by objectivating the very movement of objectivation. Self-certainty is dialectically structured because it is a movement to objectivate itself, thus know itself, experience itself as a unity that cannot happen in a single moment of time. It is pure reflection. It is pure freedom too, which becomes evident when we foreground the dialectics of human-being rather than cognition.

Knowing as being

Much of the above on the "I" as pure negativity had cognition in the foreground. But the cognitive is dependent upon, embedded within, forms of life. In the form of human-being, rather than the form of cognition, we find self-certainty to be the standard by which, among many other things, cultural oppression is lived and experienced as oppression. It is an idea crucial to critical theory and critical research (whose most direct instantiation is critical *action* research). From lived oppression, which involves the movement from experience to awareness of experience and back to experience within the routines of everyday life, the critical practitioner explicates. Implicit ideas about what a person is and can be, what the purpose of life is, what is good and bad and right and wrong and beautiful, are made discursively explicit and contrasted with self-certainty. This is the first stage of critique. It is knowledge already in the form of being.

By the end of *Phenomenology*, Hegel's claim that knowing is finally identical with being becomes the beginning platform for his *Science of Logic* (1991). In earlier sections of *Logic*, he several times explains that he has established the unity in his earlier *Phenomenology* and thus can begin *Logic* with the category of Being. Here are just two of many such statements:

> This pure being is the unity into which pure knowing withdraws, or, if this itself is still to be distinguished as form from its unity, then being is also the content of pure knowing. (1991, p. 72)

> If pure being is taken as the content of pure knowing, then the latter must stand back from its content, allowing it to have free play and not determining it any further. Or again, if pure being is to be considered as the unity into which knowing has collapsed at the extreme point of its union with the object, then knowing itself has vanished in that unity, leaving behind no difference from the unity and hence nothing by which the latter could be determined. (1991, p. 73)

Today few thinkers would agree that this is possible. Few today would regard the being of rocks and trees as an alienation of the self-certain of *Geist* in forms of actualized being. But when it comes to specifically human being, many thinkers agree with the central insight that enables us to understand knowing as being. It is a theme in the many various forms of existentialism—both religious and secular—and it is a theme as well in many traditions of spiritual thought and practice that have existed for millennia in the East. It is something that any compelling critical theory must have room for.

Critical Knowledge Typology

Habermas's work in *KHI* makes sense of the internal connection between knowing and being, for human-being, in ways that I believe can be much further developed. Habermas argues against ontology in that book, but in his later work developing communicative action theory he argues for three formal ontological domains. They are "formal" because they are necessarily claimed as distinct from each other with every communicative act. All claims involving some sense of "existing" fall within one of the three categories (objective, subjective, and normative). This actually makes a good deal of sense and, I think, can be filled out more through integration with his earlier *KHI*. Knowing, experiencing are the same at the origins of communicative competencies and thus of abstract, communicatively structured thought. Knowing takes the form of knowing about and predicting once there are communicative competencies and concepts can be considered in separation from their roles in integrating experience. The separation of experience from concepts enables the observational-empirical sciences because theories of external relations between events require the difference between data and theory vocabularies. But in the case of hermeneutic inquiry, knowledge is about socio-cultural dynamics and its milieu—which ontologically includes knowledge. Knowledge is a social phenomenon that can be set aside for observational-empirical work (when not examining scientific paradigm changes) but is the actual "object of inquiry" for hermeneutics. Knowledge is being here; associated with the ontological category of "the social" as Habermas calls it, with normativity foregrounded.

And in the case of self-knowing, the dialectical identity among experience, knowledge, and being remains as it was at the origins, before communicative competencies differentiated these things from within. Kant and especially Hegel are steps toward understanding this. A Habermasian and communicative-pragmatist critical theory advances our understanding of them.

Hence the trajectory of this essay has led us to the subject-subject mode of understanding as the self-understanding of knowing in general, an area directly involved with critical research and theory, including the existential limits of the being of human.

Subject-Subject Knowing as Being; Limits to Knowledge as Existential Conditions of Being Human

We move next from subject-object thinking to the subject-subject framework as developed by Habermas and communicative pragmatists like Robert Brandom to examine limits to knowledge more fundamental than those arising within the subject-object framework. These are existential limits of human being that also limit the knowledge that can be produced through qualitative social research whose method is primarily hermeneutic.

Explorations in this area can show that critical action research works directly with the limits of human knowing and being, producing knowledge as changes in human existence and its milieu of culture and social relations. This is because of the "action" in critical action research. Limits of human being are transcended continuously as human life is in movement towards greater freedom in its many senses.

The subject-subject relation of knowing and being helps us to understand human identity in terms of "I," "me," "we," and self-narrative. It clarifies the difference between reasons and causes—reasons only are what they are through the assumption of a free other subject. It shows knowledge to be a form of power only if it is ideological and thus false or distorted. Empowerment is different than power, and knowledge is empowering in both utilitarian and ontological ways.

Critical social research and theory, and critical action research in particular, has everything to do with themes prominent for millennia within religious and spiritual traditions. The dependency of human identity on the principle of a free other subject has a religious dimension to it. The "I" as pure negativity is an articulation that is more than just congruent with many Buddhist and yogic teachings.

The Limits to this Essay on Limits to Knowledge

And I did originally intend to include a final major section detailing points about the subject-subject framework woven throughout this chapter. The above discussion of the subject-object framework creates context for an equally detailed discussion of subject-subject thinking: that is, it provides necessary ground clearing for a substantive shift in thinking. And, having created the context, I actually wrote several versions of a concluding segment exploring the subject-subject framework. However, there is too much to say and too little space remaining in this chapter to say it. It will have to follow my earlier thoughts (Carspecken, 2009) with a detailed publication on the subject-subject framework in the future.

Notes

1. *The Critique of Pure Reason* (*CPR*) was first published in 1781 and a significantly changed edition was published in 1787. There are a number of English translations of *CPR*, all of which present Kant's writings in both editions for each section of the treatise. It has become customary to use "A" to indicate that a passage is from the first edition and "B" to indicate second-edition versions. When I quote Kant in this essay I use the 1965 Norman Kemp Smith translation. The *Critique of Practical Reason* was published in 1788, three years after a work devoted to the same topic of moral-practical reason titled *Groundwork of the Metaphysics of Morals*. In 1790 Kant published his third critique, *The Critique of Practical Judgment*, and he published *The Metaphysics of Morals* in 1797. Details of English translations are given in the bibliography.

2. In Greek-European history an example of transcendent metaphysics would be the four temperaments (melancholic, choleric, sanguine, and phlegmatic) that were related to the proportions of the four humors (black bile, yellow bile, phlegm, and blood), which in turn were related to the four fundamental elements of air, fire, water, and earth. One of many examples from India would be the three gunas: satva guna, raja guna, and tama guna. Uses of yin and yang in various medical and dietary theories of ancient China and cultures influenced by China are another example.

3. I won't spend time on the concepts of transcendent realities discussed by Kant even though at least one of them, the thing-in-itself or *noumenon*, can be studied as a form of those limits to knowledge that have relevance to critical theory

(I hope to include an examination of this in a future work). But here I will just say that one can divide concepts of transcendent realities appearing in Kant's philosophy into types. Some are of realities we cannot know to exist, of course, but nevertheless cannot help but hope for or postulate (God is an example). Some have been used in metaphysical systems of the past but are the products of the misuse of reason, pushing reason beyond what can be grounded in sensations. As representative of yet another type, the "thing-in-itself" is transcendent, but there are arguments made by Kant, not considered valid by many people today, that the thing-in-itself can be shown logically, necessarily, to exist but without any specific knowledge of its nature possible.

4. This is Kant's term.

5. This remains arguably true after Einstein's paradigm-shifting work on the concepts of space and time, even though empirical measurements can show us whether or not space is curved; see Strawson, 1966, for an excellent discussion. However, there are philosophical ways to understand space and time without the concept of "transcendental." I reason I suggest thinking of transcendental conditions of possibility with the space and time example as a paradigm is not because space and time truly are transcendental categories but because it is relatively easy to get the general idea of transcendental conditions this way.

6. I got this definition from the online *Merriam-Webster* dictionary after reading lots of other online definitions that are basically the same. See http://www.merriam-webster.com/dictionary/empirical

7. I use the word "structure" deliberately, with a sense drawing upon three sources: linguistic and anthropological structuralism, cognitive and moral developmental structuralism, and the structuration theory of Giddens (1979). A structure is not a system although human social systems work through structures. Culture is not a structure; when we use the word "culture" a number of differentiable but related structures are referred to but I cannot go into details in this essay.

8. The idea of transcendental-like features of culture catches things best when thought of with Anthony Giddens's expression: "medium and outcome of action" (1979). They are not like a canopy under which people act, interact, and think; they rather only exist as instantiated over and over in human practices, including discursive practices and thinking. Thus they can drift, change without awareness or plan as do spoken languages over time. Their instantiation, moreover, can be thought of as tacit claims about the most basic structures of being-in-the-world—the "certainty" that Hegel discusses in terms of self-progressing forms of life, the topic of another section of this essay.

9. In the case of the feminist movement I know that the project of critique and activism is far from complete. The structures involving gender distinction in patriarchal form are not yet dismantled. But the feminist movement that gained much visibility during the 1960s and 1970s did change many people, women and men, significantly.

10. In the *Critique of Practical Reason* and related works, Kant addresses issues related to what I've listed. His work on moral-practical reason has important insights for critical theory, but I am not going to examine them in this essay. Instead I will examine implications of his concept of the transcendental unity of apperception in *CPR*.

11. There are a number of English translations of Kant's *Critique of Pure Reason* but when I quote Kant in this essay I am using the Norman Kemp Smith translation published in 1965.

12. Existentialism can be articulated through the subject-object framework only—arguably Buddhism and some of the teachings in yoga (but not all) and similar teachings/perspectives/philosophies result. Or it can be articulated through the subject-subject framework that usually results in monotheistic versions of existentialism, the necessary Other Subject to our human being represented in limit case form as God (see Barrett, 1962, for arguments that early Western forms of existentialism originated from the encounter of Greek rationalism with Judaic monotheism).

13. I am having difficulty in finding words that convey what happens when we *awaken* to the transcendental "I." I use "awaken," "notice," "intuit" but all of those terms can be misleading. We do not sensually experience the unity of apperception but, Kant's restrictions on the concept of experience aside, awakening to this unity definitely involves experience. We do not in any way experience this unity as an "it," as an experiential content, but our state changes when transcendental unity is noticed.

References

Barrett, W. (1962). *Irrational man: A study in existentialist philosophy.* New York: Anchor.

Brandom, R. B. (1994). *Making it explicit; Reasoning, representing, and discursive commitment.* Cambridge, MA: Harvard University Press.

Carspecken, P. F. (1996). *Critical ethnography in educational research: A theoretical and practical guide.* New York & London: Routledge.

Carspecken, P. F. (2003). Ocularcentrism, phonocentrism and the counter-enlightenment problematic: Clarifying contested terrain in our schools of education. *Teachers College Record, 105*(6), 978–1047.

Carspecken, P. F. (2006). Limits of knowledge in the physical sciences. In K. Tobin & J. Kincheloe (Eds.), *Doing educational research: A handbook* (pp. 405–438). Rotterdam: Sense.

Carspecken, P. F. (2009). Limits to knowledge with existential significance. In R. Winkle-Wagner, C. A. Hunter, & J. H. Ortloff (Eds.), *Bridging the gap between theory and practice in educational research: Methods at the margins* (pp. 47–62). New York: Palgrave Macmillan.

Carspecken, P. F. (2012). Basic concepts in critical methodological theory: Action, structure and system within a communicative pragmatics framework. In S. R. Steinberg & G. S. Cannella (Eds.), *The critical qualitative research reader* (pp. 43–66). New York: Peter Lang.

Csikszentmihalyi, M. (1991). *Flow: The psychology of optimal experience*. New York: HarperCollins.

Foucault, M. (1970). *The order of things: An archaeology of the human sciences*. New York: Vintage.

Foucault, M. (1979). *Discipline and punish: The birth of the prison*. New York: Vintage/Random House.

Foucault, M. (1980). *Power/knowledge: Selected interviews and other writings, 1972–1977* (C. Gordon, Ed.; C. Gordon et al., Trans.). New York: Pantheon.

Foucault, M. (1983). The subject and power. In H. Dreyfus & P. Rainbow (Eds.), *Afterword to Michel Foucault: Beyond structuralism and hermeneutics* (2nd ed., pp. 208–226). Chicago: University of Chicago.

Giddens, A. (1979). *Central problems in social theory: Action, structure and contradiction in social analysis*. London: Macmillan.

Habermas, J. (1968). *Knowledge and human interests*. Boston: Beacon.

Habermas, J. (1981). *The theory of communicative action; Vol. 1, Reason and the rationalization of society* (T. McCarthy, Trans.). Boston: Beacon.

Habermas, J. (1987). *The theory of communicative action; Vol. 2, Lifeworld and system: A critique of functionalist reason* (T. McCarthy, Trans.). Boston: Beacon.

Hegel, G. W. F. (1977). *The phenomenology of spirit* (A. V. Miller, Trans.). Oxford: Oxford University.

Hegel, G. W. F. (1991). *The science of logic* (A. V. Miller, Trans.). New York: Humanity.

Johnston, A. (2014a). *Adventures in transcendental materialism: Dialogues with contemporary thinkers*. Edinburgh: Edinburgh University.

Johnston, A. (2014b). Jacques Lacan. *The Stanford encyclopedia of philosophy* (Summer 2014 Edition), Edward N. Zalta (Ed.). Retrieved from http://plato.stanford.edu/archives/sum2014/entries/lacan/

Kant, I. (1952). *The critique of judgment* (J. C. Meredith, Trans.). Oxford: Clarendon.

Kant, I. (1965). *The critique of pure reason* (N. K. Smith, Trans.). New York: Macmillan.

Kant, I. (1993). *The critique of practical reason* (L. W. Beck, Trans.). Upper Saddle River, NJ: Prentice-Hall.

Kant, I. (2002). *Groundwork for the metaphysics of morals* (A. W. Wood, Trans.). Binghamton, NY: Vail-Ballou & Yale University Press.

Kim, J. (1993). *Supervenience and mind: Selected philosophical essays*. Cambridge: Cambridge University Press.

Kim, J. (2000). *Mind in a physical world: An essay on the mind-body problem and mental causation*. Boston: MIT.

Leibniz, G. W. (1890). *The philosophical works of Leibniz* (G. M. Duncan, Trans.). New Haven, CT: Tuttle, Morehouse & Taylor. Public Domain Archive & Reprints. Retrieved from https://archive.org/details/philosophicalwor00leib

Nisargadatta, M. (1973). *I am that; Talks with Sri Nisargadatta Maharaj* (M. Frydman, Trans.). Bombay: Chetana.

Priest, G. (2002). *Beyond the limits of thought*. Oxford: Clarendon.

Priest, G. (2005). *Towards non-being: The logic and metaphysics of intentionality*. Oxford: Oxford University Press.

Priest, G. (2014). *One*. Oxford: Oxford University Press.

Rosenblum, B., & Kuttner, F. (2011). *Quantum enigma: Physics encounters consciousness* (2nd ed.). Oxford: Oxford University Press.

Strawson, P. F. (1966). *The bounds of sense: An essay on Kant's 'Critique of pure reason.'* London: Methuen.

Vygotsky, L., & Luria, A. (1994). Tool and symbol in child development. In R. van der Veer & J. Valsiner (Eds.), *The Vygotsky reader* (pp. 99–194). Cambridge, MA: Basil Blackwell.

Xie, X., & Carspecken, P. F. (2008). *Philosophy, learning and the mathematics curriculum: Dialectical materialism and pragmatism related to Chinese and American mathematics education*. Rotterdam: Sense.

PART TWO

Critical Teacher Research in Urban Contexts

Introduction

Teacher Research, Urban Contexts, and the Emergence of the Critical from the Practical

P art 2 offers a look at teacher research (frequently called teacher inquiry), a form of action research conducted by one or more practitioners in their classrooms. It has long been advocated as an effective form of professional development—and has also long been criticized by critical theorists and pedagogues as a technical or practical form of action research seeking to find only "what works" in a classroom. For example, "If I do x, will students' reading test scores improve?" However, teachers can design action research projects serving critical—rather than or in addition to—utilitarian goals. And, as Kinsler points out in Part 1, classroom projects frequently dismissed as technical can be considered empowering in that students who are academically successful within the existing educational system gain valuable cultural capital.

An important second argument against dismissing technical classroom research is that it frequently evolves (perhaps as a common developmental progression?) into critical work. As Tripp pointed out long ago, teachers who undertake technical classroom research frequently encounter questions and difficulties in their work that lead them to recognize, and then to oppose, institutional and social forces working against the interests of their students:

> [F]ew teachers set out to embark upon a socially critical action research project. Rather, they tend to begin with projects that are of a technical or practical nature. They set out to deal with improving such matters as discipline, inquiry learning, spelling, and learning in heterogeneous classes, but ... they find socially critical questions emerge as they proceed. (Tripp, 1990, p. 164)

As they find their efforts limited or impeded by structural barriers, teachers frequently begin looking beyond the walls of their classrooms and asking very different kinds of questions. Part 2 offers several teacher research articles that illustrate this progression; two introductory articles set the stage for the teachers' work.

In the first of the stage-setting articles, Jennifer Esposito and Venus Evans-Winters argue in Chapter 7 that while all students need teachers who work against anti-democratic elements of schooling, the need for critical teacher researchers is particularly acute in urban contexts. The authors point out that, although many rural schools serve impoverished students, urban schools often serve students who are not only poor but who are also often members of racial, ethnic and language minorities. And, since the U.S. teaching force continues to be predominately white and middle class, they point to a likely cultural mismatch between teacher and urban students that often short circuits relationships and derails pedagogies. Moreover, many urban schools are under intense pressure to raise test scores, increase student attendance, and reduce dropout rates—and to do so despite a constantly changing roster of students, teachers, and administrators. In short, the urban context presents a host of challenges for both teachers and teacher educators. After detailing these challenges, the authors document their own successes and disappointments as teacher educators who assign action research projects in the interest of nurturing critical consciousness in their students.

Next, in Chapter 8 Eduardo Lopez—who mentored the featured teacher researchers—discusses his work with teachers in Los Angeles schools, where many of the challenges Esposito and Evans-Winters describe are common. Lopez speaks from a multilayered perspective: as a former urban student who experienced racism and classism during his own education and began resisting school in an effort to maintain personal dignity; as a former social studies teacher at an all-boys Catholic high school in the Watts section of Los Angeles; and as a teacher educator in UCLA's master's program in urban education, which requires students to complete critical action research projects in their classrooms. The stated mission of the program is to encourage K–12 teachers "to develop critical perspectives on teaching, curriculum, instruction, and the social, political, and cultural issues facing their schools and neighborhoods … [and to create] democratic classrooms, where the lived experiences of bicultural students are not only validated but also utilized to foster critical consciousness and social transformation." In discussing details of his program, Lopez highlights principles guiding his work, which can serve as guideposts for teacher educators who share his critical goals. Of course, since good teaching in any context incorporates some basic principles (such as respect for students), much of what Lopez discusses is also applicable to critical pedagogy outside the urban context.

The remaining articles in this Part 2 come from Lopez's students—the teacher researchers—who have varied backgrounds and teaching contexts. Each tells the story of an action research project undertaken in the urban master's program Lopez describes. Questioning what is lost when test scores alone drive teaching and learning, Jennifer Zapata in Chapter 9 reports on a project in her upper-elementary school classroom to employ literature circles as a way to insert relevance, enhance learning, and counteract the dehumanizing effects of a skill-and-drill environment, especially for English language learners. Among the several lessons she takes away from the project is that when a teacher trusts students enough to share power with them, important and surprising learning results as students "grow like vine tendrils—in unexpected directions and at their own rate." In Chapter 10, aware of inequity and other issues associated with high school AP courses, Rachel Klimke reports on her attempt to decrease competition and to promote intercultural communication among her students by introducing social justice topics into her AP world history class. She takes away from the project a deepened understanding of the way that mandated curriculum and testing serve to discipline teachers and students to stay within routines that preclude critical thinking; she also realizes that to effect substantive change, her efforts will have to turn toward school policy. In Chapter 11, dismayed by her third graders' acceptance of test scores as a meaningful measure of their intelligence, Nien N. Tran sets out to persuade them to see themselves and other members of their community as knowledgeable persons. As she works to transform their self-image, she develops a heightened awareness of other dehumanizing school routines; that awareness ultimately leads her to speak out against new behavioral protocols she describes as "an orange jumpsuit and metal shackles away from being in prison." The last of these master's papers comes from health educator Inga Wilder, who, in Chapter 12, undertakes revision of a high school health curriculum to make it more relevant to student needs. The project results not only in a better understanding of the students and the community but also in Wilder's firm conviction that school–community collaborations must be formed.

The work of these teachers across disciplines and grade levels stands as testimony to the transformative potential of critical teacher action research even in highly restrictive environments, and especially if it is thoughtfully mentored in teacher education programs. It also demonstrates how naturally teachers' critical gaze and their efforts at reform shift from the classroom to the school and community beyond. Overall, the work in Part 2 argues for the potential of teacher action research in classrooms to make substantive contributions to critical goals—in and beyond urban communities.

Reference

Tripp, D. H. (1990). Socially critical action research. *Theory into Practice, 29*(3), 158–166.

CHAPTER 7

Contextualizing Critical Action Research
Lessons from Urban Educators

Jennifer Esposito and Venus Evans-Winters

Background

The aim of this article is to call for an action research that is more applicable to teachers and teacher educators who teach in urban school communities. Many urban educators face challenges in their classrooms and school buildings that may appear to be beyond their pedagogical reaches. Therefore, if the purpose of teacher-driven action research is to define, study and change classroom practice, many practitioners may have ambivalent feelings toward engagement in meaningful action research. Furthermore, many urban educators may experience affective and palpable obstacles in the action research process. Although many of the challenges that we face in the millennium are related to the social and academic development of poor and minority students, very few theoretical frameworks have looked at critical approaches to action research that are specific to urban contexts and urban students. Consequently, teacher educators have to work in the realms of action research while designing a process that is more conducive to urban educators and the students and communities they serve. We address the following questions: How can action research be more applicable in urban contexts? How can action research be used in processes of urban education reform? How can educational researchers (both university faculty and teacher-researchers) continue to advocate for an action research that is critical, emancipatory and empowering to all stakeholders?

Introduction

Lisa was a white female English as a Second Language middle school teacher in an urban school, who wanted to improve her ESL students' attendance rates. Lisa was fairly new to the teaching profession, and was enrolled in my Master's level research course. I was excited about Lisa's study, because I thought she would ground it in the idea of difference since she had students from 14 different countries. Throughout the semester, I was continually disappointed in her journal reflections because they lacked attention to race and class. I had hoped Lisa would start her project by self-studying. How did her whiteness and her American citizenship affect her relationships with students and their parents? I thought this might be central to student attendance rates. I suggested Lisa spend time reflecting on this and I was astonished upon reading in her journal that she thought, 'Being a white female teacher has nothing to do with how I interact with my ESL students. The only impact I personally have is that I don't speak their language. Once students learn English, I will have an easier relationship with them.'

The above excerpt from one of the authors' reflective journals illuminates a problem both authors faced while teaching action research to teachers in urban school communities. As colleagues from different institutions, we shared our pedagogical struggles in teaching action research and worked together on solutions to enhance the experience for ourselves as teacher educators and the teachers whom we worked with in our educational research courses. As teacher educators, we both believe that issues of power, privilege and difference have to be central to educational research and believe action research should be empowering to all involved, especially the students and teachers who will immediately experience its possible effects. In our university classrooms, we had hoped to create an atmosphere where teacher-researchers became skilled in thinking 'critically and creatively, within a context that is built on a model of collaboration and mediation' (Marsh & Vagliardo, 2002, p. 288). The action research course offered the rare opportunity for teachers, especially urban educators, not only to examine their own classroom practices but also to voice their views about those practices and contexts in which they teach. Pedagogically, we believed our role in the action research process was to introduce teachers to the methods involved in this type of educational research and to help guide the teachers in the self-reflection process that has become an essential aspect of action research.

Using lessons from our experiences teaching urban educators, we address some of the challenges that teacher researchers and teacher educators may encounter during the research process, and we propose possible solutions that can lead toward empowerment for everyone involved in the action research experience. Drawing from these lessons we call for an action research that critically examines the intersections of race, class and gender as they relate to education as an institution (location) and as a process (a systematic series of actions directed towards some end). Both authors have personal and professional experiences teaching, researching and being schooled in urban school communities. As practitioners and instructors of action research, we utilized participant observation, journaling, course evaluations and analysis of student writings to reflect upon our experiences in teaching practitioners how to carefully journey towards action research.

We argue that attention to context is crucial to conducting empowering action research; therefore, it is appropriate for us to contextualize who we are as writers, researchers and educators. We are women of color, professors of educational research and social foundations, and advocates for those disenfranchised by structures of domination. As critical action researchers, we think that empowerment is an act of liberation. Similar to Freire (1970), we believe that education can free people from structures of domination. We also believe that critical urban action research can be a liberating and empowering act.

One author bases her experience in teaching action research from experiences teaching graduate courses at a midsize liberal arts institution in the Midwest of the United States. In order for teachers to qualify for admissions into the Master's-level education program, they had to have at least three years of professional teaching experience in the state where the university was located and be employed full time in a classroom setting. The cohort of students referred to in this paper were primarily made up of white female teachers, working in urban (central city) public schools, with a few teachers working in more rural or suburban contexts. The other author bases her discussion for this article on experiences teaching action research and other education courses in a Master's-level graduate program, located in the northeastern part of the United States. Like the first researcher, the students enrolled in her education action research class were also predominately white females yet had been teaching for at least one year in urban, suburban and rural school communities.

Both authors found that most of the educators enrolled in the courses identified as urban educators, even though some were teaching in urban communities reluctantly due to extenuating circumstances such as employment patterns or residential patterns. Admittedly, we viewed action research as an opportunity to open discussion about *how* where one taught might influence a teacher's approach to practice, perceptions and attitudes about students and families, and overall educational outcomes. We have come to the understanding from interaction working alongside educators from diverse settings that critical action research is a viable vehicle for understanding how educational policy affects one's views about teaching in certain social contexts, whether that context is urban, rural or suburban. Most of this understanding is derived from viewing firsthand what urban educators in our action research courses were not *willing* to examine or were not *allowed* to examine.

Action Research

Action research has been conceptualized in many different ways to many different people in the research community. Action research has been defined as the systematic collection of information that is designed to bring about social change (Bogdan & Biklen, 1992). In action research that utilizes the spiraling model, teacher-researchers are encouraged to identify a problem, systematically collect data, engage in personal and professional reflection, analyze the data collected, take action based on the data, and revisit the solution and original problem (Kemmis & McTaggart, 2000). In this type of action research, the practitioner deliberately and consciously examines classroom practices, curriculum and students' learning.

According to Mills (2003), the geographical locations and sociopolitical contexts where action research takes place have varied, but its primary goal in education is to focus on the development of the student. Even though here we acknowledge the contributions of Mills's work and the intent of the above statement, it is this *laissez-faire* attitude about the significance of context in action research that has presented challenges for us as teacher educators. The problems current conceptualizations of action research present are: (a) teachers' attitudes and perceptions appear to be separate from implementation of methods and modes of teaching (and research questions and topics); (b) teachers are viewed as objective beings simply participating in the act of teaching; (c) geographical location, political constraints and social and economic conditions are viewed as irrelevant to what students might learn and what teachers might teach; and (d) students are consequently taken as inactive agents in the learning process.

Even more, 'context aside' action research may unintentionally lead teacher-researchers to view students' learning outcomes and development as separate from larger social forces outside of the immediate classroom setting (i.e., location, socioeconomic status, institutional racism, deculturalization processes, etc.). Traditional action research frameworks place at the center of the action research process the classroom teachers' pedagogies, but with an even larger gaze on the student. For example, most teacher-research focuses on increasing student achievement (i.e., standardized test scores), improving student grades, and/or changing student behavior. It appears that, in their efforts at examining their own classroom practices, teachers often place many times the burden of change on their students.

Starting from the standpoint of liberatory educational practices, in our research courses we needed to re-examine what is the purpose of teacher research, in particular, action research. In addition, we needed to examine how might its meaning and purposes shift in different contexts, especially in those spaces occupied by marginalized individuals and groups. As teacher educators of urban educators, we did not have the luxury of ignoring the socio-historical context in which the teaching and learning process unfolded. When working from a social justice framework, disconnecting student development or teacher development, for that matter, from location and context, is too narrow a view of education and its purpose. Student development had to be witnessed/measured alongside the social, political, economic and historical conditions in which students and teachers were developing.

How do we focus on teacher empowerment in the research process without grounding the research rationale in student pathology? How do we encourage teachers to question their own assumptions about student culture without blaming teachers for the problems and challenges they face in their classrooms and school buildings? At what point in the action research process do we address how teachers' perceptions of students (and their families) affect teacher–student relationships and the teaching and learning process? Furthermore, how do we critically guide teachers in the action research process at a time when curriculum is being constrained by public policy and 'scientifically based' research? These are important questions not only for advocates of urban action research but also for those who embrace the possibility of the emancipatory function of education. In agreement with Noffke et al.'s (1996) discussion on multicultural education and action research, we believe that both have 'the capacity to be cooptive rather than transformational, when clear analysis of power and purpose are not embedded in their practices' (p. 171).

Critical Approaches to Action Research

One of the most celebrated volumes to examine critical action research was *Becoming Critical*. Carr and Kemmis (1986) discussed three kinds of action research with critical action research intending to emancipate people. Although their book was groundbreaking, it was not without its flaws. Noffke (2005) articulates one of these flaws:

> A huge flaw in the Carr & Kemmis work, while not often audible to 'white' scholars 20 years ago, was very prevalent in the scholarship of women and other non-dominant groups. This has to do with what has been referred to as identity politics, in particular, gender and 'whiteness' studies, and what these might mean in relation to both the substance and process of educational practice. A major point of this is that the role of teacher is again in need of careful definition. Identity matters. (p. 324)

This means, then, that action research has to take up issues of race, ethnicity and gender. We cannot conduct research outside of these contexts. Noffke (1994) is careful to point out how placing action research within current epistemologies may make it less critical because privileged standpoints might be further reified.

To begin to create a critical urban action research that met our needs and the needs of our students and their communities, we turned to the tenets of critical social theory and postmodern theory. According to Kincheloe and McLaren (2000):

> a critical social theory is concerned in particular with issues of power and justice and the ways that the economy, matters of race, class, and gender, ideologies, discourses, education, religion and other social institutions, and cultural dynamics interact to construct a social system. (p. 281).

Critical social theory examines processes and relationships of domination and oppression, whereas postmodernism provides the analytical tools to (re)examine ideas of metanarratives, universal truths and rational objectivity. In education, postmodernism advocates for research that challenges the 'taken-for-granted assumptions of daily classroom life and presenting truths that are relative, conditional, situational, and based on previous experience' (Mills, 2003, p. 6). A critical research informed by postmodernism understands that individuals' view of themselves and the social world is influenced by social and historical forces (Kincheloe & McLaren, 2000). Critical action research proposes that all educational research should be democratic, equitable, liberating and enhancing (Mills, 2003). More specifically, critical action research entails the following components:

- Participatory and democratic.
- Socially responsive and takes place in context.
- Action research helps teacher researchers examine the everyday, taken-for-granted ways in which they carry out professional practice.
- Knowledge gained through action research can liberate students, teachers and administrators and enhance learning, teaching and policy making. (Adapted from Mills, 2003, p. 8)

Again, while we agree with Mills's conceptualization of critical action research, we add a critical lens that forthrightly examines the intersection of race, class and gender and believe the intersection in every possible aspect must be central to critical action research. We also believe critical action research must not fear difference or change, and must extend its focus to include fostering change outside of the school building. The only way to ensure that action research continues its goal of social change is to implement research that is context specific, critical, reflexive and democratic. There is also a need for an action research that specifically and deliberately considers the context in which teachers teach, especially those who teach in politically and socially isolated contested spaces, probably urban and rural school communities. Carr and Kemmis (2005), in evaluating their earlier work, argue for a critical action research that is continually 'reinterpreted and reconstructed' (p. 355) to meet changing needs of stakeholders. Drawing from our experience teaching educational research to white middle-class women working in urban public schools, we argue that now is the time to reinterpret and reconstruct critical action research to fit particular urban contexts.

Focusing on Urban Context

Although we are aware that rural schools face some of the same challenges as urban schools, we believe that urban educational contexts have a common particularity that is not necessarily present in rural education contexts. There exists a more likely cultural mismatch between teachers and students in urban contexts in the United States than exists in rural or suburban schools. Such a cultural mismatch means misunderstandings are more likely as students and teachers try to navigate across racial/ethnic borders. Because whiteness is normative and many schools propagate white middle-class cultural values, urban students of color continually negotiate practices, policies and expectations that may be unfamiliar, different or culturally incongruent with their everyday realities (Nieto, 1992; Ladson-Billings, 1994; Miron, 1997; Noguera, 2003; Kincheloe, 2004; Evans-Winters, 2005). It is for this reason that we argue for attention to the urban context. Of course, urban contexts can be as varied as the people who live within them. We recognize each research context is distinctive in its own right. There are, however, some commonalities (like cultural mismatch) within urban settings that necessitate a critical urban action research approach.

For example, teachers in the United States who teach in public urban schools are more likely to teach in high-poverty neighborhoods and in school communities with low test scores, high dropout rates, high mobility rates and high absentee rates (Fine, 1991; Wilson, 1996; Anyon, 1997). Also, urban educators are more likely to be responsible for teaching racial/ethnic and language minorities (Nieto, 1992; Gay, 2000; Noguera, 2003) while working in school districts with high staff and administrative turnover rates (Noguera, 2003). Those same urban educators are more likely to teach in a school that has been labeled as a 'failing' school under the U.S. government's federal mandates. During the action research process, teachers have to take into consideration the set of circumstances or social facts that will affect the teaching and learning process and the research itself. It is the teacher educator's responsibility to guide the teacher-researchers in the process of contextualizing the research problem, as it relates to the socio-political conditions that affect positive educational development.

Furthermore, research supervisors may have to learn to accommodate those teachers who teach in urban settings. Below is a reflection shared by one of the authors that emphasizes the obstacles that urban teacher-researchers and university faculty may experience when working in urban school communities:

> One of the biggest struggles I face in teaching action research is how to make my course relevant and appropriate to my urban educators. In the city I teach in, the majority of schools are 'failing schools', according to the U.S. federal government. The administration is under pressure by the district and state to raise test scores. The urban educators I've taught have complained that they are either being given scripted lessons that have little room for change, or they are being pressured to teach with repetitive

worksheets in the hopes that repetition will raise test scores. These educators have very little flexibility with or control of their pedagogical choices. This means that the very premise of action research, 'to effect change' is not a realizable goal for many of my urban educators.

Both authors have had experience supervising teacher-research projects that were scrutinized by the local school district or building principals, because the proposed project did not meet the requirements of 'scientifically based' research as defined by the U.S. government's No Child Left Behind educational policy. As it has been explained, teachers are not allowed to adapt curriculum or introduce curriculum in a school that has been labeled as low performing. The district is required to only use curriculum or teaching material that has been 'researched' (often by researchers not connected to the community) and shown to be effective in raising student test scores.

The next example demonstrates one instructor's efforts to advocate for her urban educators and the 'spirit' of action research:

> I went to the school district and inquired more about what type of research projects teachers who taught at a 'low-performing' school were allowed to implement in their classrooms. After being told again, that practically no new material or methods could be introduced, I asked if the district could benefit from having their already chosen curriculum evaluated by actual classroom teachers. I was told 'yes', as long as the currently used material was not adapted in any way. Because many of my teachers were justifiably not excited (and frustrated) about studying already in-place curriculum, I convinced a few to not only study if a certain curriculum was effective or not effective with their particular group of students, but also to study their own, students', colleagues', and parents' personal feelings about the enforced current curriculum.

In the above example, the teacher-researchers learned not only that sometimes researchers cannot choose the type of research questions they ask or problems they must study but also that research is inherently context specific. Both examples show how context directly and indirectly shapes the research process. The examples also illustrate how a basic premise of action research, to effect change, is often incompatible with urban educators' goals and responsibilities. To address this issue, we quickly learned to encourage our teacher-researchers to study what is already being implemented in classrooms across the United States and begin to understand their effectiveness at the local levels.

Our Own Pedagogical Choices Examined

As feminist instructors, we both strive to be student centered. To this end, we always make changes to our syllabi and approaches after we reflect on the work of each semester in the hopes of improving student experience and enhancing student learning. We each utilize a practitioner-oriented action research textbook but supplement it with readings that we find help engage students in the development of a critical consciousness and an understanding of alternative approaches to action research outside of the traditional practitioner project. Our courses are similar in format, content and structure to the course described by McKernan (1994) with the exception that we encourage a critical consciousness around issues of race, class and gender within the teaching and learning of action research. In both programs, the teachers have one semester to implement their research projects, and like McKernan (1994) we believe our students would be better served by a two-semester course because of the time constraints inherent in learning methodology and method as well as completing an inquiry cycle. Because it is not possible to change the semester format of the courses we teach, we spend the initial class periods discussing the history of and various approaches to action research. We have students begin their projects as they continue to learn about data collection and analysis. Such an approach entails flexibility on the part of us, as instructors, but also on the part of students. We also strive to create a trusting relationship with our students so they will feel supported as they begin an endeavor fraught with uncertainty (see Esposito & Smith, 2006).

To create trust in a short period of time, we offer our time in terms of face-to-face meetings about project topics, struggles and progress, a sympathetic ear and constructive written comments on assignments. We require students to keep a reflective journal. We read and assess the journal over the course of the semester. We also utilize research groups (students are given time each class period to work with the same group of students, who offer ideas and additional support for individual projects). As researchers invested in urban public education, we see our students as change agents, and we see ourselves as conduits for change. Often we have the resources and authority that come with being positioned as university faculty that we willingly share.

We struggle with the notion of how to encourage change without disempowering our students. For example, once after a class on participatory action research (PAR) and Tripp's (1990) conceptualization of socially critical action research (SCAR), one of the authors struggled with ways to encourage teacher researchers to work for social justice within the confines of their school districts:

> My students seemed so passionate about and attracted to the empowering aspects of PAR and SCAR but the discussion soon turned to claims that social justice was not within their reach. As part of a small group activity, I asked them to design a SCAR project and they created thoughtful and important research questions. Treneka was the first to present her group's design. She prefaced it by saying that this project would not be feasible in the urban district she taught in. I saw the majority of the class nod their heads. Her district utilizes a proscriptive school reform model as a way of trying to increase student test scores. The school reform models leave little room for pedagogical choice. Betsy stated that she wanted to do a SCAR project but feared she would lose her job because such a project would mean she would have to deviate from her scripted lessons. The majority of the class chimed in. Disheartened and frustrated, they complained about their situations and refused to view SCAR or PAR as viable options.

After validating the students' frustration, strategically the discussion was moved toward the topic of how teacher researchers can utilize SCAR or PAR given the constraints they face. Students were encouraged to become the change agents they thought they could be upon entering teaching. A few of the students tried and created projects that included some form of social justice as the ultimate aim. As an example, one student created a PAR project to enhance community literacy. The high school students he taught served as tutors for adults in the community who wanted to learn to read for the first time or to read English as a second language.

As reflective practitioners, we are constantly exploring ways our courses could be improved to better meet the needs of our urban educators. We have found that exercises geared toward developing a critical consciousness about race, class and gender oppression enable our students to see action research as an approach to emancipation for themselves, their students and the communities within which they teach. As an example of such an exercise, one course instructor required her students to ride the public transit system from the south of the metropolitan area to the north. During this ride, students see the changes that occur due to racial and socioeconomic stratification across neighborhoods that are really only 10–15 miles apart.

Another example directly related to teaching action research and understanding its role in the research process is evidenced below:

> Students were told to research, using current school district data, government census data, and school report cards the demographic make up of their classroom, school building, neighborhood and school district. After gathering such data, students were required to report that data to the entire class. The teachers reported feeling shocked at the discovered similarities and differences across contexts. For example, the rural and urban teachers shared the common reality of the number of students living below the poverty line, as measured by those receiving free and reduced lunch. However, the urban teachers reported having higher mobility, suspension and expulsion rates. Interestingly enough none of the teachers was surprised to discover that the school districts they worked in were very segregated by race. Yet, white teachers in rural and suburban communities were more likely to work (and live) with white

students, while white teachers in urban schools were more likely to teach black students. After gathering and reporting these observations, the teacher-researchers began themselves to put possible race and class differences at the center of their analyses.

Critical Lenses

Even in the example above, it is still necessary to be careful that teacher-researchers do not fall into cultural-deficit models of thinking. For instance, teachers are typically pushed to find fault as they articulate a research problem or rationale for the study. Who is pushing them to find fault? The influence of positivist paradigms on action research encourages instructors and teachers to begin research questions with the premise that there is a problem (hence the term research problem). Usually action researchers follow up the question 'What is the research problem?' with the question 'What may be causing the problem?' It has been our experience that teachers usually find fault with their students' ways of learning or the ineffectiveness of their own teaching strategies. However, through a critical approach to urban action research, it is not enough to simply find fault with issues such as students' lack of learning, inability to learn or lack of motivation. Moreover, it is not enough to find fault or point the finger at the ineffectiveness of the teacher's teaching methods. All of these issues occur in particular contexts and, thus, the fault finding extends beyond teacher and student. For example:

> Becky, Jeff, and Janice taught at an alternative school, serving middle and high school students. The school was located in the middle of the city, across from a low-income housing project. The student population was made up of majority African American low-income students, who had been expelled from the local school district's regular public schools, due to violent behavior or persistent insubordination. The alternative school was the court's and district's method of giving these youth a second chance at education, with the possibility of entry back into the mainstream student population. The three teachers admitted that their students did not readily trust them. Often white authority figures were viewed as the enemy by these children who had negative experiences with white school personnel, social workers, and police officials.

> Because of students' perceptions of teachers, the teacher-researchers decided to develop and implement a research project that focused on increasing student attendance and classroom participation, and decreasing negative student behavior, by first changing their own behavior and attitudes toward their students. First the teachers developed a pretest that assessed students' perceptions of their teachers' attitudes toward them. Next, the teachers developed an action plan that required them to use more positive language throughout the day to their students in the classrooms and hallways, and more frequent (e.g., weekly notes) positive communication to the parents. Their findings showed that student negative behavior decreased, while classroom participation and attendance increased over time. Post-tests also revealed that students' perceptions of their teachers were more positive at the end of the study. Even more important to critical action research, the teachers reported that their own attitudes and behaviors in the classroom positively changed, even after completion of the study.

There is no doubt that, to be less strict and verbally aggressive in an alternative school setting, like the one described above, requires some risk for the students and teacher-researchers. Teachers and students run the risk of being viewed as 'soft'. However, as the example illustrates, to be engaged in critical research requires some risk. Depending upon how one thinks about risk, it can be either an exciting endeavor or something to fear. Teachers must turn a critical lens upon themselves, their perceptions and their pedagogies. Furthermore, they may also have to look, through a critical lens, at administrators, community members, city officials, taxpayers, other teachers, curriculum developers, policy makers or even university faculty. Being an advocate of change in an educational system that refutes innovation and supports the needs of the dominant elite is a fearful endeavor. Consequently, doing so for the purposes of a grade in a Master's-level course may even raise the stakes for teacher-researchers. Nevertheless, we have encouraged our educators to understand all the dynamics of education as a social and cultural institution.

We have both struggled with the aspect of risk taking in our own teaching and research and, thus, we try to empathize with our teacher-researchers who fear risk. The fear our teacher-researchers face is real. It is difficult and uncomfortable, for example, to turn a critical lens on oneself. For instance, how am I implicated in the racism, sexism and classism that structure the institution I teach in? How does my own identity privilege me? How does who I am shape what I believe about my students? We personally believe that all of us, regardless of race, class and gender, are implicated in structures of domination. Because we have multiple identities, we may be simultaneously privileged and oppressed. Therefore, we believe that everyone involved in the process of action research (including university faculty who teach it) must engage in tough personal examinations. These personal examinations are crucial to critical action research, but they are examinations that make us painfully aware of power, difference and social justice.

As stated above, we have both struggled with risk taking in our own research and teaching. As untenured faculty members, we negotiate continuously how to stay true to our own beliefs but also simultaneously survive the 'publish or perish' mandate and secure 'good' teaching evaluations. The arguments we make in this article are arguments that we stress in our courses. We aim to teach action research methods in a contextualized manner. This necessitates a more in-depth focus. In other words, we require our teacher-researchers not only to design and carry out an action research project but also to examine and negotiate the cultural, social and historical forces that structure and shape their research projects. Because of these requirements, we have heard refutes in class or read evaluation comments that reported that our course expectations were too high and did not consider the teacher's schedule and responsibilities outside of class.

More specifically, the students complained about the feasibility of reflective journal writing, reporting that it was time consuming and they did not necessarily see its relevancy to what they do in the classroom. In the teachers' words, journaling 'took time away from their children'. Practitioners of action research (Noffke et al., 1996) have noted that sometimes teachers and university faculty may have similar objectives in the action research process but may also have different views about the utility and purposes of action research.

At the end of the academic year, we have also received comments such as 'not everything is about race and class.' Sometimes these comments do foster anxiety, because we worry how such teaching evaluations will be received. Nevertheless, we continue to look for ways to teach critical action research in ways that empower educators and their students enough that meaningful change can occur. We agree with Elliott (2005), who argued that 'becoming critical is not enough to become empowered as a change agent' (p. 362). While we want to encourage our teacher-researchers to become critical, we also need to find ways to empower them to continue to advocate for social justice.

We encourage teacher-researchers to look at the micro-level and macro-level forces that impact on the teaching and learning experience. Utilizing this approach, a critical urban action research moves teacher-researchers away from a focus on outcomes (i.e. baselines), which is grounded in positivist thinking, to more in-depth understandings of the immediate and larger contexts in which they teach. Critical urban action research should be characterized by careful evaluation and judgment of the social forces that have contributed to the social construction of urban schooling and the resulting positive and negative consequences that play out in the classroom and/or school building.

Reflexivity

It is expected during the action research process that teacher-researchers examine their own practices and beliefs and how they affect the teaching and learning process. In essence the teachers themselves become a part of the 'object' or subject of study. By definition, reflexivity should be an automatic impulse. Reflexivity is nearly taken for granted in critical action research. The critical researcher views it as a part of ethical practice to examine and re-examine her/his role in perpetuating and combating the *status quo* as it relates to social life. Action research with urban school teachers may not be as impulsive as it purports. Even when urban schools do not fit the blighted social conditions described previously, it has been found that the media, politicians and researchers distort the public's perceptions of public urban schools and their students (Payne, 1984; Miron, 1997). It is very difficult to argue that these negative portrayals do not also distort teachers' perceptions of who they teach, where they teach and whom they work with on a daily basis. In fact, it has been our experience that these perceptions creep into the action research process even when teachers believe they are being reflexive.

For example, one of the author's students, a young white woman teaching in an urban school, hoped to complete her action research project on ways to improve her students' 'lack of social experiences'. When the author inquired about what she meant by 'lack of social experiences', the student explained 'my students have never gone to a museum, been to a zoo or even planted a flower. They are missing all of the experiences we had as children'. Below, the author recounts how she handled the situation:

> When Lindsay told us her students lacked social experiences, I really wasn't sure what she meant. At first, I thought it might be a new education buzz word. When she explained, I could feel myself tightening up. The kids she was talking about were similar to me. I didn't feel I lacked social experiences. I tried to explain to Lindsay that just because the students didn't have the experiences she had as a child, did not mean they 'lacked social experiences'. I told her that I had never planted a flower in my life and I did not attend a museum until I became an adult. I hoped my comments did not offend her or make it seem as if she put me down, but her comments did sound so disparaging and displayed a lack of knowledge about cultural difference.

This was a clear example of negative perceptions about urban students affecting the approach to action research. Because a teacher-researcher's research questions are strongly grounded in how he/she perceives his/her ability to change or engage in the problem he/she raises in her study, it is imperative that he/she is also guided by the research facilitator to consider all the possible personal, social, political, economic, cultural and historical conditions that may impact the teaching and learning process. This pursuit and discovery process may be a daunting and uncomfortable task for most urban teachers, because the students are no longer seen as simply a part of the problem. Students in fact, like the teacher, may be victims (or survivors) of the problems that exist in many urban public schools and communities. Then the ultimate goal of urban action research is to figure out how to aid teachers, parents and students in becoming resilient and/or resistant under such social conditions, thus helping make education a liberatory practice (Freire, 1970; hooks, 1994).

Democratic

Work with urban educators may require more advocacy on the part of the university instructor and the teacher-researcher. Practitioners involved in action research engage in the process of inquiry in the hopes of solving an educational problem. Action research is reflective in nature (Arhar et al., 2001) and involves holding a mirror up to cultural and social practices that are part of our everyday lives. This paradigm intends to blur the boundaries between the researcher and the researched whereby both stand to gain from the process as well as the product of the research. Thus, empowerment for teachers and students should be inherent in action research. In addition, interpretive action research allows the expert knowledge of the researcher/practitioner to stand alongside the knowledge and experiences of those 'Others' who are implicated in the research setting (Stringer, 2004). This is especially essential in instances when the social and/or cultural background of the researcher differs from that of the research participants, as is the case in many urban schools.

For some reason, even those teachers who teach in high-performing schools continue to focus on aspects of student behavior. In one group of elementary school teachers' action research projects, for example, the teachers maintained that students in their classrooms simply did not know how to behave in the classroom. The following discussion stresses the point.

> As they argued, while attempting to 'state the problem', their low-income students simply did not know how to behave in middle class schools. Somehow our course readings and discussions on how American schools are reflective of white middle class values, transferred into black children simply cannot conform to the rules of white middle class teachers. Instead of focusing on how to change the cultural climate of the school to meet the social and cultural needs of the students, the teachers decided to develop and implement a project that served to change and mold the students into more disciplined-bodies (Foucault, 1984). Two of the teacher-researchers involved in the research project were third grade teachers, and the other teacher was a fourth grade teacher. Their school building was operated by a private company that was financed by the local school district. The company referred to their schools' discipline protocols as behavior modules.

> As a part of the action plan, the teacher-researchers were to tally negative student behavior displayed in the classrooms, such as talking out of tern, leaving one's seat, etc. for a given period of time. The next step in the action plan was for each teacher, over a period of time, to review each day at the beginning of class, the behavior modules or school rules. The teachers during this time period recorded daily the number of undesirable student behaviors. In the action research project, they concluded that there was a significant decrease in unwanted student behavior, during the observation period. This project was disappointing for at least three reasons: (1) the teachers never questioned the motives of the company's uniform behavior modules; (2) Furthermore, no one questioned the long-term consequences of instilling unspoken obedience in children who are a part of marginalized social groups; and (3) the teachers did not find it necessary to ask the students or parents their perceptions about the school rules and what purposes they might possibly serve in the role of student growth and development. It was taken for granted that the school's rules, and relationships within the school, functioned to serve the needs of the students.

Currently, as it stands, action research has a strong focus on empowering and motivating teachers. Traditional research has been purported to be on and about teachers without actually engaging practitioners in the research process. Schools and teachers have been described as being on the 'receiving end of manufactured research products' (Quigley, 1997, p. 3). Very few supporters of action research have questioned the role of the student in action research. Most action research focuses on university researchers, teachers, principals, community members, and curriculum consultants (Kemmis & McTaggert, 2000). We argue that teacher-researchers should strive to empower themselves and their students through the democratic process of action research. For example, in the case above, because the school's standardized test scores were found to be in compliance with federal and state guidelines, the teachers may have overlooked a rare opportunity to involve students in the process of reflecting on the purposes and possible outcomes of classroom and school expectations of behavior. Obviously, based on the original purpose of the project, students must have been resisting the stated school rules.

We have found in teaching action research that most teacher-researchers are taught through conventional texts on action research to focus on their experiences (i.e. what worked or did not work in a classroom setting), needs (i.e. an extra teacher in a reading classroom) and wants (i.e. a decrease in negative student behavior). Very little attention in teaching and implementing action research appears to focus on the student needs. In fact, it seems that teachers and institutions of higher education are embracing action research for its feasibility and immediate usefulness to (suburban) teachers. While, as advocates of action research, we believe that it can be utilized to empower teachers, we also believe students need liberation as well. Urban education provides a site rife with social and cultural differences. Many of our current preservice teachers and advanced-level teachers are preparing to teach in urban locales. Those of us who teach action research to these groups of educators have the advantage of forwarding a more progressive action research, which critically examines issues of domination and oppression. It is up to us to ask action researchers to critically examine how they negotiate the many raced, classed and gendered identities of themselves as well as their research participants.

Conclusion

Given that, in many educational settings, students are embedded within institutions that uphold Eurocentric middle-class values, how can researchers who are implicated in these values be sure they are interpreting experiences from multiple lenses? For instance, Delgado (1996) cautions that 'false empathy' is a condition by which a 'White (person) believes he or she is identifying with a person of color, but in fact is doing so only in a slight, superficial way' (p. 12). This type of false empathy can hinder action research in that it limits the liberatory process of understanding the different perspectives of those involved in the research process, and thus restricts the ways in which practices can be improved and changed. We argue that courses on action research need to incorporate attention to issues of race, class and gender. Such attention will help create action research projects that are more emancipatory and critical. By making visible relationships of power, we believe that the research produced will be more likely to effect change for students, especially historically marginalized students, than research produced by researchers who continue to take for granted such relationships. Such educational reform is one way to empower all stakeholders involved. Also, by not including students' voices in the research process, socially and politically contested classrooms continue to be sites of differentiated power instead of sites of transformation and resistance. Action research that ignores systems of power relationships and student voice sustains the teacher as knower and the student as receiver of knowledge. A more critical contextualized action research would consider how to involve students and teachers, while advocating for both to understand hegemony and domination in context.

We have argued that action research in urban educational settings in particular can be useful, but the researcher/practitioner must proceed with caution. Because the interrogation of race and racial domination should be at the forefront of educational research with dominated people (Duncan, 2002), it must be incorporated into the teaching of action research at the university level. By way of conclusion, we will present a framework of urban action research.

We propose a critical urban action research that is characterized by the following:

1. puts students' needs first;
2. pays particular attention to social and cultural contexts of students' lives;
3. is participatory and strives to include students and parents; and
4. requires that the practitioner continually reflect on his or her assumptions including but not limited to assumptions about the contexts in which they teach.

We believe that research faculty can pedagogically engage teacher-researchers in urban action research by (1) engaging teachers in urban communities; (2) having teachers interact directly with urban adolescents; (3) implementing programs/curriculums with urban residents (at school, in the community, etc.); (4) encouraging teacher-researchers to be more reflexive; (5) teaching educators to evaluate the effectiveness of their own programs/curriculums; and (6) encouraging teacher-researchers to become more familiar with urban education and social science literature. In actuality, the above model is useful for most teachers and teacher-educators who teach and research across race and class differences (i.e., rural educators). Such a contextualized action research experience holds the possibility of meaningful empowerment for all stakeholders.

It is worthwhile to report here that one of the above-mentioned school districts actually threatened to break all ties with the university the teachers were enrolled in during the action research course. The school district threatened not to honor the teachers' original contract, which promised to reimburse teachers for any courses related to teacher development and promotion. According to school officials, it was impossible for teachers to meet the research requirement, and the university's research agenda was not in alignment with the school district's policies and goals. This issue was eventually taken up by the teacher's union and has not been recently discussed publicly. Apparently, context has become even more important under the current political climate. We are in the midst of cultural wars, where students and teachers alike are being objectified for others' political gains. Therefore, we call for a critical action research that extends metaphorically beyond the classroom and into the very political and social spaces that (re)produce and (re)structure teacher and student identities. We must acknowledge that context plays a significant role in student and teacher development and therefore should play an even bigger role in the types of action research questions and topics proposed and implemented.

References

Anyon, J. (1997). *Ghetto schooling: a political economy of urban educational reform* (New York, Teachers College Press).

Arhar, J. M., Holly, M. L. & Kasten, W. C. (2001). *Action research for teachers: traveling the yellow brick road* (Upper Saddle River, NJ, Merrill Prentice Hall).

Bogdan, R. C. & Biklen, S. K. (1992). *Qualitative research for education: an introduction to theory and methods* (2nd edn) (Boston, MA, Allyn & Bacon).

Carr, W. & Kemmis, S. (1986). *Becoming critical: education, knowledge and action research* (London, Falmer Press).

Carr, W. & Kemmis, S. (2005). Staying critical, *Educational Action Research, 13*(3), 347–357.

Delgado, R. (1996). *The coming race war? And other apocalyptic tales of America after affirmative action and welfare* (New York, New York University Press).

Duncan, G. A. (2002). Critical race theory and method: rendering race in urban ethnographic research, *Qualitative Inquiry, 8*(1), 85–104.

Elliott, J. (2005). Becoming critical: the failure to connect, *Educational Action Research, 13*(3), 359–373.

Esposito, J. & Smith, S. (2006). From reluctant teacher to empowered teacher-researcher: one teacher's journey toward action research, *Teacher Education Quarterly, 33*(3), 45–60.

Evans-Winters, V. (2005). *Teaching black girls: resiliency in urban classrooms* (New York, Peter Lang).

Fine, M. (1991). *Framing dropouts* (Albany, NY, SUNY Press).

Foucault, M. (1984). in: P. Rabinow (Ed.) *The Foucault Reader* (New York, Random House).

Freire, P. (1970). *Pedagogy of the oppressed* (New York, Continuum).

Gay, G. (2000). *Culturally responsive teaching: theory, research, & practice* (New York, Teachers College Press).

hooks, b. (1994). *Teaching to transgress: education as the practice of freedom* (New York, Routledge).

Kemmis, S. & McTaggart, R. (2000). Participatory action research, in: N. Denzin & Y. Lincoln (Eds) *Handbook of qualitative research* (2nd edn) (Thousand Oaks, CA, Sage Publications).

Kincheloe, J. L. (2004). Why a book on urban education?, in: S. R. Steinberg & J. L. Kincheloe (Eds) *19 urban questions: teaching in the city* (New York, Peter Lang).

Kincheloe, J. L. & McLaren, P. (2000). Rethinking critical theory and qualitative research, in: N. Denzin & Y. Lincoln (Eds) *Handbook of qualitative research* (2nd edn) (Thousand Oaks, CA, Sage Publications).

Ladson-Billings, G. (1994). *The dreamkeepers: successful teachers of African American children* (San Francisco, CA, Jossey-Bass Publishers).

Marsh, M. M. & Vagliardo, M. (2002). The commingling of teacher researcher identities: a mediated approach to teaching action research, *Educational Action Research, 10*(2), 275–289.

McKernan, J. (1994). Teaching educational action research: a tale of three cities, *Educational Action Research, 2*(1), 95–112.

Mills, G. E. (2003). *Action research: a guide for the teacher researcher* (2nd edn) (Upper Saddle River, NJ, Merrill Prentice Hall).

Miron, L. (1997). *The social construction of urban schooling: situating the crisis* (Cresskill, NJ, Hampton Press).

Nieto, S. (1992). *Affirming diversity* (New York, Longman).

Noffke, S. (1994). Action research: towards the next generation, *Educational Action Research, 2*(1), 9–21.

Noffke, S. E. (2005). Are we critical yet? Some thoughts on reading, rereading and becoming critical, *Educational Action Research, 13*(3), 321–327.

Noffke, S. E., Clark, B. G., Palmeri-Santiago, J., Sadler, J. & Shujaa, M. (1996). Conflict, learning, and change in school/ university partnership: different worlds of sharing, *Theory into Practice, 35*, 165–172.

Noguera, P. (2003). *City schools and the American dream: reclaiming the promise of public education* (New York, Teachers College Press).

Payne, C. (1984). *Getting what we ask for: the ambiguity of success and failure of urban education* (Westport, CT, Greenwood Press).

Quigley, B. A. (1997). The role of research in the practice of adult education, *New Directions for Adult and Continuing Education, 73*, 3–22.

Stringer, E. (2004). *Action research in education* (Upper Saddle River, NJ, Merrill Prentice Hall).

Tripp, D. H. (1990) Socially critical action research, *Theory into Practice, 29*(3), 158–166.

Wilson, J. (1996). *When work disappears: the world of the new urban poor* (New York, Alfred Knopf).

CHAPTER 8

From Disillusionment to Hope
Bicultural Practitioner Research

Eduardo Lopez

As a young child I would often leave my Los Angeles home to spend my summer vacations with my grandmother in Mexico City. I always looked forward to these trips because I knew each one would hold new wonders for me. Determined that I would learn Mexican history and culture, my grandmother and aunts arranged visits to museums and other Mexican states; time and again I returned from such visits amazed by what I had learned. In fact, I still vividly remember the day I visited Mexico's National Museum of Anthropology and first saw the Aztec stone of the sun: a monolithic 12-foot, 24-ton sculpture that stands as testimony to Aztec mastery of geometry and mechanics. Emotionally overwhelmed, I started to cry at the realization my ancestors had built this ancient artifact.

Imagine my disappointment, and confusion, when I asked my fourth grade teacher when the class would study the history of Mexico and heard her respond that Mexico had no history worth studying.

Despite the very best efforts of my family to instill a strong cultural identity, my schooling experiences taught me to feel ashamed of and confused about my Mexican heritage. These feelings persisted throughout elementary and secondary school, and they intensified when I entered the University of San Francisco (USF), where I tried very hard to erase my past and fit in to my new environment. I joined a predominately white fraternity; I asked everyone to call me Ed instead of Eduardo; and, I tried my best to speak "standard" English. However, my trips back home to East Los Angeles and Mexico City constantly reminded me of the richness of my history and culture. These experiences made me feel schizophrenic. I constantly felt at war with myself—an experience richly captured in W. E. B. Du Bois' (1897) concept of "double consciousness":

> It is a peculiar sensation, this double-consciousness, this sense of always looking at one's self through the eyes of others, of measuring one's soul by the tape of a world that looks on in amused contempt and pity. One ever feels this two-ness,—an American, a Negro; two souls, two thoughts, two reconciled strivings; two warring ideals in one dark body.

Eventually, in an effort to sort out my ongoing struggle, I joined a program at USF called the Phelan Multicultural Community.

Each year, a group of 24 students was selected to spend a year living together exploring topics such as multiculturalism, intercultural communication, and cultural diversity. Throughout the year speakers were invited to discuss issues explored in our course readings. One of the speakers who came to campus was Antonia Darder, a critical education scholar. In preparation for her talk, we read Darder's *Culture and Power in the Classroom: A Critical Foundation for Bicultural Foundation* (1991). As I read, I became fascinated with the concept of biculturalism, which she defines as the process:

> wherein individuals learn to function in two distinct sociocultural environments: their primary culture, and that of the dominant mainstream culture of the society in which they live. It represents the process by which bicultural human beings mediate between the dominant discourse of educational institutions and the realities that they must face as members of subordinate cultures. More specifically, the process of biculturalism incorporates the different ways in which bicultural human beings respond to cultural conflicts and the daily struggle with racism and other forms of cultural invasion. (p. 48)

Up until that point of my life I did not know it was possible to adopt a bicultural identity. For nearly two decades, I had been ashamed of my own skin, language, and cultural background because my schooling experiences had been subtractive (Valenzuela, 1999). Reading Darder's work was a tremendously powerful and liberating experience. Finally, I had language to name what I had experienced in schools. Bicultural theory helped me to understand I could retain my primary cultural identity and work toward challenging racism and other forms of marginalization. Realizing the frustration, anger, and shame that the assimilation process had caused me, I made it my goal to learn more about my history and the larger socioeconomic conditions that negatively impacted the schooling of bicultural students like me. I committed my efforts to doing everything I could to spare other young people the conflicted youth I had lived.

This goal led me to enroll in a doctoral program at Claremont Graduate University, where I studied with Professor Darder and learned how to implement a critical bicultural pedagogy. Over subsequent years, I have worked to implement this pedagogy in a wide variety of educational contexts: after-school programs, college outreach programs, an all-boys Catholic high school, adult education programs, and postsecondary institutions.

UCLA's Master of Education in Urban Teaching Program

This breadth of experience has served me well in my work with the Teacher Education Program (TEP) at UCLA. Founded in 1992 as a two-year master's and credential program, TEP has an explicitly critical intent. Founded on the principle of social justice and a commitment to integrating theory and practice, coursework consistently situates the act of teaching within a moral, cultural, and political context (Oakes, 1996). TEP specifically prepares urban public school teachers to have the commitment, capacity, and resiliency to promote social justice and develop caring and nurturing spaces in working-class, urban schools. Since 1994, TEP has developed a national and international reputation for developing high-quality teachers who are motivated and driven to work in urban public school settings—and who are effective in them.

My work with TEP includes coordinating its Master in Urban Teaching program. Started in 2010, the program seeks to sustain and support the growth of urban public school teachers with two or more years of experience. Designed as a rigorous four-quarter program (summer, fall, winter, and spring), the program works to help K–12 teachers develop critical perspectives on teaching, curriculum, instruction, and the social, political, and cultural issues facing their schools and neighborhood communities. Opposing the view of teachers as technicians who should simply implement scripted curriculums and strategies, the program seeks to empower teachers to create culturally democratic spaces in which the lived experiences of bicultural students are not only validated but also used to foster critical conscious-ness and social transformation. The program argues that if teachers are to radically alter existing systems of inequality in urban public schools, they must: challenge internalized biases and develop an awareness of how these impact their practice; carefully listen to the voices of bicultural students and their families; understand the dual nature of schooling as a site that both reproduces inequality and fosters liberation; and, learn to link their practice with theory. Guided by the theoretical frameworks of critical bicultural pedagogy and teacher research, the program seeks to develop in teachers a sense of hope and possibility, a sense that conditions in urban schools may be not only challenged but also transformed.

Each year the program admits a cohort of 15–20 urban public school teachers. Candidates are selected based on having two or more years of teaching experience at schools that serve historically under-represented communities. Such schools are typically ethnically and linguistically diverse; in ad-dition, most of their students are enrolled in free or reduced lunch programs and are academically underachieving. Experience suggests that many candidates apply because they find that neither their previous credentialing programs nor their school districts provided them with understandings and tools to work effectively with working-class students of color. Other candidates have become sensitive to in-equity and apply to the program hoping to deepen their knowledge of social justice and to find ways to develop more equitable pedagogy in pursuit of a more equitable world. Most are tired and frustrated of being told over and over again to implement lessons that their students find irrelevant and, thus, resist. They yearn to see teaching as an intellectual endeavor and dream of creating classroom spaces that are humanizing.

The following course sequence is essential in our efforts to help teachers realize their goals.

Summer

- Race and Education (4 units)—examination of the role of race in educational policy making and how schools contribute to racial stratification and inequality.
- Ed454A: Action Research: Collaboration in Change (4 units)—examination of teacher re-search and action research methodology.

Fall

- Ed 454B: Action Research: Collaboration in Change (4 units)—second course in three-course sequence on learning how to do and use action research.
- Ed 498A: Teaching Seminar (8 units)—students meet with instructor to debrief field experi-ences and continue study of curriculum, instruction, and assessment issues.

Winter

- Ed 420A: Principles of Curriculum (4 units)—critical examination of basic concepts underly-ing determination of objectives, selection, and organization of learning experiences, and evalu-ation process.
- Ed 498B: Teaching Seminar (8 units)—second course in three-course sequence where students meet with instructor to debrief field experiences and continue study of curriculum, instruc-tion, and assessment issues.

Spring

- Ed 454C: Action Research: Collaboration in Change (4 units)—third course in three-course sequence on learning how to do and use action research.
- Ed 498B: Teaching Seminar (8 units)—third course in three-course sequence where students meet with instructor to debrief field experiences and continue study of curriculum, instruc-tion, and assessment issues.

Elective

- Students complete a minimum of one graduate-level elective course (4 units) before the end of the academic year. Most students chose to enroll in Ed466: Critical Media Literacy. The course prepares educators for teaching K–12 students to explore their relationships with media, technology, and popular culture by critically questioning different types of representations and creating their own alternative media messages. Media representations of race, class, gender, sexual orientation, and other identity markers are explored. Educators critically question media and technology as well as explore alternatives for creating multimedia messages in their own classrooms.

Summer: Developing Critical Questions

In a policy environment that has done much to define the role of teacher as technician (Giroux, 2012), the first goal of this master's program is to help teachers redefine themselves as public intellectuals. The program's strategy centers on engaging students with individual research projects, in part to foster within them the understanding that they need not be passive recipients of information but instead can themselves become researchers and change agents: they can become public intellectuals. Because their work lives are busy, complex, and exhausting, we know that few teachers have time built into their schedules for planned, intentional, and systematic reflections (Dana & Yendol-Silva, 2003). The first course of the sequence, then, Ed 454A Action Research: Collaboration in Change, not only introduces the transformative goals of critical action research but also explains how intellectual work can be built into a work schedule that already feels overwhelming.

Within the course, teachers take the first step toward bicultural, critical action research by exploring Cochran-Smith and Lytle's (1992) definition of teacher research as "systematic and intentional inquiry about teaching, learning, and schooling carried out by teachers in their own school and classroom" (p. 27). This action research framework allows teachers to develop questions based on their own curiosities and to engage in a yearlong process of collecting and analyzing data, identifying and reflecting on findings, and sharing their findings with others (MacLean & Mahr, 1999).

As the advisor on their teacher inquiry projects, I caution teachers not to structure their projects in a way that would reinforce asymmetries of power and privilege. This caution has become increasingly important as more teachers who enter the program come from schools and teacher education programs that focus narrowly, and often exclusively, on raising test scores. While current federal policy means that teachers often face the practical challenge of raising test scores in their school environments, the program works to help teachers understand that the emphasis on testing is entwined with much larger social, political, and economic issues that impact urban schools. Public schools are not neutral institutions.

To nurture an understanding of schools as sites of political and cultural struggle, class discussions pose questions like the following:

- What are the functions of schools in a capitalist society?
- What are the experiences of working-class students of color in urban schools?
- What is the relationship between power and knowledge?
- How can education become a vehicle to improve conditions in urban spaces?
- What role can teachers play in helping students become change agents?

To help teachers reflect on these questions and develop critical frameworks for their action research projects, they read the most recent edition of the book that so transformed my own thinking, Darder's *Culture and Power in the Classroom* (2012).

In the book, Darder outlines eight essential principles of critical bicultural pedagogy:

1. Schooling both reproduces inequality and is a space for liberation.
2. Schooling is the foundation for learning about participating in a democratic society.
3. Teachers should work toward mediating, reconciling, and integrating the lived experiences of bicultural students into the curriculum in an effort to retain primary culture and also work to transform the dominant society.
4. Teachers should reinforce the home and school relationship.
5. Teachers should provide opportunities to learn in one's own primary language.
6. Teachers should work to change the educational style of the school through greater parent participation.
7. Teachers should develop student voice (the process of providing opportunities for students to enter into dialogue and engage in a critical process of reflection from which they can share their thoughts, ideas, and lived experiences with others in an open and free manner).
8. Teachers should challenge racism, sexism, and homophobia in the classroom.

After discussing and reflecting on these principles, teachers refine their original ideas for the research question so that they focus on disrupting inequality in their classrooms or schools.

For example, an initial question a middle school math teacher asked at the start of the summer course was, "Why do my students not turn in homework?" This question essentially casts the teacher as authority charged with maintaining traditional classroom routine and defines the role of the students as simply doing what they are told; whether the homework activity is meaningful or relevant, or what other responsibilities working-class students assume when the school day ends are made irrelevant by such assumptions. The processes of dialoguing with classmates, reflecting, and reading theory led the teacher to transform the apparently simple—but ideologically charged—question about homework to two questions that instead recast the teacher's responsibility to design meaningful educational experiences. The initial homework question was rewritten: "How can I integrate a problem-posing pedagogy into my classroom to make instruction more relevant to my students' lives and to increase student participation?" and "How can I help students understand mathematics as a useful tool to challenge oppressive aspects of their world?"

Fall: Learning How to Systematically and Critically Observe the Classroom

In the fall quarter candidates enroll in Ed 454B, Action Research: Collaboration in Change. In the second course in a three-course sequence on action research theory and methodology, teachers focus on developing their ethnographic skills. Teachers are asked to keep a journal and write at least two or three observations a week about their practice or student interactions. Cochran-Smith and Lytle (1992) argue:

> Similar in some ways to ethnographic filed notes, journals capture the happening with students in their classrooms and what this means for their continued practice. Furthermore, because journals stand as a written record of practice, they provide teachers with a way to revisit, analyze, and evaluate their experiences over time and in relation to broader frames of reference. (p. 26)

Similarly, William Ayers (2010) argues that recording observations allows teachers to "look unblinkingly at the way children really are and struggle to make sense of everything that we see in order to follow along and to teach them" (p. 46). Journals not only provide teachers a record of events they can analyze to better understand both their own and their students' experiences and classroom habits, but they also nurture the habit of ongoing analysis of classroom life. Class discussions stress in particular the importance of striving to understand students' learning, perspectives, and lived experiences.

To practice such analysis and begin moving toward building a conception of teachers as a collegial professional community, teachers periodically share journal selections with small groups, discussing what prompted them to write about a particular observation and what insights they are developing as they capture classroom life in their journals. Although observational data collected from the journals helps teachers to gain valuable insights into their focus questions, class discussions insist that analysis move beyond describing events and also include theoretical reflection. If teachers are to work toward understanding the web of political, social, and economic interests shaping schools and classrooms, they need to grapple with the complexity of theory.

Darder (2012) argues that to create liberating classrooms, teachers must develop not only a language of description but also a language of theory because all human activity requires theory to illuminate it.

> The language of theory constitutes a critical language of social analysis that is produced through human efforts to understand how individuals reflect and interpret their experiences and, as a result, how they shape and are shaped by their world. Although it is a language generally connected to the realm of abstract thinking, its fundamental function of praxis cannot be fulfilled unless it is linked to the concrete experiences and practices of everyday life. Such language also encourages the use of more precise and specific linguistic representations of experience than is generally expected—or even necessary—in the course of everyday practice. (p. 107)

Participants in the program are therefore asked to identify theories that help explain what they are observing in the classroom and to ask themselves how these theories help deepen their understanding of issues around the specific question each is studying.

Winter: Aligning Theory with Action—Praxis

Having spent some time critically observing, analyzing and understanding the issues that impact their classrooms, in the winter quarter teachers enroll in Ed 420A: Principles of Curriculum and begin to design curriculums that address their inquiry questions and are explicitly aligned with the critical theories that they have been examining. Praxis is critical at this stage because it represents "an approach to social change in which interventions (actions) are grounded in the best available theories, and theories are amended based on the careful evaluations of the results of interventions" (Schurman, 2007, p. 38).

Curriculum plans are developed in two stages. The first stage asks teachers to reimagine their practice through a social justice framework. The following questions from Ayers (2010) are used to help teachers assess their ideas as they explore possibilities for action.

1. Are there opportunities for discovery and surprise?
2. Are students actively engaged with primary sources and hands-on materials?
3. Is productive work going on?
4. Is the work linked to student questions or interests?
5. Are problems within the classroom, the school, and the larger community part of the student consciousness?
6. Is work in the classroom pursued to its furthest limits? (pp. 104–105)

The second stage asks teachers to identify relevant theory/research that supports the proposed curriculum plans. Class discussions stress that if teachers are to understand teaching as intellectual work, they need to move away from only using the language of practice and instead adopt the language of praxis—understanding how practice informs theory and theory informs practice.

Throughout the first few weeks of the quarter, teachers with interests in a particular issue or topic are organized into small groups, in which they provide important support and resources for each other. Collectively, teachers brainstorm and share lesson plan ideas, discuss theory, provide critical feedback, and help select appropriate data to be collected.

Once implementation of the curriculum plans begins, teachers reconvene in these small groups to discuss what they notice about student engagement and the evolution of their plans. The following questions are used to facilitate discussions: What are the successes and challenges you have experienced? What specific examples/evidence from your journals illustrate these reflections? Do you see any need to make modifications to your plan? If so, what needs to change? Why? I believe it is critical to make the possibility of change as the plan unfolds explicit, so that teachers experiencing difficulties will not define themselves or their projects as *failures*. If the teachers are truly to change their classrooms and the world beyond, then they must have every encouragement to persist as teacher researchers long after the program ends. Therefore, every potential discouragement must be assiduously avoided. Making clear that research frequently unfolds much differently than the researcher originally planned helps to demystify the action research process and to promote the teachers' conceptions of themselves as researchers and intellectuals.

Spring: Analyzing the Data, Determining Findings, Reflecting on the Future

For many novice researchers, data analysis is the most daunting element of the research process. At the end of the year they have collected large amounts of data and are overwhelmed with attempts to find patterns, insights, and new understandings from the data. Therefore in Ed 454C, the last course in the three-course sequence of action research, activities related to analysis are highly scaffolded to provide both a supportive audience and supportive feedback. Participants bring to class examples of data to share and examine with a partner. Each teacher initiates discussion of the data by answering the following questions:

1. Why did you choose this particular form of data collection?
2. What were you hoping to understand?
3. What specific evidence supports your conclusions?
4. How do your conclusions help you reflect on the theory used to design the action plan?

After this presentation by one partner, the other provides feedback by answering the following questions:

1. Are your partner's conclusions supported by the data presented?
2. Is your partner's discussion of theory connected to conclusions drawn from the data?
3. What additional insights can you share about your partner's data?

The first person listens to the feedback and shares closing reflections:

1. What did I learn from my partner that was interesting or surprising?
2. What new perspectives did my partner offer about my data?
3. How did the yearlong research process impact my growth and understanding of what it means to work for social justice?

At the end of the discussion, the second person shares his or her data and the cycle of questions begins anew.

Ending the Cycle: Publication

Teachers in the program are required to present their teacher research projects at a yearly conference organized by TEP in June. The purpose of the conference is for participants to share their findings beyond the members of the cohort. Teachers are encouraged to invite students, colleagues, administrators, and loved ones. Each time I watch and listen to the presentations, I am filled with admiration and humility for the work teachers in the program have done in rethinking their pedagogy and transforming their classrooms. This process is often not easy because it requires them to look inward. Despite their progressive politics, they often knowingly or unknowingly have played a role in reproducing oppressive practices. One teacher reflected:

> Doing this inquiry was as much about searching for a math curriculum as it has been about uncovering the beliefs, attitudes, and theories that guide my teaching without me knowing it. As much as I envisioned myself to be an activist, a social justice teacher, a feminist ally, an anti-racist/anti-capitalist; this whole process has helped me look at who I envisioned myself to be and who I was in the classroom. It revealed the oppressive structures, practices, and beliefs that I had replicated in my classroom, which I had no intention of creating, and forced me to consider how my own positionality influences every decision and thought daily.

Rather than feeling overwhelmed and powerless from these reflections, teachers felt the inquiry process empowered them and gave them hope to challenge oppressive practices at their schools:

> The inquiry process has truly helped me be the teacher that I am today, the person I am today. It has given me a foundation in which I am able to build on and experiment with. It provides me hope in a world of hopelessness. Inquiry has given me the courage to push back against the hegemonic structures of the school system. Inquiry has forced me to reflect upon my practice and truly create transformational change in my classroom. It has helped me to understand that change comes from within and no matter the circumstances we are up against, with inquiry (reflection and action), I can and will fight the good fight!

Living in Hope

It is perhaps the worst of times in terms of educational context for we educators pursuing social justice in our classrooms and our world—and yet, in my own journey from confusion through theoretical reorientation to my current efforts to nurture other critical educators, it is perhaps the very best of times. The special moments I experience with program graduates at each annual conference allow me to remain hopeful about the fate of public education in Los Angeles and the nation. Despite the neoliberal agenda of restructuring and defunding public schools, the teachers in the Master in Urban Teaching Program are fully committed to improving conditions at their school sites. They are tired of working with scripted curriculums and having their students defined only in terms of their test scores.

I feel privileged to work with them in their efforts to intervene in a reductionist system that insists on pronouncing students to be failures because they reject meaningless instruction and assessment designed primarily to ensure that they do not in fact escape the dismal future elite powerbrokers have in mind for them. I believe that Darder's (2012) bicultural theory and the teacher research process help provide an escape route for marginalized students by allowing their teachers to:

- Have a better understanding of the implications of the neoliberal educational reform on the education of working-class students of color.
- Connect teaching with the lived experiences of students.
- Develop confidence in implementing a social justice framework in their pedagogy.
- Understand the importance of reflection, observations, and theory in growth as a social justice educator.
- Take actions against oppressive practices.
- Remain hopeful that conditions in urban schools may be transformed.

The following chapters are four examples of teacher research projects from the 2011–2012 cohort. These projects stand as a testament to the type of dedication, humility, and honesty with which all the teachers in the program engage. They represent windows into the yearlong process of learning how to listen and integrate effectively the lived experiences of children and young people into the classroom. This journey could not have been undertaken without a profound love for bicultural students and their families and a commitment to an emancipatory practice of classroom life—one that transforms our old disillusionments into hope.

References

Ayers, W. (2010). *To teach: The journey of a teacher.* New York: Teachers College Press.

Cochran-Smith, M., & Lytle, S. (1992). *Inside/outside: Teacher research and knowledge.* New York: Teachers College Press.

Dana, N. F., & Yendol-Silva, D. (2003). *The reflective educator's guide to classroom research: Learning to teach and teaching to learn through practitioner inquiry.* Thousand Oaks, CA: Corwin Press.

Darder, A. (1991). *Culture and power in the classroom: A critical foundation for bicultural education.* New York: Bergin & Garvey.

Darder, A. (2012). *Culture and power in the classroom: Educational foundations for the schooling of bicultural students.* Boulder, CO: Paradigm Publishers.

Du Bois, W. E. B. (1897). Strivings of the Negro people. *The Atlantic.* Retrieved from http://www.theatlantic.com/magazine/archive/1897/08/strivings-of-the-negro-people/305446/

Giroux, H. A. (2012). The war against teachers as public intellectuals in dark times. *Truthout.* Retrieved from http://truth-out.org/opinion/item/13367-the-corporate-war-against-teachers-as-public-intellectuals-in-dark-times

MacLean, M. S., & Mohr, M. M. (1999). *Teacher-researchers at work.* Berkeley, CA: National Writing Project.

Oakes, J. (1996). Making the rhetoric real: UCLA's struggle for teacher education that is multicultural and social reconstructionist. *Multicultural Education, 4*(2), 4–10.

Schurman, S. (2007). Labor deserves credit: The popular education foundations of the national labor college. In P. Finn & M. Finn (Eds.), *Teacher education with an attitude: Preparing teachers to work with working-class students in their collective self-interests.* Albany: State University of New York Press.

Valenzuela, A. (1999). *Subtractive schooling: U.S.-Mexican youth and the politics of caring.* Albany: State University of New York Press.

CHAPTER 9

Teaching Beyond the Skill and Drill

Reimagining Curriculum and Learning in a High-Stakes Testing Environment[1]

Jennifer Zapata

Introduction

Sometimes I cannot help but wonder, after particularly hectic weeks at my charter school, what my fourth- and fifth-grade students will remember about their school year with me. Ten years from now, will they understand that I wanted to give them thoughtful memories about themes or ideas that they can connect to their own lives? Will memories of our discussions about the Trayvon Martin case reemerge in a different classroom someday? Will I have helped my students build a deeper understanding of the larger issues embedded in our society through my current decisions in curriculum, assessment choices, and instruction? These questions and others have been negotiating themselves with the other questions that arise from working in a test- and data-intensive work environment. My concern for my students' well-being, my desire to sustain their enthusiasm for learning, and my commitment to strengthening their positive self-perceptions led me to my research focus on creating and validating more meaningful learning experiences for my students, who are also confined within a high-stakes testing environment.

As an upper-elementary school teacher, I am aware of the role I play in preparing my students for more rigorous academic expectations as they get older each new school year. More and more, I have witnessed how standardized testing and data results have become normal aspects of evaluating our youngest learners, especially in charter school settings. Since this type of data measures certain markers of achievement and success, at times students and teachers find it useful to work with quantitative data. Such data also serves a practical purpose for administrators, who cannot be inside our classrooms at all times to see the continual progress that students make every day academically and socially. They cannot be tasked to read the writing drafts of a class of students in order to see how each person has challenged his or her previous barriers. Perhaps a student is taking more risks in her writing, or is finishing a draft up with a smile instead of in tears of frustration. Quantitative indicators of student achievement can offer quick, informative data on our students—but they certainly do not capture it all.

Despite the known weaknesses of standardized assessment, when testing is the primary basis for evaluating students it transforms the school culture so that every minute of every day becomes focused on test scores. This pervasiveness of standardized, data-driven decision making in the classroom is what led me to question the exclusivity of quantitative assessment in my charter school. If this was the predominant form of making inferences about students, their abilities, and teacher quality, I questioned what was being left out. What are we losing when we lose sight of other forms of understanding and discovery? What can we gain from adopting student-centered, qualitative forms of evaluation and instruction? Finally, how can we make these transformative changes not only co-exist but effectively counteract the effects of the mandated high-stakes testing agenda driving our charter school organization?

To be clear about terms, I intend "high-stakes testing" to mean any test that has substantial consequences or is used as the basis of a major decision for its stakeholders. In the context of an educational setting, these stakeholders can include the individual students, their teachers, class, school, and/or district. They are high-stakes tests because they are used in making decisions about which students will be promoted or retained in a grade level. They carry significance in the decisions that districts make regarding which schools they keep open, threaten to shut down, or eventually close. Due to the No Child Left Behind Act, high-stakes tests also affect teachers, their reputations, and their job prospects, as test scores are increasingly adopted (or mandated by state legislation) as key components of teacher assessment systems.

In addition, standardized data have been used to drive instructional practices, curriculum, and accountability for students, teachers, and schools (Diamond & Spillane, 2004). However: one primary form of evaluating how much a student has grown or how much dedication a teacher has shown is simply not enough. There are many other ways students can show growth, and I began to realize that my school's current practices, left unquestioned, were doing long-term, concealed harm to my students and their perceptions of how knowledge is validated and how learning takes place. Drawing on McLaren, Darder (1991) offers teachers a powerful warning about the effects of not challenging hegemonic forces in our classrooms:

> Given this view, teachers practice hegemony when they fail to teach their students how to question the prevailing social attitudes, values, and social practices of the dominant society in a sustained, critical manner. Thus, the challenge for teachers is to recognize, critique, and attempt to transform those undemocratic and oppressive features of hegemonic control that structure classroom experiences in ways that are not readily apparent. (McLaren, 1985, p. 88)

Despite the defeat that I have felt alongside my co-workers—who also question the rigid testing culture and its consequences—Darder introduces the idea that we might not be as powerless as we think. True, weekly and quarterly multiple-choice assessments would still have to happen, and data walls with public numerical rankings of standardized results would still be present in my classroom. Administration would still rely on benchmark scores and, eventually, California State Test (CST) results to determine which staff will be returning next year. But as Darder openly contends, this is a challenge to find a way to transform these oppressive spaces into inspiring ones. It is one that asks us as educators to understand the larger role that we play in a community's self-liberation, beginning with its children.

I have already seen the heartbreaking effects that come from extending the school's test-obsessed culture into one's own classroom. Students see themselves as categories; as numbers; as colors on a benchmark scale. They learn to measure their intelligence and their worth through a set of questions that were neither constructed with them in mind nor will actually ever capture all the potential of their minds. What Darder asks us to do as educators is to reclaim the classroom as a space where learning happens in a variety of forms. Even if my classroom contains the markers of a hegemonic construction of "student data," it also contains counter-hegemonic, qualitative evidence that students are growing and learning. As I began planning my project, I became excited about applying this notion of transforming my classroom into a space where student learning is active and enriched with opportunities to work outside the constraints of a standardized system of right and wrong.

School Context and Background

A better understanding of the plan I devised and a fair presentation of the constraints affecting my teaching require a closer look at the context of my classroom. For the past year and a half, I have worked for Century Charter Schools, a charter organization serving urban, low-income neighborhoods. My school serves a predominantly Latino and immigrant family base (87%), but it also has a significant representation from Filipino/other Asian/Pacific Islander families (7%) (http://www.education.com). Our school is located in a residential neighborhood, where most students live within walking distance of the school. Last year, the school's first CST score impressed the other Century schools by reaching an Academic Performance Index (API) of 933 out of a possible 1,000 (grades 2–5) straight out of the gate. The precedent that this has set for our current teachers and students (including many who are new and unfamiliar with last year's culture) has affected our own expectations for measuring success, especially in the context of our overall Century Charter school culture's emphasis on high test scores—itself linked to the No Child Left Behind Act. While that legislation continues to be hotly debated by various stakeholders, the reality is that it has affected how schools and communities approach teaching and learning. Schools have no choice but to pay attention to the law—including charter schools, whose performance is being regularly scrutinized by educational researchers.

Like many schools responding to current climate and constraints, my school has a streamlined system of weekly, quarterly, and yearly assessments, which all aim to keep student and teacher accountability high. Viewed from one perspective, this system of detailed pacing plans for computer and classroom curriculum and assessments is a practical method of monitoring performance on No Child Left Behind metrics. In many ways, it is a privilege to work in a school where the top administration is at least attempting to meet the performance goals set forth in the law, even if the law itself is questionable in its expectations and assumptions about what counts as "equitable" education. Yet the numbers-based, uniform approach to teaching and learning and the tyranny of test scores kept me not only frustrated but also worried about the kinds of teaching and learning being pushed out of my classroom.

This was my reality as a Century Charter School teacher in Los Angeles in 2012.

The Plan

I wanted to focus on an area that I felt was at an inherent position of conflict with the multiple-choice standard format of most high-stakes testing models. Also, I felt that by focusing on English-language arts (ELA) in a class with mostly English-language learners (ELLs), I would be able to better serve their needs, since I was not succeeding using the school's curriculum. My primary plan was to introduce literature circles for a class novel. I had seen literature circles in other classrooms and had read about their benefits to students, including their potential to improve literacy and a love of reading among students. Anderson and Corbett (2008) found literature circles to be "ideal for increasing oral language, reading, and writing achievement in a supportive, collaborative learning environment" (p. 25). Literature circles also appeal to me because they are designed to extend over weeks and months, and they offer many opportunities for cross-curricular connections. Compared to the weekly stories from our Houghton Mifflin anthology, a class novel gives students a chance to see the character and plot development unfold more naturally and to appreciate more substantive literature than an abridged version of a story. Such circles also give students a chance to work within a small group in a deliberate way and rely on each other for new information, questioning, and discoveries about the text. In short, literature circles serve as a teaching tool that focuses on the student's growth in self-confidence in literacy with the direct support of their peers.

For our class novel, I used Pam Munoz Ryan's *Esperanza Rising*. The story is about a young and wealthy Mexican girl named Esperanza, who essentially goes from "riches to rags" and faces adversities as she immigrates to America during the time of the Great Depression. She starts the story as the spoiled and privileged daughter of a generous and rich landowner. As events begin to worsen for her and her family, she confronts a lot of wake-up calls about reality, and themes of poverty, immigration, and racism begin to emerge. Overall, it is a very student-friendly portrait of a girl's journey into a stronger self, and I like how relatable it can be for my students, who have diverse ethnic, immigration, and socio-economic backgrounds (although mostly Latino immigrant backgrounds). To help spark student discussions, I used a chapter-by-chapter *Esperanza Rising* Reading Guide from a Teach for America Resource Exchange website (http://tfanet.org), which offered short-answer and interactive prompts that asked students to make connections between the novel and themselves, other texts, and the world and society at large.

There were several modifications that took place as the project progressed. Most notably, I originally planned to have our class novel completed in a few weeks, imagining that we would meet regularly and finish within a given time frame. However, the combination of pausing for benchmarks and other curriculum, along with our own needs to slow down and explore the major themes, made our literature circles extend well after the planned weeks were over.

The second major modification came from the unexpected addition of several qualitative, imaginative approaches to teaching the curriculum. Although the central focus of my plan was to incorporate literature circles into an otherwise regimented curriculum, I began to explore how to make other English and language arts topics, and later, science curriculum, come alive to my students. This led to the addition of smaller projects, namely newspaper study sessions, figurative language plays, and more hands-on experiments that connected to our science classes.

Data Collection

My data collection methods were primarily qualitative. I observed student dialogues at every literature circle session and recorded notes on them in a teaching journal. In addition, I collected students' individual literature journals as well as group reflection sheets, where groups recorded the larger themes emerging in their discussions. I also supplemented my data collection with occasional video recordings of certain groups, in order to transcribe their word-for-word interaction about a certain chapter, reaction, or other point of discussion. By the end of the planned six-week time frame, I had collected a diverse group of student data that highlighted students' growth as readers, writers, and speakers in a way that had yet to be seen in their ELA standardized testing results. As for the other, smaller projects that grew out of my original action plan, I collected several samples of student work (including, for example, scripts from figurative language plays and reflection sheets) and pictures as well as video recordings of their work in action.

Emerging Understandings

Before this action plan, I had never done literature circles in my classroom. I had been to professional development workshops and read online resources about their benefits to students, but I always felt too intimidated to jump in the water for myself. But I am really glad that I did because it was my first conscious step into purposefully seeking to challenge the assumptions I had been taught to make about "student data." As an alumna of the non-profit program Teach for America, I came into the teaching profession understanding student data only one way—quantitative calculations about student mastery. At the end of each year as a corps member, I would nervously anticipate my meetings with my program director, because I knew the goal was for my class to reach 80% or above on their end-of-year assessments. I never really understood how this was supposed to happen, and even if it did, what this truly meant for my students. In many ways, like many other teachers, I never fully got to challenge the assumption that these multiple-choice assessments were thoroughly representing what my students were capable of, or even how much I taught them that year. Even if I were to have asked my program director these questions two years ago, I wonder what she could have responded with. Comparing my experience at Teach for America to the one at my current charter school, I see and hear much of the same defensive rhetoric surrounding standardized, high-stakes testing.

I have thought a lot about the lack of room for questioning in the quantitative system being prioritized and privileged. But as Paulo Freire (1970) says in *Pedagogy of the Oppressed*, "No oppressive order could permit the oppressed to begin to question: Why?" (p. 86). I think now that when high-stakes testing is so closely tied to our children's self-perceptions as "smart" or "dumb" students, it is crucial to question the exclusive privilege that quantitative markers hold in our understanding of student success. Once I began to ask more "Why?" questions in my classroom and curriculum, I saw more student engagement, participation, and changes in relationship dynamics.

My choices for data collection meant that I had made a conscious effort to seek out student data that relied heavily on written reflection, observation, and dialogue. Initially, I presumed that students' literature journals would primarily reflect conclusions drawn from group sessions. As it turned out, the literature journals showed students' individual abilities to summarize what they were reading and to make insightful predictions or conclusions about events happening in the novel. I also had originally assumed that the entries would include personal connections between the story's events and real-life situations—and that the larger themes, heated discussions, and instances of symbolism and figurative language that I heard and observed students make in their literature circle group talks would be carried over into their written entries.

I realized later, however, that I had never explicitly taught or modeled such habits, so it was presumptive of me to think that they would happen as purposefully as I hoped for. This taught me that even as I steered the class agenda to a more free-form, written-response direction, I had actually held on to similar expectations to those of multiple-choice assessments. Specifically, I wanted there to be a certain type of reaction to the text, in the same way that I imagined students "getting it" versus "not getting it" in my head. It made me think about how as much as I wanted to reflect on seeing "how" my students were learning and showing me evidence of their learning, I was still resisting the possibilities that students will grow like vine tendrils—in unexpected directions and at their own rate. This initial new understanding helped me see how ingrained the ideology behind high-stakes testing can be, even when I actively tried to reinterpret ways for students to show their learning in more meaningful ways. With this in mind, I made a point of seeing their written reflections as part of their portfolio of growth, and I spent more time sitting in and listening to focus groups during their discussions.

Here is where I began to see another insight begin to emerge. The student trios, selected at random with some discretion, went through some struggles while working together, providing me with some insight into how literature circle time changed their relationships with one another. During my sit-in observations and recordings of two selected focus groups, I captured dialogues and behavior that were as much a part of their learning as the content of the book. Although these two groups were not the only trios that faced internal conflicts with each other while trying to read and discuss the novel, these two groups contained students who already struggled with behavior and social relationships. Also, both groups (subsequently referred to as Group A and Group B) had the dynamic of two relatively high-performing, academically strong females, with one male student. Both male students have histories of resisting classroom expectations; they have academic potential but do not always show commitment or responsibility. While on the surface this is what other students see, the truth is that there are deeper issues that cannot be disclosed here still developing and affecting both male students. But the general dynamics from both groups during literature circles often became negative due to the conflicts arising between the two girls and the boy in each group.

There were times when I heard the dialogue move from sharing to interruptions and to refusals to read or participate. For Group A, the conflict would mostly become about choosing where to sit during literature circles. Students spread out around the room, and the male student in that group would often choose a location without consulting the other two students. There was a clear power struggle happening, and the two girls, who are generally not outspoken in the classroom, struggled to affirm their position to him about taking turns on deciding where to sit. Observing this conflict occurring repeatedly, I itched to step in and assign the group a permanent seating place to stop the arguing. But against my inclination, I decided to let them work it out themselves, and then I began to make the need to share in decision making a central theme (or stated objective) in my remarks to the class as they prepared to split off into groups.

In Group A, individual actions began to change the group dynamic. Rosie,[1] the soft-spoken fourth grader in her group, sat next to Simon, the fifth grader who had been mandating the group's meeting area for the past several sessions, and firmly explained to him what she found unfair in this situation. To paraphrase, she explained that when they sat by the library and began to take turns reading, Simon would let his eyes travel to the book titles on the shelf of the library and get so distracted that it became distracting for the whole group. She said that because of this, sitting next to the library, as he always insisted, was not going to work anymore. For Rosie to ever say anything like that by herself, and for Simon, who was apt to resist commands from others more often than not, to go along with her showed tremendous progress in their relationship and in their character growth, too. When I saw how Simon listened to her, and how he proceeded to follow her to the table that she chose for their spot, it also showed me another side of Simon: a side that was not only accepting of another's ideas but also respectful of Rosie, who had never previously spoken to Simon or anyone else so directly before.

I have wondered if I made the right decision by stepping back on this group-dynamic issue. Wasn't this interfering with the goals of discussing a novel? Or was this also teaching an important lesson to my students? Were they feeling supported enough by my encouragements to "work it out as a team" or were they feeling abandoned? I made a point of meeting with all three members of the group individually after observing how Rosie handled the conflict. I expressed my admiration for how the group faced a problem that needed to be solved, and was solved, through careful conversation and compromise. Mostly, I said that it took lots of courage (one of our class expectations) and maturity to communicate how something is unfair, and also to realize when someone else has a valid point and to accept their feedback with actions as well as words.

This brought me back to what Freire (1970) says about problem-posing education: that it affirms us as "beings in the process of becoming," constantly stretching our own self- or socially-imposed limits on ourselves as we face new challenges (p. 84). As the morning of this transformation unfolded, Rosie and Simon both faced the unpredictability of a problem-posing reality. Specifically, Rosie was confronted with the idea that conflicts are going to happen whether we want them to or not and ignoring the problem was never going to make literature circles an enjoyable time for her. She beautifully demonstrated how problem-posing education is a process of becoming, from realizing how frustrated she was with Simon's stubborn control of the group's sitting area to her reflection on how she would approach him with her problem to the way she asserted her needs for the improvement of the group's productivity. In other words, she was submerged in a problem from which she began to emerge, and eventually she intervened to find her own solution (Freire, 1970). This process of developing into a stronger, more assertive Rosie was a very real and tangible result from her time spent in literature circles. Outside of a space where peer dynamics are integral to creating cohesive dialogue, adults (like teachers) often intervene too early in the process and miss out on opportunities to see students work things out together and benefit from it.

Group A's dynamics were not exclusive to that group. In fact, by making problem solving and teamwork part of our daily objectives for literature circles, I learned to let go a lot more in conflict resolution. And I began to see relationships change and strengthen for students who earlier did not have relationships. Group B also shared a set of conflicts, mostly arising from someone reading ahead, but through a slow progression and some intervention from me, the group grew into another example of students working out their differences and allowing great debates and exchanges to grow out of it all. This entire conversation about group dynamics and personal student growth was not something that I originally anticipated as a larger theme of my innovating. But, it emerged within the six weeks as clearly something worth analyzing. There was a change in the way students treated each other and even in the way they expressed themselves with one another. Rosie's articulation of her feelings and conflict-resolution idea was one among many other instances where I saw students step outside of their comfort zones to communicate with one another, as if for the first time.

It is interesting that this apparent sidestep brought me back to my original questions: What are we losing when we lose sight of other forms of developing understanding and discovery? Without the extended time spent working with their peers, running into conflicts, and finding their own solutions, would my students have missed out on character-building opportunities not conceivable through independent work time or lecture-based lessons? I think so. This space for dialogue and peer-teaching became a space where the shy became outspoken, and the usual high participants were not competing for the attention or approval of a teacher.

Of course, in the current environment, gains in character might easily be sacrificed if academic gains didn't come with them. So, what happened academically? I think that student-centered evaluation and instruction really helped my students gain a deeper understanding of the interdisciplinary nature of literature/learning in general. Often, students would raise their hands in science, math, or social studies class, and proclaim, "I have a connection to *Esperanza Rising!*" The connections were varied, but I especially took note of the connections they made to skills within the reading comprehension strand. They compared and contrasted the living conditions of Esperanza in Mexico and her new life as an immigrant in California, and they compared her access to education with that of students in Pakistan. In our daily language warm-ups they highlighted examples of figurative language, using pages from the novel to demonstrate similarities. After some time, I began to notice the phrases "I have a text-to-text connection" or "I have a text-to-self-connection" and "I have a text-to-world connection" spring up a few times per day. I saw a distinct change in my students' understanding that everything we learn is intertwined with prior knowledge, and we can use that knowledge to help us gain deeper appreciation for a different subject. I showed them my own academic papers, demonstrating that even I need to cite my sources and follow a specific format. Their own writing became clearer and more interesting, noticeably in their use of expressive language to communicate. And I noticed that when students shared their new insights with me, they were excited, proud, and sometimes would actually reference their lit circle discussion as a source for their information.

For me, these developments provided strong evidence of benefits from student-oriented changes in the curriculum and instruction. The more I began to talk to certain members of my staff about it, the more I learned that most of us were looking for more stimulating approaches to teaching. I think I made one of my more important discoveries related to my staff and my research during a recent conversation with my curriculum specialist (CS). She is an administrator in training and is often the one who most aggressively pushes the data-driven model at our school site. It took me a few weeks after the initial timeframe was over to share with her what I had been doing in the classroom. We were discussing the CST preparation practices that the school recommended during the last few weeks before the exam, and she brought up creating motivational posters or using song lyrics as posters. She harkened back to a charter-wide professional development day, when she was in charge of the ice breaker and introduced a song called "Beautiful Day" as something we can use in our classrooms to motivate students for CSTs. I remarked:

> Yeah, I remember that day. I *really* like how one of the lyrics goes, "Life is a journey, not a competition," and then we immediately proceeded to show our benchmark data on the big screens. Then Mrs. Marks [a principal at a different school site] cheerfully remarked, "Look at the grade-level teachers at your site. Who has the highest scores?" (journal entry, April 20, 2012)

I shared that snide remark to point out the contradiction between the song lyric and the reality of our school's high-stakes testing culture. But to my surprise, my curriculum specialist responded with:

> I know. Honestly, I hate this constant push too. But this is the way it is becoming at every school, more and more. So, we work within that and make the best of it. (journal entry/personal communication, April 20, 2012)

Before this exchange, I had not really approached my CS with this issue that I have struggled with, because I did not think she would be open to using class time on activities that might venture away from the standard curriculum. Yet after hearing her also express frustration and having her share other ideas on making the classroom a more humanizing space for students, especially around CST times (when they are getting the heaviest high-stakes testing pressure from home and school), I began to see her as an ally in this struggle.

Working in the Quantitative Paradigm

A remaining question from my initial planning was that of how educators might make transformative changes not only co-exist but also effectively counteract the effects of the mandated high-stakes testing agenda. Here, I really began to reevaluate what I could have done differently if I were to do this project again. I noticed that my plan never intended to include quantitative markers of progress since I wanted to get away from quantitative assessment. However, after reflection, I think I might have designed a form assessing students' original reading attitudes as well as some form of diagnostic on current ELA skills, especially on reading comprehension. I would like to see how this numerical data would work alongside the qualitative work that I collected. As much as I enjoyed seeing students' growth in multiple arenas, my curriculum specialist has a point.

We need to work within a system that may certainly change in the future but is currently entrenched in the notion that quality learning and teaching are best evaluated through standardized questions and answers. I feel very privileged to have seen my students express themselves in ways that illustrate the many facets of their personalities and multiple intelligences. Now, I am also seeing how numerical data can help me speak the same language as administrators, who—for the most part—want this form of data. Although the actual construction of these exams and accessibility is still controversial (Gasoi, 2009), there may be ways to use quantitative data to support more student-oriented approaches to curriculum and instruction. If I had also used a more traditional diagnostic to chart progress, I might have gathered more persuasive evidence to support my approach. Instead, I have only quantitative data from our benchmarks taken on a schoolwide basis to use as a comparison. However, even this data is worth looking at alongside the qualitative student data.

Below are results for the fifth-grade students (Table 9.1) and the fourth-grade students (Table 9.2) from the October 2011 ELA benchmark and from the March 2012 ELA benchmark. At that time, my innovations had been underway for four weeks.

Performance Level	Number of Students October 2011	Number of Students March 2012	Gain/Loss
Advanced	1 (8%)	1 (8%)	0
Proficient	4 (33%)	9 (69%)	+36%
Basic	7 (58%)	3 (23%)	-35%
	(12 students)	(13 students)	

Table 9.1. Performance Levels for Fifth Grade, October 2011 to March 2012, Benchmark Results in English Language Arts

Performance Level	Number of Students October 2011	Number of Students March 2012	Gain/Loss
Advanced	5 (71%)	5 (83%)	+12%
Proficient	1 (14%)	1 (17%)	+3%
Basic	1 (14%)	0 (0%)	–14%
	(7 students)	(6 students)	

Table 9.2. Performance Levels for Fourth Grade, October 2011 to March 2012, Benchmark Results in English Language Arts

It is apparent that since the beginning of the year to March, students in both grade levels improved on the whole in the English-language arts benchmarks.[2] How much of this gain came from my students and how much of my students' gains came from my innovations I cannot tell. I am keenly interested in how I might start to gather evidence on those topics in the future. I do know what I observed during literature circles, and I do know how events unfolded. My definite focus was in the ELA curriculum, even as I began exploring how to apply these student-dominated opportunities to science as my action plan progressed.

I end with more questions: Are there ways to define learning or to "display" it in ways other than data walls that I have not explored yet? I bet there are! How can I ensure that literature circles keep a privileged place in our schedule, even when faced with big interruptions, like charter-wide benchmark exams? How can I transfer the insights and growth that I witnessed, read about, or recorded throughout my action plan into a medium or language that can mean something to administrators or other stakeholders in the high-stakes-testing culture? I have only begun to scratch the surface of my research interest area.

Moving Forward

This project attempted to empower my students by impacting their perceptions of themselves and their abilities. To complete it, I had to stretch my thinking and challenge myself to move beyond the standard and set expectations of my curriculum and administrators. It required me to rethink even subtle assumptions about what I thought "success" was supposed to look like, and it had me going back to rethinking everything I seemed to learn as "good teaching" from my credentialing program, Teach for America, and other sources to reevaluate how I felt about these ideas, given my classroom experiences.

As a result, I believe that I have moved forward into a more confident and risk-taking teacher than I was before I began this school year. I also feel that my history and personal experience as a third-year teacher, second-year upper-elementary teacher, and Teach for America alum contributed to my overall willingness to challenge the aspects of teaching that I felt conflicted about. That is, I do not know if it is the constant change in school site, grade level, and lessened pressure of not having to answer to the TFA requirements and expectations, but I do notice that this history has affected my current willingness and enthusiasm to keep exploring my area of research. I am still within a space where high-stakes tests are a predominant marker of so much of a student's identity, and for the longest time, I attached that same pressure to perform at 80% for myself. There have been dark times in my teaching career that have arisen from a sense of inadequacy, which I am sure is all too common. Being evaluated, evaluating our students, facing the hostility directed to all of our results: it can become overwhelming and can directly seep into one's own self-esteem and happiness. I felt a direct connection to my students as I reflected on why this action plan research was important to me and to my students.

As mentioned earlier, I know that my students experienced opportunities to interact with one another in a way that is not always a given in our classrooms. The development of relationships, mutual understanding, and appreciation for each other's thoughts and insights came from a long-term, trust-building time together that was made possible through literature circles. Even their fluency levels were remarkably improved through the quality time spent reading on a regular basis. That slow build-up is very different to me from the objective exam that gives you one opportunity to show your mastery. In their daily group reading, students mentored one another, listened to the pronunciation and intonations of their partners, and really provided that extra support when someone made a mistake.

One of my final reflections was that to be the best version of my teaching self, I needed to use all tools and methods that work for my students in supporting them. I think my view is currently in a state of shift toward understanding that qualitative and quantitative data both serve their own purposes and using both within my practicc is needed, as long as I continue to reflect on and question their implications, starting with the question "Why?" Why am I choosing to use this type of data for this topic? Why are my students feeling stressed out this week? Why did you choose B as your answer? Working within this system is the first step. But presenting my students with the possibility of more, of seeing their words and hearing their connections on recordings, helps them see their learning in forms beyond a bar graph or percent. It's empowering to see how large our minds can expand and how this shows up (and gets validated) in our classroom, even within a high-stakes testing environment, school wide.

As I mentioned earlier, I truly felt that there was an interdisciplinary nature to our work with literature circles and, later, with science experiments, figurative language plays, and article studies from the *LA Times* newspaper. Particularly with literature or current events, students find a lot of home connections or prior knowledge that they can draw on. Once they make these types of connections, they keep them tucked away for later use, when they can make a new connection. I saw this often with students who would surprise me with causc-and-effect examples we learned about through the events of *Esperanza Rising* to cause-and-effect examples of the chemical reactions labs we conducted. What may look initially unrelated becomes exciting and cross-curricular to students. It becomes a type of unintentional learning game that always keeps their minds active. It was a beautiful trend that I want to reproduce earlier in the year next time and, of course, improve on. For my future practice, I can imagine integrating cross-curricular activities, projects, and interactive opportunities that challenge students to see larger themes or patterns like power, struggle, opportunity, changes, and so on.

The work I report here has been significant in my process and growth as a social justice educator because it gave me an exciting reason to keep on exploring how much potential my students and I have. If I had stopped at the idea that knowledge, growth, and learning success only show up in one form of data, and I did not see a student budge from Basic, I might feel helpless or negative about my prospects for positively affecting that student. Because I had a chance to explore the other possibilities beyond A, B, C, and D for mastery, it was stimulating for me to see how much more learning I have to do. I think that this is always a goal not only for social justice teachers but also for teachers, and humans in general. We should always find new ways to innovate and create opportunity for growth. Especially if it's about our students and ourselves, how can we not?

Notes

1. Adapted from an unpublished master's thesis at the University of California, Los Angeles, 2012.
2. Student names have been changed for confidentiality.
3. There were two slight changes in each group between October and March: a new fifth-grade student was added, while a fourth-grade student left in January.

References

Anderson, P., & Corbett, L. (2008). Literature circles for students with learning disabilities. *Intervention in School and Clinic, 44*(25), 25–33.

Darder, A. (1991). *Culture and power in the classroom: A critical foundation for bicultural education*. New York: Bergin & Garvey.

Diamond, J., & Spillane, J. (2004). High-stakes accountability in urban elementary schools: Challenging or reproducing inequality? *Teachers College Record, 106*(6), 1145–1176.

Freire, P. (1970). *Pedagogy of the oppressed*. New York: Continuum International.

Gasoi, E. (2009). How we define success: Holding values in an era of high-stakes accountability. *Schools: Studies in Education, 6*(2), 173–186.

CHAPTER 10

Big History, Little World

The Politics of Social Justice Curriculum in Advanced Placement World History[1]

Rachel Klimke

Theory into Practice

I teach high school history at the Learning Academy, a Title I school located in the Mid-City neighborhood of Los Angeles. It is an integration magnet and part of a large school district. Students who are bused in every day from all over Los Angeles represent the vast socioeconomic and racial-ethnic diversity of the city.

On the surface, the Learning Academy seems like an excellent institution. It is safe; it has a reputation for quality academic instruction; and, it regularly produces good results on state and national tests. However, because the school is very much a place where test prep is the goal, students have been unable to engage in critical conversations about their school community, adding to deep segregation, rifts, and intense competition among students. My students have the benefit of a multicultural environment, yet they are isolated from one another by the way they are tracked into AP and regular classes, as well as through self-segregation. The AP program at my school divides students and generates instances of racism, competition, and self-doubt, replicating colonial and imperialist traditions. As a result, the Learning Academy is a highly competitive environment where personal goals are put above the needs of the community.

Such individualism and indifference strongly characterize the four sections of AP World History I teach, affecting the experience of the 142 students enrolled in the courses. This project involved my effort to modify the curriculum in a way that would allow my most marginalized students to find voice and empowerment and that would help my most dominant and successful students to learn empathy. I wanted to establish a culture of care and to deconstruct issues of inequality and racism in the classroom and at the school site.

My first thought was to make the AP program at my school more equitable, since it is well known that advanced courses have traditionally been sites of educational inequality and exclusion for African-American and Latina/o students. However, I came to realize that simply enrolling more students of color was not going to actually improve conditions. Rather, I realized that the experience of students after they enrolled was critical to long-term change. My hope was that if I motivated students to think more critically about their experiences, they would begin to question the exclusive emphasis on competition, learn to care for one another, and begin to develop new insights into the discipline of world history. I wanted students to begin linking classroom learning to larger social issues and to issues within our school. In short, I wanted to create an environment where my students could rethink their position in the world and their relationship to how knowledge is constructed. My questions became:

- How might students begin to develop an understanding of themselves and each other in an environment that fosters compliance and competition, so that they might become empowered to consciously reconsider and reconstruct their identities?
- How might students begin to see the divisions between students at our school as being related to the AP program and embedded colonial norms?
- How might I change the AP curriculum so that the experiences of all my students are represented?
- How might I use the AP curriculum to create instances of care and empathy in the classroom?
- How might students take action, addressing emerging issues at school and in their communities?

Curricular Modifications

Eventually I developed a theme that my students would use to examine the units on global interactions from 1450 to 1750 and industrialization and global integration from 1750 to 1900. The emphasis of lessons would be to explore the ways human beings tend to develop identity in opposition to people perceived as different, as "the other." At the center of this theme is a deep-rooted history of colonialism and imperialism (Said, 1978). As Narayan (1997) writes:

> Colonialism as an historical phenomenon does not only connect and divide Westerners from subjects in various Third-World nations in a series of complicated and unequal relationships. It also connects and divides mainstream Western subjects from Others in their *own* societies whose unequal relationships to the mainstream are themselves products of Western colonial history. Colonial history is not only the history of Western domination of "non-western" populations, but is also a history of the creation of racially distinct and oppressed populations within Western countries such as the United States. (p. 44)

Understanding the roots of oppression and the historic implications of colonialism and imperialism might, I hoped, allow my students to assess elements of their identity that are legacies of these processes. Throughout the unit students were asked to answer the following essential questions: How do I view myself in opposition to others? How have the historical processes of colonialism and imperialism shaped these views? What is my identity as a global citizen?

I created a sequence of topics and concepts for students to explore, including first contacts, race as a social construction, racial oppression, dominant ideologies, gender oppression, institutional oppression, economic oppression, and imperialist ideologies. In each week-long segment, readings about historical events were followed by discussions and assignments intended to help students forge linkages between the concept under discussion and the world in which they were living. For example, after discussions of historical examples of race serving to separate people and structure inequality, students took pictures of places they socialized in school and then analyzed them in class, which demonstrated how race structures our school environment. After readings and discussion of the function of patriarchy in various societies, students brought in and analyzed examples of contemporary media portrayal of women. I hoped such activities would steadily build students' understanding that the history we were reading reflected important problems evident in their own environment and world. I intended to close the units by having students generate oral history projects and create a video titled "Where I Come From," with the intended result of affirming culture and teaching others.

To promote individual reflection, students also wrote frequent essays and kept reflective journals. To help capture events, I also kept a teaching journal, which, along with student-produced work, provided the data for my analysis.

As It Turned Out …

Because I realized that for the past three years I have not been preparing my students for anything more than the AP test, I wanted to provide a course of study in AP World History that was more reflective and student centered. My goal was to reimagine the AP curriculum to support critical social science instruction, as well as to deconstruct issues at my school that I perceived to stem from the AP program. After enacting eight units incorporating social justice themes and analyzing materials from the class, I was able to uncover several findings—none of which I was anticipating. Three in particular stand out. First, that because of the limitations of the AP situation, I never really changed my teaching style and my students never fully engaged with the social justice lessons. Second, despite the challenges of the situation and mistakes I made, there were opportunities for, and glimpses of, changes in student thinking. Third, the current high-stakes testing environment—and the AP system that is part of it—contributes to institutional racism. At first I thought these realizations insignificant, but I now believe them to be important to my practice and to my school site.

To begin, I found that the limitations of the AP curriculum and the expectations of my students and the school community were more severe than I had imagined. My students were focused on passing the AP exam and were not looking for much more. Throughout the year they repeatedly requested that I just lecture and tell them what they needed to know, a situation much different than I expected.

At first I had grand ideas that my students would quickly engage with the social justice themes in my lessons, relate the content to their lives, and become empowered. In a way I needed them to react this way, to show my success as a teacher and to prove that moving away from the AP standards was a good idea. However, it soon became clear that my students were having a difficult time grappling with the social justice lessons, specifically with letting go of the test-prep portion of the AP curriculum. In class a few of my students would make good connections between such themes as racism and economic oppression and their own environment, and I chose to focus on these as evidence of my success. However, after reading through my students' reflective journals on these topics, I found that the majority of my students wrote eerily disconnected entries that showed a lack of connection to these issues. I pigheadedly felt that because a few of my students were making some connections that all my students were absorbing these ideas. My journal entries and my writing reflect my neglect of the majority of my students who weren't making connections or breakthroughs.

Following are examples of how I chose to gravitate toward work that showed my success as a teacher rather than the work that was representative of the majority of my students. The first entry gives a basic description of racism but fails to provide any other insight. In fact, 28 of my 35 students turned in papers like this. But I chose to focus on the shining examples as represented in the second journal entry, because they made me feel like I was successful and that veering away from the AP curriculum had value.

> Race is a tool made up by a society to describe, judge, and oppress other people by their looks and/or their culture. Different societies have constructed race by a certain type of feature that makes them different from themselves. They used this to enslave a certain type of people and make them feel less human just because they are different. (student journal, 2/25/12)

> We Koreans have our own culture and region of the city. At school we only hang out in our own groups. There are many racists in my community and family. We Koreans have been brought up to think we

are superior to other races. In Korean culture we do not mix with people who are not Korean. (student journal, 2/25/12)

I suppose the reason I chose to focus on limited success was because I was not ready to admit to myself that I was having difficulty doing social justice work within the AP space. My journal entries and writing from this period reflect a failure to acknowledge this issue and focus very systematically on what I did as the instructor. In addition, my choice to focus on the few students who were making connections illustrates my insecurities about moving away from a program that had for the last three years been marked with success, in the institutional sense, with high AP scores and pass rates.

In trying to think through why this happened, I have come to believe that there was a problem with the way I presented social justice ideas to my students. I was presenting my "radical" curriculum as if it were an extension of the AP curriculum. After analyzing events, I do not believe students felt as if they were engaging in anything outside the norm. They were still involved in the same process, in which I simply gave them information and they received it. I was presenting radical ideas in a non-radical and non-political way. Presenting social justice ideas in this sanitized way allowed me to feel like I was acting within the AP program rather than subverting it. It seems I am not alone. Speaking of her time in university settings, bell hooks (1989) notes a similar phenomenon among professors:

> Everyone seemed reluctant to talk about the fact that professors who advocated radical politics rarely allowed their critique of domination and oppression to influence teaching strategies ... In retrospect, it seems that my most radical professors were still educating for domination. And I wondered if this was so because we could not imagine how to educate for liberation in the corporate university. (pp. 100–101)

I acted much like the professors with radical philosophies hooks describes.

Because of my inability to trust my students, my fears of failure, and the constraints of the AP curriculum, I basically adapted my social justice curriculum to the banking model (Freire, 2011). Because I was so fearful of keeping up with the AP program, I felt I had to continually stick to a strict pacing plan and move students quickly through ideas and curriculum. Teaching AP World History basically requires being a very good timekeeper and coach, and I see now the pacing of the course is utterly incongruent with the time it takes to do social justice work. There was little time for reflection and discussion as we could barely move through the content. As a result, I spent a lot of time leading my students toward concepts and making connections for them, forcing them through the social justice curriculum and giving them little opportunity to reach realizations on their own. I was not asking for their input into what they wanted to learn: I was telling them what they needed to know.

I understood and envisioned intellectually what I wanted to do, but executing it was a challenge. Below is a fairly unsophisticated field note that illustrates my frustration.

> I am so disappointed about having to knock off the oral history video project. This is probably the most important part of the plan. All I do is lecture. We are so behind. (field notes, 4/20/12)

I realize now that my students and I were in a state of oppression imposed by the AP program: time and the need to pass the test kept us captive. Consequently, my ability to find liberation in this institution has been minimal. In March I received a layoff notice from my school district, providing me with a unique opportunity to move past the regimentation of the AP program since I had nothing to lose. But even with the potential freedom my RIF notice gave me, I continued to have a difficult time shedding the expectations of the AP program. I remained compliant.

I began to question if it is possible to exist within an oppressive system and not oppress. Ironically, one of the themes I incorporated into my lessons was centered on this theme, yet I was living it out unaware in my own classroom. As Freire (2011) cautions:

Discovering himself to be an oppressor may cause considerable anguish, but it does not necessarily lead to solidarity with the oppressed. Rationalizing his guilt through paternalistic treatment of the oppressed, all the while holding them fast in a position of dependence, will not do. (p. 49)

Freire's work informed much of my plan and in time taught me a great deal about my role in oppressive systems, but awareness did not mean I entered solidarity with my students. I kept my students dependent on me. They needed me to pass the AP exam.

But the more I thought critically about myself as an oppressor, the more aware I became of the space I was working in and the expectations I faced. While I struggle with the fact that I was unable to escape the role of the oppressor in my classroom and I initially lamented my failure constantly, I have come to the conclusion that it is Advanced Placement testing that is oppressive. It fosters severe competition and has clear capitalist goals. I believe the competition and free-market forces that are a part of this process tricked me into blaming myself for my failure to make meaningful change in an oppressive institution. While I cannot escape some culpability for my behavior, I am also acknowledging the complications for teachers acting within oppressive systems.

My second finding attends to the ways in which I encountered amazing glimpses of transformative possibilities as a result of the curricular changes I implemented, despite the limitations of the situation. I encountered great possibilities as well as great challenges. The AP World History curriculum is broad and inclusive—both its biggest asset and biggest curse, and it did offer some limited opportunities for students to grapple with social justice concepts through media assignments, reflective journals, and class discussions. Although these were done as sort of asides to the AP curriculum, students did at least begin to explore social justice concepts. Their early journal entries showed an intellectual grasp of the concepts, although there was a lack of reflection as to how an issue such as racism has affected them personally. I know they deal with issues of racism, poverty, and privilege in their lives, but they rarely talked about their own experiences. As I reflect on this now, I am not surprised that this was the case. The low levels of consciousness I initially saw in my students' responses are a clear reflection of the fact that students in the AP track at my school are rarely, if ever, asked to relate content to their lives, and they are rarely given time in classes to explore such topics.

> The reflective journals on racism were terrible. I thought students would be more forthcoming about their experiences. For the most part their writing was void of any attempt to talk about racism in their own lives. (field notes, 3/1/12)

Eventually, however, more and more of my students did use the reflective journal to relate content to their lives and to explore themes from class on a personal level. The photographs they took, however, may have been the most successful part of the coursework.

Students were always eager to see the pictures, which frequently prompted productive thinking and discussion. For example, after viewing photos of students socializing in school spaces, they engaged in a meaningful conversation about racial separation in our own society and racial separations that have existed historically, specifically after the colonization of the Americas.

> I was surprised to see how honest students were about the racial separations they face in their lives; however, they were not willing to chalk any of it up to actual racism. In a way they felt that their racial separations were part and parcel of just wanting to be around people who are like you. I asked them why don't you just go and hang out with people who are different from you? What keeps you from doing this? Finally Jeremiah said there are really clear racial separations at the school. I asked, were you all not aware of this? Almost in unison the students said, "yeah we know." I think the visual of this was most important in that it really allowed students to see clear separations. (field notes, 2/24/12)

Students in the AP program self-segregate into mono-cultural groups; I believe that seeing the photographs that so obviously depicted self-segregation may have moved them to a new awareness of the implications of a habit they took for granted as normal. Changing behavior is difficult even after awareness is raised, but it is impossible without awareness. Even small steps count as progress, and I found this exercise allowed students to see each other a little differently and understand more about the ways they act within this institution.

I also found I could build classroom community by providing spaces for students to have meaningful interactions outside their cultural groups. As more students brought their cultural truths openly into the classroom, student separations began to diminish. After these lessons I found a wider variety of students participated in class and that students chose to sit in cross-cultural groups.

> I decided to allow students to assign their own seats in class. As they walked in I asked them to sit where they like. I had done this at the beginning of the year and students sat in mono-cultural and mono-gender groupings. The desks in my room are arranged in pods of four. Students sat in groupings that were noticeably more cross-cultural, however, they still sat in same-gender groups. There are also more students participating in class. Usually Jordan and George are the only people to offer opinions, but more students are now volunteering to speak. (field notes, 3/16/12)

I believe such activities as a cultural food day, a successful event that created an environment where all students saw their culture and identity recognized and celebrated, contributed to such growth. All of my students with European ancestry were able to bring a dish from their family and talk about it. This helped address the "I don't have a culture" statements that characterized some of our class discussions (field notes, 2/16/12). And, it affirmed discussions we had been having about cultural diffusion and how it relates to colonization and identity.

More important, it set the framework for addressing identity and culture in an inclusive manner. My goal was obviously not to compartmentalize students into cultural groups, giving vague and universal descriptions of what it's like to be "South Asian." Instead, I wanted my students to explore themselves and their histories and teach each other their individual cultural truths and experiences. It was important that they understand there is no universal truth but rather that humanizing each other creates spaces where we can build community and collective knowledge, moving away from competition and self-segregation. As Gramsci writes:

> The starting-point of critical elaboration is the consciousness of what one really is, and "knowing thyself" is a product of the historical process to date which has deposited in you an infinity of traces, without leaving an inventory. (1971, p. 324)

I would like to think that I moved at least some students to the starting point of the kind of thinking that might lead to increased consciousness.

My third finding addresses the racial separations I found so troubling at my school site. One of the issues that we spent the most time on in class and that most interested my students was the segregation in our school. It became clear that cultural separations and segregation exist in part because my students are constantly engaged in acts of cultural preservation against dominant ideologies. In analyzing our discussions and student journals, I found that one way students respond to the intense competition of our environment is by forming mono-cultural groups to create safe havens and to preserve their culture. The nature of the AP program breeds deep competition and resentments. I saw this as students were segregated by race between AP and general education courses, and also within AP classes as same-cultural students banded together. As we started to deconstruct these issues and we began to learn more about culture in the classroom, I realized that students do not have a lack of cultural affirmation. Rather, they are quite culturally affirmed and steeped in cultural practices. As a result, they seek out mono-cultural interactions.

> After I graduated elementary I came to the [Learning Academy] and it was a lot different than what I had experienced in the past. The school itself was so diverse. In the beginning, I hung out with the white

kids but as time passed I gradually began to fit in the Asian crews. It wasn't that hanging out with the white kids was uncomfortable but I just fitted in more with the Asian kids because they were more like me. We speak the same language, have the same tradition, and eat the same things so I didn't have to explain anything about my culture because they already knew. (student journal, 2/27/12)

We can see this in the pictures that we shared during class because we see that many people of the same race shared the same ideas. We all shared the same idea of American culture. We all thought of America as a place that feeds their people bad food. The food that we eat leads to obesity. That was the funny thing. We think so highly of our culture and we don't really care much about the culture of the society we live in. But why is that? I believe it is because we want to preserve our culture and make it look good. It's who we are and American culture is only a place where we live in. (student journal, 3/9/12)

The issue really stems from the fact that students do not see each other or interact with people who are different from them. Instead of building and affirming cultural identity, I found my students needed space to interact in a cross-cultural way.

I realized that through the AP program, issues of cultural separation were exacerbated as students were forced to see each other through competition only. Overall I found that mono-cultural interaction is an act of resistance against a system that fosters competition above humanization, where mono-cultural groups make students feel safe in an environment that constantly pits them against each other. Several journal entries on racial separations addressed this issue.

There is always lots of ways that make people not want to be with people who are different. I get annoyed because everyone is against each other at school. Either you are a smart kid or not, so you just want to be with people who you know and who you trust. And yes those people are from my culture. (student journal, 3/15/12)

I like to be with my own group because we don't have to one-up all the time. Everybody at the [Learning Academy] is always one-upping. (student journal, 3/15/12)

People always ask me—how many AP classes are you taking? I say 1. And they are all like, oh. Like that's bad or something. (student journal, 3/12/12)

One student said that AP classes are really competitive. She said testing and AP classes were a game and you played this game with your friends. Many students chimed in with similar responses. Several students said so many people at our school take AP classes that you have to do it so you can be competitive for college. Over the semester I have received numerous answers reflecting this point and lamenting the competition at the school. (teacher journal, 4/9/12)

Competition is an obvious and critical theme at my school. So many of my students see no inherent value in their coursework but rather are searching out tips and skills necessary to pass the national AP exam. They find it important to excel and leave others behind.

I believe their attitude to be a direct result of the high-stakes testing environment that is so prevalent in public schools. Darder (2011) is one of many theorists who has deconstructed the motivations and outcomes of standardized testing—which includes AP exams. As happened in my class, "students and teachers as subjects of classroom discourse … are systematically silenced by the need for the class to 'cover' a generic curriculum at a prescribed pace" (p. 169). AP courses, including the world history course I teach, require teaching to a test and, as Darder notes, such tests themselves create "the conditions within school that perpetuate a culture of elitism, privilege and exploitation" (p. 171). It is this culture that helps explain how competition has nurtured the divisions manifested at my school.

While I firmly believe that rejecting the capitalistic high-stakes testing regime for a humanizing approach would be the most empowering approach for my students and for me, the goal of passing the AP test turned out to be an insurmountable object. None of us could break free from the pressure of the looming exam.

Over the last month students have been interacting more in class. I feel this has to do with our push to create a space within the AP class that allowed students to see one another in a more humanizing way. When I provided my AP students with a practice AP test on a Saturday in the cafeteria, I saw that students were nervous, they felt the competition creep back into their lives and they self-segregated by culture in a way I have seen diminish in the classroom. (field notes, 4/28/12)

As soon as high-stakes testing comes into play, students immediately retreat to mono-cultural groups as a way to provide safety from competition. For me this represents a significant finding, the beginning of a larger discussion I think needs to happen about the impact of high-stakes testing and competition.

Looking Back and Thinking Ahead

I wish I had not taken for granted the idea that I could so easily revamp a very structured and entrenched course of study—but my hindsight is better than my foresight. If I were more realistic about how difficult it would be for me to depart from the expectations of the AP course, I would have done things differently. While I would keep my goals, I would have done more thinking about how to work within the time constraints of the course. I should have made it a priority to spend the majority of class time exploring the social justice curriculum rather than covering content. I realize now that, for the most part, content can be obtained at home, and class time should be reserved for exploring personal and collective connections to the subject.

Despite the difficulties, this experience has profoundly changed me as an educator. It has forced me to ask serious questions about myself as a person working for social justice. I struggled so deeply to balance the needs of my students with the goals of the AP program—but I am not sure if I can act within an oppressive institution without oppressing. I need to continue trying to understand how I dealt with the problems I faced. I seemed to react in three ways to setbacks, none of which were very helpful. I blamed myself instead of looking at the larger context of the system I was working in. I dropped meaningful lessons to prepare for the AP test. And I chose to focus on students who provided me with positive examples of how I was doing as a way to negate my own insecurities and fears.

If I remain at my school site and continue teaching AP World History, I know now that from the first day of class it has to be my goal to foster an environment where my students are able to truly interact with the content of the AP World History course and relate it to their lives. It will be my goal to work against the high-stakes testing regime with the hope of helping students create connections and meaning in their learning. I believe that creating noncompetitive spaces in AP classes could have important implications for my school site and student learning because it may create a space where students can interact outside their cultural groups and begin undermining institutional culture. I would also advocate a two-year AP course as a way to create a course of study over ninth and tenth grade that would allow students to have more time to explore issues and engage in action. Several schools already do this, and I believe it could radically alter the way this course is taught, allowing for the time needed to pursue student interests and to foster an active community.

I think it is important for educators and other stakeholders elsewhere to understand that high-stakes and competitive environments for students replicate systems of institutional racism and capitalism in such a way that it makes collaborative learning difficult to implement. But not impossible.

Reflections on Social Justice

I romanticized the concept of social justice educator. I thought it would be easy to dislodge the curriculum I have been teaching for the last three years and incorporate changes that challenged my students intellectually. This is by far one of the most difficult tasks I have embarked on. Through this process, more than anything, I have come to the realization that this work is messy. Theoretically and ideologically I can make conclusions about what needs to be changed in education and at my school site, but achieving this is something completely different. I thought of myself as someone who, for the last 12 years, has worked to understand systems of oppression and speak truth to power. In fact, I have devoted much of my life to these pursuits. However, it has been difficult for me to enact this in my own classroom. Having awareness is one thing, but truly living out these principles means taking significant risks. I thought I was prepared to take them, but in the end I had devoted myself too deeply to institutional success. I realize that teachers cannot be neutral or apolitical actors, but for the last three years I have been teetering on this line. This choice I have made has been oppressive to me and to my students. I made choices I am not proud of, and I had a difficult time reconciling them. That aside, I began to realize how oppressed I have been at my school and as part of the AP regime. To continue this work, my students and I must act together to promote our mutual liberation.

As for the future of my classroom practice, I am starting to realize that I may not be able to do the kind of work I wish to accomplish at my current school site. It is clear to me that incorporating a social justice curriculum into the AP World History course is a needed reform. History courses need to serve as locations where students can explore their lives and their communities in a cooperative environment. My school has a very rigid environment, and it is hard to go beyond the expectations of high test scores and AP pass rates. It is competitive for both teachers and students. Second, students and parents have very specific expectations of what an AP class is. Mostly, that it is preparation to pass a national exam, and if teachers do not do a good job of preparing students, they are deemed ineffective educators.

I know that I would like to continue the work of trying to understand if it is possible to work within an oppressive system and not oppress. I find this to be a fundamental question that has important implications for my future as a social justice educator and the path I choose to take. Second, I find it important to continue to explore and research the connections between segregation and cultural preservation in high-stakes testing environments. I believe these ideas will have an important impact on students if we are able to think about the implications for each as educators.

Note

1.   Adapted from an unpublished master's thesis at the University of California, Los Angeles, 2012.

Bibliography

Darder, A. (2011). *A dissident voice: Essays on culture, pedagogy and power.* New York: Peter Lang.

Delgado, R., & Stefancic, J. (2001). *Critical race theory: An introduction.* New York: New York University Press.

Finn, P. (2009). *Literacy with an attitude.* New York: State University of New York Press.

Freire, P. (2011). *Pedagogy of the oppressed* (30th anniversary ed.). New York: Continuum.

Gramsci, A. (1971). *Selections from the prison notebook.* London: Lawrence & Wishart.

hooks, b. (1989). *Talking back: Thinking feminist, thinking black.* Boston: South End.

hooks, b. (1994). *Teaching to transgress: Education as the practice of freedom.* New York: Routledge.

Lorde, A. (2001). *Sister outsider.* Freedom, CA: Crossing.

Narayan, U. (1997). *Dislocating cultures: Identities, traditions, and third world feminism.* New York: Routledge.

Noddings, N. (2005). Caring in education. *The Encyclopedia of Informal Education.* Retrieved from www.infed.org/biblio/nodding_caring_in_education.htm

O'Connor, C. (2002). I am usually the only black in my class: The human and social costs of within-school segregation. *Michigan Journal of Race and Law, 8*(1), 221–248.

Oakes, J. (2005). *Keeping track: How schools structure inequality* (2nd ed.). New Haven, CT: Yale University Press.

Peterson, R. (2003). Teaching how to read the world and change it: Critical pedagogy in the intermediate grades. In A. Darder, M. Baltodano, & D. Torres (Eds.), *The critical pedagogy reader* (pp. 365–387). New York: Routledge.

Said, E. (1978). *Orientalism.* New York: Random House.

Solórzano, D. G., & Ornelas, A. (2002). A critical race analysis of Advanced Placement classes: A case of educational inequality. *Journal of Latinos and Education, 1*(4), 215–229. Retrieved from http://dx.doi.org/10.1207/S1532771XJLE0104_2

Solórzano, D. G., & Ornelas, A. (2004). A critical race analysis of Latina/o and African American Advanced Placement enrollment in public high schools. *The High School Journal, 87,* 15–26. Retrieved from http://muse.jhu.edu/journals/hsj/summary/v087/87.3solorzano.html

Tatum, B. D. (2007). *Can we talk about race? And other conversations in an era of school resegregation.* Boston: Beacon.

CHAPTER 11

Challenging Standardized Curriculum

Recognizing, Critiquing, and Attempting to Transform the Learning Process[1]

Nien N. Tran

Positionality and School Context

I was twenty-one years old and had just graduated from the University of California, Berkeley, when I started teaching third grade at a high-performing, bilingual charter school in downtown Los Angeles. As a Teach for America corps member, I had six weeks of preparation and training before I stepped into a real classroom with real students, real lives and futures in my hands. I was both fearless and fearful; the adrenaline of having the opportunity to make positive contributions to public education made me feel invincible, but the anxiety of planning and executing day-to-day teaching made me feel nauseous. Aside from being exceedingly excited, I had no idea what I was doing.

I was given a pacing plan and a blueprint to follow, but since I was inexperienced, the documents meant relatively little to me. My proactive self printed out the third-grade California standards and California Standards Test–released questions for English Language Arts and Mathematics. I figured since I did not understand the pacing plan, I would "backward plan," using those materials in addition to the teacher-created quarterly benchmarks from the previous year. Fresh from college, I planned to use the available questions as a final exam and the quarterly benchmarks as midterms to teach my students what they needed to know to be successful in third grade. It sounded so simple.

I followed my plan, and my students got used to the culture of testing. They were given an exit ticket at the end of every lesson. They were also given a weekly assessment on Fridays to review the objectives and standards taught during the week. I tracked student progress using these exit tickets and weekly assessments to figure out what I needed to review or re-teach. I also used these tests to pull small groups of students who struggled with specific standards. By the third quarter, the art of teaching became a science. My students and I were checking off the list of standards and celebrating when, as a class, we achieved 80% or above on power standards.

But student learning was disjointed, to say the least; none of it was coherent nor was it cohesive. This whole "teaching" thing seemed simple because I was not actually teaching at all. Instead, I was preparing my students for the third-grade version of a college final—the CSTs—without much of the critical thinking, reading, and writing evident in a college course.

But: the current reality of my school dictates that my students take benchmarks every ten weeks. Benchmarks are held in such high regard because they speak volumes when it comes to student-retention conversations. Our school uses the students' benchmark results as well as their reading levels to determine whether students should be retained. In second grade, students begin to take benchmarks because it is the first grade level where CSTs are administered. The rationale is that the benchmarks serve as training wheels for students to succeed on the CSTs in May. My third graders were well aware of the implications of their performance on benchmarks. They realized the repercussions of not doing well: they might have to repeat third grade instead of moving on to fourth grade.

What struck me was my students' internalization of the tests as the spearhead of their education. The power seemed to be in the hands of the tests. The tests were in charge of their future and dictated how they felt and saw themselves. I was saddened by this realization because my students were merely eight-year-olds but they already understood that assessments determined their academic futures. If they did well, they would move on to the next grade. But if they failed the benchmarks, they might be retained.

Students themselves had no input into how their performance was to be evaluated. Instead, metrics were created by an educational system that is inherently biased against students of color or from a working-class background. I am fully aware of this system and aware of being part of it, because I wrote the benchmarks by using CST–released questions, modeling all of my question stems on CST format. My administrator then combed through the test, double-checking the language of the CST sample questions to the language in my benchmarks to vouch for the benchmarks' validity and reliability.

I began to realize that my students and I were stuck in a paradigm. I taught my students to be excellent test takers because I attributed my academic success and my ability to climb the social ladder to my good test-taking skills. I taught them to be successful on tests because I knew their academic futures depended on these scores. In time, my students equated learning with performing well on assessments because I had been teaching to the test. I wasn't aware that what I was doing was actually belittling my students' knowledge and seeing them as empty vessels needing to be filled.

Posing a Problem and Developing an Action Plan

Reading and thinking about Freire (1993) and Darder (2011) helped me clarify my purpose as an educator. Despite my original emphasis on the tests, I realized that test scores do not reflect my most important classroom values. I want to inspire my students to develop a passion for learning. I want learning to be a thirst that they can never quench. I want my students to be curious about anything and everything, asking questions about why this is and how that becomes. I hope that curiosity will eventually lead them to be passionate, educated advocates and leaders. Moreover, I do not want to instill in my students the idea that assessments are definitive measures of their intelligence. The numbers do not define them and should not confine them. I do not want my students to be demoralized by terms like "basic," "below basic," or "far below basic."

This thinking led me to some key questions: How can I challenge the standardized curriculum? How do I integrate a culturally relevant pedagogy? How do I get my students to realize that knowledge comes from within?

Freire (1993) insists on "a pedagogy [that] must be forged with, not for, the oppressed (whether individuals or peoples) in the incessant struggle to regain their humanity" (p. 48). He explains that banking pedagogy dehumanizes and oppresses students. But what teaching practices exactly constitute banking and fake schooling? And how do I challenge myself to build a different type of curriculum? What resources do I need to truly invigorate my students' learning so that they are critical about any and all information presented to them?

Such questions arose in part because my first year of teaching experience led me to agree with Darder (2011), who has shown that in high-stakes testing the "emphasis of learning shifts away from intellectual activity toward the dispensing of packaged fragments of information" (p. 169). As she describes, in my classroom standardized testing was "turn[ing] the education of working class and poor students of color into 'drill and kill' exercises of teaching-to-the-test and highly scripted literacy" (p. 164). Moreover, I agreed with her that the real purpose of tests is not to assess knowledge but to rank students; as a result, many questions are purposefully written in ways sure to trick many test takers (Darder, p. 165). Not understanding this, my students internalized ideas about whether they were smart or stupid based on the test scores.

I needed to prepare my students for the standardized tests because that is my school's expectation—but I wanted to do it in a way that was conducive to meaningful learning. How could I balance the pressure of state tests with authentic instruction? How could I show my students that they are "the master[s] of [their] fate and the captain[s] of [their] soul"? How could I get my students to realize that knowledge is a way of life, that knowledge comes from within them, and that they can generate knowledge?

I devised and executed the best plan I could within the parameters of my limitations. First, I attempted to challenge the standardized curriculum by incorporating relevant themes in my literacy units to undermine the banking model. I was using an anthology from Houghton Mifflin for reading selections because it was required. Unfortunately, while the stories in it are of high caliber, they may not be most relevant to my population of students in an urban setting. So I complemented the selections with appropriate activities to enrich students' learning experiences.

The second component of my plan was to integrate culturally relevant pedagogy by inviting parent speakers to broaden my students' perspectives and understanding of the themes we were studying. Four parents came to speak to the class, each highlighting different aspects of their immigration experience as they moved from their respective native countries to Los Angeles, California. I also invited my own father to address the class and share his experience of emigrating from Vietnam to the United States.

The final component of my project was to convince my students that they had, and could create, knowledge. In response to my students' interest in hearing more stories, I decided to create an elaborate culminating assignment. I asked students to interview someone in their family or community who had immigrated to the United States, generating 21 more stories for my students to share with each other.

Reflection and Evaluation

Over the course of my inquiry, I learned to be patient with myself as a researcher and a practitioner, to trust in the process, and to have hope. I must preface the evaluation of my action plan with a disclaimer. I do not believe that the work I have done is monumental to changing the current state of public education. It merely scratches the surface of a giant renovation project that requires demolition, rebuilding, and remodeling. Nonetheless, I have come away with two insights or themes as I analyze my data and implementation, which have led me to have more questions about the current theoretical or research-based understanding of education and the implications of my work in the classroom.

The first has to do with my understanding of the learning process, especially its purpose, and my reevaluation not only of what is considered knowledge but of who is knowledgeable. During my first year of teaching, I felt students were acquiring knowledge and learning from me when they sat silently in their desks, copied down notes, and followed along as I provided instruction. I talked and my students listened. I had all the knowledge in my head and power in my hands and every day, I was giving some of that precious knowledge and power away to my students, who took it without questioning me or challenging the information. However, I no longer see what my students were experiencing as learning. I have remembered, or maybe re-imagined, the purpose of learning or the process of knowledge acquisition as a person's ability to gather information, think critically about its impact, and take a firm stand while clearly articulating the rationale and evidence for the stance. Learners of all ages can think and articulate, including my eight-year-old third graders. In the banking model I first employed, there was no room for students to think or speak for themselves.

Having parents come into the classroom and teach my students about their immigration experiences opened a space for student thinking and helped undermine the notion that the teacher, and only the teacher, has worthwhile knowledge. I de-centered myself and put attention on my students' parents instead, showcasing them as knowledgeable individuals. The first parent I invited to my classroom to talk to my students about her immigration experience was Yasmin Arias, an English-speaking parent. In fact, Yasmin felt more comfortable speaking in English than in Spanish because she grew up in the United States. Her family fled El Salvador during the 1980s, in the midst of a war and political turmoil. She was merely two years old. Her recollection of the journey was sparse because it was as if she did not experience the immigration firsthand. She was too young and her story was short and sweet.

Nonetheless, the students reacted positively to the experience. They were completely engaged. They asked many questions that Yasmin did not have answers to. I noticed that my students began making connections with Yasmin's skeletal story because she did not give a lot of details (field notes, 02/17/2012). They wanted to know more but Yasmin could not give more, so they contributed what they knew about the topic of immigration. It turned into an open discussion that gave students an opportunity to function as knowledgeable members of the classroom community:

Maria:	She traveled here because there was a war in El Salvador too.
Lisbeth:	A mom was carrying her baby and they were walking and she did carry the baby and she didn't have no more food. The man was telling them which way to go and he got mad and frustrated. If she doesn't quiet her baby, he would leave them back. That happens … they're called smugglers that bring people. Coyotes.
Lisbeth:	When they travel on the Beast [a nickname for the freight trains that people from Central America and South America ride] to Los Angeles. I have a stepbrother that came on the train and he fell off the train and he had a big scar.
Anthony:	My aunt went on the train too.
Sophie:	My grandma came from El Salvador to Los Angeles. She didn't have enough money. She came with my mom.
Lisbeth:	My mom told me a story about her that my grandpa came to the United States for find a house for my grandma and my mom can live. But then the police, he didn't let. His friend helped a little. (field notes, 02/17/2012)

The discussion that we had with Yasmin made it evident that my students were competent thinkers and held relevant knowledge. When Yasmin did not have many details to offer, my students carried on the conversation with their own understanding and experience of immigration journeys.

Aida, another mother who volunteered her story, sat on a chair in the front of the classroom while my students quietly positioned themselves on the carpet by her feet and intently listened to her story. Aida showed no fear. She started talking and did not take any long pauses until her story was completely over. None of the students interrupted her. Her story was suspenseful, filled with gruesome and heart-wrenching details. I felt my students holding their breaths at various points of her plot because they were so enthralled and captivated by the information. They were hearing from a primary source: someone they knew walked and crossed the *frontera* (border). They were utterly amazed and flabbergasted. When she finished talking, I sensed my students' bodies finally relaxing because they had been so tense for the nearly 20 minutes she had been speaking (field notes, 02/24/2012). It was as though they felt so glad that her journey had ended positively; she had made it to the United States safely.

After Aida answered my students' questions, I asked them to write and reflect. I did not give them a prompt; I simply wanted them to write down whatever they were thinking and feeling. Many shared a common sense of relief after hearing Aida's story.

> Estoy contento porque nos contó su historia en forma de un cuento o narración. Estoy agradecido de que haya venido a CNCA. Disfruté mucho la historia que contó a la clase, fue muy linda y aprendí mucho de ella. (field notes, 02/24/2012)
> *(I am happy because you told us your history and left it like a story and I am grateful you came to Camino Nuevo. I enjoyed the story you told the class, it was beautiful and I learned a lot.)*

> Me sentí tan bien de que todos sobrevivieron. Eso fue increíble. Mi parte favorita fue cuando pudieron cruzar la frontera. Me gustó su historia pues es muy parecida a la de mis padres y tíos. (field notes, 02/24/2012)
> *(I felt so happy that all of you survived! That was great. My favorite part was when you were able to cross the border. I liked your story; it is similar to the one of my uncles and parents.)*

> Me sentí contento con su aventura y que pudo llegar hasta acá pues si no yo no hubiese conocido a Edwin. (field notes, 02/24/2012)
> *(I felt happy with your adventure because you could make it here, if not I would have never met Edwin.)*

My students were reacting to Aida's story and coming up with their own conclusions. Many of them commented that their favorite part was when Aida was finally able to cross the border, most likely because they had a sense of how difficult it was for Aida to come to the United States. Even though most of my students had family members who shared a similar story, few had heard the story told so openly and honestly or had thought much about the commonalities binding their individual families into a cultural community. More important, my students realized the reason that so many of their community members had made the treacherous trek across the border was the children themselves. Their parents hoped for a better future for their children. I wasn't responsible for teaching my students the concept of hope. Aida's story did that and the idea of hope arose from self-reflection and group discussion. When one of the students commented that "[his] favorite part was when [Aida was] able to cross the border," it showed that he understood the potential of that successful crossing. He realized that the happy ending to Aida's story was the beginning of hope for her child, Edwin. Knowledge came from our collective classroom community.

My students do not need me to tell them what to think and how to think. They clearly can do so themselves, as was evident in the discussions and reflections following parent speakers. My role in the learning process should be to set up the structures for such learning experiences to take place, not to spoon-feed my students with information that tests designate as valuable knowledge. Learning occurs when my students talk to the members of the community and talk to each other to make sense of the world. If I am constantly feeding them what I perceive as the truth or what test makers consider important, then they will never realize their own abilities, their own humanity and power.

With a change in my understanding of the learning process has come a second fundamental change in how I see standardized curriculum and standardized testing—no longer as an integral part of teaching and learning, but as antithetical to meaningful learning and, in fact, harmful to students. According to Darder (2011), the standardization of curriculum and assessments is to blame for the shift from thinking about information to the mechanical dispensation of fragmented information. I have experienced firsthand what testing does to my students, how it humiliates them, breaks their spirits as learners, and devalues them as human beings. Tests are like prisons that confine my students to permanent cells; proficient and advance prisoners have the best amenities, basic prisoners get the most attention, and below-basic and far-below-basic prisoners are abused with neglect.

I began this inquiry by giving my students a survey containing three questions: What does it mean to be smart? How does one become smart? Are you smart, and why or why not? A majority of my

students responded to the survey as Anyon (1981) describes: teachers are the only knowledgeable beings in the classroom, and test scores determined if one were smart or not.

> One can become smart by paying attention to your teacher. Remembering all the things your teacher
> has taught you. To answer the questions quickly because you already know the answer. (field notes,
> 02/17/2012)

> I'm smart because I put my effort on my work and I know math and all of the things. I'm also smart
> because I work hard to pass grade. (field notes, 02/17/2012)

> I'm not smart because I don't know how to do a lot of things like math and my reading level is low. And
> because I get low in my percentage of the test. (field notes, 02/17/2012)

> I am smart because I think I'm really focused. I always finish my work. I get high scores on my test. I
> follow directions first time given. And I study a lot. (field notes, 02/17/2012)

My students' responses made me realize how much pressure these children felt from standardized
tests and how much their test scores affected how they saw themselves. High scores made them think
they were smart, while low scores convinced them they were unintelligent.

This revelation was not news to me; I was a student once and am a student still. I felt good about
myself when I got good grades and retook the SATs when I wasn't satisfied with my scores. However,
getting good grades and high scores happened to me more often than not. But what about my students
who were consistently doing poorly on standardized tests? My inquiry led me to think more critically
about the impact standardized testing had on students who perform poorly on standardized assessments, especially when test results are the only measurement used to determine intelligence and gauge
mastery over subject matter.

In fact, the combination of standardized testing and banking education creates a vicious cycle of oppression for both teachers and students. Because of standardized testing, teachers rely on banking education to ensure student performance. Banking education continues in public schools because students fail
to perform—but students fail to perform because banking education does not challenge them to think,
read, or write critically. Its purpose is simply to get students to memorize and regurgitate disjointed bits
and pieces of information to satisfy standardized tests. The rationale is that if there is a problem, it is not
with the tests or banking pedagogy; it must be the students and teachers who are not up to par.

But we know that poor students of color are disadvantaged by design. They are blamed for being
lazy and stupid when they do not perform well on standardized tests, the very same tests that are purposefully created to rank students and to create winners and losers, with the ultimate goal of ensuring
that people in power stay in power and people not in power stay disenfranchised. The tests are not opportunities for students to show what they know but to catch them out at what they don't know. My
students were able to make connections between the literature we read and the parents' oral accounts
of immigration, to draw upon various sources of information and to use that information to think
critically about the world around them. They were able to identify the root causes for migration as they
conducted their own interviews with immigrants. They could tie in elements of their family history and
explain it as a source of intrinsic motivation for obtaining higher education and changing what they see
as injustices in their community. Can such important learning be captured on a standardized test with
a standardized curriculum? The answer to this rhetorical question is a resounding no.

In addition, standardized tests deskill and demoralize teachers because teaching becomes a science
instead of an art. Pacing plans and lesson plans are based on grade-level standards and test-released
questions instead of student needs and interests. Teachers are teaching for the benefit of the hegemonic
forces rather than doing right by their students. At the end of the day, teachers may be rewarded or
punished based on their student performance on standardized tests. In this environment, teachers are

being forced to make a choice. They can be moral and adopt a culturally relevant curriculum—or they can comply, teach to the test, and keep their livelihood.

I choose to be ethical because my decision affects the lives and futures of young people. I look to Ayers (2010) for hope that I can develop meaningful curriculum to address the needs of my students instead of the needs of the CSTs. I will keep his crucial questions in mind as I plan learning themes for my students: "Are there opportunities for discovery and surprise? Are students actively engaged with primary sources and hands-on materials? Is productive work going on? Is the work linked to student questions or interests? Are problems within the classroom, the school, and the larger community part of student consciousness? Is work in my classroom pursued to its furthest limits?" (Ayers, 2010, pp. 104–105). I will focus less on how a standard will be tested on the CSTs and more on how such learning experiences will enhance my students' awareness of the world we live in, trusting that critical consciousness will eventually lead to action.

No Going Back

My craft has grown in two ways as a result of my action research. First, quality instruction and meaningful learning experiences have become the forefront of my thoughts when I put together my curriculum and units. For example, I recently put together a unit asking my students to explore global issues that stem from poverty. Right now, impoverished children and families are homeless or live in shanty shelters, do not have adequate clothing and shoes, suffer from hunger, have no access to health care, and have no opportunity to obtain an education. I am aware that these problems exist within my students' community, but I want my students also to see themselves as connected to citizens across the globe, as part of a global human family. We will explore our own privilege, build our awareness of the global issue, and recognize philanthropic organizations. My students will be exposed to the works of nonprofit organizations such as Oprah Winfrey's Leadership Academy for Girls, Doctors Without Borders, Feed the Children, Habitat for Humanity, and Toms in order to help them understand that it is possible to make choices based on values other than competition—and greed.

I will, of course, make sure to address academic standards in reading and writing alongside our thematic learning and deep discussions. We will be reading expository texts, ranging from news articles to online websites, about the global issues that stem from poverty. I will highlight the importance of attending to text features and determining the main idea and supporting details in reading materials, but I will do it as students are reading about a world much larger and more diverse than the one commonly found in commercial textbooks. They will also put together presentations that reflect their learning to make sense of the world we live in and that teach their peers about specific global issues. Because of my action research, I have realized that teaching is an art where broad learning themes should be the epicenter and the standards are seamlessly incorporated into daily lessons.

In addition, treating my students humanely has become the core of my daily interactions with them. Because this new habit requires honest and open communication, I find myself providing a rationale for why it is that we do things in certain ways. For example, I took the time to explain why we do not run up and down the stairs. Our school is small and it is unsafe for us to run because we might trip, tumble, and fall, causing us immense pain and suffering. On top of that, we would have to miss school to go to the doctor's office and then stay home and rest. We would miss out on important learning and time with our classroom community. This domino effect all began because we were running up and down the stairs. We can avoid all that if we simply walk. I have done more explaining than yelling and controlling student behaviors lately and it feels good. I feel like I am treating my students humanely rather than imposing arbitrary rules simply because I can, and I know they are more than capable of understanding my rationale.

Being more transparent with my students has also been beneficial for them. When they disagree with each other, they try to give each other reasons instead of simply retaliating. On a rainy day, my students had lunch in the classroom instead of the courtyard. Atziri was giving away her juice to Anthony because she did not want it. She tossed it across the room to Anthony instead of walking it over to him or passing it, causing her classmates to protest loudly. They all gave her reasons it was not okay for her to do that. She could have missed and hit another student. She could have destroyed the projector and Elmo equipment. She could have hit Anthony in his eyes and his glasses could have shattered. What made me proud of this moment was that my students were not waiting for me to take action and reprimand the culprit. Instead, they understood the danger of tossing juice across the room and took it upon themselves to explain it to Atziri, who I'm sure will never throw juice at anyone again.

I have been struck by the fact that changes in my perception that affect my behavior are not, and cannot be, confined to my classroom. In the concluding week of my project, I attended a staff meeting on the topic of behavioral expectations for students that proved especially emotionally draining. The middle school recently underwent a "behavioral reset." The leadership team and the middle school teachers spent an entire instructional day retraining students in how to transition between classes, how to walk up and down between the lower school and the upper school, and how to properly get their lunches. The dean of culture showed pictures of the students moving from place to place as evidence of success, attributing it to the efforts behind behavioral reset day. He announced that soon, K–3 teachers and students would be doing the same at the lower-school campus.

When I saw the pictures, I was shaken with fear, disappointed and petrified. In one picture, middle school boys were walking in a straight line, in uniform, from the lower school to the middle school. I could not see the students' expressions because the picture captured their back side but I can guarantee that they were not jumping for joy. They were honestly an orange jumpsuit and metal shackles away from being in prison. I was floored. The images devastated me and made me feel helpless. I raised my hand to voice my concerns but the image was so powerful that I broke down in tears in front of the entire staff, leadership team, and additional support staff. The only sentence I managed to get out was that the picture made me feel like we were disrespecting our students and treating them like prisoners.

My reaction definitely caught the attention of everybody in the room. My principal spoke up and defended the position of the school because our students needed to learn how to move around in our limited space safely and reassured me that a lot of thought went into the behavioral reset. The dean of culture invited teachers to join the Improving School Culture Task Force to continue the conversation. I asked to be included. The Task Force is responsible for reexamining the discipline code; finalizing a list of norms, school-wide procedures, and classroom expectations; and identifying positive culture-building practices and components that can be systemized. I appreciate my leadership team for their willingness to take feedback constructively and meet the needs of teachers and students, and I am glad for the opportunity to try and spark new thinking on such important issues.

My reaction at the staff meeting made me realize how passionate I have become as a social justice educator. I cannot be pushing an agenda of respect for individual students and what they know and can do in my classroom and then stand by while they are mistreated and disrespected in the school at large. I feel proud of myself for standing up for my students, even though I did very little speaking and a lot of crying. I have become more critical and vigilant of what is happening at my school. I do not want to be antagonistic, but I do want my colleagues and leadership team to question the things that we do and ask whether those things send the right messages to our students, because the impact of our decisions is enormous. I know and trust that the educators at my school have the same mindset as me; they believe in our students and want the absolute best for them. Therefore, I will continue to ask those difficult questions, reflect and reexamine the humanity of my own teaching practices, and engage in conversations when the occasions arise.

My inquiry and my findings have made me realize that this work is an arduous process and will yield slow progress. But I must never lose hope. My influence will increase with each set of students that walks through my door. My students will continue to teach me, and I will continue to learn from them.

We will grow together. This year, what I have done is not enough but the change in attitude, tone, and attention on standardized testing and standardized curriculum has fundamentally transformed me into a social justice educator. I will continue my efforts to teach with humanity, compassion, and love.

Note

1. Adapted from an unpublished master's thesis at the University of California, Los Angeles, 2012.

References

Anyon, J. (1981). Social class and school knowledge. *Curriculum Inquiry, 11*(1), 3–42.

Ayers, W. (2010). *To teach: The journey of a teacher.* New York: Teachers College Press.

Darder, A. (2011). *A dissident voice: Essays on culture, pedagogy and power.* New York: Peter Lang.

Freire, P. (1993). *Pedagogy of the oppressed.* New York: Continuum.

CHAPTER 12

Perceptions of Health Education among Adolescents in an Urban School

A Project to Promote Empowerment and Health Literacy in an Underserved Community[1]

Inga Wilder

Rationale and Research Questions

In addition to teaching high school health education, I am also a medical student in the Program in Medical Education-Health Equity (PRIME-HEq) at UC San Diego. PRIME-HEq is a special dual-degree program that prepares medical students to work with underserved or at-risk populations across California. Students in PRIME-HEq are given the opportunity to obtain a master's degree in addition to a medical degree. I chose a master's degree in education because I believe that if I am equipped with the knowledge and skills of an educator, I will be able to teach others how to live healthy lives.

I know from personal experience that urban communities face many challenges, especially when it comes to educational and health care needs. I grew up in Compton, California, which is an inner city in Los Angeles County. Compton is a city that is terribly underserved, and my experiences growing up there helped me to realize how the social problems and health disparities of my city impact the health-care needs of minority communities. Growing up, I always questioned things. I asked, "Why do so many obstacles plague inner-city communities?" "Why are African Americans and Latinos who live in urban environments more likely to get sick?" "Why are *we* more likely to suffer from certain diseases?" However, the question that I reflected on the most was, "What can I do about this?"

In order to understand these issues more deeply and to better serve my community, I decided to learn how to become a more effective teacher. As a medical student, I take the health of my patients very seriously, but I am also passionate about teaching my patients. Historically, physicians were teachers who taught patients about various diseases and how to take better care of themselves. But medicine today is in a state of emergency, especially in underserved communities. Patient education is no longer a priority and, unfortunately, many communities are suffering. Therefore, I decided that as a physician I would try my best to make patient education a priority in my clinical practice.

As a health educator, and future physician, I want everyone to be healthy. However, I know that underserved communities have unique struggles, especially when it comes to educational and healthcare needs. Low-income, underserved communities often have a short supply of physicians (Grumbach, Vranizan, & Bindman, 1997). Poverty plagues these communities, many of these neighborhoods are unsafe, and there are few medical resources available to community members. In medicine it is well known that racial and ethnic minorities who live in urban communities are more likely to develop preventable conditions such as Type 2 diabetes, obesity, and heart disease (Office of Minority Health and Health Disparities, Centers for Disease Control and Prevention, n.d.). Therefore, people who live in these communities should be more aware of how they can prevent these types of illnesses from occurring.

There are many public health campaigns directed specifically at teenagers. However, since teenagers spend most of their time in school, the most accurate information they receive about preventative medicine is in health education classes. But adolescents living in urban, underserved communities may have unique healthcare needs that might not be reflected in the health curriculum they receive at school. This study investigated whether or not students attending an urban school believed their current health curriculum met their needs. This study also aimed to use student input to create a new health curriculum to address the students' concerns about their health education course.

Additionally, it is known that health, education, and literacy are intricately linked (St. Leger, 2001). Low literacy rates in underserved communities may affect people's access, acceptability, and use of health care resources. Since there are strong correlations between literacy and future health outcomes, the second goal of this study was to improve my students' "health literacy" by incorporating fun classroom activities into the health curriculum. Health literacy is a person's ability to read, understand, and use health information to make healthy decisions. Health literacy affects all of the interactions that people have with the medical field. It affects how well a person can follow instructions for treatment and it also includes how well a person can communicate with medical personnel. Students were introduced to the idea of health literacy and asked to suggest how they would like to see math and reading used in health education classes to promote health literacy. Therefore, the goal of this project was to promote health literacy and empowerment by incorporating the students' experiences and opinions about health education, as well as their suggestions for including basic math and reading skills, into the health curriculum at their school.

I hoped to answer the following questions during this project:

1. Do teenagers attending an urban high school feel that their existing health curriculum meets their health needs?
2. How can basic math and reading skills be integrated into a health curriculum? What impact would these skills have on students' health literacy levels and learning needs?

These research questions addressed current gaps in health education theory because they take the perspectives of the teenagers who are currently living and attending school in the communities into account. In the past, health education was "done 'on' or 'to' people, rather than 'by' or 'with' people" (Nutbeam, 2000). Also, traditional health education curricula are designed using a one-size-fits-all model. These curricula do not address issues within the community and they do little to influence or improve future health outcomes for students. This project aimed to address this discrepancy by incorporating students' suggestions, opinions, and experiences into the health curriculum. This project adopted a newer, more empowering educational model for promoting health awareness and health literacy. It was designed to address issues of adolescent health and health literacy with—not for—the teenagers involved. In order to accomplish these goals, I developed a conceptual model that depicts how teachers and administrators could develop a student-centered health curriculum (see Figure 12.1). The cyclical nature of this model implies that health education is dynamic and it should always be revised and updated to meet the students' needs.

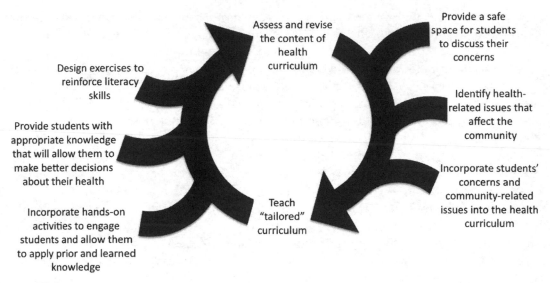

Figure 12.1.

Context: Community and School Snapshot

I taught health education classes at two public high schools in East Los Angeles, hereafter referred to as School A and School B. The community where I worked was home to a large Latino working-class population (see Table 12.1). According to the *LA Times* (n.d.), many households in the community around my schools made less than $20,000 per year. To put this number into perspective, in 2011 the U.S. Department of Health and Human Services set an annual income of $22,350 for a family of four (living in California) as one of its poverty guideline markers (U.S. Department of Health & Human Services, 2011). In the school community, then, many families live below the poverty line.

	School A (*N* = 339)	School B (*N* = 419)
Race, %		
Hispanic or Latino	96.76	97.85
Asian	0.88	0.95
African American	1.48	0.48
American Indian	0.29	0.48
Caucasian	0.59	0.24
Home Language, %		
Spanish	71.68	79.00
English	27.73	20.76
Other	0.59	0.24
English Language Learners (ELL), %	20.06	26.01
Students with Individualized Education Programs (IEPs), %	11.80	16.23

Table 12.1. Demographics of Students at School A and School B

As is often true in poor communities, residents of East Los Angeles are much underserved. There are few grocery stores in the neighborhood, an inadequate number of affordable housing options, hardly any youth programs, and only two adult educational centers. However, there is a huge police presence in the community. Although it includes fewer than 10 square miles, it is home to three LAPD police jurisdictions (*Los Angeles Times*, n.d.). The students who participated in this project were recruited from mandatory ninth-grade biology courses: 58 students from School A and 67 students from School B joined the study. To enroll in this study, students had to have written parental consent and they also had to provide signed student assent.

Methodology

To answer my focus questions I divided my inquiry project into 4 phases (Figure 12.2). During the first phase of my project, I taught students at School A the existing health education curriculum. Afterward, I held four focus groups with some of the students to get more information about what they thought about the health curriculum. Ultimately, 27 students from School A participated in four after school focus groups: two Latino groups and two Latina groups (each group had between six and eight participants). I allowed students to choose which lesson in the curriculum they wanted to discuss: exercise and nutrition; drugs/substance abuse; sex and birth control; or healthy relationships. In addition, at the end of each focus group, I showed the participants a brief presentation about health literacy and asked them how they would like to see math and reading used in health education class. All of these 1.5-hour sessions were recorded and the audio was transcribed and analyzed for themes. After revising the health curriculum based on feedback from students, I taught the course to a new group of students at School B.

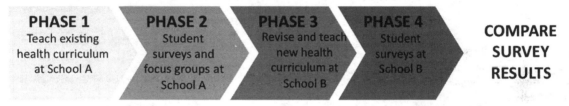

Figure 12.2.

At the end of the courses, both student groups completed the same satisfaction survey and the same two health literacy assessments: the Short Test of Functional Health Literacy in Adults (STOFHLA) and the Newest Vital Signs (NVS). I compared survey results for some insight into whether the new curriculum seemed more relevant to students and/or seemed more effective in improving students' health literacy. While the comparison is not perfect (given that the student groups were not statistically matched for comparison), I believe the findings are at least suggestive.

Focus Group Findings: Love and Coping

The focus group sessions proved very informative. I had no idea how much some of my students were struggling with issues related to drugs, love, sex, and relationships. Although I thought I had a good idea of what my students needed to learn, I soon realized that they had much more complicated needs.

Table 12.2 illustrates the type of questions I used in focus groups to elicit student thinking. Analysis of transcripts from each session revealed themes common to all of the groups; specifically, students expressed clear interest in learning more about drugs, sex, and relationships. They reported that drugs are hard to escape in the community and are used as a coping mechanism and that sex is viewed as a rite of passage. Peer pressure to try drugs and have sex was common. Table 12.3 shows all seven of the themes identified, but I soon realized that they could be distilled into two common themes. My students wanted to know (1) how to love and (2) how to cope.

Before the focus groups I thought the idea of love was simple and straightforward, but during the conversations that I had with my students I realized that they were confused about what it means to love someone else and what it means to love yourself. It is interesting that both male and female groups thought that in order to show your love to a significant other (boyfriend or girlfriend) you had to have sex with them.

Lesson	Questions
Exercise and nutrition	1. *Why* don't a lot of teens who live in LA exercise? Do you think they're all just being lazy? 2. What places do you have to exercise? 3. *Why* do you think there are so many cheap, fast food restaurants next to high schools? 4. Many teens know that fast food is unhealthy, but they still like to eat it. *Why* do you think they do it instead of choosing healthier food?
Drugs and substance abuse	1. What's going on with teens nowadays that makes so many of them want to do drugs and drink alcohol? 2. Do you think some drugs are better than others? 3. How would some of your friends answer this question: When is it a good time to do drugs? When is it a bad time to do drugs? 4. Who do you talk to if you have questions about drugs?
Healthy relationships, sex, and birth control	1. *Why* do some teens have sex when they aren't ready? 2. How is love related to sex? 3. Where do you get your information about sex and birth control? 4. Do you think your friends are being pressured to have sex? 5. *Who* do you talk to about relationships?

Table 12.2. Sample Focus Group Questions

Themes	Sample Quotations	
	Female Focus Group	**Male Focus Group**
Drugs are used as a "coping mechanism"	*Miss, because they have problems at home and then once you do it, it like calms you down […]* *It's like you know how when adults, they get all stressed out, instead of, oh, some people do smoke weed, but like others they actually smoke tobacco or smoke cigarettes.* *Mary Jane is like your only friend. Everyone is fake Miss. I don't trust no body. I just trust Mary Jane.*	
Drugs are hard to escape	*It's hard 'cause I'm always around it. Like my whole family, like, you know. Damn. We're like drug dealers and cholas and I'm around that all the time.* *In school you just see, like, people doing it. You just enter into the restroom and they be blazing it.*	*Moderator: [During the lesson on substance abuse] You guys named a lot more drugs than I thought you would.* *Boy: We even showed you some new ones, huh?* *Boy: 'Cause this is [name of the community] Miss.*
Teens are pressured into trying drugs by other teens	*Some do it because they're afraid that if they don't do it they're goanna lose their friends.* *For a lot of them, Miss, they're just trying to fit in.*	*Question: Why do you think there's so many kids at this school who do marijuana?* *Boy: Just to be with the crowd.* *Moderator: Why are so many kids doing drugs?* *Boy: Because they pressure them! They'll be like, "Oh, you're still a little kid. You're a mama's boy."* *Moderator: Who's pressuring?* *Boy: Friends.*
Sex is seen as a "rite of passage"		*Because we're guys Miss. We're supposed to lose our virginity.* *[When discussing sex in relationships] Some girls are like, 'Let's do this shit. You're lagging.'* *Because Miss, you don't want to be called names. You don't want to be a virgin.*

Table 12.3. Focus Group Themes and Sample Quotations

According to my students, having sex was how you showed your love to someone you cared about. One male even exclaimed, "Lack of sex. No love!" (male focus group #2, December 15, 2011). I was flabbergasted by this! Since my students had this misconception that "sex equals love" they were putting themselves at risk for acquiring a sexually transmitted infection, and they were also more likely to become teen parents. I knew that this belief was something that I definitely had to address in the new health curriculum. Therefore, one of my goals was to teach my students that there are other ways to love someone without having sexual intercourse.

Peer pressure was another theme that kept coming up in the conversations with my students and I believe it is related to self-love and inner strength. I realize that it is very difficult to stand up to peer pressure. Many of my students said that teens do drugs and have sex *because* they are being pressured to do so by other teens. Therefore, to improve adolescent health and to improve health education for my students I tried to think about how I could help my students figure out ways to stand up to peer pressure. Again, love seemed to be the answer. I figured that if I could help my students learn how to love themselves, then they would be able to stand up to peer pressure because if you love yourself you would be less inclined to do or try things that would be detrimental to your health, no matter how hard others might be pressuring you.

The focus group sessions also helped me to realize that my students wanted to learn how to cope with the issues that they were dealing with. My students are mostly ninth graders and I think the transition to high school was difficult for some of them. Also, the majority of my students are between the ages of 14 and 16 so they are all going through the ups and downs of puberty. Their hormones are changing and their bodies are changing, and I believe that they are all curious about these new changes. In addition to their physical changes, their social circles were also changing. These new social interactions, which included interacting with much older students, making new friends, and dating, presented my students with a range of situations that impacted their physical and mental well-being. In addition to the stress and challenge of just being a teenager, I also learned that many of my students had outside stressors they had to deal with. For example, during one of our discussions, I asked, "Why do teens do drugs even though they know it is bad for their health?" The following is one of the responses that I received:

> It's [for] so many reasons. It depends, like, if you're going through a lot of things in your house or whatever, it's 'cause of that. Or if you're like, if everything's good at your house and you're happy, you shouldn't be doing that because, I guess that's what got me into it. Problems at my house. Well, yeah, my cousin got me into it. He's older though. (girl focus group #2, December 12, 2011).

Unfortunately some of these stressors were things that no child (or adult!) should have to deal with. My students were weighed down with financial concerns and they were worried about how their families would make it. From our discussions I concluded that my students were also dealing with violence at home and in the community. In this community, narcotic and alcohol use are rampant, and I discovered that these substances are commonly used to self-medicate. I also learned that my students were struggling with isolation, which is a clinical condition rather than a fleeting emotion.

Isolation (also known as "isolation of affect" in medical literature) is a psychological defense mechanism:

> *Defense mechanisms* (or coping styles) are automatic psychological processes that protect the individual against anxiety and from the awareness of internal or external dangers or stressors. Individuals are often unaware of these processes as they operate. Defense mechanisms mediate the individual's reaction to emotional conflicts and to internal and external stressors. (American Psychiatric Association, 1994, p. 751)

In other words, defense mechanisms are subconscious ways that our bodies try to protect us. There are many different types of defense mechanisms, but the one that I noticed most often in my students is isolation:

> [Isolation occurs when] the individual deals with emotional conflict or internal or external stressors by the separation of ideas from the feelings originally associated with them. The individual loses touch with

the feelings associated with a given idea (e.g., a traumatic event) while remaining aware of the cognitive elements of it (e.g., descriptive details). (American Psychiatric Association, 1994, p. 756)

In short, isolation occurs when the individual separates his or her feelings from surrounding events. Isolation is common in people who have experienced significant traumatic events. For example, veterans who can describe horrendous war events without an emotional response are said to be in "isolation." Although I am still in the process of completing my clinical training, I feel fairly confident that I noticed isolation in many of my students. This observation echoes Jeffrey Duncan-Andrade's work on posttraumatic stress disorder among students who live and attend school in the inner city. He notes:

> The fact that witnessing or experiencing physical violence contributes to a person's traumatic stress load is common sense. What is not often clear to educators is the frequency and intensity with which this happens to urban youth and the medical research that suggests this may be one of the biggest inhibitors to academic success. Recent studies suggest that as many as one-third of children living in urban poverty show the symptoms of posttraumatic stress disorder (PTSD), a rate nearly twice that found in soldiers returning from Iraq (Tucker, 2007, p. 1). Complexifying the issue is the fact that while soldiers leave the battlefield, young people do not. This suggests that for youth that are repeatedly exposed to violent traumatic events, modifiers like "perpetual" or "persistent" would more accurately describe their experiences than the commonly used "post" traumatic stress. (2011, pp. 314–315)

I believe all of the conflict and stressors that my students face on a day-to-day basis reflect deeper social issues that the community is plagued with. I also believe that these stressors contribute significantly to the widespread use of illegal substances, like marijuana, among students at my school. Therefore, another concern in the curriculum was helping teens deal with their problems without turning to harmful substances and developing toxic behaviors and habits.

Revisions: From Educator to Tailor

Designing a new health curriculum for my new students often felt like a very daunting task, and I worried I was not medically prepared to address emerging issues. Still, I forged ahead and revised first the substance abuse lesson. My thinking was recorded in my weekly journal:

> I find it amazing that so many of my students smoke marijuana. I am even more amazed by how open they are about it with me (sometimes, I wonder if they have these conversations with their other teachers …) … Unfortunately, we didn't talk about marijuana much in my [previous] substance abuse lesson and I've been trying to figure out how I can do things differently. First, I think I'm going to focus the lesson entirely on marijuana and addiction. Also, I realize that it would be silly for me to only talk about prevention, because a lot of my students already have some serious drug habits. To address this, I would like to incorporate "harm reduction" strategies into the lesson. Harm reduction is something that is done a lot in medicine. It is not focused on eliminating the "unhealthy" behavior, but it is more focused on managing the situation until things can be improved. Giving free condoms and birth control to sex workers or needle-exchange programs for IV drug users are examples of harm reduction. In other words, harm reduction is mainly focused on minimizing "damage" in a "less than ideal" situation … My goal for my revised substance abuse curriculum is to: 1) help the students who are marijuana-free remain so; 2) encourage the occasional users to consider giving it up completely someday; 3) encourage the heavy users to transition into occasional use. (January 20, 2012)

The harm-reduction strategy I mention was the method I used to revise all of my health lessons (Resnicow, Smith, Harrison, & Drucker, 1999). I decided to stick with this strategy because it is known to be effective. Therefore, in the substance abuse lesson we focused on staying safe if students did use drugs. I also emphasized the importance of cutting back on drug use and I stressed the importance of being drug free.

To address issues of peer pressure and trying to cope, I thought it would be more powerful to let my students teach each other. Therefore, we role played, with students working in groups to figure out how they would intervene in situations where close friends were being pressured to try new street drugs by older cousins or where a friend was self-medicating because she was having problems at home (these scenarios were pulled directly from the focus group discussions). All of the groups acted their resolutions in front of the class, and I think it was a very powerful experience for students to see and hear how their peers would respond in those situations.

I revised the other lessons in the health curriculum in a similar fashion. I tried to lecture my students less, and I gave them more time to share their experiences with the class. I did not try to scare them into being compliant, because most students in the focus group said that my "scare tactics" would not work. Also, they wanted to see more pictures, so I included more visuals in all of the presentations that I made. I gave them more time to reflect on the information that I shared with them (this was especially important when we talked about sex and I had them reflect on different reasons teenagers decided to start having sex). Pregnancy was a new topic that I added to the lessons. My students wanted to know "what happens after the sperm goes inside" (girl focus group #2, December 12, 2011) so I showed them pictures of what the fetus looks like at various stages of the pregnancy. At the time I had two students who were pregnant so I included a section where we talked about what happens during the labor and delivery process. I also included a very extensive section on birth control options and I informed the students how they could get birth control when they decided that they were ready to have sex.

In order to improve my students' health literacy skills I gave them simple vocabulary words at the beginning of each lesson (I chose words that were mentioned in the focus groups like love, cope, depression, peer pressure, addiction, self-esteem, violence, abuse, relationship, etc.). It is interesting that the majority of students in the focus groups said that they did not like math and they did not want to do math in health class, but I decided to incorporate math in the curriculum regardless (this was the only time I included something they did not want). They did, however, provide me with some fun ideas for incorporating more reading activities in the health curriculum and I used all of their suggestions— word puzzles, scrambles, and crossword puzzles.

Findings: Comparing Outcomes

My goals were to determine whether I might make the curriculum more relevant and might improve health literacy outcomes. The survey comparison data in Table 12.4 shows that, generally, students at School B were more satisfied with the content of the revised health curriculum, although the gains seemed somewhat modest.

	School A (*N* = 48) Mean (SD)	School B (*N* = 62) Mean (SD)
I think learning about health in school is important.	4.46 (0.54)	4.52 (0.70)
I learn a lot in my health class.	4.19 (0.70)	4.23 (0.88)
I think the information I learn in health class is useful.	4.44 (0.65)	4.52 (0.76)
I feel comfortable talking about health topics in class.	4.44 (0.65)	4.12 (0.93)
I talk with my friends about information I learn in health class.	3.23 (1.10)	3.53 (1.29)
I share the information I learn in health class with my family.	3.23 (1.24)	3.45 (1.33)
My health class makes me more confident about decisions I make about my health.	4.06 (0.86)	4.25 (0.94)
My health class teaches me everything I need to know about my own health.	4.15 (0.82)	4.26 (0.85)

*Statements assessed using a 5-point Likert scale (5 = Yes, I strongly agree; 4 = I agree; 3 = I don't know; 2 = I disagree; 1 = No, I strongly disagree).

Table 12.4. Survey Results Assessing Satisfaction with Relevance of Health Curriculum

Figures 12.3 and 12.4 also indicate gains in scores on the two health literacy surveys, and these gains appear stronger. Although this data is not statistically significant, it implies that students who are exposed to concepts, like reading and mathematics, multiple times (and in different settings) retain more of the information they learn. It also suggests that students can benefit from learning different topics in different settings.

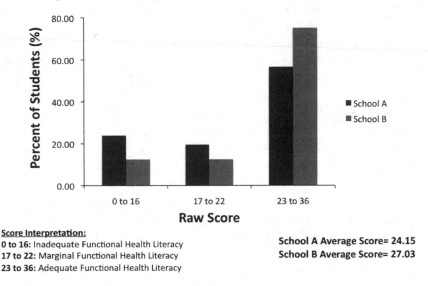

Score Interpretation:
0 to 16: Inadequate Functional Health Literacy
17 to 22: Marginal Functional Health Literacy
23 to 36: Adequate Functional Health Literacy

School A Average Score= 24.15
School B Average Score= 27.03

Figure 12.3.

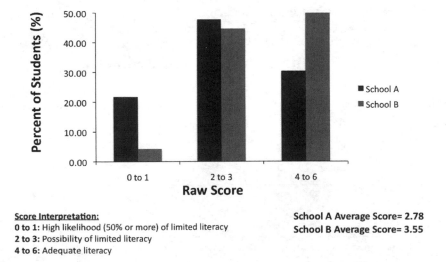

Score Interpretation:
0 to 1: High likelihood (50% or more) of limited literacy
2 to 3: Possibility of limited literacy
4 to 6: Adequate literacy

School A Average Score= 2.78
School B Average Score= 3.55

Figure 12.4.

Discussion: Toward a More Relevant Curriculum and a More Just Community

During the course of my project I learned a lot about my students and myself. Admittedly at times I was not sure if I was the right person to do this kind of project, but with time to reflect I have come to believe that I was destined to work with these kids, in this community, and on this project. This project showed me that students in this community had healthcare needs that were not being addressed in school—and I believe this statement is true for other students at other schools in similar communities. I also learned that pressures to use drugs and to have sex were common in this community, so I tried to address these issues in the revised health curricula to promote more responsible behaviors. Also, the improvement in NVS and STOFHLA scores suggests that the incorporation of fun math and reading assignments into the health curriculum my students were learning helped to reinforce their math and reading literacy skills in other classes.

I believe this inquiry project points to a new direction in the field of health education because there is not much information in the literature that shows the importance of tailoring health curricula for students in urban communities. More research is needed to investigate whether long-term health outcomes can be affected through curriculum modifications. Also, in my own location, students in each school should be consulted so that curricula respond not only to common areas of need but to unique challenges in particular locations. If health courses aren't helping create improved community health, they serve little or no purpose.

My work this year has revolutionized how I will practice medicine in the future. It has also revolutionized how I will educate my patients. This project provides evidence that highlights the importance of learning the story behind our students and each patient. It shows the importance of listening, not being judgmental, and of using this information to guide educational practices and patient care. Now I realize that in order to provide the best medical care I need to spend extra time listening to my patients and getting their history. In medical school the emphasis is always on developing an extensive differential diagnosis and learning how to treat individual health problems. But now I have learned that I cannot treat individual health problems without listening to and treating the entire individual, who is, after all, enmeshed in a community beyond a physician's office walls. The health challenges of that community, which sadly have historically been overlooked, must also be integral to my concern for the individual patient.

In essence, my views on how to realize more equitable health outcomes have changed significantly. I now realize that students and teachers cannot do this type of revolutionary work alone. To have the greatest impact, we need community-wide interventions to address the issues that plague inner-city communities—issues like violence, drug use and acceptability, and social responsibility. I am now convinced that before lasting change can occur educators and researchers have to work with community members to develop solutions that are sustainable and that empower the community to be catalysts for their own change. Actors can show students how to overcome their fears and improve self-confidence. Musicians can help students express themselves creatively in addition to helping students improve their math skills. Artists can help students learn how to think critically about the world around them. Doctors and other medical professionals can help students learn that the decisions they make about their health today will eventually affect them in the future.

We must find ways to build bridges in the community if we are to attain the goal of a healthier America—especially a healthier urban America.

Acknowledgment

I would like to thank Drs. Eduardo Lopez and Raymond Perry for their guidance and mentorship as I developed this research project and brought it to life. I would also like to thank all of the teachers who are working in disadvantaged communities and are struggling to change the world around them.

Note

1. Adapted from an unpublished master's thesis at the University of California, Los Angeles, 2012.

Bibliography

American Psychiatric Association. (1994). *Diagnostic and statistical manual of mental disorders DSM-IV*. Washington, DC: Author.

Duncan-Andrade, J. (2011). The principal facts: New directions for teacher education. In A. F. Ball & C. A. Tyson (Eds.), *Studying diversity in teacher education* (pp. 309–326). Lanham, MD: Rowman & Littlefield.

Grumbach, K., Vranizan, K., & Bindman, A. B. (1997). Physician supply and access to care in urban communities. *Health Affairs, 16*(1), 71–86.

Los Angeles Times. (n.d.). Mapping L. A.: The Eastside. Retrieved from http://projects.latimes.com/mapping-la/neighborhoods/region/eastside/

Nutbeam, D. (2000). Health literacy as a public health goal: A challenge for contemporary health education and communication strategies into the 21st century. *Health Promotion International, 15*(3), 259–267.

Office of Minority Health and Health Disparities, Centers for Disease Control and Prevention. (n.d.). *Minority Health Determines the Health of the Nation*. Retrieved from http://www.cdc.gov/omhd/

Parker, R., Baker, D., Williams, M., & Nurss, J. (1995). The test of functional health literacy in adults: A new instrument for measuring patients' literacy skills. *Journal of General Internal Medicine, 10*(10), 537–541.

Resnicow, K., Smith M., Harrison L., & Drucker E. (1999). Correlates of occasional cigarette and marijuana use: Are teens harm reducing? *Addictive Behaviors, 24*(2), 251–266.

St. Leger, L. (2001). Schools, health literacy and public health: Possibilities and challenges. *Health Promotion International, 16*(2), 197–205.

Tucker, J. (2007). Children who survive urban warfare suffer from PTSD, too. *San Francisco Gate*, pp. 1–7.

U.S. Department of Health & Human Services. (2011). 2011 Health and Human Services Poverty Guidelines: One Version of the [U.S.] Federal Poverty Measure. Retrieved from http://aspe.hhs.gov/poverty/11poverty.shtml

Weiss, B., Mays, M., Martz, W., Castro, K., DeWalt, D., Pignone, M., Mockbee, J., & Hale, F. A. (2005). Quick assessment of literacy in primary care: The newest vital sign. *Annals of Family Medicine, 3*(6), 514–522.

PART THREE

Participatory Action Research (PAR)

Introduction
Participatory Action Research (PAR) and Youth Participatory Action Research (YPAR)

Part 3 explores participatory action research (PAR)—the strand of critical action research that assigns participants the role of respected co-researchers. When co-researchers are drawn from youth populations, the work is typically referred to as youth participatory action research (YPAR). Often, though not always,[1] participants are drawn from marginalized populations. The researcher leading a project typically contributes expertise on the action research process and serves as facilitator. Participant co-researchers contribute expertise from their life experiences—essential for identifying critical questions, gathering and interpreting data, and devising strategies for change. One notable characteristic of this strand of critical action research is that it requires tolerance for a high level of uncertainty as a project unfolds under the direction of its many participants. Another is that among all forms of action research, PAR perhaps yields the most innovative strategies for sharing findings and pursuing substantive change.

The first chapter following this overview is by Caitlin Cahill, whose work is well known in the PAR/YPAR field. This rich piece serves as a useful introduction to the field for two reasons. First, Cahill details principles of participatory action research,[2] which include not only a social justice orientation but also an insistence that participant co-researchers have real voice in the research—requiring close monitoring of power sharing as work progresses. Researchers must be willing to share substantive control. Second, in detailing a project with young women in New York City who found negative stereotypes to be an important challenge, Cahill also provides a detailed illustration of elements and challenges of YPAR in practice. Among the benefits of participatory work including marginalized youth, she notes that "it recognizes young people's agency and competency and very directly privileges their voices and develops their capacities, and is potentially open enough to allow young people to challenge accepted points of view." Here is a hallmark of participatory research: rather than the researcher speaking on behalf of the population researched, participants typically speak for themselves. In this well-known research project, young women of color devised innovative ways to confront and challenge negative stereotypes. These included producing posters they placed strategically throughout their neighborhoods and creating a website featuring their voices and inviting others to share their voices as well.[3]

Chapter 14 is by prominent participatory researchers Madeline Fox and Michelle Fine. Here, the focus is on strategies for advancing change. The imperative for social change combined with the reconfigured role of "researcher" in the participatory model prompts new ways of thinking about—in fact, demands new ways of thinking about—how to share data strategically, in formats more likely to have practical effect than the traditional article in an academic journal. In this case, researchers shared data in dramatic performances, with audiences including "teachers, parents, school administrators, young people, social scientists, community members, police, Department of Education officials, and policymakers." At issue was unjust treatment of certain populations based on class, gender, race-ethnicity, sexuality, immigration status, disability status, and neighborhood. The authors share both details of the project (part of a large-scale project designed by an adult and youth research collaborative) and its theoretical basis.

Next, in Chapter 15, Carolina Muñoz Proto details a participatory project exploring how the incarceration of parents or close relatives affects youth. In addition to "challenging the fantasy that research for critical purposes is a neat, linear endeavor," results of the project included what the author terms "self-education," which "confirmed many intuitions and debunked others, empowered the members of the team, and inspired [the researchers] to reframe the work at various points in order to avoid otherizing narratives of redemption." Clear in this piece is the value—and challenge—of conscientization, so often the concern of critical researchers.

In the final chapter in Part 3, Jennifer Ayala illustrates the complexities of conducting participatory action research within educational institutions, which often are the workplace of critical action researchers. And she makes clear that PAR generates strong emotional as well as intellectual engagement, including "[l]ove, anxiety, conflict, depression, euphoria, [and] disappointment." Ayala uses a novel "split-screen" approach to report on two different research projects in which students served as co-researchers: one exploring the experiences of "vulnerable" college students and one exploring the experiences of students in a high school with a reputation for violence and for serving "remedial students with no future." Perhaps most important, Ayala illustrates the many tensions that arise when work that ultimately challenges existing power arrangements plays out in settings where those arrangements are firmly in place. There is danger in speaking truth to power, for students and faculty alike, and there are ethical uncertainties for faculty who recruit students into critical research projects which may—or may not—influence hoped-for change.

Taken together, the chapters in Part 3 illuminate what participatory action research is as well as some of its particular challenges—and potential rewards.

Notes

1. For an example of YPAR with a privileged population—and the challenges of such research in an elite location—see Stoudt, B. G. (2009). The role of language & discourse in the investigation of privilege: Using Participatory Action Research to discuss theory, develop methodology, & interrupt power. *The Urban Review, 41*(1), 7–28.
2. Elsewhere, Cahill explicates ethical complexities of PAR. Readers may find the following article a useful complement to the work included here: Cahill, C. (2007). Repositioning ethical commitments: Participatory action research as a relational praxis of social change. *ACME: An International E-Journal for Critical Geographies, 6*(3), 360–373.
3. See http://www.fed-up-honeys.org/

CHAPTER 13

Doing Research *with* Young People
Participatory Research and
the Rituals of Collective Work

Caitlin Cahill

We know little about the 'spaces that youths engage with a kind of deliberate agency, sometimes an urgency … [where] voices can be heard, and differences can be articulated; deficit models are left at the door' (Weis and Fine, 2000, p. xii).

While youth research is a burgeoning field, there is still not enough research on young people's everyday lives from a youth perspective (cf. Ginwright *et al.*, 2006; Rios-Moore *et al.*, 2004; Torre and Fine, 2006a). Young people are under increasing pressure to adapt to the requirements of the 'new economy' and as young people attempt to negotiate this neoliberal context, society's anxieties about political and economic changes are projected onto their bodies and they get blamed for emergent social problems (Hall and Jefferson, 1976; Harris, 2004). This is especially true of poor, working-class, young people of color, whose challenges in achieving 'success' implicitly expose the failures of our society. If young people are seen as analogous to the canary, whose malaise alerted miners to the presence of poison in the air, then their distress should be seen as 'the first sign of a danger that threatens us all' (Guinier and Torres, 2002, p. 12). *Listening* to youths' concerns is therefore critical to both understanding and participating in social change.

This is an exciting juncture at which to bear witness to the growing, multidisciplinary support for youth participation and more inclusive collaborative research practices in geography and the social sciences. Participatory action research (hereafter PAR) approaches pry open a space for youth agency, making them 'subjects [and] architects, of research … researchers [not just] the "researched"' (Torre and Fine, 2006a). In this contribution, I offer a broad overview of the principles of participatory research and reflect on my own experience of doing a participatory action research project with young people (see also Cahill, 2006, 2007). I will discuss three themes: a 'collective praxis approach' (a set of rituals and practices for sharing power within the research process), the role of that facilitator, and processes of collective data analysis. While most attempts to use participatory approaches with children and young people draw upon visual methodologies (increasing accessibility and transcending barriers of language and literacy—PLA Notes 1988 – present; Hart, 1997; McIntyre, 2000; Driskell, 2002), the methods I discuss focused on written and verbal expression. These *techniques* may be especially useful for researchers working with teenagers; however, the principles of the PAR approach are relevant to all doing research with children and young people.

Principles of Participatory Action Research

At the center of a participatory action research program is a commitment to break away from traditional research conventions by involving the 'researched' in some or all stages of the research process (Pain, 2004). PAR starts with 'the understanding that people—especially those who have experienced historic oppression ... hold deep knowledge about their lives and experiences, and should help shape the questions, [and] frame the interpretations [of research]' (Torre and Fine, 2006a).

In a PAR project there is an emphasis upon process, a commitment to research contributing and 'giving back' to community collaborators, and a recognition of the power of knowledge produced in collaboration and action (Breitbart, 2003; Pain, 2004; Kesby *et al.*, 2005). Including young people as partners in research reveals an understanding of young people as not only assets, but as 'agents of change' (Ginwright and James, 2002), reflecting contemporary conceptualizations of youth (Holloway and Valentine, 2000; Skelton, 2007).

PAR is rooted in grassroots and international liberationist, feminist, antiracist, activist, social justice movements (Freire, [1970]1997; Fals-Borda, 1979; Smith, 1999; Bell, 2001; Rahman, 2006; Fine *et al.*, in press). Participatory practices are already widely used by child rights advocates, critical educators, youth workers, and community organizers working on the problems of educational inequities, media portrayals of youth, violence in the community, police brutality, and discrimination based on sex/race/class (Ginwright *et al.*, 2006; Torre and Fine, 2006a).[1] There is also a small, but growing, group of researchers who are using PAR with young people to study issues that matter to them. This work builds on and complements work within geography and the related social sciences, where scholars have worked closely with young people to investigate their everyday lives (Bunge and Bordessa, 1975; Lynch, 1977; Hart, 1978; Williams and Kornblum, 1994).

PAR offers a promising new framework for researchers committed to social justice and change. Engaging young people in research helps challenge social exclusion, democratize the research process, and build the capacity of young people to analyze and transform their own lives and communities. Nevertheless, not enough consideration has been given to evaluating the practice of doing collective research with young people. One critical concern is that the term *participation* is often used indiscriminately to refer to a wide variety of practices (Cahill and Hart, 2006). Roger Hart's (1992) 'Ladder of Participation' offers a useful way to differentiate between the very different roles and degrees of decision making young people take up in various 'participatory' projects (see also Driskell, 2002; London, 2006).

We need to be wary of broad applications of the term 'participation' because it often masks tokenism and the illusion of consultation that may, in fact, advance dominant interests (Hart, 1997; Cooke and Kothari, 2001; Mohan, 2001). This danger is heightened where participation is presented as a set of *techniques* rather than as a political commitment. Used in this way 'participatory methods' can reproduce rather than challenge unequal power relations (Kothari, 2001; Kesby, 2005). Thus, it is important to articulate more clearly what we mean by youth participation in collaborative research and to specify the degrees of participation in our practice. My focus is on participation as an approach (as opposed to a method) which takes seriously young people's agency and capacity. It is crucial to ask what domains of research and action are young people involved in (or excluded from) and what is the purpose of their involvement? There is a qualitative difference between a project in which young people are intimately involved in framing research questions and one in which they just assist in the collection of data.

To advance the field of youth participatory research, we also need self-reflexive accounts of practice evaluating what works and what does not. The analysis of power dynamics within a youth research collective is important especially as many projects are undertaken with marginalized young people (Christensen, 2004; Cahill and Torre, 2007). We need to articulate how issues of race, gender, and class are addressed within projects (Torre, 2005; Breitbart and Kepes, in press; Cammarota, in press). Beyond the personal benefits of involvement, how have young people been able to contribute to social change through participatory research (Chawla *et al.*, 2005; Cahill and Hart, 2006; Ginwright *et al.*, 2006; Torre and Fine, 2006b; Youth Speak Out Coalition and Zimmerman, 2006)? I am not espousing a 'singular vision' of 'usefulness' (see Horton and Kraftl, 2005) nor proposing that participatory research is the only valid approach for young people's geographies. Rather, I am arguing that engaging *with* young people in research might in fact create more vibrant research agendas, new *theoretical* possibilities, and push scholarship in new directions. In this regard, PAR offers the potential for challenging the false dichotomy between research 'of use' and theoretical engagement (Beale, 2006). As researchers know better than most, if you ask a different question, you get a different answer. Thus, it is important to identify the new questions and concerns that young people can contribute to scholarly inquiry. A critical concern in this regard is how to help young people make deeper analyses, including understanding how their local research and action is connected to broader global conditions (Katz, 2004; Fine *et al.*, in press). This is particularly relevant for geographers because PAR processes foreground contextualized knowledge whilst creating opportunities for an analysis of issues and problems at different scales (Cameron and Gibson, 2005; Kesby, 2005).

Building a Community of Researchers

My discussion here refers to a PAR project that I developed with six young women (aged 16–22) who all lived in the same neighborhood (the Lower East Side) in New York City. Participants were paid a stipend for their commitment to the project (initially only four weeks). We met daily at the Graduate Center of the City University of New York (CUNY) and at various sites in their home community. I was concerned with engaging the young women as fully as possible in every stage of the research project and helping them to take ownership over the whole process. For the program to be fully participatory, and for the young women to 'own' the process it was imperative that they were involved in defining the focus and purpose of the project from the ground up. To this end, the project was initially presented as a broad study of the 'everyday lives of young women in the city,' leaving it very open to follow their lead. After much deliberation and debate the young women decided to focus our research on the issue of stereotypical (mis)representations of young people of color and the relationship between these images and processes of financial disinvestment from their neighborhood. They entitled the project 'Makes Me Mad: Stereotypes of Young Urban Womyn of Color'.

In order to create a space where the co-researchers would express themselves and take control, the issue of their ownership of the project was developed from the outset. Reflecting upon lessons from grassroots social movements such as the civil rights movement, Myles Horton, the radical educator/activist and co-founder of the Highlander Research and Education Center, explains the significance of this principle:

> I think it's important to understand that the quality of the process you use to get to a place *determines* the ends, so when you want to build a democratic society, you have to act democratically in every way. If you want love and brotherhood, you've got to incorporate them as you go along, because you can't just expect them to occur in the future without experiencing them before you get there. [Horton, 1990, p. 227, my emphasis]

Rather than 'establishing trust' with 'informants' simply in order to gain information, making the co-researchers comfortable in the space of the university and creating a warm collegial atmosphere was understood along the lines of hospitality. I wanted my co-researchers to feel at home and not feel intimidated by the unfamiliar institutional setting. Welcoming the young women was taken seriously.

At the outset I made it clear that I considered the young women equal partners with me in the research, as competent agents and experts in understanding their own lives. Their experiences and perspectives would guide the project: 'What matters to YOU?' I asked at the first meeting. They interpreted the openness of the research agenda as a lack of structure, which was an unusual and different experience for most involved, as expressed in the following retrospective reflections (Cahill *et al.*, 2004, pp. 237–238):

Indra: The fact that we had a very loose idea of what we were there to do gave us an opportunity to make the space our own and to express our thoughts and ideas more freely … Because we were at CUNY, clearly an educational setting, there was potential for us to feel intimidated or feel that there were going to be specific expectations of us, but because we only knew we were going to be there to do some level of discussion and because our activities were loose enough to be group directed they resulted in shared thoughts and ideas that were particularly unique to us as a group.

Tiffany: If it was more structured it would have felt like school to me, and I know Caitlin was worried about coming off as a teacher but she wasn't. She gave us the opportunity to speak our minds about every and anything even if it was racial … For me the unstructuredness helped me to develop ideas on what to do and made it easier to work knowing there were no barriers. The most important thing for me to be able to do this work was it not feeling like school. (see Cahill *et al.*, 2004, pp. 237–238)

In fact, while the project was undefined, it was not unstructured. However, precisely because it *was* collaborative I could not plan and structure the process ahead of schedule and the research evolved in a slightly messy, organic way. This different way of working was unsettling at first for some who were used to following directions and who were not sure how to contribute to a very open process.[2] I purposely left room in the process for the unexpected to occur and for co-researchers to fill gaps (literally and theoretically) with their bodies, desires, and concerns.

The PAR process followed a Freirean model, starting with the concerns and questions of participants (Freire, [1970] 1997 hooks, 1994). Freire (1974) proposed a radical reassessment of education as the 'practice of freedom' … and a 'practice *with*, not *for*, the oppressed in their incessant struggle to regain their humanity' (Freire, 1997, p. 30). This practice is conceived as an ongoing process of dialogue and critical reflection towards the goal of 'conscientizacao' (the awakening of critical consciousness) which starts with a reflection upon the conditions of one's own life.

'Deep' participatory research *with* rather than *on* participants requires that we take seriously the processes of collaboration and building a community of researchers, and that requires the development of research proficiency among all participants (Torre *et al.*, 2001; Lykes, 2001). The development of skills is significant because it helps to equalize the power relationship between the facilitator and participants (and between participants with varying levels of experience) in the PAR process. In addition, this may also be in itself 'emancipatory' and personally transformative (Lather, 1986; Hart, 1997). I therefore developed an integrative youth-centered approach to training the co-researchers and started by building upon the existing knowledge and experience of the young women. Our project began with the young women investigating what they shared in terms of what it meant to be a young woman growing up in their neighborhood. Through the process they 'learned through doing' and developed research skills in an applied way.

I introduced my co-researchers to multiple methods: we employed mental maps, behavior mapping, a guided tour of the Lower East Side, a social map of roles, responsibilities and expectations in their everyday lives, and daily focus groups/brainstorming sessions. This preliminary research/training in turn informed the development of research questions. The young women were involved in each step of the research process from problem identification through data collection, data analysis, and the presentation of research findings (action!). The research process was complicated, cyclical, and 'layered' and each turn pushed us to ask new questions and re-think our interpretations (Fallis and Opotow, 2003, p. 107). Below I focus on the role of the facilitator in guiding this process, on methods of writing and reflection which were at the heart of our collective praxis, and on our approach to doing participatory research and data analysis.

Facilitating Collective Research

A collaborative research process necessarily shifts the role of the academic researcher who may be identified as a facilitator, training participants to do research, or as a collaborator, who researches alongside participants providing technical assistance (Lewin, 1948; Hart, 1997). The relationships between the researcher and participants and between the participants themselves are the subjects of critical scholarship which is concerned with the challenge of negotiating underlying and sometimes unspoken power dynamics within a collaborative process (Cooke and Kothari, 2001; Kesby, 2005; Stoudt, in press). How do you create a 'democratic space of radical inclusivity' (Torre, 2005) despite social inequities along lines of race, gender, class, etc. (Maguire, 2000; Fine *et al.*, 2003)? And, despite differential skills and proficiency in research and self-expression? In youth research there is the additional problem that young people may identify researchers as adult authority figures (Matthews, 2001). In my own case I was aware that most of the adult white women the co-researchers had come into contact with were teachers from outside of their community. Early on, therefore, it was critical for me to openly address my positionality and identify my standpoint, paying special attention to my whiteness and related privileges. Acknowledging race was not only a step towards creating space for discussing differences, it also served to disrupt the power connected to the 'invisibility' of whiteness (Fine *et al.*, 2004b).

As our project involved addressing power in the community, it was crucial to also address power within the research process.

Given these significant considerations, I had a very particular interpretation of what my role as a facilitator and collaborator should be within the collective research project. I wanted to establish a very open structure for participation, and transparency in the research process was my primary concern. This was especially important given my overlapping roles as project initiator, co-researcher and facilitator, and the obvious differences in age, race, and educational levels and research experience between me and my co-researchers. To this end, my strategy involved a conscious and ongoing explication of every step or decision made. In practical terms this meant sharing with the co-researchers all the nuts and bolts of doing research from financial issues to my own struggles and thought processes. When possible all decisions were made collaboratively, and we discussed everything from how long we should take for lunch to the research agenda to deciding what to do with a $1000 grant and how to develop a project budget.

A primary role as a facilitator was to create 'a safe space for honest dialogue,' an environment where everyone involved would feel comfortable to express themselves and contribute (see Stoudt, in press). At times this involved actively facilitating everyone's involvement, at others, interrupting silences (e.g. 'Alice, what do you think?') or disrupting dominant voices by creating regular opportunities for group reflection (e.g. 'Do we all agree? Why/why not?'). Part of my role involved modeling this practice (e.g. being an active listener, working to validate people's contributions, checking in my understanding of what was being said). Such practice became especially important when we were trying to articulate and understand abstract and theoretical interpretations offered by individual research team members. This, in turn, enabled richer analysis of our data.

However, my role was *not* simply to be a passive facilitator of others' participation. Deep participatory research is *collaborative* and reciprocal. As a co-collaborator I was also involved in the research process and had opinions about our heated conversations. However, I had to balance my contribution so as not to dominate or derail discussion. The key issue, however, if one is to participate in ways that do not silence others, is to be very careful about the grounds on which you make a contribution. When I did disagree, I made sure to first clarify I was speaking from my own experience and standpoint, without making any claim to authority. I also regularly shared my interpretations with my co-researchers confirming and clarifying my understanding with the group in order to gain further understanding and challenge my assumptions. Not only was this 'good science,' a tried and true qualitative research practice to ensure against the misunderstanding of the young women's contributions, it also served to reflect back to the young women their own interpretations in a way that drew out political/social/ethical implications. For example, Carmen suggested that other students at her school brought failure upon themselves. I asked, 'Do you mean that they don't try because they don't care? Or they do try but still don't succeed because they aren't capable?' Later, another co-researcher asked Carmen why she didn't think the students cared and then, how she thought she fitted into this understanding given that she was also having a hard time in school. In other words, while it was initially my role to support connections between participant's interpretations and social and political theory, co-researchers soon began to play this role for each other. Through this process we collectively developed theory in the Makes Me Mad project.

A Collective Praxis Methodological Approach: Rituals to Share Power

We began our collaborative work with a set of 'agreements' that guided our collaboration. These included being present on time to participate, respecting others' opinions (which we interpreted to mean actively listening and disagreeing with each other only in a way that was constructive or explicative of one's own point) and taking our work together seriously. Because there is a danger that participatory work can prioritize *consensus* (Kothari, 2001), it was crucial to create an environment in which differences could be aired constructively. For example, while the researchers agreed that their neighborhood was disinvested, they disagreed about how to deal with this issue at a personal level; some wanted to leave the community, while others wanted to stay and improve it. Rather than avoiding this fault line, co-researchers kept returning to it, excavating it as they constructed their personal and collective analyses of urban restructuring across multiplicity.

In order for the project to be open and inclusive, it was necessary to establish a series of complementary methodological strategies, practices or 'rituals' that were collaborative, facilitated group ownership, and move towards the concrete application of knowledge generated by the group. In the spirit of Patti Lather's (1986) call for 'research as praxis' that advances emancipatory knowledge in 'an unjust world' (cf. Zusman, 2004) I call this the 'collective praxis approach'. It builds upon critical pedagogical approaches that emphasize the relationship between dialogue, critical reflection, and action, and on Gramsci's ([1971] 1999) and Freire's ([1970] 1997) action-oriented approach to knowledge production and social transformation.

The collective praxis approach draws upon complementary methodological strategies or 'rituals' which were embedded within the participatory epistemological approach. A key praxis involved writing and reflecting in personal journals. This offered co-researchers a private space/time for reflection, and the opportunity to develop their own perspective on an issue or topic (e.g., 'what I like in my community') or to reflect upon what we had (or hadn't) accomplished during the day. Writing can be an important generative and productive process through which one can start to make sense of feelings and experiences. This is particularly important for young people who may be experimenting with different identities; providing a space to 'try on' different selves and to re-write one's personal narrative. It is a constructive space for participants to formulate their perspectives and in so doing develop their critical consciousness. Writing thus also served as a preparation for public participation. We frequently shared journal excerpts with each other. This was an effective way to start a group discussion, compare perspectives, jump-start a decision-making process, or bring closure to the day. It also established a process by which to move from personal to shared experiences. A related practice was 'reflective note-taking.' As the co-researchers shared their writings I would take notes on what they were saying on 'our wall'. I would constantly seek clarification (e.g. 'is this what you were saying?').[3] The notes documented our conversation and could be referred back to. This enabled rigorous analysis. For example, I might ask: 'it seems like everyone likes the fact that the neighborhood is diverse but yesterday some of you expressed some problems with the newer residents. Do you want to talk about that?' Our collective wall was a point of reference and a public memory of shared knowledge production from which we could build new ideas and construct our project together.

Another important practice was informal agenda setting at the beginning or end of each day. We would discuss issues such as: What did we accomplish so far? What do we want to do next? How much time should we spend on each thing we want to do? Is this realistic? Do we need a timekeeper? (as I was failing in this role). New agenda items often grew out of journal discussions. We would also check in periodically on overall process (e.g., 'we have only 2 weeks to collect data, do analysis, and whatever else we decide to do! Oh my god! How are we going to do this!?'). This also fed back into the practice of setting our agenda and a backwards planning process (e.g., if we want to accomplish *this* we need to do *this* first). So, not only were participants involved in framing the research from the outset, they were also engaged in research organization (setting both short- and long-term goals), analysis, planning future collaborations, and building new research agendas.

Methodologically, the collective praxis approach established a set of rituals that facilitated deep participant involvement and collective ownership over the research process. While I initially determined the topics for discussion after a short time reflections and issue identification grew organically. Rather than 'purifying knowledge' or 'tidying up' people's messy lives (Kothari, 2001), the collective praxis approach to participation was also open to redefinition by participants.

Writing as a Method of Inquiry

Writing itself can be understood as a form of *praxis* as Freire ([1970] 1997) defined it, because it generates a critical space of reflection and action. My approach was informed by the 'writing-to-learn' and 'critical thinking' movements in educational practice. These argue, first, that learning involves an active engagement with problem solving (Britton, 1970; Elbow, 1973; Fulwiler and Young, 1982; Bean, 1996; Gilyard, 1996) and, second, that writing is itself a process of inquiry and is closely linked with thinking; when 'we struggle with writing we are struggling with thought itself' (Bean, 1996, p. xiii). Writing is a 'method of inquiry,' not only a mode of 'telling' but also a way of 'knowing' (Richardson, 1994, p. 516). *How* we choose to write and represent reveals different aspects of ourselves.

'Free-writing', the practice of writing continuously whatever comes to one's mind, is a way of starting to give shape to what psychologist Lev Vygotsky (1978) identifies as 'inner speech', which mediates between thought and language, 'a dynamic, shifting, unstable thing, fluttering between word and thought' (1962, p. 149, in Fulwiler, 1983). Because it is through 'language [that] we come to represent, come to know and understand the world' (Fulwiler, 1983, p. 276), writing is an act of discovery that allows us to make our thoughts concrete and allows us to interact with them (ibid., p. 277). In a similar vein, 'meaning is not what you start out with but what you end up with. Think of writing not as a way to transmit a message but as a way to grow and cook a message' (Elbow, 1973, p. 15).

In the 'Makes Me Mad' project, writing allowed participants to process their thoughts and clarify their positions. Through the process the young women ended up challenging the meanings they originally assigned individually to their neighborhood and collectively reworked their initial interpretations (Cahill, 2007).

There are, however, limitations to a methodology that emphasizes and requires a substantial amount of writing. People have different capabilities when it comes to writing, and some may find it a barrier to personal expression. In our project we worked around these drawbacks, and although some were initially uncomfortable, they became more at ease with writing over time and expressed pride in being paid for their writing as part of their work. Others relished writing and a few even started using their journals for personal use. More generally, however, we need to be flexible in order to maximize everyone's participation. Different people learn in different ways (Gardner, 1993); some are more visual, others more verbal. What works for some may alienate others. Thus, it is important to collectively identify and validate the different capacities co-researchers bring to a project and to create opportunities for these diverse strengths to be mobilized. This may be particularly true for working with younger people and children (see Hart, 1997).

Notwithstanding the emphasis upon writing, in our collective praxis approach writing functioned as a means to prepare for conversation and dialogue. Carmen in particular, (who was much more comfortable talking than when she was writing) used writing time as an opportunity to make notes from which she expounded freely (rather than verbatim) during feedback sessions. Like writing, talking is a way of processing and understanding our thoughts. We use speech 'more to shape [our] own experience than to communicate with others: the words give concrete form to our thinking and so make it more real' (Britton, 1970). This 'shaping at the point of utterance' (ibid., 1970, p. 53) helps us discover the meaning (our own meaning) of our everyday experience (Fulwiler, 1983, p. 277). Collective dialogue offered another space for individual and collective inquiry and a means for participants to make sense of and align themselves with particular subject positions.

Only Alice (who had emigrated from China two years before) found verbal communication uncomfortable. In fast-paced group discussions, she often had to ask for explanations of terms. This was actually useful as it forced others to be more precise with their language and to define terms. However, more often than not, Alice was quiet, actively listening. Thus, by comparison with Carmen, who used writing as a prelude to the main business of speaking, for Alice, writing was the place where she could most readily express herself and articulate her opinions. Here the flexibility and multi-method aspect of the collective praxis approach worked to allow this participant's perspective to be heard because she could read aloud verbatim from her journal, which was easier than expressing herself extemporaneously. Again, here is another example of the need for identifying different ways for participants to contribute and express themselves in the ways that feel comfortable for them.

A Collaborative Autoethnography

Grounding their project in the concrete details of their everyday lives at the neighborhood scale, the researchers proposed an analysis that engaged issues of power and self-representation. The 'Makes Me Mad' project was a response to all-too-common and oppressive stereotypes of young women of color, and was conceived of as a strategic intervention into the ways in which outsiders perceive them. It aimed to 'force a dialogue in which many (westerners) would not willingly engage' (Pratt, 1999, p. 47). As such the co-researchers developed a collaborative 'autoethnography', in which they re-present 'themselves in ways that engage with the colonizer's own terms' (rather than an ethnography in which a dominant group 'represents to themselves their (usually subjugated) others') (Pratt, 1992, p. 7; see also Butz and Besio, 2004). This, then, was a theoretical, practical, and methodological decision. It is at once 'a critique from below' and a conscious shifting of the terms of engagement intent on making visible the processes of erasure that represent young women in dominant discourse (Ladson-Billings, 2000; Fine et al., 2003). The autoethnographic project is about the struggle for self-determination and control over the terms and conditions of material local/global practices (Pratt, 1999).

'This project is about us'; the young researchers repeatedly returned to the fact that their own life stories could serve as evidence challenging reductive stereotypes. After developing the research focus, we realized that we had already collected a lot of information relevant to the study through our journal writings, personal investigation, and 'wall' summaries. This was also a practical decision given the time limits and ethical Institutional Review Board constraints (which would have made it impossible to do research with anyone else who had not signed a consent form).[4]

Data Analysis

In a PAR project, data analysis is integral to the research process, an ongoing part of a cyclical approach (Cahill, in press). Moments of analysis emerged organically at multiple and regular points as part of our reflective praxis rather than being a set 'phase' of research. Analysis also fed directly back into our project as part of a looped process of critical reflection. Crucially, therefore, the analysis process was not external to the process but an integral part of it in which all the co-researchers participated and learned. Similar to the 'listening guide', developed by feminist psychologists who read through transcripts for different voices (Brown *et al.*, 1988; Way, 1998), in a collaborative data analysis process researchers engage in a process of comparing perspectives, actively listening, contributing, and explicitly taking into account the subtle differences between points of view (Bhavnani, 1994). This represents a participatory develop-ment of grounded theory (Strauss and Corbin, 1994) with the women building an understanding of themselves as they study themselves. For example, it was through this practice that the co-researchers realized that it was not just 'outsiders' (defined variously as white, wealthy, and powerful people, people from outside their community) who stereotyped young women of color, but also sometimes they were also implicated in reproducing the very stereotypes that marginalized them. This finding complicated the ways in which the researchers conceptualized their project (turning their gaze inward), led to new research questions about how and why young women themselves adopted stereotypes, and in turn a deeper analysis. This fed into the development of research products and dissemination strategies which included a website (www.fed-up-honeys.org), a sticker campaign, and a report (see Cahill, 2004; Cahill and Torre, 2007).

The research team also engaged in a variation of content analysis procedures (Auerbach and Silverstein, 2003) in order to be able to write a report of their findings. Co-researchers repeatedly read through the various journals and wall diagrams looking for themes. They initially coded themes indi-vidually, then after reflection we did this collaboratively, paying attention to our differences and the contradictions within our writing. It could be argued that engaging the co-researchers in the process offers an even deeper level of analysis because the young women's 'inside perspective' creates an op-portunity to confirm interpretations and because they have insights an outsider lacks. In our case this process was especially complex because the co-researchers were analyzing what *they* themselves had written throughout the project. It was quite intense to read through one another's writings while sitting next to each other and to consider how various group members' writings betrayed the ways in which these stereotypes had become accommodated and even accepted.

While everyone was trained and understood the mechanics of the coding process, the process felt somewhat convoluted and insular. Soon enough we realized that our analysis only captured what we were thinking and writing at a particular moment in time, and of course we were always changing our perspectives. We realized therefore that it was important for us to try to record how we had changed as a result of our collaboration. For example, at the beginning Carmen had blamed the poor quality of her school on other students and their parents: 'how people bring up their children and how people act; that has nothing to do with the school'. Later in the project, however, not only did she acknowledge the problems endemic to her school, she also ended up leaving the school.

It seemed somewhat problematic to ignore the ways all of us shifted our perspectives over time. How to account for both perspectives? Perhaps by suggesting that the process of data analysis recon-firmed our complexity, and the ways in which we both accept and reject stereotypes, day in and day out. While this was another finding, it was something we already knew. We wondered aloud: Did we really need to do this systematic analysis to prove it? Why? Who does it serve? It felt like a hoop we needed to leap through to prove we were doing research (and the hoop, like the ones the lions jump through at the circus, was on fire).

This points to the potential tensions in doing participatory research. On the one hand, it seemed important for the co-researchers to gain academic research skills doing data analysis. But on the other hand, because we didn't have the distance from our data usually afforded to researchers, it felt like we were taking a very formal approach to the more free therapeutic and reflective practice we usually engaged in collaboratively. Another tension was between my own training as to how to generate academically worthy 'results' and our collective desire to do analysis for action.

After already having gone through the conscientização process of problem identification (an emotionally difficult process) to analyze our own writings involved knowingly revisiting this process, studying oneself under a microscope. However, the process was important and helped us to see the ways in which hegemonic logic has found its way into the everyday ways we make sense of ourselves, our language and our micro-level interpretations. Data analysis involved sorting through distorted characterizations, and coming to terms with the violence of these stereotypes on our everyday lives (Cahill, 2004). Thus, far from being an under-theorized practical 'technique', participatory action research can provide opportunities for young people to engage with complex (and often inaccessible) theoretical approaches in ways that makes sense to them (Kesby, 2005).

Conclusion: Including Excluded Perspectives

The research collective made their own assessment of the value of the participatory approach in a retrospective reflection:

> Womyn of color are all the more in need of the space and the encouragement to start shaping their paths within society. Part of the journey starts with young womyn of color smashing the skewed pictures of themselves that they see being constantly portrayed and reified in the world that they live in. Participatory action research is one such method of making sure that we, as young womyn of color, could control how our voices and our thoughts would be portrayed and interpreted through the lens of research. (in Cahill *et al.*, 2004, p. 239)

Self-analysis leading to a reworking of self-representation is one of the most critical contributions of a PAR process (Cahill, 2007). The 'Makes Me Mad' project is an example of how a small group of young working-class women of color chose to self-identify and speak back to reductive mischaracterizations. Aside from its principal objective as a research approach 'of use' outside of the academy (Fine and Barreras, 2001), PAR's role in producing new knowledge is less understood. Committed to bringing new and underrepresented voices into the academy, PAR acknowledges the intellectual power of what Gramsci (1999) identifies as 'organic intellectuals' whose critical perspectives are developed from everyday experiences (Fine *et al.*, 2003). Starting with the understanding that all people, including young people, develop social theory in the course of their life experiences, PAR foregrounds the perspectives of marginalized groups, opens up critique and troubles the status quo (Bell, 2001; Torre *et al.*, 2001; Guinier and Torres, 2002). While certainly not all young people are marginalized, as a group their voices are not often taken seriously and they are excluded from many decisions that affect their lives.

What happens when underrepresented perspectives (for example, those of women and people of color) enter the academy and participate in the production of 'official' knowledges? Not only might they transform themselves, they might also transform the academy (see Kelley, 1998; Collins, [1990] 2000). This is the ground upon which new knowledge can take root, pushing scholarship in new directions, asking new questions, challenging old assumptions, 'thinking outside the box' and moving beyond the privileged perspectives of the ivory tower. Participatory action research creates an opportunity for exchange, for academic researchers to engage responsibly with communities and use their expertise as well as be open to learning from communities (Fuller and Kitchin, 2004; Zusman, 2004). A participatory approach to research offers a 'bottom-up' approach which is especially relevant to the critical study of youth geographies: it recognizes young people's agency and competency and very directly privileges their voices and develops their capacities, and is potentially open enough to allow young people to challenging accepted points of view. In this case, the 'Makes Me Mad' project contested the academic literature's preoccupation with young women of color's bodies, sexuality, and pregnancy, highlighting that the existing literature persistently begins from a position that such young women are 'problems'.

At the same time, a PAR approach could be understood to be more rigorous, and likely to generate 'better' data because insiders 'simply know things that outsiders don't' (Torre *et al.*, 2001). Without romanticizing 'inside' knowledge as the 'truth' or erasing differences between diverse young women of color, there is an understanding that 'insiders carry knowledge, critique, and a line of vision that is not automatically accessible to outsiders' (Fine *et al.*, 2003). Young people are less likely to romanticize their experiences and more likely to be aware of the ways in which different parts of their lifeworlds are connected (Fine *et al.*, 2003). 'Inside' cannot, of course, be defined statically as a singular place; it is a shifting, multivalent perspective. This complexity is especially evident within a collaborative work when *your* 'inside' is different than *mine*. PAR values the perspective gained from a particular standpoint (Hardstock, 1983; Collins, 2000), such as a shared interpretation of discrimination across multiple different experiences. 'Inside' could be identified as an emotion, what it *feels like*, and at the same time addresses the banal negotiations of everyday life invisible to those 'outside', and that might slip below the radar of 'data.' For example, one researcher, Ruby, pointed out how only two of the classmates that she started ninth grade with were still in her homeroom, their missing bodies invisible in quantitative reports of dropouts since they were purged from the attendance rolls. Or Jasmine, another researcher, reported how she was surveilled in one store and ignored by a salesperson in the next, an experience corroborated by the other researchers which collectively begins to paint a portrait of the hypervisibility and invisibility of racial discrimination. Another common shared experience was identified by Annissa, who observed how the neighborhood bodegas were being replaced by more expensive 24-hour Korean markets catering to newcomers in the area. In a PAR process observations of everyday life become validated as data.

How can research function as a site for 'counter work'—'where what could be, is sought; where what has been, is critiqued; and where what is, is troubled' (Torre *et al.*, 2001, p. 150)? Engaging young people fully in the research process offers a starting point for a more inclusive research agenda, one which recognizes young people as social actors and creates an opening for their concerns to influence new knowledge production.

Acknowledgements

Together with the Fed Up Honeys I experienced just how powerful collaboration in action could be. Thanks to each of you—your collective energy and insight continue to inspire. Sincere gratitude to Mike Kesby for his incredibly generous editorial guidance and critical feedback. Thanks also to the referees whose insights informed my revision. I am most appreciative of the encouragement and constructive critique of Cindi Katz, Michelle Fine, and Roger Hart on earlier drafts of this paper. This work was supported by a fellowship from the American Association of University Women and a CUNY Writing Fellowship at Medgar Evers College.

Notes

1. For websites see Youth Together 2006 *www.youthtogether.net*; Kids as Self Advocates 2007 www.fvkasa.org/; CAAAV Youth Leadership Project, 2007 *http://www.caaav.org/projects/ylp*; Youth Organizing Communities 2007, http://www.innercitystruggle.org; Youth & the World Urban Forum 2007, http://eya.ca/wuf/for_research.html; RedWire 2007, *http://www.redwiremag.com*

2. This highlights absences in highly structured educational settings where young people are rarely asked their opinion, much less engaged in producing knowledge.

3. Sometimes the researchers would take turns doing reflective note taking, but most often this was my role as I wanted to enable co-researchers to contribute to the discussion.

4. Most likely, if we were able to do research with other people, the researchers might have taken another approach and interviewed other young women, for example.

References

Auerbach, C. F. and Silverstein, L. B. (2003). *An Introduction to Coding and Analyzing Qualitative Data*, New York: New York University Press.

Beale, N. (2006). The practicalities of theory: Engagement, relevance and application, *Children's Geographies*, 4(2), 219–224.

Bean, J. C. (1996). *Engaging Ideas: The Professors Guide to Integrating Writing, Critical Thinking and Active Learning in the Classroom*, San Francisco, CA: Jossey-Bass Publishers.

Bell, E. E. (2001). Infusing race in the US discourse on action research, in: P. Reason and H. Bradbury (eds) *Handbook of Action Research: Participative Inquiry and Practice*, London: Sage, 48–58.

Bhavnani, K. K. (1994). Tracing the contours: Feminist research and objectivity, in: H. Afshar and M. Maynard (eds) *The Dynamics of 'Race' and Gender: Some Feminist Interventions*, London: Taylor & Francis.

Breitbart, M. (2003). Participatory research, in: N. Clifford and G. Valentine (eds) *Key Methods in Geography*, London: Sage, 161–178.

Breitbart, M. and Kepes, I. (in press). The youth power story: How adults can better support young people's sustained participation in community-based planning, *Children, Youth & Environments*, 17(2).

Britton, J. (1970). *Language and Learning*, Harmondsworth: Penguin.

Brown, L. M., Argyris, D., Attanucci, J., Bardige, B., Gilligan, C., Johnston, K., Miller, B., Osbourne, R., Ward, J., Wiggins, G. and Wilcox, D. (1988). *A Guide to Reading Narratives of Moral Conflict and Choice for Self and Moral Voice*, Monograph #2. Cambridge, MA: Center for the Study of Gender, Education and Human Development, Harvard University.

Bunge, William and Bordessa, R. (1975). *The Canadian Alternative: Survival, Expeditions and Urban Change*, Toronto: York University.

Butz, D. and Besio, K. (2004). The value of autoethnography for field research in transcultural settings, *The Professional Geographer*, 56(3), 350–361.

Cahill, C. (2004). Defying gravity? Raising consciousness through collective research, *Children's Geographies*, 2(2), 273–786.

Cahill, C. (2006). 'At risk'? The fed up honeys re-present the gentrification of the Lower East Side, *Women Studies Quarterly* (special issue *The Global & the Intimate* edited by Geraldine Pratt and Victoria Rosner), 34(1&2), 334–363.

Cahill, C. (2007). The personal is political: Developing new subjectivities in a participatory action research process, *Gender, Place, and Culture*, 14(3).

Cahill, C. (in press). Participatory Data Analysis, in: S. Kindon, R. Fain and M. Kesby (eds) *Participatory Action Research Approaches and Methods: Connecting People, Participation and Place*, London: Routledge.

Cahill, C. and Hart, R. (eds) (2006). Translating global participatory practices with youth 'Pushing the Boundaries: Critical Perspectives on Child and Youth Participation', *Children, Youth & Environments*, 16–17.

Cahill, C. and Torre, M. (2007). Beyond the journal article: Representations, audience, and the presentation of participatory research, in: Sara Kindon, Rachel Pain and Mike Kesby (eds) *Participatory Action Research Approaches and Methods: Connecting People, Participation and Place*, Routledge.

Cahill, C., Arenas, E., Contreras, J., Jiang, N., Rios-Moore, I. and Threatts, T. (2004). Speaking back: Voices of young urban womyn of color using participatory action research to challenge and complicate representations of young women, in: A. Harris (ed.) *All About the Girl: Power, Culture and Identity*, New York: Routledge.

Cameron, J. and Gibson, K. (2005). Participatory action research in a poststructualist vein, *Geoforum*, 36(3), 315–331.

Cammarota, J. (in press). A map for social change: Latina/o students engage a praxis of ethnography, *Children, Youth & Environments*, 17(2).

Chawla, L. (2002). *Growing up in an Urbanizing World*, London: Earthscan.

Chawla, L. *et al.* (2005). Don't just listen—do something! Lessons learned about governance from the growing up in cities project, *Children, Youth & Environments*, 15(2), 53–85.

Christensen, P. H. (2004). Children's participation in ethnographic research: Issues of power and representation, *Children & Society*, 18, 165–176.

Collins, P. H. ([1990]2000). *Black Feminist Thought: Knowledge, Consciousness, and the Politics of Empowerment*, New York: Routledge.

Cooke, B. and Kothari, U. (eds) (2001). *Participation: The New Tyranny?*, London: Zed Books.

Driskell, D. (2002). *Creating Better Cities with Children and Youth: A Manual for Participation*, London: Earthscan.

Elbow, P. (1973). *Writing without Teachers*, New York: Oxford University Press.

Fallis, R. K. and Opotow, S. (2003). Are students failing school or are schools failing students? Class cutting in high school, *Journal of Social Issues*, 59(1), 103–120.

Fals-Borda, O. (1979). Investigating the reality in order to transform it: The Colombian experience, *Dialectical Anthropology*, 4, 33–55.

Fine, M. and Barreras, R. (2001). To be of use, *Analyses of Social Issues and Public Policy*, (1)1. Retrieved July 3, 2004 from: http://www.asap-spssi.org/issue2.htm)

Fine, M., Torre, M. E., Boudin, K., Bowen, I., Clark, J., Hylton, D., Martinez, M., 'Missy', Rivera, M., Roberts, R. A., Smart, P. and Upegui, D. (2003). Participatory action research: Within and beyond bars, in: P. Camic, J. E. Rhodes and L. Yardley (eds) *Qualitative Research in Psychology: Expanding Perspectives in Methodology and Design*, Washington, DC: American Psychological Association, 173–198.

Fine, M., Roberts, R. A., Torre, M. E., Bloom, J., Burns, A., Chajet, L., Guishard, M. and Payne, Y. (2004a). *Echoes: Youth Documenting and Performing the Legacy of Brown v. Board of Education*, New York: Teachers College Press.

Fine, M., Weis, I., Powell-Pruitt, L. and Burns, A. (2004b) *Off White: Readings in Power, Privilege, and Resistance*, New York: Routledge.

Fine, M., Tuck, J. E. and Zeller-Berkman, S. (in press). Do you believe in Geneva?, in: N. Denzin, L. T. Smith and Y. Lincoln (eds) *Handbook of Critical and Indigenous Knowledges*, Beverly Hills, CA: Sage Publications. Freire, P. ([1970]1997). *Pedagogy of the Oppressed*, Harmondsworth, Middlesex: Penguin Books.

Freire, P. (1974). *Education: The Practice of Freedom*, London: Writers & Readers Publishing Cooperative.

Fuller, D. and Kitchin, R. (eds) (2004). Radical theory/critical praxis: Academic geography beyond the academy?, in: *Radical Theory, Critical Praxis: Making a Difference beyond the Academy?*, 1–20, ACME e-book series/Praxis (e)Press: Vernon and Victoria, BC, Canada. Retrieved July 15, 2004 from http://www.praxis-epress.org/availablebooks/radicaltheorycritical-praxis.html.

Fulwiler, T. (1983). Why we teach writing in the first place, in: P. L. Stock (ed.) *FFORUM: Essays on Theory & Practice in the Teaching of Writing*, Upper Montclair, NJ: Boynton/Cook, 273–286.

Fulwiler, T. and Young, A. (1982). *Language Connections: Writing and Reading across the Curriculum*, Urbana, IL: National Council of Teachers of English.

Gardner, H. (1993). *Multiple Intelligences: The Theory in Practice*, New York: Basic Books.

Gilyard, K. (1996). *Let's Flip the Script: An African American Discourse on Language, Literature and Learning*, Detroit, MI: Wayne State University Press.

Ginwright, S. and James, T. (2002). From assets to agents of change: Social justice, organizing, and youth development, *New Directions for Youth Development, 96*, 27–46.

Ginwright, S., Noguera, P. and Cammarota J. (eds) (2006). *Beyond Resistance! Youth Activism and Community Change: New Democratic Possibilities for Practice and Policy for America's Youth*, New York: Routledge.

Gramsci, A. ([1971]1999). *Selections from the Prison Notebooks*, New York: International Publishers.

Guinier, L. and Torres, G. (2002). *The Miner's Canary: Enlisting Race, Resisting Power, Transforming Democracy*, Cambridge, MA: Harvard University Press.

Hardstock, N. (1983). *Money, Sex, and Power*, New York: Longman.

Harris, A. (2004). *Future Girl: Young Women in the Twenty-first Century*, London: Taylor and Francis. Hart, R. (1978). *Children's Experience of Place*, New York: Irvington Publishers.

Hart, R. (1992). *Children's Participation: From Tokenism to Citizenship*. Vol. 4, *UNICEF Innocenti Essays*. Florence, Italy: UNICEF/International Child Development Centre.

Hart, R. (1997). *Children's Participation: The Theory and Practice of Involving Young Citizens in Community Development and Environmental Care*, New York: UNICEF.

Holloway, S. and Valentine, G. (2000). *Children's Geographies: Playing, Living, Learning*, London & New York: Routledge.

hooks, b. (1994). *Teaching to Transgress: Education as the Practice of Freedom*, New York: Routledge.

Horton, J. and Kraftl, P. (2005). For more-than usefulness: Six overlapping points about Children's Geographies, *Children's Geographies, 3*(2), 131–143.

Horton, M. (1990). *The Long Haul: An Autobiography*, New York: Doubleday.

Katz, C. (2004). *Growing up Global: Economic Restructuring and Children's Everyday Lives*, Minneapolis, MN: University of Minnesota Press.

Kelley, R. D. G. (1998). Check the technique: Black urban culture and the predicament of social science, in: N. B. Dirk (ed.) *In Near Ruins: Cultural Theory at the End of the Century*, Minneapolis, MN: University of Minnesota Press, 39–66.

Kesby, M. (2005). Re-theorising empowerment-through-participation as a performance in space: Beyond tyranny to transformation, *Signs: Journal of Feminist Theory, 30*(4), 2037–2065.

Kesby, M., Kindon, S. and Pain, R. (2005). 'Participatory' approaches and diagramming techniques, in: Flowerdew and Martin (eds) *Methods in Human Geography: A Guide for Students doing a Research Project*, London: Longman, 144–166.

Kothari, U. (2001). Power, knowledge and social control in participatory development, in: B. Cooke and U. Kothari (eds) *Participation the New Tyranny?*, London: Zed Books, 139–152.

Ladson-Billings, G. (2000). Racialized discourses and ethnic epistemologies, in: N. K. Denzin and Y. S. Lincoln (eds) *Handbook of Qualitative Research*, 2nd edition, Thousand Oaks, CA: Sage, 257–278.

Lather, P. (1986). Research as praxis, *Harvard Educational Review, 56*(3), 257–277.

Lewin, K. (1948). *Resolving Social Conflicts*, New York: Harper & Row.

London, J. K. (in press). Power and pitfalls of youth participation in community action research: Lessons from community design in San Francisco, *Children, Youth & Environments, 17*(2).

Lykes, M. B. (2001). Activist participatory research and the arts with rural Mayan Women: Interculturality and situated meaning making, in: D. L. Tolman and M. Brydon-Miller (eds) *From Subjects to Subjectivities: A Handbook of Interpretative and Participatory Methods*, New York: NYU Press, 183–199.

Lynch, K. (1977). *Growing up in Cities*, Cambridge, MA: MIT Press.

Maguire, P. (2000). *Doing Participatory Research: A Feminist Approach (4th printing)*, Amherst, MA: Center for International Education, University of Massachusetts.

Matthews, H. (2001). Power games and moral territories: Ethical dilemmas when working with children and young people, *Ethics, Place & Environment*, 4, 117–178.

McIntyre, A. (2000). Constructing meaning about violence, school, and community: Participatory action research with urban youth, *The Urban Review*, 32(2), 123–154.

Mohan, G. (2001). Beyond participation: Strategies for deeper empowerment, in: B. Cooke and U. Kothari (eds) *Participation the New Tyranny?*, London: Zed Books, 153–167.

Pain, R. (2004). Social geography: Participatory research. *Progress in Human Geography*, 28(5), 1–12.

PLA Notes (1988–present) (Participation, Learning & Action) Issues 1–49 can be retrieved from the website of the International Institute for Environment and Development: http://www.iied.org/NR/agbioliv/pla_notes/backissues.html (accessed 12.0307).

Pratt, M. L. (1992). *Imperial Eyes: Travel Writing and Transculturation*, New York: Routledge.

Pratt, M. L. (1999). Apocalypse in the Andes: Contact zones and the struggles for interpretive power, *Américas*, 38–47.

Rahman, A. (2006). The praxis of participatory research, in: P. Reason and H. Bradbury (eds) *Handbook of Action Research*, London: Sage Publications.

Richardson, L. (1994). Writing: A method of inquiry, in: N. Denzin and Y. Lincoln (eds) *Handbook of Qualitative Research*, Thousand Oaks, CA: Sage, 516–529.

Rios-Moore, I., Arenas, E., Contreras, J., Jiang, N., Threatts, T, Allen, S. and Cahill, C. (2004). *Makes Me Mad: Stereotypes of Young Urban Womyn of Color*, New York: Center for Human Environments, Graduate School and University Center, City University of New York.

Skelton, T. (2007). Children, young people, UNICEF and participation, *Children's Geographies*, 5(1–2), 165–181.

Smith, L. T. (1999). *Decolonizing Methodologies: Research and Indigenous Peoples*, New York: Zed Books, Ltd. Stoudt, B. (in press) The co-construction of knowledge in 'safe spaces': Reflecting on politics, power and the use of participatory action research to study violence in an independent boys' school, *Children, Youth & Environments*, 17(2).

Strauss, A. and Corbin, J. (1994). Grounded theory methodology, in: N. Denzin and Y. S. Lincoln (eds) *Handbook of Qualitative Research*, Thousand Oaks, CA: Sage.

Torre, M. E. (2005). The alchemy of integrated spaces: Youth participation in research collectives of difference, in: L. Weis and M. Fine (eds) *Beyond Silenced Voices*, 2nd edition, Albany, NY: State University of New York Press, 251–266.

Torre, M. E. and Fine, M. (2006a). Participatory Action Research (PAR) by youth, in: L. Sherrod (ed.) *Youth Activism: An International Encyclopedia*, Westport, CT: Greenwood Publishing Group, 456–462.

Torre, M. E. and Fine, M. (2006b). Researching and resisting: Democratic policy research by and for youth, in: S. Ginwright, P. Noguera and J. Cammarota, in: S. Ginwright, P. Noguera and J. Cammarota (eds) *Beyond Resistance! Youth Activism and Community Change: New Democratic Possibilities for Practice and Policy for America's Youth*, New York: Routledge.

Torre, M. E., Fine, M., Boudin, K., Bowen, I., Clark, J., Hylton, D., Martinez, M., Roberts, R. A. M., Rivera, M., Smart, P. and Upegui, D. (2001). A space for co-constructing counter stories under surveillance, *International Journal of Critical Psychology*, 4, 149–166.

Vygotsky, L. S. (1978). *Mind in Society: The Development of Higher Psychological Processes*, John-Steiner Cole, Scribner & Souberman (eds) Cambridge, MA: Harvard University Press.

Way, N. (1998). *Everyday Courage: The Lives and Stories of Urban Teenagers*, New York: New York University Press.

Weis, L. and Fine, M. (2000). *Construction Sites: Excavating Race, Class, and Gender among Urban Youth*, New York & London: Teachers College Press.

Williams, T. and Kornblum, W. (1994). *The Uptown Kids*, New York: A Grosset/Putnam. Youth Speak out Coalition and Zimmerman, K. (2006). Making space making change: Models for youth-led social change organizations, *Children, Youth & Environments*, 16(2).

Zusman, P. (2004). Activism as a collective cultural praxis: Challenging the Barcelona Urban Model, in: D. Fuller and R. Kitchin (eds) *Radical Theory, Critical Praxis: Making a Difference beyond the Academy?*, 132–156, ACME e-book series/ Praxis (e)Press: Vernon and Victoria, BC, Canada. Retrieved July 15, 2004 from http://www.praxis-epress.org/available-books/radicaltheorycriticalpraxis.html

CHAPTER 14

Circulating Critical Research
Reflections on Performance and Moving Inquiry into Action

Madeline Fox and Michelle Fine

I n times of economic, educational and racial "crisis," as the inequality gap widens and youth of color are targeted by social policies that further erode their opportunities, we are interested in the design, analysis and activist possibilities of participatory youth studies. Thus, we start at the end, at a performance of Polling for Justice, a participatory action research project surveying youth experiences of education, criminal justice and health care across communities, sexualities, genders, race/ethnicity and class in New York City, in order to theorize how critical research can circulate through the academy, communities, youth organizing and social policy—and maybe even theatre.

The Polling for Justice (PFJ) research performance opens with a lone bespectacled academic-looking person standing on stage in a white lab coat and fumbling through a sheaf of papers, mumbling:

> Hello. My name is Dr. Researchy, and I am going to be presenting a paper to you on "The Urban Teen" and a theory I developed that is a framework for looking at one of the major problems that growing urban U.S. city centers have been faced with—namely the adolescent ...

Played by PFJ artistic director Una Osato, the character is designed to represent traditional positivist academic research where older White men visually represent the privileged status of expert. The Dr. Rebert Researchy character reads his paper on "The Urban Teen" in a slow, monotonous ramble. Before long, the audience hears the voices of the Polling for Justice researchers discussing Dr. Researchy's talk from offstage.

> "This is boring!"
> "What is he saying?"
> "I think he just said something about the 'urban teen'."
> "Ohhh he's talking about you!"
> "No I think he's talking about you!"
> "I got no idea what he's talking about, all I know is this is boring."

"No one understands him but himself."

"You know what, I'm going to go up there and say something."

One by one, Polling for Justice youth researchers walk up on stage, interrupting Dr. Researchy by taking the microphone and insisting that he sit down and listen to the results of their youth research on youth experiences in New York City. In the last moment, as Dr. Researchy is being escorted off stage, one of the youth researchers, Darius Francis, admires Dr. R's lab coat and takes it for his own, wearing it for the rest of the performance.

The depiction of Dr. Researchy was meant to critique and provoke. As a caricature of the disembodied and "objective" researcher who studies *on* but not *with* youth, he pushes audiences to rethink their assumptions about where expertise lives, troubling notions of objectivity, validity and the celebrated distance of academic research. In their initially disruptive presence, the PFJ researcher-performers raised equally compelling questions about critical research, participation, social representations of youth and social justice. By modeling talking back and speaking out from their seats, they encouraged other audience members to do more than watch, to engage actively in the production.

We offer this chapter to introduce the notion of "circuits" into the grammar of critical research, inviting a sharp turn away from the individualism that saturates most U.S.-based social inquiry—whether quantitative or qualitative in design. Instead, here, we want to argue that critical inquiry take seriously the circuits of dispossession, privilege and possibility that run between us, across zip codes and dangerous power lines, through youth bodies, connecting, in this case, youth researchers/actors and audiences of privilege.

While our participatory action research approach (Torre et al., 2008; Tuck et al., 2008) derives from social scientists and practitioners including Orlando Fals-Borda, Paulo Freire and Ignacio Martin-Baro, as performative researchers we align ourselves, as well, with Augusto Boal's recognition that there are no spectators, only spect-*actors*, linked in the social drama of witnessing and responsibility. We introduce circuits as foundational to our theoretical perspective on *circuits of dispossession, privilege and possibility*; to participatory methods and analytic "camps"; and to our thinking about how critical inquiry travels into popular culture, social movements and policy.

Theorizing Circuits of Dispossession in Critical Youth Studies

Political theorist David Harvey writes on neoliberalism and dispossession: "Accumulation by dispossession is about dispossessing somebody of their assets or their rights ... we're talking about the taking away of universal rights and the privatization of them so it [becomes] your particular responsibility rather than the responsibility of the State" (Harvey, 2004, p. 2). In the United States, public resources, opportunities, dignity and therefore aspirations are being redistributed by public policies, from poor communities to elites. Youth of color, those living in poverty, and youth who are immigrants are increasingly denied access to or detached from public access to high-quality education and health care as their families and housing are destabilized. Shamefully, at the same time the state has invested heavily in their criminalization and surveillance.

In 2009 Fine and Ruglis migrated Harvey's theoretical work into critical youth studies to understand how neoliberal policies activate what we call "circuits of dispossession" in the lives of low-income youth of color, such that they are increasingly *detached* from public institutions of development such as education and health care and *attached* to public institutions of containment such as criminal justice and the military. In the original article Fine and Ruglis (2009) document, for instance, how the simple condition of being a high school drop-out/push-out cascades into a flood of negative outcomes in education and economics, of course, but also health outcomes, parenting practices, voting and community participation and criminal justice involvement. Fine and Ruglis document that these outcomes are dramatically worse for drop-outs/push-outs who are Black or Latino than those who are White or Asian.

Just as dispossession *accumulates* within communities and across sectors, it is also the case that dispossession is unevenly distributed across communities. The loss of resources, human rights, dignity, legitimacy and opportunities in one community corresponds with their respective accumulation in another. As the *inequality gap* widens across communities, social outcomes worsen—for all of us. Thus we should be interested in understanding and undermining circuits of dispossession and privilege for purposes of progressive solidarity and perhaps even for self-interest.

British epidemiologists Richard Wilkinson and Kate Pickett published *The Spirit Level: Why Greater Equality Makes Societies Stronger* (2009), in which they argue that severely unequal societies produce high rates of "'social pain": adverse outcomes including school drop-out, teen pregnancy, mental health problems, lack of social trust, high mortality rates, violence and crime, and low social participation. Their volume challenges the belief that the extent of poverty in a community predicts negative outcomes. They assert instead that the size of the *inequality gap* defines the material and psychological contours of the chasm between the wealthiest and the most impoverished, enabling various forms of social suffering to saturate a community, appearing natural. In societies with large gaps, one finds rampant state and socially reproduced disregard, dehumanization, policy neglect and abuse. As you might guess, the inequality gap of the United States ranks among the highest in their international comparisons.

Moving these notions of cross-sector dispossession and cross-community dispossession into critical youth studies, Maddy Fox and Michelle Fine, collaborating with the Urban Youth Collaborative of the Annenberg Institute for School Reform and other colleagues, developed Polling for Justice (see M. Fox et al., 2010), a multigenerational, participatory action research project designed to document youth *experiences of dispossession* and *sites of youth resistance* in New York City.[1] PFJ surveyed more than 1,000 NYC youth about their experiences in schools, with police and health care (see Fine, Stoudt, Fox, & Santos, 2010) toward four ends:

1. document the *geography and demography of dispossession and privilege* by detailing empirically where and for whom social policies, institutions and practices enable and constrict opportunities for youth development across the boroughs of New York City;
2. track the *cross-sector consequences of dispossession* by investigating how dispossession in one sector (e.g., not earning a high school diploma) adversely affects outcomes in other sectors (e.g., economic, health and criminal justice outcomes);
3. chronicle the ways in which youth and adult allies *mobilize to resist,* negotiate and challenge collectively these policies and practices;
4. design activist *scholarship to "be of use"* in varied organizing campaigns for youth justice and human rights policy struggles.

And then, most recently, given the radical assault on public education, the hyperreliance on school closings and charter openings, we added a fifth goal:

5. to examine the extent to which *school closings and charter openings map onto zones of dispossession*; that is, to assess the extent to which high drop-out/discharge rates are associated with heavy police presence/surveillance/criminalization of youth (a link that the youth researchers emphasized and insisted that we study) and then to consider the extent to which these are communities declared educational disasters by the DOE, where schools are being closed and selective-admissions/charter schools opened.

As U.S. public policy floats resources and opportunities upward toward a gentrified community of young people viewed as "entitled" to public support, social suffering anchors the aspirations and mobility of poor youth. New York City may be a caricature of these global dynamics. In our research, presented briefly below, we were interested in theorizing and documenting how the retreat of the state from social welfare, mobilized since the Reagan years, has swollen the stress load on poor and working-class youth while disabling the very relationships and institutions that might provide support for youth in crisis. We were interested, further, in the capillaries that could carry critical, participatory research from the halls of the CUNY Graduate Center into theatre, theory building, youth organizing, community life and social policy circles.

Design, Methods and Analysis Camps: Circuits of Collaboration

Polling for Justice is a large-scale, participatory action research project designed by a research collective of youth and adults, focused on youth experiences of (in)justice in education, criminal justice and health. An interdisciplinary collaboration among faculty and students at the City University of New York, a committed group of youth co-researchers, Brown University's Annenberg Institute for School Reform and the Urban Youth Collaborative,[2] our primary methodological instrument was a (rather lengthy) text-based and Internet-based survey co-constructed by youth and adults. With participation at the heart of theory, methods, crafting questions and analyzing the data, we gathered data from more than 1,000 New York City youth.

In the early spring of 2008, PFJ embarked on designing a citywide survey. Noting the fraught political, social and educational context for youth in the city, we were interested in amassing a public archive/database of youth knowledge and experiences to speak back to neoliberal forces aimed at privatizing and/or cutting publicly funded resources. Designed with colleagues from inside and outside the academy, with young people, and with advocates from the field of public health, we structured the work through circuits of collaboration across research, advocacy and organizing.

The PFJ researchers set out to study, theoretically and empirically, what we call *circuits of dispossession* (Fine & Ruglis, 2009) and *pools of youth resistance* in New York City, the ways in which social policies, institutions and practices systematically deny youth of color key human rights across sectors (education, criminal justice and health care) and the ways in which youth mobilize to resist, negotiate and challenge collectively these very forms of dispossession. We sought to investigate how urban youth, living with rapid gentrification, intense police surveillance in communities of color, privatization of schooling under the guise of choice, the deportation of massive numbers of immigrants, shrinkage of the supportive public sphere and expansion of the "disciplining" public sphere, experience, respond to and organize against the profoundly uneven opportunities for development across the five boroughs of New York City in three sectors: education, health care and criminal justice. PFJ was explicitly designed to gather and funnel social science evidence into organizing campaigns for youth justice—violence against girls and women, police harassment, college access, high-stakes testing and access to comprehensive sexuality education, to name just a few.

In 2008, at our first gathering, more than 40 youth arrived, recruited from activist organizations, public schools, detention centers, LGBTQ youth groups, foster care, undocumented youth seeking college and elite students from private schools, joined by educators, representatives of the NYC department of adolescent health, immigrant family organizers, lawyers, youth workers, psychologists, Planned Parenthood researchers, geographers, psychology and education doctoral students, in the basement of the Graduate Center of CUNY.

We posed a single, simple challenge to the group: We would like to collectively design a large-scale, citywide research project, creating a youth survey of standardized and homegrown items and conducting a series of focus groups, to document youth experiences across various public sectors of the city. We explained that the youth and adults were recruited because of their distinct experience, knowledge and expertise, and the young people and adults formed groups to pool their knowledge about prisons and their impact on youth, about foster care, immigration and deportation, homeless shelters, peer relationships, access to health education, worries about feeling safe, and concern for communities. Once groups were formed, jackets and hats came off and the groups began their work. We created a graffiti wall where youth could jot down the questions they would want to ask of other NYC teens.

We organized groups across certain experiences of urban youth: In one corner was a young man whose father was in prison, a girl worried her mother would be deported and a ninth grader expressed concern about gentrification; they designed questions about the real homeland security. In another corner, youth were reviewing standardized health items, such as the Youth Behavior Risk Survey (YRBS) and the National Longitudinal Study of Adolescent Health (AddHealth) about sexuality, reproduction, health and nutrition. Angry about these surveillance systems asking questions that are "none of their business" and equally concerned with "risky" health behaviors without accounting for questions and issues of access, resources, opportunity (educational or otherwise), and cultural differences, we worked to understand why it would be important to track the relation of unsafe sex practices with type, quality and access to comprehensive sexuality education (versus abstinence only, or none at all) or violence in a relationship or dropping out of school. But these workgroups also helped to stimulate critical youthful discussions on the meaning of "health"; societal fears of and judgments about adolescence; cultural influences on health; reified and racist perceptions of "urban" youth and youth of color; and about how health behaviors cannot be divorced from opportunity structures and the social, economic and political contexts into which one is embedded.

Down the hall, yet another group was talking about where they felt safe. At home? On the streets? In school? And a fourth group discussed youth experience with the criminal justice system. Together, in a participatory approach to survey construction, this group created a long checklist of contacts with police. What grew out of this was the most politically mobilized set of questions contained within the survey. In fact, nearly all of the criminal justice survey questions were developed by the youth. It became overwhelmingly evident that existing measures of youth experiences with policing in New York City failed to capture their realities.

Our work was designed as a contact zone (Torre, 2005) among youth from varied communities and ethnicities; between young people and adults; advocates, educators, practitioners and researchers from education, criminal justice and public health. Within our research team, questions of privilege, power and oppression were interrogated collaboratively; youth experiences led the inquiry and adult skills surrounded and supported; expertise was democratized and the "right to research" assumed fundamental (Appadurai, 2004). The process wasn't always smooth, but we tried to create spaces in our youth research camps where diverse forms of experience, analysis, theory and affect could be held, and explored delicately.

Within the Public Science Project at the Graduate Center, CUNY (Torre, Fine, Stoudt, & Fox, 2012; Torre & Fine, 2010), research camps have been crafted as a third space/process for building the democratic capacity of a research collective where questions of difference, power and solidarity can be engaged. We begin our first sessions with exercises designed to strip away misconceptions about what constitutes scientific inquiry and who can engage in social research, democratizing notions of knowledge and expertise. We design scavenger hunts to reveal the distinct insights that differently situated researchers import. For instance, we are always amazed (and yet, by now, never surprised) that it is often the least *formally educated* members of our collectives (e.g., students in special education classes) who most astutely read between the lines of dominant storylines. We develop exercises and activities in the traditions of critical pedagogy and popular education to extract and honor multiple perspectives—not just one designated right answer. Acknowledging many forms of intelligence is sometimes resisted by students who have been "at the top" of their schools or privileged or professionals who believe it is their job to teach the youth what they do not know. We spend much time helping young people explore themselves as intersectional; defined at once by culture, neighborhood, gender, class, adolescence, interest in books, music, politics, sexuality, gender, language, humor, how people treat them, how they resist and how they embody their worlds.

We read psychological theory, critical race theory and methods, newspaper articles and listen to music to "hear" how youth are represented, and to search for voices of dissent, challenge and resistance; we "take" standardized scales and try out new survey questions; we learn to conduct interviews and role play focus groups; we watch films and create questions; we spend time writing, discussing issues on the streets, in their schools, homes, meeting other youth researchers from other regions; building research skills, designing the survey, piloting items, collecting and analyzing qualitative and quantitative data; presenting findings across New York City and at professional meetings.

In PFJ, we launched "seminars" for youth researchers and doctoral students in which everyone took a set of questions to investigate the growing PFJ data. The collective was trained to approach their questions inductively using the philosophy and techniques of Tukey's (1977) exploratory data analysis (Stoudt, 2010). And all participating researchers—both youth and adult—took on the responsibility to "train" the next generation of youth researchers on future projects that grow out of the Public Science Project at the Graduate Center of CUNY.

Over 18 months, PFJ organized a series of multigenerational research camps focused, at the beginning, on building research expertise, sharing readings on the issues, histories of injustice and political struggles of resistance, refining our research questions, specifying the design and sample, exploring intersectional analyses of qualitative and quantitative data and generating provocative ideas for products, actions, scholarly papers, testimony, white papers and performances.

Analyzing/Embodying the Circuits—Bodies of Data Analysis

By the time we closed the survey in August 2009 we were swimming in data. We organized the data to examine what we called *cumulative dispossession*, trying to understand the extent to which youth who have been pushed out/dropped out of schools, for instance, and also have no health insurance, have had negative encounters with police and disrupted home lives were more likely to report depression, risky sexual engagements, involvement with violence and lower levels of psychological well-being. The youth researchers were adamant that PFJ *not* simply report racial "disparity" data, for they knew too well how such data were used to smear their communities, racial groups and individuals who were victims, but discursively turned into perpetrators of injustice through victim-blaming analyses. We were, instead, interested, as a collective in how policies of dispossession affect the lives, aspirations and care that different groups of youth engage as they navigate lives in communities made treacherous by these reckless social policies. And indeed, for every indicator we studied, those youth who scored as "highly dispossessed" by educational, housing/family, criminal justice and health care policy reported much higher rates of negative outcomes (for detailed findings see Fine, Stoudt, Fox, & Santos, 2010).

We also arrayed our survey material so as to create citywide maps to display the dramatically uneven geographic implementation of policies for youth development and policies for youth containment. With an analytic eye on class, gender, race/ethnicity, sexuality, immigration status, disability status and neighbor, we reviewed the geography of police harassment.

Bronx	Manhattan	Queens	Brooklyn
LGBTQ = 87.5%	LGBTQ = 52.4%	LGBTQ = 31.6%	LGBTQ = 69%
Straight = 53.8%	Straight = 35.0%	Straight = 44.7%	Straight = 50.7%
33.7% pt. diff	17.4% pt. diff	13.1% pt. diff	18.3% pt. diff

Negative Police Contact

Once we developed a preliminary analysis of the quantitative mapping of youth experiences of cumulative and community dispossession, we launched a set of data-driven focus groups in the neighborhoods where we found "hot spots" of dispossession (e.g., high rates of school push-out; high rates of criminalization of youth of color; high rates of surveillance on LGBT youth). In these focus groups, young people were asked to interpret, for and with us, the distributions and circuits of injustice we had documented. Conducting focus groups with youth who sit at the intersections of our statistical findings, we hear that young people remain buoyant through a sense of solidarity, critical understandings of unjust arrangements to stay positive, and through actively imagining a different tomorrow.

In one focus group with youth who identify as lesbian, gay, bisexual, queer, questioning and/or transgender, as they pored over findings about negative youth interactions with police, they discussed their anger in response to experiences like getting ticketed on the subway for putting their feet on a seat, for sitting in a playground after dark, or getting harassed for wearing the wrong clothes ("gay wear") in the wrong neighborhood.

They explained that outrage at these conditions is paired with an understanding of limited potential for appeal, and therefore, they find ways to dissipate their anger and move forward with their lives. As one focus group participant put it,

> It's like an everyday life in the city. It's like cops are mean, we just have to deal with because it's really like, there's really not much I can do with arguing with a cop. So it's like move on and keep on going, and it's every day. So it gets to the point where you no longer, it's not as shocking to us anymore. It just goes away after a while, you know, you walk it off, you watch TV, take a shower, and then it's like, okay, just another day in New York City.

The focus group participants offered up their critique of current realities and their vision for the kind of world they wish exists, a world rich with supports, access and resources for all young people (Brewster, Billies, & Hyacinthe, 2010).

The PFJ analyses provided evidence of circuitries in the form of cumulative dispossession of youth of color in low-income communities and then across communities: low-income young people of color from poor communities and LGBQ youth have the lowest rates of graduation, the highest rates of negative interactions with police, the most experiences of violence and the most alarming reports of depressive symptoms (Fine, Stoudt, Fox, & Santos, 2010). As PFJ youth researcher Jaquana Pearson always makes sure we emphasize, our data shows how young people are resisting oppression, redefining reality, aspiring to greatness and insisting on change. We also see evidence of the positive impact meaningful relationships with adults and participation in youth organizations can have in young people's lives.

Circuits of Analysis

From our participatory stance, in PFJ, we pencil a distinction between methods for *data collection* and methods for *analysis*. Participatory action research projects make use of both qualitative and quantitative methods. When participatory projects use quantitative methods, the *collaboration* that is inherent in a PAR approach adds new dimensions to analysis. The diverse nature of our research teams means that we must take multiple perspectives into account in relation to the interpretation of quantitative data, and this can sometimes pose challenges for finding approaches to collaboratively analyze quantitative data. In our case, when faced with a largely quantitative data set as a multigenerational research team, we were pushed to develop innovative methods for analysis—critical methodologies that include using qualitative (inductive, artistic, consciously subjective) methods to understanding our "bodies" of data.

As a research team, we spent time developing mathematical and statistical skills to be able to understand percentages and interpret cross-tabulation tables. It was one thing to intellectually understand what *87.5%* means; however, it was another thing to make sense of *87.5% of LGBQ youth living in the Bronx report negative experiences with police*. We decided that we would use embodied approaches to developing analyses of our largely quantitative data. In the beginning of July 2009, our research team retreated to a college campus for five days to steep in the data and learn an improvisational theatre method that emphasizes audience participation called Playback Theatre (H. Fox, 2007; J. Fox, 1994; Salas, 2007).

Circuits of Affect Within and Across Bodies

We turned to embodied methodologies in part because we needed an approach to quantitative data analysis that made room for multiple ways of knowing. However, we also used embodied methodologies because we wanted to find ways to communicate our findings that made explicit that the justice work and responsibility for action is held collectively in the bodies of both audience *and* performer, reader *and* researcher, adult *and* youth. Through drama and art, the PFJ researchers performed our findings on circuits of dispossession in a way that moved the work into the audience meaningfully— not as youth ventriloquy, but as intimate communication of the material and engagement with the audience. We used drama and other embodied methods to make meaning from the survey data within our research collective. Our research meetings began with personal updates and physical, playful warm-ups that brought whimsy (creativity) into our research space. Without minimizing the seriousness of our roles as knowledge producers, we played games to establish a dynamic in which everyone was invited and urged to contribute—to play (Boal, 1997). In fact, the more we all contributed, the more the "game" succeeded. We found there was power in play—our approach encouraged collaboration and creativity that opened up new insights about our data. Maxine Greene writes on the powerful potential of imagination and the arts to pry open fresh awareness of what's possible (1995). Through the warm-up process we were reminded that our data needed our brainpower, yes, but also our life experiences, and the knowledge stored deep in the muscles of our bellies, arms, calves and shoulders. The ritual reestablished our research space as collaborative and shared and developed our capacity for thinking critically together, as an ensemble.

In order to dive into the survey data, we started in front of a large projection screen running statistical analysis in real time, *Stats-in-Action* (Stoudt, 2010). In order to make sense of the data, we moved the data off the screen and put the numbers "on their feet," creating scenes and human images of the data. We found that when we put the numbers in our bodies, through sculptures or scenes, we made room for differences in understanding and experience to come into our research collective.

An illustration: The survey data showed that level of mother's education was a powerful indicator of survey respondents' school experiences, mental health, and involvement with violence and police. For instance, of the 1,110 people who took the survey, more than half of those who had dropped out also had a mother who dropped out of high school.

When we looked at the table, we could understand the data intellectually as powerful evidence of cross-generational fallout of inadequate access to education. When we moved this data *to its feet* the analysis became more complex and delicate. As we worked data over months and through images (digital photos), personal stories, scenes, and human sculptures, we came to understand the impact of the level of a mother's education from multiple perspectives.

Several members of the research collective could identify intimately with this finding, and as we theorized from the data, our personal experiences kept us accountable to ourselves, the survey respondents, our communities, our mothers, and our social justice goals. Embodied methodologies were elastic enough for us to be able to make sense of the survey data, reconciled with what we knew from our diverse personal experiences. Through art, we found a means to uncover and express various kinds of knowledge—including affective ways of knowing. The embodied methodologies made room for pain and shame, for anger, for frustration, making visible circuitries of affect orbiting the data. As a result, our group developed a critical analysis of educational betrayal that moved blame from the individual to the structural.

Finding creative ways to dramatize the data during analysis was especially effective for creating a highly collaborative space and for developing complex, layered analyses of the survey data. In Polling for Justice, we conceptualized the shift from the intimate backstage of our research space to the public stage of research dissemination as a moment of action and an opportunity to explore together with audiences *what is* and *what is possible* (Gallagher, 2007; Greene, 1995; Salverson & Schutzman, 2006).

Circuits of Representations and Responsibility—The Performance Lab

Ignacio Martín-Baró conceptualized public opinion polls as *social mirrors* designed to provide a scientific reflection of lived realities that might speak to power and disrupt injustice (1994; Torre et al., 2012). In PFJ, in line with our commitment to do social research of use (Fine & Barreras, 2001), we turned to performance methodologies that might interrupt hegemonic (mostly negative) representations of adolescence and adult complacency. We imagined our performance spaces as *labs* where we played with and dismantled the wall that can separate audience from performer-researcher. We thought of performances as opportunities for the PFJ researchers to hold up a "social-mirror-in-the-round," making visible the link between youth, adults and structural inequalities.

We took this turn to drama and performance allied with social scientists who insist on doing research with social relevance and space and the particular community of scholars and social scientists who incorporate the arts into their research process and products. In our case, we self-consciously followed in the footsteps of the performance work of W. E. B. Du Bois.[3]

Although this line of Du Boisian work is little known, as a social scientist, Du Bois used pageantry, performance and circus theatre in order to explore alternative possibilities about African American history and reality. He conceived of art, the stage, drama and theatre as a vehicle through which to educate, inspire and unite Black audiences (Horne & Young, 2001). Through theatre, Du Bois was able to share histories, and historical figures, to audiences without reliance on literacy. Committed to theatre with Black people, for Black people, he used the stage to insert productive stories of African Americans into the public discourse and imagination (Krasner, 2001).

Humbly following in this tradition, the Polling for Justice project turned to dramatic performances of our research project as a way to disseminate our research and engage with audiences. In Polling for Justice, our turn to art and performance grows out of a similar commitment to social justice,[4] and we build not only on the Du Boisian legacy and other social science research entwined with the arts (Gallagher, 2007) but also the work of community art projects that make social justice claims. The discipline of community-based art has much overlap with participatory action research, as illustrated by Jan Cohen-Cruz: "Community-based art is a field in which artists, collaborating with people whose lives directly inform the subject matter, express collective meaning" (2005, p. 1). In line with these commitments, we took seriously the *performance* of our data, as well as the *process* of encountering and analyzing the data through embodied methods as well.

We turned to performing the PFJ data in order to incite engagement from the audience but wary of arousing a simply empathic response. Megan Boler (1999) cautions that empathic readings permit the reader to go under the false assumption that it is possible to fully imagine others and allow for a passive consumption of the subject's experience/emotions without also having to examine the reader's social responsibilities. She calls instead for an active empathy, or a "testimonial reading," where the responsibility for action lies with the reader. In PFJ, as a group of mostly African American and Latina young people, we were especially concerned that we not encourage our predominantly White, adult, middle-class audiences to want to save or rescue poor Black and Brown youth. We used playful, nuanced, powerful embodiments of our data as one way to guard against portraying youth of color as suffering and as victims. We worked to avoid a performance setting where rows of comfortable audience members reenacted the watching of others' pain as onlookers. We understood bystanders, witnesses, and non-victims, though seemingly unaffected, as actually being in potentially powerful, liminal roles

(Fine, 2002). Our hope was to facilitate our audiences to notice, that is, to incite a recognition that their contribution towards collective responsibility could be to do a careful interrogation of their own story/future actions and recognize the cross-circuits of dispossession, privilege and responsibility coursing through the performance space. We wanted to make visible the power lines and the braiding of our collective circuits (Salverson & Schutzman, 2006).

The PFJ performances were conceived as an extension of the ethic of participation across the inequality gap. Audiences included teachers, parents, school administrators, young people, social scientists, community members, police, Department of Education officials and policy makers. In order to activate the participation of audience members, the performances had three phases. The researchers started with a presentation of the PFJ data in embodied, visual, storied ways that employed metaphor, humor, maps, graphs and numbers. In the second phase audience members were invited to respond and react to the data using Playback Theatre improvisation (J. Fox, 1994; Salas, 2007) to transform the audience members' affective responses into theatre on the spot. Finally, in the third phase, the PFJ researchers invited audience members to contribute their own expertise and experience in generating knowledge and visions for action in light of the PFJ data.

Provoking a Politic of Solidarity

According to Augusto Boal's theoretical frame, we are all actors. In Boal's theatre form, Theater of the Oppressed, no audience member simply watches; there are no spectators, only spect-*actors* (Boal, 1997). Theatre of the Oppressed dramas are designed to simultaneously be productive for transforming real issues of social injustice and as an allegory for the kind of democratic, participatory politic possible in the world outside the performance space. In PFJ we too did not want our audiences to remain passive. We wanted audience members to grasp the analyses we presented on youth social psychological experience of circuits of policy dispossession, and we wanted audience members to recognize their own roles in the arrangements that produced the conditions we performed. Towards the end of the PFJ performances, once the audience had seen embodied interpretations of the survey data, we broke the fourth wall of the performance space, turned up the house lights and explained that it was time for the audience members to take on a more active role in the performance lab. We passed a microphone around and heard audience members' affective responses to hearing the data: "That was powerful, I feel shocked by some of the data"; "Amazed at how many police are in the NYC school system"; "I feel frustrated and lost. How do I keep going as an educator?"; "I feel inspired by seeing young people full of knowledge and critique." After each response, the PFJ researcher-performers would turn the responses into theatre on the spot in the form of a human sculpture that could simultaneously hold multiple interpretations.

The purpose of the Playback Theatre was to make visible some of the circuitry of emotion swirling around statistical representations of life for young people in New York City. The human sculptures opened fissures in the divide that usually exists between performer and audience, researcher and reader and youth and adult. These openings made space for more meaningful collaborations to germinate and grow.

In the PFJ performances, audiences had to make sense of the paradox between the data on dispossession and negative experiences they were hearing and the sophisticated work of the youth researchers presenting/performing the research. Through a small scene or a physical sculpture, the researcher-performers could quickly communicate multiple and complex perspectives. The ultimate goal of the PFJ performances was to provoke a sense of solidarity between audience, researchers, youth and adults. In the presentations of our data, as in our research camps, we made strides to create spaces that allowed for interaction and exposed (explicitly and implicitly) the circuitry that connects us all. With performance, we stretched the web of participation to include the outer circle, the audience, as those who bear witness, in the hopes that we would engage. In this way, our research itself was an intervention in the institutional and policy-based production of adolescent experiences of injustice. Through PFJ performances the audience could identify with youth of color in new ways, across power, suggesting a shift in collective identity, and perhaps making political engagement more likely.

At the very end of the PFJ performance, Dr. Researchy is brought back on stage. He has been watching, thinking, and he has had an awakening. He says,

> Well I was just thinking that we should really ask teens what they think the questions we should ask are and find out their ideas on the best solutions to some of these problems. I mean, you all are the ones living it each day, and together we can think about we can do next...

The PFJ researcher-performers, glad Dr. Researchy finally "gets it," invite him into the research collective. But their final move is to turn questions of "what next" back to the audience; to re-place responsibility collectively.

Thus, in the final scene of the PFJ performance, the youth researchers explained that there was no ending to the show. Instead we insisted the audience take responsibility for imagining what should happen next. Audience members popcorned suggestions for future research, policy change and organized community responses:

> I'd like to see some opportunity for other young people to do research like this with allied adults and for it to go viral worldwide, standing up together to change policy.

> Let's show the data to police departments and police officers and figure out how to change the policies and realities.

The performances were not designed to be solutions. Instead, they were meant to expose, provoke and motivate people to contend with their own/our own collusion in the inequality gap, worsened by policies that privilege those already privileged. Theatre allowed us to collectively hold the complexity, particulars, the broad analysis, the contradictions and the dream—all at the same time. With policing data, we could know the numbers, the discrimination, and still communicate the need for protection, or share our aspirations to be a police officer in what could be a stable career. With education or economics, we could critique capitalism or privatization but still explain why we advocate for our younger brothers and sisters to get into the new charter school on the block with better resources.

As an art form, our performances were at once an encounter and a metaphor—the performances slowed down time somewhat to allow for a close examination of particular realities, and through art we invited audiences and performers to experiment with what is and expand what is possible. Outside the performance space, PFJ data circulated in more concrete ways. The research findings traveled into public hearings, policy reports, community speak-outs and academic papers on education, safety reforms and social critique. In every arena, the aim was to maintain the live-wire connection between the findings, the researchers and audience. The PFJ data made evident how the impact of certain policies ripple out in young people's lives along circuits of dispossession, and our approach to disseminating the data made sure that audiences of the research felt their own location in that roughly circular arrangement we call a revolution.

Notes

1. Polling for Justice was made possible thanks to the Surdna Foundation, Overbrook Foundation, Hazen Foundation, Glass Foundation, Schott Foundation, Urban Youth Collaborative and the Public Science Project and the Youth Studies Research Fund at the CUNY Graduate Center.
2. Polling for Justice research collective includes Niara Calliste, Michelle Fine, Madeline Fox, Darius Francis, Candace Greene, Jaquana Pearson, Una Osato, Dominique Ramsey, Maybelline Santos, Brett Stoudt, Paige Taylor, Jose Torres, Isabel Vieira and Jessica Wise.

3. In November 1913, *The Crisis* magazine published a detailed description (nearly a script) of a pageant of African American history written by W. E. B. Du Bois. The pageant was performed as a celebration of the Emancipation Proclamation, was titled *The People of Peoples and Their Gifts to Men* (Du Bois, 1913, p. 339) and was produced by over 300 and performed by over 1,000 people (Du Bois, 1913; Horne & Young, 2001).

    The sketch of *The People of Peoples and Their Gifts to Men* begins with four heralds yelling, "Hear ye! Hear ye! Men of all the Americas, and listen to the tale of the eldest and strongest of the races of mankind, whose faces be Black. Hear ye, hear ye, of the gifts of Black men to this world, the Iron Gift, the Gift of Faith, the Pain of Humility and the Sorrow of Pain, the Gift of Freedom and Laughter, and the undying Gift of Hope. Men of the world, keep silence and hear ye this!" (Du Bois, 1913, p. 139). The pageant continues, telling the history of the successes and strengths of African people. Through dramatic effect, Du Bois and colleagues told audiences about early African technologies, of ancient civilizations in Egypt, of old roots of modern religions, of survival, of pain, and of "Struggle Toward Freedom" (Du Bois, 1913, p. 340). This pageant, later called *The Star of Ethiopia*, was "a great human festival" with a cast of 1,000 African Americans using procession, story and extravagant costumes (Du Bois, 1915).

4. Du Bois was explicitly uninterested in art for art's sake; he was interested in art as propaganda (Krasner, 2001). He turned to performance and art in order to take action with scholarship and reach masses of people.

References

Appadurai, A. (2004). Capacity to aspire: Culture and the terms of recognition. In R. Vijayendra & M. Walton (Eds.), *Culture and public action* (pp. 59–84). Stanford, CA: Stanford University Press.

Brewster, K., Billies, M., & Hyacinthe, Z. (2010). Presentation: LGBTQ youth experiences with police in neighborhoods, subways, and to and from school. Syracuse University Queering Education Research Institute (QuERI) Roundtable on LGBTQ Issues in Education. New York, NY.

Boal, A. (1997). *Games for actors and non-actors*. London, England: Routledge.

Boler, M. (1999). *Feeling power: Emotions and education*. New York, NY: Routledge.

Cohen-Cruz, J. (2005). *Local acts: Community-based performance in the United States*. New Brunswick NJ: Rutgers University Press.

Du Bois, W. E. B (1913, November) *The Crisis, 6*, 339–345.

Du Bois, W. E. B. (1915, December). Star of Ethiopia. *The Crisis, 11*.

Fine, M. (2002). 2001 Carolyn Sherif Award address: The presence of an absence. *Psychology of Women Quarterly, 26*, 9–24.

Fine, M., & Barreras, R. (2001). To be of use. *Analyses of Social Issues and Public Policy, 1*, 175–182.

Fine, M., & Ruglis, J. (2009). Circuits and consequences of dispossession: The racialized realignment of the public sphere for U.S. youth. *Transforming Anthropology, 17*(1), 20–33.

Fine, M., Stoudt, B. G., Fox, M., & Santos, M. (2010). The uneven distribution of social suffering: Documenting the social health consequences of neo-liberal social policy on marginalized youth. *European Health Psychologist, 12*(September), 30–35.

Fox, H. (2007). Playback theatre: Inciting dialogue and building community through personal story. *The Drama Review, 51*(4), 89–105.

Fox, J. (1994). *Acts of service: Spontaneity, commitment, tradition in the nonscripted theatre*. New Paltz, NY: Tusitala.

Fox, M., Mediratta, K., Ruglis, J., Stoudt, B., Shah, S., & Fine, M. (2010). Critical youth engagement: Participatory action research and organizing In L. Sherrod, J. Torney-Puta, & C. Flanagan (Eds.), *Handbook of research and policy on civic engagement with youth* (pp. 621–649). Hoboken, NJ: Wiley.

Gallagher, K. (2007). *The theatre of urban: Youth and schooling in dangerous times*. Toronto, ON, Canada: University of Toronto Press.

Greene, M. (1995). *Releasing the imagination: Essays on education, the arts, and social change*. San Francisco, CA: Jossey-Bass.

Harvey, D. (2004). Conversations with history: A geographer's perspective on the new American imperialism [Webcast transcript]. Berkeley: University of California Institute of International Studies. Retrieved May 10, 2007, from http://globetrotter.berkeley.edu/people4/Harvey/harvey-con0.html

Horne, G., & Young, M. (2001). *W. E. B. Du Bois: An encyclopedia*. Westport, CT: Greenwood Press.

Krasner, D. (2001). "The pageant is the thing": Black nationalism and *The Star of Ethiopia*. In J. Mason & E. Gainor (Eds.), *Performing America: Cultural nationalism in American theater* (pp. 106–122). Ann Arbor: University of Michigan Press.

Martín-Baró, I. (1994). *Writings for a liberation psychology*. Cambridge, MA: Harvard University Press.

Salas, J. (2007). *Improvising real life: Personal story in playback theatre*. New York, NY: Tusitala.

Salverson, J., & Schutzman, M. (2006). Witnessing subjects: A fool's help. In J. Cohen-Cruz (Ed.), *A Boal companion: Dialogues on theatre and cultural politics* (pp. 146–157). New York, NY: Routledge.

Stoudt, B. (2010, June). *Testing circuits of dispossession: An exploratory look*. Presentation to Pathways to Resilience II: The social ecology of resilience, The Resilience Research Centre, Halifax, NS, Canada.

Torre, M. (2005). The alchemy of integrated spaces: Youth participation in research collectives of difference. In L. Weis & M. Fine (Eds.), *Beyond silenced voices* (pp. 251–266). Albany: State University of New York Press.

Torre, M., & Fine, M. (2010). A wrinkle in time: Tracing a legacy of public science through community self-surveys and participatory action research. *Journal of Social Issues, 67*, 106–121. doi:10.1111/j.1540–4560.2010.01686.x

Torre, M., Fine, M., Alexander, N., Billups, A., Blanding, Y., Genao, E., … Urdang, K. (2008). Participatory action research in the contact zone. In J. Cammarota & M. Fine (Eds.), *Revolutionizing education: Youth participatory action research in motion* (pp. 23–44). New York, NY: Routledge.

Torre, M., Fine, M., Stoudt, B., & Fox, M. (2012). Critical participatory action research as public science. In P. Camic & H. Cooper (Eds.), *Handbook of research methods in psychology.* Washington, DC: American Psychology Association.

Tuck, E., Allen, J., Bacha, M., Morales, A., Quinter, S., Thompson, J., & Tuck, M. (2008). PAR praxes for now and future change: The collective of researchers on educational disappointment and desire. In J. Cammarota & M. Fine (Eds.), *Revolutionizing education: Youth participatory action research in motion* (pp. 49–83). New York, NY: Routledge.

Tukey, J. W. (1977). *Exploratory data analysis.* Reading, MA: Addison-Wesley.

Wilkinson, R., & Pickett, K. (2009). *The spirit level: Why greater equality makes societies stronger.* New York, NY: Bloomsbury Press.

CHAPTER 15

In Search of Critical Knowledge
Tracing Inheritance in the
Landscape of Incarceration

Carolina Muñoz Proto

When I was younger, people said, "You're going to end up like him." I would like to end up like him, now. So now you could say all of that … because now you know he's doing the right thing. This is a positive time in his life. He's not in jail no more. So, hopefully, I can be like him now. (Rebuilding Communities life story interview with Sam, 19, African American)

Sam is the son of a formerly incarcerated father who, after completing a 12-year prison sentence, became a graduate student and a social service professional. Like most youth with formerly imprisoned parents, Sam cannot narrate his life without contending with two notions that frame public discourses about incarceration: inheritance and transformation. The Rebuilding Communities Project (RCP) is a multi-method, participatory study that traces the meanings of inheritance and transformation across individual lives, family dynamics and social discourse.[1] For 18 months, the RCP team carried out a case study of the College Initiative (CI), a post-prison college program located within the City University of New York that works to "rebuild lives, families and communities through higher education."[2] Since 2002 CI staff have supported nearly 500 men and women as they pursue a college or graduate education after prison. By offering services that are seldom available to this population, the CI opens an opportunity to learn about how former prisoners and their children fare in the presence of policies that increase their access to educational opportunities, resources and networks, thus capitalizing on a strengths-based model (Boudin & Zeller-Berkman, 2010). Deficit-based models, on the other hand, pay "an inordinate amount of attention to the assumed 'pathologies' of ghetto residents" (Wacquant, 1998, p. 348), emphasizing social exclusion, trauma, academic detainment, and risk of criminality (Foster & Hagan, 2007). Many studies about the injustice of mass incarceration imply that its causes and consequences live *within* individual prisoners, their families and their children. To avoid this trap, the RCP was based on participatory action research (PAR), which denounces master narratives about what the world is and could be (Brydon-Miller, 2001; Fals-Borda & Rahman, 1991; Fine, Roberts, Torre, & Upegui, 2001). PAR researchers distinguish between empirical-analytical knowledge—needed for survival, produced by positivist approaches and concerned with causality and determinism—and critical knowledge, rooted in social action and concerned with multiple relationships over determinism (Brydon-Miller, 2001; Fine, Roberts, Torre, & Upegui, 2001).

The search for critical knowledge led the RCP in a recursive journey through intimate stories of imprisonment and macro-level structures that sustain the violence of mass incarceration. In the spring of 2008, Professor Michelle Fine and CI founder Benay Rubenstein brought together trained researchers from the Public Science Project at the CUNY Graduate Center and an advisory board of CI staff, CI students, and teenaged children of CI students to discuss the goals of the study. It was decided that the project would explore *how post-prison college contributes to rebuilding the lives, families and communities of formerly incarcerated adults.* Methodologically, the challenge was to (1) interrogate the meaning of post-prison college in the lives of students, their children, and communities; (2) go beyond evaluations that compare recidivism rates among CI students to those of the general population of former prisoners; and (3) produce knowledge that would have an impact on current debates about incarceration and education.

Tracing Inheritance

A First Approach: Self-education and Action

The RCP youth team brought together trained researchers, educators/filmmakers and New York City youth who have experienced the incarceration of a parent or close relative. We initially planned to carry out focus groups with children of CI students between ages 16 and 21 to explore how youth experience their parents' transition from prison to college. However, my co-researchers refused to make CI families look like isolated cases and quickly broadened our research question to the strengths and challenges in the lives of youth with incarcerated parents. This broadening vitalized the self-education and action aspects of the PAR process, during which we collaborated with educator and filmmaker Jeremy Robins on a video documentary about the impact of parents' incarceration on New York City youth, titled *Echoes of Incarceration.*

As part of this work, we drew from various sources to develop memos with facts about incarceration like the following:

> According to the World Prison Population List (Walmsley, 2009) a fourth of the world's prisoners are in the United States (2.29 million). Based on a recent report by the Pew Center on the States (2008), incarceration and correctional control are raced, classed and gendered experiences. While one in 100 adults is incarcerated in the US, incarceration rates are higher for blacks and Latina/os than for whites, and higher for males than for females: One in 15 black men is imprisoned as compared to one in 106 white males over 18; and one in 100 black women is incarcerated as compared to one in 355 for white women over 18. According to the Bureau of Justice Statistics (2000), incarceration has important consequences for the children of prisoners who in 1999 amounted to 2.1% of the 72.3 million minors in the country. According to the *From Prison to Home* conference report (2002), 7% of African American children have a parent inside compared to 2% of all children in the country. Over 43% of parents in federal facilities are held more than 500 miles away from their children.

These memos reaffirmed the team's goals, which were reflected in the following mission:

> We are a team of youth researchers and adult allies who are documenting the impact of incarceration and post-prison college on New York families. The goal of this project is to get a message across to young people who are experiencing the incarceration of their family members and friends. This project also hopes to educate the general public about what is going on in the country when it comes to incarceration and education. These goals are very important because the incarceration of young people's relatives is happening at high rates nation-wide. This affects young people's lives and must be changed.

Through self-education the youth research team came to a shared sense of urgency about mass incarceration as a form of collective punishment for underprivileged communities. Although the information had always been there, as facts in books and as individual intuitions and experiences, our shared learning allowed this knowledge to infuse and inspire the research. This process, which echoes Freire's notion of conscientization (1970/1990), inspired me to write about my position in the project:

> I've lived in the US for 7 years but I've been blind to mass incarceration until recently ... At some point, I reached a critical level of information that makes one unable to forget this open wound ... Racial and political surveillance, imprisonment, and mass punishment are not easy for me to accept because I grew up [during] Pinochet's dictatorship ... Given my experiences in Chile, I would like to think that the reality of mass incarceration would be more obvious to me. This [tells me that], as a privileged visitor, one can live in the US for a long time, even years, without giving any thought to the one in one hundred people who lives behind bars. [Also], having three friends and many acquaintances whose parents are/ have been in prison does not make me immune to ignorance.

Over the months, our self-education work began to suggest that most studies and representations of youth with parents in prison highlight negative outcomes. The RCP, however, wanted to acknowledge the fact that CI students have wisdom to offer and that youth can take an active role in their lives as they take up useful advice from others. To this end we developed a written questionnaire asking CI students to provide an anonymous "statement of advice for a young person whose parents are or have been inside." Twenty-four CI students answered our questionnaire. Because the goal was to find new understandings of parental incarceration, we used a grounded theory approach (Charmaz, 2006) to look for emerging themes in the answers, first individually and then as a group. *Breaking the chains of despair* and *the strained parent–child relationship* emerged as important themes.

Regarding *breaking the chains of despair,* the statements of advice described three types of challenges that may cause young people to feel despair:

(1) a fear that they might repeat their parents' mistakes;
(2) a relative lack of guidance and protection compared to other youth;
(3) painful stereotypes and emotions.

The statements also conveyed a strong sense of possibility in the form of concrete advice. CI students encouraged youth to focus on their positive goals ("Remain true and strong and do not give up on your dream regardless of how long it takes to materialize"), find positive role models ("Seek positive, strong and caring role models that will guide you through this disturbing time"), and reject the feeling of being doomed to repeat parents' mistakes ("Do not allow the stereotypes to take precedence"). Finally, CI students emphasized how education provides resources and opens horizons ("Education is very important. It shines some light and gives meaning to life"). In relation to the strained parent–child relationship, CI students highlighted: (1) the remoteness of prisons; and (2) the emotional distance, anger and pain felt when a parent is convicted. The advice told youth to take an active role in the parent–child relationship by communicating openly and often during incarceration and after release ("Communicate daily with them. Let them know how you feel and probe their feelings as well") and providing support and encouragement ("Do not give up on them. Continue to support and love them with all your heart"). Similar themes emerged from interviews with siblings of the co-researchers during the making of the video documentary, as well as from three focus groups with a total of 20 youth, aged 16 to 21, from local community organizations. Focusing on their expertise, the focus group data took the form of life maps, stories about their communities, recommendations to policy makers and leaders and word maps about family and incarceration (see Table 1).

During the self-education and action phase, we learned that *both* the challenges of incarceration and the possibilities created by education are salient issues in the lives of youth with incarcerated parents (for a detailed discussion of the topic, see Harris, Graham, & Carpenter, 2010). From this initial round of data collection we concluded that the incarceration and release of a parent can weaken young people's sense of hope and also take away emotional and material resources needed for a successful transition into adulthood. In addition, youth are often burdened by negative stereotypes but lack safe spaces where they can process their experiences. Finally, the parent–child relationship suffers from physical separation, feelings of anger, disappointment and sadness, and the disapproval of those who view parents as negative influences. From these challenges, however, youth can build a sense of determination towards their dreams, learn how to find positive role models, gain perspective about their own life choices, and find the motivation to grow in resources, purpose and pride through their own education. Although these findings are exploratory, they were a step towards more complex understandings of how inheritance and transformation relate to post-prison college.

Incarceration	Jail/Bars/Loneliness/No freedom/Abuse/Finding themselves/Lack of attention/ Redemption/Goals/Justice
Family + incarceration	Hurt/Educated/Forgotten/Dysfunctional/Lost/Distance/Wanting better/ Looking for love in the street/Motivation/Foster care/Single parent/Hardship/ Raising siblings/Hustle/Understanding/Secret/Bad grades
Family	Love/Commitment/Patience/Fun/Loyalty/Caring/Trust/Fights/Help/Home/ Looking out/Being close—Being far/Respect/Reunion

Table 1. Word map about families and incarceration. Example of a word map from a focus group with 10 Latino/a, African American and South East Asian youth, ages 16 to 21

A Second Approach: Inheritance in Discourse

The self-education and action phases raised important questions about how to address race, class and power without perpetuating the notion that poor people of color are prisoners and that prisoners are poor people of color. Reporting the challenges and achievements of our participants in a socio-cultural vacuum or through the lens of disparities research was not a satisfactory solution to this problem. It was vital to move beyond the redemption story that we were ready to gather, our participants ready to tell, and the world ready to hear. Otherwise, our well-intentioned research would portray at-risk youth whose lives can be saved through their parents' post-prison education. An important challenge was that our approach to the data gave us limited information about the power dynamics and discourses surrounding parental incarceration and post-prison college. Looking for clues, I began to re-read my notes in search of answers and wrote the following:

> In the teams' discussions about youth with incarcerated parents [there is] a tension between a sense of hope that is infused with dreams of a college education, and the feeling of being doomed to a future of convictions ("They don't let me see my father cuz I might turn out like him"). Another tension is the relationship between shame ("I let people believe my foster mom's my real mom") and pride ("My friend tells everyone her father's inside and he's a Latin King") … So what is the "common sense" that surrounds incarceration? … What is really being inherited? Is it the role of "out of control"/"incorrigible"/"anti-social"/"super-predator"/"morally bankrupt" other?

Borrowing from Hole's (2007) work on narratives of deafness, I began to conceptualize the RCP and all other claims about prisoners and their children as part of the *discursive landscape of incarceration*. Hole argues that "surrounding any phenomenon there may be a variety of discourses … the set of meanings, metaphors, and representations, images, statements and so on that produce a particular understanding of an event, person, or experience … a different way of representing it to the world" (2007, p. 262). Within this framework, incarceration and inheritance are contested phenomena about which various discourses compete for legitimacy. In order to explore these meanings I decided to shift the unit of analysis away from the individual child-of-prisoner in order to ask the following questions:

1) *How do experts construct the intergenerational significance of incarceration through narratives of inheritance?*

2) *How do youth whose parents attend college after prison negotiate the intergenerational meaning of incarceration through their stories of post-prison college? What is at stake when youth speak of pride, shame, transformation and fate?*

To answer these questions I built a body of data from three purposive samples of experts who are differently positioned around the issue of incarceration. The first sample includes the expert sources that had informed our self-education and video work (Table 2), including five large-scale reports by research institutions and excerpts from the relevant chapters of nine criminal justice textbooks selected at random from the library catalogue of the John Jay College of Criminal Justice. These texts are worth examining because, as the voice of scientific objectivity, criminal justice experts affect the families of prisoners and the public opinion on parental incarceration through social policies and programs. The second sample includes song lyrics about incarceration by artists in the United States (Table 3). The sample stands in contrast to criminal justice textbooks in genre and in the social position of its authors, since hip hop, blues and jazz have historically been central to storytelling and self-representation by criminalized voices (Chang, 2005; Rose, 1994). Finally, the third sample includes the life stories of five young people—Charles, Sara, Jonathan, Marcus and Sam—who are 18 to 20 years of age and who, except for Charles, have seen their parents' transition from prison to college thanks to the CI. Their stories were co-constructed during audiotaped interviews using the Life Story Interview (McAdams, 1995), which invites interviewees to share their own analysis of the internal and external forces shaping their lives. Narrative research holds that "it is through the minutiae of daily life that human beings access the political ripples, and tidal waves, of their times" (Andrews, 2007, p. 2). Listening to these life stories in the context of other voices was a means to trace inheritance and learn about how the children of the "disposable" (Bauman, 2004) build lives of meaning (Hall & Fine, 2005) and thrive in double consciousness (Du Bois, 1903) This approach was inspired by the work of critical youth researchers whose work bypasses narratives of pathology (Brotherton & Barrios, 2004; Conquergood, 1992; Mendoza-Denton, 2008) by "bear[ing] witness to the ways in which young people are volunteered by their culture as a canvas for global economic, racial, cultural, gendered, and sexual conflicts" (Fine & Sirin, 2007, p. 34).

With these ideas in mind, I carried out a discourse analysis of the representations of what youth inherit from their parents at the material, symbolic, psychological, biological, legal and other levels. Using a code-book grounded on the data (Charmaz, 2006), I moved across the samples to understand contrasting representations as cultural tools (Vygotsky, 1978a, 1978b) used to celebrate or deny transformation. The analysis reveals parental incarceration and post-prison college as liminal spaces where determinism, hope, redemption and revision co-exist and also compete. The song lyrics represent inheritance in the context of raced and classed patterns of surveillance and conviction, highlighting the strengths of those who are criminalized and inscribing deficits on structural factors rather than on individuals and communities. In "Behind Enemy Lines," for instance, Dead Prez claims that Khadejah's father is incarcerated due to systematic race- and class-based repression of political leaders (see Table 4). Parental incarceration is represented as a part of oppressive structures in which the mass incarceration of poor black people is more a matter of fate than of personal choices:

> You know they got me trapped in this prison of seclusion/Happiness, living on tha streets is a delusion … Can barely walk tha city streets/Without a cop harassing me, searching me/Then asking my identity/Hands up, throw me up against tha wall. (From "Trapped," by Tupac, 1998)

In contrast, criminal justice experts weave inheritance into representations that highlight individual-level deficit in order to speak of the unjust causes and consequences of mass incarceration:

> The majority of female inmates are members of racial or ethnic minorities … *Only* four in ten report having had full-time employment at the time of the arrest, and *nearly* 30 percent were on welfare before incarceration, compared to just under 8 percent for male inmates … Health experts believe that [high]

levels of abuse are related to the significant amount of drug and/or alcohol addiction that *plagues* the female prison population ... (Gaines & Miller, 2008, p. 342, italics added)

This focus on individual outcomes hides the fact that employment and self-reliance can be the exception rather than the norm among the urban poor whose jobs have been relocated to more profit-able places (Bauman, 2004). The lyrics of prison songs, on the other hand, complicate the notion of inheritance; they reject intergenerational damage (see Cross, 2003) and locate the sources of disparity at the level of structural oppression. Consider the following lyrics by Tupac:

When I was conceived, & came to be in this position/My momma was a panther loud/Single parent, but she proud/When she witness baby boy rip a crowd .../Will my child get to feel love/Or are we all just cursed to be street thugs/Cause being black hurts/And even worse if you speak first. (From "Letter to My Unborn Child," by Tupac, 1998)

Prison lyrics fracture narratives of urban primitivism about the urban poor (Conquergood, 1992) and portray children of prisoners who inherit a sense of pride from being part of a community that can be powerful and resilient despite oppressive circumstances—all indicators of an identity rooted in posi-tive marginality (Hall & Fine, 2005; Unger, 2000). The lyrics also speak of loss but introduce another dimension to it: it is the state that has failed the children of prisoners and put them at risk, rather than their criminalized parents.

The contrasts and tensions that make up the discursive landscape of incarceration give us a sense of how much is at stake when Charles, Sara, Jonathan, Marcus and Sam speak of what they have inherited from their parents. It is with these insights in mind that I now turn to a more detailed discussion of the meaning of incarceration and post-prison college in the life stories of youth with formerly incarcerated parents.

Title	Author	Year
Criminal Justice: A Brief Introduction	Schmalleger	1999
American Criminal Justice: An Introduction	Bartollas & Jaeger	1988
Criminal Justice	Adler, Mueller & Laufer	2000
Criminal Justice in Action	Gaines & Miller	2008
Criminal Justice in America	Barlow	2000
Criminal Justice	Reid	2006
Introduction to Criminal Justice	Bohm & Haley	1997
Criminal Justice	Inciardi	1999
Crime and Justice: An Introduction	Abadinsky & Winfree	1992
World Prison Population List	Walmsley	2009
One in 100: Behind Bars in America	Pew Center on the States	2008
Incarcerated Parents and Their Children	Bureau of Justice Statistics	2000
Bringing Families In	Christian et al.	2006
From Prison to Home	Department of Health and Human Services	2002

Table 2. Purposive sample of criminal justice textbooks and reports

Compilation Title	Label	Year
No More Prisons 2	Raptivism	2003
Tupac's Greatest Hits	Death Row Records	1998
In Prison: Afro-American Prison Music from Blues to Hip Hop	Trikont	2006

Table 3. Purposive sample of song lyrics

Song Lyrics	
Pride	"Yo, little Khadejah pops is locked … And she be dreamin bout his date of release … Her fathers a political prisoner, free Fred/Son of a Panther that the government shot dead/Back in 12-4-1969" *Dead Prez, "Behind Enemy Lines"*
Resilience	"Even as a crack fiend mama,/ya always was a black queen mama … ya always wuz committed, a poor single mother on welfare/tell me how ya did it" *Tupac, "Dear Mama"*
Textbooks and Reports	
Stigma	"Problems in school may be directly related to the alienation and stigma a child feel because a parent is incarcerated." *Christian et al., 2006*
Criminality	"Inability of children to adopt productive coping mechanisms over time typically results in delinquency and adult criminal behavior." *From Prison to Home Conference: Background Paper, 2002*
Risk	"The children, families and former prisoners impacted by incarceration may represent a group more at-risk than any subculture in the country." *From Prison to Home Conference: Background Paper, 2002*
Life Stories	
Inspiration	"It was inspirational. I wanted to follow in [my father's] footsteps … That was why I really wanted to go to college." *Sam*
Resilience	"I remember Christmas … and this is a tough year but my mom had bought me a bunch of gifts. I remember her telling me my father couldn't be there, but he loves me, and he supports me." *Sam*
Pride	"I'm proud of him for staying clean, for getting back on his feet, helping other people." *Sara*

Table 4. Representations of inheritance

A third look at data: Listening to the ripples and the tidal waves

With the findings from the discourse analysis of inheritance, I went back to the life stories by Sam, Sara, Jonathan and Marcus and carried out a content analysis. Focusing on the impact of their parents' transition from prison to college and their involvement with the College Initiative, I searched once more for both strengths and challenges. In their stories, Sam, Sara, Jonathan and Marcus describe a new framework through which to tell their families' stories with pride, allowing them to speak of inspiration and guidance, solidarity and newfound stability. From them we learn that higher education makes CI students into legitimate mentors who inspire their children and provide guidance about life decisions, employment and educational opportunities ("And as far as the applying [to college … my father told me what to do and where to go"). A parent's transition from prison to college or graduate school inspires youth to grow as individuals and motivates them to begin or complete their own college education:

It was inspirational. I wanted to follow in [my father's] footsteps ... He did 15 years in [prison]. He didn't even finish high school. You know, I finished high school, so I know if he could go, I could go. That was why I really wanted to go to college. You know, he's coming home, and going to college ... That's one of the major reasons I decided to go [to college]. *Sam*

In Sara's family "now we are all racing to see who finishes first since we all started around the same time." As parents and children attend college or graduate school around the same time, they are bonded by mutual support and healthy competition that brings them together despite living in different states or neighborhoods. Jonathan now sees "my aunt, my grandmother, cousins, uncles, everybody's all happy for [my father]. A lot of people come home and go back, so you know, everybody's happy for him. He's going to school, he's working."

This positive influence travels cities, households and generations, reinforcing the lives of young people who, like Sara and Sam, have excelled in high school and also opening new horizons for youth who face considerable challenges. Her father's example "gave [Sara's] sister the nudge to go back to school" at age 27 after becoming a mother at age 19 and finding herself overwhelmed by new responsibilities. Similarly, Jonathan's brother found in his father "a big incentive that he can [go to college], that 'if my father can do it ... then I can also do it.'" This inspiration also travels outside the family, as the children of CI students become role models to their friends and schoolmates. Sam believes that "seeing me going to school and getting a degree will help [my friend] decide he wants to go back to school." Similarly, he sees himself as a role model for his 13-year-old half brother, to whom he tells, "Maybe one day you're going to want to go to college."

These experiences make post-prison college not only a source of inspiration but also an opportunity to tell a new story to teachers, friends and generations to come. This new story of achievement and transformation buffers the toxicity of negative stereotypes about parents as "ex-convicts" who are a weight on society and youth as future criminals:

Sam:	... when I was younger, people said "you're going to end up like [your father]," ... It wasn't a good feeling at all. I knew, at the time, I wasn't going to end up like that. It was a positive time in my life. And people telling me I'm going to end up like him. I just didn't know how to get to it ...
Carolina:	What do people say [now]? How does it feel?
Sam:	It feels good. I would like to end up like him, now. So now you could say all of that, whatever you want, because now you know he's doing the right thing. So you can't say you're going to end up like him no more, because he's moving forward. This is a positive time in his life. He's not in jail no more. So, hopefully, I can be like him now. I can receive my degree.

Jonathan, whose girlfriend was pregnant at the time of the interview, also finds himself with a new story to tell to his child: "Grandpa's life was kind of crazy, but it was very cool. It showed his inner strength. The strength of the mental." Through redemption narratives, youth can safely speak about the strengths that have always existed in their families and about the many possibilities that can open up during life after prison. This is clear in Sara's story:

He used to be a paralegal before prison. He said now he wanted to become a counselor to help other people in his position. So he started the College Initiative process. I'm proud of him for staying clean, for getting back on his feet, helping other people ... Having him back has been great because it shows there is hope, that there's life after jail. People say that there are no jobs, no love. But there is life after being incarcerated.

Their parents' experiences have taught the children of CI students about the value of educational opportunities and have made them aware of the need to overcome prejudice and to support formerly incarcerated individuals as they rebuild their lives and their communities through education. Jonathan believes that "[we] should have more programs for [college after prison] because it's pretty much a big advancement in civilization itself to [have been] in prison [and] know that you need to have your education."

Telling and living this new family story gives children of CI students a deep sense of pride in their parents' ability to give back to their communities. Jonathan and his siblings "are proud of [our father] for going to college." For Sam, silence about his father's incarceration has turned into pride:

> I feel more open to talking about [my father] … now he's home, doing the right thing. Working. Going to school. It feels great, because all this time he was in jail. So it's not like he came home and ended up right back in jail.

These accounts highlight the importance of including education as part of reentry policy. At the level of methodology, they also show how crucial it is to study the children of prisoners not only in their dispossession at the hands of defunded schools and a swollen prison system (Torre & Fine, 2005) but also in the face of opportunity. It is clear that Sara, Jonathan, Sam and Marcus would be telling different stories in the absence of the College Initiative program. Sara feels that if her father "wouldn't have went [to college], I wouldn't have had that talk with him. I wouldn't be going." Similarly, Jonathan believes that if his father had not become a student after prison, this "probably would have led me to follow in his actions because that's what I would have seen him as doing." Sam, Jonathan and Sara base these answers on what they see in their communities:

> I know some people who haven't gone back to school and are back in jail or in a dead end job. It's hard for the children. One of my friends, he feels like his father doesn't care, doesn't love him, "because he couldn't make those changes for me." Another friend, he's working, and his mom is working too, and his dad is looking for a job, but it's hard without a degree. *Sara*

> Being from where I'm from, once [parents] come out pretty much within a reasonable amount of time go back [to prison] … So somebody going to school would be pretty abnormal. *Jonathan*

College, however, is not an antidote against dropping standards of living in the country. Parents who do go to college after prison must work hard to rebuild their lives and their communities. For Jonathan's father, being an MA student is challenging: "To be a parent, to go to school, to go to work, bills—everything is just hectic." For Sara, having her father back from prison and in school for a Master's degree "is hard … because he works a full-time and has a part-time job, and is a full-time student, so during the school year there isn't much communication." This suggests that successful post-prison programs must consider the needs of students' families. Only in this way can formerly incarcerated adults successfully meet their responsibilities and dreams as college students, parents and community members despite shrinking social services and rising costs of living. In the absence of affordable education, health, housing and well-paying jobs, lives become hectic, and parents often drop out from school to address other pressing responsibilities.

Discussion

The positive intergenerational impact of higher education has been well documented among the families of non-traditional City University of New York students (Attewell & Levin, 2007). The life stories of children of College Initiative students suggest that such impact is also experienced among families of formerly incarcerated students, an important subcategory of non-traditional students. The life stories of the children of CI students teach us that higher education after prison can be a nutritious additive that protects youth at material, socio-psychological and also symbolic levels. The transformative power of higher education radiates from individual CI students and travels generations, households, neighborhoods and cities, touching the lives of their children, relatives and friends. This, in turn, nurtures the adult during and beyond reentry as in a virtuous cycle. Post-prison education interrupts intergenerational cycles of dispossession, disempowerment, social exclusion and despair as new resources and opportunities become available; stability, hope and trust grow among family members while the parent–child relationship finds new legitimacy.

Post-prison college helps fulfill the material and emotional needs identified in the self-education and action phases of the project. At the material level, educational achievement enables formerly incarcerated parents to obtain good employment and enter new social networks, thus breaking cycles of poverty and conviction and making new resources available to their children. At the socio-psychological and symbolic levels, youth experience their parents' educational achievements as a source of pride in their families and a new platform upon which to tell their stories. The transition from prison to college or graduate school gives parents new legitimacy as role models who can guide and inspire their children as they pursue a better education, employment and personal growth. The toxic effects of prejudice and stigma are buffered as children see their parents build meaningful lives after prison. However, it is not only individual youth who gain trust in their own ability to build meaningful and productive lives. Post-prison college also brings about new meanings to discourses of inheritance and reminds us, as a society, that ongoing positive transformation is possible for all.

Conclusion

Recursive and participatory methods are at the heart of the RCP project and its study of post-prison college. At the policy level, the project queers the notion of inheritance by complicating deficit-based discourses about incarceration and post-prison college. At the methodological level, the project challenges the fantasy that research for critical purposes is a neat, linear endeavor.

Three lessons about critical knowledge are worth mentioning. First, participatory methods enabled us to document individual achievements and struggles without turning incarceration and reentry into issues that are relevant only to *them*—prisoners and their families. This, in large measure, is due to the fact that design of the RCP focuses on how adults, their families and their communities come to thrive and embody counter-narratives of inheritance of school readiness, persistence and ongoing positive transformation in the presence of opportunity.

Second, collective self-education was a central aspect of this participatory approach. Conscientization carries the research towards critical knowledge and action because it reshapes the questions, methods, analyses and dissemination strategies. Self-education confirmed many intuitions and debunked others, empowered the members of the team, and inspired us to reframe the work at various points in order to avoid otherizing narratives of redemption. Changing ideas about what should be asked and from/of whom revealed parental incarceration and post-prison college as moving targets whose meanings cannot be understood solely through prison headcounts and surveys.

Finally, working between thematic and discourse analyses allowed the research to take on a more critical nature. This meant abandoning initial intentions to treat the experiences of youth and CI students as "data" to be inspected through criminal justice frameworks and instead using accounts by different kinds of experts (academics, musicians and youth) *both* as data and analytical frameworks. In this manner, we came to see inheritance as a place of struggle between strength and deficiency where youth with incarcerated parents negotiate between expert discourses and their lived experiences. Similarly, we recognized inheritance also as a place of struggle between otherizing and humanizing research recipes.

Tracing the methodological journey of the RC project offers some insights into the challenges of generating knowledge about normalized and invisible forms of dehumanization and inequality. These insights can help us unpack what we know about prisoners and their children and also produce new knowledge towards more humanized ways of advocating for, serving, and accompanying them in their struggles. These reflections take individual and social transformation beyond the limited possibilities of redemption narratives; they highlight how emancipatory praxis and the constant process of becoming are defining aspects of the human experience.

Notes

1. The project, Rebuilding Urban Communities and Families through Higher Education: The Economic, Educational and Civic Impact of Post-Prison College on Adults and Their Children, was made possible by the generous funding of the Ford Foundation between January 2009 and January 2010.
2. The RCP youth team included B. J. Coleman, Carolina Muñoz Proto, Mayra Pacheco, Dominique Ramsey and Isabel Vieira, who were honored to collaborate with the College Initiative, the Polling for Justice Project, the Public Science Project of the CUNY Graduate Center, the Urban Youth Collaborative, Teen College Dreams, the Osborne Association, Exodus Transitional Communities, and the Center of Human Environments at the CUNY Graduate Center. The author and the RC youth team also thank Dr. Michelle Fine and Dr. Suzanne Ouellette for their valuable contribution to the development of this chapter.

References

Andrews, M. (2007). *Shaping history: Narratives of political change*. Cambridge: Cambridge University Press.

Attewell, P. A, & Levin, D. (2007). *Passing the torch: Does higher education for the disadvantaged pay off across generations*. New York, NY: Russell Sage Foundation.

Bauman, Z. (2004). *Wasted lives: Modernity and its outcasts*. Cambridge, MA: Blackwell.

Boudin, K., & Zeller-Berkman, S. (2010). Children of promise. In Y. R. Harris, J. A. Graham, & G. J. Carpenter (Eds.), *Children of incarcerated parents: Theoretical developmental and clinical issues* (pp. 73–102). New York, NY: Springer.

Brotherton, D., & Barrios, L. (2004). *The Almighty Latin King and Queen Nation: Street politics and the transformation of a New York City gang*. New York, NY: Columbia University Press.

Brydon-Miller, M. (2001). Participatory action research: Psychology and social change. In D. L. Tolman & M. Brydon-Miller (Eds.), *From subjects to subjectivities: A handbook of interpretive and participatory methods*. New York, NY: NYU Press.

Chang, J. (2005). *Can't stop, won't stop: A history of the hip-hop generation*. New York, NY: Picador.

Charmaz, K. (2006). *Constructing grounded theory: A practical guide through qualitative analysis*. Thousand Oaks, CA: Sage Publications.

Conquergood, D. (1992, April). On reppin' and rhetoric: Gang representations. Paper presented at the Philosophy and Rhetoric of Inquiry Seminar, University of Iowa, Iowa City.

Cross, W. E., Jr. (2003). Tracing the historical origins of youth delinquency & violence: Myths & realities about Black culture. *Journal of Social Issues, 59*(1), 67–82.

Du Bois, W. E. B. (1903). *The souls of black folk*. New York, NY: Dodd, Mead & Company.

Fals-Borda, O., & Rahman, M. A. (1991). *Action and knowledge: Breaking the monopoly with participatory action research*. New York, NY: The Apex Press.

Fine, M., Roberts, R. A., Torre, M. E., & Upegui, D. (2001). Participatory action research behind bars. *International Journal of Critical Psychology, 2*, 145–157.

Fine, M., & Sirin, S. R. (2007). Theorizing hyphenated lives: Researching marginalized youth in times of historical and political conflict. *Social and Personality Psychology Compass, 1*(1), 16–38.

Foster, H., & Hagan, J. (2007). Incarceration and intergenerational social exclusion. *Social Problems, 54*(4), 399–433.

Freire, P. (1990). *Pedagogy of the oppressed*. New York, NY: Continuum. (Original work published 1970)

Gaines, L. K. & Miller, R. L. (2008). *Criminal justice in action*. Belmont, CA: Wadsworth.

Hall, R., & Fine, M. (2005). The stories we tell: The lives and friendship of two older Black lesbians. *Psychology of Women Quarterly, 29*(2), 177–187.

Harris, Y. R., Graham, J. A., & Carpenter, G. J. (2010). *Children of incarcerated parents: Theoretical developmental and clinical issues*. New York, NY: Springer.

Hole, R. (2007). A poststructural analysis of three deaf women's life stories. *Narrative Inquiry, 17*(2), 259–278.

McAdams, D. P. (1995). The life story interview. Retrieved from http://www.sesp.northwestern.edu/foley/instruments/interview/

Mendoza-Denton, N. (2008). *Homegirls: Language and cultural practice among Latina youth gang*. Malden, MA: Blackwell.

Rose, T. (1994). *Black noise: Rap music and black culture in contemporary America*. Hanover, NH: University Press of New England.

Torre, M. E., & Fine, M. (2005). Bar none: Extending affirmative action to higher education in prison. *Journal of Social Issues, 61*(3), 569–594.

Tupac. (1998a). Trapped. On *Tupac's Greatest Hits* (CD). Los Angeles, CA: Death Row Records.

Tupac. (1998b). Letter to my unborn child. On *Tupac's Greatest Hits* (CD). Los Angeles, CA: Death Row Records.

Unger, R. (2000). Outsiders inside: Positive marginality and social change. *Journal of Social Issues, 56*, 163–179.

Vygotsky, L. S. (1978a). Tool and symbol in child development. In *Mind in Society* (pp. 19–30). Cambridge, MA: Harvard University Press.

Vygotsky, L. S. (1978b). Internalization of higher psychological functions. In *Mind in Society* (pp. 52–57). Cambridge, MA: Harvard University Press.

Wacquant, L. (1998). Three pernicious premises in the study of the American ghetto. *International Journal of Urban and Regional Research, 22*(3), 507–510.

CHAPTER 16

Split Scenes, Converging Visions
The Ethical Terrains Where PAR and Borderlands Scholarship Meet

Jennifer Ayala

Episode I: PAR as a New(er) Hope for Social Research

Split screen

Scene 1: Left	Scene 2: Right
INT. An administrative office at an ethnically and socioeconomically diverse 4-year college. Three college youth researchers in their sophomore year and their faculty advisor are meeting over data, reflecting on the work that has transpired over the course of a semester. Each is holding a set of interview transcripts and some markers. They first 'check in' by discussing how their final days of the semester are going: what exams are coming up, what papers are still due (or, on the part of the faculty advisor, how many papers still need to be graded), and what negotiations were underway with bosses during this busy time of year.	INT. A high school cafeteria in a city that parallels the college study. A panel of five high school youth researchers, four young men and one young woman, is seated in a long table in the front, a large screen displaying a PowerPoint presentation in the back. Seated as audience members are 100 or so teachers and administrators. There are two adult members of the team: one is handling the technology so that the PowerPoint slide transitions go smoothly.
The other is seated at the end of the panel along with the student researchers. The students are poised to present their research, work that has transpired over the course of a year.

I open here with a split screen, depicting scenes from two separate research studies falling along different points of the participatory action research spectrum. These scenes, positioned side by side, are a backdrop from which tensions in conducting PAR from *within* educational institutions emerge: in this case, a high school and a college. Based on actual events but fictionalized details, research scenes/screens are extended, continuing throughout this paper as concurrent storylines. They act as grounded examples of the theoretical bridging attempted here between PAR and borderlands scholarship. PAR is positioned as a new(er) hope for socially relevant, hierarchy-disrupting, counter-hegemonic research.

But there are splits that we all contend with in doing this work: splits, though not necessarily unique to PAR, between its hope or promise, and its potential for social reproduction and cooptation (Cooke and Kothari 2001). The connecting line is a border space of creative contention where tensions of doing work inside schools, as Stoudt (this volume) has discussed, can reveal broader underlying choques, collisions between epistemologies and situated structural realities. In this paper, I labor specifically in the *sitios* where possibilities flow and constraints and terrors can sit frozen (Fine, personal communication)—living in the souls of people's border knowledge and the maze of institutional protections/deceits.

Backstory on the Projects

The College Study

The first scene begins towards the end of one participatory project. As part of course credit or simply on a volunteer basis, three undergraduate students identifying as African American or Haitian American and I, an adult researcher/college administrator identifying as Latina, were co-researchers in a study that focused on the experiences of first-generation students and students of color in a 4-year college.

Given the persisting inequities in full access to a college education, access that involves not only getting in the door but staying through graduation and developing networks of opportunity along the way, this study examined the individual and institutional dynamics that impacted student experiences. Specifically, we interrogated the barriers and supports but also the multiplicity and border skills present in the bodies of students most vulnerable in this setting and in their interactions with other college community entities. With this research focus, I worked between traditional literatures on persistence (Cabrera et al. 1992; Pascarella et al. 1996; Paulsen and John 2002; Tinto 1982) infused with conversations with critical race theory (Rendon 1993; Solorzano and Yosso 2001; Tierney 2000) and borderlands/mestiza consciousness scholarship (Anzaldúa 1987; Delgado Bernal 2001; Elenes 2001). Seeking methodological approaches that were open, exploratory, and that reflected *mestizaje*, I adopted a participatory stance and invited students the college worried about losing to academic/economic pressures as co-researchers.

At the time, I was employed in an institution of higher education, facilitating a support program for students the college deemed not academically prepared, many of whom were students of color and first-generation college students. From this group, I recruited co-researchers through flyers and mailings, inviting students to investigate the research area I had broadly formulated, with an invitation for further input. Out of this larger group, three students were able to commit to the project for the following semester, when data collection was to begin. We met weekly and during this time, students were trained in qualitative research methods, interviewing in particular, wrote in a "research journal" (a diary of sorts documenting the research process and observations), and discussed what we were learning about the institution and the issues that emerged. Student researchers revised a first draft of the interview protocol, and each was encouraged to add questions of most interest to them, broadening the focus of the study. One student was interested in asking others about "outside obligations" they faced and how they navigated these responsibilities with the demands of college. Another was interested in how "financial status" affected their experiences as a college student as well as what teachers inspired them. The third, influenced by the Echoes of Brown piece (Fine et al. 2004), wanted to inquire whether students felt their "cultures were respected at the college" and whether they felt the college should do more to help students stay once there. One student also took photographs as a way of capturing data.

The student co-researchers recruited all student participants and conducted all student interviews. I conducted all staff interviews, classroom and ethnographic observations and later archival analyses. At our meetings, we would discuss the process and content of the interviews. Toward the end of the semester, once interviews were transcribed, we met to analyze the data. This analysis was preliminary and consisted of discussing quotes/data that were most meaningful to the co-researchers. This was the last time we met as a research group; after this meeting, students moved on to their other college responsibilities. I coded the data, identified other themes and wrote a report on the findings. I also put together a brief outline of key points to a top-level administrator. The group was invited to speak on a few occasions and discussed their research in two venues—an urban education conference and an audience of high school students.

The High School Study

Scene two describes an action by a group of high school student researchers. This group came together as part of a grant-funded initiative that focused on the experiences of students in urban high schools in low-income neighborhoods about to undergo educational reform. It was a project initiated from outside the high school, as a collaboration between the City University of New York and the Education Law Center in New Jersey. Two Abbott high schools in New Jersey, designated as such because of a landmark finance equity decision in which low-income urban neighborhoods receive school funding equal to that of wealthier neighborhoods, were selected and received funding to develop youth research teams. The purpose of developing these teams was to add youth voices to the school reform process by investigating an area of interest to them as high school students. I was invited to work with one of the high schools to help form a youth research collective. I absolutely welcomed the opportunity to work on a participatory project that I had hoped would really have teeth, where the collaborative process would start with identifying a research area. A guidance counselor, a recent graduate of the high school, and I interviewed a number of students the vice principal identified as being interested/eligible to participate in this after-school project. An initial team of ten students, diverse in terms of race/ethnicity, gender and academic experience was selected.

This initial group, joined by a youth research team from another high school, was trained in developing research questions, provided an overview of research methods, learned from other established youth researchers, was given information on the urban school reform initiative underway in New Jersey, engaged in hands-on activities, and worked on a question particular to their school. Unlike scene one, this group of students, who at the first convening named themselves the Chilltown Researchers (CTR), were not operating under a pre-determined research question. Instead, the youth were invited to identify/investigate a question they deemed important related to improving the school experience. They decided to focus on a critical analysis of the inside of the school and, more explicitly, its reputation as a school of violence for "remedial" students with no future.

This all took place at the end of school year. By the following year, when data collection really began, this initial group significantly decreased in number, and the students invited one more member, resulting in a core group of five high school juniors and seniors who attended meetings and conducted research. The high school students were diverse in terms of race/ethnicity, identifying as African American, Latino/a, Asian, and combinations of these identities, but not diverse in terms of gender, with four young men and one young woman. This group of students chose to study the high school's image within and outside its walls, its relationship to racism, teacher–student relationships, and media portrayals. The goal, as the students put it, was not only to identify factors related to image but to also take steps to "heal" it. Working together after school either in their high school or in the college where I now work, CTR conducted teacher, staff and student interviews, a focus group of students from other urban high schools, and an archival analysis of newspaper clippings dating back to the 1970s, also including yearbooks, and school report cards that describe various outcomes on school accountability measures. By the end of the school year, CTR presented their findings to a variety of audiences: teachers and staff within the school, professional conferences, and in a gathering of educational policy makers. CTR now has three core members, all from the same academic track, and continue their work by producing a video for the community in order to raise awareness about some of the issues identified in their research. They felt that this was a good way to communicate their findings to a wider audience, including new or prospective teachers and students. Now seniors, CTR wants to see an ongoing research group at the high school, and current members are interested in recruiting and interviewing a new team of researchers to take up new questions and issues of importance to the school now. Funding, however, is an ongoing concern.

Crafting Questions/Analysis as Theorizing PAR

Scene 3: College study	Scene 4: Chilltown researchers
"OK, so now how should we do this? We have all the transcripts in front of us and pictures ... who took pictures?" "I did. I could talk about that first." "Sounds good. Why don't you show us the pics and talk about what they mean, like why you took them and stuff." The college student researcher pulls about ten pictures from inside his backpack, shuffles them around a little, then holds one out and explains. "Ok, this is a picture of the line at the registrar's office. I took it because you see people all the way down the hall, pissed off and stuff, sometimes arguing with the people in the front." "Hmmm. Yeah, the line was that long for me when it was time to register for next semester." "This is a picture of the main buildings. This is that spot on campus where the students hang out for lunch ..." He went through all of the pictures and brief explanations for them, admitting sometimes the he wasn't clear what exactly he should photograph. After discussing the pictures, the facilitator suggesting going through the transcripts and for the first run, pointing out what quotes or ideas stood out to everyone.	*Flashback. One year earlier.* Eight students and the facilitators are sitting together in a computer lab. The college student co-facilitator stands with marker in hand by a flip chart, writing down people's thoughts as they brainstorm. "I think we should research home life because that has a lot to do with how people do in school." Two of the girls nod their heads in agreement. "What about the discipline policy the school has. I think it sets us up for failure." "We're here to learn and that's just one thing that stops us." "I think we should do it on the school's image. Our school is stereotyped." "Yeah, people assume that because this is a mostly Black school, that it's bad." "Ok, these are all really good ideas. How should we decide what research area to focus on? Is there a way we can combine these ideas into an overall question?" "Well, I think we should let the community decide what they want us to research. We should do a poll or something to ask them what we should do then decide for sure." "I like that." "Yeah, let's do that." "Great idea. OK, so let's come up with some short pilot questions to ask around. A pilot question is like ..."

Both these scenes have a foot in the world of participatory action research and land on different points of the PAR continuum (Torre 2003). The CUNY PAR Collective best describes PAR as "a methodological stance rooted in the belief that valid knowledge is produced only in collaboration and in action ... [A central belief is that it] recognizes that those 'studied' harbor critical social knowledge and must be repositioned as subjects and architects of research" (http://web.gc.cuny.edu/che/start.htm). PAR can represent a trilogy of inquiry, collaboration and mutual transformation, taking seriously social justice goals not only in the results but in the process of research itself (Torre and Fine 2006). Seeking to challenge models of research that reinforce hierarchical arrangements and hegemonic power structures, those once marginalized by research become the knowledge holders, collectors and actors (Torre and Fine 2006). Rather than being a static set of methods, PAR is a stance and, depending on the project, shapes different parts of the research process (CUNY PAR collective).

Researchers following a PAR stance can include participation at various levels. At the full participation level, or PAR with a Torre (2003), co-researchers take part in all phases of the research process—identifying research areas, collecting and analyzing data, creating products (be they written, visual, performance) and conducting actions. In other projects, research questions are already developed and what is participatory is the data collection, interpretation, or action/product (Torre 2003). In the context of this study, the first research scene would be considered "Small P" while the work of the CTR might be closer to the "Big P." What unites all these variations of PAR is the underlying critical stance, reflexivity and ideological commitment; it is the explicit wrestling with power dynamics that operate from within and outside the group (Torre and Fine 2006).

Such power dynamics vary also according to the "launching site" of the study. Working *with* schools on such projects introduces a set of complexities that can impact/constrain what gets studied, how questions are cast, and what type of actions follow, as Stoudt found in his study with boys in an environment of privilege. The youth and schools discussed in this paper have very different social locations from those of Stoudt's study, as urban schools in diverse and low-income communities, where the schools and students are held suspect, highly scrutinized and vulnerable to structural constraints. Yet despite these differences in social class and privilege, there are parallel tensions in doing PAR work inside the schools, as will be discussed further in this paper.

A sister concept, perhaps more of a madrina, in the family of PAR is that of borderlands and mestiza consciousness. Borderlands scholarship originates from the struggles within the physical borders between the U.S. and Mexico. Moving the borderlands from a physical to a symbolic space, Anzaldúa (1987/1999) explains that "psychological borderlands, the sexual borderlands and the spiritual borderlands … are not particular to the Southwest. In fact, the Borderlands are physically present wherever two or more cultures edge each other, where people of different races occupy the same territory, where under, lower, middle and upper classes touch, where the space between two individuals shrinks with intimacy" (p. 19). The borderlands discourse is one of "fluidity, migration, postcolonialism, displacement" that "speaks against dualism, oversimplification, and essentialism. It is a discourse, a language, that explains the social conditions of subjects with hybrid identities" (Elenes 1997). Borderlands as third space of possibility and conflict characterized by hybridity and complexity makes it an appealing concept for those living in and/or studying "subaltern identities" and multiply marginalized social locations. It is a literature that informs scholarship in education with its interruption of dichotomous thinking in favor of "multiple subjectivity and difference" (Elenes 1997, 2001).

Borderlands is described as an in-between space—physical, symbolic, discursive—and from within this space emerges a psychology of hybridity located in the bodies of women of color: the notion of mestiza consciousness. Mestiza refers literally to mixed-ancestry women, usually indigenous and European but also different combinations, the key element being "mixed." Finding home and alienation in multiple, overlapping places, la mestiza develops a set of strategies, an understanding of the world, a psychology that helps her cross imposed borders and be able to live in the interstices between them. A mestiza consciousness, also based on Anzaldúa's work, is referred to as "the ability of an individual subject to understand her position in a world that undervalues subaltern communities and how she uses this knowledge to transform society" (Elenes 2001, p. 692). It is framed as an individual skill, ability, strategy or understanding that allows her to function across social worlds as well as within what Saldivar-Hull (2000) calls the "warring ideologies" inside her. This understanding not only is grounded in gender and race politics but also involves sexuality and social class awareness (Saldivar-Hull 2000, p. 61).

Mestiza consciousness houses multiplicity, hybridity, conflict and collaboration, within the bodies of women of color. It is a way of being, a life approach and understanding that springs from inside the crevices that separate social worlds. From this consciousness, knowledge is presumed as existing within the flesh, with theorymaking as part of the collective existence for women of color. Anzaldúa (1990, p. xxv) writes,

> theory then is a set of knowledges. Some of these knowledges have been kept from us—entry into some professions and academia denied us. Because we are not allowed to enter into some discourse, because we are often disqualified and excluded from it … it is vital that we occupy theorizing space, that we not allow whitemen and women solely to occupy it. By bringing in our own approaches and methodologies, we transform that theorizing space…Necesitamos teorias that will rewrite history using race, class, gender

and ethnicity as categories of analysis, theories that cross borders, that blur boundaries—new kinds of theories with new theorizing methods. In our mestizaje theories we create new categories for those of us left out or pushed out of the existing ones. If we have been gagged and disempowered by theories, we can also be loosed and empowered by theories.

It is in this site, this call to use theory and research as a way to reclaim and legitimize our knowledges, this urging to do what Tuck (2007) calls "theorize back" where PAR can intersect with borderlands scholarship. If "without the hand, the voice is helpless" (Anzaldúa 1990, p. xxiv), perhaps PAR is a way of providing hands to the multiple voices of the canción mestiza. In doing this type of research, an important first step is to recognize the knowledge holders and border travelers in ourselves and around us.

When PAR Meets Mestiza Consciousness: Rethinking Who Are the Knowledge Holders

---

Scene 5: College study

AR1: OK, so what stands out to you in reading these interviews?

CR1: With the unfair situations (looking at the interviews) maybe there really isn't anything unfair going on at this school, but I don't know, I kind of find that hard to believe. But they don't seem to talk about it.

CR2: I know one person I interviewed that said there were no racial problems here, but then we were walking and she saw something and said, see that's like the question you asked. I was like, why didn't you say that on the tape? Maybe because the school is so mixed, people think there are no racial issues, and it's not as bad as in other campuses where it's mostly white, but it comes out in other ways here.

CR3: Money and family responsibilities are big. Financial holds, registration and all that. Some people think the college should do more to help students stay.

AR1: To me it's a lot of what the staff said—you don't have those interviews in front of you, but some of the things you were just talking about came up.

In a study about college experiences, who are the knowledge holders? Reviewing the literature on this topic area, legitimate knowledge holders are typically identified as faculty/teachers and to varying degrees students themselves. A mestiza consciousness asks us to look at the in-between spaces of different social worlds. What are the borderlands of the academy, and are they held or located between students and faculty only? This is a question that I considered in the college study. As part of our sampling strategy, we included what I later called code-breaker staff, another (in)version of knowledge holders, in our interviews. The women who served lunch, the departmental secretaries, technological and academic support gurus, gatekeepers to the administrators and faculty, the front-line staff at the registration and financial offices. People who were at both the margins and the center of recognition. Students knew who they were as did faculty and administrators. But faculty and administrators in general were not always cognizant of the code-breaker services or of the depth of their border knowledge. They are often not recognized as such in the higher education literature, in university reward structures as the lowest-paid employees, or in administrative decision making, often because of their position and (sometimes assumed) credentials. In part for these reasons, these college community members were invited to share their border knowledge. It was an act of recognition/validation, by asking questions where rarely anyone else asks, and as a way for all of us to learn from this knowledge. Indeed, each of the staff interviews revealed a complexity of perspectives, knowledge and theorizing about what was happening with and between students and faculty.

The reciprocity of staff and students' gifts was most apparent in these interviews. For example, a woman who worked in the cafeteria was a self-described "campus mother" who had two lines at her cashier's corner: a food line and a counseling line. The food line was for students/staff paying for their food; the other line was more informal, and was for students to relate their troubles. The multiplicity of her roles in this context is evidence of her border skills but also of the gifts students offer.

You can't not love them. You can't because they'll open up their hearts to you ... I'll never make a lot of money here, I'll never even make enough to pay my own bills here but ... what they [the students] give you ... makes it worth it.

From the staff interviews, we were able to hear about the depth of students' gifts to the college community in ways that perhaps the students themselves were not as aware. Couched in a critique of institutional reward structures and challenged notions of economic meritocracy, staff described student gifts as "something they give you"; like when another staff member shared, "I've learned [from students] how to persevere. Because when I was taking classes, they say to me, 'Oh, you could do it, you could do it because we know you could do it, you'll graduate.'" The inspiration work students offered as gifts to the community were made most clear here.

Border staff were also able to articulate, perhaps with the greatest risk, the trouble spots, rough terrain in the spaces between student and adult interactions. In the same conversation on how students taught her to persevere, Tamara described the institutional injustices she observed.

I know a student here for a fact, [who came in with a relatively prestigious merit- and need-based scholarship] and the College pulled his money back and his mother doesn't make over $15,000 a year so it's a hardship, you understand. I told him what to do, "write a letter to the president telling him if you knew that before you came you would have not come here. Tell him just like that." They didn't have to pull the money back ... I was just so angry with this school ...

Tamara is describing the common practice in Higher Education of readjusting need-based aid awarded by the college if outside scholarships are earned. As a staff member, she was able to observe firsthand the effects of this type of decision for students, as one of the people that had to explain the situation to them. As she expressed her anger and disappointment, identifying race/ist underpinnings to these policy choices, she used her code-breaker skills to explain to students actions they could take. Coupled with her vocal opposition to such policies, many times, her voice and action put her at odds with supervisors who saw her as "complaining all the time." It is the kind of work, with a mixture of risk, reward, and some uncertainty, that happens in the borders between staff, student, and institution interactions. This border work is made clearer when consulting with unacknowledged community knowledge holders.

From Knowledge Holder to Knowledge Builder

Scene 6: CTR

As the CTR prepare their lines for the presentation, they look up with pride and nervousness at the PowerPoint above them—filled with images from photographs they took at the high school, statistical graphs, quotes from students, teachers, and staff, and their own illustrations and designs. An administrator walks over, whispering, "You tell 'em like it is." They begin:

"Good Morning ... We are the Chilltown Researchers, a group of high school students who are trying to make positive changes in our school and community through research ..."

Followed by a discussion of the methods and some themes as well as questions, some quotes/slides read: "One teacher said: 'its students are wonderful people but the media and those outside the school walls see us as a troubled school.'"

"A staff person said 'I heard that it's a very violent school and that I shouldn't work there.'" "Race has everything to do with its image."

Alongside some charts and photographs, the group asked the audience why the number of students who are classified as special education in this school is so much higher than neighboring schools and towns.

CTR offers suggestions:

"Some students don't feel like they matter in the school. More opportunities are needed for students and also for teachers to support students ..."

At the close of the presentation, there is silence in the room, and the students ask "Do you have any questions?" hoping that the audience cares enough to ask.

When young people are identified as knowledge holders, they may be condescended to and positioned as receptacles holding information for academic researchers to uncover, harvest and interpret *for them* (Josselson 2004). Within a youth PAR framework, students are framed as knowledge holders but also builders because they become part of the research process with responsibility for framing, collecting and interpreting data alongside adult researchers. So what can it look like to include the participation of youth in this context?

With the CTR, a collective of high school students was invited to develop a study that revolved around a question or area of their choosing. There were several options the students considered and after many meetings, discussions, and piloted questions, the collective ultimately decided to focus on the high school's image, as described in scene four. I talk about this decision because research, from question formulation to findings distribution, involves a series of decisions, negotiations, and reflections. With a PAR stance, decision-making power is shared, distributed among group members rather than sitting in one governing individual. This type of participation is one way of taking seriously, acknowledging and legitimizing the power of knowledge holders and builders.

Recognizing on multiple levels who are the knowledge holders is an important part of PAR. What mestiza consciousness and borderlands theory offers to this are the three-dimensional lenses needed to recognize knowledge holders–looking. Looking not just horizontally but underneath (in some cases at the tips of) power hierarchies, in the spaces that are often overlooked or not legitimized. Who can contribute to building, constructing funds of knowledge (Velez-Ibanez and Greenberg 1992) are traditionally seen as those in power, dominant ideologies, but also as elders within communities. However, a PAR stance invites us to look at the construction of knowledge as embodied in the spaces between youth *in their negotiations with* elders. If PAR and borderlands/mestiza scholarship moves us from holding to building knowledge, then the methodologies suggest a collaborative enterprise, a participatory research stance.

Episode II: The Empire Strikes Back
Confidentiality as institutional barrier and ethical responsibility

---

Scene 7: College study—flash forward to a conference

It's a medium-sized room in a relatively small conference on urban education. Approximately 20 people were sitting in a circle. Three groups, including the college youth researchers, are part of the panel.

Faculty facilitator (whispering): "Remember the confidentiality stuff we talked about." "oh right, yeah" nods of agreement by college youth researchers

Panel facilitator: "Thank you all for coming. We look forward to this exciting conversation between three groups who have been working on higher education research. We will begin with each group introducing themselves and what institution they're from"

"Hello, I'm a student from [name]—uh, oops—I mean, I'm a college student from … mmmm … a college in New Jersey. We're not supposed to say the name, so … Well anyway, we worked on a project …"

"Yes, and I, my institutional affiliation is, well I graduated from right here and I now work at … um … this … college … *withnoname*. But it's in the urban northeast and I have had the pleasure of working with these amazing young people that attend [name]" (under breath) "damn … ok … um"

Looking off camera, so that the conference participants can't hear "this is so ridiculous. What am I doing?"

When talking about the promise of using a PAR stance, the word *promise* has multiple, troubling meanings. It is a stance that holds promise, in the sense of the possibility alive in this approach. Then there is the promise made by PAR, in that this sense of possibility holds a set of ethical commitments, responsibilities and vulnerabilities that both are and are not unique to PAR. Torre and Fine (2006) describe this well: "As with all social movements, and all research approaches, PAR carries questions of ethics, vulnerabilities, and negotiations of power. The dynamics vary based on the nature of the work, the situatedness of the struggle and launching site for the research. Methods and strategic moves differ when PAR emerges from within community organizing, where allies and targets are clear, in contrast to PAR launched centrally from within inequitable (schools) or oppressive (prisons) social institutions." The PAR studies described in the scenes are examples of projects launched centrally from within schools; contexts with (sometimes) clear layers of hierarchy and power differential. This episode builds on recent work on the ethics of PAR (see ACME 2007; Denzin and Giardina 2007; Tuck et al. 2007) in its discussion of the responsibilities and vulnerabilities in carrying out PAR projects; specifically, this notion of promise as it interacts/collides with institutional interpretations of ethics.

The assurance of confidentiality, one of the arms of informed consent, is a given for any human subjects review board. Working inside institutions of education, a promise is often made (by an outside researcher trying to gain access) before research has begun that the identity of the school, college, program or organization will be kept secret to protect their right to privacy and to fulfill our desire to do research within their space. Not only the names but often "identifying characteristics" are protected under the cover of confidentiality. For example, in order for me to conduct or facilitate research within high schools, I typically have to write multiple proposals: to my college's human subjects review board as well as to the high school's superintendent's office. In these proposals, I make certain that I promise to maintain the school's name confidential in any work that could be disseminated; otherwise, I know I may not be permitted to do research there. I also consider that many schools are struggling to improve and are quite vulnerable under punitive accountability mandates. I have to be sensitive to this struggle while also working for change inside the schools alongside the student co-researchers.

However, what happens when the action portion of research bumps up against the institution's confidentiality protection? As the action unfolds, whether it's in speakouts or publications, co-researchers'/participants' own public identities can "out" those of the institutions of which they are a part. How can student's work, for example, be public while keeping private the institutions they are housed in? There have been a few instances where revealing the names of co-researchers or my own position within an organization simultaneously exposed the name of the institution in which we were conducting research. I faced a similar dilemma in working with the CTR. As is typical of this type of research, I put together an IRB proposal for my home institution and for the district superintendent before I could even get access to the school. In it was the usual promise of confidentiality, not only for the participants but for the school. Once the research reached the point of disseminating findings to the outside, conflicts between my promise for confidentiality and their/our expectations for action arose. For instance, the collective wanted to create a website about the work and wanted to proudly display the high school name all over the site. In introducing themselves, they were sure to include prominently what high school they attended. They also wanted this to appear on the high school website. Now, what do I, as part of the collective do here? On the one hand, I could say, "but, we (I mean I) promised not to reveal the name of the high school for confidentiality reasons." In fact, I did some of this and the response was what I expected. "How can we work to change our image if we can't talk about the good things we are doing? It's going to be another good thing that doesn't get talked about." This is absolutely true. Is it their promise in the first place because it is one that I made beforehand? Should this promise interfere with the action? Whose promise should be legitimated: the promise for action that never materializes or the promise for protecting the secrets of an institution under siege? The website is actually up with the high school displayed, as the collective wanted it. At the moment, this is not problematic because we have support from the principal and the website only has a description of the process of the research, not the findings.

The dilemma forces our attention onto an irony of this work: what if action calls for making public the very privacy we promised to protect? Who then is confidentiality protecting? In the name of confidentiality, we can find ourselves at times protecting the institution over the needs of participants. But in a self-sustaining collective, decision making is not tied to the university researcher. There are times when our positionalities can hinder the work of the group. Perhaps that is where we learn to step back (Pedraza, personal communication). This situation applies specifically to working within institutions and may be more of a "problem" for the university researcher than for the remainder of the research team. In PAR, collective decision making can determine what is confidential.

In the future, perhaps I will not be as quick to promise the institution confidentiality or will make it contingent on the group's decision to be negotiated once it is formed. One way to avoid this as well is to invite participation across sites in terms of PAR work, so that it doesn't feel like a betrayal to a particular institution and can be framed as findings shared across settings. Another idea is to work with district and CBO partners within the same project, so that actions are built into the design in a way that helps it survive and live past the immediacy of the project's needs.

The ethical considerations surrounding confidentiality in a PAR context read as a bureaucratic nuisance instead of the social justice image this should conjure (ACME 2007). Perhaps this occurs because it is so couched in the legalistic language of ethics reflected in institutional review boards (Cahill 2007). Going beyond these framings of protection of participant rights, PAR considers its own ethical obligations as determined not solely by the university researcher but by the group of participant researchers and extends to an ethical commitment to action and change. What else should be protected? Recent work on the ethics of participatory action research document related struggles and offer other ways of framing responsibility and confidentiality. For instance, Cahill (2007) critiques the model of ethics represented by IRBs as carrying assumptions that run counter to the "ethic of care" represented by PAR. Tuck (2007) suggests we consider "sacred knowledge" produced within a group as an ethical responsibility in PAR.

This work collectively asks us to consider ethical responsibilities beyond general formulas, and doing this can involve absorbing a clash of voices. The voices of institutional needs, desires, inequities, alongside, but not in equal share, those of the community. As Mosse (2001) points out, institutional systems and procedures can act to constrain some of the critical, creative and exploratory nature of PAR work (see also Stoudt, this volume). "New concepts of 'process' have not obviated institutionally grounded needs" (p. 24) such as budgeting/project timelines, and as focused on in this section, procedures for access and approval. Moving away from the critical towards what is perceived as being safer/more attainable is what he calls an adverse "side effect" of institutional factors (p. 24). How then do we stop voice from becoming voiceover when it comes to including institutional voice? Perhaps one response lies in a space of conflict and ambiguity, a conversation that traditional social science has eschewed but borderlands scholarship can help us navigate.

Episode III: Return of the Mestiza
Epistemological intersections between PAR and borderlands

Scene 8: CTR

There is a pause at the close of the presentation. A few hands were raised. "What suggestions on best practices in teaching can you offer?"

"Would you be available to talk to my freshman class about this?"

In an agitated tone, one person commented,

"You didn't ask anyone in my office. What you have to understand is that there is a complex process involved in identifying special education students; there are legal issues here …"

A colleague interrupts,

"You did a great job in your presentation and that is a good question. Now the next step for you is to go out and do more research to answer that question."

Silence.

CTR asks, "Is that it?"

The presentation comes to a close and the presenters have a mix of frustration, anger, with a sprinkling of satisfaction. As the students keep talking, the faculty facilitator speaks into the camera …

"Maybe this wasn't a good idea. Everyone here, except for me, will have to face the teachers and staff here in school tomorrow. Oh God, will the teachers hold it against them when they see them in school? What about the guidance counselor—is she gonna have to hear it from her peers. Oh man. Should I have just said in the beginning that we shouldn't do this? I really hope they'll all be okay tomorrow. Ugh. I really put them in a bad position."

The invitation to participation and action, particularly within inequitable institutions, can come with a fine print of cost and contradiction. In many ways, the invitation for students to do research inside schools is an invitation to risk making themselves more vulnerable in an unequal system. As adult facilitators, we encourage and support youth to explore and critically analyze their schools in ways that may be uncomfortable or unwelcome for those inside it. It is "asking them to expose the elephant in the room, knowing they may get trampled in the process" (Fine, personal communication). With PAR, the goal is to trouble notions of hierarchy and expertise; to share power, and to research and speak out and back. But we can't guarantee that others will listen or do something about it (Chawla 2005). Thus, by sharing the power over decisions, questions, methods, we also share the risk.

In scene eight, I describe one such instance. Ultimately, the students, though initially feeling frustrated, described future interactions with the adults in their school in different ways. Reported reactions ranged from irritation at some of the material or at the inadequate facilitation to invitations to take student leadership positions in the school—noting the courage and analytic skill the students demonstrated. There were other opportunities where CTR presented: to an audience of policy makers and progressive educators, for example. In this setting, students felt their work was validated, as audience members provided sincerely felt feedback throughout the presentation, and in the moments afterward, when it prompted principals to discuss with one another possible reasons for some of the disparities CTR brought to light. My worries somewhat allayed this time, I nonetheless still ponder this question and consider the border space of conflict and contradiction, responsibility and power in PAR. As Anzaldúa (1987) writes, it's a struggle of borders, a struggle of the flesh …

> Cradled in one culture, sandwiched between two cultures, straddling all three cultures and their value systems, la mestiza undergoes a struggle of the flesh, a struggle of borders, an inner war …The new mestiza copes by developing a tolerance for contradictions, a tolerance for ambiguity. She learns to be an Indian in Mexican culture, to be Mexican from an Anglo point of view. She learns to juggle cultures … Not only does she sustain the contradictions, she turns the ambivalence into something else …" (p. 101)

Anzaldúa writes about how this multiplicity of consciousness born out of the borderlands both houses and transforms conflict, ambivalence. Because of the "clash of voices" representing disparate (but at times overlapping) cultural frameworks, it is not always a harmonious multiplicity. It is a multiplicity that can be contradictory, uncomfortable, because of the forces that try to splinter it and stratify the pieces according to dominant power relationships (Moraga and Anzaldúa 1981). Juggling identities, commitments, responsibilities with two hands but many eyes can sometimes bring about "un choque," a collision of cultural frameworks living within one body (Anzaldúa 1987). Un choque whose consequences vary depending upon the context, since the different cultural frameworks are also differently valued in society's power structure. In this way, areas that offer the mestiza the strength to thrive can also pose difficulties, just as the ways in which she engages the struggles can build up her strengths. Living with all these contradictions, she develops flexibility, a "tolerance for ambiguity," and an understanding that the sometimes conflicting messages, stances, frameworks are what make up the whole of her mestiza consciousness. Drawing parallels to the college study findings, students and adult allies evidenced a mestiza consciousness, transforming the contradictions, uncertainties, and choques encountered as they traversed the borderlands between the education system and home into bridges. Learning from this space of in-between, pointed to a closer examination up the power hierarchies, with a fuller view of institutional tensions and opportunities floating in the increasingly corporatizing fog of the system of higher education (Bok 2003; Kirp 2003).

As mentioned earlier, in PAR, you find similar spaces of conflict, ambiguity, and contradiction described by borderland theorists, especially working inside schools and in increasingly corporatizing universities. El choque, the clash, is between the "warring ideologies" that are positioned on the outside and from within the collective process. PAR works to push out of the grip of corporatization, coloni-zation and hegemony that holds structures and situations surrounding the collective in place but/and that can also operate from within the collective. It influences what participation looks like in a given context, what shapes decision making, what ethics and responsibilities are most closely observed, what emotions erupt or fizzle. Borderlands scholarship can tell us how this institutional voice is included—in recognizing it within the process and collective, and not just in the outside. It is this choque that in part defines these border spaces; it is what makes up its contradictory nature as both possibility and danger. Such multiplicity is messy work (Josselson, personal communication) that doesn't fit linear stories with neatly packaged processes and outcomes, a clear us and them (Torre, this volume). This is where mestiza consciousness lives, in a space of promise, ambiguity, discomfort that can be, particularly with PAR approaches, hopefully transformed into something more.

Connections between mestiza consciousness and PAR can best occur at the level of epistemology. Going beyond PAR as a methodological approach, in this volume we suggest that in order to engage in PAR, we have to take it up a level, at the basis of how we see knowledge constructed. This under-standing also implicates a more political, social justice orientation, even though there is a stream of studies, just as with all tools, that demonstrates its misuse toward hegemonic rather than humanistic ends (Cooke and Kothari 2001). PAR is an epistemological stance that is ultimately tied to research, while mestiza consciousness is more of a life orientation. With PAR, how the work is organized, in the sample, question, methods, and analysis, can reflect a mestiza consciousness when there is not just one storyline but multiple, often split narratives lined with the contradictions inherent in all our lives. As PAresearchers, we carry these epistemological conflicts across borders and in our bodies, navigating a sea of contradictions, with the youth as the most vulnerable and most brave for daring to throw stones in uncertain waters.

Final shot: a convergence of scenes and epistemologies

Scene 9	Scene 10: A week after the presentation
"OK, so what are next steps for us?"	"Some teachers came up to me to say what a good job we did."
"Finals." (laughs)	
"Yeah but what can we conclude with the work that's been done.?"	"But I can't believe she went off like that."
"And what about the college—what should the administration do about the stuff we're talking about?"	"Sometimes you have to piss people off to get them to listen."
"By the way, we were invited to speak to high school students about college. Interested?"	"Nothing really happened."
"OK. Yeah, let's think about actions."	"I have to show you an article in the paper—it talks about what we were saying. It's about how too many African Americans are put in Special Ed."
"What should	we DO now?

The line dividing the split screen expands to form a third image at its borders. In it, all participants start talking. This part is not rehearsed but improvised. Floating between questioning looks, smiles, and interactions is a subtitle that reads, "Does this work really matter?"

From a split screen can emerge a new image. Having described the convergences and split pathways of borderlands scholarship and PAR, we turn to the questions of "for what?" and "so what?" How do these stances, be they in step or about face, matter in a world marked/marred by collective traumas?

I find it difficult to answer this question; perhaps my own experiences are not sufficient. Taken together, however, the pieces in this volume offer up different ways in which PAR can both blur and clarify,[1] phase-change from solid to liquid and back—changing some of its surface or physical properties, but not its underlying chemistry. Not a singular approach that follows a linear trajectory, nor a miracle drug that cures or even tries to erase the deepest of society's wounds. But it does demand a critical reflexivity, a multiplicity of perspectives, a shift in discourse, critical engagement with power, difference and the "in between" that can itself be healing actions, even as it reveals the vulnerabilities in all of us who engage it. It matters because it is one way to name and act on the forces of constraint mounted on the backs of those most marginalized, as well as the equal and opposing forces propelling privilege further forward. In the studies I describe in the scenes, I think it mattered because it got conversations started, and the instigating force for the actions came from sources not typically expected (or sometimes welcomed). Even housed within disapproval, there was recognition. It mattered to me personally, even in the self-doubts and struggles, because I feel it as social justice work, as collective spirit work, in a way that other forms of research do not.

Also implicated in our discussions of how PAR matters are our own bodies and emotions as they operate through the choices, responsibilities and vulnerabilities of this work, as Guishard so eloquently reveals. We sit in the "creative contention" (Tuck, this volume) nestled inside the splits in all our narratives, so this is deeply personal/political work (Guishard). PAR can be seen as the "revolutionary love" that Guishard and Payne talk about, as giving back and forward, with affection and critique. Love, anxiety, conflict, depression, euphoria, disappointment, doubt are and should be part of the conversation with PAR. It is an approach where liaisons between ideology, discourse, intellect, body, spirit and emotion are not closeted but instead are made explicit, even embraced, though at times dangerously.

Perhaps PAR is a vessel swimming in border waters.[2] A new mestizaje can be seen as a traveler in this makeshift vessel moving between exile, escape, liberation. A traveler piecing together a mezcla of materials/identities to create something that holds us and protects us from waters that switch between choppy and serene but help us travel between territories. The implication is that it is not land that is traversed, a hard, relatively unchanging surface but a space of fluidity that flows, with changing currents, but always moving.

Acknowledgements

I would like to acknowledge all the hard intellectual and emotional work that my co-researchers engaged in throughout our time together. Working with this amazing group of young people and their allies has really challenged and changed me: Malan Bullock, Edric Engalla, Carolyn Garcia, Devon Gleason, Chris Hammonds, Jonathan Irizarry, Paulette Pierre-Paul and Damian Stewart, and the generous support of our allies and fellow facilitators: Sweety Patel, Esster Maxey, Larry Odoms, Ms. Andrews, David Surrey. A special thank you to Michelle Fine and Stan Karp for initiating this work and offering all the support and resources at their disposal throughout the projects. Finally, for the insightful feedback on this draft from Maria Torre, Eve Tuck and the other members of the CUNY PAR collective who provide insight and inspiration in this PAR movement.

Notes

1. Eve Tuck talked about PAR as blurring and clarifying.
2. Thanks to Eve Tuck and Michelle Fine, who asked me to think about the idea of border waters.

References

ACME: An International E-journal for Critical Geographies. (2007). In C. Cahill, F. Sultana, & R. Pain (Guest Eds.), *Special thematic issue: Participatory ethics*. Retrieved December, 2007 http://www.acme-journal.org/Volume6-3.htm

Anzaldúa, G. (1987/1999). *Borderlands: The new mestiza*. San Francisco: Aunt Lute Press.

Anzaldúa, G. (1990). *Making face, making soul, haciendo caras: Creative and critical perspectives by feminists of color*. San Francisco: Aunt Lute books.

Bok, D. (2003). *Universities in the marketplace: The commercialization of higher education*. Princeton: Princeton University Press.

Cabrera, A. F., Castaneda, M. B., Nora, A., & Hengstler, D. (1992). The convergence between two theories of college persistence. *Journal of Higher Education, 63*(2), 143–164.

Cahill, C. (2007). Repositioning ethical commitments: Participatory action research as a relational praxis of social change. *ACME: An International E-journal for Critical Geographies, 6*(3), 360–373.

Chawla, L. (2005). Don't just listen, do something! Lessons learned about governance from the Growing Up in Cities project. *Children, Youth, and Environments, 15*(2), 53–88.

Cooke, B., & Kothari, U. (2001). *Participation: The new tyranny?* New York: Zed Books.

Delgado Bernal, D. (2001). Learning and living pedagogies of the home: The mestiza consciousness of Chicana students. *International Journal of Qualitative Studies in Education, 14*(5), 623–639.

Denzin, N., & Giardina, M. (2007). *Ethical futures in qualitative research.* Walnut Creek, CA: Left Coast Press.

Elenes, C. A. (1997). Reclaiming the borderlands: Chicana/o identity, difference, and critical pedagogy. *Educational Theory, 47*(3), 359–375.

Elenes, C. A. (2001). Transformando fronteras: Chicana feminist transformative pedagogies. *International Journal of Qualitative Studies in Education, 14*(5), 689–702.

Fine, M. (2006). A brief history of the CUNY PAR collective. Retrieved 2007 http://web.gc.cuny. edu/che/start.htm

Fine, M., Roberts, R. A., Torre, M. E., Bloom, J., Burns, A., Chajet, L., Guishard, M., Payne, Y., & Perkins-Munn, T. (2004). *Echoes of Brown: Youth documenting and performing the legacy of Brown v the Board of Education.* New York: Teachers College Press.

Josselson, R. (2004). The hermaneutics of faith and the hermaneutics of suspicion. *Narrative Inquiry, 14*(1), 1–28.

Kirp, D. L. (2003). *Shakespeare, Einstein, and the bottom line: The marketing of higher education.* Cambridge, MA: Harvard University Press.

Moraga, C., & Anzaldúa, G. (1981). *This bridge called my back: Writings by radical women of color.* New York: Kitchen Table Women of Color Press.

Mosse, D. (2001). "People's knowledge," participation and patronage: Operations and representations in rural development. In B. Cooke & U. Kothari (Eds.), *Participation: The new tyranny?* (pp. 16–35). New York: Zed Books.

Pascarella, E. T., Whitt, E. J., Nora, A., Edison, M., Hagedorn, L. S., & Terenzini, P. T. (1996). What have we learned from the first year of the National Study of Student Learning? *Journal of College Student Development, 37*(2), 182–192.

Paulsen, M. B., & John, E. P. S. (2002). Social class and college costs. *The Journal of Higher Education, 73*(2), 190–236.

Rendón, L. I. (1993). *Validating culturally diverse students: Toward a new model of learning and student development.* University Park, PA: National Center on Postsecondary Teaching, Learning and Assessment. URL: http://eric.ed.gov/ERICDocs/data/ericdocs2sql/content_storage_01/0000019b/80/15/b6/b0.pdf

Saldivar-Hull, S. (2000). *Feminism on the border: Chicana gender politics and literature.* Los Angeles: University of California Press.

Solórzano, D. G., & Yosso, T. J. (2001). Critical race and LatCrit theory and method: Counterstorytelling. *International Journal of Qualitative Studies in Education, 14*(4), 471–495.

Tierney, W. G. (2000). Power, identity, and the dilemma of college student departure. In J. M. Braxton (Ed.), *Reworking the student departure puzzle.* Nashville: Vanderbilt University Press.

Tinto, V. (1982). Limits of theory and practice in student attrition. *Journal of Higher Education, 53*(6), 687–700.

Torre, M. (2003). *The power and potential of recognizing PAR as a contact zone … moving towards the Big "P."* Paper presented at the 24th Annual Ethnography in Education Research Forum, University of Pennsylvania.

Torre, M. E., & Fine, M. (2006). Participatory action research (PAR) by youth. In L. Sherrod, C. Flanagan, & R. Kassimir (Eds.), *Youth activism: An international encyclopedia* (pp. 456–462). Westport, CT: Greenwood Publishing Group.

Tuck, E. in conversation with Fine, M. (2007). Inner angles: A range of ethical responses to/with Indigenous and decolonizing theories. In: N. Denzin & M. Giardina (Eds.), *Ethical futures in qualitative research: Decolonizing the politics of knowledge* (pp. 145–168). Walnut Creek, CA: Left Coast Press.

Tuck, E., Ayala, J., Guishard, M., Stoudt, B., Boudin, K., Zeller-Berkman, S., Torre, M. E., & Fine, M. (April, 2007). *In the particulars: Critical dilemmas and radical possibilities of participatory action research.* Presented at the Annual Meeting of the American Educational Research Association, Chicago, IL.

Vélez-Ibáñez, C., & Greenberg, J. (1992). Formation and transformation of funds of knowledge among U.S. Mexican households. *Anthropology and Education Quarterly, 23*, 313–335.

PART FOUR

New Bottles for
New Wine—Report
Formats

Introduction

Innovation in Research Report Formats

I n Chapter 17 following this introduction, A. Suresh Canagarajah asks, "Can we pour new wine into old bottles?" Or, far less eloquently: Can—or should—the results of research based on a new set of assumptions and principles be rendered in the traditional format of research articles? As Part 3 illustrates, many PAR researchers have long since answered, "No." Even in the limited sampling of PAR presented there, it is obvious that new formats for reporting include innovations like websites and public performances.

One reason for such innovation is that, as illustrated in Part 1, critical action researchers are typically aware that journal articles generally have little (if any) impact on events, and so they have been working toward finding more creative and effective strategies to spark change. In addition to this practical motivation, however, is the issue of theoretical coherence: it makes no sense to change the assumptions and methodology of traditional research and not reconceptualize research reports. However, while participatory researchers point the way to genres beyond written reports, those reports are unlikely to disappear any time soon, especially in the oh-so-traditional academy. Part 4, then, introduces work that rethinks and reimagines written reports, striving to better align formats with the assumptions and goals of critical action research.

In the first chapter, Canagarajah explicates the theoretical difficulties that traditional written formats pose for critical action research reporting. These include their assumed objectivity, which "conveys the impression of infallible scholars mechanically driven along by their methodology and data to the inevitable findings." Other issues involve (mis)representation of research subjects/participants, who speak not for themselves but are spoken for and about by the researcher. Efforts to move beyond these difficulties, Canagarajah notes, include works that rely heavily on the voices of research subjects or participants; co-authored and dialogic texts reflecting more than one voice; and narratives, which eschew any pretense of objectivity and often employ a first-person, introspective voice. The author deconstructs examples of each, pointing to the many difficulties of adequately crafting reliable accounts of new forms of research within constraints of the written word. As the author notes, "[T]his process involves breaking the limits of language and textuality"—no small challenge. The remaining chapters in Part 4 illustrate the innovative ways critical action researchers have wrestled with that challenge.

Kath Fisher and Renata Phelps, in Chapter 18, take up the question of format issues within the academy, where graduate students are increasingly encouraged to conduct action research projects. Now supervisors of graduate students themselves, the authors report on their earlier experiences as graduate students who chose to write narrative theses. Highlighting what they term "the tensions and incongruities between conventional thesis presentation and the principles of action research," they illuminate the special challenges of casting the revered thesis or dissertation in a radically new format. Although the discussion makes clear that "flying in the face of academic convention is not for the fainthearted," the authors offer both encouragement and advice likely to help students—and their supervisors—develop the courage to chart new paths. While the content in this piece focuses on narrative as a genre worth exploring, its own format models yet another possibility: the report takes the form of a play script, complete with three acts and a curtain call. In both their claims and their written performance, the authors effectively contend that genres traditionally considered fictional might (as is often said of art itself) more faithfully represent lived experience than purportedly objective accounts.

Chapters 19 and 20 are taken from graduate theses and are samples of the kind of work that results when students and supervisors screw their courage to the sticking place and take the narrative path. In the first, Jessica Blanchard details how and why she emerged from the straitjacket of scripted teaching. In the author's own words, the narrative documents "a climatic clash between the author's vision of the critical teacher she wanted to be and the teacher she was becoming and being in reaction to a challenging environment." Any teacher who has taken on a difficult class in an environment that positions teachers as puppets—pulled by the strings of mandated curriculum, absurd accountability requirements, and relentlessly ticking clocks—will identify with her wish to get out from under:

> If only I could off-load this pressure, these worries and assumptions, like a sack of used clothes in a Good Will box. I've had my use of them. I don't want them anymore. Let someone else take them. Or not. Just as long as I can drop my load and leave it all behind.

The detailed account of classroom events that follow in the wake of such distress may do more to deepen understanding of teacher attrition and dysfunctional classrooms than mountains of traditional research articles.

In Chapter 20, Lisa Sibbett demonstrates a more hybrid approach, interweaving personal narrative with more traditional references to and discussion of research literature. Perhaps of particular interest here is the author's explanation of how her work evolved from a conventional approach to an unconventional analysis and report of the research. Frustrated as she tried to find meaning in data collected from students in traditional questionnaires and interviews, Sibbett ultimately realizes that the difficulty lay not in the data but in her own assumptions. Her account does much to illustrate why narrative—which frankly acknowledges the role of the researcher's subjectivity—has become increasingly popular as a genre for critical action research reports.

Shifting from prose to narrative to poetry—and between and among them—in Chapter 21 Rebecca Luce-Kapler seeks to capture what is gained as well as what is lost in the effort to breathe lived experience into words. As she works to transform a research transcript into a faithful research report, she points to the ways in which every depiction of any event is inescapably incomplete or inescapably misleading:

> In writing research, I try to reconstruct the experience, anchoring the writing in the transcript's words which I shade with my own intentions even as I invite the reader to join us in the room, to see for her or himself. But I can never choose all the possibilities, or even the best possibilities.

Much more is lost in translation than the precise scent of a pot of raspberry tea: the influence of particular social position that makes the conversation possible; what each speaker meant to say; other voices in the writer's head—from a radio program about women, from the glorified male writers who might (or might not) confess some debt to some woman … on and on. Indeed, no writer ever can choose all the possibilities, or even the best possibilities. And yet, Luce-Kapler makes clear how very much can be rendered through the imperfect choices open to any writer.

The final chapter in Part 4 is a co-authored chorus of voices—Antoinette Olberg, Joy Collins, Colleen Ferguson, David Freeman, Rita Levitz, Mary Lou McCaskell, and Brigid Walters—orchestrated by Antoinette Olberg. This piece illustrates an effort to allow participants in a research activity to speak for themselves, with minimal interpretation and intervention. In putting the article together, Olberg reports that she "disassembled each person's writing and reassembled the entire collection of parts, interspersing one person's writing with another's" with the intention of suggesting the nonlinear nature of emergent thinking and of highlighting emerging themes. Some of the voices tell stories; some speak in prose; and some nearly sing in poetry. Together they document how they "came to see and hear themselves, their students, their families, and others in their social and cultural contexts in ways they had not done before"—in words that come from the speakers' hearts rather than the researcher's pen.

Writing: the medium of endless possibility—for the novelist, poet, and playwright, of course. And for the critical researcher as well.

CHAPTER 17

From Critical Research Practice to Critical Research Reporting

A. Suresh Canagarajah

Recent discussions on qualitative and critical research orientations in the pages of this journal reflect and encourage the wide range of research approaches emerging as an alternative to, and in some cases in opposition to, traditional scientific-empirical approaches that have dominated most disciplines in the academy. But the modes of reporting research have been left out of consideration. Though research methods have been insight fully reconstructed for their hidde n assumptions and interests in keeping with a poststructuralist/postmodernist perspective on knowledge (see Peirce, 1995b; Pennycook, 1994), the ideological nature of research report ing has been overlooked. We must note that even if a study is carried out according to the emerging realizations, one can defeat or contradict these assumptions when presenting the findings according to the traditional conventions of academic research reporting. (Can we pour new wine into old bottles?)

It is understandable, therefore, that in many disciplines outside TESOL much attention is being given today to critiquing the governing assumptions of research writing at the same time that a critical research practice is being developed. There is energetic experimentation with alternate forms of research reporting that would better reflect our emerging realizations on the nature of research and knowledge production. In light of these developments, it is significant that in a recent introduction to ethnographic methods in *Research in the Teaching of English,* Steven Athanases and Shirley Brice Heath (1995) are compelled to include a discussion on strategies of reporting research findings. Developing a feminist approach to composition research, Gesa Kirsch and Joy Ritchie (1995) find that encoding such concerns will require nothing less than new forms of academic writing and proceed to consider the rhetorical changes this will entail. It is therefore important for scholars in TESOL to explore directions for more critical research reporting.

We must first realize that writing/reporting research findings is no insignificant appendage to the research process. It is the written document that embodies, reflects, and often constitutes the whole rese arch activity for the scholarly community. Because the reams of field notes, audiotapes, transcripts, and statistical printouts are never conveniently available to the scholarly community, and the lengthy research process in the many sites is rarely accessible for readers, it is understandable that the report is treated as proxy for the study. It is of some concern, therefore, if the genre conventions of research reporting can modify/corrupt/eclipse the reported data. In a very revealing statement, seasoned ethnographers George Marcus and Michael Fischer (1986) confess that "given the sort of heightened critical self-consciousness with which fieldwork is undertaken and conducted, the usual dissonance between what is known from fieldwork and what is constrained to report according to genre conventions can grow intolerable" (p. 37).

Natural scientists have come to a position of acknowledging that genre conventions can have a predictive function and actively shape the research process. Peter Dear (1991) has noted the "ways in which literary forms can direct the cognitive content of science through constraining problem-choice or through requiring ... particular kinds of theoretical and experimental formulation" (p. 5). This insight reflects the radical awareness of contemporary scholars that "science is indeed fundamentally rhetorical, drenched as it is in language" (Selzer, 1993, p. 13). It is not surprising therefore that certain disciplinary communities go to the extent of arguing that explorations into research reporting feed into central concerns of their field, not excluding theoretical development: "Theory-building in social and cultural anthropology at present is a simultaneous function of devising textual strategies that modify past conventions of ethnographic writing" (Marcus & Fischer, 1986, p. 67). The genres of academic writing are thus much more integral to intellectual practices than we have traditionally assumed. If the written document holds such importance, it is necessary to understand the values it embodies and the ways in which it mediates the research process.

Reconstructing Research Reporting

The genre that enjoys almost paradigmatic status in scholarly circles (including our own) constitutes the four-part report of introduction, methods, results, and discussion, belonging to the scientific-empirical tradition. It is interesting that even qualitative research reports often adopt a variation of this structure (see, e.g., the categories for reporting the data under Qualitative Research Guidelines for authors in the *TES OL Quarterly*). The teleological structure—beginning from the tentative hypotheses and moving to the research inquiry, the discovery of the results, and the application of the findings for solving prior problems and confusions—embodies a triumphalistic movement that reflects the heady mood of positivism in the early days of empirical science. The passive syntax and impersonal tone, together with the inductive structure, serve to maintain the pretense of objectivity, detachment, and neutrality, suppressing the agency of the researcher. The written product conveys the impression of infallible scholars mechanically driven along by their methodology and data to the inevitable findings.

Although this genre is most typical of natural sciences, variations of the above empirical-scientific rhetoric (also called *realist writing* in these circles—see Lay, 1995, p. 296) influence research reporting in other academic disciplines. For example, historians value the *realist narratives* in their discipline in which detached prose is supposed to ensure an accurate representation of past events (see White, 1973). Marcus and Fischer (1986) characterize the dominant genre of ethnographic reporting in the following way:

> Realist ethnographies are written to allude to a whole by means of parts or foci of analytical attention which constantly evoke a social and cultural totality. Close attention to detail and redundant demonstrations that the writer shared and experienced this whole other world are further aspects of realist writing. In fact, what gives the ethnographer authority and the text a pervasive sense of concrete reality is the writer's claim to represent a world as only one who has known it firsthand can, which thus forges an intimate link between ethnographic writing and fieldwork. (p. 23)

The notion that the text reflects the real world, with the multitude of concrete details photographically depicting the research context, is the mimetic view of art/literature that derives from the 19th-century empirical tradition. This genre is also influenced by the "window pane" theory of language—that is, language as a transparent medium that reveals unproblematically the material world outside. Because these linguistic and philosophical assumptions were popularized by the Realist movement, paralleling the rise of empirical science, it is apt that the appellation *realist* is widely used in different disciplines to describe this genre of academic writing.

Although Carol Berkenkotter (1993) has questioned the appropriateness of this genre for qualitative studies that do not conduct controlled experimental research, the values fostered by this mode of presentation are questioned even in psychometric and natural science circles today. The recent access to Louis Pasteur's diaries and the discovery of the matters he chose not to report in his papers have raised serious ethical and ideological concerns about research reporting among scientists (see Geison, 1995; Porter, 1995). What they realize is that "realist" writing hides huge chunks of reality, apart from embodying values and ideologies, despite its claim of transparency.

Let us consider therefore the shaping of research knowledge by the values behind reporting conventions. The need for coherence in the report—achieved by the closure, the tight structure, and seamless writing—can hide the false starts, wrong moves, misleading tracks, and interpretive gambles that usually characterize the research process. There is a similar suppression of the gaps, contradictions, and conflicts in the data for the sake of textual coherence. The report thus gets considerably removed from the existential conditions of research. The genre conventions of objectivity and detachment can also function to suppress the mediation of various levels of discourses in the research process—such as the values of the researcher, the values of the research methodology, the values of the discipline, and the values of the academic community concerned.

Such abstraction and detachment have profound implications for the representation of the knower/researcher in the report. For all practical purposes, the researcher is absent from the report, looming behind the text as an omniscient, transcendental, all-knowing figure. This convention hides the manner in which the subjectivity of the researchers—with their complex values, ideologies, and experiences—shapes the research activity and findings. In turn, how the research activity shapes the researchers' subjectivity is not explored—even though research activity can sometimes profoundly affect the researchers' sense of the world and themselves. Furthermore, the shifting/conflicting interests of the researcher—that is, professional, personal, ideological—in carrying out the study are not acknowledged. Realizing the significant place of the "personal" in the construction of knowledge (see Rich,1989; Harding, 1991, for the politics of location), recent feminist scholarship has called for a complex reflexivity from researchers to interrogate how they influence and are influenced by the research process. However, such concerns are typically deemed irrelevant by the traditional report genre.

The scope for adequately representing the researched/subjects is similarly limited. Because the subjects exist in the report only through the voice of the researcher, there is a natural tendency for their complexity to be suppressed and their identity to be generalized (or essentialized) to fit the dominant assumptions and theoretical constructs of the researcher and the disciplinary community. The power relationships between the researcher and the subjects also get concealed in the objective report. If any production of knowledge demanding codification, systematization, and categorization involves a measure of control and colonization (as poststructuralists argue), studying and analyzing powerless groups like minority groups or students becomes highly political. Minority scholars like bell hooks (1990) have protested against the practice of academic researchers using knowledge of/from subordinate groups for their own intellectual, academic, or professional agendas. Furthermore, research frequently involves a measure of manipulation and deception as interviewers and participant-observers make subjects feel friendly, comfortable, and powerful in order to reveal their intimate thoughts and experiences. But such ethical and political concerns in the "process" of the research activity are suppressed in the "product" of the report. In fact, feminist scholars have also called for a caring, reciprocal relationship with subjects in the research process (see Oakley, 1981). They would encourage active involvement in the life of the subjects, to the extent of taking measures to improve their social and material conditions. But such close involvement is discouraged by the research report because it serves to prejudice the researcher and pollute the findings. A studied detachment towards the subjects and contexts of research is the preferred relationship in this genre. Therefore, the rigorously self-examining attitude of the researcher and a caring personal investment in the life of the subjects demand new reporting conventions.

Constructing Alternate Modes of Report

Among the initial shifts in research writing is the more relaxed use of the first-person pronoun. But this perfunctory "I-dropping" (see Raymond, 1993) is too weak a gesture to incorporate the complex splits and shifts in the subject positions of the researcher, characterized by a mixture of divided interests and values influencing the research process. Another rhetorical move has been to open the report with an announcement of the subject positions occupied by the researcher: "I am a white male tenured liberal from the Midwest." I have myself resorted to a similar rhetorical strategy—albeit at paragraph length in the middle of the analysis (see Canagarajah, 1993, pp. 620–621). But critical research calls for a more sustained and rigorous exploration of the ways the researcher's subjectivity influences the research process. Boxing this concern into a single section in a largely detached, univocally authored, realist text is unsatisfactory.

Much of the research reporting in fields like composition and anthropology today is even more experimental in negotiating the values that mediate research reporting. These are polyphonous or dialogic texts that encode multiple voices/perspectives simultaneously and engage the reader more actively in the interpretive process. These texts illustrate developments in new ways of reading and writing in postmodern literature. Marcus and Fischer (1986) refer to experimental texts in their field as *modernist ethnographies* (to contrast with realist ethnographies), whereas some composition scholars call these *multi vocal texts* (see Cushman, 1996).

For example, Kevin Dwyer's (1982) *Moroccan Dialogues* attempts to build into the text the complexity of the fieldwork/research situation and the polyphony of voices in the research context to encourage readings from multiple points of view. Through a series of lightly edited interview transcripts, Dwyer dramatizes the exploratory, hypothetical, recursive, cumulative interpretive process of the researcher. Through this mode of presentation, he exposes how the neat linear textualization of ethnography distorts the immediacy of the fieldwork situation and hides the researchers' shaky control over their understanding of the culture about which they later write with authority. The readers are similarly taken through the process of arriving at a deeper understanding of the new cultural system—while also acquiring an understanding of their own values and predisposition which motivated the partial initial readings. Gesa Kirsch observes that confronted with an informant who was decidedly against her own feminist perspective, she resorted to providing lengthy excerpts from the interview transcripts to voice the other's opinion, accompanied by her own explanation and theorization (Kirsch & Ritchie, 1995, p. 19).

We must note, however, that even in such presentations there is little room for "authentic" representation of the informant's views, as the researcher eventually holds the pen. It is the researcher who enjoys the authority to choose and organize the words of the informants, apart from providing coherence for the text with an overarching generalization or theory (that would neutralize any tensions). A more promising strand of experimentation has focused on coauthoring texts. Such texts are jointly written by the researcher and the informants/subjects and, therefore, considered *collaborative reports*. They attempt to dramatize the tensions between the perspectives of the researchers and subjects. Keeping in check the usual authority of the researcher/author to offer solutions to contradictions generated by the data, such texts invite the readers to struggle with these tensions. *Birds of My Kalam Country* (Majnep & Bulmer, 1977) and *Piman Shamanism* (Bahr, Gregorio, Lopez, & Alvarez, 1974), where Western academics collaborate with native informants to explicate indigenous cultural practices, are early examples of such texts. In English studies, Susan Miller has coauthored a study on academic underlife with several of her undergraduate students (see Anderson, Best, Black, Hirst, Miller, & Miller, 1990). The process of writing such texts can be very tense as researchers and subjects negotiate their footing and attempt to reach a common platform to address the readers. Though the project can face the danger of being abandoned altogether due to irreconcilable differences—as confessed by Ritchie regarding a text she attempted to coauthor with two of her ESL students (see Ritchie, Kaur, & Meyer, in press)—the experience can be richly educational in its own right.

A variation of the above genre is the *dialogic text* that consists of counterpoised dialogues between the researcher and informants/subjects. Although the text more authentically explores the conflicting voices of the subjects, resolving the ensuing interpretive tensions is the responsibility of readers. The article by Magda Lewis and Roger Simon (1986) on their differing student/teacher perspectives on male discourse in the classroom in a graduate course is one of the earliest exemplary texts in this regard. Beverly Clark and Sonja Wiedenhaupt (1992) have coauthored a report on writer's block, with the researcher and student telling their stories from opposing standpoints.

Furthermore, narratives are gaining prominence in research publications because they represent holistically the local knowledge of the communities studied. In opposition to grand theories and global knowledge structures, narratives represent knowledge from the bottom up; in opposition to explicit forms of theorization, they embody implicit forms of reasoning and logic; in opposition to positivistic scholarly discourses which are elitist in their specialized and abstract nature, narratives represent concrete forms of knowledge that are open to further intererpretation. Narratives, then, represent the research process in all its concreteness and complexity, remaining open-ended for creative theorization. It is also worthy of note that marginalized groups such as women, Blacks, and traditional oral communities, who widely practice empathetic ways of knowing, are considered to conceive/embody knowledge in narrative forms (see Royster, 1996, on the intellectual role of narratives in the Black community in an essay written in narrative form). Narratives open up possibilities for these groups to participate in knowledge construction in the academy.

Another form of writing gaining ground in English studies is more introspective and personal, voicing the inner thought processes of the researcher in engagement with the context and subjects. A recent refereed publication in composition research proceeds as follows: "OK, so I was a little annoyed at Elizabeth—who I thought was trying to get me to help write her paper for her. And when I saw the draft she had written I was further displeased. Oh this is so lifeless and conventional, I thought. I looked at Elizabeth as 'a cheerleader of the middle class' (this is the phrase from my field notes)" (Dixon, 1995, pp. 265–266). With such stream of consciousness appearing in research writing, we have certainly come a long way from mechanical scientific prose. In fact, this mode of presentation can accommodate a narrative progression with the personal voice. Arleen Schenke (1991) has similarly reflected on her ESL students, employing a series of episodes in classroom and community.

The lines of textual experimentation outlined above make us consider how they can invigorate ESOL research reporting. Take, for example, participant action research, much publicized in recent ESOL scholarship for the democratic manner in which it ensures the active contribution of the subjects in the research process (see Auerbach, 1994; Barndt, 1986). However, if solely the researcher presents the findings from the study, the potential for the subjects' perspectives to emerge from the report will be limited. The researchers' understanding of the subjects (usually relatively powerless students) will find a privileged position through their authorial control. It is necessary, therefore, to see reports co-authored by ESOL researcher/teachers and students. Rather than the researchers filtering the students' divergent positions through their own perspectives, it is important to let the students' views remain in tension (if necessary) with the researchers' positions.

To take an ideologically more sophisticated example, consider the case of Bonny Norton Peirce's (1995a) classroom-based social research. Peirce employs a theory of subjectivity very similar to that outlined in this chapter, providing a much-needed challenge to notions of identity in language acquisition. However, the construction of the research report in the traditional genre with an unobtrusive author begs many questions. Though the writer applies the notion of split, shifting, multiple subjecthood insightfully to her subjects, the report fails to show a reflexive application of this notion to the researcher herself or the researcher's interactions with the subjects. Furthermore, because developing a sensitivity to those social contexts where learners negotiate identities for language acquisition is the thrust of the article, and because the interview/research situation is one such context, it is important to know how the subjects negotiated subject positions with the researcher. This issue can become more engrossing in the case of disempowered immigrant ethnic women interacting with a researcher from a relatively more privileged background in a study that perceives identities as a "site of struggle" (p. 15). How were such cultural and political tensions handled? Moreover, a study that highlights the importance of "investment" in language acquisition may be expected to explore the desires of the subjects in participating in the study. What was the contribution of the researcher to the socioeconomic struggles of these women to survive in the new setting—besides listening to their stories and plotting their language development? In the only place we hear the voice of the researcher (transcript of an interview in Peirce, 1995a, pp. 24–25), we listen to a voice that cuts subjects short in the middle of their turn, poses solely questions for subjects who solely answer, suggests answers, knowingly elicits further information. Given the pedagogical goals of this research, is it not valuable to make students aware that such research situations too exemplify "how opportunities to speak are socially structured" (p. 26)? The point here is not that the researcher failed to attend to these issues in her research; she very well might have. What is more important is that we need a genre of presentation that will encourage us to articulate and explore such concerns.

Such unrelenting reflexivity and critical open-endedness in research reporting need not drive us to despair on our ability to represent knowledge and experience. Although this process involves breaking the limits of language and textuality, the challenge is to strike the right balance between acknowledging the multiple values and conditions that impinge on the research process while explicating the significant thematic strands for readers. Needless to say, researchers cannot change their reporting conventions overnight. Gatekeeping processes of academic/research institutions and editorial boards, which institutionalize the scientific-empiricist assumptions of knowledge production and transmission, can exert considerable pressure on writers to conform to the dominant conventions. Furthermore, disciplinary communities respond differently to such concerns—within the humanities, some like linguistics are more resistant, whereas those like composition are less so. Readers, too, should acculturate themselves to the new interpretive responsibilities. We must hope, therefore, that the TESOL professional community, academic institutions, and publishing houses will grow sensitive to the politics of research reporting and accommodate more critical and creative writing.

References

Anderson, W., Best, C., Black, A., Hurst, J., Miller, B., & Miller, S. (1990). Crosscurricular ablex: A collaborative report on ways with academic words. *College Composition and Commun ication, 41,* 11–36.

Athanases, S. Z., & Heath, S. B. (1995). Ethnography in the study of the teaching and learning of English. *Research in the Teaching of English, 29,* 263–287.

Auerbach, E. R. (1994). Participatory action research. *TESOL Quarterly, 28,* 693–697.

Bahr, D. M., Gregorio, J., Lopez, D. I., & Alvar ez, A. (1974). *Piman shamanism and staying sickness.* Tucson: University of Arizona Press.

Barndt, D. (1986). *Just getting there.* Toronto: Participatory Research Group.

Berkenkotter, C. (1993). A "rhetoric for naturalistic inquiry" and the question of genre. *Research in the Teaching of English, 27,* 293–304.

Canagarajah, A. S. (1993). Critical ethnography of a Sri Lanka classroom: Ambiguities in student opposition through ESOL. *TESOL Quarterly, 27,* 601–626.

Clark, B., & Wiedenhaupt, S. (1992). On blocking and unblocking Sonja: A case study in two voices. *College Composition and Communication, 43,* 55–74.

Cushman, E. (1996). Rhetorician as an agent of social change. *College Composition and Communication, 47,* 7–28.

Dear, P. (Ed.). (1991). *The literary structure of scientific argument: Historical studies.* Philadelphia: University of Pennsylvania Press.

Dixon, K. (1995). Gendering the "personal." *College Composition and Communication, 46,* 255–275.

Dwyer, K. (1982). *Moroccan dialogues: Anthropology in question.* Baltimore, MD: The John s Hopkins University Press.

Geison, G. (1995). *The private science of Louis Pasteur.* Princeton, NJ: Princeton University Press.

Harding, S. (1991). *Whose science? Whose knowledge? Thinking from women's lives.* Ithaca, NY: Corn ell University Press.

hooks, b. (1990). Choosing the margin as a space for radical openness. In *Yearning: Race, gender and cultural politics* (pp. 145–54). Boston: South End.

Kirsch, G., & Ritchie, J. S. (1995). Beyond the personal: Theorizing a politics of location in composition research. *College Composition and Communication, 46,* 7–30.

Lay, M. M. (1995). Rhetorical analysis of scientific texts: Three major contributions. *College Composition and Communication, 46,* 292–302.

Lewis, M., & Simon, R. (1986). A discourse not intended for her: Learning and teaching within patriarchy. *Harvard Educational Review, 56,* 457–472.

Majnep, I., & Bulmer, R. (1977). *Birds of my Kalam country.* Auckland, New Zealand: Oxford University Press.

Marcus, G., & Fischer, M. M. J. (1986). *Anthropology as cultural critique: An experimental moment in the human sciences.* Chicago: University of Chicago Press.

Oakley, A. (1981). Interviewing women: A contradiction in terms? In Helen Robert (Ed.), *Doing feminist research* (pp. 30–61). New York: Routledge.

Peirce, B. N. (1995a). Social identity, investment, and language learning. *TESOL Quarterly, 29,* 9–32.

Peirce, B. N. (1995b). The theory of methodology in qualitative research. *TESOL Quarterly, 29,* 569–576.

Pennycook, A. (1994). Critical pedagogical approaches to research. *TESOL Quarterly, 28,* 690–693.

Porter, R. (1995, June 16). Lion of the laboratory—Pasteur's amazing achievements survive the scrutiny of his notebooks. *Times Literary Supplement,* 4811, pp. 3–4.

Raymond, C. I. (1993). I-dropping and androgyny: The authorial I in scholarly writing. *College Composition and Communication, 44,* 478–483.

Rich, A. (1989). Notes on a politics of location. In *Blood, bread and poetry* (pp. 210–231). New York: Norton.

Ritchie, J., Kaur, M., & Meyer, B. C. (in press). Women students' autobiographical writing: The rhetoric of discovery and defiance. In E. Jessup & K. Geissler (Eds.), *Valuing diversity: Race, gender and class in composition research.* Portsmouth, NH: Heinemann.

Royster, J. J. (1996). When the first voice you hear is not your own. *College Composition and Communication, 47,* 29–40.

Schenke, A. (1991). The "will to reciprocity" and the work of memory: Fictioning speaking out of silence in ESL and feminist pedagogy. *Resources for Feminist Research, 20,* 47–55.

Selzer, J. (Ed.). (1993). *Understanding scientific prose.* Madison: University of Wisconsin Press.

CHAPTER 18

Recipe or Performing Art?
Challenging Conventions for Writing Action Research Theses

Kath Fisher and Renata Phelps

Introduction

As action research and practitioner-based inquiry is increasingly adopted as a basis of doctoral study, issues arise for students, supervisors and examiners alike as to what it means to produce and judge an action research thesis in relation to traditional thesis presentation criteria (Winter, Griffiths & Green, 2000). Indeed, the question of what constitutes 'quality' action research has resulted in important paradigmatic debates across the humanities and social science disciplines, debates that problematize the nature of 'knowledge' and question the need for uniform criteria of validity (Bradbury & Reason, 2001; Winter et al., 2000). Furthermore, 'one of the great problems with all qualitative research is the constant need to seek its justification within someone else's language game and in relation to someone else's definition of suitable criteria' (Green, cited in Winter et al., 2000, p. 30).

The quality of PhD- or Master's-level research is ultimately judged by the dissertation or thesis; the primary mode of exposition, even in the creative arts. It is this writing task that is our focus in this article. Most research candidates seek advice in relation to this task to ensure they are meeting the all-important examination requirements. Traditional approaches to structuring theses, especially in the sciences and social sciences, have resulted in the familiar 'five-chapter model,' comprising introduction, literature review, methodology, analysis and conclusions. To borrow Bob Dick's (2002) terminology, this is writing by 'recipe' and, as a rule, supervisors will be anxious to ensure their students are following accepted approaches to reduce the risk of alienating examiners. But what of the student who has undertaken action research? Do these conventions apply? Can their less conventional research process be made to 'fit' the five-chapter recipe and still be true to its practice? Do they take an unacceptable risk by straying outside the mainstream? Or can they write their thesis more in keeping with the 'performing art' that is action research (Dick, 2002)?

In this article we contemplate these questions through the stories of our own experiences as doctoral action researchers. We present some insights which may be of interest to other students undertaking action research who are considering challenging the conventions of the academy. As academics now supervising students undertaking action research and remaining committed to improving our own and our students' research and writing practice, we propose that these insights might also contribute to the ongoing debate about the quality, authenticity and integrity of action research.

In keeping with the spirit of viewing research (and in our case, writing) as performing art rather than recipe, we have adopted the metaphor of a play to structure our article, playing with the notion of presenting research as a form of performance text.[1] We see our approach in this article as an example of 'presentational knowing' (Heron, 1996; Heron & Reason, 2001), which, while rarely seen in academic journal writing, allows the text to 'speak out' and challenge convention. A good performance text 'must be more than cathartic, it must be political, moving people to action and reflection' (Denzin, 2000, p. 905). It is our hope that our 'performance' produces this effect through a deeper and more active reflective engagement with our audience than a more conventional exposition may offer.

A tale of two theses

(A play in three acts)

Prologue: in which the audience is revealed and we meet the main characters

A single spotlight shines on the middle of the closed curtain as the narrator, a figure in top hat and tails, emerges onto the stage.

NARRATOR: Ladies and gentlemen, we invite you to take your seats as we prepare to take you on a journey of intrigue and adventure—some might even say foolishness! Let me assure you, this is not a voyage for the fainthearted. Before we get underway, though, how many of you here tonight are research candidates? … Wonderful! We think there might be some important lessons for you here, if not cautionary tales. What about students doing action research? … Excellent! You may find that some of the dilemmas you are facing in the writing of your thesis will be echoed in the stories you hear tonight. Any supervisors in the audience? … Aha! If you have been challenged to consider how your students might best structure their action research theses, then this play may provide some inspiration and, perhaps, reassurance.

Now, I'm wondering if there mightn't be an examiner or two out there as well? … It's great to see you here! Action research candidates will no doubt be pleased to know that you are interested in being challenged regarding the conventions of thesis presentation. Finally, there might be some action research practitioners out there who are reporting on their research outside the formal academic examination process … would you raise your hands? Ah, good. You are most welcome. While this play is more about writing theses than research reports, I'm sure you will find relevance to your own writing context.

Some of you will be fortunate enough to be studying and researching from innovative academic faculties with strong traditions of participatory inquiry and action research. Such places may well already promote creativity and breaking with convention in thesis presentation. For you, some of the messages in this play may not be all that new; however, we are glad to have you here with us, and we welcome your participation. I suspect, however, that a good proportion of you will be from contexts where action research is little understood or reluctantly tolerated. We hope our play will offer some alternative strategies as you embark on the significant undertaking of writing your thesis.

In this play we will not be reiterating the foundational tenets of action research, as we are assuming that you have come here tonight with some background already in this area. In any case, action research is discussed extensively in various seminal and current works (for instance, Altrichter, Kemmis, McTaggart & Zuber-Skerritt, 1991; Carr & Kemmis, 1990; Grundy, 1982; Kemmis & McTaggart, 1988; Passfield, 2001; Reason & Bradbury, 2001; Wadsworth, 1998; Zuber-Skerritt, 1996). In producing this play we do acknowledge that there are a range of approaches to action research, from the more technical focus on organizational or educational change (where the researcher is 'expert') to emancipatory and participatory processes that aim to engender radical social change and where all participants are equal as coresearchers. The characters who will be performing here for you tonight each have their own understanding of action research practice and appreciate that there is no one 'correct way' to do action research.

The time has now come to introduce the characters and allow them to speak for themselves. The two protagonists in this play are researchers who found that conventional social science thesis presentation constrained the way they wanted to present the complex and non-linear nature of their research. Our protagonists, MCR and CRK,[2] are both higher education teachers who conducted their (quite different) research projects in the course of their professional work. They will now introduce themselves, describing their research projects and their values and perspectives on action research. Our first is Dr. MCR, currently a teacher of learning technologies to pre-service teachers:

MCR: Thank you and good evening to you all. My thesis is the story of an action research initiative underpinned by my strong belief in the importance of approaches to computer education which foster lifelong computer learning. In my thesis I trace the journey of a reflexive process of change and iterative development in the teaching of an information computer technology (ICT) unit to pre-service teacher education students. Over a period of three years I pursued a central research question, namely: 'How can I develop my teaching practice to better facilitate the development of capable computer users?' My research explored the distinction between a 'competent' and a 'capable' computer user and trialled a range of teaching and learning approaches to facilitate the development of capable computer users (Phelps, 2002; Phelps & Ellis, 2002a, 2002b, 2002c). From the research I developed a metacognitive approach to computer education, an approach which is founded on the premise that adoption of ICT is influenced by an individual's attitudes, beliefs, motivation, confidence and learning strategies and which promotes learners' active engagement in directing the learning process.

In my approach to action research, I concur with Bob Dick (2002) who refers to action research as 'meta-methodology'. Like Lau (1999, p. 2), I equate doing action research with a 'commitment to an underlying philosophy of social science' and deeply relate to the view of action research as a 'living practice' (Carson, 1997). While my research certainly represented a process of critiquing, informing and developing my own teaching practice (the 'first-person' focus),[3] it also represented a significant opportunity for students to self-examine and redefine their relationships with technology (the 'second-person' focus). A 'third-person' focus inevitably emerged as we collectively challenged the traditions of directive-style computer training and ultimately provided a more complex understanding of the computerlearning context.

While my unconventional writing approach was somewhat challenging to my supervisors, they were willing to support it given my fairly persuasive justification of the approach in the introduction to my thesis.

NARRATOR: Our second main character is Dr. CRK, who currently supervises and mentors postgraduate students within the same institution as MCR.

CRK: Thank you—and great to see such an enthusiastic audience here tonight. My PhD explored how economics could be taught within an emancipatory framework to students in two different institutions—those studying welfare at TAFE (Technical and Further Education) and those undertaking social science at university. The TAFE students became collaborators with me (the 'second-person' focus of the research) in developing an empowering curriculum that demystified conventional economics and introduced students to a range of alternative economic theories. The process of critical reflection emerged as a key research interest for me, which I explored in detail with the university students who were encouraged to reflect critically on how economics impacted on their lives as well as on the wider society and ecological systems (the 'third-person' focus). One of the outcomes of my personal reflection was to critically examine the role of activism in the face of globalization and how I personally constructed my own activism (my 'first-person' work), drawing on critiques of critical social science put forward by postmodern writers (Fisher, 2000, 2003a, 2003b).

My philosophy in relation to action research is located in the emancipatory and critical tradition. In my view, critical action research involves a commitment to political action. I concur with Kemmis (Kemmis, 1996; Kemmis & McTaggart, 2000) that a criterion of 'success' of an action research process is the politicization of the participants. Thus I perceive the role of the action researcher as an activist who must be critically reflective of her own activist position, being careful not to impose her own 'liberatory' agenda (Lather, 1991) on those with whom she researches and works.

I undertook my research in a university department which supported the paradigm of 'action inquiry', exemplified in the work of Reason (1988), Reason and Bradbury (2001) and Torbert (1991). My supervisor supported unconventional thesis presentation, particularly emphasising the importance of the subjective presence of the researcher.

The characters and the narrator leave the stage.

– Curtain –

Act I

In which the narrator and protagonists set the scene and describe the 'existential choices' faced by action research candidates

As the curtain rises, the audience sees a set on two levels. Towering over the stage, but in the background, is a series of five large symmetrical grey blocks lined up in a row. In the foreground, and at stage level, is a colourful montage of moving and interacting spirals. The narrator walks on, gazing up at the towers and moving in and out of the spirals. MCR and CRK follow, taking up their positions on the opposite side of the stage.

NARRATOR: This is a play about challenging orthodoxy; in particular the orthodoxy of writing up research. Many of you will have consulted, at some stage, the wealth of literature available for research students on how to write a thesis (for example, Rudestam & Newton, 1992; Van Wagenen, 1991). Such 'self-help' manuals generally offer what has come to be an accepted approach to writing a thesis: the standard, formulaic 'five-chapter' structure—introduction, literature review, methodology, analysis of data, and conclusions and implementations, followed by the bibliography and appendices. While this model undoubtedly provides a valuable resource for postgraduate students learning the research writing process, it tends to be considered by novice researchers as the *only* approach to thesis writing.

But what if the straight-edged, linear blocks of orthodoxy restrict and impair the authenticity and integrity of a research process that is dynamic, non-linear and emergent? How does the PhD student doing action research proceed? Although alternative approaches have been considered by some researchers (for example, Creswell, 2003; Denzin & Lincoln, 2000; Koro-Ljungberg, 2004), candidates submitting the culmination of several years' research for examination by an unknown academic often consider it 'safer' to follow established convention. Supervisors, who are likely to have structured their own theses in the conventional way, may feel hesitant in recommending or supporting alternative approaches. Indeed, some action research candidates have run afoul of the examination process (Hughes, Denley & Whitehead, 1998), and one of our main characters, CRK, had a challenging experience of examination in this regard, as we shall see in Act III. Our focus tonight is to present the story of how our two researchers tackled the challenge of presenting action-based research in the context of a still-conservative academy.

MCR: When I was seeking guidance in structuring my PhD, I found little had been written on how to present action research theses. Those papers that did consider it tended to argue that action research be treated like any other methodology and accommodated within conventional structures and university presentation guidelines (Zuber-Skerritt & Perry, 2002). Perry (1994), for instance, noted that sticking with the five-chapter model can allay concerns regarding the 'messy' and 'inconclusive' impression provided by action research, and he recommended including reflections on the action research study in the body and restricting discussion of practical and experiential aspects of the research to appendices.

Within my institution action research had a strong profile; however, the conventional thesis structure had been widely adopted by action researchers, and adherence to convention seemed to be preferred by my own and other action research candidates' supervisors.

CRK: That could be because much action research within our institution was predominantly focused on organizational change and was technical rather than emancipatory.

MCR: You could be right, CRK. I did find some papers presenting an alternative perspective. Bob Dick (1993, 2000, 2002), for instance, notes that universities often structure higher degrees on the assumption that 'good' research is 'theory driven' rather than 'data driven.' Acknowledging that some examiners 'may be surprised by data-driven research because it does not fit their notion of legitimate higher degree research' (Dick, 2002, p. 160), he provides justification and motivation for action researchers to be creative, arguing that conventional thesis structures do not do justice to action research. Bob's articulation of the 'existential choice' that needs to be made by research candidates left a particularly strong impression on me:

> Do you want to be an apprentice who will learn thoroughly, from your supervisor, committee and literature, a particular approach to research? That is, will your learning be primarily propositional? At the conclusion of such a research program you can expect to know how to do one form of research. To overstate the situation, this is research by recipe. Or do you expect to engage in research with whatever resources and understandings you can bring to bear, learning from your experiences? That is, will your learning be primarily through questioning inquiry, with supervisor and committee functioning as mentors rather than as teachers? Such an approach will engage you in examining your assumptions about the nature of knowledge and of methodologies. This is research as performing art. (Dick, 2002, pp. 161–162)

CRK: This is certainly a pertinent quote for our purposes, but I wouldn't want to give the impression that research or even thesis writing falls neatly into one of these two categories. The 'academic norm' for research reports is only one possible format, and conventions and expectations regarding writing structure have been, and are, continually changing (Winter, 1989). Since action research emerges from a different context and different relationships (collaborative and action oriented rather than authoritative and observation oriented), Winter argues that there is good cause for reports of action research also to be different. He proposes two specific variations: a 'case study' of the process of the work, in narrative form and a 'plural text' where the voice of a single author is partially replaced by an interplay between the voices of participants in the research. Winter goes further by stating that some stylistic features of academic writing can be seen to be 'inappropriate' for action research, particularly where style, tone and vocabulary express an 'expert' role or a withdrawal from personal involvement or sustained abstraction from concrete detail.

MCR: Like Winter (1989) I would argue that the ideological aspects of action research cannot be separated from the perceived 'necessities' of thesis structure and presentation. To do so would undermine the very foundations of action research and hence the integrity of the thesis which depicts and conveys the research. If action research is truly seen by the researcher as a 'living practice' (Carson, 1997) then the life and practice of the research cannot, and should not, simply be 'appendicized'.

NARRATOR: This sets the scene for our play. Let's watch while our protagonists tell their stories of how they attempted to write their theses more in keeping with the moving montage of cycles and spirals than the fixed and immovable blocks of convention.

– Curtain –

Act II

Scene 1: in which the writer/researcher takes centre stage

The curtain rises to the same backdrop as in Act I, but in the front of the stage MCR and CRK, dressed in plain black, are seated on a comfortable garden seat that overlooks a pond reflecting the surrounding trees and sky. The narrator stands to one side of the stage, in front of the curtain.

CRK: One of the conventions of academic thesis writing that has come under sustained challenge from a number of disciplines is the use of the third person, often in passive voice, which renders the researcher invisible, giving the impression of an 'objective', dispassionate stance. The use of a first-person active voice in research presentation is now supported by ample precedent and theoretical debate (Onn, 1998), and the contribution of postpositivist and poststructuralist analysis, particularly feminist epistemology, has meant that the 'objective' researcher has been revealed to be a myth (Alcott & Potter, 1993; Guba, 1990; Lather, 1991; Reason, 1988; Schwandt, 1990).

In action research the researcher is also 'the researched' (Wadsworth, 1998). This requires the researcher to account for the way in which the research both shapes and is shaped by them, not just because they conduct it but because they *are* it (Sumara & Carson, 1997). Epistemologically it is simply not consistent to write a text which does not bear the traces of its author (Lincoln & Denzin, 2000). How did you confront this challenge, MCR?

MCR: I found it quite artificial to separate my voice as writer and researcher from the action research process and the findings. The centrality of reflection itself made this separation impossible. While some action researchers revert to the use of third person in some chapters, such as the introduction or conclusions, I maintained first person throughout. I'll read from my thesis conclusion to illustrate:

> "For me, as teacher, the research has evoked significant growth. Aside from the tangible changes in teaching approach … a number of more subtle changes have occurred. The research has necessitated my conscious 'letting go' of teacher control and centrality in the learning process … to step back and recognise the importance of explicitly acknowledging the breadth of authentic support structures which are important for lifelong and non-institutionally-based learning and fostering students' help-seeking strategies."

CRK: I also made my presence as researcher explicit from the outset of my thesis. As action research (and, indeed, any research) is inevitably formed and influenced by the researcher's values, attitudes and beliefs, I saw it as important to articulate these. After all, situations do not just happen; they are historically and temporally directed by the intentionality of the participants (Clandinin & Connelly, 1994, p. 417). In the second chapter of my thesis, titled 'Positioning the researcher: The constructing of an activist identity', I made my subjective position explicit and articulated the influences that led to my chosen research:

> "Embarking on research within the paradigm of humanistic inquiry in which social ecology is embedded meant that from the outset I was required to reflect on personal sources of my passion for my chosen research area. This process itself was revealing as it allowed me to take a particular perspective on my life and identify a 'path' that had led me to my (activist) interest in demystifying economics and making a

difference in the world … This chapter tracks the sources of my framing of such an activist intention, identifying major family and cultural influences as well as the influence of discourses of adult education, co-counselling, living in an intentional community and Heart Politics."

Such exploration would seem to be an essential aspect of reflexivity (Gergen & Gergen, 2000), as the researcher/writer exposes their own historical and geographical situation, their personal investment in the research and the biases they bring to the project.

MCR: Yes, and I'm sure you'd agree that action research theses can successfully draw on the research traditions of personal narrative (Ellis & Bochner, 2000) and self-research (Bullough & Pinnegar, 2001), within which subjectivity is 'the basis of researchers making a distinctive contribution, one that results from the unique configuration of their personal qualities joined to the data they have collected' (Peshkin, 1988, p. 18). In fact, personal narrative can enhance the relevance and impact of the research, allowing readers 'to feel the moral dilemmas, think with our story instead of about it, join actively in the decision points … and consider how their own lives can be made a story worth telling' (Ellis & Bochner, 2000, p. 735).

CRK: This idea of using reflexivity within personal narrative is illustrated in this excerpt from the second chapter from my thesis:

"When I reflect on that time in my life [dropping out of a prestigious coursework Masters of Economics at the age of 24], it is clear to me now that I was subjected first-hand to the very same alienating experience of that dehumanised, mechanistic, value-absent ideology that has provided the core motivation for this thesis. Despite my inexperience, my lack of training in critical analysis, my devotion to fulfilling my father's (and others') expectations, I wonder if at some level I recognised that there was something seriously wrong with a social science that seemed so devoid of humanity, spirit, ethics and justice."

MCR: I too defined my position as both researcher and teacher up front in my introduction, and made my values and beliefs very explicit. This helped set the tone of reflexivity throughout my thesis:

"In my approach to both my research and my teaching I firmly identify as a constructivist. I believe that we can only 'know' through interaction with the world … I have a strong passion for learning and change. I tend to challenge existing practices and to strive constantly towards improvement … I view our social existence in the world as highly complex and … challenge the capacity of traditional research to adequately address many social problems."

I also structured reflexivity into my thesis through the device of a brief section at the end of each chapter titled 'Stepping Back and Looking Forward,' which enabled me to reflect on the chapter and outline how this drove the research forward into the following research cycle.

CRK: I presented my iterative reflexive process through the use of different 'voices', similar to Winter's (1989) concept of the 'plural text', as explained in the following extract from Chapter 6 of my thesis:

"The three voices are: first, a relatively 'neutral' reporting voice that relays the 'facts' of what happened; second, the 'reflective practitioner', the voice I used in conversation with the students demonstrating my reflective practice at the time, informed by the requirements of critical action research and supported by a critical community of peers; and the third voice, the 'critical reflector', offers a 'commentary' on the sometimes naïve voice of the reflective practitioner from a vantage point that names the assumptions made and reflects on some of the silences and absences in the narrative."

NARRATOR: This connection between reflexivity and narrative leads us into the next scene, which highlights the importance of representing the unfolding research story within the writing process.

– Curtain –

Scene 2: in which the thesis stays true to the narrative

The curtain rises. The backdrop of grey blocks and garden seat remain, but the reflective pond has been replaced by a semi-circle of listeners seated on the ground at the feet of the characters.

NARRATOR: All research is a form of storytelling (House, 1994), although traditionally researchers shy away from using the term 'story' given its connotations of unreliability or lack of rigour. Let us see what our protagonists have to say on this subject.

CRK: I would argue that there is no more appropriate approach to understanding action research than to see it as an unfolding narrative. An action research endeavour *is* the story of individual and/ or group change: change in practices, beliefs and assumptions. Personal narrative and the notion of research as story repositions the reader as an active and vicarious co-participant in the research (Ellis & Bochner, 2000).

MCR: Yes, I agree. Winter et al. (2000, p. 36) have, in fact, stated that one of the important criteria for a 'quality' PhD is to 'tell a compelling story'.

CRK: I would suggest that documenting the cycles of planning, acting, observing and reflecting should be done iteratively since each cycle of the research is only understandable in terms of the systematic and self-critical learning gained through previous cycles.

MCR: Wanting to remain true to the story of my research, I presented the chapters of my thesis in the same chronological order as the research itself. I did not have separate chapters covering the literature review, the methodology or the data analysis. Instead I allowed the research process to unfold for the reader, reinforcing the notion of research as personal, professional, methodological and theoretical 'journey'. What was your experience, CRK?

CRK: I also utilized a chronological format, finding that without staying true to the changes that I experienced during the research process, I could not demonstrate the emergent nature of that process, which cycle after cycle of reflection produced. I reflected at the conclusion of my thesis:

> "The very nature of action research is an unfolding and emergent process, inevitably because of the reflection that is embedded within it. The thesis is therefore framed in a way that mirrors the unfolding research journey ... Reflection has permeated every stage and has emerged as a primary focus of the research itself. It seems to me that action research itself invites this—what emerges is what needs to be researched. In a way, this reflects a direct antidote to positivism and its ontology of prediction and control. Engaging the spirit of action research almost demands a letting go of having things go a particular way."

MCR: I believe that this narrative approach also supports validity since it consciously works against camouflaging or failing to acknowledge pragmatic realities, iterative learning and the inevitable weaknesses that frequently remain unacknowledged in traditional research presentation. In my research I explicitly acknowledged that action research represents a journey down many roads, some of which inevitably prove to be dead ends. Sometimes these mistaken paths have been taken for justifiable reasons, while others may be traversed through simple error or mistaken assumptions and beliefs.

CRK: I agree. In conventional research there is a culture of leaving these dead ends unacknowledged— we don't hear about the mistakes that often lead to significant rethinking or insight. In action research, however, these apparent 'dead ends' are a critical part of the learning, change and theory development process. As highlighted in Scene 1, reflexivity permits us to reveal such weaknesses or 'untruths' and requires us to 'own up' to our responsibility in the knowledge-construction process (Hall, 1996). Mellor (2001), for instance, refers to his 'messy project' (p. 465) as an 'honesty trail' (p. 479).

MCR: So for us, a chronological approach to thesis presentation supports the researcher's acknowledgment of this iterative and unfolding learning process and represents a more rigorous and truthful presentation of how the research proceeds.

NARRATOR: This reference to research as a journey is an example of how metaphor can be used productively and imaginatively to enhance understanding. This leads us nicely into the next scene.

– Curtain –

Scene 3: in which metaphor dresses up the thesis

The scene is identical, but the characters have changed from their plain clothes into travellers' costumes, complete with suitcases, cameras, binoculars, maps, guidebooks, hats and walking boots.

NARRATOR: As Mason Cooley once said, 'Clothes make a statement. Costumes tell a story' (Cooley, 1993). The use of metaphors in a thesis is like the wearing of costumes in a play—they bring meaning to the story, meaning that is generated through the image with more efficiency than the literal relaying of information.

CRK: Various writers have explored the use of metaphor and its integral role in the generation of meaning and the construction of social and political reality (for instance, Hovelynck, 1998; Lakoff & Johnson, 1980; Ortony, 1979; Taylor, 1984). In fact, metaphors are among our principal vehicles for understanding, permeating communication and perception at individual, cultural and societal levels (Mignot, 2000). Yet metaphor is often perceived as 'unscientific, untrustworthy, a linguistic embellishment' (Mignot, 2000, p. 518), arguments which Lakoff and Johnson (1980) refer to as the 'myths of objectivism and subjectivism'. Metaphor can provide not only a richer description of research as experienced by the researcher(s) but also allows a deeper exploration of the meanings generated by collaborating participants. You used metaphor to good effect in your thesis, MCR.

MCR: Yes, I found that metaphor provided a powerful vehicle for portraying the 'journey', the 'adventure', the 'saga' that was my action research process. For me the cycles of personal engagement over time represented a personal and professional pilgrimage through both familiar and unfamiliar terrain. The title of my thesis, 'Mapping the complexity of computer learning: Journeying beyond teaching for computer competency to facilitating computer capability', established the metaphor from the beginning. I also used my chapter headings to demonstrate the unfolding research journey:

- Charting the context of research and practice (Chapter 1);
- Journey origins and point of departure (Chapter 2);
- Embracing reflection as navigation: Postcards from cycle 1 (Chapter 3);
- Encountering a theoretical bridge: Crossing to a metacognitive approach (Chapter 4);
- Integrating metacognition: Planning for cycle 2 (Chapter 5);
- The journey continues: Postcards from cycle 2 (Chapter 6);
- Encountering turbulence: Postcards from cycle 3 (Chapter 7);
- Complexity as window on the research (Chapter 8); and
- Journey ending as journey beginning (Chapter 9).

I continued to use the journeying metaphor as part of my reflexivity, exemplified by the following extract from my final chapter:

"My research has involved me challenging my expectations and re-designing the maps which I brought to my initially envisaged itinerary. My thesis charts my 'discoveries' and individual and cultural encounters. It provides a 'diary' of my changes in direction and the influence of my travels on my own assumptions."

CRK: While I described my research as a journey I did not use metaphor explicitly to frame my thesis structure. I wish I had! I wonder if, for many academics, constructing research as 'journey' would be considered unacceptable, since the thesis is generally perceived primarily as an 'argument'?

MCR: This is likely to be the case for many supervisors. However, I believe such a perception is inconsistent with the epistemic foundations of action research. Action research is *not* about testing preconceived hypotheses or generalizing about research 'findings'. It is about depicting the context, change processes, resultant learning and theorizing of individuals or groups in a process of mutual change and inquiry. Metaphor is like a costume—it enhances meaning through imagery and colour. The author (actor) can dress her argument in a way that indicates the meaning of the process to her. Using the play metaphor has clothed this otherwise conventional journal article in a way that (we hope) brings the arguments we are making alive to our imagined audience.

NARRATOR: Let's move now to the final scene of this act, a scene in which our protagonists make a case for presenting the literature throughout the thesis rather than in the single 'literature review' chapter, as demanded by the conventional five-chapter structure.

– Curtain –

Scene 4: in which literature is woven throughout the thesis

The curtain rises to a scene of movement. The hitherto passive listeners, who have been seated at the feet of the storytellers, join together with MCR and CRK in a process of dismantling the five large blocks (which are now revealed to be made up of smaller blocks), taking the ribbons that make up the spirals and interweaving them among the blocks to produce an impression of flow and harmony.

CRK: Taking a chronological or narrative approach to thesis writing has implications for the presentation of literature and theory. In conventional research the literature review aims to build a theoretical foundation upon which issues are identified as worth researching (Perry, 1994). However, in action research the issues pursued are those which arise from a cluster of problems of mutual concern and consequence to the researcher(s) and collaborators (Kemmis & McTaggart, 1988).

MCR: This means that in an action research thesis, the explanation of the origin of the research and the justification for its need lie not in the literature but in the personal narrative of the participant researchers. Literature is more important in shaping the ongoing *development* of action research (Green, 1999) than informing its initial foundation or relating its findings to other research.

CRK: In conventional thesis formats, the literature review is presented up front in its entirety, implying that all the literature was familiar to the researcher at the beginning of the research. This is usually a misrepresentation of the research process. The requirement to present an up-to-date literature review at the time of submission itself necessitates that the review is in constant flux until submission. Moreover, it is not humanly possible to expect that a researcher, no matter how familiar they are with their disciplinary context, will have covered all relevant literature *before* they begin their research.

MCR: Action researchers seek theory to partially answer their questions, to challenge their assumptions, to widen their perspectives and to inform their practice. Green (cited in Winter et al., 2000) argues that relevant literature cannot be 'predetermined' and that quality action research will show how the writer has engaged with the literature and how this has challenged their views. For this reason there is a good case for presenting the literature as part of the cyclical structure of the research and thesis, situating it temporally in the action research cycles themselves. A similar recommendation has been made by Dick (1993, 2000), who recommended that literature be reported adjacent to the relevant findings. In another paper, Green (1999) notes the value of sharing with the reader the excitement experienced by the researcher in encountering new and challenging literature.

CRK: It is also relevant to note that literature encountered throughout the research will either support the researcher's current actions or challenge their perspectives, assumptions or approaches. As Brewer and Hunter (1989, p. 18) note, 'evidence from two sources is intuitively more persuasive than evidence from one'. If 'evidence' is interpreted as encompassing prior research, then the discovery of research which supports one's own interpretations might be seen as 'triangulating' the data, but only where such research was not known to the researcher beforehand. Thus it can be valuable to explicitly acknowledge any literature that has influenced the research process or its interpretation *as it is encountered* in the process. How did you tackle this issue of literature presentation, MCR?

MCR: I consciously presented literature iteratively and chronologically throughout my thesis. For instance, in Chapter 4, I describe a transition that occurred in the research, prompted by encountering a body of literature which acted as a new 'road map'. I not only outline this literature at that point in the thesis, but I include reflections on the literature, its relationship to the first cycle and how, as a researcher, I perceived its value in shaping my second cycle. Towards the end of my candidature, I embraced a fresh body of literature, complexity theory (Waldrop, 1992) that assisted me in 'making sense' of my data and experiences. I chose not to present this literature until Chapter 8; to do otherwise would have detracted from the integrity of my research presentation, implying a theoretical window on the research I did not hold at the time. How did you justify your literature approach, CRK?

CRK: I'll quote from my introduction, where I argued for this approach to literature in terms of honouring the unfolding nature of my research:

> "The thesis is framed in a way that reflects the emergent process that was produced through conducting action research … Literature is woven through the developing argument, reflecting how my reading informed different stages of the research process … Th[e] unfolding process of research, reflection and insight leading to further research and reflection provides the framework for structuring the thesis."

NARRATOR: Our protagonists have now finished presenting their case for a different sort of thesis presentation consistent with the spirit and epistemology of action research. Please give them a big round of applause as they leave the stage.

In our final act we will hear how their approaches to thesis writing were greeted by their examiners.

– Curtain –

Act III

Enter the critics!

The curtain rises to darkness. The narrator enters stage left, illumined by a spotlight.

NARRATOR: One of the objections supervisors are likely to raise against adopting these less conventional approaches to thesis writing is the negative response of examiners, especially those unfamiliar with action research. Let's find out from the examiners of these two theses what their responses were.[4]

Tell me, Dr. A., what do you think of the format adopted by MCR?

Another spotlight lights up Dr. A., MCR's first examiner, standing stage right.

Dr. A.: The candidate makes a persuasive argument for the format of the report and then follows this with a superb demonstration of why her initial decision was appropriate.

NARRATOR: And you, Dr. B.?

Spotlight on Dr. A. fades and Dr. B. is lit by a spotlight centre stage.

Dr. B.: The metaphor of a journey integrates the parts of the thesis in a complete story. This structure avoids an artificially neat intellectual edifice, which would disguise the messy and brilliant process of research.

NARRATOR: Overall, MCR's examiners were well satisfied with her thesis, recommending it for an outstanding thesis award. CRK's thesis, however, received a more mixed reception. Dr. C., how did you find the structure of this thesis?

Dr. C.: The thesis had a linear quality to it while capturing the dynamic dialectic of critical reflection … I kept reading to find the research questions and realized they were truly emergent … the research questions, placed where they were, was like an 'aha experience'.

NARRATOR: And you, Dr. D., how do you respond to its weaving and dynamic quality?

Dr. D.: … it is striking in the way the thesis exemplifies the critical reflexivity it sets out to explore … It continually weaves together its analytic threads in a most convincing way … [There] is a good, progressive unfolding of the research, first opening up themes and then deepening the analysis.

NARRATOR: So now to you, Dr. E. I believe you were irritated by the method, interpreting it as sloppy and lacking in rigour.

Dr. E.: I found the way literature was treated in the thesis to be most unsatisfactory. For instance, there was no definition or discussion of the nature of ideology until Chapter 3, and only a superficial discussion of reflection in that chapter.

NARRATOR: And yet the candidate returned to a more detailed discussion of critical reflection in Chapter 8, in keeping with the emergent nature of the research process, which she foreshadowed in her introduction. The candidate responded in her defence that '[Dr. E.'s] reading of … the whole thesis seemed partial and fragmented rather than integrated and holistic. He did not seem to be aware of the connections that were being made throughout and the way the thesis was crafted as a whole integrated entity'. Now let us take an example where your perceptions were very different from those of Dr. D.— the use of the different 'voices' in Chapter 6 (described in Act II, Scene 1).

Dr. E.: I found this device problematic and thought that the voices were used inconsistently and selectively with no explanation for the choices made.

Dr. D.: I beg to differ, Dr. E. The candidate made her rationale very clear at the beginning of the chapter. I thought her use of this strategy was impressive, very effective and a creative and practical resolution of a key difficulty of practitioner-based research.

The light fades on all examiners.

NARRATOR: Ultimately CRK was able to mount a successful defence against Dr. E.'s criticisms, using the comments from the other two examiners and the support of her supervisor to substantiate her claims.

Our protagonists would argue that the most effective ways to overcome potential examiner resistance are to make strong justification for the presentation format from the outset *and* to choose examiners sympathetic to action research and unconventional formats. Many examiners *do* appreciate freshness and originality, not only in thought and expression but also in presentation. While there is always the risk of an unsympathetic examiner, by explicitly structuring the thesis consistent with the epistemological, methodological and ethical aspects of action research, postgraduate students can provide a clear and rigorous justification for their choices.

– Curtain –

Curtain call

The narrator comes to the front of the stage in front of the curtain to converse with the audience.

NARRATOR: Now that we have come to the end of our performance, it is time to take stock and reflect on what has arisen here tonight, in the spirit of a reflexive engagement with our practice. How might these different writing approaches contribute to improved action research practice? Our protagonists would suggest that they contribute to greater honesty and authenticity in the research process; honour the reflective and iterative processes at the heart of action research; demonstrate heightened awareness of self for both researcher and collaborators; highlight the importance of contextual influences; and support increased engagement with complexity at personal, inter-personal and global levels. Furthermore, they would argue that encouraging honest reporting of research and the deep reflection it engenders builds competencies for all those engaging in research.

However, as our play has shown, flying in the face of academic convention is not for the fainthearted. If you are a PhD student, you may wish to reflect on whether you would consider taking an alternative approach to writing up your research. Is your writing practice consistent with the way your research proceeded? Have you been able to incorporate your own reflective process and that of your collaborators? To what extent has your perspective changed throughout your research process, and can you represent that in your writing? How important is it to you to record the research *process* as much as the outcomes or results? How open is your supervisor to a different writing format? Does your research context lend itself to this sort of writing? What would be the main constraints for you in adopting such an approach? How might conforming to convention deaden your creativity? And are the risks worth taking in terms of what you might receive at the hands of power?

Those of you who supervise action research students will be aware of the problems of exposing students' work to unsympathetic examiners. One possible risk is that the thesis becomes too 'wordy,' with too much narrative detail at the expense of clarity and strong theoretical argument. Examiners may not appreciate the 'suspense format,' feeling that they are labouring up an incline to reach the punchline (Brown, 1994) or they may be surprised by the introduction of new ideas late in the thesis. Another risk is that students over-identify with their own stories and indulge in too much 'confessional narrative'. As supervisors you might consider: how can I help my student(s) recognize what is worth reporting in their dissertations? How can I help them distinguish authentic inquiry and understanding from indulgent navel gazing? How can I assist in identifying key turning points in the narrative rather than giving 'blow-by-blow' descriptions?

CRK and MCR enter and stand beside the narrator.

To conclude, we are not suggesting that the approaches outlined here are essential for students writing action research theses. We certainly do not want to give the impression that this presentational form becomes a 'new potential orthodoxy' (to quote one of our reviewers). We would, however, wholeheartedly encourage you as students and supervisors to experiment with any form that seems analogically appropriate to your research material, being always careful to be aware of how the form you use might preclude certain perspectives and how the form itself may constrain your interpretations. For instance, attempting to maintain coherence within a particular chosen metaphor may lead to being too identified with the metaphor itself and prevent disconfirming 'truths' being voiced. We found this an interesting dilemma in re-presenting our article as performance. Did we sacrifice too much by being too enamoured with the form in which we presented our arguments? We found ourselves debating and considering the balance required to walk such a tightrope. Ultimately, we leave it to you, our audience, to judge how well we have achieved this balance.

As a parting word, in the true spirit of action research, we would encourage a 'meta-reflection' on the form of presentation as well as the substance of the research itself. Above all, strive to be simultaneously playful and rigorously reflective. Farewell for now, and we hope to meet some of you on your own adventurous journeying.

All bow. Applause.

– Curtain –

Notes

1.   We are indebted to the reviewers of our original submission, who inspired us to 'walk our talk' and produce a more creative exposition of our ideas. We also acknowledge and appreciate the editors of *Action Research*, who are prepared to support innovative writing and thus fly in the face of convention themselves.
2.   MCR stands for 'Meta Cognitive Renata' and CRK is 'Critical Reflection Kath'. The names represent our key theoretical interests (and who we were) at the time we were writing up our PhD dissertations.
3.   In response to a request from a reviewer of our original submission, we have introduced our individual projects through the lens of 'first-, second- and third-person' research practice as articulated by Bradbury and Reason (2001, p. 449). First-person research suggests the impact of the research on the researcher herself (the 'I'); reflections on practice as well as inner changes that occur through reflection and action. Second-person research is how the participants/partners in the research (the 'you') are influenced and changed through the process. Finally, third-person research encompasses the implications of the research for a broader world beyond the immediate locus of action (the 'they').
4.   Examiners' responses are either taken directly from their reports or paraphrased.

References

Alcott, L., & Potter, E. (Eds.). (1993). *Feminist epistemologies*. New York: Routledge.
Altrichter, H., Kemmis, S. W., McTaggart, R., & Zuber-Skerritt, O. (1991). Defining, confining or refining action research? In O. Zuber-Skerritt (Ed.), *Action research for change and development* (pp. 13–20). Aldershot, Hants: Gower.
Bradbury, H., & Reason, P. (2001). Conclusion: Broadening the bandwidth of validity: Issues and choice-points for improving the quality of action research. In P. Reason & H. Bradbury (Eds.), *Handbook of action research: Participative inquiry and practice* (pp. 447–455). London: Sage.
Brewer, J., & Hunter, A. (1989). *Multimethod research: A synthesis of styles*. Newbury Park, CA: Sage.
Brown, R. (1994). The 'big picture' about managing writing. In O. Zuber-Skerritt & Y. Ryan (Eds.), *Quality in postgraduate education* (pp. 90–109). London: Kogan Page.
Bullough, R., & Pinnegar, S. (2001). Guidelines for quality in autobiographical forms of self-study. *Educational Researcher*, *30*(3), 13–22.
Carr, W., & Kemmis, S. (1990). *Becoming critical: Education, knowledge and action research*. Geelong: Deakin University.
Carson, T. R. (1997). Reflection and its resistances: Teacher education as a living practice. In T. Carson & D. Sumara (Eds.), *Action research as living practice* (pp. 77–91). New York: Peter Lang.
Clandinin, D. J., & Connelly, F. M. (1994). Personal experience methods. In N. K. Denzin & Y. S. Lincoln (Eds.), *Handbook of qualitative research* (pp. 413–427). Thousand Oaks, CA: Sage.

Cooley, M. (1993). *City aphorisms*. New York: Eleventh Selection. Quote retrieved 23 May 2005 from http://www.bartleby.com/66/29/13529.html

Creswell, J. (2003). *Research design: Qualitative, quantitative and mixed methods approaches*. Thousand Oaks, CA: Sage.

Denzin, N. (2000). The art and politics of interpretation. In N. Denzin & Y. Lincoln (Eds.), *Handbook of qualitative research* (pp. 500–515). Thousand Oaks: Sage.

Denzin, N., & Lincoln, Y. (2000). *Handbook of qualitative research* (2nd ed.). Thousand Oaks, CA: Sage.

Dick, B. (1993). *You want to do an action research thesis: How to conduct and report action research*. Retrieved 1 June 2000 from: http://www.scu.edu.au/schools/gcm/ar/art/arthesis.html

Dick, B. (2000). *Approaching an action research thesis: An overview*. Retrieved 1 July 2000 from: http://www.scu.edu.au/schools/gem/ar/arp/phd.html

Dick, B. (2002). Postgraduate programs using action research. *The Learning Organization, 9*(4), 159–170.

Ellis, C., & Bochner, A. (2000). Autoethnography, personal narrative, reflexivity: Researcher as subject. In N. K. Denzin & Y. S. Lincoln (Eds.), *Handbook of qualitative research* (pp. 733–768). Thousand Oaks, CA: Sage.

Fisher, K. (2000). A wealth of notions: *Reflective engagement in the emancipatory teaching and learning of economics*. Unpublished PhD, University of Western Sydney, Richmond.

Fisher, K. (2003a). Activism in the face of globalisation: Lessons from emancipatory action research. *Action Learning and Action Research Journal, 8*(2), 3–25.

Fisher, K. (2003b). Demystifying critical reflection: Defining criteria for assessment. *HERD: Higher Education Research and Development, 22*(3), 318–335.

Gergen, M. M., & Gergen, K. J. (2000). Qualitative inquiry: Tensions and transformations. In N. K. Denzin & Y. S. Lincoln (Eds.), *Handbook of qualitative research* (pp. 1025–1046). Thousand Oaks, CA: Sage.

Green, K. (1999). Defining the field of literature in action research: A personal approach. *Educational Action Research, 7*(1), 105–124.

Grundy, S. (1982). Three modes of action research. *Curriculum Perspectives, 2*(3), 23–34.

Guba, E. C. (1990). The alternative paradigm dialog. In E. C. Guba (Ed.), *The paradigm dialog* (pp. 17–27). Newbury Park, CA: Sage.

Hall, S. (1996). Reflexivity in emancipatory action research: Illustrating the researcher's constitutiveness. In O. Zuber-Skerritt (Ed.), *New directions in action research* (pp. 28–40). London: Falmer Press.

Heron, J. (1996). *Feeling and personhood: Psychology in another key*. London: Sage.

Heron, J., & Reason, P. (2001). The practice of co-operative inquiry: Research 'with' rather than 'on' people. In P. Reason & H. Bradbury (Eds.), *Handbook of action research: Participative inquiry and practice* (pp. 179–188). London: Sage.

House, E. R. (1994). Integrating the quantitative and qualitative. In C. S. Reichardt & S. Rallis (Eds.), *The qualitative-quantitative debate: New perspectives* (pp. 13–22). San Francisco, CA: Jossey-Bass.

Hovelynck, J. (1998). Facilitating experiential learning as a process of metaphor development. *The Journal of Experiential Education, 21*(1), 6–13.

Hughes, J., Denley, P. & Whitehead, J. (1998). How do we make sense of the process of legitimizing an educational action research thesis for the award of a Ph.D.? A contribution to educational theory. *Educational Action Research, 6* (3), 427–451.

Kemmis, S. (1996). Emancipatory aspirations in a postmodern era. *Curriculum Studies, 3*(2), 133–168.

Kemmis, S., & McTaggart, R. (1988). *The action research planner*. Geelong, Victoria: Deakin University Press.

Kemmis, S., & McTaggart, R. (2000). Participatory action research. In N. K. Denzin & Y. S. Lincoln (Eds.), *Handbook of qualitative research* (pp. 567–605). Thousand Oaks, CA: Sage.

Koro-Ljungberg, M. (2004). Impossibilities of reconciliation: Validity in mixed theory projects. *Qualitative Inquiry, 10*(4), 601–621.

Lakoff, G., & Johnson, M. (1980). *Metaphors we live by*. London: University of Chicago Press.

Lather, P. (1991). *Getting smart: Feminist research and pedagogy with/in the postmodern*. New York: Routledge.

Lau, F. (1999). Toward a framework for action research in information systems studies. *Information Technology and People, 12*(2), 148–175.

Lincoln, Y. S., & Denzin, N. K. (2000). The seventh moment: Out of the past. In N. K. Denzin & Y. S. Lincoln (Eds.), *Handbook of qualitative research* (pp. 1047–1065). Thousand Oaks, CA: Sage.

Mellor, N. (2001). Messy method: The unfolding story. *Educational Action Research, 9*(3), 465–484.

Mignot, P. (2000). Metaphor: A paradigm for practice-based research into 'career'. *British Journal of Guidance and Counselling, 28*(4), 515–531.

Onn, K. W. (1998). *An action research study on project management in an engineering organisation in Singapore*. Unpublished PhD, University of South Australia.

Ortony, A. (Ed.). (1979). *Metaphor and thought*. London: Cambridge University Press.

Passfield, R. (2001). Action learning for personal and organisational transformation. In S. Sankaran, B. Dick, R. Passfield & P. Swepson (Eds.), *Effective change management using action learning and action research: Concepts, frameworks, processes, applications* (pp. 39–44). Lismore: Southern Cross University Press.

Perry, C. (1994). *A structured approach to presenting PhD theses: Notes for candidates and their supervisors*. Paper presented at the Australian and New Zealand Doctoral Consortium, University of Sydney. http://www.scu.edu.au/schools/sawd/arr/arth/cperry.html

Peshkin, A. (1988). In search of subjectivity: One's own. *Educational Researcher*, October, 17–21.

Phelps, R. (2002). *Mapping the complexity of computer learning: Journeying beyond teaching for computer competence to facilitating computer capability*. Unpublished PhD, Southern Cross University, Lismore.

Phelps, R., & Ellis, A. (2002a, 6 December). *Helping students to help themselves: Case studies from a metacognitive approach to computer learning and teaching*. Paper presented at the International Conference on Computers in Education (ICCE 2002), Auckland, New Zealand. http://icce2002.massey.ac.nz/

Phelps, R., & Ellis, A. (2002b, 11–13 July). *A metacognitive approach to computer education for teachers: Combining theory and practice for computer capability*. Paper presented at the Linking Learners: Australian Computers in Education Conference (ACEC2002), Hobart, Tasmania. http://www.pa.ash.org.au/acec2002/

Phelps, R., & Ellis, A. (2002c, 8–11 December). *Overcoming computer anxiety through reflection on attribution*. Paper presented at the Winds of Change in the Sea of Learning: Charting the Course of Digital Education: Australian Society for Computers in Learning in Tertiary Education (ASCILITE) 2002, Auckland, NZ. http://www.unitec.ac.nz/ascilite/

Reason, P. (Ed.). (1988). *Human inquiry in action: Developments in new paradigm research*. London: Sage.

Reason, P., & Bradbury, H. (2001). *Handbook of action research: Participative inquiry and practice*. London: Sage.

Rudestam, K. E., & Newton, R. R. (1992). *Surviving your dissertation: A comprehensive guide to content and process*. Newbury Park, CA: Sage.

Schwandt, T. R. (1990). Paths to inquiry in the social disciplines: Scientific, constructivist and critical theory methodologies. In E. C. Guba (Ed.), *The paradigm dialog* (pp. 258–278). Newbury Park, CA: Sage.

Sumara, D., & Carson, T. R. (1997). Reconceptualizing action research as living practice. In T. Carson & D. Sumara (Eds.), *Action research as living practice* (pp. xiii–xxxv). New York: Peter Lang.

Taylor, W. (Ed.). (1984). *Metaphors of education*. London: Heinemann.

Torbert, W. (1991). *The power of balance: Transforming self, society, and scientific inquiry*. Newbury Park, CA: Sage.

Van Wagenen, R. K. (1991). *Writing a thesis: Substance and style*. Englewood Cliffs, NJ: Prentice Hall.

Wadsworth, Y. (1998). What is participatory action research? *Action Research International*. http://www.scu.edu.au/schools/gcm/ar/ari/p-ywadsworth98.html Waldrop, M. (1992). *Complexity: The emerging science at the edge of order and chaos*. London: Penguin.

Winter, R. (1989). *Learning from experience: Principles and practice in action research*. London: Falmer Press.

Winter, R., Griffiths, M., & Green, K. (2000). The 'academic' qualities of practice: What are the criteria for a practice-based PhD? *Studies in Higher Education, 25*(1), 25–37.

Zuber-Skerritt, O. (1996). Introduction: New directions in action research. In O. Zuber-Skerritt (Ed.), *New directions in action research* (pp. 3–12). London: Falmer Press.

Zuber-Skerritt, O., & Perry, C. (2002). Action research within organisations and university thesis writing. *The Learning Organization, 9*(4), 171–179.

CHAPTER 19

Narrative Study in the Classroom— Knowing What Was, What Is, and What Could Be[1]

Jessica Blanchard

I stumble into the second nine weeks carrying the weight of first quarter's baggage. Class sizes, curriculum requirements, systemic pressures, assumptions about students, about myself, and the uneasy feeling that maybe I'm just not cut out for this anymore. If only I could off-load this pressure, these worries and assumptions, like a sack of used clothes in a Good Will box. I've had my use of them. I don't want them anymore. Let someone else take them. Or not. Just as long as I can drop my load and leave it all behind.

But it doesn't happen that way.

Mid-August—Identifying Bubble Kids via Measure of Academic Progress

I start the year in a new position teaching READ 180, a Scholastic reading intervention program geared toward students our principal refers to as "bubble kids." Her expressed assumption is that "bubble kids" have the ability and know-how to read but are out of practice and so do not demonstrate proficiency in reading as measured by standardized reading assessments. My immediate task is to identify bubble kids and move them into the READ 180 class.

I look up students' scores and schedules. I look up parent-guardian contact information and make calls. I leave messages and return messages. I explain to hesitant parents and guardians why enrolling their children in the reading class is a good idea. I assert that yes, they can make this decision for their children. When they don't and instead tell me it's up to their children to decide, I track down students directly and try to convince them to be in the class. A few kids say yes, most say no. I write and hand deliver letters to students whose phone numbers are disconnected or whose parents' voice mailboxes are too full to receive one more call. Then I track these same students down and bug them to bring their letters back because they don't. I spin my wheels and my words trying to fill seats. And yet, not one class is full.

But I know better.

I know this is best.

Our principal sees me in the hall. She asks, "How's it coming getting those classes filled up?"
I smile and say, "I'm working on it." I begin to avoid her in the halls.

September—Sharing Stories and Silence with Strangers

It feels awkward in our classroom. Eighty-two minutes. This is the length of time I spend with students each period as we say our names and write letters of introduction, knowing we will only write what we feel comfortable sharing with strangers.

This is what we are. Strangers.

I don't know how soon it will be before I have enough students to start the crucial induction phase of "the program." I am anxious to start and get it over with. I feel like I'm about to take an exam I didn't prepare adequately for and so will fail. My anxiety builds. I pull out the short stories I know so well. I find comfort in their familiarity. We read together and discuss the whos and whats and whys of it all. We write about our experiences, our connections and disconnections to the text. I do my best to engage students in conversation, to prompt them to share their ideas and respond to one another. Sometimes they speak, but in bits and pieces. I am patient. I wait. They wait, too. They wait for me to forget about them and move on, but I don't. Instead I restate, reprompt, reread, retry. I want to hear what they think and have to say. I want them to listen to one another and to respond to each other. I tell them so.

Their eyes get big and they stare at me, at each other, at strangers.

I continue the tedious cycle of enrolling students in class. New students come in every few days, their presence both a threat and a welcome to those who want or need someone else to share my attention with, to shift my focus. An unstable weirdness permeates the air in our classroom. I feel it. Do the kids? What's next and for how long?

One day in mid-September our principal rushes by me on her way to somewhere else and asks me if I'm still enrolling students. I tell her it's few and far between, considering scheduling conflicts, parent-guardian refusals, and non-responses. She raises her hands and says, "We're good. Don't worry about enrolling students anymore."

Relief consumes me. The time has come. It's do or die. I'm ready for it.

READ 180 Mantra—"Teach With Fidelity" and "Stay On Model"

The program comes with a video asserting that students who presumably struggle with reading but who work within the program's structured model will do a "180" by improving their reading skills and thus, learn to enjoy the act of reading. The program also comes with a manual dedicated to the first three weeks of instruction. It's during this initial three-week period that I am supposed to show this video to students and teach follow-up lessons designed to familiarize students with the rotation model. The rotation model is as follows:

> Whole Group Concept Introduction–10 min.→ Small Group Instruction w/Teacher to Reinforce Concept–25 min.→ Skills Building Lessons on Computer–25 min.→ Independent Reading–25 min.→ Whole Group Wrap-Up–5 min.→→→**Total 90 Minutes Every Day**

The program is designed and scripted for 90-minute classes. Our classes this year are 82 minutes long from bell to bell.

Our READ 180 director does not like this.

We're "off model" before we've even begun a lesson.

Being "off model" is taboo in the READ 180 world. I learned this during my first READ 180 training session, which happened to take place on the first day of summer vacation. Talk about taboo! I came to the training with at least twenty pounds of books and supplemental materials in my arms, all of which are part of the program, all of which we flipped through and highlighted and studied and discussed, all the while the director impressing upon us this mantra:

Teach with fidelity. If you don't teach with fidelity, you are off model. If you are off model, students will not have success.

The Book Tells Me What to Say and Do—How Hard Can It Be?

In our first-day-of-summer training session we learned that all we have to do to "teach with fidelity" and "stay on model" is follow the steps in the teacher's book. Each page is an explosion of words and color. Blue words tell me what to say and black words tell me when to say it. Pink words tell me what students should tell me or write down in their books after I tell them what the blue words tell me to tell them. Then there are more black words telling me which resource titles and page numbers to go to for students who don't tell me what the pink words say they should tell me. There are Skills Check pages and Professional Development pages, Timeline pages and Supplemental Lessons pages.

It was too much.

Overload.

My eyes glazed over and my thoughts drifted to summer vacation.

I didn't look at this book again, nor any accompanying materials, until our next READ 180 training session, which happened to take place on the last two days of summer vacation. Go figure.

We listened to our director remind us of the necessity for teaching on model and with fidelity. We listened to her speak of the implicit dangers in teaching off model and how doing so won't work. We studied the materials closer than before. We went to this page in this book and that page in the other book. We looked at a myriad of reports, comparing these ones here to different ones there.

I tried my best to remember what I am supposed to do.

If one report tells me A, B, and C, then I should look at a different report for 1, 2, and 3. After I ascertain the 1, 2, and 3, I should know the X, Y, and Z of any given student. But just to make sure, there are three more reports I should compare this to before making any final judgments.

So many reports. So much to remember. The director made it sound so easy in her soft Texan drawl. But I couldn't make sense of it all.

It was too much.

Overload.

My eyes glazed over and my thoughts drifted to how this was the fastest summer vacation to ever fly by.

Following the Script, Going through the Motions

So here I am, a month into the school year and I am just barely getting to the point where we will officially start the READ 180 program. The amount of information I have to remember overwhelms me. I turn to the "First Three Weeks" manual for guidance. It tells me what to do and say. It's simple. I just have to follow directions. Except I'm so preoccupied trying to "say" exactly what the book tells me that I come off like a bumbling robotic fool—unprepared, unintelligent, unnecessary. Anyone could do what I am doing, and with better ease, probably.

I show students their portion of what I've come to think of as the "brainwashing video." In it, a narrator informs her student-audience how students just like them used to struggle in reading, but now, after participating in the READ 180 program, enjoy reading and overall success in school. The video shows students working at the various rotation stations and in Whole Group with a teacher. It shows interview clips of students commenting on their increased reading skills ability and their increased sense of confidence and self-esteem.

It all sounds so easy.

I wonder about the students watching this video. Many are disgruntled because they are in this class instead of an elective class with their friends. Will the video convince them to give this class a shot? Will they buy into it? Or will they resist and rebel?

I do my best to augment the video by telling students that they will have lots of opportunities every day to practice and improve their reading skills and that I am here to support them in this endeavor. I tell them we all have a job to do and if we do it to the best of our ability, then we will all have success.

I am sincere when I say this. But I don't feel like I am at my best just yet. This video, these books, the script, the busyness of it all doesn't feel right. It feels unnatural, like I am trying to be somebody I'm not.

I don't like it.

It puts me on edge.

October—Succumbing to Pressure to "Teach With Fidelity" and "Stay On Model"—Losing Students and Myself in the Process

We move on to the first round of rotations. I forget I am a veteran teacher with experience and knowledge. Instead, I grip the manual in my hand like a life preserver. I move my eyes over the pages to see what I'm supposed to say and do next. I don't trust myself. I feel inadequate. As we move through the days, I lose my place in the book again and again. I forget to set the timer and so lose track of time. I lose my train of thought trying to get back on track. I lose my temper when students distract me from concentrating on what I am doing or trying to remember to do.

I lose it and yell at students. I yell at them for not taking this as seriously as I think they should. "Don't you want to improve?" I yell at them for talking to and distracting one another, which in turn distracts me. "Don't you want to raise your reading scores?" I yell at them for wasting time wasting time wasting time. "Don't you want to raise them so you can go back into your electives?"

Forget about teacher–student rapport. Forget about relationships and getting to know one another and learning about who we are as individuals and as a group. That doesn't matter—only the scores matter! Only the scores will prove whether or not students make gains in their reading proficiency!

I turn inward on myself. *What if students' scores don't show a rise in reading proficiency? Don't they know my job depends on it? Don't they understand???*

I tell myself that I don't understand students' seemingly apathetic mindset and behavior.

But really, I do.

Who am I to these students? Just another teacher telling them what they need, how they need it, and why. Just another teacher assuming I have to be heavy-handed, stern, strict, mean, just so they can't pull one over on me.

Our interactions begin on a presumption of failure. I ingrain this sense of failure further by unfairly placing the burden of the pressures I feel on the shoulders of students who I forget are as new to this as I am. I place upon them the burden of my assumptions that I can't trust them and so must protect myself by being emotionally, intellectually, and physically distant.

I forget they are not the same group of students from last year or the year before. They are a new group of students.

But I forget.

I forget we are still strangers.

In my forgetting, they react. And so do I.

October—Still Empty Seats

The READ 180 program cost thousands of dollars. Empty seats equal unused licenses. Unused licenses equal wasted dollars. Wasted dollars equal an unjustified teaching position. Uh oh! Why did I have to get picked to do this job?

The fact that a few students recently "tested out" or transferred to another school exacerbates my worries, as their absence means more empty seats. On the other hand, I like the fact that the classes are smaller. Having smaller class sizes allows me to provide students with greater opportunities for intense and focused one-to-one instruction, especially during small-group instruction where I work with only four or five students at a time. I really couldn't ask for a better situation than this.

Disempowered Teacher, Disempowered Students—A Recipe for Resistance

But in the thick of it all, I forget how lucky I am to have this opportunity to work so closely with students. Instead of working with students in ways that allow us to reveal who we are and what we're all about and to learn about each other's sense of being in relation to one another, our surroundings, and our work, I lose myself in the "rBook"—the teacher's edition of the student-version workbook. I pressure students and myself to think and speak and write what the blue and pink words say we should.

I try to make it look like I know what I'm doing, but I get hung up on all the words. There are so many of them. Blue ones mixed in with the black ones. I try so hard to concentrate on it and not mess up. But then a student at the computers distracts me by singing along with the READ 180 theme song so loudly I swear the people next door can hear it. All the other students turn to look and laugh. I yell to him from across the room.

"You are distracting us from our work!! Can't you see that?!"

I look back down at the book. I run my hand through my hair and furrow my brow in concentration. *What am I supposed to say again?*

I stumble with my words. My frustration builds. I wing it until I find my place again.

But they know. They know I am not very good at this. How will they respect me now?

Students write answers in their workbooks.

For some crazy reason, I've lost my ability to trust in my own judgment and so I turn to my teacher's edition to see if students' answers are right. I prompt and guide them until their responses match the answers in pink. Students express frustration when they have to erase and erase and erase.

"Is this right?"

"Is this right?"

"*Is this right?*" they ask.

I tell them I want them to think for themselves and to trust what they know.

I believe the lie.

But when I look down at the teacher's book to compare answers, I speak again, my tongue thick with guilt and apology. "Well, what about saying it this way ..."

Only when students' answers match the pink words in my book do I write 100% at the top.

Only then do we move on.

While we work, students from other stations come to the table and interrupt us to ask if they can go to the bathroom because they "really need to go!" Students at the computers call out to me because they "can't log on!" or their "computer froze!" or their "headphones aren't working!" A couple of students sing the READ 180 theme song while others at the table turn to look at them and laugh, laugh, laugh! Students in the independent reading station argue about who gets to sit on the couch before they call out to tell me that "it's not fair because it's my turn today!" Students at the table watch with dull eyes and listen and wait for me to tell them their answers are *"RIGHT!"*

They want to finish already.

So do I.

We've spent enough time today on page 17. I check their answers and write "100%" at the top. Some students smile and verbalize a self-congratulatory remark, while others flash an indifferent *whatever* expression.

The timer goes off.

Everyone expresses relief when I tell them to close their books and move to the computers. I motion for the next group to come over.

Going "Off Model" and Finding Relief

I perform this ritual nine times per day. It feels forced, fake. I don't like this feeling at all. A few days later I decide to put the teacher's book away and instead just teach from the student workbook. This is "off model." I am not teaching "with fidelity."

But I don't care.

There aren't a thousand words telling me what we are all supposed to think and say and write. Only simple directions, a few questions, and blank lines.

Aahhh … this feels better. Not so many words and rules. No script. No prefabricated answers.

I begin to relax.

4th Block Class—A Saving Grace at the End of the Day

Some days are better than others. On good days students focus on and attend to their work with little to no disruption. It is rare to have a day where all the classes go this well. In fact, I don't think that has happened, yet. It seems to happen more often, though, in fourth block, the last class of the day. Students in this class display a positive energy—they are enthusiastic about what we do, they get along with each other, they seem to want to work together, they are cheerful and happy, and they don't mind talking with me or each other. They respond to prompts for conversation from me and from others in ways that are not defensive or antagonistic. They are eager to help each other out and welcome the opportunity to give and receive help.

It is amazing how different this class feels compared to the others. I enjoy this class. I've started teaching from the teacher's edition more and more and I feel we are getting into a groove. Students seem to appreciate the consistency of the routine and it seems, too, that I have an easier time of teaching the lessons. Perhaps this is due in part because of the fact that I've already had two other classes in the day before this one in which to work out the kinks. I think a large part of it has to do with the fact that this class is all sixth graders. There are no seventh or eighth graders in here. I look forward to this class every day and I am thankful it is the class I end my day with.

Lingering Assumptions Fuel Mistrust, Sabotage Love

My experiences from the previous two years haunt me still. As a result, I have the lingering assumption that I can't trust students. On the surface, this assumption serves as a measure of emotional and physical protection. If I distance myself from students, I minimize my risk of being hurt. But when I peel back the layers on both of these assumptions, I grapple with the fact that this entire group of students is different and I see this difference every day. I feel the difference. I also feel my desire to trust. I want so much to let go of the past and trust the students I work with now.

But I am afraid to do so.

How, then, can I open myself up to give and receive love? I remind myself again and again that this is a different group of students. They deserve better than this from me. They deserve the best I have to offer.

Notwithstanding, my assumptions about students and my self-perceived need for protection keep me from loving students and from acknowledging any semblance of love students give to me or to each other. If students extend themselves to me or each other in a loving way, I do not see it. I choose not to see it. I remain on guard so they don't "pull one over on me."

Starting to Let the Past Go, Starting to Trust and Smile

And yet, I find myself enjoying the kids and looking forward to seeing them, despite my assumptions and self-perceived need for protection. As time goes on, I feel myself beginning to trust. In conversations with friends and family, I refer to students with whom I work as "good kids!" I haven't said this in a long, long time. It feels good to say it. I smile when I do.

But Still, I Yell

On the not-so-good days, I still respond to disruptions by yelling at students across the room or at the table with me, when only moments before I was calm and patient, and seemingly satisfied with how things were going. Ironically, I participate in disrupting class by calling everyone's attention to myself and whomever I'm calling out to. The volume and tone of my voice reflect my frustration and inform everyone that someone pushed my buttons. Then I feel even more frustrated because I don't want to be a teacher who YELLS!

A part of me believes that yelling is the only way to get through to some of the students in this class and that my attempts at being calm, patient, and reasonable get us nowhere. It seems that for some students the only way to get a preferred response out of them is to yell and be mean about it. In the meantime, the students who are not the focus of my tirade look uncomfortable, as if waiting for me to turn on them next.

I try to focus on our work, but now I feel bad about yelling, I feel frustrated with the students I yelled at, and I'm frustrated with myself for getting off track and having to spend time regrouping my thoughts and remembering what we were doing and where we were headed. All the while, I'm ready to pounce on anyone who tries to disrupt the flow of things.

This is the part of me that still holds on to my assumptions about not being able to trust that students can handle disruptive situations on their own. Instead, I jump in on a moment's notice to reprimand and redirect, thus taking responsibility away from students to self-monitor and self-regulate their behavior or that of each other. It's as if I look for every reason not to trust students. I'm on edge looking for reasons to convince myself why I can't or shouldn't trust them. Then, when I feel they've given me reason not to, the resentful voice in my head affirms this belief.

There! You see? I knew this would happen!

Innocent bystanders respond to my behavior with uneasy silence. They look at each other with wide eyes, relieved at the fact it's not them I'm yelling at. The others respond in a variety of ways. Sometimes they get back to work immediately without further incident. Sometimes they get back to work momentarily before engaging in further disruptive behavior until I yell at them again. And sometimes students yell back and tell me I'm picking on them "all the time!" and yelling at them "all the time!"

Some students aren't sure how to interpret my yelling—do I yell at them because I care about them and their learning and so I am strict, or do I yell at them because I am mean? In my mind, I am not yelling, but rather, I'm talking in a stern voice. Regardless of how I justify it or interpret my voice and behavior, though, some students interpret both as me picking on them and so I must pay attention to that.

Struggling with Destructive Intolerance

The seventh-grade boys in our second-block class gang up on Manny, a sixth grader who, at times, demonstrates the emotional and behavioral maturity of a child just starting school. When he contributes his ideas in whole group, several of the seventh grade boys outwardly express their dissatisfaction by rolling their eyes and letting out exasperated sighs or speaking words of disapproval loud enough for everyone to hear. I've talked to them individually about accepting and respecting Manny for who he is and helping him to feel that he is part of the group in our classroom. But each time I do, the boys respond by telling me that Manny bugs them and that they get tired of it. They tell me I don't see it because he does it when I'm not looking.

"I will pay closer attention to Manny's behavior," I tell them. "But I can't sit and watch him all period long. You need to let me know when this goes on so I can address it then and there. In the meantime, I want you to stop rolling your eyes and making *jetas* [faces] at Manny. He deserves your respect as a fellow member of our class who has the right to share his ideas without being made to feel like what he says doesn't matter."

They leave our conversations feeling frustrated because I ask them to do something they simply do not want to do. They do not like Manny. They don't want to give him the respect they feel he doesn't show them. They certainly don't want to be his friend. They don't want anything to do with him.

As time goes on, nothing changes. I call parents and ask them to please talk with their children about being respectful toward one another in class. I pay closer attention to Manny, but I don't see any reason for the other students' continuing display of mean-spirited behavior toward him. By this time, some of the girls are taking part in it. And worse yet, it seems this behavior is now also being directed at the other two students who share self-contained special education classrooms with Manny throughout the rest of the day.

Rather than resorting to office referrals to stop this behavior, I address it by talking to students as a group. I tell them I am frustrated because of how the situation doesn't seem to be getting better and I feel like I am the only one who is willing to speak up and defend Manny and now, the other two. I ask them to consider how they would feel if they were treated the same way by me or others. I tell them I am angry because I feel they are ganging up on certain students who express themselves differently from everyone else.

I am angry. I am frustrated. I feel bad for the students being picked on, especially Manny. And so I talk loud. I talk with anger in my voice. I want things to change, but I can't do it alone. We are in this together. I tell them so. But I don't think they believe me. I imagine they get tired of hearing me go on and on about this. But I will continue to go on and on about it, as long as they continue with this kind of behavior.

I so much want to bring in literature we can read and discuss and write about in relation to ourselves and our experiences as a way to address this problem.

But there is no time.

We've got pages in the rBook to complete. Computer lessons, quizzes, and reading logs to complete. I'm going to be observed next month and we are barely still in the first half of Workshop 1.

The timer goes off.

Time for rotations.

Authoritarian Behavior Breeds Reciprocal Mistrust

Time constraints and pressure to "stay on model and teach with fidelity" fuel my tendency to get impatient and react impulsively to what I consider to be disruptive student behavior. Students see me as nice and calm one moment, then *Whammo!*—angry and explosive the next. Students wait on edge for the moment when I lose it and lash out. They don't trust me. They don't know what to expect and when. This serves to create a nervous, uneasy environment for all of us.

I have a commitment to work with students in building and maintaining a classroom environment conducive to successful teaching and learning. But this isn't something I can do alone. It isn't just my classroom, it's our classroom. I want and expect for students to assume ownership of their learning by coming to class on time, being prepared, and committing themselves to their progress in reading. This means being committed to not only themselves as individuals, but to each other as members of a group, a community. I've discussed this with students at the beginning of the year, and then again, as more students came in later.

However, I don't think I've spent much time teaching students how to self-monitor and self-regulate their behavior. I've only assumed they know how to do this and when they don't do it, I blame them and get mad. At the same time, if they do know how to do it, I haven't given them space to do so. I haven't trusted them to do this for themselves. I always step in and take over. I've done so from day one.

Decentering Self in Effort to Shift Control to Students to Self-monitor and Regulate Behavior—But Still … Floundering in Futility

I take a different approach and talk with students about how to self-monitor and self-regulate their behavior by recognizing and addressing distractive and disruptive behavior in themselves and each other. I remind them that we are in this together, that we have to work with each other to make our classroom a successful teaching and learning environment for us all, and that this cannot be only my responsibility. I tell them I have a responsibility to the people I'm working with at the table and so everyone else in the room must work together to get their job done without my intervening every time someone disrupts class. I suggest that they tell someone who is distracting them or disrupting class to please stop and, at the same time, to redirect her or him to focus back on the assignment.

I envision students being belligerent in their manner of redirecting one another, so I talk with them further about how to go about redirecting one another in a calm and respectful manner. I also suggest that if a student continues to try and distract them from their work, they should get up and move to another spot in the room.

We move on. We have rBook pages and computer segments and reading logs to get to. I remind students as we break into our small group rotations that I expect them to self-monitor and self-regulate their behavior. Students seem agreeable to this and ready to take on the challenge. I am more than ready.

We give it a shot.

Things do not go well.

To be fair, students are used to things being a certain way in here. They are used to me taking the lead and responding to any and all distractions and disruptions. When I don't do this, they look at each other, then at me, expecting me to get up and go over to where the problematic situation is taking place or to yell to whoever is causing it from my spot at the table.

But I don't.

Instead, I carry on at the table as if nothing is wrong. I ignore the distracting behavior and hope that the students with me at the table ignore it, also.

But they don't.

They turn and look at the source of the distraction. Sometimes they laugh. Then they turn back to stare at me, waiting for me to do something about it. They no longer focus on their work before us. I ignore the behavior, hoping the disruptive student will self-regulate her or his behavior and get back to work. I redirect students at the table to focus on our work.

As the disruptive behavior continues I ignore it, hoping another student in the room will calmly and respectfully redirect the disruptive student back to focusing on her or his work so that I don't have to.

But nobody makes a move.

I guess this wouldn't be so bad, except that other students are not focused on their work anymore, either. They stop working and stare at me, waiting for me to do something. My frustration builds. I don't want to have to leave the group at the table and take time away from their learning opportunities to deal with someone who is messing around.

The timer counts down the seconds. We still have half a page to go and there's only seven minutes and thirty-nine seconds left before we rotate. Seven minutes, thirty-eight. Seven minutes, thirty-seven. Seven minutes, thirty-six. Tick tock. Tick tock.

Tick.

Tick!

TICK!

The next thing I know, I take over by yelling out to whoever is *"screwing around!"* I give this student and, by default, everyone else in the class, a lecture about how she or he is "cheating everyone else out of their learning by being disruptive!" Then I gripe at everyone else in the room about how they need to "step up and take charge of their learning by redirecting anyone getting off track!"

"We all have a job to do," I say, "and we need to work together to make sure we get it done!"

Stepping Back to Listen, Responding with Patience

Students are confused by my yelling. They are not sure how to make sense of it. Do I yell at them because I care about their learning? Because I am a strict teacher? Or is it simply because I am annoyed with them? They are not sure and so do not trust my actions.

I tell students I want them to take charge of their learning, but then I take over and gripe and yell at them for not doing it the way I think they should. I must be patient and allow for students to try. I must remember they are not used to doing this, and so if and when I see they aren't responding after a reasonable amount of time, then I do need to step in and take care of the situation. However, I must make time to talk with students in a calm and patient manner about whether or not they are self-regulating and self-monitoring their behavior and if so, discuss how they are successful in doing so. If not, then we must discuss what measures they can take to be successful in this endeavor.

Pressing My Buttons Equals Distractions and Disruption—A Desirable Thing?

Perhaps some students simply prefer distractions. If the acts of reading and writing are a struggle, then any distraction might be welcome. On the other hand, perhaps some students simply enjoy the amusement factor of pressing my buttons and watching me react the way I do when I go off on someone or on the group. The bottom line here is that when this happens, for whatever reason, we are not engaged in the acts of reading and writing. We are not maximizing our opportunities for teaching and learning.

Battle for Attention and Control—A Way for Students to Force Me to Know Them on Their Terms

I feel there is a power struggle between me and a couple of students who get and maintain other students' attention. Is this a battle for control? I suppose so. I want so much for students to share the responsibility for ensuring we all stay focused and on task, but right now it seems as if they give me no choice but to use my authority to assume control.

This is not how I want us to function in here. I want students to value the time we have together, to value the teaching and learning opportunities they have in here and the impact they might have on their efforts to strengthen and improve their reading skills. And yet, how can I ask students to care about their learning and what I ask them to do when I haven't made a consistent effort to know them, to really know them? How will students take ownership of their learning and assume responsibility for not only their own individual learning but for that of their classmates as well, if they don't feel I care about who they are as individuals? Perhaps this is why they act out—as a way to get me to notice them as individuals, to get me to know them on their terms, even if they have to force me to know them by misbehaving and being disruptive.

Epiphany in Mid-October—Hearing What Students Have to Say—Acknowledging an Absence of Love

Students say they care about me and worry about me when I'm not here. Yet, I am shocked when CF tells me this. How can I be unaware of the care students say they have for me? Am I resisting it? If so, is it out of fear of getting hurt? Perhaps students care about me in ways that I do not perceive as care, but yet, they do. I have a loving responsibility to recognize students' gestures of care and to acknowledge and receive their care with an open heart. I feel bad for not noticing and worse still for any pain I may have caused because of it.

Students say I show and give them care by working with them individually until they understand what we are working on and by working with them to raise their reading levels. Beyond this, though, they have a difficult time articulating how they know and believe I care about and for them.

"It's just a feeling," they say.

On the other hand, CF tells me that students say I don't have a clue who they are or what they're all about when they leave our school every day. I am ashamed of this. This is not me, not the teacher I want to be or know I can be. How can I ask students to care about their learning and the work we do when I don't love them and care about them in ways that they know? How can students receive love if they don't know it's there?

I let students down. I know this. I am ashamed. And yet, although it's happened right under my nose, I feel shocked that I've let it come to this, considering how differently I feel about this entire group of students. But I haven't allowed myself to show it. Instead, I've taken them for granted. I've only thought about myself and my pressures and my feelings. I've placed an unfair burden on students to complete the READ 180 program requirements just so that I can look like I know what I'm doing to the people who are watching me. And what it is doing to me is turning me into someone I don't want to be. I don't like myself for treating students this way and ignoring who they are as people. They deserve better than this from me.

Relying on and Trusting in Love

Love means telling the truth, even when it hurts. Students say I don't have a clue of who they are. This is their truth. In my act of listening to CF share this with me, it becomes my truth.

Perhaps this is my first real act of love in the classroom. I listen. And it hurts. I cry. I cry because this is not the kind of teacher I want to be. I cry because I am not teaching with and through love. I cry because I have failed after all. But not for the reasons I thought I would fail in the beginning, when I worried about teaching "on model" and "with fidelity." I failed because I have not connected with students in ways that matter. I've not worked with them in building and sustaining loving relationships built on trust and respect, knowledge and responsibility, care and commitment.

Making Amends and Starting Over—Sharing Truth and Forgiveness

I decide to put the rBook away and focus instead on providing opportunities for us to connect with one another and to learn about each other beyond what little we've managed to do thus far. I begin by talking with students about how I've become aware that they feel I don't have a clue who they are. I share with them that hearing this jolted me into realizing how little attention I've paid to providing all of us with opportunities to connect with and among one another.

In being honest with them, I explain how I allowed myself to become preoccupied with learning the ins and outs of the program and, in so doing, succumbed to the pressures therein. "This," I say, "is one of the driving forces behind my eruptive behavior. But that isn't all of it."

I admit to students that I have negative assumptions about them and explain how these assumptions stem from previous experiences in the classroom. I tell them how ashamed I am that I allowed these assumptions to cloud my judgment and that my holding these assumptions over their heads is not fair to any of us.

"Doing so," I tell them, "doesn't allow for us to build meaningful and loving relationships with and among one another. Rather, it diminishes our spirits and tears us down."

I apologize and ask for a second chance, not just for me, but for all of us, to begin building relationships based on mutual respect, trust, and a desire to come together as a team working toward success for all.

"I can't do it alone," I tell them. "We are in this together and we all have a responsibility, not only to ourselves, but to each other to accept and support one another with respect and a desire to succeed in our work. If we all commit to working together in this way, we will succeed."

I stop talking. I look around at each student and I wait. They look back at me, mostly in silence. In this silence, they seem to let out a collective and relaxing sigh of relief. I see forgiveness in their smiles and hear it in their words when those who do speak say, "It's okay, Mrs. Blanchard."

I ask students to share any thoughts they have on the matter, comments, questions, and criticisms alike. When they are silent, I say that I understand why they may not trust me right now to say what's on their minds.

"That's okay," I tell them. "But please believe me when I say that I *did* listen when CF told me that you feel like I don't have a clue of who you are. I *did* listen and I do intend to turn things around, starting now with this conversation."

It is time to move on. Not because I set the timer, but because I said enough. Students appear ready to move on, too. I segue into discussing the *I Am From* writing project we will start the very next day. I share with students that I am "so excited and happy!" about starting this project with them. By the time I finish explaining the project, students seem excited and happy to put the rBook away and to focus on them for a change. We begin tomorrow.

So ends our first nine weeks of school.

Note

1.   Adapted from Blanchard, J. A. (2012). *Critical love praxis in a middle school classroom—Exploring the struggles, outcomes, and possibilities of loving practice through critical practitioner action research and autoethnography*. New Mexico State University. ProQuest, UMI Dissertations Publishing, 2012. 3534117.

CHAPTER 20

From Deficit to Abundance in the Classroom; Or What I Learned From Jayda[1]

Lisa Sibbett

*M*idmorning at Martin Luther King, Jr. High School, and I am hurrying from Portable 98, where I am a teacher intern in Language Arts, all the way across campus to Room 173, where I am assigned to U.S. History. Some of the students I teach are headed the same direction, gleefully cussing and hollering with their friends. Some cuss and holler back and forth to each other in English and then Spanish, while others slide fluidly between Somali and Arabic. I am learning to hear the difference. The hallway is all jostling and jockeying, some kids sneering at each other, others high fiving, while teachers, administrators, and security guards alternately hassle and cajole: "Get to class, Kadir, hurry up! Let's go, Serena!" I dart through the crush, apparently going the opposite direction of everyone else. And now ahead of me coming through the din I hear the lovely plunking of ukuleles, and now the throng parts a little, and here are some members of the football team, longhaired and ambling and grinning as they strum their tunes. As I finally approach the North wing, the halls begin to empty. A few kids are practicing breakdancing moves outside the Proyecto Saber room. "Let's go!" a security guard shouts behind me, and the bell rings. The dancers and I grin at each other as we duck into our separate rooms—we're all late for class again.

Again. I am battling wills with Jayda again.[2] I've tried everything I can think of—engaging her in friendly conversation before class, pulling her out of the room when she's disruptive during class, giving her a hard time, giving her an easy time, modifying assignments, asking her opinions and using her suggestions, asking other teachers for advice—all to no avail. The strategies I try sometimes work for a day or two, but then we're back where we started, with Jayda refusing to participate, distracting classmates and trying to incite rebellions, and shouting "This is stupid!" in response to just about everything we ever do in class. Today I am asking students to do an image analysis, writing about what they notice in the photograph I've brought in, and discussing their observations and interpretations with the group.

"This is stupid!" Jayda exclaims (again). "I'm not doing it. Why you always wanna make us do this boring effed up stuff?" Other students stop what they're doing and turn to watch, or chime in.

I've been trying to get her on board with the lesson all period. It's time for another one-on-one talk.

As we stand in the rain outside the portable, arms crossed in cold and frustration, I rack my brain for some new strategy. Why is Jayda so angry? Is it me? Why does she seem to hate everything we ever do? How can I defuse the situation and get her to engage with what we're doing? How can I help her learn when she refuses to try anything I ask?

Now she is glaring off into the middle distance, angrily snapping her gum. I take a deep breath. "What's going on?" I ask her, again …

What Got Me Thinking: Deficit or Abundance?

The two scenes I have just described represent contradictory phenomena that I experienced often during my teacher internship. The first experience is joyful: life, energy, and youth abound in the hallways, and different ways of knowing, speaking, and existing flourish. Such cultural, communal, vibrant resources permeate the school and are precisely why teachers, students, and families take enormous pride in their community. But the second phenomenon is deeply troubling: despite the abundant resources they bring with them, many students are profoundly alienated from school. Some, like Jayda, go to war with the institution, battling teachers, administrators, and other students until they are undergoing repeated disciplinary actions. Others give up, check out, or drop out.

This article charts my attempt to understand the problem more fully, an attempt that ultimately took an unexpected direction. What started out as a practitioner research project became a kind of autoethnographic, self-reflective narrative. I wanted to investigate how students learn but discovered that I had first to search my own assumptions and practice. I begin this chapter by contrasting two ways of thinking about education: the deficit view, which I reject, and what I am calling the abundance view, which I embrace. From the beginning of this project, I strove for an abundance approach, inquiring into a particular learning strategy I thought students might already be using. When I started analyzing the data I collected, however, I discovered a pattern of deficit in my own ideas, rhetoric, and behavior. This is the story of how I learned more than I had expected from my students; and it is my attempt to understand how to use what I learned to build a classroom in which all students—even the most disaffected—can flourish.

This chapter draws a sharp distinction between two ways of understanding how students learn and what school is for. The first of these is the deficit view of education, wherein students are understood to lack skills, knowledge, and resources and the role of school is to fill students up and repair the deficit. The second is the abundance view, wherein students are understood to carry with them plentiful knowledge and resources. In this view, the role of school is to support students in using these resources to bloom and grow.[3]

In most public schools and classrooms there are measures of both approaches, while some learning communities live out the abundance approach thoroughly. But every day, all across the country, entire educational communities are attempting to teach and learn in a world of perceived deficit. In these districts and schools, consensus holds that there is not enough: there are not enough resources, teachers are not doing enough, students are not prepared enough and not learning enough. With such scarcity, the only option is to compete, and the scarcer the resources, the more losers there must inevitably be. I do not want to diminish the often-staggering challenges faced by underfunded schools, undereducated teachers, and underserved students, but I do also believe that this epidemic of "underness" is, to some extent, false. We have more resources than we think we do.

What I Want to Reject: The Deficit View of Education

While there are certainly many individuals and communities in schools across the country that reject the deficit perspective, it nonetheless dominates public discourse about education. Teachers and principals are said to be underqualified, undertrained, and underprepared to deal with their jobs, as at the Rhode Island high school where, in February 2010, the entire teaching and administrative staff was fired (Zezima, 2010). Twenty-five years after the infamous *Nation at Risk* report (National Commission on Excellence in Education, 1983), *A Nation Accountable* (U.S. Department of Education, 2008) claims that we are "at even greater risk now," because "our education system is not keeping pace" (p. 1). In short, we are all presumed not to be living up. Standards must be raised, we are told. The deficit must be filled.

In schools and classrooms, the deficit perspective manifests in the twin assumptions that learners essentially lack knowledge and that school is for meeting that lack. As Freire (2008) puts it in his description of the "banking concept" of education, students are "receptacles" to be "filled" (p. 72). Both Freire and Dewey (1966) highlight the passivity and obedience this view of learning requires of students. Often, instead of accepting this worldview, students choose to resist (Hinchey, 2004; Kohl, 1994). Thus teachers, even those of us who want to reject deficit thinking, spend much of our energy on classroom management.

Perhaps the most insidious incarnations of the deficit perspective are beliefs that students' homes, families, communities, cultures, languages, lives, experiences, interests, and aptitudes are either irrelevant to their learning or actively detrimental to it. In my experience most critical educators now share, quite rightly, in condemning racist ideas about "cultural deficit," and we do our best to be alert for it in our own schools and classrooms (Delpit, 1995; Lee, 2007; Nieto, 1999). But rejecting such theories is only part of the battle. I have often been guilty of imagining that students' home lives are lacking, and I have treated students' daily lives and friendships and interests as detrimental to their learning: "Ana and Michelle, I don't want to have to separate you"; "Ethan, please stop looking up basketball scores; we're in the lab to do research."

My expectation has been that Ana and Michelle and Ethan will do as I ask: in essence, I expect them to obey my requests and be receptive to the knowledge I think they need to acquire. But I have doubts about how much authentic and meaningful learning is really going on, even when students do stay on task (Purpel, 1989). Furthermore, I am dogged by Freire's suggestion that teaching obedience and passiveness amounts to teaching people to accept oppression. Maybe I am teaching Ana and Michelle that they are wrong to laugh and talk loudly together in Spanish when they are "supposed to be working." Maybe I am teaching Ethan to keep his attention on his task and not worry about what might be going on around him. I worry that when I attempt to socialize students to my behavioral expectations—even if I believe I am empowering them with a form of cultural capital (Bourdieu & Passeron, 1977)—what I am really doing is, in Freire's words, "adjusting" them, perpetuating the very systems of oppression I so passionately want to transform (2008, p. 74).

What I Want to Embrace: The Abundance View of Education

An appropriate alternative to the deficit view is the abundance view, wherein all students are presumed to carry with them enormous intellectual, aesthetic, physical, interpersonal, cultural and intercultural, spiritual, and communal resources. Far from being empty receptacles to be "filled" with the knowledge they "lack," our students already are experts: they are experts in the things they love, they are experts in the workings of their communities, and they are experts on the subject of their own lives and experiences. Regardless of their track records in school, all students are good learners because learning is what humans do. Humans are good knowers because we dwell in and deal intimately with language, culture, and people every day of our lives.

Students' cultural backgrounds and experiences, including family and community practices, stories, languages, and religion, as well as daily activities such as sports or extracurricular activities, provide a particularly rich set of resources for teachers and learners in the abundance classroom (Gutierrez & Rogoff, 2003; Lee, 2007; Rodríguez, 2001; Yosso, 2005). Building on what students have means inviting their lives into the classroom, in all their cacophony, energy, and adolescent emotion; and it means co-constructing meaning out of that din, in cooperation with our students (Christensen, 2009). This requires enormous trust from teachers: in order authentically to partner with students and give them real autonomy in cooperative decision making, we must trust that they have good ideas and can make good decisions about their learning (Apple & Beane, 2007; Dewey, 1966; Freire, 2008; Meier, 1995).

Wholly to make this leap of faith constitutes a sea change in classroom practice. It means that class assignments encourage Ana and Michelle to talk to one another about what is going on in their lives; it means Ethan's basketball scores are academically meaningful, a possible site of learning about human lives and the ways we might improve them; it means that when students are "off task," I assume that the task may be at fault and that the students may be in the process of having "wonderful ideas" I had not foreseen (Duckworth, 1987); it means that I view students' behavior as an expression of their needs. It means that my professional and personal authority is "on the side of freedom, not against it" (Freire, 2008, p. 80). Abundance is for freedom, liberation, and transformation; deficit opposes these things. When we most perceive deficit in our classrooms, this is when abundance is most vigorously clamoring to be liberated (Rosenberg, 2003).

Who I Worked With: The Students of MLK High School

For my teacher internship, I worked for several months at Martin Luther King, Jr. High School, an urban Pacific Northwest high school with a tremendously diverse student population: ethnically Asian and Pacific Islander, Latino/a, Black, and White students are about equally represented at this school. Many students come from middle-class communities, but most live in relatively low-income neighborhoods; and the school has a large population of English language learners, including many students born in Central and South America, and many students from East Africa, most of whom are practicing Muslims and contribute to the religious and linguistic diversity of the school.

In my experience, students, staff, and families have pride in their cool, urban, diverse school, which has recently been designated an International School, but the perception in the larger community is that MLK's population is essentially underprivileged. The percentage of MLK students "meeting standard" is conspicuously lower than the state average (for example, in 2009, according to the school's annual report, 76.7% "met standard" in reading, compared to the state's 81.2%, and 71.6% "met standard" in writing, compared to the state's 86.7%). Meanwhile, disciplinary action and dropout rates at the school are conspicuously higher than the district average (according to the same report, in 2008–2009, MLK had a 15.1% suspension rate, compared to the district's 6.4%). One of the key contentions of this article is that few or no students can accurately be described as "underprivileged," but it would be appropriate to say that much of the student population at MLK is, as Wilhelm (2008) puts it, "severely labeled" (p. 38).

At the time I conducted the research for this project, I had nearly completed my teacher internship. The following week would be my last week in the school. I had grown to care deeply for my students, but my relationships with them were still developing. With many students, every day, I still did not know if things would go well or poorly. Of the fourteen students who participated in this study, most were at that time coming into regular conflict with teachers and administrators. Most also struggled to maintain passing grades.

What I Thought I Would Do, What I Actually Did, and Why

I use reflective personal narrative as a key mode for conveying my findings and the meaning I make of them, although this was not originally my intention. In this section, I describe how data was collected, briefly sketch why I changed my approach partway through, and explain the methodology I used thereafter.

At the outset, I planned to conduct a conventional practitioner research study, in which I would use a form of problem-based methodology in order to improve my teaching practice (Robinson & Lai, 2006, p. 15). Namely, I would use qualitative tools, including questionnaires, interviews, and documents, to collect data from my students; I would then analyze the data I had collected in order to develop a "theory of action" for my classroom (Robinson & Lai, 2006, p. 18). My research question was: "How can I support my students in transferring their outside-of-school knowledge and expertise into school for academic success?"

Participants spent part of a 50-minute class period filling in a questionnaire that elicited information about their cultural identity, their present self-concept as learners and knowers, their positive experiences using their outside knowledge for academic success in school, and their recommendations for how teachers might support them in using this expertise in the future. The rest of that session was spent discussing what participants had written, and the discussion was digitally videotaped. On the second day, participants were asked to write an essay discussing in detail a positive learning memory of their choice. I had planned to use at least a week to collect the data for this study, but for a number of reasons, including conflicts with the upcoming statewide standardized assessment, only two days were available.

Although I understood and accepted these constraints, I came away from the data collection feeling frustrated. I thought students would enjoy participating in this study, but as I will explain, things did not go as well as expected, and I attributed this to a lack of time. As I began to organize and code data, the feeling of deficit persisted: participants seemed to have given me little to go on as I sought answers to my research question. And it was too late to fix it: my teacher internship had ended. I did not have enough data.

Or rather, I had plenty of data, but it did not seem to be answering my question of how students transfer their outside knowledge into school. What the data did indicate, I finally understood, was how the participants in this study behave and talk under deficit conditions—the very conditions that had been shaping the project, and my practice, all along. Participants had plenty of messages they wanted me to hear; they simply were not the messages I expected.

In the rest of this chapter, I tell the story of what happened in my classroom when I attempted to collect data from students under deficit learning conditions. I use what Nash (2004) calls "scholarly personal narrative," enacting my recognition that I am "an integral part" of what I "observe, study, interpret, and assert" (p. 26). Such an approach recognizes that, as researchers, we are not separate from the research we do or the way we interpret our findings (Miles & Huberman, 1994; Robinson & Lai, 2006). Similarly, teachers are not separate from students or from the lessons we teach them: as Palmer (1997) puts it, "we teach who we are" (p. 15). I have come to see that this narrative reflection about my experience aligns with my argument. If I want my students' learning to be grounded in their experiences, then it is fitting that my learning operate in the same way.

Much of the data in the rest of this article is reconstructed from memory, since some of the most important information was not systematically collected. My findings are, therefore, not only narrative but also hybrid: part officially recorded, part remembered. In selecting what I present and how I interpret it, I have tried to stay mindful of Nash's (2004) ten "postmodern truth criteria" for scholarly personal narratives: "openmindedness, plausibility, vulnerability, narrative creativity, interpretive ingenuity, coherence, generalizability, trustworthiness, caution, and personal honesty" (p. 41). However successful (or not) I have been in meeting these criteria, I can say that I have attempted to apply these tests to my findings and analysis as rigorously as I can, and in good faith.

Finally, all of the data I select and unpack have two features in common. First, they illustrate the pervasiveness of the deficit view in my own beliefs and practice and the pernicious effects of this view on students. And second, they contain—as deficit always does—those clamorings for liberation and for meaning that are a sure sign of abundance.

What Happened, Part 1: Deficit Intrudes

Thursday morning, questionnaire day. I reviewed the instructions, handed out questionnaires, and expected students would get to work. I thought they would enjoy answering questions about themselves, their experiences, and their preferences. I was wrong. Only a few immediately got started. Many sat chatting. Others got up and walked around. Some did not have a pen or pencil and sat, saying nothing, or put their heads down and tried to go to sleep. I variously exhorted them, reminded them of the benefits they would get, and asked them to do it for me as a personal favor. At one point my cooperating teacher got frustrated enough to intervene.

"Ms. Sibbett is doing this study for you, guys! Now you need to please show her some respect and get to work."

Things finally did settle down, although not entirely. When twenty minutes of class remained it seemed everyone was more or less finished, so I reconvened us for a class discussion. I began by asking what had gone wrong.

Me:	I noticed that some people were like "oh, this is dumb," so can you explain—if you were feeling kind of annoyed, like "this is not a valuable use of my time," can you explain a little bit why or why not? I'm really going to listen to what you say.
Kenneth:	This isn't going to do anything.
Me:	Why's that?
Kenneth:	Because this is for you, it isn't for all the teachers in the universe.
Me:	Okay, so you wish that teachers in general would—
Jayda:	Even if teachers in general did [inaudible], nothing really would change.
Me:	Well, so let me ask you this: have you guys—my guess is this—that you guys have been asked these kinds of questions before.
A few students:	Yeah.
Me:	Yeah? And you felt like nothing really happened?
Kenneth:	Put it this way: [inaudible] a lot of talk.[4]

Kenneth had a point: I was going to change my practice on the basis of my findings, which is what I told the class when I responded to this exchange, but everyone in the room knew I was leaving next week, so no matter what future changes I made to my practice, for this group the research probably was not "going to do anything." Not only that, but although I launched the conversation by telling students I was "really going to listen," my behavior sent a clear message that I was not listening closely at all.

One problem was that I was in an enormous rush. We had only twenty minutes of class remaining, and there was so much I wanted students to hear from one another. I hypothesized that students often transfer their outside knowledge into school unconsciously, so I thought it was important for them to share their insights and generate ideas for tomorrow's essay. I felt we needed to have this conversation, fast. They needed to be filled up with ideas, fast. Despite my professed intention to "really listen," what I did instead was rush.

Me:	Does anybody else want to share about "are you a good student, not a good student?" What other things did you say about that?
Leticia:	I said yes 'cause I'm a hard worker. Failure is not an option.
Ana:	I said sometimes.
Me:	Sometimes you're a good student? Okay, so here's a question that I really want to know the answer to. It's question 8. Do you think of yourself as smart? Who put yes?

I cringe every time I read how blatantly I brushed Leticia and Ana off. The whole transcript of our class discussion reveals a similar pattern: I ask a question, a few students volunteer their answers, and then I move quickly on. The amount of actual learning occurring under these conditions—for me or anyone else—is unclear. Many students were checked out; some had their heads down; one was reading a novel. Because we lacked time I did not intervene or investigate but, rather, forged ahead.

I knew very well at the time that I was engaging in bad pedagogy, and almost immediately, I was filled with regrets. I wished I had asked students to put their chairs in a circle and just talk about what they had written and thought. I wished I had gotten out of the way. But I did not do those things because I felt I couldn't. After all, who knew where the conversation would go? How would I get my data about how students transfer outside knowledge into school if I just let them … talk? Who knew what they would talk about? I was tangled up in deficit and believed I had no choices. Students responded with skepticism, goofing off, or checking out. The next day, the situation got worse.

Friday morning. The standardized test would be administered next week, so students were to prepare (and participate in my research) by responding to this essay prompt, which I had modeled on a common standardized test prompt:

> Think of a time when you used your outside knowledge to have a positive learning experience in school. Write a multi-paragraph essay for your teacher *explaining* what happened, why this experience was so positive for you, and how you can have more positive learning experiences like this in the future.

Like the day before, I thought that students would enjoy writing about their learning experiences and preferences; and like the day before, I was wrong. Some students did begin right away, but the battles I had fought the previous day got worse. Five minutes went by, then ten, and very few had gotten anything down on paper at all.

I had to ask Ana and Jayda again and again to get started. No matter how many times I walked by, tried to give them support, or exhorted them to get going, the next time I came by they would be giggling again and disrupting everyone around them, with no new words written down. Finally, I tried to separate them; they both refused to move. Jayda was especially upset with me for expecting them to write when other students were also off task. She shouted, "This is stupid!" and crossed her arms and glared angrily around, hoping the rest of the class would join in her protest. I asked her to step outside so we could talk—

Now, as my introduction suggests, this was by no means the first such clash with Jayda. In fact, her loud and regular proclamation "this is stupid!" had started to run through my head every time I was planning lessons. "This is stupid!" Those words, in Jayda's angry voice, kept me up at night. No matter what I did, I could not win her trust. Every day we seemed to be back to square one.

—And now we were standing in the rain outside the portable again, valuable writing minutes ticking by as Jayda first ignored, then angrily accused me.

"Teachers always pick on me! Other people are talking and not doing their essays, too!"

"I know, and it's really frustrating to me," I remember replying. "What do you think I should be doing differently? What's going wrong?"

I cannot recall her words. I know we stood in the rain talking for several minutes, making little headway. I explained again why we were doing this project: to help make it so classes feel more relevant to students. I wanted her to have a cool idea, something she could write passionately about so the project would not feel like a waste. I wanted to see the tension smooth from her face; I wanted to see the anger go out of her eyes. Finally, it did, sort of. It was the best I could do. We went back in. She started writing.

Meanwhile, it seemed few other students had made much progress. Many seemed to be messing around or just doing nothing. I kept thinking, "Really? You don't want to take this chance to explain what school should be like?" I went over to Tyrell and Kyle's desk, where neither had written anything.

"What's going on, guys?"

"No ideas," said Tyrell.

I asked what they were good at. I already knew how they would answer.

In unison: "Basketball."

"Okay, so in basketball you have to be able to focus, right? You have to know where your team is and where the other team's players are, so you have to be aware of what's going on around you even when you're not looking. You have to not give up when it gets hard, right? Do you ever use those skills in school?" We had used the basketball example as a class already, but apparently it had not connected before, because now both boys' eyes lit up.

"I can write about that!" Kyle exclaimed. They bent over their papers, pencils flying.

So I fed them an answer. It was far from perfect, but at least, as Nieto (1999) puts it, the light had come into their eyes. Soon the bell rang, students turned in their essays and filed out the door, and I sat looking at a stack of papers, chin in my hand.

What Happened, Part 2: Abundance Breaks Through

In the days that followed, I began organizing and coding students' work. I was looking for how students transfer knowledge into school, but I could not find it. Some students' questionnaires had little written at all. Many gave one- or two- or three-word answers. Tyrell wrote "don't know" for four questions in a row. And I had to rely on students' own reporting of their areas of expertise: I noticed again and again their failures to list knowledge and skills I knew them to possess. Tyrell, who is one of the friendliest, most easygoing, popular, and generally socially gifted students I have met, wrote "football, basketball"—and nothing else. Or Jayda, who listed by far the most areas of expertise of any participant (17), and included a lot of great skills and areas of knowledge (such as "poetry," "boys," and "church/religious"), did not include anything about her skills of analysis—her highly developed BS-detector, for example. I had not had enough time to do the research, and now I did not have enough data. There was never enough. Deficit, deficit, deficit.

The breakthrough finally came when I noticed a pair of phenomena that did not seem to add up. First, students expressed a more positive self-concept as learners and knowers than I had anticipated. Hoping to set up some context for the questions that followed, I had included four questions eliciting information about whether students viewed themselves as smart and as good students, and also about their sense of how teachers view them. These turned out to be findings in and of themselves. Most students were positive about their capacities. Some identified themselves as smart but "lazy," or suggested they could do better in school if they only "worked harder," and some were just unequivocally, glowingly positive. Tyrell wrote, "I am one of the smartest in the world"; Leticia, during our class conversation, said, "I think I'm f—in' brilliant. I am a genius, dawg"; and Darius expressed incredulity at the very question itself, wondering, "What student does not think they are smart?"

The second thing I noticed seemed somehow to contradict the first. Namely, most students indicated they rarely got to use their knowledge, skills, and talents in school. This information arose spontaneously in the class discussion. I had not asked this on the questionnaire, but as students erupted in a rare moment of enthusiasm, shouting out areas of expertise like "video games!" and "cooking!" it had occurred to me:

Me:	Cooking, all right. So, how much—this is so important—um, do you get to use your skills in school very much?
Jayda, Darius, Leticia, others:	No!
Jayda:	Because we don't do enough stuff to get to where our skills are—
Me:	Okay, well, can you put this on your questionnaire? On a scale of 1 to 10, 10 means always, 1 means never, how much do you get to use your skills in school? What are you putting?
Jayda:	2!
Michelle:	1!
Another student:	3!

Although not every student put a number on his or her questionnaire, the results were striking for those who did. The highest number indicated was 5 (from Amir, the only student in the class to consistently get high grades in all of his classes). There were two 4s, one 3, and four 2s. Michelle put 1. When later I asked if students had done school projects on subjects they were interested in, only two students raised their hands. Kenneth observed, drily, "It's kind of a rare occasion."

These two phenomena together—students' reported high self-concept, paired with their reported low opportunities to use their outside expertise in school—allowed me finally to see how students' abundant resources come springing forth in spite of school's rhetoric of deficit. Even though they rarely get to show it in school, students know very well that they are capable of brilliance. The issue was not so much how teachers could help students bring in outside knowledge; it was how we could stop stopping them from doing so.

Once I started viewing my findings this way, I was able to make more sense of what had gone wrong during the study: I wanted students to reflect on their abundant resources, but my behavior undermined my suggestion that those resources were valuable. I did not listen well when students spoke, I hurried us along and shushed the group when too many people started speaking at once, and I actively interfered with students' ability to talk to one another. Sure, students' side conversations were not always on topic, but from the abundance point of view, their discussions expressed the overflowing resources they *did* bring into the classroom that day. And on the flipside, it showed the deficit behaviors I was imposing: I wanted them to share with me what they valued and needed as learners, but I did not show them the same trust. Instead, I tried to control their behavior and our discussion, rushing to fill their minds with the knowledge I believed they needed.

Accustomed as they are to deficit classrooms, students participating in this study demonstrated little trust that their abundant interests and areas of expertise and ways of knowing would really be honored. Instead, to use Kohl's (1994) term, they "creatively maladjusted." Kohl explains: "When it is impossible to remain in harmony with one's environment without giving up deeply held moral values, creative maladjustment becomes a sane alternative to giving up altogether" (p. 130). In an environment that treated what they wanted to do and talk about as either irrelevant or detrimental to their learning, instead of giving up altogether, the students in my class resisted, in small ways (tuning out and reading during class discussions) or large (shouting, "This is stupid!").

After months of standing in the rain with Jayda, this project helped me finally understand what the fight was about. She wanted me to stop stopping her from bringing her abundant resources into school. The piece she wrote after our talk is a pointed testament to the abundance she possesses and the ways in which school and teachers, with their rhetoric of deficit, of "not enough" and "not allowed," suppress that abundance. Jayda wrote:

> A time when I used my outside knowledge to have a positive learning experience in school is in Middle School when we did a Black History skit. There was a church scene and since everybody knew that I went to church, they called me to be the church choir director. So when that part came we were extra sharp on that part. This was a positive experience because I felt like for once I was appreciated for going to church. Because how in public schools, you can't talk about religion because it offends people. But what people fail to realize is that it offends us too when we get told that we can't talk about our religion.

Jayda's choice to focus on religion is a powerful one. By selecting a subject that shapes many students' daily lives, communities, and understandings of the world, and that is widely treated as taboo in school, she vividly illustrates how learners' abundant resources and ways of knowing are actively shut out. Of the many participants in this study who come into regular conflict with teachers and administrators, Jayda is perhaps the most obviously at odds with school. Or, from the abundance perspective, she is the most passionate resistor of her own domestication, the most vocal protector of her own and her communities' ways of knowing. The final paragraph of her essay shows this:

> Ways I think I can have a more positive learning experience is if the teachers would allow us to bring more of our outside nature into school. Because teachers fail to realize that what and where we are started outside of school like in our homes, churches, and communities, and more. But I believe that we

as students would be more successful if we wouldn't get shut down when we try to bring in our outside learning.

Jayda knew very well who her audience was for this essay: it was me. I wanted to study students' abundance, but I could not see past what I perceived as their deficits, and she was letting me know it.

What I Learned from Jayda: Some Ideas for Liberating Abundance in the Classroom

The findings of this study point to at least two areas in which teachers might support students as they learn better to harness their abundant resources. First, I have said that students who participated in my research were "creatively maladjusting," but that label was not precise. Rather, Kohl (1994) might say that most of the students in this study were thoughtlessly maladjusting, failing to reflect on their methods of resistance and thereby damaging both their learning and their credibility. In order to maladjust to a disharmonious environment creatively, students must behave in accordance with their own values and needs while at the same time staying out of trouble and continuing to learn. Teachers can support students in learning to do so. It could be as simple as brainstorming with students the kinds of situations in which they feel they need to maladjust, working as a group to imagine what some creative solutions might look like, and making those strategies part of the class behavioral norms. And teachers ourselves might creatively maladjust. For example, I know a teacher who talks with students about how to have successful side-conversations—those that will not distract others or diminish students' own learning. Another colleague instructs students how to write a good essay at the last minute.

Second, teachers might focus on helping students learn to convert tacit to explicit knowledge. Tyrell and Kyle already knew what skills basketball requires of them; their eyes lit up when I clumsily fed them that information because they instantly understood the application to academic learning. If I had not been operating under the specter of time deficit, it would have been simple to ask them a few questions, and support them in activating the abundant knowledge they already have. The project of making visible, reflecting upon, and then revising and reconstructing our tacit understandings of how the world works, our cultural values, and the significance of our experiences—this in itself could take the whole school year. Indeed, the endeavor is infinite. Placing such a project at the center of our curriculum is precisely what is needed.

Stopping students from bringing their abundant outside resources into the classroom does not have to equal chaos. It does not mean letting students do whatever they want. Rather, it means that instead of spending all our time as teachers attempting to suppress the abundance that constantly erupts into our classrooms, we can use students' interests and cultural expertise and ways of knowing to support authentic, meaningful learning. Many educators are already doing so. Lee (2007) offers one compelling approach through "cultural modeling," which draws "cultural data sets" from "the routine practices and attendant belief systems" of communities of color and low-income communities (p. 35). Christensen (2009) has described a whole array of practices for the language arts classroom that draw on students' experiences and expertise. And democratic educators, including Apple and Beane (2007) and Meier (1995), have demonstrated how effective teaching and learning can be when the voices of students—and their families and communities—are meaningfully included in educational decision making.

This is not to say that putting the abundance view into practice will be easy: on the contrary, I expect that, in the beginning especially, it may be very challenging. I will need to be able to make a case for my abundance-based classroom practices even when my school faces enormous pressure to operate on assumptions of deficit. Moreover, it will take time for both me and my students to learn how to trust and listen to one another and build understanding and meaning together. But I also believe that it will be surpassingly worthwhile: my students (and I) will learn better and will learn more. We will learn authentically and lastingly. Stephen, a participant in this study, points out an additional benefit:

although the transition from a deficit to an abundance classroom may be challenging, as students' learning becomes more meaningful, Stephen wisely argues, "Teachers [will] have an easier time." I believe this is true. My job will be incomparably easier when the Jaydas in my classroom are busy, not distracting their neighbors or shouting, "This is stupid!" but rather engaging in the reliably fascinating act of genuine learning.

Abundance gushes endlessly into school, no matter how much the culture of deficit attempts to keep it out. It tumbles into our classrooms with our students jostling in off the basketball courts after lunch, still carrying the ball under their arm; it spills over every time our students' emotions and feelings about what's going on in their lives affect how they are learning, which is to say unceasingly; and it erupts in our classrooms when, faced with the demand that they become passive, obedient receptacles of knowledge, our students resist in whatever ways they know how. My job is to let abundance in.

Notes

1. Adapted from an unpublished master's thesis at the University of Washington, Bothell.
2. Participants' names have been changed.
3. I am deeply indebted to Bert Hopkins, a teacher at Seattle Girls' School, who first introduced me to the idea of classroom abundance.
4. Here and throughout, exchanges with students presented in this transcript form (with the speaker identified at the head of each line) are drawn from officially collected data. Where exchanges are presented in conventional dialogue format (with quotation marks), they have been reconstructed from my memory.

References

Apple, M. W., & Beane, J. A. (Eds.). (2007). *Democratic schools: Lessons in powerful education* (2nd ed.). Portsmouth, NH: Heinemann.

Bourdieu, P., & Passeron, J. (1977). *Reproduction in education, society, and culture*. London: Sage.

Christensen, L. (2009). *Teaching for joy and justice: Re-imagining the language arts classroom*. Milwaukee, WI: Rethinking Schools.

Delpit, L. (1995). *Other people's children: Cultural conflict in the classroom*. New York: Free Press.

Dewey, J. (1966). *Democracy and education: An introduction to the philosophy of education*. New York: Free Press.

Duckworth, E. (1987). *'The having of wonderful ideas' and other essays on teaching and learning*. New York: Teachers College Press.

Freire, P. (2008). *Pedagogy of the oppressed* (M. B. Ramos, Trans., 30th anniversary ed.). New York: Continuum International.

Gutiérrez, K. D., & Rogoff, B. (2003). Cultural ways of learning: Individual traits or repertoires of practice. *Educational Researcher, 32*(5), 19–25.

Hinchey, P. H. (2004). *Becoming a critical educator: Defining a classroom identity, designing a critical pedagogy*. New York: Peter Lang.

Kohl, H. (1994). *"I won't learn from you" and other thoughts on creative maladjustment*. New York: New Press.

Lee, C. D. (2007). *Culture, literacy, and learning: Taking bloom in the midst of the whirlwind*. New York: Teachers College Press.

Meier, D. (1995). *The power of their ideas: Lessons for America from a small school in Harlem*. Boston: Beacon.

Miles, M. B., & Huberman, A. M. (1994). *Qualitative data analysis: An expanded sourcebook* (2nd ed.). Thousand Oaks, CA: Sage.

Nash, R. J. (2004). *Liberating scholarly writing: The power of personal narrative*. New York: Teachers College Press.

National Commission on Excellence in Education. (1983). *A nation at risk: The imperative for educational reform: A report to the Nation and the Secretary of Education, United States Department of Education*. Washington, DC: National Commission on Excellence in Education.

Nieto, S. (1999). *The light in their eyes: Creating multicultural learning communities*. New York: Teachers College Press.

Palmer, P. J. (1997). The heart of a teacher: Identity and integrity in teaching. *Change, 29*(6), 14–21.

Purpel, D. E. (1989). *The moral and spiritual crisis in education: A curriculum for justice and compassion in education*. Granby, MA: Bergin & Garvey.

Robinson, V. M., & Lai, M. K. (2006). *Practitioner research for educators: A guide to improving classrooms and schools*. Thousand Oaks, CA: Corwin.

Rodríguez, L. J. (2001). *Hearts and hands: Creating community in violent times*. New York: Seven Stories Press.

Rosenberg, M. B. (2003). *Nonviolent communication: A language of life*. Encinitas, CA: PuddleDancer.

U.S. Department of Education. (2008). *A nation accountable: Twenty-five years after A Nation at Risk*. Washington, DC. Retrieved from http://www2.ed.gov/rschstat/research/pubs/accountable/accountable.pdf

Wilhelm, J. D. (2008). *'You gotta BE the book': Teaching engaged and reflective reading with adolescents* (2nd ed.). New York: Teachers College Press.

Yosso, T. J. (2005). Whose culture has capital? A critical race theory discussion of community cultural wealth. *Race Ethnicity and Education, 8*(1), 69–91.

Zezima, K. (2010, February 24). A jumble of strong feelings after vote on a troubled school. *The New York Times*. Retrieved from http://www.nytimes.com/2010/02/25/education/25central.html

CHAPTER 21

Reverberating the Action-Research Text

Rebecca Luce-Kapler

We only know to begin in the centre where it is still
where we can try to find our way out through words
colours
there is silence and fear and loneliness in this place
where we do not age

Opening Up the Text

I look at the transcripts and realize that they are my interpretations filtered from a memory of being in that room with two other women,

> I turned the heat up so it was warm and cosy. I pulled the chair close to the coffee table across from the couch so we were in this comfortable circle. We talked about what the group would be like—we all agreed to be open, flexible and see what occurred—

and I realize there is a responsibility to tell my story, but to be clear that it is my story of this time, in this room, in this group as I sat across from two women with a maple coffee table, a pot of raspberry tea, and a plate of oatmeal cookies between us.

Can research ever be anything more than a subtle form of writing the self?[1] Or not so subtle. Perhaps it is time to reveal the writer of the research as much as the data. The writer is the data; the data is the writer. The writer who initiates the research, creates the space, becomes implicated. The research bespeaks her; she bespeaks the research.

The words are spoken—no not spoken—woven among we three through gesture, smile, giggle, guffaw, a wave of the wrist, a passing of paper, a pouring of tea, a downturn of the eyes, a toss of the head, a listening (ear cocked; eyes dreamy). Later, hearing the tape through muffled headphones there are only disembodied voices and hollow laughter, but it is enough to return memory to the room where there are the three of us: three become dimension; three-dimensional. A raspberry bush blooming from the teapot. I watch the raspberries thicken, drip red juice. The reverberations of memory are the folds of fabric I saw woven in that room.

Reverberate: to shine or glow on with reflected beams[2]

So I can listen to the tapes, bask in the pleasure of remembering that hour or two of listening to and speaking of writing. But that is not where it can end. I want to tell others: This is what I saw in that room. This is what I heard. What do you think? Continue the dialogue. Come to understand what I know, who I am, by speaking/writing to others. To point to, to show: bespeak. Belie the neutrality of research textuality.

Textuality and intertexuality. The voices that sound through the transcript; the voices that whisper; the voices that mouth words; texts that rebound words.

Reverberate: to resound, re-echo, rebound

When I reread the transcripts, typed from the tapes, the voices seem silenced; the page dead. There is no space for the reader to take a sip of tea, to laugh where the text reads [General laughter], to sigh at the [Long pause]. Now that I have killed that day—made it colder than it was even for a February—why would anyone want to read this text, except those of us who were there who can hear the voices re-echo in our memory. Is this research for ourselves alone? Maybe. Maybe research is always for ourselves, no matter what we say.

I wonder about writing a story, just a short fictional reconstruction, which will invite readers to be present in that room, taste the oatmeal cookies, see the snow blowing outside the window, smell the raspberries. Then I remember my voice on the tape from our first meeting. I sounded like I was directing traffic. If I open up room for this narrative voice, it will begin to take over: arranging characters, dipping into thoughts, sorting through motivations. I'm reluctant to see friends become full-blown characters. I know the dangers of that from writing. When I'm creating a fictional character, I feel no hesitation to step inside them, feel what they are feeling, take liberties. Of course, if I've created memorable characters, eventually they begin to shut doors in my face and tell the narrator what to do, but there is an initial commingling that would seem invasive and disrespectful of persons who live not wholly in my imagination. Maybe what I'm looking for in telling the story of this research is something else.

> The holistic sense of life without the exclusionary wholeness of art. These holistic forms: inclusion, apparent nonselection, because selection is censorship of the unknown, the between, the data, the germ, the interstitial, the bit of sighting that the writer cannot place. Holistic work: great tonal shifts, from polemic to essay to lyric. A self-questioning, the writer built into the center of the work, the questions at the center of the writer, the discourses doubling, retelling the same, differently.[3]

In writing a poem, a poet searches for and anticipates a pattern to emerge from her perceptions, sensations, and emotions.

> You begin with the chaos of impressions and feelings, this aura that overtakes you, that forces you to write. And, in the process of writing ... the order-the marvelous informing order emerges from it.[4]

After the first white heat of writing, I choose the shape and rhythm of the line, the diction, the sound. How things are said matters as much as what is said. A poem filled with profound images falters if it is carelessly constructed.

There is possibility in poetry for shaping the words of a research transcript, of revitalizing the words. Not creating new words, still using what was said, but revealing the researcher's interpretation of those words through rhythm, juxtaposition, and placement on the page. A page where a "pause" is not written but revealed, where laughter unfolds from the break in the line, the speed of the phrase, the space left for the reader.

Reverberate: to subject to the heat of a reverbatory furnace

By not writing a new poem, but by reading the transcripts as poetry reveals what was hidden before. Makes the expected, unexpected; the usual, unusual; the polemic, lyrical. Reveals the researcher/

writer. Bespeaks her in ways she cannot imagine. Tells about the poet's ability to convert experience into vision.

Research Re-textured

THREE WOMEN SEARCH FOR TIME TO WRITE

I do more writing, but in snatches.
Caroline says to me
you have to put aside
     Caroline in her way says
you have to put aside half an hour everyday
or one hour everyday
and then I'm:
putting aside one hour to find time to go for a walk,
to find time for a nap,
to find time to read a book so I'm ready
for what I'm doing tomorrow
and there's so many hours
               I put aside
I don't have anymore hours for writing.

So what happens is that I get invited to something
and I don't have anything new
so I'm pressed for time and I whip something up.
Which isn't bad because
I work okay under deadline but
this takes more time
This takes crafting.
The deadline.
               I agree. I can't–I can't
               just sit like I couldn't
               just sit down last night
               and write something
               for today
               because I just had too many other
               things
               going on in my head
               and it's not,
               it's not my real writing,
               it's not real.
               I don't know.
I had only minutes to write
     I like some of those pieces,
     but they are really
     bereft of imagery.

     I think anyway.
               this year
               I've had time to spend with Emily.
               So I think what you're saying
               about time is really
               an important thing.
               That being able to be there
               and yet I mean I've struggled
               with this for so long—
               how to find the time and still live

and–

raise a family and–
>   I don't know. I just don't know
>   how to do all the things. I
>   don't know. I just
>   don't know
>   how to do it very well. Sometimes
>   there's little windows
>   like right now for me
>   where I can do it,
>   but I know this won't last.

So how can
I guess you learn to write
under those constraints.
I mean—look—
out of incredible horrible circumstances,
great literature is born
but my god.

Con-text: With the Texts[5]

As writer/first reader of this research text, I begin by interrogating my situatedness, my embodiedness, embeddedness in the text.

> Not positing oneself as the only, sol(e) authority. Sheep of the sun. Meaning, a statement that is open to the reader, not better than the reader, not set apart from; not seeking the authority of the writer. Not even seeking the authority of the writing. (Reader could be writer, writer reader. Listener could be teacher.)[6]

I am in the text like I was in that room in February. The feel of upholstery beneath my fingers, thick wool socks resting on the edge of the table, the light weight of pages resting on my lap. They rustle as I search to revisit the image that shook me. I am in that room with my awareness of earlier writing groups hovering on the edges. A radio show about women that I heard last night while driving home is not far behind my other thoughts, and the edginess from yesterday's poetry class is still evident in the way I hug my poem to my chest. Voices of others intertwine with mine as I speak about the story one of the women just read to us; they color my thinking.

Rereading this retexturing of the transcript stirs me to emotional memories even stronger than our discussion during our meeting. I remember my edge of desperation to find space to write.

> When I first began to write at home with two small children, it was an effort of will some days to make it to my typewriter, but gradually a rhythm of working was found that could accommodate my children and their emergencies. I learned to type and breastfeed at the same time. If I kept the angle of my knees just right, I could even use both hands. I wrote when they napped and when they would no longer nap, I wrote while they played by my feet. I also learned to keep a thought, a character, a storyline in my head while we went for walks or when I bandaged a bloody knee. The writing streamed through my head constantly; my world was lived on two planes.

In reading the words from the transcript, in letting them sink into me, things begin to stir. When I arrange the transcript into poetic form, the line breaks suggest the edge of desire/despair

I put aside.
>   I can't—I can't

>   but I know this won't last

that was there in the conversation between the three of us, but my returning shades it deeper, darker as my own history interacts with the words again and again.

Some resentment lingers here too: Women searching for time; sometimes spinning in circles. Threads of request, need and obligation tugging all the time and the desire for writing, to write, to be a writer.

> Why was it so difficult to be a teacher and writer? Part of the difficulty, I think, lay in being a mother too. My life seemed forever in a web of relationships. I interacted with at least 150 students a day; when I came home, I had two more children who wanted my time. Immersed as I was in the midst of young people, it was difficult to form a relationship with fictional characters. There was not enough time to disconnect and reconnect. But time was only part of the difficulty within this relationship-rich world. The other part was the expectation and evaluation of what I did as a woman. And because my writing was about my life as a woman, those expectations and judgements also coloured that aspect of my work. I was experiencing what many women before me have experienced—a sense of worthlessness about what I was doing.

At the same time because I can write, because I am a white, middle-class woman of some privilege compared to other women, I can write this desperation, write out this resentment. Then show the text to the other two, have another conversation among three relatively fortunate women. Do we hear the whispers through our walls of women less fortunate than we? I wonder. Still, it is a beginning perhaps.

> There is no more subversive act than the act of writing from a woman's experience of life using a woman's judgment.[7]

My writing, my poetry can't stay out of this research. My writing is the research; the research the writing. Poetry is subversive; reverberates.

Reverberate: to recoil *upon*, to appeal responsively *to*, rebound

Pre-text: Before the Text

Our conversation and the text of this conversation arises from a tangled world of voices, texts, textual strategies and interpretations all colored with social and cultural significance. We three are women struggling to write from what has been a largely patriarchal world and from a history where women have not been seen as important writers.

Hear John Gardner after confessing that his wife Joan is a collaborator in his writing with her imaginative suggestions for his characters:

> I use a lot of people, Joan in particular. She hasn't actually written many lines because Joan's too lazy for that. But she's willing to answer questions. The extent of her contributions doesn't quite approach collaboration in the modern sense.[8]

I want to hear Joan's side of the story. Was she like Dorothy Wordsworth whose talent was overshadowed by her brother's need? Or was she like Colette whose husband locked her away in a room to ghostwrite for him?

What we have valorized as great writing, as "real" literature, has been a particular way of seeing and responding to the world. And written mostly by men who feel that to create great art is to withdraw from the world into garrets and ivory towers and to use the language of the father tongue that creates gaps and distance between the experience of relationship and the word.

> … a man finds it (relatively) easy to assert his "right" to be free of relationships and dependents, a la Gauguin, while women are not granted and do not grant one another any such right, preferring to Jive

as part of an intense and complex network in which freedom is arrived at, if at all, mutually. Coming at the matter from this angle, one can see why there are no or very few "Great Artists" among women, when the "Great Artist" is defined as inherently superior to and not responsible towards others.[9]

Those are the conditions for women writing under masculine constraints. Adrienne Rich calls for the need to re-vision women's writing. It is a matter of survival, she says, that we see with fresh eyes and enter the old text in a critical new direction.

Until we can understand the assumptions in which we are drenched we cannot know ourselves.[10]

Women need to begin to share their private and painful experience, despite others' efforts to dismiss it by calling it confessional writing.
Reverberate: of flames: To strike upon, to pass over or into, as the result of being forced back
Make no mistake in thinking there is one female aesthetic.

I favour an understanding of femininity that would have as many 'feminines' as there are women.[11]

If I simply present the transcript as what "really happened" in that room among three women, if I remain silent about my role in this process, then what does that say? I can detach the story from my fingers, wash it from my eyes and pretend that it is some profound truth floating at large in the world. But that also suggests that I (as researcher) am the keeper and releaser of truth.

Many of us are beginning to recognize that representation in its traditional sense has had to do with the exercise of power. It has been, ordinarily, arbitrary and dependent on false assumption. This applies not merely to the taking for granted of the referential status of words, images, symbols, and the like.
It also applies to any person's being thought to be representative of a gender, category, ethnic group, as if there were "essences" to be embodied or exemplified.[12]

If I remain hidden in the research text, then I can be a woman speaking for other women, relating "our" experiences of writing in the world. But that is to write from the patriarchy; to leave oneself open to assumptions. I have to add my voice to many, but stand up and be heard. Take responsibility for the research I am writing; the writing I have researched.
Is the struggle for time and the desire to write that is revealed in the research text saying more? Is there a desire to find space to write about experience in a world that still has walls that try to narrow women's possibilities?

it's not my real writing
how to find the time and still live and
raise a family
I just don't know how to do it very well

Perhaps that is why the poetry is important. It begins to reopen space. Poetry has space for questions to echo. Poetry can threaten the organization of the symbolic order and the stability of meaning. It demonstrates the temporary, the fleeting in

… a process of semiotic generation which constantly challenges and seeks to transform the apparently unitary subject of the symbolic order. [This semiotic chora] is manifest in symbolic discourse in such aspects of language as rhythm and intonation and is at its strongest in non-rational discourses which threaten the organization of the symbolic order.[13]

Reverberate: to send back, return, re-echo.

Sub-text: Beneath the Text

Put your ear to the line, closer to the words. Listen. There are other texts called and recalled in the research text. The intertexuality shadows, hovers, and sometimes illuminates. Hear the echoes below the text of multiple voices, multiple discourses. Smell the other contexts in which these words have lived.[14] Underneath every line of the research text, voices speak about what we should and shouldn't do. As people(?) Women(?) Who writers are and aren't; can and can't be. But in listening we gain

> Knowledge of more than one discourse and the recognition that meaning is plural allows for a measure of choice on the part of the individual and even where choice is not available, resistance is still possible.[15]

Resistance. Subversion. A text reverberating with possibility.

Reverberate: to appeal responsively *to* Time. Writing. Women. Women writing in time, for time, through time, without time.

> putting aside one hour to find time to go for a walk
>   just sit like I couldn't
>   just sit down last night
>   and write something
>   So I think what you're saying
>   about time is really
>   an important thing.

Reverberate: to shine or reflect *from* a surface.

And below the surface. Sounding the depths, dredging the bottom, hearing the echo below the words.

Women writing? To be a writer, you must overcome resistance; you must want it enough to shove aside the room; to be a writer, you must be goal driven and organized; to be a writer, you must give up all else.

> Whip yourself into shape. A writer is committed, driven, obsessed. Shoves aside time for it.
> What kind of writer do you want to be? Give yourself five years. Write down where you want to be at the end of that time. Then do it. It's just that simple.
> Writing is a part of your life set aside, separate. Keep that time precious, holy; a time of communion with the spirit.

Writing as athletics; writing as business; writing as religion. The language of the father again.

But writing in spite of. Writing anyway. Even writing between time. In no time. Writing as you walk down the street, drive the car. Never in training to write, but always writing. Not praying to write, but writing. Writing of our experience.

> The mother tongue is language not as mere communication but as relation, relationship.[16]

Three women writing, speaking of writing, in relationship with one another. Weaving a text, choosing colours from other voices, soaking the threads with their own dye: indigo, violet, cerulean, ochre, lemon. A reverberation of color.

Hearing the subtext so

> The *meaning* of the sign is thrown open—the sign becomes 'polysemic' rather than 'univocal'—and though it is true to say that the dominant power group at any given time will dominate the intertextual production of meaning, this is not to suggest that the opposition has been reduced to total silence. The power struggle *intersects* in the sign.[17]

The mother tongue speaks.

Re-text: Returning Another Time

Inscribing a specific context for a text does not close or fix the meaning of that text once and for all: there is always the possibility of reinscribing it within other contexts, a possibility that is indeed in principle boundless, and that is *structural* to any piece of language.[18]

There are many other readings or writings of this text. It seems that research is even more like poetry than I thought. I see possibilities unfold even as I choose some possibilities. I don't use all I can see; don't see all I can use. With poetry I try to reconstruct experience using words from other contexts, hoping to offer readers a vivid taste of my particular vision in a poem. In writing research, I try to reconstruct the experience, anchoring the writing in the transcript's words which I shade with my own intentions even as I invite the reader to join us in the room, to see for her- or himself. But I can never choose all the possibilities or even the best possibilities.

I exclude. Because of the complexity of language, of research, I must use the page as a boundary for this moment. If the words weren't written on this page for others to read, the language would scatter, become other meanings in other contexts.

My hope for multiple readings of this research text is merely to begin a process of playing within the spaces, of trying to recreate a situation where the reader can spot the researcher, can drink the tea, can nibble on the cookies and leave, being able to describe her or his own story of being in that room in the text for that time.

> always dancing in that one place of revelation
> the vortex where all is still
> and we can contemplate in endless fascination
> the forest the prairie
> tucking them into our bodies leaving
> our petal-strewn dresses behind
> our prints trailing through the sand

Notes

1. Robin Usher and Richard Edwards, *Postmodernism and education* (New York: Routledge, 1994), 148.
2. All definitions of reverberation in this text come from *The compact edition of the Oxford English dictionary.*
3. Rachel Blau DuPlessis, "For the Etruscans," in *The new feminist criticism: Essays on women, literature, and theory,* ed. E. Showalter (New York: Pantheon Books, 1985), 79.
4. Maxine Kumin, *To make a prairie: Essays on poets, poetry, and country living* (Ann Arbor: The University of Michigan Press, 1979), 23.
5. I am indebted to Usher and Edwards for their explication of different textualities of the research text: con-text, pre-text, and sub-text, *Postmodernism and education,* 153.
6. Rachel DuPlessis, "For the Etruscans," 75.
7. Ursula K. Le Guin paraphrasing Virginia Woolf in *Dancing at the edge of the world: Thoughts on words, women, places* (New York: Delacourt, 1978), 222.
8. Tillie Olsen, *Silences* (New York: Delacourt, 1978), 222.
9. Ursula K. Le Guin, *Dancing at the edge of the world,* 236.
10. Adrienne Rich, *On lies, secrets, and silence* (New York: W. W. Norton, 1979), 43.
11. Julia Kristeva quoted in Toril Moi, *Sexual politics: Feminist literary theory* (London: Routledge, 1990), 169.
12. Maxine Greene, "Postmodernism and the crisis of representation," *English Education* (December, 1994), 209.
13. C. Weedon, *Feminist practice and poststructuralist theory* (New York: Basil Blackwell, 1987), 89.
14. This is a paraphrase of Bakhtin's words, "Every word smells of the context and the contexts in which it has lived its intense social life …" Quoted in Tzvetan Todorov, *Mikhail Bakhtin: The dialogical principle,* trans. Wlad Godzich (Minneapolis: University of Minnesota Press, 1984).
15. Ibid., 106.
16. Ursula K. Le Guin, *Dancing at the edge of the world,* 149.
17. Toril Moi, *Sexual textual politics: Feminist literary theory* (London: Routledge, 1985), 158.
18. Ibid., 155.

CHAPTER 22

Sojourning
Locating Ourselves in the Landscape

Antoinette Olberg, Joy Collins, Colleen Ferguson,
David Freeman, Rita Levitz, Mary Lou McCaskell
and Brigid Walters

Joy Collins:

Desks and chairs
Haphazardly arranged in a circle
Students/adults/learners
Listening intently
To the speaker's voice,
Hearing their own melody.
Knobby knees stretch out,
Legs crossed, ankles bare.
Nikes, slip-ons, flip-flops,
Oxfords.
Our shoes a symbol of our differences.
A glimmer of recognition
Awakens in our eyes
Of the enormity of the task
We have undertaken.

Antoinette Oberg: The task undertaken by the owners of those shoes was to locate themselves in the landscapes they inhabited as professional educators. This task presumed that the landscape is constituted by our ways of seeing and hearing. While the land itself may be given, a landscape is what is seen and heard from a particular location. In other words, a landscape is an expression of reality shaped by the ways of seeing and hearing available to us from our current position in time and space.

As much as we inscribe our landscapes, they also inscribe us. Our sensibilities are inherited from our forebears and reinforced by our contemporaries. Yet our current sensibilities are neither exhaustive nor immutable. By attending carefully to what is around us, we can come to be able to see and hear what was before invisible and inaudible. We produce a different reality. We take up a different position in a different landscape.

The term "sojourning" is chosen to suggest the temporariness of a location. Every position is open to reconsideration. Locating ourselves in a landscape is a continuous struggle. "Sojourning" is chosen instead of "journeying" or "questing" to indicate that neither the goal nor the method of movement is known in advance. This does not mean the inquiry is aimless or formless, but rather that it is undetermined, producing itself according to its own requirements. Setting out is deceptively simple: it begins with writing about what we are in the midst of, what interests us deeply *(inter esse*—to be in the midst of). By paying careful attention to what is taken for granted in our descriptions, usually with prompting from another sojourner,[1] we can begin to reconsider our locations and rewrite our topographies.

The selections of writing in this chapter are pauses in the sojourns of six educators. These six were part of a larger group of twenty-three educators who enrolled in a two-year master's program in Curriculum Studies and Educational Administration through the University of Victoria. This paper is not about that master's program, although it must be acknowledged that the community of inquiry that formed within it was important for the writing that was done. This paper focuses on the inquiries of six people[2] whose sojourns took them into landscapes different from their accustomed ones. Each of them came to see and hear themselves, their students, their families, and others in their social and cultural contexts in ways they had not done before. They came to speak and write differently, to live differently, as they will continue to do again and again.

I have disassembled each person's writing and reassembled the entire collection of parts, interspersing one person's writing with another's, partly to suggest the non-linear, discontinuous nature of sojourning and partly to allow certain themes to stand out through both similarity and contrast. Collins's writing directs our attention to the ordinary events of everyday life and keeps returning us there, reminding us of the requirement to seek understanding first from within rather than from without. Levitz shows how a voice that has been silenced may eventually speak again, a theme sketched on a larger scale by Freeman. Both Freeman and McCaskell deal with problematic relationships with First Nations peoples, Freeman in terms of difference and McCaskell in terms of similarity. Like McCaskell, Walters illuminates her own life by seeing the lives of her students from a shifted vantage point. The poetry of Levitz and the story Ferguson received from Margaret Jackson show how it is possible to reinvent a landscape, liberating ourselves from unknowing complicity in our own subjugation.

I have intentionally avoided more specific interpretations of these writings, preferring instead to allow each reader her own reflections. For me personally, they prompt reflections about our embeddedness—the ways we are implicated in and inscribed by dominant cultural practices—and the attendant requirement for continuous doubting of our analyses. I am also struck by our connectedness to others—the other in the self as well as others with whom we live—and the paradoxical requirement for detachment in order to discern the depth and complexity of these relationships. Doubt and detachment characterize a way of living different from the one I learned from my elders, a landscape different from the one in which I used to locate myself.

Joy Collins:

Ten past nine
Home at last
Daughter to bed.
I pooed my pants Mom.
You didn't put in any underpants Mom.
The fault becomes mine.
No, I guess I didn't.
She's been at her Dad's—smoky, littered
Her hair smells
And we washed it just last night.
I should have married a rich man.

Margaret Jackson (told to Colleen Ferguson[3]): *My name is Margaret and I am an alcoholic. I am an Indian woman who grew up on a reserve with two brothers, five sisters and alcoholic parents. I started to drink at the age of twenty-four. I got into a lot of trouble from drinking too much.*

I had a really fast life, no time to grow up. My mom and auntie always told me what could happen if I continued to carry on and that my babies would be deformed. I "cooled it," but only for a while. When I carried, I was on my best behaviour. I was scared.

After my fourth baby was born and a year and a half old, I hit the booze again, hard and heavy. After all I deserved a good time. I was a good mother, only the man I lived with drank a lot and roamed all over. It was catch-up-and-get-even time so I drank and roamed all over too.

Whenever I could, I sold household items. Drunken Indian, yes, that is exactly what I was. I was always trying to be someone I wasn't. I could talk all night when drunk; sober I was shy and ashamed and hid. Blackouts were many. Broken promises to my children were many.

I would tell them, "Mom is going to town for groceries and I will be right back with something good for you." But mom never did. I only came home when I had no place else to go, and never with food, only booze. I used to leave my children—sometimes for a week. I needed lots of attention and booze; it was time for me to get out and get even again.

Rita Levitz:

Voice and Silence were born together,
Born attached.
Their mother, at first, was pleased.
She loved her child Silence, and was excited by Voice.

But soon, a split appeared between them,
And one of the offspring,
Silence,
Became favoured.
Silence did not embarrass;
Silence knew how to act.
Voice did not.
Voice carried the wildness of her birth, still saw the
stars   and wind and
water she
                                                had come from,
And gave it sound.
But Voice was not nurtured;   Silence was.
Silence grew strong, felt important.
Voice grew weak and unsure.
Silence watched, and what she saw, Voice forgot how to say.
Silence wore grays, plaids and pleats, had hair in bobby pin curls.
Silence smiled, people smiled around her, and she forgot about
Her sister Voice.

Mary Lou McCaskell: I thought I'd tell you about a school district I once knew. When I first became acquainted with the children and parents of this area, a school district didn't exist. Local schooling was delivered by a national level of government up to grade seven. Students who wanted to continue had to leave their homes and go to nationally (later provincially) sponsored facilities at various regional locations. Parents told me the lucky ones had relatives to stay with. The others were boarded with strangers. The changes (electricity, plumbing, buses, food, a barrage of unfamiliar stimuli) were heartfelt by all. Some could come to terms with their new situation, some could not.

From time immemorial The People had lived beside the river. It had fed them, transported them, bathed them inside and out, and occasionally washed clean the land they chose to live on. It was the latter ability of the river that set the stage for The Choice. Certainly there had been village moves in the past to other spots along the river. Knowledge of an ancient village passed from ancient elders to present-day elders. As a young teacher I wandered the gutted school building wondering what memories my older students had of their times spent in this relatively new-looking structure. (Local hearsay reported this structure had cost a half million dollars, even then.) I wandered the overgrown paths and derelict wooden sidewalks that ran along sagging picket fences surrounding the vacant but still handsome Victorian and post-1930s houses. I envied the sense of community the physical setting bespoke.

Some of the older children remembered the evacuation and had told me stories of their fears during the final flood. Reverence was in their voices as they spoke of "the old village." The old fellow who had seen us and fetched us from the far side of the river just now told of older people like him returning in the summer to live, planting their gardens in the river's rich loam and preparing the river's fish for winter sustenance. On the return journey he was silent. He deposited his cargo on the far side of the river where a road connected the valley to another world and to the new village.

I was never sure who chose the spot, the elders or government agents. The story was told both ways. Perhaps it was both. On the hillside there would be no repetition of a flood nor sight of its cause. Nor would there be gardens to grow in the clay-based earth. Paths and wooden sidewalks gave way to earthen roads for people and cars alike. Electricity brought to the valley by a logging camp farther north was available on this side of the river. Although radio and television wouldn't be available for several years, two outdoor telephones connected the village to anywhere. A school was built with money that had not been available for rebuilding at the flooded site.

David Freeman: People were milling about the hall and the din of conversation reverberated off the walls of the large banquet room. Many of the people seemed to know each other and small nodes coalesced, dissipated and reformed again. I am never comfortable in large groups, but I was able to pick out of the crowd one or two individuals that I knew and gravitated toward them.

I was in Prince Rupert for the Community Futures Association's annual meeting. People from all over British Columbia interested in community development were meeting for three days to discuss community economic development issues and Native–non-Native partnerships, the theme of the conference. It was the evening banquet and the room was filled with white-covered tables. An announcement was made that dinner would soon be served and people began to sit down. I picked the closest table and sat down. Throughout the room polite dinner conversations soon ensued.

On my left sat a man, younger than I by about ten years. I commented on his black jacket with a gold eagle and the words "Gwa'sala 'Nakwaxda'xw Nation" proudly embroidered on its back; it was striking. We talked about where he was from and where I was from, polite dinner conversation. He told me he was born in a remote village up near Rivers Inlet and now lives in Port Hardy where he works for one of the Native Bands. When I told him I worked in Alert Bay, a troubled expression came over his face; I left it at that. We talked some more, about the conference, the workshops and speakers. I told him I worked for North Island College. "Where in 'the Bay' is that?" he asked. "Namgis House, old St. Mike's," I replied. He turned away and began to eat.

Later we began to talk again. "I don't like to visit Alert Bay," he said with a pained expression on his face. He told me how he had had to leave his village to attend the residential school in Alert Bay, how that experience has continued to haunt him. He told me that when he was young he believed that he must have done something terribly wrong to be sent away from his home, family and village. Why did he have to leave when the white kids down the inlet could go to school where they lived? He said that every time he sees that school building he is reminded of how terribly he missed his family. From what he told me, he wasn't a compliant student and was often in trouble. He said that the school was very strict. "I often had to wash the stairs with a toothbrush," he told me. "Every time I see that building I'm reminded of the most terrible time of my life," he said just as the banquet speaker was introduced.

Rita Levitz: Soon Voice could not remember the sound of water,
                    the sound of stars, and light
                                                  and laughter.
                    Voice could only remember
                    The sound of anger.
                    Silence grew stronger and stronger, and Voice hid
                    herself away.
                    Eventually
                    Even Voice's anger grew dim,   and
                    She forgot the sound   that was her own voice.

Mary Lou McCaskell: In the valley three modern, well-equipped schools staffed by qualified personnel from without and increasingly within The People impart a provincial curriculum to which has been added studies of local language, pictorial artifacts and occasionally, traditional cultural ways. Modern group homes staffed by "parents" from home villages house secondary students. Classes have been graduating for over a decade. Some graduates have sought participation in post-secondary institutions. Some have succeeded and many have returned. At a mid-1980s Valley Education Conference a deep sense of frustration was publicly expressed by a spokesman of The People. Had the system failed them? Had the teachers failed them?

David Freeman: As the ferry rounds Yellow Bluffs, a broad bay comes into view. "Yalis, spread-leg beach" is what it used to be called before the white man came; now it's called "Alert Bay." Low buildings, docks, fishing boats, and houses line the shore that once hosted "big-houses" and welcomed dugout canoes.

First-time visitors watching expectantly from the ferry usually ask, to no one in particular, "What's that?" pointing to the large, three-story brick building that dominates the left side of the bay. Sometimes I look up from what I'm doing and answer, "That's the old residential school—St. Michael's." The brick monolith looks incongruous in a land of sea and cedar, the bricks brought by boat from some far-off place to a shore that was accustomed to houses made of hand-split red cedar boards. Did the builders intend the building to be so alien or was it built that way for some other reasons?

This is the building in which I work. I climb those same stairs that were washed as punishment by the man I met in Prince Rupert. Our classrooms are the dormitories that were once filled with young people who missed their families. It is a building filled with ghosts that I can't see or hear but that others can.

There are some who would like to tear down the building brick by brick; they say that it is a symbol of the worst of white colonialism with its systematic policy of assimilation. Others want to keep it; they say that it represents the transformation of something bad into something good. I have my own feelings about what should be done with the building, but I don't express them. This decision must be made by those who lived in, went to school in, or were in other ways affected by the building and all that it symbolizes.

Years ago the brick exterior was painted white. This, of course, caused it to stand out even more against the blues, greens and grays that characterize this coast. Now the paint is flaking off and the building looks like it is molting. Visitors that accompany me often suggest that it should be sandblasted. I once thought so too, but not anymore. Now I see it as symbolic: an alien institution, constructed out of foreign materials, covered by a thin veneer of white paint. As the paint is flaking off, a culture is rebuilding itself and both are revealing their inner selves.

Each day, before entering the building, I look to see how much more of the original red I see. It reminds me of the efforts that the Kwakwaka'wakw have made rebuilding their culture. It also reminds me of the strength of their spirit and the power of their culture that is the basis of their cultural regeneration. Watching this natural process is much more satisfying and appropriate to me than seeing the paint blasted off.

This building, renamed the Namgis House, now belongs to the institutions that are fostering this cultural revival. This building, built with the sole intention of destroying a culture, now houses the offices of the Nimpkish First Nation, the Band School, and the Musgamagw Tsawataineuk Tribal Council. Here are located the forces at the heart of the cultural regeneration of the Kwakwaka'wakw. Where once Native art and culture were derided is a carving studio where young artists are taught and masks and bent wood boxes are made. Where once youngsters were severely punished for speaking their language, Kwakwala is now taught. North Island College is also located in the Namgis House, and it is here where I have had the opportunity to learn many lessons about myself, as a white educator of First Nations students.

Rita Levitz:

> My silence is passionless, dry and white
> When I am alone, I like quiet,
> No music, radio or T.V.
> But that is not the kind of silence I wish to speak
> Of.
>
> My silence is hollow, fearful, clammy
> Easily saddened
> Easily caught
> Brittle to hold
> Opens and falls in little pieces
> Rolls off in many directions
> And cannot be picked up.
>
> In bargains with myself
> There has been a loser
>
> Until now.

Margaret Jackson (told to Colleen Ferguson): *One winter evening in January, a meeting for parents was called at school and I went. There sat three AA members who told me about a disease called alcoholism, and these members spoke words I will never forget. "An alcoholic is incapable of love." God how I tried to justify my drinking. I loved my children, but some form of sanity came through and I knew I loved alcohol more. That's why I left my children. I knew I was sick and I needed help.*

I started to go to AA meetings. I sat with scorn on my face, so no one would dare bother me. I hated everyone and everything, but I went. Some unseen force kept me going. These feelings of shame were great. I shamed my family and my people. I got a sponsor and wrote down what I was capable of facing. I got active in AA, prayed, and argued with AA members. I wanted so much to be right and not be an alcoholic.

Finally after my first year, I woke up. I learned to listen and do what I was told to maintain sobriety and gain peace of mind. After five years, I still kept an open mind. I could make some positive decisions. After six years, I went back to school to get some education. I made it; I got accepted in school. I am teachable.

Brigid Walters: When an adult returns to school after a period of years, she is making a change in a system which has been orderly in some way, even if the order is not immediately apparent. Each term I have a group of students in biology who have been out of school for several years and who are returning in order to train or retrain for a career. Most often they are women—housewives, single mothers, waitresses; some are men—commonly loggers or fishermen who have been injured or whose job has disappeared.

They have decided to return to school in order to change something in their lives—most often they want to improve their financial situation. Many are living on social assistance or are working at hard, poorly paid jobs and are bringing up children. The men are on Unemployment Insurance or disability coverage, also most often trying to support a family. So they have reached a decision to become a nurse, a dental hygienist, a forestry or fisheries technologist, after several months of exploration, advising, and conversation with the counselors, the workers at Manpower or at the Ministry of Social Services, and me. The decision has been difficult but has been made. We all try to help the student to consider realistically the changes that will occur, in terms of the time commitment and the commitment to school work that has to be made. But planning for change and going through change are not the same thing at all; it is only later as the reality begins to be understood that a student most often gives up.

Joy Collins:
My mind excited by the evening workshop,
What I've heard
Connecting with what I'm reading
Connecting to my classroom practice.
The responsibility becomes mine.
The drive there and back.
What does next year hold?
You're transferring? You've applied where?
Pro-D day coming up—schedule's a mess
Someone should complain
But we can't.
I should have married a banker—Mom likes bankers.
Or maybe a doctor. A doctor is good.

Mary Lou McCaskell: When I first read Burble's "The tragic sense of education,"[4] I thought of this school district, the teacher, the parents, the students I once knew. I thought it was just the article to mail to the district's superintendent, a member of The People himself. It said what I felt should be said but never had been said or perhaps even thought by any of us: education comes with no guarantees, it doesn't make a predictable product like a factory does, it's a process and schooling is only one facet. But thinking about this a little more I know I wouldn't presume to mail anything of the sort because the story within this school district is my story, too.

No, I'm not of these people, but my people made a choice, too. In the early part of this century my maternal grandmother with her five children, and later as a young man my father chose to cross not a river but an ocean. My life is speckled with snatches of a language, pictorial artifacts, and traditional ways of my ancestors. It is not what it would have been had that ocean not been crossed. In that old village on the other side of the river, I envied not the Victorian houses, picket fences, or tangled gardens but the sense of community, of belonging, of counting not because of anything you might achieve through schooling or any other form of public acclaim but because you are one of the people. And so it is not so difficult to look at this old village and see what also might have been mine.

Brigid Walters: So the new student returns to college, full of hope and anticipation, coming from a background of being in control of his or her life, of being part of family and community, of having a schedule of activities which has been worked out over a long period of time. She has been responsible for looking after her children and husband, for going to work, for running her house. He has been working in a resource industry in a job which is male identified and is carried out in company of other males and has been responsible for family support and structure.

The first change, and it is a shock, especially for the men, is that they lose control. Now someone else is setting the schedule, determining what will be done when, what is acceptable performance, and who will be the members of the new group. The next change is the concrete alteration in their lives required by the demands that I and the other instructors place upon them: the *idea* of ten hours of school work is not the same as the ten hours as they really happen.

In addition to the new experience of sitting in class for an hour and a half and working in the laboratory for three hours, there is a necessity after class to sit at a desk, at home or at school, and read attentively, usually making notes. What is this like for someone who has perhaps never done it? To me it is a comfortable habit, a common way of working, but to these students it is unfamiliar and difficult. And they are faced with being evaluated by me, in ways foreign to them, on how well they manage to guess how much they are expected to know and how they should tell me about it.

They begin to experience the tension between desire for change and desire for stability, and unless the change is perceived as positive, as worth the pain of losing the stability, they disappear back to their old, orderly, familiar system. This happens early in the process. How can I invite and encourage such a student to remain physically present so that he or she can begin to open up and to receive the "spreading change" which is part of and which leads to learning?

Joy Collins:

> Kettle's home ten minutes.
> I pull the blind too hard;
> It wraps around the rod.
> Damn. Now I have to get the stool.
> The phone rings.
> It's Lois. I was just thinking of you.
> I know you've had a long day; I won't keep you.
> I listen, undressing with one hand
> Slip into my pajamas and lay back on the bed.
> There's just a couple of things I thought you should know.
> Met with Beau's Mom—that went well.
> That's good.
> *A doctor works too hard. Maybe a lawyer.*
> *Do they make jokes about the wives of lawyers?*

Brigid Walters: I have gained some insight over the last two years into the problems that my students face when they return to school. Like them I decided to change; the reasons included, certainly, a financial reason: with another degree, I would be qualified to apply for other positions in my institution which would pay more. I think (and hope) that a desire to expand my areas of thought was an equally important reason. As I have read, thought, and written, the first reason has receded and the second one has become paramount; I had forgotten the satisfaction and pleasure which comes from intellectual work in a different mode from that which is essential in teaching.

Like my students, I have a family, a full-time job, and a structured life, into which I was inserting another activity. The difficulties that I encountered are similar to the difficulties that my students encounter, with the difference that at least I am used to the method of working. I have found that the necessity to restrict family activities, to work on weekends and during the summer is a greater problem than I had anticipated. Even having to refrain from professional activities that normally I would involve myself in has been hard, and assigning priorities to the various demands made on my time has not been well done.

We expect a lot of our students and often do not give credence to their priorities, arrogantly assuming that course work comes first, and everything else comes second. I must always remember that life comes first for them, as it does for me—an aging parent, a sick child, or an unhappy partner will not wait until a more opportune time.

Joy Collins:

Tara's writing notes again.
I took one off of Shanna and had to tape it together
After school.
It said, She's getting meaner.
I'll mention it to her Mom. She's coming in tomorrow.
Daniel peed on the bathroom floor,
Rick from grade five saw him do it and made him clean it up.
That's good.
The principal wants to see him tomorrow.
Why?
There's nine items on the staff meeting agenda Nine?
Yeah and Spring Things are sixth on the agenda
And there are eight things under it.
Then there's Learning for Living with three things under it
And computers with three things under it.
Oh my God, can't we miss?
An engineer is even better
My brother is an engineer and he's a nice guy.

Did you start any of the new things we talked about?
No, not yet.
You probably need to give it some thought.
Well, I guess I should go.
O.K. see you tomorrow.
I'll come in early and talk to you before you have to leave.
There were some good things that happened too
About Scott and Justin.
That's great.
Bye.
Bye.

I would never marry a teacher.
A rich man maybe.
Someone to rub my neck and
Bring me a sherry
And tell me to sleep in tomorrow
Or maybe we should catch the last of the snow
At Mount Washington.

My tea is finished
The taco chips devoured
My sense of control restored.
I'll do my day plan
And I'll dream of another day
When things slow down and
I can do what I want to do.
There really are those kind of days, aren't there?
I don't care if he's rich or not

I just want him to make my lunch for tomorrow.
I'll work and support him.

You did that once, remember?
Oh yeah.

Rita Levitz:

Before, I did not know I was lost
Before, I knew I was lost but was too busy
Before, I knew but could not look any further

the unknown rested quietly
motionless, undisturbed,
in a musty, old, wooden trunk,
whose creakings and cobwebs warned me
when I got too close

And now ...
uncovering my eyes
unsealing the silence
unleashing the voice

> I know when I am lost
> The discomfort, too great to be ignored
> Has become my valued companion.

Appendix

As observer and supporter of these sojourners and many like them over the last 20 years, I have observed the following conditions to be conducive to sojourning. First, sojourners themselves must possess a disposition to question, even if it has not been acted upon in the past. They must also have the courage to seek for and to acknowledge the often elusive connection between their inquiry and an interest buried deep within their psyches. They must be able to imagine a different landscape from the one they first see. And they must have the persistence to keep going in the face of uncertainty and difficulty and also after the satisfaction of arrival.

Second, an environment that encourages sojourning usually includes at least one other sojourner. Ideally there is a community of sojourners, who provide each other moral support and inspiration. Vicarious learning takes place as people learn from seeing others doing their work, seeing what is possible and how one might come to it.

There must also be a context within which sojourners can give meaning to what they see and hear. This context is created not only by others in the immediate community of inquirers, but also by distant others whose writings we read. It is important to read in multiple modes: not only to grasp what the writer is saying, but also to appreciate her location as she speaks. We read not only to accumulate information, but also to extend our own understanding. Choosing texts that attract us, we open ourselves to them and allow them to work on us, literally to (in)form and to inspire us. We do this by continually coming back to our own landscapes, incorporating the texts of others into our own web of understanding. This means coming back to what we have written and writing again. It is crucial that writing precede reading in order for this process to occur. Otherwise, the risk of sliding out of our own landscape and into the landscape of the other's text is too great.

There must be an audience for our own writing, one who receives the writing without judgment. An audience is valuable firstly as an impetus to write and secondly as respondent. The readers of our writings may simply acknowledge them, or say how they connect to their own lives, or ask questions born of genuine curiosity about what is at work in the writing. Sojourners judge the quality of their work themselves using standards immanent in the work, namely, the extent to which it furthers their understanding of where they are located in their landscapes. (It is important to note that evaluation by a reader becomes an issue only when grading is required.)

An arena of legitimacy is also required, usually in the person of an Other in front of whom the work is validated. Validation comes not from judging the product of an effort but by acknowledging the work as valuable and by prompting the sojourner to keep going.

Finally, there must be continuity over time in order for the inquiry to develop and gain momentum. Patience is required in the face of ubiquitous deadlines. Sojourning is sporadic: we often rest in one place for a time. There is no way to speed up the process. Once it begins, however, it continues indefinitely with greater or lesser intensity and with more or less evident material effects.

Notes

1. Conditions conducive to sojourning are outlined in the appendix.
2. The writings included here were chosen by their authors, who were themselves se!se!f-selected from the larger group of 23 inquirers. The excerpts included here were extracted from a longer piece of similar woven form produced by the six inquirers themselves for presentation at the 1994 JCT Conference on Curriculum Theory and Classroom Practice in Banff, Alberta. The text of that presentation is available from David Freeman, Box 71, Sointula, British Columbia, Canada VON 3EO; e-mail FREEMAN@NIC.BC.CA
3. This story is included here with Margaret Jackson's permission.
4. N. C. Burbles, "The tragic sense of education," *Teachers College Record* 91, no. 4 (1990): 469–479.

PART FIVE

Complexities

Introduction

No One Ever Said It Would Be Easy

As the preface suggested, nothing in this text is intended to be definitive. In various strands of critical action research, participants, locale, purpose, and report format vary widely. It should be no surprise, then, that the types of challenges that emerge from projects vary widely as well. While some are not surprising (as when a politician shows interest in research that appears critical of local industry), others often are (as when a researcher learns something unsettling about him- or herself). Part 5 offers a glimpse of such complexities.

In Chapter 23, Edward J. Brantmeier reports on his sojourn as a peace builder in a high school where "racism, sexism, militarism, and classism were an everyday reality." Part of a university research team working with school staff to improve conditions for newcomer students, Brantmeier approached his work with teacher inquirers in a spirit of openness:

> Understanding a research site, from the inside-out, requires allowing one's own sense of what is right and wrong, what is good and what is true to be questioned by the logic and everyday meaning-making of participants in the research process. It's not easy, but essential. [A]n approach of vulnerability ... allows the researcher to more fully understand oppressive conditions and the flipside—related privileges.

However, as the author illustrates, a critical researcher can be fully committed to equity and yet concurrently blind to elements of personal privilege. In the author's own words: "The unraveling of my own myth of meritocracy was part of the critical inquiry process. Hard work alone doesn't propel one in social and economic mobility." For those of us who occupy privileged positions and who have worked hard, the realization that we cannot claim full responsibility for our own achievements comes slowly, and it is a bitter pill to swallow. A second realization that Brantmeier reached is equally difficult to take in: attaining the social equity critical researchers so vocally support will require sacrifices from them, too. That is: not only will some distant owning class, some *they*, have to yield their power: we in the academy will have to give up unearned privilege and power as well. The author speaks the truth, and speaks it plainly, when he says that embracing critical work with openness and vulnerability is "not easy"—but is "essential." How far forward can critical workers move society if we ourselves do not honestly confront the practical implications of our own privilege?

In Chapter 24, discussing "disruptions," Janet L. Miller also offers a candid account of a painful lesson in the difficulty of exorcising a privileged perspective. As a university researcher, Miller worked for some years with several teacher researchers to collaboratively design innovative classroom curriculum. In such situations, university researchers typically assume—as Miller did—that all participants in the project were equal partners and that the teacher researchers were fully empowered to make their own decisions. However, as events unfolded, Miller was challenged by the fact that her teacher research partners did actually feel empowered ... so empowered, in fact, that they felt free to make choices in direct opposition to her own most cherished beliefs. Even worse: they felt secure in making choices without considering her point of view at all. Her dismay over the situation and her subsequent analysis of it led Miller to some difficult realizations:

> I now also must acknowledge that not only did I anticipate that my perspectives as university researcher might have some influence on Pam and Julie's decision, but also that I *wanted* my perspectives and theories to provide some basis for their decision. The ... episode highlighted ways in which I still *expected* to be listened to as the expert ... I couldn't deny the intentions of power [in my actions] ... Nor could I deny my slight impatience and incredulity [with the teachers' own rationale].

Miller wanted the teachers to be free in their practice—but free only to choose those things she would have chosen for them. Like confronting the questions of whether we critical researchers are willing to acknowledge that we haven't earned all we have, or of whether we are ready to yield some of our own privilege and power, confronting the fact that we often secretly assume that others will follow in our footsteps is not an easy or happy experience.

Pamela Konkol and her colleagues, Simeon Stumme and Isabel Nuñez, report on another type of personal challenge for critical researchers within the boundaries of the academy. Offered an opportunity to re-examine online programs, the authors found an existing capstone experience in their online master's program to be an "impersonal, sterile, and cumbersome task" rather than a meaningful educational experience. As part of their work to reconceptualize and recast the programs, they devised a capstone experience intended to be a "transformational encounter," with students repeatedly examining their emergent thinking throughout their coursework and eventually rendering their most important new understandings and visions in a final capstone project. As the article details, student learning did reflect the goals of critical pedagogues. These included questioning of the status quo; a willingness to take on advocacy on behalf of their students; and a commitment to engage more fully with their own students' communities in which they worked. Despite such success, however, a change in leadership led to a change in institutional vision of what constitutes *learning*: the faculty's embrace of constructivism has been replaced by a new administration's commitment to positivism. Expansion of the online program fueled by a marketing firm's stress on practical ("how-to") solutions to classroom problems further eroded support for the faculty's innovations.

Now teaching in a program out of alignment with their professional commitments, the authors struggle both to genuinely understand the positions of those well-intentioned administrators and colleagues responsible for the shift in emphasis and practice ... and to decide what actions are open to them if they are to be true to themselves:

> Our moral compasses tell us that it is our duty, our responsibility, to serve not just our candidates, but more important, the children and families that they serve as educators themselves. To *not* assist them is to be complicit in those practices and affirming those perspectives that contribute to the destruction of the very fabric of education as we know it. This is a dilemma of professional practice that none of us are sure we signed up for, but believe have a moral obligation to engage.

Unfortunately, too many teacher educators will recognize the authors' dilemma. Because we are in a time when politicians and their allies in the business sector are increasingly attempting to discipline practice in higher education as well as in pre-K–12 education, it is nearly inevitable that critical educators engaging in program design and self-studies of pedagogy will face the complexities these authors so thoughtfully illuminate.

In Chapter 26, Jeanine M. Staples and co-authors Talia Carroll, Donna Marie Cole-Mallot, Jennifer Myler, Corey Simmons, Julie Schappe, and Theresa Adkins touch on other types of challenges that they and their students encountered as they worked together in a course designed to address another problem all too familiar to teacher educators: how to erode white teacher education students' negative perceptions of students of color. In their effort to influence students' perceptions, the authors asked students to approach their experience guided by four specific principles—the Four Agreements—from the work of Don Miguel Ruiz. As the course unfolded, instructors found themselves challenged first by students' doubts about the Agreements. For example, students had difficulty accepting the idea that words substantively influence experience; they also doubted whether it is desirable—or even possible—not to make assumptions about others. In short, instructors were challenged by students' lack of faith in the instructors' approach.

Other difficulties arose for and with students who did accept such ideas. For example, working consciously not to make assumptions about angry parents of color, but at the same time working alongside others who confidently did make negative assumptions, students who embraced the Agreements began to feel themselves out of touch with their colleagues. That is, in enacting different ways of being in the world, they began to feel "weird." And, as the authors note, "The cognitive dissonance and social awkwardness immediately imposed by comprehension and appropriation of the Agreements served as a deterrent" to students' continued adherence to them. The authors' experiences remind us that students, too, face difficult personal challenges when we ask them to embrace a critical stance in their work—and the students' challenges in turn generate challenges for instructors. Again: the work is not easy. But it is essential.

Whereas the other chapters deal with various emotional challenges, Stephen R. Couch, in Chapter 27, explores the practical perils of conducting action research that supports critical ends in the context of a major research university. Couch facilitated a project involving collaboration between graduate students in an action research course and a grassroots community environmental group. In light of the fact that they knew various industries in the community were producing toxins, the environmental group developed health-related questions for the students to research. As a result, one student group identified elevated levels of brain cancer in the county, and another found an elevated level of childhood learning disabilities. Research reports from both groups noted that, although there was literature relating the presence of such toxins to those particular health problems, the toxins were only one possible cause—and not necessarily the most likely. They were clear about not suggesting a definitive cause-and-effect relationship. Despite their caution, however, when the findings became public, Couch was contacted by a high-level university administrator—who in turn had been contacted by a local congressman, complaining that the research was flawed and insisting that the university disavow the study. All's well that ends well, and this story ends well (as readers will see in the piece). Nevertheless, as the author explains, because the desire to bring about positive social change is inevitably political, researchers—including faculty who orchestrate action research projects as well as the students who conduct them—need to be prepared for the sort of political challenges generated even by such modest projects as the one reported here.

Emotional as well as practical and political challenges are an inescapable element of critical research of any kind. They cannot be avoided. However, as the authors in Part 5 make clear, they can serve as a catalyst to deepen our understanding of our students, our research partners, our contexts—and ourselves.

CHAPTER 23

Wounded in the Field of Inquiry
Vulnerability in Critical Research

Edward J. Brantmeier

> Now I've been crying lately, thinking about the world as it is
> Why must we go on hating, why can't we live in bliss?
> Cause out on the edge of darkness, there rides a peace train.
> Oh peace train take this country, come take me home again.
> "Peace Train" by Cat Stevens

In the mornings of 2003–2004 I would gas up, fuel myself with coffee, and drive my Subaru an hour or so to my dissertation field research site—Junction High School. As I drove on narrow asphalt country roads, cornfields edged by small woods and streams whizzed by. When I finally arrived at Junction High School, I was greeted by drab gray slate walls of Indiana limestone and a windowless aluminum front door. No longer an English teacher, no longer a university supervisor of student teachers, I entered the school with a new identity—educational researcher. My task was to help change prejudicial attitudes and discriminatory behaviors enacted by mostly white students toward newcomer students from Central and South America. My goal was to raise awareness about this oppression and then foster culturally responsive and inclusive teaching practices. In short, I was a peace builder. Work for peace does not necessarily come without costs, though.

Wounded in the Field

"Wounded in the field," a term rooted in the critical ethnographic research tradition (McLaren, 1992), describes a researcher's transformation of a sense of "self" and "other" from her dialogic encounters with places, people, and institutional processes in the field—the research site. In order to "be wounded," one must be open to understand and experience the world of research participants through a dialogic process (Korth, 2002) that requires de-centered position taking with multiple viewpoints. It may require a change of one's own identity and meaning making. Carspecken (1996) puts it simply: "You must be prepared to be threatened and to change through your field work" (pp. 169–170). Understanding a research site, from the inside out, requires allowing one's own sense of what is right and wrong, what is good and what is true to be questioned by the logic and everyday meaning making of participants in the research process. It's not easy, but essential. In short, an approach of vulnerability, or being open to cognitive, emotional, and behavioral change from engagement in oppressive research contexts, allows the researcher to more fully understand oppressive conditions and the flipside—related privileges.

Similar to a pedagogy of vulnerability (Brantmeier, 2013) in teaching, vulnerability in research requires researchers to open up their frames of knowing, thinking, and feeling to describe the positions of multiple cultural actors in a given research site. "Mutual vulnerability" (Kcet, Zinn, & Porteus, 2009) on the part of both researcher and participants creates intersubjective spaces where dialogical exchange can take place. In this process, the researcher comes to know her own preconceived judgments and knowledge paradigms while delving more deeply, and with more validity, into the process of reconstructing meaning from the positionalities of research participants. Critical researchers, in self-reflective processes, embark on a journey of understanding self and other in oppressive contexts, and in that process, they sometimes emerge wounded and transformed.

Being open to the beliefs, norms, and everyday practices of some members of the dominant Euro-American population at Junction High School was not an easy task; racism, sexism, militarism, and classism were an everyday reality. As part of a larger Indiana University team of researchers who were asked to help with the challenges of newcomer student integration in a historically homogenous school system, I facilitated seven teacher inquirers in an intercultural peace curricula development and implementation project at Junction High School for my dissertation project (Brantmeier, 2005). Our general goals were to lessen the degree of prejudice and discrimination experienced by newcomer students whose first languages included Spanish, Japanese, Mandarin Chinese, and Arabic through two different phases of research. First, I attempted to raise consciousness of peaceful and nonpeaceful attitudes and behaviors that impacted newcomers. Second, we attempted to develop intercultural curricula to address the lack of empathy for the situation of newcomers by several members of the white, mainstream population at the school.

Some comments made by Euro-American students to or about newcomer students included: "Don't speak Spanish here, go back to Mexico"; "All Hispanics are knife carriers"; "Why don't you ride your camel [said by a white student to an Arabic-speaking student] back to your country!"; "They [newcomer students] don't belong here, we [Euro-Americans] made this country"; and, "Hispanics are bringing crime and gangs to our community—just look at the newspaper." These prejudiced and racist comments, expressed by members of the dominant white student population, surely reflected wider Unityville community attitudes and beliefs. During the research process, it was reported that one white community member commented, "Hispanics are the new niggers of Unityville."

It was deeply painful for me to hear these racist comments, but the comments were not altogether nonfamiliar from my own experiences growing up in a rural Wisconsin town—though my memory tells me that people in Hilbert seemed less blatantly racist and blunt and, generally speaking, a little more open to diversity. At Junction High School, I strived to remain open to understanding why members of the dominant white population held these attitudes and enacted discriminatory practices against perceived "outsiders." Why do members of dominant groups create boundaries and patrol those boundaries with various cultural practices? What undergirds this strong need for a solid group identity, one that is often juxtaposed or in binary tension with another group of "others"? What cultural and human need does this in-grouping and out-grouping fulfill? Does it come from a place of fear, a habit of otherizing, an epistemological position or need for superiority? How is this form of white supremacy similar to and different than other forms enacted in different historical contexts across space and time (segregation in the American South, Apartheid in South Africa, British colonization in India, Fiji, Australia, etc.)?

Trying to understand the ideology of white supremacy was one part of my ethnographic endeavor, yet I did not see it as a form of white supremacy in 2004 as I see it now ten years later and with much thought, research, and consideration. Another part of the critical ethnographic endeavor was trying to understand why some white folks stand up to prejudice and discrimination. I strived to understand the intentions and actions of teacher inquirers who identified these attitudes and practices as non-peaceful and who committed to change them. We encountered several roadblocks and a few insights along the way.

Insights along the Way

My task was to facilitate a change process via a peace curricula development process. In collaboration with an administrator and staff member, we formed an interdisciplinary group of teacher inquirers who were reported to be "dedicated to the cause" of creating more positive conditions for newcomer transnational students. While "us" and "them" rhetoric strewn with contentious binaries and rigid dichotomies from the wake of the 2004 U.S. presidential campaigns filled the airwaves, we worked to break down barriers of prejudice and discrimination that seriously hampered transnational newcomer student adjustment at Junction High School. We aimed to build intercultural peace, or positive relationships, characterized by mutual understanding, trust, diversity affirmation, and a sharing of both decision making and available resources—characteristics of a healthy, democratic school. I share two major insights from the approximate eight-month process that deeply impacted the way I view peace building in schools. In particular, these insights lefts some wounds.

Insight One: Power, Privilege, and "Giving it up"

After teacher inquirers identified nonpeaceful behaviors in their classrooms and school that needed to change in initial group meetings, I facilitated the generation of goals for the intercultural peace curricula. Teacher inquirers wanted to make students and staff multiculturally aware; to decrease ignorance; to increase feelings of empathy and compassion for each other; to overcome resistance by [Euro-American] students; to make the school one community where people are people; to see the person through the black and white; and to recognize that all people, even Euro-Americans, have differences (Brantmeier, 2005, p. 165). Teacher inquirers desired to make the school climate more aware, more caring, and more accepting.

In one meeting in particular, teacher inquirers were asked to reflect on readings in peace and multicultural education that I had provided for them. With a lot of emotion, Julianne enthusiastically began discussing a "Valuing Diversity" chapter from Lantieri and Patti's (1996) *Waging Peace in Our Schools:*

> Knowing, that to create an equal society, we [white U.S. citizens] would not (**stresses**) grant privileges to everyone, those people we would all have to meet somewhere in the middle. Which would mean they would have to give up (**heavily stresses** last two words). And that's what they're not (**accented, stresses**) willing to do. And I think that's their greatest fear, is that equality means, "I give up." Not "I bring them up to me." I mean I just, that was extremely (**stresses**, elongates) to say "We should not accept any of them [racial and class privileges]."

Prior to the meeting, Julianne had shared that she had an epiphany when reading the book chapter on valuing diversity. Her reflection above about racial privilege and equality highlights that epiphany. Equality, in this light, will require members of the white majority in the United States to give up some of the economic, social, and political privileges that they presently hold. It will not require a "leveling of the playing field" as the often-used analogy states. It will require a relinquishing of power and privilege and a new playing field altogether.

I was very emotional when Julianne was discussing her epiphany because I felt the power of her transformational insight into dominant and subordinate group relations in the United States. When Pam began to speak about racism in the same meeting, my tears started to flow:

Because there's a lot of people out there that will say no they are not a racist. Every single person on this planet, you cannot (**stresses**), nobody can say that they are not a racist. So, it's the coming in the individual awareness, how do we get these kids, how do we get people to start (**stresses**) acknowledging where do they stand, in, in the whole issue of racism? And be acknowledgeable within themselves, and then start to grow from that? I think that's a major (**stresses**) step to get. First, where am I in this continuum of racism? Where do I stand? And where do I go from here?

Teacher inquirers were making sincere, heartfelt realizations when reading the articles that I had provided for them; and I was learning how to better lead these honest, open dialogues.

In the past ten years of my teaching experience since my dissertation research in 2004, I have walked many mostly white, middle-class students through a process of understanding racism not only as derogatory comments or discriminatory behaviors but also as an endemic structural phenomenon that is pervasive in social, economic, and political institutions. I now more deeply understand why I was overwhelmed by the insight that Pam was expressing. Racism is a form of structural violence—social, political, or economic arrangements that privilege some at the expense of others. If members of the white majority group in the United States begin to deeply and sincerely reflect on racism, power, privilege, and "giving it up," can we create a new democratic playing field where people are not dehumanized and where nonviolent relationships and participatory democracy flourish?

Reflecting on my 2004 tears now in 2014, 10 years after the interview where Pam and Julianne came to grips with their white privilege in a systemically racist social and economic order, I realize at that time I was increasingly aware of my own white racial privilege in the United States and, as a result, my notions of meritocracy—that all people advance by honest, hard work—were being crumbled by a growing awareness of legacies of racial privilege, from which Pam, Julianne, and I benefited. The unraveling of my own myth of meritocracy was part of the critical inquiry process. Hard work alone doesn't propel one in social and economic mobility. There are institutional, social, and structural layers of privilege that provide access, opportunity, and advantage to me simply because I am white, male, and heterosexual. In essence, my own frames of knowing were being directly challenged and changed alongside research participants in our process of vulnerability—of opening to realities of institutional, societal, and structural racism, sexism, classism, and linguicism. I was being wounded in the field of inquiry, and I have emerged a more aware researcher and teacher, committed to social justice, cultural competence, and sustainable peace.

Since this time, I have walked hundreds of future teachers, teachers, educational leaders, and university faculty in processes of becoming aware of their privileged and oppressed social identities, which matter in relationship to access, opportunity, and advantage (Brantmeier, Aragon, Kees, Peila-Shuster, & Anderson, 2011). In addition, I have worked with university faculty who do the same as we build our toolkits to be effective educators committed to transformative learning on the topics of power, oppression, and privilege. However, each semester I am reminded of the pain involved in individuals becoming more aware of how they participate in systems of power, privilege, and oppression. I am also more aware of how in certain aspects of our social identities we are all oppressed. Through this oppression, we can build empathetic bridges to other forms of oppression—not in a minimizing, assimilating kind of way, but in a way where we are able to examine our own oppression, become empathetic with others, and then choose to engage in acts that disrupt systems of oppression. Understanding how to rehumanize one another in the context of privilege, power, and oppression is a lifelong journey—this seems obvious now.

Insight Two: In-group and Out-group Dynamics

Imagine having recently immigrated, having brown skin in a 95% white population where many whites do not want you there, and imagine speaking a different first language than most white citizens of your town. Most of the intercultural peace curricula process focused on building bridges of understanding, intercultural empathy for peace (Brantmeier, 2008) between members of the white dominant group and newcomer student groups at Junction High School. When teacher inquirers were asked to identify words that go with nonpeace, it was clear that dominant (in-group) and minority (out-group) relations and boundaries were embedded in the word choices of teacher inquirers. Nonpeace was conceived in a relational we-to-other manner where the "we" was the predominantly white population and the "other" were students of color. Group superiority and inferiority were part of a boundary-maintenance process.

For example, one of the teachers, Lisa, identified an attitude of superiority that was based on the "other" being different, or not the same. Implicitly, she talked about an attitude of a white superiority over other groups. Similarly, Jennifer talked about "exclusion" as nonpeaceful and described it as "keeping people at bay." She explained that the basis for exclusion was an attitude of superiority and that it implied boundary maintenance. Jennifer spoke of a boundary-maintenance behavior in the form of exclusion, "We are the exclusive group. We won't allow you to come in." Mary, who identified herself as biracial/bi-ethnic, chose "division" as the most important word that went with nonpeace and referred to "something that's keeping two or more groups apart"—again alluding to a divisive boundary. Binary constructs of them and us were prevalent in teacher inquirer perceptions of the antithesis of peace at Junction High School.

In-group and out-group dynamics were strong. Different skin colors, different languages, different cultural behaviors, values, and belief systems—all of these accentuated the dichotomies of "us" and "them" between members of the dominant white, English-speaking group at Junction High School and the perceived "outsiders"—transnational newcomer students with countries of origin that included Mexico, Guatemala, Puerto Rico, Venezuela, Ecuador, El Salvador, the Dominican Republic, Israel, Taiwan, and Japan. Linguistic normative monitoring practices (Brantmeier, 2007) realized in repeated demands on newcomers by select members of the white student population and some teachers to speak English in class and in school were a method of border patrolling—of ensuring that newcomers knew the rules of how they should participate in the racial and linguistic space of Junction High School.

As a researcher in this context of this discrimination and border patrolling, I was often struck by the insensitivity of members of the white population to the difficult circumstances of being a newcomer in a foreign land. So were several teacher inquirers who were wanting to see change in the oppressive context. Lack of empathy for the plight of newcomers was identified as the most important nonpeaceful attitude exhibited by members of the dominant local population. As part of their intercultural peace-building process, a few teacher inquirers conducted a unit on U.S. Japanese internment camps during World War II and asked students in a few classes at Junction High School to imagine what it felt like to have to leave your homes, everything you owned, neighborhoods—with only what you could carry on your back. The purpose was to create intercultural empathy for those people who were Japanese/Japanese Americans who were forcibly removed from their homes during World War II.

Another teacher created a unit involving the movie *Remember the Titans* (2000). She asked students to analyze why a white football player stood up against other racist whites in their discriminatory efforts to stop racial integration on a high school football team in the South during the period of desegregation. I was touched by how this teacher inquirer used a movie from the past to create courage for white bystanders to stick up for newcomers who were experiencing present-day discrimination at Junction High School. As a researcher who consciously entered a context of oppression to try to work with allies to create intercultural peace—conditions where people of different primary cultures could get along and also gain access to the same opportunities and resources—I was touched by the ingenuity of several teacher inquirers in addressing modern day issues with historical vignettes that spoke powerfully to deconstructing past injustice. The past was an opportunity to reflect on the present and the opportunities that individuals and groups have to change their circumstances. I was wounded by the compassion and the know-how of these white teachers in the field of inquiry. I cried during our last teaching inquiry meeting together when a teacher inquirer asked if my expectations for the project had been met.

Though the radical school change I had hoped for did not come about, positive seeds for growth and change were planted (Brantmeier, 2009).

In pluralistic schools in democratic societies, what are the best ways to foster intercultural peace? Intercultural peace can be understood here as positive relationships and collective participation in decision making and the distribution of resources among groups of people with distinctive primary cultures. "Us" and "them" attitudes hindered the development of deep intercultural peace. A professional development day devoted to breaking down "us" and "them" binaries and to building empathy for the plight of newcomer English language learners at Junction High School was conducted by members of the Indiana University research team because teacher inquirers recommended that we do that. Intercultural peace curricula that attempted to build empathy, to promote common understanding, and to instill courage for some white members of the student body to stick up for newcomers was developed and implemented (Brantmeier, 2007). Overall, we had modest results in our peace-building efforts.

Toward Closure: Healing the Wounds

As a white male who immersed himself in the cross-cultural conflicts, conundrums, and challenges at Junction High School, I emerged a wounded educational researcher. My whiteness and maleness afforded me privileged access; I used that privileged access to attempt to promote positive change for those who were marginalized and relatively powerless. Being an empathetic person, I took on the pain of newcomer students who felt threatened, harassed, and unsafe during the school day. I tried to take on the fear of change exhibited by members of the dominant white group who resisted the presence of multilingual newcomer students at Junction High School; this was hard to do given the hateful and uninformed attitudes that I encountered. I identified mostly with teacher inquirers who had sincere intentions for building positive relationships among students with diverse backgrounds—the same teachers who faced considerable constraints when trying to develop and implement peace curricula in their classrooms. We had lofty goals that were met by the constraints of the wider U.S. outcome-based educational policy climate, teacher time and energy, and negative attitudes of certain white faculty members toward catering toward the needs of newcomers (Brantmeier, 2005).

Wounds can make one stronger. I was wounded by the stories I had heard and the behaviors that I had witnessed in a critical ethnographic inquiry process. I was wounded by sincere teacher inquirer intentions that met administrative and policy constraints. Yet life is about learning from our challenges and moving forward with insight—the couple of granules of wisdom that we might garner from our wounds. I am certain that if I had not conducted this critical inquiry project, I would not have as deeply explored the complexities of power, oppression, privilege, and social dominance theory in the ways that I did to understand and learn from my wounds in my dissertation project.

Now, I am more fully dedicated to research and to teaching that tries to explain and transform educational and social problems. The purpose of educational research, in my mind, should be to more deeply understand societal problems and move toward positive democratic change in our schools; sometimes one has to be wounded in the field in order to deepen her or his dedication. With a growing white middle-class teaching force and a growing nonwhite U.S. public school population, I dedicate my research and teaching efforts to promote intercultural peace building, cross-cultural competence, and culturally responsive and inclusive teaching and learning.

My wounds from working at Junction High School were not from bullets or shrapnel; they were from taking on the pain of both those who oppressed and those who were oppressed. Both suffered deeply, even if they were not conscious of their suffering. Those who resisted newcomer transnational students felt the pain of fear, isolation, and rigid identity maintenance. Those who experienced the prejudice and discrimination felt unwanted, alien, and defensive at times. The oppressive conditions caused all to suffer, all to be dehumanized (Freire, 1972).

One of the overarching purposes of public schooling can be to forge common understanding amid diverse ways of perceiving and experiencing the world. It also can be to attain acceptance and transformational insight about how diversity makes us all stronger. Diversity can be recognized as a critical asset for societies to encounter the changing problems we all face as a species. Diversity can be understood as a selective advantage to the changing circumstances, and it can increase our capacity to adapt, adjust, and thrive. Public schooling brings diverse people together in a nonviolent environment so that we can learn, grow, and actualize as individuals, groups, and democratic citizens in a pluralistic society. I remain hopeful that through education we can transform our world. We all have immigrant stories, dependent on how long we look back in time. I often wonder what made Margrethe and Andrew Brandmeier leave Haussen, Germany, in the 1850s. How did they survive and thrive in America? Who did they displace in doing so? Sometimes critical ethnography, in the end, is a journey into the self. For me, this has been the case. For others, I only hope that critical ethnographic power analysis can lead to access, opportunity, dignity, and happiness for the most vulnerable in society. For future critical researchers, please carry the torch forward, wounds and all.

References

Brantmeier, E. J. (2005). *Constraints and possibilities for intercultural peace curricula: A critical case study of teacher involvement in multicultural change at Midwestern high school.* Unpublished doctoral dissertation, Indiana University.

Brantmeier, E. J. (2007). "Speak our language … abide by our philosophy": Language and cultural assimilation at a U.S. Midwestern high school. *Forum on Public Policy, 2007*(2). Retrieved from http://www.forumonpublicpolicy.com/paperssspr07.html

Brantmeier, E. J. (2008). Building empathy for intercultural peace: Teacher involvement in peace curricula development at a U.S. Midwestern high school. In J. Lin, E. J. Brantmeier, & C. Bruhn (Eds.), *Transforming education for peace* (pp. 67–89). Charlotte, NC: Information Age.

Brantmeier, E. J. (2009). Teacher insights from an intercultural peace curricula development project. *Inter-American Journal of Education for Democracy (IJED), 2*(2), 295–319. Retrieved from http://scholarworks.iu.edu/journals/index.php/ried/article/view/163/257 (Published in both English and Spanish)

Brantmeier, E. J., Aragon, A., Kees, N., Peila-Shuster, J., & Anderson, S. (2011). Examining the inner circle: Unpacking white privilege. In M. Pope, J. S. Pangelinan, & A. D. Coker (Eds.), *Experiential activities for teaching multicultural counseling classes and infusing cultural diversity into core classes*. Alexandria, VA: American Counseling Association.

Brantmeier, E. J. (2013). Toward a critical peace education for sustainability. *Journal of Peace Education 3*(10), 242–258.

Carspecken, P. F. (1996). *Critical ethnography in educational research: A theoretical and practical guide*. New York: Routledge.

Freire, P. (1972). *The pedagogy of the oppressed*. New York: Penguin.

Keet, A., Zinn, D., & Porteus, K. (2009). Mutual vulnerability: A key principle in a humanising pedagogy in post-conflict societies. *Perspectives in Education, 27*(2), 109–119.

Korth, B. (2002). Critical Qualitative Research as consciousness raising: The dialogic texts of researcher/researchee interactions. *Qualitative Inquiry, 6*(8), 381–403.

Lantieri, L., & Patti, J. (1996). *Waging peace in our schools*. Boston: Beacon.

McLaren, P. (1992). Collisions with otherness: "Travelling" theory, post-colonial criticism, and the politics of ethnographic practice—the mission of the wounded ethnographer. *Qualitative Studies in Education, 5*(1), 77–92.

CHAPTER 24

Disruptions in the Field
An Academic's Lived Practice with Classroom Teachers

Janet L. Miller

Enacting research as a lived practice is daily work for me. I constantly have to work against my academically induced tendencies to romanticize, generalize, or technologize the purposes and forms of collaborative action research. Fortunately, the classroom teachers with whom I research usually disrupt any of these tendencies. These disruptions, in fact, are what constitute the lived practice of our research. For, no two days in the classroom are the same and no one theory holds together the disruptions in the work in which classroom teachers and I are engaged. I *must* pay attention to these disruptions in the field, then, for they daily reconfigure not only the curriculum theories that frame my work but also the ways in which I conduct research with teachers.

Disrupted Researcher Roles

I have been working with five elementary classroom teachers for the past four years. Here, I want to pursue some aspects of our collaborative action research that have disrupted particular perspectives in curriculum theory as well as in research orientations that I bring to my work with these teachers. And I want to examine how disruptions of some of my theoretical perspectives by these same teachers encourage me to perform action research as a living practice.

The five women teach in an alternative program within their elementary school. The program is a multiage, activity- and project-based integrated curriculum for children in grades one through three. This program initially was conceptualized and then implemented during its first year by two of the teachers, Pam and Julie.[1] They, along with a third teacher, worked with seventy-seven children during each of the program's first three years. In the third year, a fourth/fifth grade combination was added to the program, and two new teachers who support the philosophies and goals of this program were hired to teach this age grouping.

The multiage program represents this school district's commitment to providing alternatives to traditional self-contained classrooms that typically conceptualize separate subjects, skills acquisition, and linear and sequential mastery of predetermined content as "curriculum." Instead, parents and children choosing the multiage program know that a project-based and child-centered orientation frames its curricular and pedagogical approaches. Parents also know that their children will receive the attention of all three teachers in the 1–3 program every day, and of the two teachers for those in the 4–5 combination.

In my initial work with the teachers in this program, I responded to the school district administrators' as well as the teachers' request to provide a long-term qualitative study of the program's first year. The teachers asked me to pay special attention to the intersections of curriculum and teaching issues that emerged within and because of the program's frameworks.

In its second year, I conducted an interview study of the multiage program. I interviewed many of the program's students, parents of children both in and out of the program, and the teachers in the program. As well, I talked with teachers who work with children in self-contained classrooms in the same building and district and building administrators. These interviews provided feedback to both the teachers and administrators about issues, problems, and successes within the multiage program. During the program's third year, I observed and documented the 4–5 combination, although I also continued to observe in the 1–3 classrooms as much as possible.

Other teachers in the elementary school, parents, administrators, school board members, and interested community members have read my "formal" reports. These include analyses of field notes, of interviews, and of overarching themes and issues of the multiage program identified by myself and the program's teachers, students, and parents. Further, I participated, with the teachers, in yearly meetings with the district's administrators and program's parents to present my research reports as well as to engage in discussions of program issues. These discussions have contributed to ongoing revisions of the program's curricula and of the teachers' interpretations and implementations of those emphases.

Now, what I've just described is an "official" detailing of my research activities, with no inklings of any deviations from a traditional university researcher role (that is, an "outside" and thus "objective" observer). But of course my overt "researcher" relationship with the five teachers quickly and dramatically shifted as I spent time in their classrooms and in countless meetings with them after school. I was often positioned in differing ways by the five teachers, depending on what issues were prevalent during any particular segment of time. For example, variously and sometimes simultaneously, I was a sounding board, a confidante, a curriculum "expert," an evaluator, a representative of Pam and Julie's conceptions of the program, or a representative of the two new teachers' concerns and fears. And I positioned myself in differing ways, too, sometimes serving as the teachers' advocate in discussions with administrators, or as mediator when frustrations erupted among the teachers.

And always, as I discussed my "official" observational field notes of the program, the teachers changed, corrected, elaborated, and questioned my versions of what was "happening" within their classrooms as well as within the overall structure of the multiage program.

Now, I could have considered these interactions and various (re)positionings to be examples of working toward reciprocal and equitable research relationships between university professor and classroom teachers. After all, I listened to the teachers, they listened to me, and our interactions changed each other's readings of data and experience. So, our process could be seen as a successful example of what some educational theorists claim to be good and possible in collaborative action research.

But there was nothing easy, linear, predictable or necessarily successful about any of our disruptions of each other's assumptions and interpretations. The teachers' and my own disruptions of one another's fixed notions of what was "going on" in their classrooms or our collaboration belied romanticized ideals. The disruptions of my data interpretations, of any one "researcher" and/or "teacher" role, and of one another's perspectives on the creation and implementation of the multiage program also interrupted any easy or smooth lived relationship to collaboration. Disruptions, then, were a daily reminder that the relationships and methodologies of teaching and of collaborative action research are ambiguous, contingent, and shifting. And research, within and because of disruptions across power positions, interests, and goals, is a living and constantly changing practice.

A Disruptive Example

Thus, by the fourth year of our collaboration, we were analyzing not just my field notes but six sets of field notes, questions, reflections, and constructions of ourselves as teachers-researchers-collaborators. Here I want to describe in some detail why I now understand action research as a living practice. Focusing on relationships and on the shifting and contingent nature of power relations within our collaboration, I have not been able to ignore the constant disruptions of myself as teacher, researcher, theorist.

Near the completion of the program's third year, the five teachers began to discuss their possible participation in the creation of an elementary Charter school in the district. District-level administrators and the parents who supported the Charter school effort were encouraging these teachers to consider moving their whole multiage program into the Charter configuration.[2]

During Charter school discussions, the district superintendent presented the possibility of the Charter school's potential association with a very large publishing company. This company, if the teachers agreed, would provide much of "the curriculum" and its related materials, including hands-on and manipulatives, for the Charter program. In addition, the district superintendent proposed the possibility of working with members of a school of education faculty at a nearby university. Among a variety of research agendas, some faculty members supposedly had interest in researching the implementation of this publisher-generated curriculum within the multiage program.

And so here I was, positioning myself as the "outside" researcher in this situation, and thus sitting to the far outside edge of the table in the superintendent's conference room. I listened as the five teachers, who were facing me, and three of their district administrators discussed the future of the multiage program. As the superintendent outlined their possible move into the Charter school and their alignment with the publishing company and its prepackaged curriculum, I slowly, quietly gestured, signaling miniature *No, Stop, Cut, Never* signs to the teachers. All veteran teachers, they smiled through the administrators at me while never fully disengaging their eyes from the superintendent's forehead.

A few days later, Julie, Pam, and I gathered around one of the trapezoid tables in Julie's classroom. The three other teachers in the multiage program had by then announced their hesitancy in joining the Charter school, even though the parent who was spearheading the Charter effort and the superintendent appeared quite supportive of their participation. I thought that here, in our informal meeting, Julie and Pam would echo their fellow teachers' sentiments. But Julie and Pam surprised me by beginning to talk about the possible advantages of being in the Charter program and working with the publishing company and its curriculum. I was more than surprised, actually, because these two have taken fierce pride in their own creation and implementation of the curricula of the multiage program. But I tried to remain quiet, to listen to their points of view about the possible advantages for their students as well as themselves of joining the Charter initiative and of working with the publisher's curriculum materials.

Pam and Julie talked at length about the relief that they might feel if they didn't have to reconceive every aspect of grade-specific content to accommodate their multiage students' needs and the program's philosophies. And they reminded me of the countless weekends when they not only created hands-on activities but also planned opportunities for children to create and to engage in their own projects. They talked about the difficulties of conceptualizing forms of assessment that did not depend on standardized and "objective" forms of measurement and of the work that it took for them to continually realign their curricula to address the differing needs of their children.

But as they talked, multiple critiques and analyses of prepackaged, technocratic, linear and sequential versions of curriculum, defined only as predetermined content, reeled through my mind. These critiques, analyses, and alternatives, which have emerged in curriculum studies, during the past twenty years especially, influenced the questions and objections that I now wanted to raise: what of teachers and texts? what of the power relations between and among teachers and administrators inherent in the superintendent's support of the Charter and its publisher-generated curriculum? what of possible gender issues inherent in the five women teachers' responses to the superintendent's urging that they participate in that Charter? what of social, cultural, historical, economic, and political influences in this particular middle-class, rural-to-suburban setting on teachers' constructions of their work with students and of themselves as teachers, as researchers? what of curriculum as intersections of national educational and local community expectations? what of curriculum, too, as intersections of individuals' educational expectations, assumptions, and experiences?[3]

What was most disturbing to me as I listened to Julie and Pam's descriptions of the possible advantages of linking with a major publisher and with university faculty who would research the publisher's program implementation, was that Julie and Pam were not talking about doing less work. These two teachers are outstanding professionals, dedicated to their students and to their teaching. These are teachers who conceptualize and enact versions of curriculum that conceive of content as well as identities in the classroom as influenced and framed by political, historical, economic, social, and cultural intersections.

For example, Pam and Julie constantly try to identify where and when and how they are replicating someone else's version (including mine) of what they want to be doing. They try to trace the ways in which their educational philosophies and conceptions of curriculum are the result of community or national reform pressures rather than enactments of their own professionally informed judgments and beliefs about the needs of their specific students. And these teachers try to monitor the ways in which others (including me) are trying to reshape their educational philosophies and pedagogical approaches in order to reflect various political stances within the district or even within the field of education, writ large.

Further, these two teachers willingly give time during evenings and weekends to the continuation of the multiage program. In fact, much of their dedication is a source of concern for some other teachers in the elementary school who feel that they can't spare the same amounts of time that Julie and Pam devote to implementing an innovative program.

But during that conversation with the three of us in Julie's classroom, Pam and Julie weren't talking, from my curriculum perspectives, as the two committed, creative, energetic, and courageous teachers with whom I had worked for three years. Instead, they were talking, I thought, as teachers who were ready to relinquish their authority as curriculum creators, as generators with their children of the contents and processes that had become the lived curriculum of the multiage program. During their discussion of the advantages in joining the Charter school, it seemed to me that Julie and Pam might be willing to sacrifice their autonomy for the support and external validation that a major publishing company's version of elementary curriculum supposedly would provide for their teaching and for their multiage program. And I just couldn't imagine that they would be willing to do that.

But of course, that was my invested perspective, a perspective grounded in particular arenas of curriculum theorizing. These feminist and postmodern arenas call attention, for example, to the idea, articulated by Judith Butler, that "power pervades the very conceptual apparatus that seeks to negotiate its terms."[4] From these views, power is inherent in language, in constructions of meanings, identities, and relations. And one project of many feminist and postmodern curriculum theorists is to question underlying assumptions in curriculum design and development in order to expose the privilege granted to some ideas and persons over others.[5]

At the moment in which I was silently grappling with my own curriculum perspectives in relation to Pam and Julie's, they began to express fears that replicated some of my own concerns. Ah, here we go, I thought. Now we could really begin to discuss these issues in some substantive ways, calling on the curriculum studies that so informed my work with them.

And Pam and Julie did ask the following questions as we watched the early spring light fade into darkening landscape outside Julie's classroom windows: How would it affect the teachers' work and inquiry into their work if we all would have to relinquish an in-depth chronicling and examination of the multiage program, of teaching, and of research? (And I had to ask myself how that relinquishing would affect my work and inquiry, my investment in these teachers and their work, and my investment in pursuing my own lines of academic interest in collaborative action research.)

Those long-term inquiries enabled sustained reflection on the teaching and learning episodes that constituted the lived curriculum of the multiage program as well as the lived practice of our collaborative action research. What would their teaching and constructions of curriculum look like without that aspect? (And what would my teaching, research, and conceptions of curriculum look like?)

Would the supposed validation provided by the university research team, with what was described to us as its largely quantitative orientation, override the long-term qualitative inquiries into the multiage program and its curriculum constructions that our work together had produced? (Would these teachers finally find such research to be more valuable to them than the qualitative action research in which we had been engaged?) Were they just responding to subtle pressures from others to join the Charter? (And was I just raising objections, supposedly grounded in feminist and postmodern perspectives on the nature and circulations of power, out of my own self-interest?)

What constituted a disruption for me during our conversation was that part of Pam and Julie's questioning did not arise particularly from their alignment with my concerns or curriculum and research perspectives. On one level, they both explained, they were deeply weary of having to daily reconstitute and create curriculum with their students that was congruent with their educational philosophies about how children learn and what they should learn. According to them, and of course supported by my perspectives on curriculum, textbook versions still leave much to be desired in terms of curriculum conceptions that attend to the complexities of various aspects of differences between, among, and within children in any one classroom. But more importantly, Pam and Julie declared that they were weary of having to constantly defend their conceptions of curriculum to a larger public of parents and school administrators and community members. Many of these individuals still only conceive curriculum to be a syllabus or a textbook or "content to be covered." And they conceive evidence of children's mastery of that content only to be a high standardized score.

So, these two teachers, who had worked so hard to implement this innovative program and who had struggled for support from their peers and their administrators, appeared to be taken with the possibilities of working with the publishing company's representatives and the university research team. They seemed relieved by the possibilities of external validation and of measurable students' "success" promised by the publishing company and the university curriculum researchers. And I of course supported work in the curriculum field that *challenged* such promises. But these teachers expressed the possibility that such validation might ease some parents' expressed concerns about their children's progress as compared to children in self-contained classrooms or about the lack of spelling lists in the multiage program or about the emphasis on reading and writing as processes and not as skill acquisitions, for example.

So even when I thought that Pam and Julie were asking questions that emerge from theoretical conceptions, critiques, and positions with which I am theoretically aligned and which I had shared with them, their reasons were different. And I had to seriously consider those reasons and these teachers' resulting perspectives, even if they didn't coincide with my own. Research as a living practice.

At the end of our meeting, Pam and Julie had not in any way finalized their vote to join the Charter School. And as we jotted down lists of questions to bring to the superintendent, such as "what do these curriculum materials look like? what are the philosophical and curricular orientations of the people who have developed them and of the people who will be researching them?" I wondered too about my own involvement in this deliberation. My commitments to particular conceptions of curriculum studies and forms of curriculum theorizing had been quite evident in my subdued but subversive gesturing to the teachers, in my concerns expressed in our meetings, in my insistence that they find out more before they committed to joining the Charter school.

But the conversation among the three of us in Julie's classroom that late afternoon forced me yet again to question, as all work with classroom teachers forces university professors to question: Do my curriculum theorizings and my perspectives on what curriculum is and should be as a field of study have any relation to the daily political, personal, social, and cultural dynamics, situations, and pressures upon these teachers? Does what constitutes research as well as curriculum theorizing and construction as a living practice vary in both form and substance for classroom and university teachers? And how might I attend, as a university researcher and teacher, to those differences in ways that do not replicate the very unequal power relations against which I write and research?

A Confluence of Disruptions

A few weeks after our meeting in Julie's room, the five teachers decided that they and the multiage program would remain within their elementary school. They would not join the Charter school. When I discussed that decision with Julie during a pause in my observations of her classroom, she noted that there were numerous reasons for their decision. These included the fact that they did not receive what they considered to be substantive answers to their questions about the role of the publishing company in determining curriculum for their multiage program. Nor did they receive detailed descriptions about the roles and emphases of the university researchers in assessments of both "the curriculum" and their students' "mastery" of that curriculum or about issues of faculty governance, development, and certification.

And, in a survey of multiage-program parents by the five teachers, many of the parents indicated that they felt reservations about the Charter school, especially in relation to the time, effort, and energy that the five teachers already had committed to the existing multiage program. Many parents were fearful that the teachers would have to start all over again, and these parents did not want conceptual or philosophical changes in the basic pedagogical approaches and curriculums that undergirded the multiage program.

Julie indicated to me that the parents' reservations, especially, were a strong influence, but not the only influence, on the teachers' decision. And she also indicated that she and Pam felt relieved that the decision had finally been made and that they in fact wouldn't have to be worrying about potential conflicts with the publishing company's versions of curriculum, for example. She continued:

> I guess that we've done enough now in three years that the parents have confidence in us and what we've developed. And going into our fourth year, with all five of us returning, maybe it won't seem to be so energy-draining and all-encompassing. It's nice to hear and read so much parent support and acknowledgment of what we've created here.

So it wasn't particularly that Julie and Pam had considered or reconsidered or realigned the curriculum perspectives that I had presented both implicitly and explicitly throughout our three-years' work together. For example, it wasn't particularly that the five teachers had rejected the prominent ways in which a major publishing company and a corps of quantitative university researchers could lend credibility to their work. It wasn't particularly that they were concerned about the possible gendered power relations that circulated between and among the superintendent and his supervisors and teachers. And it certainly wasn't the teachers' reluctance to potentially relinquish the collaborative research relationships that we had forged. In fact, it wasn't any one particular emphasis or reason or influence or person or theory that could be identified and traced as *the one reason* that these teachers made the decision to not join the Charter school. Rather, a confluence of reasons, circumstances, and questions led to their decision.

And that confluence constituted a major disruption in the field for me. In that confluence of many reasons for the decision the teachers made, I didn't recognize any of *my* reasons or theoretical perspectives. Where was *I* in their decision and reasoning? As much as I thought I welcomed disruptions as a way of constructing and reconstructing my research as a living practice, I had not anticipated the twists and turns that configured this particular disruption and my reactions to it.

Part of constructing (and here reconstructing) my research as a living practice involves looking closely at the ways in which my own expectations for myself as researcher/teacher/feminist curriculum theorist are intertwined with institutional, personal, social, and cultural assumptions about how I should be conducting myself and my work. Certainly, constructions of theory as well as conventions of academic writing and researching are such that university theorists/researchers often work under dominant expectations: One expectation, derived from hierarchical constructions of who can engage in knowledge production, is that university theorists/researchers will be able not only to name but also to supply the theories, the causes, and the directions for particular actions, decisions, and constructions of curriculum. But if classroom teachers identify and construct other and multiple reasons and theories for their decisions and curricular constructions, as in this case of Pam and Julie and the Charter school episode, the university researcher who subscribes to hierarchical notions of who can construct theory certainly risks disruptions in the field.

But I didn't align my work with such conventions. Instead, I have worked, along with many others, against traditional hierarchical constructions of the university researcher as "expert" among classroom teachers and as singular knowledge producer. At the same time, from my previous long-term collaborative research efforts,[6] as well as from much current research that challenges any simplistic notion of equitable and constant relationships among university and classroom collaborators,[7] I knew that I could not assume that my voice would be regarded as only one among six in our collaborative action research efforts. For example, I still was introduced, in meetings with parents and students and administrators, as the university professor, with title and degree listed before and after my name. And even though I had established close working relationships with the five teachers, and especially with Julie and Pam, I knew that they still sometimes looked to me for answers, support, theories, and explanations as we examined the work of the multiage program as well as the processes of action research.

So, even though I still at times wished for the romanticized possibility of equitable relationships among all teacher-researchers, I knew that such a version could not attend to the complexities of power relations between and among individuals working together. Yet the Charter school episode provided profound disruptions of what I supposedly had crafted as my "collaboratively inclined" yet "power-relations aware" researcher stance. The Charter school episode, in fact, harshly illuminated for me Butler's contention that "power pervades the very conceptual apparatus that seeks to negotiate its terms."

To illustrate this disruption in the very terms I was utilizing in my initial framing of the Charter school episode, I need to trace those terms. So here's an encapsulated version of my thinking as I entered into the Charter school episode. Acknowledging my theoretical alignment with collaborative goals of equitable and reciprocal research relationships, I felt that I should not be the only one to provide an answer or theory or direction for these teachers' decisions about the Charter. At the same time, acknowledging my own and others' critiques of idealistic and romanticized versions of totally equitable collaborative research processes, I also recognized that, because of my university professor designation, my perspectives probably would have some influence on Pam and Julie's thinking about the Charter school.

Attempting to enact my research as a living practice forces me to trace multiple and often contradictory expectations for myself as collaborative researcher. So in reviewing and deconstructing the Charter school episode, I now also must acknowledge that not only did I anticipate that my perspectives as university researcher might have some influence on Pam and Julie's decision but also that I *wanted* my perspectives and theories to provide some basis for their decision. The Charter school episode highlighted ways in which I still *expected* to be listened to as the expert, as the one who knew of the curricular pitfalls of standardized and prepackaged versions of curriculum and instruction, for example. I couldn't deny the intentions of power evidenced in my negative hand signals during that meeting with the teachers and district administrators about the Charter possibility. Nor could I deny my slight impatience and incredulity when Julie and Pam indicated that they might want to join the Charter in order to obtain visible and "objective" evidence of the validity of their teaching.

But given the ways in which Pam and Julie delineated their reasons for not joining the Charter, not only must I necessarily relinquish any construction of myself as the only one who can theorize about the influences on, obstacles to, or framing of conceptions of curriculum. I also have to consider that my theoretical positions and collaborative research goals were at best peripheral to their decision.

Theoretically, as I have noted, I situate my work within feminist and postmodern perspectives that constantly call attention to the shifting, multiple, unrepeatable, and contingent nature of teaching, research, theorizing, and the power relationships inherent within these. But at the same time, and in the context of the Charter school episode, I continued to work in terms of an either/or position. I saw myself as *either* having to work against assumptions that accompany the traditional researcher as "expert" *or* having to work against assumptions that I indeed could automatically be one among equals by just engaging in the supposedly democratic processes of collaborative research. In fact, I needed to work these two positions simultaneously. And, in the Charter episode, a third possibility was thrown into the binary that not only disrupted my either/or stance but also provided stark evidence that neither position mattered much to Julie and Pam in terms of the decision that they had to make about the Charter school.

So given my theoretical stances, I "knew" that I must work within the ambiguities, uncertainties, contingencies, and multiple influences that characterize any university- and school-based collaborative action research. But the Charter school episode disrupted that theoretical orientation by calling my attention to the ways in which I still positioned myself as researcher in an either/or stance. Multiplicities, contingencies, ambiguities become visible and usable when I see myself as *both* combating the romanticized version of collaboration as always equitable *and* combating the traditional researcher role of "expert."

Further, that Charter episode revealed to me ways in which I still assume that contradictions in my theoretical orientations and research practice can become obvious to me if I just reflect on my practice, that those contradictions only appear in binary form, and that, once realized, they are able to be permanently exorcised. For, in fact, in the Charter episode, it didn't matter, in the ways I thought or expected, that I worried about static constructions of curriculum, or of power relations within teaching, administration, and research, or of binary oppositions that maintained certain power relations within collaborative and teaching contexts. And it didn't matter, in ways I thought it would, to the teachers' decision making or the ways in which they continued with their action research, that the Charter episode provided a major disruption in the field for me. The very fact that these things mattered differently to Julie and Pam, even though I wanted them to matter the same, disrupted the very binary (expert researcher/equitable collaborator) that constructed the research tensions with which I heretofore had grappled. Butler: "Power pervades the very conceptual apparatus that seeks to negotiate its terms."

Even after the Charter school episode, I still think that my work with Pam and Julie and the other three teachers has connections to their teaching, curriculum perspectives, and collaborative action research about the multiage program. But those connections are not ones that can be presumed from the theories I work with and through, nor are they connections that can be controlled, predicted, explained or accounted for by those theories or by my particular intentions or concerns or political commitments as a researcher. In the Charter school episode, Pam and Julie were not engaging with me in the terms that I had been using to theorize curriculum or research relationships—such as when I worked either against romanticized versions of always-equitable collaborations *or* against a conception of university researcher as the powerful knowing expert.

But what Julie and Pam *were* doing was engaging with me based on the then three-year history that we had constructed together as collaborative action researchers. They did seek my counsel, they did use me as a sounding board, they did rehearse their arguments and questions to the superintendent with me, they did draw on countless discussions we shared about constructions of curriculum and about the intentions and forms of the multiage program. But what they turned to in the Charter school situation was not any analytical perspective that I had provided on our research of the program. Rather, what Julie and Pam turned to was our shared history—not our identical experiences—but our lived history of questioning and challenging together, which was so complex and nuanced that it exceeded any single theoretical frame. And that lived history enabled the disruption of the static researcher binary corners into which I had backed myself.

For me, then, what prevents the notion of action research as a living practice from becoming a technology or a romanticized process is the unpredictable and necessarily changing nature of that practice. I have found it impossible to approach collaborative action research with any fixed or unitary notion of the ways in which the classroom teachers and I might approach our work together or of the curriculum theories which might frame and guide our research. Classroom teachers often do question who and what constitutes and constructs curriculum, theory, and research in any given educational situation. But they often raise such questions in different forms and for different purposes than those proposed by university professors.

Therefore, as a curriculum theorist working with classroom teachers, I risk disruptions in the field, not only of my traditional hierarchical position as the one who theorizes but also of the ways I think about and see things. And sometimes disruptions provide a harsh reminder of the ways in which I still often remain entrenched within traditional academic contexts and expectations even as I work against them. Such disruptions, even when encouraged by the theoretical stances that I take, jerk my attention in unanticipated directions, thus leaving action research open to the surprise of a lived practice.

Notes

1. These teachers' names are pseudonyms, given possible political entanglements within their school district that could arise from the power relations described here.

2. In the United States, the concept behind charter schools is that they provide a real mechanism for change by creating new kinds of schools within the public domain. In Wisconsin, Charter schools, initially established in August 1993, were conceived as instrumentalities of the public school district. Efforts to privatize public education by allowing school boards to contract with private organizations to run these schools thus far have been thwarted by the Wisconsin Education Association Council and the Wisconsin Federation of Teachers.

3. Such critiques and inquiries have proliferated in curriculum studies during the past twenty years, especially within the curriculum movement initially known as the Reconceptualization. For comprehensive discussions of the emergence and development of reconceptualist perspectives in the curriculum field, see William F. Pinar, ed., *Curriculum theorizing: The reconceptualists* (Berkeley, CA: McCutchan, 1975); William F. Pinar, ed., *Contemporary curriculum discourses* (Scottsdale, AZ: Gorsuch Scarisbrick, 1988). For current discussions of mappings of the traditional as well as contemporary field of curriculum, including views of contemporary curriculum scholars as simultaneously closer to both "practice" and "theory," see William F. Pinar, William M. Reynolds, Patrick Slattery, and Peter M. Taubman, eds., *Understanding curriculum: An introduction to the study of historical and contemporary curriculum discourses* (New York: Peter Lang, 1995). Briefly, other varied and influential examples of curriculum theorizing that critique relations of power in education include Michael W. Apple, *Teachers and texts: A political economy of class and gender relations in education* (New York: Routledge and Kegan Paul, 1986); Deborah Britzman, *Practice makes practice: A critical study of learning to teach* (Albany: State University of New York Press, 1991); Henry Giroux and Peter McLaren, eds., *Between borders: Pedagogy and the politics of cultural studies* (New York: Routledge, 1993); Madeleine R. Grumet, *Bitter milk: Women and teaching* (Amherst: University of Massachusetts Press, 1988); Linda M. McNeil, *Contradictions of control: School structure and school knowledge* (New York: Routledge and Kegan Paul, 1986).

4. Judith Butler, "Contingent foundations," in *Feminists theorize the political,* ed. Judith Butler and J. Scott (New York: Routledge, 1992): 3–21.

5. Very briefly, influential feminist and postmodern work within the curriculum field includes: Elizabeth Ellsworth, "Why doesn't this feel empowering? Working through the repressive myths of critical pedagogy," *Harvard Educational Review* 59 (1989): 297–324; Henry Giroux, *Bordercrossings* (New York: Routledge, 1992); Patti Lather, *Getting smart: Feminist research and pedagogy with/in the postmodern* (New York: Routledge, 1991); Carmel Luke and Jennifer Gore, eds., *Feminism and critical pedagogy* (New York: Routledge, 1992); Jo Anne Pagano, *Exiles and communities: Teaching in the patriarchal wilderness* (Albany: State University of New York Press, 1990); William F. Pinar and William M. Reynolds, eds., *Understanding curriculum as phenomenological and deconstructed text* (New York: Teachers College Press, 1992).

6. For extended discussions about a six-year collaborative teacher-researcher group in which I participated, see Janet L. Miller, *Creating spaces and finding voices: Teachers collaborating for empowerment* (Albany: State University of New York Press, 1990).

7. Briefly, again, for discussions of difficulties centered around power relations in teacher–university researcher collaborations, see Caroline Clark, Pamela A. Moss, Susan Goering, Roberta. Herter, Bertha Lamar, Doug Leonard, Sarah Robbins, Margaret Russell, Mark Templin, and Kathy Wascha, "Collaboration as dialogue: Teachers and researchers engaged in conversation and professional development," *American Education Research Journal* 33 (1996): 193–231; Allan Feldman, "Promoting equitable collaboration between university researchers and school teachers," *Quantitative Studies in Education* 6 (1993): 341–357; Marilyn Johnson and Richard M. Kerper, "Positioning ourselves: Parity and power in collaborative work," *Curriculum Inquiry* 26 (1996): 5–24; Chrysoula Kosmidou and Robin Usher, "Facilitation in action research," *Interchange* 22 (1991): 24–40; Judith Davidson Wasser and Liora Bresler, "Working in the interpretive zone: Conceptualizing collaboration in qualitative research teams," *Educational Researcher* 25, no. 5 (1996): 515.

CHAPTER 25

Who Says We Can't Make a Silk Purse out of a Sow's Ear?

Transforming Market-based Programs into Critical Education

Pamela J. Konkol, with Simeon Stumme and Isabel Nuñez

> If we focus on the kinds of reflection-in-action through which practitioners sometimes make new sense of uncertain, unique or conflicted situations of practice, then we will assume neither that existing professional knowledge fits every case nor that every problem has a right answer. We will see students as having to learn a kind of reflection-in-action that goes beyond statable rules—not only by devising new methods of reasoning, as above, but also by constructing and testing new categories of understanding, strategies of action, and ways of framing problems. (Schön, 1988, p. 39)

Better, Stronger, Faster: Building a More Meaningful Capstone Experience

When we joined the faculty of our current institution, our state-required master's capstone process was comprised of a standardized online portfolio using a commercially available portfolio builder. Among many challenges (interruptions in service, issues of scale and personnel, software problems), candidates and faculty felt that the capstone process was an impersonal, sterile, and cumbersome task and regarded the enterprise as merely another "hoop to jump through" rather than a meaningful learning or developmental experience. Schön's (1988) concept of "technical rationality" captures the positivistic undertone of what was merely a pseudo-reflective exercise. This wasn't surprising; the college had been experiencing a period of rapid growth in graduate enrollment, and senior faculty often joked about the "office counter conversations" that generated many a program and course of study while standing around the countertop that separated office workstations from the walking aisle. In an effort to be responsive to institutional needs and to capture the market share, this once-tiny college of education became expert at getting new programs off the ground quickly.

Very early in our tenure here, we were given the opportunity to reconceptualize the product, the process, and the pedagogy involved with our two graduate Curriculum and Instruction programs (one straight C and I and one that included a state ESL endorsement) and the concluding capstone. We were ecstatic and our colleagues at the time were supportive of taking it to a new level of engagement and personal/practical value for our candidates. Our own disciplinary groundings were in curriculum studies and the social foundations, and the importance of balancing the practical (what candidates came to the programming wanting) and the philosophical (what we knew the candidates needed, even if they initially disagreed) was high on our priority list. We endeavored to build a program that provided a space for our candidates, nearly all of them practicing teachers, to develop in multiple directions—practical, theoretical, and conceptual. We wanted our candidates to both experience and actualize in their own practice Lather's (1991) vision of pedagogy, a "transformation of consciousness that takes place in the intersection of three agencies—the teacher, the candidate and the knowledge they together produce" (p. 15). We also worked to build a program that not only encouraged but demanded that candidates become cognizant of the dominant power structures, develop an understating of how schools serve as agents of socialization and social control, and develop the ability to understand and describe how educational problems are often rooted in and symptomatic of social arrangements and broader social ills (such as poverty, discrimination, and segregation) that extend well beyond the classroom or schoolyard and impact families, communities, and local and national economics and politics.

We started by thinking how the capstone could be a holistic reflection of our candidates' learning experience throughout the whole of their ten-course master's programs. Our focus was to create an inquiry-based curriculum with the goal of gaining a deeper understanding of teaching and learning by explicitly connecting theory with practice (Samaras & Freese, 2006) in each course as well as in the capstone. We took care to ensure that methods were not taught in isolation and that along with class-room practice and application, candidates were asked to consider the underlying theoretical assumptions about teaching and learning in which these methods were grounded. We carefully structured the programs such that candidates were continually asked to translate their thinking work into action and built in specific opportunities for both Schön's (1983) reflection-in-action and reflection-on-action.

Early in the development process, we knew that if we were going to push candidates toward self-study and critical action planning at the end of the programs, we needed to start engaging them in these activities at the beginning. Instead of thinking of the capstone as, at best, the end product and, at worst, another add-on, we took Gray's (2003) advice to heart; we developed each course and capstone component as a transformative encounter, woven through the whole program rather than standing alone as a discrete project or paper to be completed at the end. For example, the first course in the program was Foundations of American Education. In addition to "helping candidates develop richer and more systematic interpretations of the historical, philosophical, and social foundations of American education and schooling," it was important that this course asked candidates to commit to several things through-out the program. First, it asked them to reflect deeply on their own sociocultural autobiography and to consciously return to it throughout the program to consider how their own contexts impact how they en-vision and actualize educational worlds for their students. Second, it provided them with a set of touch-stone philosophical questions (briefly, about the aims and purposes of education and schooling, the roles and responsibilities of educators, and the concepts equal-equitable educational opportunity) to apply to both their practical and theoretical work—again, questions to be returned to throughout the program. Third, at the end of the course (and subsequent courses as well), it required candidates to "craft a vision of what is possible and to articulate a plan for action in their own classroom, school, and educational context." Candidates were compelled to explicitly link their intellectual meaning making in the course and experiences and issues in their classrooms and schools with concrete manifestations for provoking change in practice—and to engage in a similar cycle of reflection and action planning at the end of each eight-week course experience. Within these pieces, candidates often explored and provided examples of how the course materials and experiences impacted their beliefs and practices and discussed issues they were grappling with and plans for working through difficulties. Candidates were encouraged not only to be mindful of the authors and texts they were encountering but also to include critiques of the scholarship. Increasingly, candidates became empowered to discuss both how their practice supported the conclusions of the scholars as well as how their experiences indicated that there was more to the story.

We also structured the program such that candidates were constantly switching between courses that were oriented toward deeper understandings of theory and perspectives and those focused more on developing concrete classroom practices. In this way, linking the intellectual with the practical was both micro (within the course contexts) and macro (across the program as a whole). Fast-forward to the last course in the program, Seminar in Critical Practice, where the final capstone project was completed. This course provided a space in which candidates were asked to bring all of the threads of the program together into a final project, which became their state-mandated capstone (explained in greater detail later in this chapter).

In addition to asking our candidates to commit to what amounted to a two-year process of near-constant engagement with their developing philosophy and practice, we asked faculty members to do the same. In order to provide consistency and structure for candidates as they progressed through the program and this process, the instructor for the first course (typically foundations faculty and a cadre of amazing adjuncts) would commit to two key elements: one, returning as facilitator of the final, capstone-generating course, and two, providing feedback and guidance to candidates throughout the program via their end-of-course reflections and action plans. To do so, we built in three checkpoints throughout the program. At these checkpoints (the first at the end of the second course, the second at the end of the sixth course, and the third at the end of the program), candidates and what became known as their "capstone reader" would engage around the candidates' experiences thus far. What kind of connections were being made between the program material and individual teaching practices? Between and across the courses and course material themselves? What theoretical assumptions were being challenged or further developed? What sorts of changes were happening (or not) regarding personal ideology, teaching philosophy, classroom practice, relationships, among others? What questions did candidates have, and even more important, what questions did they continue to return to? How were candidates putting the pieces of this program together and, importantly, what was the resulting picture beginning to look like?

The requirement to engage in explicit reflection and action planning at the end of each course and program as a whole prompted both excitement and initial concern from our candidates—and some of our colleagues. And truth be told, for as eager as we were to embark on this revisioning of the program, we had our concerns as well. We were all accustomed to graduate work that was comprised of bounded, and in many ways finite, course experiences. This program asked both candidates and faculty to do more than take a class, do the work, get a grade, and move on; this program required a sustained state of engagement with the intellectual and practical work of this program. (There was one eight-week recess in late summer, plus standard two-week winter and one-week spring breaks in the academic year.)

Despite the initial grumblings of "this seems like a lot of work," we quickly began to see encouraging results of the programmatic changes. As candidates moved through their coursework, their ability to make clearer connections between the theoretical work they were encountering in their courses and the practical work they engaged in every day in their classrooms continued to develop. End-of-course reflections provided a space in which faculty and candidates could engage in conversation around the conceptual material of the courses and the practical application of that material in the classrooms. The checkpoint structure allowed for faculty to both observe and help cultivate their skills in this regard, and it allowed for faculty to see changes in practice as well. Further, the required interaction between candidates and faculty provided an opportunity for a long-term thinking through of the implications of the work that was being engaged in, and allowed ample opportunity for candidates to begin envisioning what their final capstone might look like at the end. Anecdotally, both candidates and faculty indicated they benefited from the processes.

Important to all of this work is Griffiths's (1993) notion of how one's sense of identity and personal values impacts how one sees his or her role as an advocate and agent of change. Explicitly calling for the joining of "biography and history" that Bullough and Pinnegar (2001) emphasize as crucial to critical self-study research, candidates were asked to explore how "private experience can provide insight and solution for public issues and troubles and the way in which public theory can provide insight and solution for private trial" (p. 15). To this end, we asked candidates to engage in both critical self-study and reflective action planning throughout the program and employ action-oriented methods for executing their capstone project. As will be illustrated more clearly later in this chapter, the final capstone became a unique reflection of each candidate's experience during the program as a whole as well as his or her cumulative endeavor.

As Krol (1997) notes, there is abundant evidence that "as a conception of best practice, reflective practice is deeply embedded within state teacher licensing agencies, teaching, and teacher education programs" (p. 96). Further, the importance of reflective practice is often codified through reform efforts, teacher preparation and professional development, and standard-bearing and accreditation agencies. It has become "common sense" that teachers who are purposefully reflective in their practice are "good" teachers. Despite this lip service, however, we know from Schön's (1988) work that, by and large, in-service programs have not conceptualized truly meaningful ways of developing reflection-in-action through clinical experiences. McLaughlin (1999) notes that while "reflective practice" is both good practice and intuitively appealing, it is important to remember that the concept is also seductive and fashionable and often "used as a vague slogan rather than as a concept whose meaning and implications are well thought through and worked out" (p. 9). We were well aware of these dangers. For this reason, candidates were challenged throughout the capstone process, and particularly in the culminating seminar, to recognize the difference between authentic and superficial engagement, to push themselves to continually ask critical questions of their context, perspectives, and practice, and to use the their ever-increasing funds of knowledge to critically inform their future practice—and clearly articulate how they plan to do it.

What Was This Final Capstone Project, Anyway?

At the end of the program, candidates were required to produce a program-culminating project and to present that project at the Graduate Research Symposium, held at the end of each term, in which the Seminar in Reflective Practice was taught. Although the first symposium started with a mere 25 candidate presentations, quickly that number increased to better than 100 participants—per symposium. The capstone, as noted earlier, was transformed from a commercially available online portfolio builder into a project that was unique to each individual.

As mentioned in the beginning of this chapter, the college had become quite adept at moving new programs from inception to on-the-ground and deliverable in very short timeframes. As a result, the first students enrolled in the revamped program and began their coursework before we had the opportunity to completely conceptualize what the final capstone would, should, or could look like in real life. Other than three broad categories in which candidates would be asked to demonstrate understanding and competence (briefly, educational foundations and policy issues; curriculum, instruction and pedagogy; and teacher leadership, advocacy, and school change), we hadn't made a decision as to what the final project should look like. Although the scholarly side of us was inclined to require a thesis-like paper (despite the fact that our program was marketed as a thesis-free environment), we were also pulled toward candidates producing a final project that had real practical implications and knew that the practitioner research course that immediately preceded the final seminar could be a promising site of imagination.

Reflecting back, perhaps this lack of planning was a good thing, because we were developing the capstone as we were still developing the program, and as candidates and faculty were engaging in the coursework and the checkpoints together, we were able to allow it to emerge as a more organic outgrowth of the program itself. That said, we certainly did experience moments of panic in that first cohort of students in which we tried to craft a structure for the final piece. But interestingly, each attempt at nailing something concrete down felt "wrong"; whether we used this as an opportunity to rationalize our tendencies to procrastinate or we were on to something brilliant, we erred on the side of having faith and allowed the reflection and action cycles to unfold before committing to a final project structure.

As the first group of candidates moved through the program, we used what they were resonating or grappling most with in their coursework (as evidenced in their end-of-course statements) to frame objectives for the final course and final product. It was our hope that in this culminating seminar, candidates would find a place in which to articulate their own beliefs and assumptions about teaching and learning—and ground those beliefs in both the literature and their own experiences, critically examine schools and institutions, explore their role and responsibility as an advocate for equity and social justice in a diverse democratic society, grapple with issues of teacher identity, illustrate an understanding of teacher agency and social change, and articulate a plan of personal action in which to bring life to these pursuits.

Developing a structure for the final capstone project was less clear; this was due in some part to our own divergent notions of what the ideal capstone should look like. For example, whereas one of us was very committed to the idea of candidates producing a traditional, scholarly piece of writing, another of us was equally committed to facilitating an environment in which candidates could express their cumulative piece in any number of alternative ways. In the end, our primary instructions were that the capstone project needed to be personally meaningful to each candidate, that regardless of how the project manifested, the candidate must attend to the course and program objectives and support their work with conventional literature, and the project must articulate some clear plan of action (which could be large or small). As a result, candidates had a choice, and as subsequent cohorts progressed through to the end, the scope of projects that were born out of this program was nothing short of amazing.

This general lack of instructions was both a blessing and curse for candidates and faculty (and administration) alike, and final capstone projects took many forms. For some candidates, the ability to imagine a culminating project that had the capacity to be very personal or academically nonconforming represented a welcome freedom that is so often not a part of the graduate educational enterprise. For others, the highly interpretable guidelines and a comparatively open evaluation rubric pushed the very limits of their understanding of what constitutes "good work" at this level.

And to say that the capstone project was unique to each individual is in some ways a bit of an understatement. For some candidates, there was a real comfort in being able to render this rather high-stakes assessment in a medium in which they felt the most comfortable. Many candidates remarked that, like many of their own students, their preferred ways of learning and expressing did not align with what was conventionally expected and honored in school environments. The opportunity to engage what was still a highly academic endeavor in a way that suited their own learning styles was a freedom they had not previously encountered. For others, the opportunity to step outside of their comfort zone and pursue something meaningful in a safe environment was a welcome challenge.

For example, some candidates chose to connect their work very explicitly to their practice and extend the work they began in the practitioner research course toward the development of a specific inquiry or initiative in their classroom. Also in this vein, some pursued critical self-study of their teaching practices, while others explored memoir, autoethnography, and narrative modes of inquiry in crafting their final projects. Other candidates chose to produce a thesis that brought together the many theoretical threads of their work throughout the program. Projects represented what seemed to be a dizzying array of topics, from deep discussions of Dewey's vision of utopia to practical analysis and critique of various theories of teaching and learning. Some candidates, in the spirit of Maxine Greene (2001), chose aesthetic routes of representation, including but not limited to using music, textiles, poetry, and other artistic modes and media to more fully and personally illustrate their development and accompanying narrative. Candidates produced short films, children's books, musical compositions, and quilts—and more—as physical representations of the learning journey they took through this program.

Although the capstone was in many ways supposed to serve as the culmination of learning through this program, it was the candidates' documentation of the journey along the way that best illustrated their day-to-day points of resonance and practical application of theory and course material.

As candidates moved through the program, we as faculty were encouraged in a number of ways. First, prolonged engagement with candidates around the whole of their coursework allowed for the opportunity to both get to know the candidate on a deeper level and to see, almost in real time, how they were making connections between the course material and their own practice. As capstone readers, we saw students for the first and last courses; we did not typically see students for their course experiences in the middle. However, the relationship that came from responding to their reflective work and meaning making in the end of course reflections gave us the chance to see how they were developing along the way—what they were struggling with, what they were resonating with, perennial questions they were troubling, and so on.

From our perspectives as program leaders and capstone readers, what was happening with candidates along the way was inspiring—and not just to us as faculty: our students emphasized this as well. In terms of their work in their own classrooms and schools, as our candidates progressed through the program, they articulated a myriad of ways to put their unique experience of the principles they have renewed or discovered into practice. For some candidates, this meant experimenting with new ideas, techniques, and content in the classroom (we should mention that the Common Core was not yet adopted in most of the contexts in which our students were teaching). For other candidates, this meant engaging more explicitly with colleagues and administration. Candidates wrote of feeling more empowered to take on advocacy or activist roles in their classrooms, schools, and districts, or to engage colleagues in discussion and dialogue around ideology, theory, and technique. Some candidates indicated a new feeling of responsibility to engage more fully with the communities in which they were teaching, whereas others cultivated the courage to approach administration regarding issues and ideas and share their perspectives and funds of knowledge.

We realize that this may seem simplistic and that this merely represents what teachers in classrooms and schools just do as a part of their everyday experience. But what was significant for both faculty and students here seemed to be the connectivity between the students and their work, the theory and practice learned in their coursework, and the ongoing dialogue with the capstone reader around this integration. Candidates indicated that the feedback and dialogue that happened outside the context of specific coursework but with a consistent faculty member was integral to their development and willingness to venture into uncharted waters. Further, candidates also indicated that the compulsory reflection statements at the end of each course, although initially annoying, served as touchstones to assist them in staying focused and engaged. Anecdotally and experientially, the program plan seemed to be working.

Engaging a More Disciplined Inquiry

Although the program seemed to have a positive impact on our candidates (at least this was what they were telling us, both in person and on course and program evaluation documents), in order to defend what was increasingly being perceived as nonessential practices by faculty and administrators higher up the chain from us, we needed to develop a better understanding of candidate engagement with the action-oriented capstone process, as well as to better understand and evaluate the process itself. We sought to demonstrate that approaching end-of-program requirements in this way was not merely an effective way to illustrate teachers' engagement in reflective practices, but as well it could encourage a disposition toward critical reflection into action and serve as an individually meaningful endeavor for our candidates. To that end, we engaged in both critical analysis and evaluation of the process, products, and outcomes, as well as considered further possibilities as well as liabilities. As the winds of change were once again wafting through our institution, we hoped that through demonstrating the benefits of this process for our candidates and the children in their classrooms, we could protect the program—and the capstone process—from being dismantled in favor of experiences that are less inventive, more "practical," and easily and explicitly aligned with "the standards."

We interrogated the following questions throughout our inquiry: How did candidates perceive and understand the program and the process? How did candidates experience the capstone process, and how did those experiences translate into their final capstone product? How was this particular process valued (or not) by candidates? In what ways was their professional practice impacted through this experience? How did they interpret and internalize this experience, and how was that reflected in their personal and professional growth? What did this process accomplish both for our candidates and our own practice? As well, we considered how to represent such a process in an accrediting body–friendly manner (NCATE was the dominant accrediting body at this time).

This inquiry explored the capstone process as a case of action-oriented practice in in-service teacher education. We sought better understandings of both our teachers' and our candidates' learning. We resonated deeply with the self-study work that the candidates were doing and thought that self-study methods could assist us in analyzing student work. As self-study involves "reflection in which teachers systematically and critically examine their actions and the context of those actions as a way of developing a more consciously driven mode of professional activity" (Samaras & Freese, 2006, p. 11), we are continually studying our practice in teacher education through this study of the practices of our candidates. Further, we employed critical hermeneutic and phenomenological perspectives to better understand how individuals created meaning throughout this endeavor. Through exploring their unique trajectories through the program, we were able to develop a deeper understanding of not only how their meaning making is related to practice but also how the process impacted them in practical, philosophical, and theoretical ways. The capstone experiences of individual candidates provided more specific, bounded cases for analysis. In the course of this inquiry, we conducted interviews and observations and collected course and program documents. We also collected data on our own experience throughout the capstone process. We kept a journal in which we reflected on our teaching, our responses to candidate work, and the mechanics of reading the candidates' capstones. We also engaged in regular discussion circles that focused on how we were interpreting the work of our candidates. Finally, we collected e-mails that we exchanged regarding the capstones; we analyzed the ways that we discussed our candidates' work and the challenges we often encountered, the administrative headaches of the capstone process, and how we sought advice from each other. All these sources of data were utilized in a purposefully engaged process of self-study.

We found that the benefits to candidates of a truly reflective, action-oriented capstone process went beyond what we had expected in two directions, inward and outward. Similarly, our own self-studies required us to examine our teaching, our scholarship, and our roles as advocates for the program and processes.

Course-culminating work from early in the program showed signs of struggle and resistance. For many of our candidates, prolonged and critical engagement with texts and ideas had never been asked of them before, nor had the explicit application of this engagement to their classroom practice. Toward the end, however, they tended to become much more adept at appropriating intellectual material—truly making it their own—and relating it to the whole of their practice and experience rather than compartmentalizing for a particular assignment or class. Such text as experience became a part of who the candidates are in a holistic way. As a result, they developed clearer visions of who they are and what they are capable of, both inside and outside of their classrooms and schools. Candidates increasingly felt—and became—empowered to identify issues, advocate for change, and, in some cases, to become activists themselves.

For many candidates, the end-of-course reflection and action cycles became an occasion for looking back farther than the beginning of the term, and there are connections made to their life narratives, their undergraduate experience, and their stories as teachers. Here, autobiographical reflection drives reconceptualization (Grumet, 1999), and candidates find that they are reading their own life stories in a whole new way. For these candidates, the capstone process gave teachers the intellectual space for a personal practice in which their own development is critical, a space where they come first. Despite the pervasive societal and media messages that teachers should be selfless (Taubman, 1997), Diller (1999) explains that all teachers need to care for self. Unless we care for ourselves, we cannot truly care for others.

While caring more deeply for self, our candidates also looked more widely out to the world. At the end of their program, the research symposium gave them the opportunity to become experts in their educational pathways before an audience of their peers. Recognizing their own intellectual work of teaching, candidates became a community of scholars rather than individuals pursuing a discrete task. Several candidates took their work to the national stage as well; candidates have presented individually on this work at the American Educational Research Association, and both individually and as a symposium at the American Educational Studies Association. Through emails, social media, phone calls and visits, candidates regularly keep us informed of how they continue to ask critical questions, work for change when necessary, and are participants in an educational milieu that extends beyond their own classrooms.

Our own self-study of the capstone process paralleled the struggles and issues in many of our candidates' program processes and culminating projects. Just as teachers face increased standardization and positivistic accountability measures, so have we as our university continues to adopt standardized assessment rubrics in an attempt to quantify the learning experience of our graduate students. We are all imperiled by the tide of data-driven decision making. This realization has opened conversations within our classrooms about the value and goals of reflective and often introspective culminating activities (such as the capstone). Knowing how valuable and transformative the experience was for our students, it also challenged us to become stronger advocates for reflective, action-oriented processes across programs within our college and university.

As professors engaged in our own self-study, we found ourselves reengaged in thinking about our practice as teachers. Studying our students' capstone process has brought our focus to the practical and personal side of scholarship: We have become students alongside our students. An article by Collins (1970) argues, among other things, that teaching requires a commitment by teachers to relearn material, to always be a student; true teaching occurs through a shared process of learning. Our self-study has transformed our teaching by inspiring us to become learners.

Self-study for us, as professors, allowed us to reinvest in our teaching practice. While we all have our own areas of research interest (and these are varied), exploring our own teaching became an additional area of scholarly pursuit. Teaching and research are often seen as separate, or worse, unconnected, endeavors in higher education. Through our self-study, we were able were able to think of teaching as scholarly. We challenged ourselves to do what we asked our students to do: engage in critical, prolonged, and personal reflection on our practice in order to best meet the needs our students.

The master's programs at our university use a cohort model in which all students take a standard set of classes. The capstone process described here offered students the opportunity to express their own connection to the material. Here, students were able to highly individualize an extremely standardized program and to articulate and actualize specific and explicit changes in their classrooms, schools, and communities.

It is important to note that ours is not a prestigious degree program; our students are regular teachers. Yet for many, something transformative happened that provided these teachers recognition and ownership of the highly theoretical work that their teaching is. Through this process of interrogating both their prior assumptions and every new text or idea, each student took on what Hinchey (2008) refers to as an identity as a critical educator.

Explicitly engaging in prolonged self-study and action-oriented inquiry for our master's degree candidates was an invaluable way to transition from their course of graduate study to the rest of their careers as educators. Our own self-study as teacher educators validated this approach to providing the culminating experience required by our state. Through this inquiry, we attempted to ascertain the quality of an experience that we hoped would be beneficial. Dewey (1938), in the passage quoted below, sets this as a crucial task for the educator:

> Everything depends on the *quality* of the experience which is had … The *effect* of an experience is not borne on its face. It sets a problem to the educator. It is his business to arrange for the kind of experiences which, while they do not repel the student, but rather engage his activities are, nevertheless, more than immediately enjoyable since they promote having desirable future experiences. (p. 27)

Of Course, It's Not All Good News: Politics and Challenges

Although we were heartened to have found the engagement, enjoyment, and impact on the future that Dewey hoped for, we are sad to say that it's not all good news; and to borrow the words of Ben Stiller (1994), "reality bites." Several years into the program changes, and well prior to the writing of this chapter, a change in college and departmental leadership resulted in the program and processes described here being fundamentally altered; students in this program are no longer engaged in prolonged self-study and action-oriented inquiry, the coursework is no longer sequential and is heavily practice-focused, and the state-required capstone is once again a discrete, end-of-program activity.

It's easy to point to several institutional factors that seem to have contributed to this subsequent overhaul of the programs, most notably, accreditation pressures, program marketing, and issues of faculty workload and responsibility. These will be discussed momentarily. However, we believe that what really happened is actually quite deeper than that—and a bit scarier. Two of the most influential and perennial questions posed by noted curriculum theorist Bill Schubert (1986) are that of "what's worthwhile" and "who benefits." Here, too, we think of Dewey's (1900/1915) discussion of what is in the "best interest" of all the members of an educational community. In many ways, these questions get at the heart of the conflicts we experienced as a result of this reimagination of the C and I programs and capstone project.

For as much support as we had initially been given regarding the redevelopment of everything, a massive reconfiguration of the college and departmental structure resulted in different people being in positions of power—people with much stronger ties to and feelings of comfort with positivistic ways of knowing and demonstrating.

What characterized the struggle in terms of accreditation pressures can superficially be understood as competing visions of what "counts" as "data" in terms of demonstrating the competence of our candidates. Pursuant to both the climate within and constraints under which we were operating, we developed an extensive evaluation rubric for the final capstone project. In developing this document (a task we were loath to engage, because we felt it was in many ways counterintuitive to the more critical processes that we were trying to cultivate in our candidates), we sought to provide the kinds of information about the candidates and their work that our accreditation process required. It is interesting that the conversations we had with candidates around the rubric were quite telling as well. Some of the most compelling of these centered around the question of whether we, as program leaders, were capitulating to a system and set of processes we were, in the words of Bill Ayers (2004), "teaching against," or whether we were merely working within the parameters of a larger system in such ways as to provide an easily understood tool of legitimization for work that was clearly coloring outside of the lines. In this regard, we found ourselves at an interesting intersection; as Adrienne Rich writes, "This is the oppressor's language//yet I need it to talk to *you,*" while at the same time, Audre Lorde warns us that "the master's tools will never dismantle the master's house." Yup.

Further, new leadership was firmly committed to standards-based models of instructional delivery at the graduate level. Here, too, we sought to demonstrate in various ways how the work that candidates were doing in the context of their courses and the capstone could explicitly be linked to the various sets of standards that the college departments sought to align with (this is a more complicated conversation, but this alignment started with National Board for Professional Teaching Standards [NBPTS] and progressed through an alphabet soup of existing and newly developed criteria).

Marketing of college graduate programs became another point of contention regarding what was, again, increasingly perceived as nonessential or "luxury" (as one of our colleagues described) practices and sites of knowledge regarding these programs and processes. It is important to note here that our graduate students, of which we have thousands across numerous programs, are primarily recruited through the efforts of a contracted marketing firm. The notion that teachers aren't interested in having to think, that they just need practical tools to use in their classrooms the very next day, became what seemed to be the default mantra by the marketing firm and, as a consequence, faculty and program leadership. As evidenced throughout this whole chapter, the C and I programs were difficult to explain in a few bullet points, and the full measure of meaningfulness of the experience often wasn't realized until the end (or even later, as some of our former students are still indicating, two years after the final cohort finished). To that end, the challenges experienced by the marketers were very real in terms of selling the program as a quick fix to what ails them in the classroom to prospective degree seekers.

In asking both candidates and faculty to commit to a long-term, engaged process of conceptualization and implementation, we knew we were asking a lot of our students, ourselves, and our colleagues. Although this could be framed as a reasonable expectation for candidates, asking faculty to do significant work outside of the context of a specific course challenged the existing professional structure and values at our institution. To this point, none of our graduate programs required a thesis, and faculty were not required to advise graduate students (or really, any students; undergraduate advising was handled by faculty outside of our college). As well, all work outside of regular teaching was subject to independent, paid contracting—including capstone portfolio evaluation, course development, and dissertation committee work. Although we structured the checkpoint system to align with the review and payment structure for the previous capstone (there were no additional costs to the department or college), this new process required a significantly greater commitment from faculty in terms of time and personal engagement. No longer could capstone evaluators click through an electronic portfolio builder and check "does not meet," "meets," or "exceeds" at the end of each section to collect their payment. The new process required establishing a relationship with candidates and their work, required narrative and connective feedback to candidates, and required a shift in focus from evaluation to advising.

Theoretically, this shift in perspective from evaluative to advisory in terms of faculty responsibility with the capstone was supported throughout the department and across the college. As previously discussed, there was widespread agreement that the existing processes were not particularly meaningful or effective for either candidates or faculty. However, for as much initial support that our advisory model of capstone evaluation was given in terms of the *theory* of what was good for students, the practical requirements of such engagement met with disfavor from a small group of colleagues. As the college moved to cut costs by eliminating payments for capstone checkpoint reviews, this increased responsibility became even more problematic for some faculty.

As previously mentioned, although the institutional issues outlined above certainly make sense with regard to what happened with this program, we can't help but fear this situation is symptomatic of a much larger malaise.

So, to What End Do We Educate?

As mentioned previously, the pervasiveness of social media has created a culture in which many of the candidates we encountered through this program remain part of our professional and personal communities. For as ridiculous as it can be, Facebook has provided a useful forum in which we can both continue the conversations with our former students and facilitate a space in which they can engage with each other—as well as thousands of other teachers fighting the same good fight (at the writing of this article, the Badass Association of Teachers had over 51,000 members—among them many former candidates). This continued engagement with our candidates has illustrated that the lessons of the program have taken root; their continued actions and commitment have manifested as a steadfast perennial garden of practice rather than an ever-changing plot comprised of showy and short-lived annuals.

Although we have not explicitly studied the candidates who have completed any one of the numerous other programs our institution offers, (for example, in addition to the current manifestation of the Curriculum and Instruction program, the college offers MA degrees in Differentiated Instruction and in Teacher Leadership), we do still teach courses across the college and encounter these candidates on a regular basis. Based on our (albeit comparatively limited) engagements, we have noticed a difference in the candidates' approaches to their coursework and programs. Generally speaking, candidates tend to encounter each course as a discrete learning module, and, not surprisingly, we do not experience students making the same kinds of linkages among the various courses. In the reconfigured program, the foundations courses come at the end; as such, they tend to be perceived (per students) more like add-ons to fill up credit hour requirements than theoretical and practical foundations upon which to build an understanding of the social, cultural, political, and other contexts of teaching, learning, and schooling. On our end of the exchange, the programs feel more mechanical, more like a process to *complete* rather than one in which to *engage*, and a means to an end rather than the beginning of something new.

Although the above is disappointing, it is not surprising. Unlike the often messy—even sometimes chaotic—intellectual treatises that comprised the course and program outcomes that we were used to, the current crop of candidates is in many ways much better at the execution of clean products with clear practical and conceptual boundaries than our former candidates. Current conversations around the "challenge to act" paper in the foundations course are more often about the required number of pages than whether or not the candidate can base their entire essay on Arendt's *The Crisis in Education* (1954) or Baldwin's *A Talk to Teachers* (1963). Our exaggeration is mild here. We would like to say that the course experiences we provide are environments in which these candidates might realize that what they are being spoon fed in terms of their program is not only insufficient for understanding the many-layered realities of teaching in an increasingly complicated and diversifying world, but it is also comprised of an unpalatable milquetoast of noncontroversial ideas, mind-numbing routines, and rubrics on developing rubrics—but given the structure of the programs and the content, it is not likely. Still, when it does happen, it gives us great hope for the future.

Here's the problem: although our existing programs might be very good at producing the kinds of teachers that the system wants and finds useful (and by "the system," we're talking not just the forces outside of education that are making decisions for education, but also the social understanding of what teaching and learning is supposed to be in society today—as molded by these forces, of course), we are not very good at producing the kinds of teachers who will take issue with that very system when appropriate or necessary; who will ask the difficult questions of "Is this good for children?" and "In whose best interest does X serve?" and who will advocate for families, communities, and schools in ways that might not conform with what the powers that be see as conduct becoming a deliverer of content knowledge. Our program is not unique in this regard; we hear similar laments of our colleagues at institutions across the land.

To place blame on our colleagues alone for creating these types of environments is unfair—they, as we all, are held hostage in many ways by the logic of accreditation and standardization agencies, the pressures of the monied and the powerful, and the not-so-random opining of individuals and celebrities with loud voices or large fan bases. These forces create an environment that almost demands that higher education conform and participate by creating programs and course experiences heavy in methods and standards alignment and that narrowly define "teaching" or "leadership" as a set of prescribed behaviors and skill demonstrations that are easily measured with clear and simple instruments.

If we as faculty members see as our responsibility the whole of our society, versus merely the candidates who contract our services, we must always ask Schubert's increasingly difficult questions of "to what end?", "what is worth knowing?", and "who benefits?" and act in accordance with the moral compact we have made with society as educators of educators—and therefore with each subsequent generation that is socialized by our system of education and schooling.

However, if we look at this from the perspective of our colleagues, we see through a different window. To our colleagues charged with developing teacher professional practice, grooming school leaders, or preparing candidates to enter public school classrooms, by openly and deliberately teaching in these ways, we are engaging in a subversive activity (Postman & Weingartner, 1971). And although we might see this as cultivating opportunities for candidates to question and contest practices that are harmful to their students and disempowering for teachers at large, our colleagues see the other side of the same coin—that we are the ones doing harm by distracting our students from concentrating on the real work of what teaching has become: aligning content to standards, developing lessons, and quietly getting in line.

Our moral compasses tell us that it is our duty, our responsibility, to serve not just our candidates but, more important, the children and families that they serve as educators themselves. To not assist them is to be complicit in those practices and affirming those perspectives that contribute to the destruction of the very fabric of education as we know it. This is a dilemma of professional practice that none of us are sure we signed up for, but believe we have a moral obligation to engage.

When Dewey's vision of a good society was questioned (much like our own visions of a good education for both teachers and their students), he cultivated dialogue across camps of agreement and difference. We believe that it is at this place of dialogue where the seeds of critical conversation are planted and an impetus toward action is born. If Dr. Seuss (1971) is right in that, "Unless someone like you cares a whole awful lot, Nothing is going to get better. It's not," then we have no moral choice but to heed Maxine Greene's (1997) call to "reach beyond [our]selves to what [we] believe should be," and to "imagine not what is necessarily probable or predictable, but what may be conceived as possible." In doing so, we hope to come close to creating a space in which to practice what John Dewey articulated as necessary in the opening paragraphs of *The School and Society*,

> What the best and wisest parent wants for his own child, that must the community want for all of its children. Any other ideal for our schools is narrow and unlovely; acted upon, it destroys our democracy. (1900/1915, p. 3)

References

Ayers, W. C. (2004). *Teaching toward freedom: Moral commitment and ethical action in the classroom.* New York: Teachers College Press.

Bullough, R. V., & Pinnegar, S. (2001). Guidelines for quality in autobiographical forms of self-study research. *Educational Researcher, 30*(3), 13–21.

Collins, P. (1970). Some philosophical considerations on teaching and learning. *Teachers College Record, 71*(3), 413–422.

Dewey, J. (1900/1915). *The school and society.* Chicago: University of Chicago.

Dewey, J. (1938). *Experience and education.* New York: Touchstone.

Diller, A. (1999). The ethical education of self-talk. In M. S. Katz, N. Noddings, & K. A. Strike, *Justice and caring: The search for common ground in education* (pp. 74–92). New York: Teachers College Press.

Gray, A. L. (2003). Conversations with transformative encounters. In G. Gay (Ed.), *Becoming multicultural educators: Personal journey toward professional agency* (pp. 67–90). San Francisco: Jossey-Bass.

Greene, M. (1997). Teaching as possibility: A light in dark times. *The Journal of Pedagogy, Pluralism, and Practice, 1*(1). Retrieved from http://www.lesley.edu/journals/jppp/1/jp3ii1.html

Greene, M. (2001). *Variations on a blue guitar: The Lincoln Center Institute on Aesthetic Education.* New York: Teachers College Press.

Griffiths, M. (1993). Educational change and the self. *British Journal of Educational Studies, 41*(2), 150–163.

Grumet, M. R. (1999). Autobiography and reconceptualization. In W. F. Pinar (Ed.), *Contemporary curriculum discourses: Twenty years of JCT* (pp. 24–30). New York: Peter Lang.

Hinchey, P. H. (2008). *Becoming a critical educator: Defining a classroom identity, designing a critical pedagogy.* New York: Peter Lang.

Krol, C. A. (1997). Reflective practice (coming to terms). *English Journal, 86*(5), 96–97.

Lather, P. (1991). *Getting smart: Feminist research and pedagogy with/in the postmodern.* New York: Routledge.

Lorde, A. (1978). *Sister outsider.* Trumansburg, NY: Crossing.

McLaughlin, T. H. (1999). Beyond the reflective teacher. *Educational philosophy and theory 31*(1), 9–25.

Postman, N., & Weingartner, C. (1971). *Teaching as a subversive activity.* New York: Dell.

Rich, A. (1971). The burning of paper instead of children. In *The will to change: Poems 1968–1970.* New York: W. W. Norton.

Samaras, A. P., & Freese, A. R. (2006). *Self-study of teaching practices.* New York: Peter Lang.

Schön, D. A. (1983). *The reflective practitioner.* New York: Basic Books.

Schön, D. A. (1988). *Educating the reflective practitioner.* San Francisco: Jossey-Bass.

Schubert, W. H. (1986). *Curriculum: Perspective, paradigm, and possibility.* New York: Macmillan.

Seuss, D. (1971). *The lorax.* New York: Random House.

Stiller, B. (Dir.). (1994). *Reality bites.* Universal Pictures, United States.

Taubman, P. (2007, April). *It's all about the kids: The lure of service and sacrifice in a master's level education course.* Paper presented at the American Educational Research Association annual meeting, Chicago, IL.

CHAPTER 26

Forming New Agreements

A Brief Critical Exploration of the Pedagogical Formations of Predominantly White, Preservice Teachers in an Urban Context

Jeanine M. Staples, Talia Carroll, Donna Marie Cole-Mallot, Jennifer Myler, Corey Simmons, Julie Schappe, and Theresa Adkins

Introduction and Statement of the Problem

> And I realized that I was afraid of him … this little black boy.
> "Kristy," a 21-year-old White woman, pre-service teaching in a third-grade classroom

The predominance of White preservice teachers working with students of diverse backgrounds is well documented (Sleeter, 2001, 2013; Flint, Zisook, & Fisher, 2011). The sociocultural mismatch between novice, White, middle-class preservice teachers and the racially, culturally and economically diverse students they are positioned to teach presents particular problems. First, these teachers are more likely to stereotype students and the spaces in which they live and to internalize low expectations for youth's multiple learning trajectories (Staples, 2010b, 2012). They are also less likely to form generative, appreciable, respectful, or empathetic relationships with such students, those who seem to be so "different" from them. These problems emerge in relation to, and can ultimately impact, preservice teachers' perceptions of students' intellectual aptitudes and behavioral abilities. Low expectations and flawed perceptions, in effect, generate disabling classroom cultures and inhibit student–teacher relationships. In order to mediate these problems, teacher educators must find ways to introduce and facilitate the assumption of meaningful, constructive perceptions, practices, and pedagogies among White middle-class preservice teachers placed in teaching/learning contexts in which they are racial minorities. In this essay, I attempt to clarify how I, an African-American woman teacher educator, intentionally took up this work with a group of teacher educators who are graduate students and co-instructors in a course titled CI 295D/A: The Philadelphia Urban Seminar.

The two-week course is intensive. It is offered, in conjunction, by the Department of Curriculum and Instruction in the Pennsylvania State University's College of Education and Penn State Outreach. In the course, students are assigned as mentees to mentor teachers within pre-K–12 schools in the Philadelphia School District. Every imaginable discipline and content area is represented via these placements (including, for example, math, English, sciences, culinary arts, physical education, and special education). Students are invited to engage in participant observation, one-on-one or small-group tutoring, curriculum inventory, assignment design and evaluation, class trips, parent–teacher conferences, and administrative meetings. Students are not required or encouraged to lead instruction, however, since this course meets the requirements of an early field experience and is a mandate to be fulfilled prior to the declaration of the education major at Penn State.

In addition to preservice teachers' experiences in schools by day, students must participate fully in academic coursework, professional development seminars, sociocultural events, and civic volunteerism nearly every evening and during the common weekend. These participations take place within and around multiple sites in the city of Philadelphia (such as a host university's campus, area parks, museums, and community centers). So, while students learn the application of educational theory (regarding instruction, assessment, behavior management/modification, etc.), they also have the opportunity to live as visiting citizens of a thriving, vibrant urban community—vis-à-vis the neighborhood and school. In the context of this course, students are required to demonstrate at least proficiency (if not mastery) of course content through various exhibitions of talk and writing. For example, course assignments include essay writing, blogging, the development of an educational case study, and evidence of sociocognitive engagements with course readings, professional development sessions, social activities, and civil service through structured and informal discussions, commentaries, questionings, and various types of sociocultural involvements.

The Emergence of a Critically Active Stance in Response to the Statement of the Problem

Our course attempts to mediate the multiple disconnects that exist between White preservice teachers and their prospective Black and Brown students in urban contexts. These disconnects have been explored before (see Ladson-Billings, 2000; Hollins & Guzman, 2005; Gay, 2010; Lee, Eckrick, Lackey, & Showalter, 2010) and many solutions have been presented to the field. Some include curricular stances (focusing on cultural relevance), behavioral stances meant to cultivate particular classroom and school cultures (such as zero tolerance and character building) and policy stances intended to institutionalize various levels of social and political governance that might police teaching-learning spaces, making it easier for teachers and students to relate to each other peacefully and respectfully. While each of these approaches has assisted in mending the aforementioned disconnects, they all fall short of stabilizing and perpetuating a meaningful change in the ways White preservice teachers perceive and relate to urban contexts and youth.

This chapter clarifies the critically active stance I have assumed, as a teacher educator, in my efforts to contribute new efforts in mediating these disconnects. Herein, I explore the impetus and rationale for my selection of *The Four Agreements* (Ruiz, 2012) as a perceptual framework through which to facilitate the formation of White preservice teachers' emergent pedagogies as they engage with urban contexts and youth. As one of many solutions to the problem noted, I see inclusion of the four agreements as a means to bridging the perceptual, experiential, and empathic gaps that exist between the army of new White, middle-class women entering the teaching profession and their increasingly Brown and Black working-class and poor students. By incorporating a perceptual frame that enables new, more complex levels of sociocultural and self-perceptions, I seek to stabilize and perpetuate meaningful change in how these novice teachers perceive, understand, and relate to urban contexts and youth by influencing first the ways they see themselves. Kristy's quote in the epigraph above reveals a hint of the beginning of this alternate perception. As she outed the results of a deeply embedded racist inclination, making herself not only aware of her toxic thoughts and feelings but also rendering herself in full ownership of them by voicing them aloud, of her own volition, she better positioned herself to uproot that which hindered understanding, respect, and sociocultural intimacies as these things relate to perceptions of teaching-learning contexts and youth. This is the very beginning of pedagogical formation (Staples, 2010a, 2010b).

In this chapter, and from the position of a critically responsive and inclusive African-American woman teacher educator, I intentionally take up this exploratory work. I do so by examining the perceptual framework chosen to inform the pedagogical formations of our predominantly White preservice teachers in our urban education course. I also address some of the ways the framework has the power to constructively influence our understanding of what it means to teach, learn, and relate to context and "other." First, I make explicit what it is I mean by "pedagogical formation." Then I introduce *Four Agreements* and Don Miguel Ruiz's work, noting what the agreements are and how they can support the amelioration of the teacher preparation problem noted here. I present, within this section, examples of how preservice teachers in our course took up these agreements and used them to support their perceptions of urban contexts and youth. Finally, I conclude with some ideas about how this framework can support further research in teacher preparation and teacher education.

Conceptualizing Pedagogical Formation

When I say "pedagogical formation," I am referring to the incremental developments of one's comprehension of instructional methodology, assessment, behavioral understanding, and interpersonal relating, in addition to one's elective personal and professional appropriation of these things. I see this comprehension and appropriation as the beginning of stance. Stance speaks to the cultivation of a praxis that can be enacted in teaching-learning contexts and with the constituents found there. To affect pedagogical formation is to inform the heart of an educator. I understand formation as a phased, developmental process comprised of intellectual, experiential, and perceptual approaches to teaching, learning, and relating. It is comprised of one's professional and personal attitudes and beliefs. It determines an approach to practice and personhood. Pedagogical formations among White preservice teachers in urban contexts are particularly important because they directly influence the ways these teachers construct and implement approaches to instruction, behavior management, assessment for, and relationship building among marginalized youth.

The Four Agreements and Teacher Preparation

I first heard of Don Miguel Ruiz's *Four Agreements* while watching *The Oprah Winfrey Show*. I read the book in graduate school and then again in my first few years as a professor. I found it intensely compatible with my Christian faith, which is why I felt drawn to it. I also found the four primary agreements very easy to remember and embed within everyday life, and so I held onto the framework with no glitches in memory or application. I began to consider how it might work in teacher preparation when the needs of this course came up in Teaching Team discussions. We needed a perceptual framework that could function as a tool for pedagogical formation. It needed to be practical, simple, critical, and broadly applicable. To be counted as practical means to be easily enacted within multiple contexts and in relation to multiple "others" who may be encountered within those contexts. To be simple means to be uncomplicated, clear, direct, and easy to retain, apply, and share. Criticality refers to the framework's ability to build sociocultural awareness, inform interpretations, and interrupt senses of normalcy from a personal vantage point. Finally, a broadly applicable framework needed to inspire reflections on how knowledge gets built and how being gets done within and across multiple teaching-learning contexts (including urban spaces and those beyond).

Ruiz's framework for lifework and "personal growth" (2012) posits that perceptual bondage can be overcome through alignment with four primary "agreements." These are agreements that one makes with one's Self (sparking an internal revolution) and extends to perceptions of "others" (sparking external revolution). The first agreement refers to the management of Self through voice and language. The second and third agreements involve management of Self through thought and emotion. The fourth agreement attends to management of Self through operative action. Preservice teachers were asked to apply these agreements to lived experiences with urban contexts and youth and reflect on the outcomes of the application through discussions and writings (Harmen & McClure, 2011).

The First Agreement: Be Impeccable With Your Word

This intrapersonal agreement is called "the most difficult one to honor" (Ruiz, 2012, p. 25). It means to speak with continual integrity. It means to say only what is meant and to understand and mean what is said. It encourages one to "avoid using the word to speak against [Self] or to gossip about others" (Ruiz, p. 25). This agreement governs voice and language. It urges one to use the power of words in the service of truth. It signals to preservice teachers the power of spoken word and also provides a way to influence and construct language in ways that are direct, clear, and appreciable. This agreement introduces the concept of love in teacher preparation (a largely novel concept). It provides preservice teachers with a guideline through which to be at once honest (about their perception of context and other) and kind or constructive (in articulating perceptions of context and other). For example, when talking about students of color, who may be perceived as culturally deprived and exhibiting behavioral challenges, preservice teachers who make this agreement with themselves are positioned to make earnest attempts to use language as a framing instrument. In this case, their voice and language can be used in the service of well-being by enacting them as a tools to frame contexts and youth in ways that affirm their humanity, value, power, and contributions. New, positive, appreciable perceptions of students can be initiated and upheld through impeccable language—language that is committed to affirmation and resistance from fear and disrespect.

For example, a student who may be called a "troublemaker" then may be renamed and repositioned as "energetic" and "comedic" (and therefore very intelligent, savvy, and astute). A classroom that might be termed "disruptive" or "disorganized" might be also reconstituted as "energetic" and "busy" or "post-systematic." Using voice and language to reframe context and youth does not nullify reality; it opens up new layers of reality. When this happens, preservice teachers are more enabled to make choices and decisions that are in the best interest of all teaching-learning constituents as they begin to see in broad, appreciable wholeness rather than in miniscule, negating parts.

The Second Agreement: Don't Take Anything Personally

This agreement clarifies that nothing anyone does is because of anyone else. What others say and do is a projection of their own reality, their own dream. Ruiz therefore contends that when one is immune to the opinions and actions of others, one will not be "the victim of needless suffering" (Ruiz, 2012). This agreement governs thoughts and emotions by pointing out our temptations to Self-center. It provides for preservice teachers a clearer understanding of positioning in the world by disrupting the impulse to place oneself in the role of object of others' words, thoughts, deeds, or desires. This displacement simultaneously inspires freedom from Self-aggrandizement and Self-loathing. Ruiz contends that whether someone praises or vilifies anyone else, the recipient of such attention is free to disassociate from taking those affirmations or insults to heart. In the midst of this agreement, preservice teachers are free to release whatever guilt, shame, anger, or resentments they have about what a parent or child may have said or done. This agreement can help to assuage whatever concerns preservice teachers have regarding relating to students and families that are so different from them. For instance, preservice teachers may feel concerned about speaking to a parent or community member in error, making an administrative mistake, fielding an unpleasant or cruel remark from a student, or letting down a colleague. When one makes the agreement to not take the outcome of such errors (or triumphs) personally, resisting the urge to make the outcome all about the Self, one can be free to learn from the experience in a whole sense, considering multiple vantage points, needs, desires, intentions, and cares. When this happens, preservice teachers are better prepared to build empathy and respect. For example, instead of nurturing a feeling of anxiety about a comment from a concerned parent, one that can easily be perceived as directly hostile and scary ("You are a bad teacher"), a preservice teacher can instead call up this second agreement with Self. She or he can decide to not take the comment personally by noting what it is really about: assertive defense of the child's safety and success as well as a search to identify and blame responsible parties for threats to the child. While it may be true that a preservice teacher invariably requires coaching for methodological improvement in instruction and behavior management, it is commonly highly debatable that she or he is totally incompetent. Therefore, while fielding constructive criticism to improve craft and skill, the teacher can understand the parents' commentary as a complex realization of a deeper desire to protect, thereby building incrementally the empathy and respect described above.

The Third Agreement: Don't Make Assumptions

This agreement also governs thoughts and emotions. It urges one to find the courage to ask questions and to express what is desired or misunderstood. By forming this agreement, preservice teachers can more effectively communicate and "avoid misunderstandings, sadness and drama" (Ruiz, 2012, p. 64). This agreement encourages inquiry. It asks preservice teachers in the daily practice of identifying perceived problems, disconnects, misunderstandings, needs, and so on to acknowledge that the onus is upon oneself to explore and investigate processes and practices that can function as solutions to problems of perceptions (assumptions that dehumanize the "other"). This agreement is about mediating or outing the prejudices, beliefs, or inferences that one makes internally in order to nullify them and root them out externally. For example, because Kristy made herself aware of whatever she assumed about the little boy in her class (that perhaps it was right to fear him, think him dirty, dangerous, unwieldy, out of control), she also gave herself permission to rebuke those assumptions when she made them public for herself and her colleagues. When this happens, preservice teachers are better able to build awareness and pursue socioculturally just inquiry from within and, eventually, without. This agreement differs from, and strengthens, the first agreement because it highlights the root of less-than-impeccable wording by insisting that its prompt (internal thoughts and feelings) be outed.

The Fourth Agreement: Always Do Your Best

This interpersonal agreement creates jurisdiction over actions and behaviors. Ruiz cautions that one's best efforts will change from moment to moment. He states that one's "best" will be different when one is healthy as opposed to sick. And still he advocates that, under any circumstance, one must simply do his or her best, and as such, avoid Self-judgment, Self-abuse, and regret. This agreement governs personal responsibility, grit, and actions. It provides for preservice teachers a goal for higher levels of situational performance in relation to context and other while also providing space for redirecting energy away from that which depreciates or stifles. When this redirection happens, preservice teachers are positioned to succeed in multiple situations and have opportunities to eliminate guilt, shame, and regret in relation to contexts and youth. For example, when a preservice teacher feels tired, perhaps disillusioned by a series of experiences that can easily be perceived as negative (a fight between two ninth-grade boys, a girl who curses an adult), he or she can recall this agreement and push through a desire to quit or retreat and master whatever pedagogical tasks remain in the day or week at hand.

These agreements are discrete and cooperative. They can each be centered in consciousness and action in efforts to build self and "other" awareness. They also each overlap each other to bolster a collective sense of heightened awareness. The final agreement governs the role of personal effort. In effect, it establishes goals for behavior and actions that are responsive and evolutionary. These goals are person and context specific and appreciate, even intensify, over time.

Some Problems in Acquisition: A Conclusion and
Implications for Future Studies in Critical Action Research

To address directly some students' concerns about implementation of the *Four Agreements* at the close of our course, I wrote an email to all students:

> I heard someone in our [Penn State] Family say that the more they attempt to learn the agreements, and embody them, the more confused they feel. Perhaps one might question the usefulness of the four agreements, or one's ability to enact them consistently. Or, someone may question whether or not they're even necessary for personal peace [sociocultural awareness and the cultivation of interpersonal intimacies]. I will refrain from responding to such questions because they are a matter of opinion. I do however, urge you to stick with [the agreements] and gauge their efficacy as more life experience is gained. Discomfort and even some bewilderment in teaching and learning [are] a part of the journey of education. The presence of these phenomena do not unilaterally signify the presence of a problem. Quite often, they signify the presence of progress and promise. When discomfort and bewilderment are in effect, acquisition and appropriation of new knowledge are also often in effect, as well.

Through the inclusion of the four agreements in our course on urban teaching and learning, we intended, as a team of teacher educators, to inspire constructive changes in White preservice teachers' perceptions of urban contexts and youth. The goals of this pedagogical initiative were to foster comprehension and appropriation of the agreements among our students and to help students then use them in relation to urban contexts and youth. Because the agreements introduce a shift in consciousness, they also simultaneously introduce a shift in positioning or perceptions of positioning. Such shifts, at first, can render feelings of loneliness and isolation. This is particularly true when others in the surround are not operating from the same perceptual frame. Assuring preservice teachers that the risks involved with such shifts were worth it was a key address that needed to be made regularly. The corresponding problems the Teaching Team faced as their students struggled to acquire the agreements are interesting to note. A brief synopsis of three primary problems follows:

Fielding Doubts

Several students responded to their first reading of *The Four Agreements* with doubt. As they comprehended the ideas presented, they doubted their origin and validity. Don Miguel Ruiz describes the origin of the agreements vis-à-vis his ethnic and religious culture, which are both endarkened (Dillard, 2012; Staples, 2011; Staples, forthcoming). To be "endarkened" means, essentially, to be governed by and to embody a racialized, gendered, and spiritual ethos in word, thought, and deed. Such an origin was foreign to many of our students because they were not yet ostensibly in touch with racial consciousness in and of itself, let alone its intersections with spirituality. Beyond origin, students doubted the validity of the agreements. They asked questions like this: Is it reasonable, or even accurate, to say that words form our worlds? Or is that a fanatical overstatement (the first agreement)? Is it really possible to not take anything that is perceived as hurtful or painful personally, ever? Or is that just a goal to strive for (the second agreement)? Is it actually helpful to not make assumptions about anything? Aren't assumptions based on largely substantiated facts and, therefore, helpful (the third agreement)? And finally: How is it possible to always do one's best? Does this pertain to every situation at all times (the fourth agreement)?

Fielding these doubts was not always possible. So, some were left to live in our teaching-learning contexts. Others were inserted into conversations reflecting on events from practicum experiences.

Feeling Weird

Once students began to comprehend the efficacy of the agreements and appropriate them in their lived experiences as preservice teachers, they often felt a sense of not quite belonging. For example, when preservice teachers from other institutions took part in parent–teacher conferences in which a Black or Hispanic parent raised his or her voice at a White mentor teacher, our preservice teachers resisted the urge to commiserate in assuming the worst about the parent and reinforcing stereotypes (the third agreement) or using disparaging language against the parent in order to descriptively categorize and disassociate from them (the first agreement). These resistances (inspired by their comprehension and appropriation of one or more of the agreements) occasionally caused students to feel left out of their cohort and be perceived as weird in the eyes of their peers.

Facing Choice

By the close of the course, students were faced with the choice of either keeping or relinquishing the agreements they made with themselves. It was a tough choice for some. The cognitive dissonance and social awkwardness immediately imposed by comprehension and appropriation of the agreements served as a deterrent. However, when students saw the greater potential benefit of the full acquisition of the four agreements, the choice became slightly easier. Many students, however, grasped the "personal freedom" (from anxiety, selfishness, sociocultural dismemberment, perceptions of failure, and self-loathing) that could be attained from full acquisition and chose to keep the agreements. Surveys gauging the impact of this full acquisition are in development.

Implications for Future Critical Action Research

This research suggests two primary implications for future critical action research, particularly as it pertains to White preservice teachers and their racially diverse students in diverse contexts. First, it is important for teacher educators to design and implement, with preservice teachers, theoretically informed methods for solving problems in daily living with self and others in diverse contexts. Additional cooperatively designed studies exploring the ways in which preservice teachers might identify their own problems in perceiving and acclimating to new contexts and with new people (all deemed very "different") is key. Such studies might include attention to White preservice teachers' voices regarding their perceptions of urban contexts (what they believe is true about them) and how these corresponding beliefs and attitudes affect their interactions with contexts and youth. This means investigating, with preservice teachers, what doubts they have about frameworks that are purported to enable their sensitivities, push forward whatever discomfort or "weirdness" they experience in relation to these things, and explore the choices that are afforded through the adoption of critically, conscious frameworks for perceiving context, other, and self.

Bibliography

Carroll, T., Staples, J. M., Myler, J., Simmons, C., Cole-Malott, D., Schappe, J., & Adkins, T. (forthcoming). *Implementing backward design: The development of an immersion urban education course for predominantly White pre-service teachers.*

Cole-Malott, D., Staples, J. M., Carroll, T., Myler, J., Simmons, C., Adkins, T., & Schappe, D. (forthcoming). *Analyzing white, pre-service teachers' desire to teach in an urban context.*

Dillard, C. B. (2012). *Learning to (re)member the things we've learned to forget: Endarkened feminisms, spirituality, and the sacred nature of research and teaching.* New York: Peter Lang.

Flint, A. S., Zisook, K., & Fisher, T. R. (2011). Not a one-shot deal: Generative professional development among experienced teachers. *Teaching and Teacher Education 27*(8), 1163–1169.

Gay, G. (2010). *Culturally responsive teaching: Theory, research, and practice.* New York: Teachers College Press.

Harman, R., & McClure, G. (2011). All the school's a stage: Critical performative pedagogy in urban teacher education. *Equity & Excellence in Education, 44*(3), 379–402.

Hollins, E. R., & Guzman, M. T. (2005). Research on preparing teachers for diverse populations. In M. Cochran-Smith & K. M. Zeichner (Eds.), *Studying teacher education: The report of the AERA panel on research and teacher education* (pp. 477–548). Mahwah, NJ: Lawrence Erlbaum.

Jackson, T. O. (2011). Developing sociopolitical consciousness at Freedom Schools: Implications for culturally responsive teacher preparation. *Teaching Education, 22*(3), 277–290.

Johnston-Parsons, M. (2012). *Dialogue and difference in a teacher education program: A 16-year sociocultural study of a professional development school.* Charlotte, NC: Information Age.

Ladson-Billings, G. (2000). Fighting for our lives: Preparing teachers to teach African American students. *Journal of Teacher Education, 51*(3), 206–214.

Lazar, A. M. (2007). It's not just about teaching kids to read: Helping pre-service teachers acquire a mindset for teaching children in urban communities. *Journal of Literacy Research, 39*(4), 411–443.

Lee, R. E., Eckrich, L. L., Lackey, C., & Showalter, B. D. (2010). Pre-service teacher pathways to urban teaching: A partnership model for nurturing community-based urban teacher preparation. *Teacher Education Quarterly, 37*(3), 101–122.

Myler, J., Staples, J. M., Simmons, C., Carroll, T., Cole-Malott, D., Adkins, T., & Schappe, J. (forthcoming). *Understanding pre-service teachers' beliefs in a community of difference.*

Ruiz, D. M. (2012). *The four agreements: A personal guide to personal freedom.* San Rafael, CA: Amber-Allen.

Simmons, C., Staples, J. M., Myler, J., Carroll, T., Cole-Malott, D., Schappe, J., & Adkins, T. (forthcoming). *Understanding white, male, pre-service teachers' perceptions of urban contexts and youth.*

Sleeter, C. E. (Ed.). (2011). *Professional development for culturally responsive and relationship-based pedagogy.* New York: Peter Lang.

Sleeter, C. E. (2013). *Power, teaching, and teacher education.* New York: Peter Lang.

Staples, J. M. (2010a). Encouraging agitation: Teaching teacher candidates to confront words that wound. *Teacher Education Quarterly, 37*(1), 53–72.

Staples, J. M. (2010b). How the bridges are falling down: A new literacies teacher negotiating "new" pedagogies in "old" spaces. *Issues in Teacher Education, 19*(1), 67–84.

Staples, J. M. (2011). The revelation(s) of Asher Levi: An iconographic literacy event as a tool for the exploration of fragmented selves in new literacies studies after 9/11. *Qualitative Studies, 2*(2), 79–97.

Staples, J. M. (2012). "Niggaz dyin' don't make no news": Exploring the intellectual work of an African American urban adolescent boy in an after-school program. *Educational Action Research, 20*(1), 55–73.

Staples, J. M. (2013). Reading popular culture narratives of disease with pre-service teachers. *Teacher Education Quarterly, 40*(4), 27–40.

Staples, J. M. (forthcoming). *The revelations of Asher: An endarkened, feminist new literacies event.* New York: Peter Lang.

CHAPTER 27

A Tale of Three Discourses

Doing Action Research in a Research Methods Class

Stephen R. Couch

Nearly forty years ago, a well-known social critic sang, "the times, they are a-changin'" (Dylan 1986). This is still true today, and nowhere is it more evident than within the institution of science and between the institutions of science, education, and politics. When Dylan first sang his song, the early salvos questioning science's autonomy and objectivity had been fired, and the battle has raged ever since. Today, it is fair to say that, while we better recognize the social nature of science and the many limitations this implies, science has not diminished in its importance to our lives. At the same time, how science is used and who uses scientific knowledge has changed drastically.

An important part of this change can be seen as the breaking down of boundaries between the discourse of science and the discourses of other institutions, resulting in, among other things, ordinary citizens developing and using scientific knowledge to a much greater extent than they had previously. Alan Irwin (1995) characterizes this as "citizen science," which consists of "... various attempts ... to place technical expertise at the direct service of the public" (p. 5). Phil Brown (1992) coined the term "popular epidemiology" to signify cases when citizens themselves conduct epidemiological research in their communities. Steve Kroll-Smith and I have written of the "new populism" in which grassroots groups make their claims based not only on moral criteria but also on scientific evidence, which often they themselves or a sympathetic scientist has found or created (Couch and Kroll-Smith 1997). A consequence of all this is that the role of the intellectual is changing, according to Michel Foucault (1984), from "universal intellectuals" who pontificate on and attempt to embody universal moral and social principles, to "specific intellectuals," who engage in specific social struggles (pp. 67–8).

The permeating of the boundaries of science coincides with a similar change in the boundaries of education. Specifically, in higher education, more emphasis is being placed on using knowledge and expertise directly to help alleviate social problems in communities. This emphasis occurs at many levels, both in relatively traditional forms of applied research as well as in more innovative uses of educational resources to serve community residents. These latter forms include collaborative research (Nyden et al. 1997), community-based research evolving from the Dutch "science-shops" model (Murphy, Scammell, and Sclove 1997), and action research (Greenwood and Levin 1998). These forms provide new ways in which the resources of education and science can be used to empower citizens to confront and alleviate the social problems they face.

In this chapter, I describe a research collaboration between a graduate research methods class I taught and a grassroots environmental group. In order to give students an opportunity to carry out part of an action research project, I contacted leaders of a grassroots environmental group to see if there was some research they would like to have done. The group leaders developed a set of questions they hoped the students could answer by carrying out secondary analysis of available health and environmental data. The students produced reports, which the group leaders gave to a local newspaper reporter. The reporter mentioned two of the findings of the reports in an article about local environmental problems and possible health impacts. This article gained the attention of the local congressional representative, who contacted the university and attempted to get the school to disavow the research.

Through the telling of this story, this chapter illustrates the differences between the discourses of science, politics, and education; the permeability of the boundaries between the discourses; and how interpretations of scientific research are shaped by the discourses in which they are used. Perhaps most importantly, the chapter reveals some interesting information about the nature and uses of power.

The Story

During the summer, I offered a graduate research methods class in action research. I assigned two books and a series of articles to be read during the six-week class. Since the class was on action research, I thought it essential that students actually become involved in doing action research, not just read about and discuss it.

Action research "is a form of research that generates knowledge claims for the express purpose of taking action to promote social change and social analysis … [It] aims to increase the ability of the involved community or organization members to control their own destinies more effectively and to keep improving their capacity to do so" (Greenwood and Levin 1998:6). Beginning with the pioneering work of social psychologist Kurt Lewin in the 1930s and 1940s, by 1997, the number of "schools" of action research exceeded 30. These numbers reflect the burgeoning interest among many intellectuals in reconstituting the relationship of theory and practice (Fals Borda 2001:32, 27; see also Argyris, Putnam, and Smith 1985; Atweh, Weeks, and Kemmis 1998; Fals Borda and Rahman 1991; Freire 1970; Gaventa 2000).

According to Davydd Greenwood and Morten Levin (1998), despite the many differences between schools and practitioners of action research, there are three elements that all action research has in common: research, participation, and action (pp. 6–8). Action researchers believe in the importance of generating new and valid knowledge through research. They believe that research should be developed and carried out with participation of members of the local community or organization being studied. Democratic values and practices underlie the collaboration between all the parties involved in the research, with all sharing in developing and carrying out the research process, and all being accountable for the outcomes. Finally, a goal of action research is to empower the community or organization to take action to improve its situation. The generation of knowledge and the production of social change are both goals of action research.

Given that the course ran only six weeks, developing and implementing a full-blown action research project was not possible. Instead, I decided to attempt to involve students in a collaborative research project with elements of an action research design. To this end, I contacted the leaders of a local grassroots environmental group to see if they would benefit from having students carry out some research for them. The leaders were delighted. They had been concerned about the health effects of toxins produced by various industrial facilities in their community and were aware of research which supported their concerns. However, there were many health-related questions that they had not had the time or expertise to answer; they welcomed the opportunity to have students do some research on these questions.

The group leaders developed a list of health-related questions that they wanted to have researched at the county level or lower. They came to the class, gave a presentation about the environmental and health problems in the community, and discussed the questions they hoped the students would answer. During the following class period, the class broke into four groups, each group taking one set of questions to answer. Specifically, the groups dealt with adult medical disorders; childhood medical illnesses; childhood learning disabilities; and women and children's health concerns.

Shortly after the students began their research, it became apparent that most of the statistics they sought were not available. They learned quickly that health statistics concerning disease rates at the county level or lower are few and far between. Therefore, while the students continued to look for those statistics, they altered their tasks so as to include environmental information for the local area, as well as a literature review of studies that looked for links between the kinds of environmental toxins found in this local area and various diseases. They also developed annotated bibliographies of all sources they used.

In the end, only two of the health statistics the students were able to find showed a significantly higher level of health problems for residents of the local county, when compared to other counties, the state, or the nation. One student group found a statistically significant higher level of brain cancer in the local county when compared with other counties in the state and the overall state and national levels. Another group found elevated levels of childhood learning disabilities. Both reports carefully noted that while toxins such as those present in the local area have been linked in the literature with these particular health problems, the data the students reported were insufficient to claim that a causal relationship existed.

At the end of the six-week period, each group produced two copies of their report. One copy was given to me and was graded. The other copy was given to the grassroots group leaders to do with as they wished. The leaders and I were very pleased with the quality of the reports, and the students indicated that they enjoyed the class and learned a lot.

Shortly after the conclusion of the class, the grassroots group leaders shared some of the findings of the reports with a local newspaper reporter. The reporter included some of these findings in an article he was writing about possible links between environmental toxins and health problems in the local area. He included the findings on brain cancer and on childhood learning disabilities. He also erroneously stated that the reports concluded that pollution was the most likely cause of these health problems.

A few weeks after the article was published, I received a telephone call from a high-ranking member of the university's administration. This administrator had received a query from a member of the university's public information office who had been approached by the congressperson representing the district in which the grassroots group is located. The representative was irate about the findings reported in the newspaper and attributed to a study by students of this university. The representative wanted the university to disavow the study. Moreover, the representative stated that a well-known scholar at another university had found a flaw in the students' work—specifically, that five-year cancer rates were reported as one-year rates, thereby inflating the actual rate. It is interesting to note that this scholar was also beginning a cancer study in the local area, a study which was supported by the congressperson and opposed by the grassroots group.

After some discussion, the administrator and I agreed that we would both respond to the congressperson. The administrator wrote a letter affirming the rights of students and faculty of the university to freely publish their research, with their conclusions standing or falling on the basis of scientific scrutiny. The administrator also emphasized that this was a student project done for a class and not a full-blown research project done by university faculty; therefore, the project was not subject to rigorous peer review. For my part, I agreed to reread the reports and respond directly to the congressperson about the concerns that were expressed.

Upon re-reading the reports, I was unable to locate the alleged error. Five-year and one-year rates were in the report, but they were reported correctly. I wrote the congressperson and shared these findings, offering to revisit the question if the congressperson or the scholar who found the alleged error supplied me with the page number in the report where the problem was said to have occurred. I also wrote that all four reports concluded that pollution was a possible cause of the health problems, not the most likely cause, as reported in the newspaper.

A few weeks later, I was surprised to receive a phone call from the above-mentioned scholar. The scholar had become aware of the fact that criticism of one of the student reports was being attributed to him. He stated that he had never criticized the reports. In fact, he had never seen them. He speculated that someone in the congressperson's office had confused our studies with a cancer study of the area conducted by yet another researcher, in which reputedly there were incorrectly reported statistics. He apologized for the misunderstanding and wrote a letter to the university administrator disavowing any connection with this criticism.

Subsequently, I contacted the grassroots group leaders and alerted them to what had happened, in case the criticism of the reports was ever made public. I also called an optional meeting with members of the class to recount what had happened and to discuss how these events illustrate many of the opportunities and pitfalls of doing action research.

A Modest Analysis

Without making too much of this story, how might we analyze what happened? What lessons can my students learn from these events? Perhaps before the times changed, one conclusion that might have been reached was that the boundaries between institutional discourses should be strictly maintained. This story would have been viewed as illustrating how political discourse intruded into scientific and educational discourses—how a politician tried to use undue influence to undermine the legitimacy of scientific information. For shame, we would have said! Keep politics out of education and science!

However, "the times, they are a-changin'." Today, we lack the ethical and methodological justification to call for the strict maintenance of institutional boundaries. The boundaries are porous, and we embrace and encourage this. A collaborative project such as this one, done as part of a class in action research, purposely crosses boundaries. We measure success not only through the learning that takes place but also through the extent to which the research projects empower the grassroots group to bring about positive social change. By their nature, the desired outcomes are educational, scientific, and political.

So rather than decry politics, it behooves those of us engaged in such projects to work to better understand what happens when institutional boundaries become porous. What social dynamics can we expect when developing and carrying out collaborative and/or action research projects? What happens when institutional discourses overlap? How can we analyze stories such as the one described here?

One approach is to analyze the meanings contained in the discourses. In this approach, discourse is defined as "a continuous stretch of language containing more than one sentence ... Discourse analysis is the social and linguistic description of norms governing such productions, and may include ... focus upon the social and political determinants of the form discourse takes ..." (Blackburn 1994:107). More broadly, discourse includes "symbolic sets that embody clear references to social system relationships" and include norms which govern behavior and the creation and transmission of knowledge within and across institutional domains (Alexander 1998:31). Discourse analysis is seen as synonymous with textual analysis and can include techniques ranging "from quantitative content analysis to interpretive analysis of abstract systems" (Edles 2002:179).

While his work is historical and genealogical, Michel Foucault's extension of the concept of discourse has relevance for analyzing present-day institutions, issues, and events (e.g., see Popkewitz 1991; Sawicki 1991). Foucault broadens discourse to include "first and foremost techniques, practices, and rules ..." (Simola, Heikkinen, and Silvonen 1998:65). He cogently points out that discourse is not only cultural but is also structural; not just the analysis of meanings but of activities. Furthermore, he argues that discourses "are implicated in and arise out of the power/knowledge relationships between the groups of people that the discourses themselves constitute and regulate" (Smith 2001:123). Power relations are pervasive, operating in every aspect of social life. Power circulates through web-like structures and can be creative as well as oppressive (Edles 2002:211). In contrast to those who focus only on the analysis of texts, Foucault (1984) writes:

> The problem is at once to distinguish among events, to differentiate the networks and levels to which they belong, and to reconstitute the lines along which they are connected and engender one another. From this follows a refusal of analyses couched in terms of the symbolic field or the domain of signifying structures, and a recourse to analyses in terms of the genealogy of relations of force, strategic developments, and tactics. Here I believe one's point of reference should not be to the great model of language and signs, but to that of war and battle. The history which bears and determines us has the form of a war rather than that of a language: relations of power, not relations of meaning. (p. 56)

If we view this story through the lens of relations of power, we begin with an instructor deciding to include a research project in an action research class. The nature of the project would be determined through negotiations between the instructor and two leaders of a grassroots environmental group, with the students concurring and having some say over how the research topics were divided. The project was carried out and adjusted along the way, based on the availability of the scientific knowledge being sought, and on ideas of the instructor about how to change the project so it would still produce useful information for the grassroots group.

Once the reports were given to the grassroots group, power relations became much more complex. Using the local newspaper was a major part of the group's strategy. Along with other data the leaders and others had collected, the leaders gave a copy of the class reports to a friendly newspaper reporter, pointing out the two significant findings contained in the reports. These were the findings reported in the newspaper article, bolstering the group's contention that there are environmentally related health problems in the community.

From another perspective, the congressperson had been busy reassuring the public that there was no credible evidence of health problems due to environmental toxins. On this point, the congressperson and the local industrial concerns had been sounding the same message. However, in order to maintain legitimacy with a wide range of constituents, the congressperson had supported the development of an epidemiological cancer study by the scholar discussed above. The congressperson was convinced that the cancer study would not show conclusive evidence of a problem. Given the low number of cancer cases likely to be found, it is unlikely that the findings will rise to a statistically significant level, even if there is an environmental cause. The study is likely to be "inconclusive by design" (Lewis, Keating, and Russell 1992). This is recognized by the grassroots group leaders, who oppose the study.

In any event, the congressperson was not pleased to see a study reporting high levels of health problems cited in the newspaper and attributed to a university. The representative made an effort to undermine the legitimacy of the study by getting the university to disavow it and by criticizing the study's content. For its part, the university held fast to the educational and scientific norms of free speech and scientific inquiry while downplaying the significance of the findings by emphasizing that these were merely student reports produced for a class. By doing this, the university was able to reaffirm its core norms while downplaying the significance and legitimacy of the reports' findings, thereby placating the congressperson and offering another line of argument that could be used to dispute the value of the findings.

The content issue turned out quite differently. A blunder in the congressperson's office resulted in attributing an inaccurate criticism of the reports to the scholar, who disavowed having even read the reports, while the instructor of the course re-read the reports to make certain the criticism was not valid. The instructor of the course reported this little controversy and its results to the grassroots group leaders, who were left with this information in their arsenal of knowledge to use strategically as they saw fit.

Finally, the instructor reassembled the students and discussed what had happened with them, pointing out some of the issues and consequences resulting from the practice of action and collaborative research, and thereby giving the students a more thorough understanding of this type of research endeavor.

Conclusions

As this story illustrates, with action/collaborative research, the boundaries between discourses are inevitably porous. A result is the clash of norms from different discourses. The norms of open and free scientific inquiry came up against the blatantly power-oriented norms of political discourse. The result in this case is not a clear victory of one set of norms over another but a finessing of norms so that scientific norms can be reaffirmed while downplaying the significance of specific findings and their legitimacy. This manner of handling the situation can be seen as a defusing of a potentially escalating conflict which would not have benefited the university.

In line with Foucault's analogy, a fruitful way of analyzing what happened is in terms of power relations and strategy. Once scientific findings enter the public discourse, they become part of webs of power relations wherein contending parties use scientific findings to enhance their own agendas. The findings become decontextualized and are focused on through the lenses of the political debates occurring at the moment. In this case, the two positive results were reported accurately. Yet taking them out of context and focusing on them gives them a high level of significance, since the "non-findings" in the reports and the qualifications about no evidence of a causal link with environmental toxins did not get newspaper coverage. The report of these two findings and their connection with a major university were enough to provoke the congressperson to attack the study and its legitimacy without anyone in the congressperson's office seeing or reading the reports.

In this case, the accuracy and legitimacy of scientific findings became points of conflict. The congressperson's office bungled the attack on the accuracy of the findings. The congressperson was somewhat more successful concerning delegitimizing the findings. While the university did not disavow the reports, they emphasized that they were merely student reports, implying that the results should not be taken too seriously.

In doing this type of research, it appears that once the research findings enter into public/political discourse, it is the rules of that discourse that come to dominate what transpires. This is not meant to imply that the norms of other discourses are not an important part of the mix but rather that the thrust of what transpires is governed by norms and actions of political discourse. In this case, the reports were not examined in detail for their scientific and methodological merit, except by me for the purpose of assigning grades. Instead, findings were reported out of context to make political points. These findings were attacked by a congressperson and mildly defended by a university administrator, neither of whom had seen the reports in question. The norms of political discourse, analogous—as Foucault points out—to war and battle, held sway, not the norms of scientific evaluation of the merits of the studies.

It is interesting to note the structural position of the instructor in this story. I can be seen as having a "weak tie" relationship with the class and the grassroots group, acting as a bridge between the two, and facilitating the growth of knowledge and power for both the students and the grassroots group leaders (Granovetter 1973). In fact, this is a common position for faculty to be in when involved in action research projects. It is a very different role from that of the traditional university sociology instructor; it involves bridging the educational, scientific, and political discourses in new and creative ways. The implications of this for education, university–community relations, and social change opportunities are worth further study.

More generally, it behooves those of us who engage in and teach this kind of research to reflect on the social processes involved. By doing so, we and our students can be better prepared for the "war and battle" that may be in the offing. Current moves toward new forms of university/community partnerships, including those involving action research, will inevitably involve the university in political discourse in ways to which it is unaccustomed. Those of us based within the walls of academia need to understand the dynamics of this discourse in order to be effective in it while protecting the core norms and values of science and education. For:

> There's a battle outside
> And it is ragin'.
> It'll soon shake your windows
> And rattle your walls
> For the times they are a-changin'. (Dylan 1986)

References

Alexander, Jeffrey C. (1998). *Real Civil Societies: Dilemmas of Institutionalization.* Thousand Oaks, CA: Sage.

Argyris, Chris, Robert Putnam, and Diana McLain Smith. 1985. *Action Science.* San Francisco, CA: Jossey Bass.

Atweh, Bill, Patricia Weeks, and Stephen Kemmis, eds. 1998. *Action Research in Practice: Partnerships for Social Justice in Education.* New York: Routledge.

Blackburn, Simon. (1994). "Discourse." *The Oxford Dictionary of Philosophy.* New York: Oxford University Press.

Brown, Phil. (1992). "Popular Epidemiology and Toxic Waste Contamination: Lay and Professional Ways of Knowing." *Journal of Health and Social Behavior 33*: 267–81.

Couch, Stephen R. and Steve Kroll-Smith. (1997). "Environmental Movements and Expert Knowledge: Evidence for a New Populism." *International Journal of Contemporary Sociology 34*: 185–210.

Dylan, Bob. (1986). "The Times They Are A-Changin'." *The Times They Are A-Changin'.* Compact disc. New York: Columbia.

Edles, Laura Desfor. (2002). *Cultural Sociology in Practice.* Malden, MA: Blackwell.

Fals Borda, Orlando. (2001). "Participatory (Action) Research in Social Theory: Origins and Challenges." pp. 27–37 in *Handbook of Action Research: Participative Inquiry and Practice,* edited by P. Reason and H. Bradbury. Thousand Oaks, CA: Sage.

Fals Borda, Orlando, and Rahman, M. A. (1991). *Action and Knowledge: Breaking the Monopoly With Participatory Action Research.* Lanham, MD: Rowman & Littlefield.

Foucault, Michel. (1984). *The Foucault Reader.* Edited by Paul Rabinow. New York: Pantheon.

Freire, Paulo. 1970. *Pedagogy of the Oppressed.* New York: Plenum.

Gaventa, John. (2000). *Learning From Change: Issues and Experiences in Participatory Monitoring and Evaluation.* Ottawa, Canada: International Development Research Center.

Granovetter, Mark. (1973). "The Strength of Weak Ties." *American Journal of Sociology 78*: 1360–80.

Greenwood, Davydd J. and Morten Levin. (1998). *Introduction to Action Research.* Thousand Oaks, CA: Sage.

Irwin, Alan. (1995). *Citizen Science: A Study of People, Expertise and Sustainable Development.* New York: Routledge.

Lewis, Sanford, Brian Keating, and Dick Russell. (1992). *Inconclusive by Design: Waste, Fraud and Abuse in Federal Environmental Health Research.* Chesapeake, VA: Environmental Health Network.

Murphy, Danny, Madeleine Scammell, and Richard Sclove, eds. (1997). *Doing Community-Based Research: A Reader.* Amherst, MA: The Loka Institute.

Nyden, Philip, Anne Figert, Mark Shibley, and Darryl Burrows. (1997). *Building Community: Social Science in Action.* Thousand Oaks, CA: Pine Forge Press.

Popkewitz, Thomas S. (1991). *A Political Sociology of Educational Reform: Power/Knowledge in Teaching, Teacher Education, and Research.* New York: Teachers College Press.

Sawicki, Jana. (1991). *Disciplining Foucault: Feminism, Power, and the Body.* New York: Routledge.

Simola, Hannu, Sakari Heikkinen, and Jussi Silvonen. (1998). "A Catalog of Possibilities: Foucaultian History of Truth and Education Research." pp. 64–90 in *Foucault's Challenge: Discourse, Knowledge, and Power in Education,* edited by Thomas S. Popkewitz and Marie Brennan. New York: Teachers College Press.

Smith, Philip. (2001). *Cultural Theory.* Malden, MA: Blackwell.

Studies in the Postmodern Theory of Education

General Editor
Shirley R. Steinberg

Counterpoints publishes the most compelling and imaginative books being written in education today. Grounded on the theoretical advances in criticalism, feminism, and postmodernism in the last two decades of the twentieth century, Counterpoints engages the meaning of these innovations in various forms of educational expression. Committed to the proposition that theoretical literature should be accessible to a variety of audiences, the series insists that its authors avoid esoteric and jargonistic languages that transform educational scholarship into an elite discourse for the initiated. Scholarly work matters only to the degree it affects consciousness and practice at multiple sites. Counterpoints' editorial policy is based on these principles and the ability of scholars to break new ground, to open new conversations, to go where educators have never gone before.

For additional information about this series or for the submission of manuscripts, please contact:

> Shirley R. Steinberg
> c/o Peter Lang Publishing, Inc.
> 29 Broadway, 18th floor
> New York, New York 10006

To order other books in this series, please contact our Customer Service Department:

> (800) 770-LANG (within the U.S.)
> (212) 647-7706 (outside the U.S.)
> (212) 647-7707 FAX

Or browse online by series:
> www.peterlang.com